THE HONG KONG FINANCIAL SYSTEM
A NEW AGE

The Hong Kong
Financial
System
A NEW AGE

SIMON S. M. HO
ROBERT HANEY SCOTT
KIE ANN WONG

OXFORD
UNIVERSITY PRESS

OXFORD

UNIVERSITY PRESS

Oxford University Press is a department of the University of Oxford.
It furthers the University's objective of excellence in research, scholarship,
and education by publishing worldwide in

Oxford New York

Auckland Bangkok Buenos Aires Cape Town Chennai
Dar es Salaam Delhi Hong Kong Istanbul Karachi Kolkata
Kuala Lumpur Madrid Melbourne Mexico City Mumbai Nairobi
São Paulo Shanghai Taipei Tokyo Toronto

Oxford is a registered trade mark of Oxford University Press

Published in the United States
by Oxford University Press Inc., New York

© Oxford University Press 2004

First published 2004
This impression (lowest digit)
1 3 5 7 9 10 8 6 4 2

British Library Cataloguing in Publication Data
available

Library of Congress Cataloging-in-Publication Data
available

ISBN 0-19-593749-X

Printed in Hong Kong
Published by Oxford University Press (China) Ltd
18th Floor, Warwick House East, Taikoo Place, 979 King's Road, Quarry Bay
Hong Kong

Contributors

Editors and Contributors

Simon S. M. Ho
Dean and Professor
School of Business
Hong Kong Baptist University
224 Waterloo Road
Kowloon Tong
Hong Kong

Robert Haney Scott
Professor
Department of Finance and Marketing 0051
The College of Business
California State University
Chico, California 95929
USA

Kie Ann Wong
Professor of Finance
Department of Finance & Accounting
NUS Business School
National University of Singapore
1 Business Link, BIZ 1 Building
Singapore 117592

Contributors

Camay Chan
Research Assistant
Department of Finance & Decision Sciences
School of Business
Hong Kong Baptist University
224 Waterloo Road
Kowloon Tong
Hong Kong

David Y. K. Chan
Associate Professor
Department of Finance & Decision Sciences
Hong Kong Baptist University
224 Waterloo Road
Kowloon Tong
Hong Kong

Matthew Harrison/Queenie Wu
Senior Vice-President,
Research and Policy—Corporate Strategy
Hong Kong Exchange & Clearing Ltd
Central
Hong Kong

George W. L. Hui
Visiting Scholar
Department of Decision Science & Managerial Economics
The Chinese University of Hong Kong
Shatin, NT
Hong Kong

Keith Lam
Assistant Professor of Finance
Faculty of Business Administration
University of Macau
Macau

Worapot Ongkrutaraksa
Assistant Professor
Faculty of Business Administration
University of Macau
Macau

Clement Shum
Associate Professor
Department of Accounting and Finance
Lingnan University
Tuen Mun, NT
Hong Kong

Robert H. Terpstra
Professor of Finance
Faculty of Business Administration
University of Macau
Macau

Hugh A. L. Thomas
Associate Professor
Department of Finance
The Chinese University of Hong Kong
Shatin, NT
Hong Kong

Md. Hamid Uddin
Assistant Professor of Finance
Institute of Business Administration
University of Dhaka
Dhaka-1000
Bangladesh

C. K. Wong
Department of Finance & Decision Sciences
School of Business
Hong Kong Baptist University
224 Waterloo Road
Kowloon Tong
Hong Kong

Jason Yeh
Assistant Professor
Department of Finance
The Chinese University of Hong Kong
Shatin, NT
Hong Kong

Paul S. L. Yip
Associate Professor
Division of Applied Economics
Nanyang Technological University
Nanyang Avenue
Singapore 639798

Contents

Acknowledgements

Chapter 5

The author is indebted to the Mandatory Provident Fund Schemes Authority, Dr Joan T. Schmit of the University of Wisconsin-Madison, and my previous Master of Science in Finance students at the Chinese University of Hong Kong: Daphne Leung, Francis Chan, Jeff Liu, Joseph Chow, and Teddy Ku. The chapter reflects only the author's personal opinion and any errors belong to no-one but the author.

Chapter 6

The author is indebted to the Office of the Commissioner of Insurance, the Census and Statistics Department, Hong Kong Federation of Insurers, Swiss Reinsurance Company, Dr Joan T. Schmit of the University of Wisconsin-Madison, and my one-time students at the Chinese University of Hong Kong: Lily Chang, Katie Cheung, Chloe Shih, Rosalyn Tang, and Peggy Wong. The chapter reflects only the author's personal opinion and any errors belong to no-one but the author.

Chapter 17

The author would like to thank participants of the Economic Policy Forum at NUS for their comments.

Foreword

It is just over a decade since the previous version of this important work appeared, and in the intervening period Hong Kong has grown and matured as a leading international financial centre.

Indeed, during the past ten years Hong Kong has witnessed many significant events and successfully weathered a series of turbulent financial storms. Our financial service infrastructure has proven its strength, showing that it is on a par with the very best in the world, with robust financial markets and sound regulatory institutions.

The financial services industry is a cornerstone of the vibrant, new Hong Kong. It is a high-valued-added, knowledge-based industry. It is an industry well suited to Hong Kong, with its long tradition of respect for the rule of law, its location at the centre of the dynamic Asian region, its efficient telecommunications and transport links, and its highly skilled and resourceful workforce.

The dedication and hard work of many individuals, both inside and outside government, have allowed us to mould our natural and man-made advantages to create the conditions that have permitted the financial services industry to flourish.

Earlier this year, the Legislative Council passed the omnibus Securities and Futures Ordinance, standardizing and modernizing all legislation relating to trading in securities and futures. The Ordinance sets high standards in order to protect investors, and provides a rational framework within which our markets may respond to new trading opportunities and new technology.

Hong Kong Exchanges and Clearing Limited (HKEx), created from the merger and demutualization of the two exchanges and their associated clearing houses in 2000, provides a modern trading environment fully able to meet the needs of all market participants.

The Hong Kong Monetary Authority, founded in 1993, has brought a new level of transparency and fair market competition to the banking industry. Measures such as the creation of the discount window, the implementation of the US dollar clearing system, and the full deregulation of deposit interest rates have helped to improve liquidity and efficiency in the market and enhance opportunities for all players.

The creation of the Mandatory Provident Fund will dramatically increase the amount of funds under management in Hong Kong. Recent moves to streamline the issuance of corporate debt issues will help to nurture the growth of the local bond market. These are just a few of the many notable advances Hong Kong has made in recent years.

Yet we do not stand still. Our markets continue to evolve; we continue proactively to enhance opportunities for companies seeking to tap our capital markets, for local and international investors, and for market intermediaries.

In the years ahead, our success will increasingly be tied to our ability to work alongside a fast-growing China. A decade ago, China's stock markets were a bold new experiment; today, they are emerging as the engine that will power China's place in the new global economy.

This volume takes stock of Hong Kong's present position and clarifies many of the key issues that will occupy policymakers and market participants in the years ahead. It makes valuable, dare I say essential, reading for all who work within our industry, and for a wider public keen to understand the dynamics that underpin the future development of the financial services industry in Hong Kong.

Dr David K. P. Li GBS, JP
Chairman and Chief Executive
The Bank of East Asia, Limited

Preface

The previous version of this book was published in 1991. The many significant improvements in Hong Kong's financial system since then have required us to write entirely new chapters. A few pages of monetary theory remain the same, and the chapter on Hong Kong's gold market will look familiar to readers of the previous book, but the remaining chapters are completely new.

We sincerely hope that this new book will be useful not only to those who work in financial markets and institutions in Hong Kong, but also to managers of international firms intent on doing business in Hong Kong. We also hope that university instructors will find this book useful for students enrolled in courses on economics, finance, accounting, and business. To this end we have attached to each chapter a set of discussion questions on materials explained within its pages to help point out to students some of the more important concepts that the chapter in question contains.

While the text of the book is, for the most part, descriptive, it also contains some theoretical sections. These are usually supplemented with brief comments on policy. By containing description, theory, and discussions of related policy questions, this book can be used as a textbook for students who wish to understand how Hong Kong's financial system works.

Each of the authors attaches his or her own views to the chapters. In this way, no single viewpoint on policy issues is presented, and each issue is raised as food for thought.

Since monetary systems are made by human beings, they often reflect human frailty. Perhaps the chief benefit of democracy is the freedom of expression of ideas that can lead to an improvement in the working of economic and financial systems. Around the world today we find many major economies in difficulty, and the impact of global imbalance is evident to some extent in Hong Kong as well. Laws in different countries that establish rules for the governance of corporations often seem ill-suited to more complicated modern financial systems. For many years international inflation seemed the norm; now we have an era of deflation in many major economies. Financial institutions and systems need to be resilient if they are to weather the storms of economic imbalances. We hope that this book will be helpful to those seeking to craft solutions to economic problems around the world.

The editors wish to thank all fourteen authors who have contributed chapters to this volume. They have brought depth and breadth of understanding to complex and exacting topics of discussion. We also wish to thank the editors of Oxford University Press for the professionalism they have brought to this publishing effort. In particular, Anastasia Edwards was very helpful to us when we first thought of the idea of publishing this new book, and we would have given up without her encouragement. Jacqueline Young offered first-class professional help in the editorial process. In addition, we thank our support staff for their efficient and generous assistance: in Singapore, Siew Eng Soh and Shuhui Teo; and in Hong Kong, Kitty Leung and Candy Tse. Their important and thoughtful contribution to the success of this project is gratefully acknowledged.

Simon S. M. Ho
Robert Haney Scott
Kie Ann Wong
4 July 2003

1. Overview of Financial Institutions and Markets and their Regulation

SIMON S. M. HO, ROBERT HANEY SCOTT, AND KIE ANN WONG

Introduction

Since the return of sovereignty of Hong Kong from the United Kingdom to the Peoples' Republic of China ('China' hereafter) in 1997 as a Special Administrative Region (SAR), the 'One Country, Two Systems' concept has been working well and Hong Kong remains an active international financial centre.

From 1977 to 1997, Hong Kong had an average of twelve per cent GDP growth rate. Like other economies in East Asia, Hong Kong was affected by the Asian financial crisis until 2000. Since then, the global economic downturn has affected these economies in a different manner. Apart from dealing with this global downturn, Hong Kong people are also facing painful economic restructuring. The bursting of the property and dot.com bubbles has led to more than four years of price deflation, and local consumption remains weak as of late 2002. Most worrying was the record high unemployment rate of almost eight per cent in late 2002. Coupled with the unexpected tragedies of 11 September 2001 and the Enron collapse, these events put pressure on and brought challenges to the Hong Kong people and their government. Fortunately, the Hong Kong stock market by and large continued to work well, although stock prices and trading volumes reacted quickly to sudden events and also to the subsequent policy measures. This also shows that the many years of hard work in upgrading the reliability of the financial infrastructure has paid off.

Hong Kong society has tackled many of these new challenges proactively and pressed ahead with structural reforms in order to move up the value chain, creating more wealth. Among the various key areas of the service sector that comprise over eighty-five per cent of the local GDP, the financial services sector has the greatest potential to create extra value and wealth. A financial system usually consists of three interrelated elements: financial instruments (assets), financial institutions (intermediaries), and financial markets. Financial institutions in Hong Kong offer a wide variety of financial products and instruments, such as cash, negotiable certificates of deposit, notes, debt, equities, funds, and their derivatives, which are traded freely in financial markets. Hong Kong's financial system has a strong infrastructure providing sophisticated electronic platforms for transactions and settlement. These facilitate the efficient production and exchange of goods and services by bringing together those who have funds to lend and those who wish to borrow these funds to finance their investments.

Hong Kong has long been an important fund-raising centre for mainland China enterprises. The successful listing of the Bank of China in July 2002 in Hong Kong, raising US$2.5 billion, highlights the strength of the Hong Kong financial system. Hong Kong wishes to continue positioning itself as an economy with the highest quality financial system in the region. This book aims to describe and analyse systematically the important financial markets, institutions, and instruments in Hong Kong and their contribution to the functioning of the economy. As financial activities affect every member of a modern economy such as Hong Kong's, it is important for each of us to have a basic understanding of the financial system.

The purpose of this chapter is to give a brief overview of Hong Kong's financial system and to consider the nature of, and need for, highly developed financial markets and institutions to promote economic prosperity. It also highlights the major challenges and prospects of the financial system. The second chapter contains a review of monetary theory and the development of Hong Kong's monetary system. There is also an analysis of the policies adopted by the Hong Kong Monetary Authority. The first two chapters are therefore introductory and serve as the foundation for further discussions. The remaining chapters contain descriptions of sectors of the financial system and a greater depth of analysis of the functions of institutions and markets.

Of central importance to a financial system is the payments system. A strong and resilient monetary system provides the foundation for economic stability. Because economies are subject to random shocks, a monetary system needs to be both strong and resilient. Like bamboo scaffolding, it needs to bend with pressure but be strong enough to hold the economy together. Part I of the book, Chapters 3 to 6, is devoted to the study of financial intermediaries or institutions in Hong Kong. These include commercial banks, investment banks, mutual funds, pension funds, and insurance companies. All of these popular institutions are intermediaries and have one thing in common: they accept funds from the public in various forms called deposits or contributions or premiums. Then the bank, fund, or company lends these funds to business enterprises in order to earn some form of return. The return is typically in the form of interest, but may be in the form of a capital gain on shares traded on the stock exchange. These returns are later paid out to depositors as interest or retirement benefits and so forth. That is, rather than investing directly in businesses, the people employ an intermediary—a middleman—to carry out the investment on their behalf.

Because people depend on their savings for retirement it is extremely important that only ethical and responsible people be permitted to operate as intermediaries. The public places trust in the managers of banks, mutual funds, and insurance companies, and these institutions have a fiduciary or prudential responsibility to care for an individual's wealth. It follows that these institutions are regulated by governments because people rely on governments to assume regulatory authority.

Part II, Chapters 7 to 14, is devoted to the financial markets in which financial instruments are traded. There are so-called 'money' markets that do not really involve spendable currency or deposits, but instead conform to an arbitrary definition: a money market is the market for securities or debts that have a year or less to maturity. They are often called short-term securities. They stand in contrast to capital markets, in which the securities being traded have maturities of greater than one year. The arbitrary one-year demarcation is adopted for convenience, perhaps because interest rates are usually based on an annual period. In any case, it is conventional to distinguish between money and capital markets by setting the 'less than one year' and 'more than one year' dividing line.

Besides money markets, this section of the book also contains chapters on the foreign exchange market, in which currencies of different countries are traded. There is a chapter on debt markets, including a discussion of the less-well-developed bond markets in Hong Kong. There are two chapters devoted to the rather more highly developed stock markets, in which shares of ownership of companies are issued and traded. There is also a chapter on what are called derivatives: financial futures contracts, option contracts, and swap contracts—or simply futures, options, and swaps.

Two other important financial markets are included here. They are: the mortgage market, in which mortgages on private dwellings are created by banks lending to homeowners; and mortages that are pooled and securitized, with bonds issued by the pooling agency and sold to investors who are in the market for bonds. In the United States these bonds are called Collateralized Mortgage Obligations (CMOs) or Real Estate Mortgage Investment Conduits (REMICS). In this way, funding for mortgage loans to homeowners ultimately comes from investors allocating funds to a special segment of the bond market for a guaranteed return.

Part III of the book, Chapters 15 to 17, deals with the rules and regulations that are extremely important to financial institutions of all sorts. First, corporations are legal institutions and operate under charters issued by the government. It is important that they govern themselves well and in the interest of their principals. Corporate boards of directors must not exploit the shareholders, but it is difficult to create incentives to ensure that they do not. Problems of corporate governance apply to all businesses, but are vital to the structure of a financial system (Scott, 1999; Ho, 2002).

Hong Kong rightly prides itself on its adherence to the rule of law. One chapter is therefore devoted to financial laws and the protection of investors' wealth positions. As an appropriate conclusion, the final chapter describes Hong Kong's position as a world-class financial centre.

The Hong Kong Monetary Authority

Institutions in Hong Kong are created and directed by Hong Kong laws which are called ordinances. Section 7 of the Banking Ordinance states that the principal function of the Monetary Authority is to 'promote the general stability and effective working of the banking system'. Under Section 5A of the Exchange Fund Ordinance, the Monetary Authority is an individual appointed by the Financial Secretary of the Hong Kong government. The powers under the Ordinance are personally vested in the Monetary Authority. That person is, by law, the Monetary Authority of Hong Kong.

In practice, of course, the Hong Kong Monetary Authority (HKMA) is an office of the Hong Kong government. Joseph Yam was appointed the first Chief Executive of the HKMA in 1993, and his record of accomplishment is long and outstanding despite occasional disputes on some controversial issues. He began his career as a government statistician after graduating from the University of Hong Kong in 1971, and became a government economist in 1976. He was appointed Deputy Secretary of Monetary Affairs in 1985 and a director of the Exchange Fund in 1991. The modern structure of Hong Kong's financial system is due principally to his guiding hand.

From an academic point of view, one of the most beneficial activities of the HKMA has been the publication of statistical data in its *Monthly Statistical Bulletin* as well as the many speeches, research findings, and position papers in its *Quarterly Bulletin*, along with other booklets devoted to special topics. There are references to these publications throughout this book. One minor, but unnecessary, offset to this generous service is that these publications are all held under copyright—but might it not be reasonable to expect that the people are the owners of official government documents, and that they should be able to use them freely as long as the sources are acknowledged and fully cited? After all, government publications in the United States, including all those of the Federal Reserve System, may be freely quoted and republished with a simple citation of the source of the material. That said, the HKMA has, from its inception, promoted what is called 'transparency' in all of its activities and decision-making processes. For this commendable behaviour it deserves the highest marks.

Money as a Medium of Exchange and Standard for Deferred Payments

The principal function of money is to serve as a medium of exchange. As such, money permits the discharge of debt that arises out of transactions. Transaction costs are far lower under a monetary system than under a barter system. Since a transaction freely entered into may be presumed to benefit both parties, it is obvious that society benefits whenever it is possible to lower the cost of transactions. Everyone agrees that monetary exchange systems, if managed sensibly, play a big role in raising the standard of life for the populace generally.

The simpler and less costly it is to create money and place it in circulation, the more efficient it is to employ money in transactions. Over the ages, commodities have served as money—but this is costly, and takes commodities away from their use as commodities. So precious metals, gold and silver, have served as money, but these too are more costly than token coin. Even less costly in larger transactions is paper money. It is usually in the form of a debt. Finally, banking deposit accounts are even less expensive to manage. Today, measured by dollar volume, most transactions are made through the electronic transfer of ownership of bank deposit balances.

Hong Kong has a full complement of coin, paper currency, and bank deposit money. Coins are issued by the government. Three banks are permitted to issue paper currency: the Hongkong and Shanghai Banking Corporation (HSBC), the Bank of China, and Standard Chartered Bank.

The second main function of money is to serve as a standard for deferred payments. People are familiar with the use of money to pay for goods and services in the markets using coin and paper currency, because most people use them every day. But as economies develop, more and more transactions are made under contracts that provide for payments to be made periodically. Contracts create debts that may be discharged immediately or paid at a later date—deferred payment.

Payments for assets, as opposed to goods and services, often call for deferred payments. The transfer of ownership of stocks, bonds, and real property does not, in itself, measure the value of new production of goods and services, but simply the value of existing assets as they change hands. Every trading day, money is exchanged on foreign exchange markets around the world in amounts of several trillion dollars. Stock exchanges and over-the-counter markets for shares and bonds also trade huge sums daily.

Financial Markets as Markets for Assets

One hallmark of a modern exchange economy such as that of Hong Kong is a highly developed set of financial markets. These markets are extremely important to the well-being of the general population. They facilitate the efficient production of goods and services by bringing together borrowers and lenders. Borrowers need funds to develop their business plans. Lenders hold excess funds and want to offer them to the market in order to earn interest. Interest rates are prices; they represent a price paid to the lender of funds and are determined in financial markets. If determined in freely competitive markets, interest rates serve to apportion the available supplies of funds among those businesses that will put them to their highest and best uses. A large portion of the supply of funds comes from businesses saving retained earnings and from personal savings.

Interest rates reflect the time value of money. When interest rates exceed the time value of money, there is an interest premium paid to the lender—a premium required to induce the lender to assume greater than normal risk. Thus, risk premiums serve to ration risk among investors and ensure that the borrowers incur the added costs in instances of more risky projects.

Three Important Functions of Financial Markets

An efficient financial system channels a nation's savings into its highest and best uses. Financial markets that are broad, deep, and resilient also impart 'liquidity' to assets that are traded in them; liquidity allows individuals to adjust their portfolios of property and securities so as to maximize the utility of their wealth. And financial markets place a price on risk so that those who are willing to accept it can assume it.

These three functions are fundamentally important to economic growth. Economic growth requires investment, which is, in turn, guided by rates of return. When socialist economies deny the free working of financial markets, the source of economic growth simply dries up. A rate of return— that is, the return for the use of capital—is often wrongly viewed as exploitative. However, it is the right return to a factor of production and is necessary to bring the services of that factor into use in the production of goods, services, and additional capital. Growth and prosperity depend on the efficient working of financial markets. It must be remembered, of course, that to be efficient these financial markets must themselves be competitive, free, and open. Regulations are necessary, but they need to be of the type that promotes free markets.

While extensive evidence supports the importance of a highly developed banking industry and efficient capital markets to economic growth, more recent research has focused more closely on the mechanics of the relationship between financial development and economic growth. In a brief article, Nicola Cetorelli (2002; see also King and Levine, 1993) asks:

> What is the role of the regulatory environment in which banks and capital markets operate? How does the quality of law enforcement, reflected in protection of creditors and property rights, affect the role played by banks and capital markets? How does the level of efficiency of these segments of the financial sector affect firms' access to investment funds and, therefore, capital accumulation? Finally, does it matter if banks are privately owned or government owned?

Her empirical studies offer evidence of 'stronger growth in countries characterized by a good legal structure, a less restrictive banking regulatory regime, efficient banks and capital markets, and a low degree of government ownership in banking'.

Real Investment and Financial Investment

Real investment goods include buildings, factories, homes, machinery, and equipment as well as inventories of materials, terraced land suitable for crops and irrigation, and so on. Human capital is created by investment in education and the acquisition of skills. If K stands for capital, and I stands for investment, then $I = \Delta K$. When we speak of investment, we are talking about the increment in real capital that is used in producing goods and services, and additional capital.

But real capital and investment differ from financial capital and investment. Financial investment occurs when an individual uses saved funds to purchase securities—such as shares of corporate stock or bonds—or lends funds to a bank in the form of a deposit. If the funds used to purchase a share of stock are directly employed by the business issuing the stock to construct a building, then that share of stock represents real investment. But when the share is sold by its first owner to a second person, the investment by the second person does not represent any new real investment; instead it represents a change of ownership of existing capital. The importance of a broad and deep market for existing shares of corporate stock is that it provides liquidity. When new companies need to expand, they can usually find a ready market for new shares. As noted earlier, individuals who hold existing shares are willing to hold them partly because they know that when they need funds to use for important purposes, such as education, the shares can be readily sold. Investment in shares is attractive, and real investment is encouraged.

Thus financial markets provide the most efficient way to create capital and expand the volume of tools with which human beings can work. Production theory clearly shows that workers who have more and better tools with which to work, as well as the skills to use those tools, will earn higher wages. Larger supplies of capital raise wages. Workers' lives improve. Growth leads to prosperity. A look at the rise in living standards in Hong Kong over the past several decades sets a positive example for all the world to see. Credit for this success goes to the hard-working people, and the free economic and financial system under which they live and work.

Shares of Stock, Bonds (Debt)

In America the words 'shareholder' and 'stockholder' mean the same thing. These investors hold a share of the ownership of the pool of assets, both real and financial, held by a corporation. In Britain 'stockholder' can refer to someone who holds bonds as well as shares, while in the US a person who holds bonds is a 'bondholder'. In any case, bonds represent debt rather than a share of ownership. The return on bonds is called 'interest', whereas the return paid to shareholders may be either in the form of dividend payments or capital gains—that is, in the form of an increment in the price received for a share of stock when it is sold over and above the price paid for it when it was purchased. The word 'return' is the most general term here, and can mean 'interest', 'dividend', or 'change in value'.

In many parts of the world, debt has, or has had, a bad reputation. In nineteenth-century England, a debtors' prison was the frequent abode of those who could or would not repay a debt. There are also provisions in the law in Hong Kong allowing a creditor to have a person who refuses to repay a debt placed in prison—however, the law also requires the creditors to pay the government for the prisoner's room and board. In the contemporary Islamic world, fundamentalists believe that creditors are evil for charging a debtor interest, and it is the creditor, not the debtor, who has sinned against the laws of Islam; whether a sin is deemed to have occurred or not depends on whether interest is charged. In the Bible, 'usury' is the old word for interest. Today, usury is a legal term that means 'excessive interest', and excessive means an amount or rate of interest that exceeds legally binding limits.

There is no doubt that debt can be abused, both by spendthrift borrowers as well as by ruthless creditors, but it is also true that funds are needed to finance investment projects. Financing decisions involve whether to borrow funds or sell shares in an enterprise (equity) and/or what proportion of each form of financing should be used. Most corporate financing is raised from retained earnings in the United States.

Debt financing is attractive for one principal reason—it is less expensive than equity financing. Because the bondholder must receive interest before the shareholder can be paid any dividends, the return to the bondholder is more certain and less risky. The returns that must be paid to bondholders are therefore lower than those required by shareholders, and the result is that it is less costly to create new investment goods through debt financing than through equity financing. Since it prohibits interest, Islamic law forces investments to carry high, risky returns of equity financing to pay for real investment projects. It would be interesting to estimate how much lower the cost of investment financing would be in places that operate under Islamic law if debt financing were permitted. Consider what this lower cost for financing real investment projects would imply for improving economic growth in fundamentalist Islamic countries.

Derivatives

Derivatives are securities, the value of which is derived from some underlying asset. One could argue that a share of stock in a corporation is a type of derivative in the sense that the value of the share is derived from the value of the productive real assets owned by the corporation. Most derivatives, though, are items such as futures contracts, options, and swaps. These are described in Chapter 12, which also provides detailed examples of each type of contract. Here it is sufficient to note that when someone buys a good, the trade is usually made 'on the spot'. Nothing prevents people from agreeing today to trade a good at a set price on some date in the future instead of on the spot—that is, for the exchange to be made on a forward date. This kind of contract is called a forward contract.

A futures contract is a special type of forward contract. Futures contracts are written for specific amounts of goods to be exchanged on specific dates, and these contracts are themselves traded on an exchange. Futures contracts may be written on commodities, currencies, or bonds. Anyone holding large amounts may use futures contracts to protect the value of his or her investment. Although futures contracts may be used by speculators, they also provide a useful function in that they allow businesses to hedge against changes in the prices of commodities. Hedges reduce the risk of doing business. To hedge a bet means to take a second bet that offsets an existing risky position. Say, for example, you bet $100 that a particular team will win a game or match of some kind. Later, you change your mind about the outlook and wish you had not made the bet. The way to get out of the first bet is to bet $100 again, but on the other team. One bet offsets the other, so you neither win nor lose and you have eliminated the risky position you got into with the first bet.

Options are also derivative contracts. Let's say that I promise to deliver ten bonds to you, each bond to be worth $1,000. I give you a piece of paper with my promise written on it. How much is this paper worth? If buyers believe that I am willing and able to do what I have promised, this contract will be worth approximately $10,000. Since the promise to deliver is for a date in the future, there will be some implicit interest involved, and the market value of the derivative will be discounted to allow for the time value of money.

Instead of using the market for derivatives to hedge, some people will buy or sell options, futures contracts, and other derivatives for the purpose of betting on price movements. Prices of underlying assets are certain to change, and if you can correctly guess the direction of change, you can make gains on your trades. So derivatives are used for speculating. Some investors buy what are known as hedge funds: funds made up of derivative securities. These are extremely risky and should be avoided by all but those who love taking unnecessary risks with their funds. The government of Hong Kong is considering whether to approve the licensing of hedge funds.

Swaps consist of a set of forward contracts under which streams of interest payments are exchanged for each other. These may also involve a series of exchanges of foreign currencies at the same time. Chapter 12 provides a complete, clear, and concise description of these markets in Hong Kong.

Financial Intermediation

Banks are financial intermediaries. They accept deposits and they make loans. Savers who do not spend all of their income may choose to place their excess funds on deposit with a bank. The bank promises to keep the funds safe, and even to pay some interest. The bank takes the funds and lends them to businesses, consumers, homebuyers, and so forth, effectively making the bank an intermediary between savers and borrowers. Bank lending has played a large role in the economic development of Hong Kong.

The Hongkong and Shanghai Banking Corporation, founded in 1864, was the only British bank with a local head office, meaning that its officers could provide service without first having to check with London. This gave it a competitive advantage. It soon played the role of a quasi-central bank for the Hong Kong government, and it maintains a prominent role in Hong Kong financial affairs to this day.

Commercial banks not only assist economic development by lending to businesses, they also create deposit money because they operate under a fractional reserves system. This money-creating power makes commercial banks a special target of government regulation. Commercial banks borrow from depositors, re-lend the funds to borrowers, and in the process create deposit money on the basis of fractional reserves. They earn income when the cost of the funds they borrow from savers is lower than the return on funds they lend.

Merchant banks, as distinct from commercial banks, evolved from prosperous merchants who were asked to lend to and participate in other enterprises. They offered financing, or to arrange financing, and became known as banks. However, since merchant banks do not usually accept deposits, and therefore do not generally create deposit money, they are far less heavily regulated than commercial banks. Changes in legal arrangements regarding joint stock companies in the mid-1800s permitted them an expanded role allowing trading partners to form companies and acquire limited liability. Risks of investments were greatly reduced. Stanley Chapman (1984, p. 142) notes that 'the most enterprising exponent of what we may term the "joint-stock subsidiary" . . . were undoubtedly Jardine, Matheson & Co., originally a merchant house in the China trade'. He further writes:

> Jardine Matheson & Co. had begun to explore possibilities in banking, insurance, silk reeling, sugar refining, mining, railways, and cotton mills. In thirty years or so of apparently boundless enterprise, they produced . . . varied joint stock subsidiaries. . . . In this way Jardine Matheson maintained its mercantile interests in the Far East, but developed rapidly into an investment house, or (in present day terms) an investment group.

In the world of finance in Hong Kong, Jardine Matheson and HSBC stood as two prominent financial intermediaries for many years. They now share centre stage with the Bank of China, the Bank of East Asia, and many other international banking institutions and investment houses as described in subsequent chapters.

The Regulatory Framework of the Financial Sector[1]

If governments did not regulate financial institutions, the public would demand that they did. Money is one of many 'stores of wealth'. People want to have their wealth protected, and for this reason governments have to make and enforce laws that dictate property rights. Money, being highly liquid, is easily stolen. Banks and other financial intermediaries request that money be given to them for safekeeping, so they must assume prudential responsibility for handling funds owned by others.

Financial regulations differ greatly from country to country. Now that the world economy is much more highly integrated and financial markets have become global in scope, the Bank for International Settlements, a club of central bankers, has worked to standardize rules for the operation of banks.

There is a variety of ways to classify regulatory structures. One is to note that some countries rely on quite rigid government laws, while others rely on informal rules. In mainland Europe, the regulations surrounding finance and business organization rely more on codified law, while in the British tradition there is a greater reliance on informal rules and the common law.

A second category of regulation is self-imposed by firms in the same industry. For example, stock exchanges establish their own listing rules and trading procedures without government direction. However, governments will act to make such rules legitimate by approving their implementation. In Hong Kong, such rules are often written into ordinances. In later chapters the development and evolution of the regulatory processes in Hong Kong will be discussed in detail. Here, an introduction to the theories of regulation is necessary.

Theories of Regulation

Several bodies of theory related to regulations are summarized here.

The Theory of the Public Interest

Basic economics textbooks usually tell us that the free and competitive market mechanism of the 'invisible hand' will lead to an efficient allocation of resources. Thus, with unrestrained entry and exit, a market will function effectively, even a financial market. However, inefficient market practices may result from monopolies or other external conditions. A government may create regulations to prevent the formation of monopoly and correct other external conditions that inhibit the market from functioning effectively. These regulations are believed to be in the public interest and are justified for that reason.

The Capture Theory

Government regulations may not be in the public interest. Consider how a government chooses individuals to be responsible for creating and enforcing regulations. If you wanted someone to regulate the banks, would you choose a farmer, a doctor, or a banker? Wouldn't it be best to choose someone who knows about banks? The answer is yes. However, wouldn't such a person be likely to put forward regulations that helped to promote the interests of bankers at the expense of the public? Here, again, the answer is yes. The regulators are often 'captured' by the regulated, and the effect is that the regulated end up *de facto* regulating themselves.

The Theory of a Market for Regulations

George Stigler (1971) put forward the suggestion that there are wealthy people who want regulations to support their own private interests. At the same time, there are suppliers of regulations—namely, the politicians who seek financial support in return for granting privilege to private interests. When there is a demand for something, and there are people willing to supply it, we have a potential market for regulations. Like the capture theory, the market theory implies that the regulators are sympathetic to the regulated.

The Dynamic Theory of Regulation

Joskow (1974) asserted that there is a dynamic interaction between consumers, regulators, and the regulated. Regulators usually have two behaviour modes. One is the equilibrium mode, in which the regulators behave passively as long as they believe that there is an appropriate balance or equilibrium between the regulated firms and the consumers. If, however, there is an unbearable imbalance or disequilibrium between the firms and the consumers, the regulators will switch to the innovative mode and search for new techniques to restore equilibrium. In this way, regulations are constantly evolving, keeping regulators busy.

A Regulatory Dialectic

An extension of the dynamic theory of regulation, proposed by Kane (1977 and 1991), is called regulatory dialectic. Regulations are constantly changing, as there is an accepted thesis, then an antithesis, and finally a synthesis in the fashion of Hegel. Because those who are regulated feel constrained by the regulations, they take steps to bypass the constraints. Soon the bypass activities become routine, forcing the regulators to change the regulations to conform with the newly routine practice—amounting to a synthesis. Firms always find ways to get around the new regulations, however, and the cycle of regulations continues. Kane's regulatory dialectic helps to explain the regulatory process of most jurisdictions, including that of Hong Kong.

Types of Regulation: Prohibitive and Preventive

Euh and Amsden (1990) describe how Korea reformed many of its financial markets by changing from a system of prohibitive rules to a system of preventive rules. Banking institutions often operate under prohibitive rules. These give the firm the licence or permission to engage in a certain set of activities, but not to do anything else. In contrast, under preventive rules the firm is prevented from carrying out a particular activity but is allowed to do anything else.

The distinction between the two types of regulation can be understood in terms of permission. A rule that gives you permission to engage in a single business but prohibits you from doing other things is restrictive. A rule that prevents you from doing one activity but gives you permission to do lots of other things is preventive, but it gives freedom. This greater freedom of preventive rules over prohibitive rules relates to the 'liberalization' of financial industries.

Figure 1.1 Regulated Activities of Business Firms

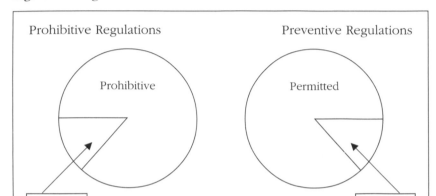

Imagine you come to a traffic intersection and a road is blocked. The traffic police tell you that you cannot go forward but you can go to the right or left or turn around. This is preventive (see Fig. 1.1, the circle on the right side). Imagine instead that you are told you must go right and you cannot go left, forward, or turn around. This is a prohibitive regulation and you are told where you can and must go and you have no freedom of choice (see Fig. 1.1, the circle on the left). Banks are often told precisely what types of deposit they can accept and what types of loan they can make. Both the bank's assets and its liabilities are regulated. Through the capital adequacy requirements, even a bank's capital structure is regulated.

Real or Fake Justifications for Regulating Financial Institutions?

There are many real justifications for regulating financial institutions. Perhaps the most important is to prevent fraud or imprudent behaviour on the part of those who purport to take care of other people's finances. A second important reason is that there needs to be some macroeconomic control over the supply of money in a modern exchange economy. A third reason is to provide information so that individuals can make rational choices. For example, inside information in securities transactions gives those who hold such information the power to make gains at the expense of others who are less well informed. As well as attempting to limit trading by individuals with insider information, the regulators require the dissemination of information so that it is no longer 'inside' information.

The need to ensure prudent behaviour is one important reason for some regulations, the need to control money-creation activities is a second, and the need to ensure the adequate and inexpensive availability of information is a third.

Many of the reasons given for regulations by those seeking to protect their own private interests are not genuine. The problem is sorting out good reasons from bad. Here is one recent example. For many years a committee of the Hong Kong Association of Banks oversaw interest rate agreements under which banks regulated the rate of interest paid to depositors on time deposits, savings accounts, and current accounts. It was recognized to be acting as a cartel and to have been operating a price-fixing agreement since its establishment in 1964. The justification for holding down (effectively placing a ceiling on) rates paid to depositors was to reduce excessive competition among banks.

After criticism by a public interest group and some members of the cartel itself, the authorities began a process of phasing out deposit rate regulation in the mid-1990s. Deposits have maturities extending from overnight to one week, one month, two months, and so on, up to one year. The first step was therefore to take away the ceiling on the interest paid out on the longest maturities, then on the next longest, and so on. Finally the time came to take away the deposit interest ceiling on deposits maturing within one week. The large banks said it should be retained, arguing that smaller banks would be put into financial jeopardy and might go bankrupt unless they were protected from their larger rivals.[2] The Legislative Council was persuaded to retain the last vestiges of the cartel from 1996 until July 2001, when an end to the system of interest rate regulation was finally declared.[3] This was an important step towards a competitive banking environment and away from the self-serving interests of larger banks. Of course, many large bankers undoubtedly still believe that their interest was the same as the public interest—it is never easy to find the truth, especially when people hold different views of what the truth is. Free and open discussion is the *sine qua non* of the search for truth.

The Regulators

Perhaps the most important of the four financial regulatory agencies in Hong Kong is the Hong Kong Monetary Authority. It was established on 1 April 1993 by the merger of the Office of the Exchange Fund and the Office of the Commissioner of Banking. Both offices were under the then Financial Secretary, Donald Tsang. The declared policy objectives of the HKMA were: to maintain currency stability, within the framework of the linked exchange rate system, through monetary policy operations and sound management of the Exchange Fund; to promote the safety and stability of the banking system by the regulation and supervision of the banking sector; and to enhance the efficiency, integrity, and development of the financial system, particularly payment and settlement arrangements.[4]

The Chief Executive of the HKMA has three Deputy Chief Executives. The first of these oversees the Banking Policy Department and the Banking Supervision Department, the second oversees the External Department and the Reserves Management Department, and the third oversees the Research Department and the Monetary Policy and Markets Department. The HKMA also has three Advisory Committees with highly qualified representatives. The Financial Secretary is the *ex officio* chairman of the Exchange Fund Advisory Committee, and the other members are appointed by the Chief Executive of the Hong Kong Special Administrative Region. There is an Advisory Committee Sub-Committee on Currency Board Operations, and a Banking Advisory Committee and a Deposit Taking Companies Advisory Committee. Readers will find the details in HKMA *Annual Reports* and other publications of the HKMA.

Securities and Futures Commission of Hong Kong

The Securities and Futures Commission (SFC) was established in May 1989 as a non-governmental agency outside the civil service. Members of the commission are appointed by the Chief Executive of the Hong Kong SAR. The SFC is responsible for the regulation of securities and futures markets in Hong Kong and reports to the Financial Secretary. The Stock Exchange of Hong Kong Limited (SEHK) was responsible for the regulation of listing requirements and other basic functions of the market for shares, but the SFC's role was to oversee the SEHK in the performance of its responsibilities. In 2000, the SEHK was merged with Hong Kong Futures Exchange Limited (HKFE) and Hong Kong Securities Clearing Company Limited (HKSCC) to become Hong Kong Exchanges and Clearing Limited (HKEx).[5]

The SFC monitors trading to detect unusual price movements and it conducts investigations of potential wrongdoing. The new composite Securities and Futures Ordinance was introduced in March 2002 to ensure fair, orderly, and transparent market activity.

The SFC has five executive directors, including the chairman, and an additional six non-executive directors. There are four operating divisions, each headed by an executive director. They are:

1. The Supervision of Markets Division. This division is responsible for the sound functioning of the trading, settlement, and operational systems.
2. The Corporate Finance Division is responsible for the regulation of takeovers and mergers and related matters.
3. The Intermediaries and Investment Products Division is responsible for the licensing of securities and commodities dealers, margin financiers, and others. It also supervises investment advisors and

other exchange participants, and the marketing activities of unit trusts, mutual funds, and other investment schemes.
4. The Enforcement Division is responsible for investigating alleged breaches of relevant ordinances, including instances of insider dealing and market manipulation offences.

Here is an example of an important responsibility that was in the hands of the SFC in the spring of 2002. The SFC, which regulates the mutual funds industry, was putting the finishing touches to a proposal to permit the sale of speculative hedge funds in Hong Kong to retail investors. High net worth investors living here could invest in hedge funds through private banks, but the investing public could not. It was up to the regulator of the industry to decide just what types of hedge fund could qualify for sale to the general public.

Insurance Authority and the Mandatory Provident Fund Schemes Authority

Two other regulatory authorities play important roles in Hong Kong's financial system. One is the Insurance Authority, which has regulatory control over insurance. The second is the Mandatory Provident Fund Schemes Authority. This was created to ensure that funds saved for retirement—five per cent of employees' wages and salaries and five per cent contributed by employers—would be invested with care. It is responsible for the overall administration of retirement funds, including the master trust scheme, industry schemes, and the pooled investment funds. However, the SFC must clear documents and marketing materials, and investment managers must be approved by the SFC.

The question of whether or not regulations help promote efficient markets or interfere with the effective creation of efficient markets is one that must be addressed by the government of Hong Kong. This is also discussed in Part III of this book.

Problems and Prospects

In the first chapter of the 1991 edition of this book, we observed that the authorities were making gradual moves towards creating a central bank. Now, one might ask, is the HKMA a central bank? Does it matter what we call it if it carries out central banking functions? There is no question that in the last decade of the twentieth century a large and important set of changes took place in the financial system of Hong Kong. The system grew in sophistication, and the regulatory structure evolved accordingly. Today we see many structures in place that were not dreamed of at the beginning of the 1990s.

We can be sure that change will continue as the structure of the financial system adjusts to technological changes and innovations in financial industry products. There is clearly a global trend in the merger and acquisition of banks, and this is bound to affect Hong Kong. In late 1999 the US Congress passed legislation that opened the way for mergers among banks of all types, and for mergers between banks and other types of financial institution, such as insurance companies and securities firms. The impact of these changes will spread to Hong Kong by way of US financial institutions. Hong Kong opened its doors to foreign banking operations in the 1970s and has not looked back. We cannot predict specific changes in Hong Kong's financial system, but we do predict that change will continue to occur at a rapid pace. Anti-globalization protests will be loud, and clearly heard, but the forces of change are irresistible.

By listing in Hong Kong, mainland Chinese enterprises which follow Hong Kong's high legal, accounting, and corporate governance standards can tap into this well-developed Hong Kong market for funds. Nevertheless, Hong Kong is facing increasing competition from other parts of the world. Mainland Chinese enterprises can also choose to list in exchanges outside Hong Kong.

Besides globalization, other challenges facing the Hong Kong financial markets include the introduction of the Euro, consolidation in the banking industry, the emergence of advanced information technology and new electronic platforms, new regulations and standards, changing customer and investor needs, and the uncertain general macroeconomic climate. The main concerns to international investors include currency risk, market liquidity, corporate governance standards, and opportunities in China.

To enhance the Hong Kong SAR's financial industry's competitiveness in the world arena, Hong Kong must constantly improve itself. The Hong Kong government and all related sectors have been reforming the securities and futures market structures. In March 2002, the new Securities and Futures Ordinance was enacted, and this will put the local regulatory regime on a par with the best international standards. The Ordinance contains a number of key initiatives to enhance the quality of the market, lower transaction costs, and protect individual investors more effectively. The Company Ordinance and the non-statutory Listing Rules have been reviewed to incorporate new initiatives for improving corporate governance and disclosures. There are also new HKMA guidelines for local banks to observe better liquidity management, risk management, and disclosure practice.

Similar efforts are being made to increase the quality and scope of the market, and to facilitate the development of new products and services in banking, equities, debts, insurance, mortgages, and the funds industry. In particular, to enhance long-term economic growth and promote financial market stability, one important policy for Hong Kong and nearby economies is the improvement of the allocation of domestic savings for economic development. This could be achieved through the development of a liquid bond market via the setting up of securitization and credit guarantee facilities in the region to reduce the over-reliance on bank loans and equity financing (Ma, 2002).

There is no doubt that there are tough times ahead for Hong Kong at the beginning of the new millennium. With the support of all related sectors, the Hong Kong SAR government is taking a number of steps to tackle the difficulties and challenges facing the Hong Kong financial system and lay the foundations for sustained growth. Alongside other reforms and initiatives, Hong Kong is sustaining itself as a major financial centre in Asia.

Discussion Questions

1. What are two important functions of money? Distinguish between measures of money and definitions of money, and give examples of each.
2. Distinguish markets for goods and services from markets for assets.
3. Explain the three important functions of financial markets.
4. Distinguish financial investment from real investment.
5. Is debt good or bad? Is interest good or bad? Discuss answers to these questions.
6. What are derivative financial instruments? Give examples.
7. Explain why financial institutions are more heavily regulated than most other businesses.
8. Five theories of regulation are introduced in this chapter. List and briefly explain each.
9. Distinguish between preventive and prohibitive regulations.
10. Using examples of preventive and prohibitive regulations in Hong Kong, how would you describe the positive non-interventionist approach to regulating business in Hong Kong?

Keywords

bonds
capture theory
Collateralized Mortgage Obligations (CMOs)
commercial banks
corporate governance
credit guarantee facilities
debt financing
debt market
derivatives
dynamic theory of regulation
economic growth
Exchange Fund Ordinance
financial development
financial infrastructure
financial institutions

financial instruments
financial intermediation
financial investment
financial markets
Financial Secretary
financial system
foreign exchange market
Hong Kong Exchanges and Clearing Limited (HKEx)
Hong Kong Futures Exchange Limited (HKFE)
Hong Kong Monetary Authority (HKMA)
Insurance Authority
insurance companies
Mandatory Provident Fund Schemes Authority
merchant banks
monetary authority
monetary system
money market
mortgage market
mutual funds
preventive regulation
prohibitive regulation
Real Estate Mortgage Investment Conduits (REMICS)
real investment
regulatory dialectic
regulatory environment
regulatory framework
securitization
Securities and Futures Commission (SFC)
short-term securities
Stock Exchange of Hong Kong Limited (SEHK)
stock market
Theory of a Market for Regulations
Theory of the Public Interest

2. Monetary System and Policies

ROBERT HANEY SCOTT

An integral part of every modern exchange economy is its monetary system. It provides an anchor for financial markets, intermediaries, and the entire financial sector of the economy. Since monetary institutions are not part of what nature gave mankind and are, instead, created by people and governments, every monetary system is governed by policy. It is inaccurate to say 'we have no monetary policy since the money supply is market-determined', because to allow the market to determine the money supply is itself a monetary policy. Since government has power to set the money supply, whether it chooses to use that power actively or not is a policy choice. Thus, taking no action is a choice of government policymakers, who must assume responsibility for whatever supply of money is generated under its monetary system. In Hong Kong the government claims that the supply of Hong Kong dollars is market-determined. But it must accept responsibility for economic conditions caused by inappropriate money supplies generated by its particular regulated market system. Let me explain.

Hong Kong's Monetary System—A Currency Board

In 1983 Hong Kong adopted what was variously called a linked exchange rate system, a pegged exchange rate system, and a modified currency board system. (These terms are used interchangeably throughout this book. It is important for the reader to note that they are fundamentally the same.) Under the new system the government guaranteed to exchange US dollar currency for Hong Kong dollar currency at a fixed rate of HK$7.8 for US$1.0. The establishment of a fixed rate of exchange of a local currency with the currency of another larger country that is a close trading partner is often referred to as a currency board. The reason is that a governing board of individuals from banks and government was typically set up to oversee the currency exchanges, so the system took on the name currency board. No governing board was set up at that time in Hong Kong; instead the already existing and operating Exchange Fund was given the task of handling the new pegged exchange rate system, so many commentators preferred to call the new system a linked exchange rate system. Today, the Exchange Fund has an Advisory Committee, and this committee has a sub-committee on Currency Board Operations. It reports regularly to the Exchange Fund Advisory Committee, so it is now, presumably, appropriate to refer to Hong Kong's currency board system. (However, the general term pegged exchange rate system more clearly differentiates the pegged and flexible exchange rate systems.)

In Hong Kong, exchanges of foreign currency, the US dollar, are made only between banks and the Exchange Fund at fixed rate. The word currency means coin and paper notes. It does not mean bank deposit account money, but it does include paper currency issued by banks and, as a practical matter, coin and notes are costly to count. This means that the market rate of exchange could vary plus or minus one per cent around the fixed rate before exchanges net of counting costs would be profitable.

The pegged exchange rate system is similar to the fixed rate of exchange system under the gold standard that was predominant in the nineteenth century. Then, market values of currencies had to differ by an amount large enough to cover transportation costs between one country and another as gold flowed between them.

Since gold circulated in coin or provided reserves for banks and thus for the issue of banknotes, a gold inflow registered as an increase in the domestic money supply. The inflow occurred when there was an excess of exports over imports (a balance of trade surplus) so that the excess was paid for through the importation of gold. Thus, the local money supply increased when the balance of trade was in surplus. In Hong Kong a balance of trade surplus (exports exceed imports) means that US dollars are flowing into Hong Kong to pay for the excess. They become cheap relative to Hong Kong dollars at the going rate of exchange, but the pegged rate system keeps the value of the US dollar from depreciating (that is, keeps the Hong Kong dollar from appreciating). Local people will then trade their oversupply of US dollars into Hong Kong dollars and the local money supply will increase.

There is also, however, a balance on capital account as well as a balance of trade. So it is necessary to observe whether local people take measures to invest in the US. If they buy investments in the US with their newly acquired US dollars then this capital outflow may act as a deficit on capital account and offset any surplus on the trade accounts. In this case there may not be an increase in the money supply in Hong Kong. Thus it is the balance of payments, including both trade and capital balances (and official balances), that determines whether there is a change in the money supply in Hong Kong.

Therefore, under the pegged exchange rate system that imitates the currency board mechanism, changes in the balance of payments determine changes in the domestic money supply.

The mechanism for maintenance of the fixed rate to the US dollar and the control system for changes in the HK dollar money supply has undergone many changes in the two decades since 1983. (See Jao, 1998 for a review of the evolution of the mechanism until 1997.)

Introduction to Chapter Topics

This chapter continues with a brief review of monetary theory and macroeconomic policy concerns in Hong Kong. It moves on to a discussion of Hong Kong's economic stability, the seigniorage it earns from its issue of HK dollar currency, and its fiscal surpluses and their management by the Hong Kong Monetary Authority (HKMA). There is a brief comparison of the HKMA and central bank operations generally. Then there is a review of a sample of articles by academic economists who comment on the financial system in Hong Kong. The chapter ends with a discussion of the relevance of a pegged exchange rate system to an international financial centre as important as Hong Kong.

Monetary Theory: A Brief Statement

David Hume's essay 'Of Money' appeared in *Political Discourses*, 1752. In it he articulated the relation between money and prices in literary form, a relation that later became known as the Equation of Exchange:

$$MV = PT$$

where M is the amount of money in circulation, V is the velocity of money expressed as the average number of times a unit of money changes hands during a given period, P is the average price of all items exchanged during the period, and T is the number of transactions during the period.

This equation is an accounting identity and must always hold by definition, but it provides a framework for analysis. Assume that T represents principally the final goods produced in an economy and offered for sale to consumers, investors, or government. This output of goods depends upon the resource base of the economy, the vagaries of nature, and the efficient operation of a free-pricing system. Thus, T is treated as given. Assume that V, the velocity of money, is also given. It depends upon the institutional structure of the pricing system—whether wages are paid weekly or monthly and how much cash and bank balance a person routinely wants to have on hand.

With V and T both fixed, it follows that changes in M will accompany changes in P. If M increases, P rises. If M rises six per cent, then P rises six per cent too, so long as V and T remain fixed. Alternatively, assume that the economy's output level represented by T grows six per cent during the year. In this case the six per cent increase in M will accommodate the six per cent increase in T and prices will remain unchanged.

When prices rise people call it inflation. Economists prefer to reserve the term 'inflation' for a rate of increase in the level of prices over time rather than a single rise in the price level. Inflation is usually expressed as an annual rate.

With the Equation of Exchange in logarithmic form, all four variables can be expressed as rates of change and the rates may be added together to represent multiplication. Thus, if V holds steady while the rate of growth of M is six per cent and T grows at two per cent, the inflation rate will turn out to be four per cent. Inflation follows when 'too much money chases too few goods'. Letting small letters represent the logarithms of the variables, the logarithmic form of the Equation of Exchange becomes simply: $m + v = p + t.$

The Early Quantity Theory of Money

The Equation of Exchange is changed into a theory of inflation when one assumes that V and T are fixed so that P depends on M and changes in M cause changes in P. The rate of inflation is the result of changes in the money supply. The early quantity theory was a theory to explain the rate of inflation.

McCandless and Weber (2001) reviewed data from 110 countries using data from the International Monetary Fund's *International Financial Statistics* on money growth for different measures of money, inflation, growth in gross domestic product, and so forth, for the period 1960–90. They calculated only long-run correlation, not short-run relations. They found that:

> There is a high (almost unity) correlation between the rate of growth of the money supply and the rate of inflation. This holds across three definitions of money and across the full sample of countries and two sub samples. There is no correlation between the growth rates of money and real output. This holds across all definitions of money, but not for a subsample of countries in the Organisation for Economic Co-operation and Development (OECD), where the correlation seems to be positive. There is no correlation between inflation and real output growth. This finding holds across the full sample and both subsamples. (pp. 14–15.)

They also examined earlier studies for comparisons of results. They concluded that the evidence is overwhelming that money supply growth determines inflation over the long run, but that it does not affect growth in real output. It does not work well to predict either inflation or output in the short run. Most economists find truth in the early quantity theory of money.

The Modern Quantity Theory of Money: A Theory of the Demand for Money

With the addition of other relevant variables, such as interest rate levels, and the rearrangement of terms in the Equation of Exchange, the demand for money can be expressed as an equation in functional form:

$$M/P = f(i, Q, X)$$

In this equation M is the amount of dollars that people wish to hold. When divided by the price level, the term on the left becomes the amount of purchasing power people wish to have on hand. M/P is called 'real' money balances to distinguish the term from 'nominal' money balances measured by M alone. The variable i represents the general level of interest rates. The variable Q represents the real quantity of output produced by economic activity. Since output and income are two sides of the same coin, Q could be called real income. In this equation Q is a proxy for transactions. The variable X represents a catch-all set of other factors that may importantly affect the quantity of money that people wish to hold.

The demand for money equation reads as follows: the quantity or real balances of money that people wish to hold is related to interest rate levels, the amount of output the economy is producing, and other exogenous factors such as the availability of money substitutes, political stability, and so on.

Graphs help interpret this equation. In Figure 2.1 the general level of interest rates, i, is measured on the vertical axis. Real balances of money, M/P, is measured on the horizontal axis. The levels of Q and other X factors do not appear explicitly, but the effects of changes in Q and X can be described by shifting the money demand curve.

Let us simplify the equation by omitting the catch-all variable X at this time. The downward sloping curve in Part (a) of the figure represents the demand for money relation expressed as:

$$f(i, Q_0)$$

where the subscript attached to Q indicates that this is the fixed amount appearing in an initial period. Since Q is fixed, the curve shows the relation between i and M/P for that size of Q. At lower interest rates people will hold a larger quantity of real balances of money. Thus as interest rate levels fall from a to b, the quantity of M/P on the horizontal axis increases, indicating a negative relation between the two variables.

The concept of opportunity cost helps explain the negative relation between interest rates and the quantity of money people wish to hold. Instead of holding money, a person has the opportunity to lend the money and earn interest. Therefore the opportunity cost of holding money is the value of the interest that might be earned. The higher the interest rate, the higher the cost of holding money, so at higher rates people hold less money. The interest rate is the price of money, or the cost of holding money. Interest rates ration the available supply of money among those who wish to hold it.

In Part (b) of the figure the dashed curve indicates how the demand for money shifts up or to the right when Q increases from Q_0 to Q_1. At each and every level of interest, the quantity of money that people wish to hold increases. This is because more money is needed in the economy to accommodate the increased level of transactions that occurs as economic output expands.

If output were to decrease, the curve would shift down or to the left. Thus the relation between output as measured by Q, and M/P in the equation $M/P = f(i, Q_0)$, is positive. Output and the quantity of real balances of money tend to rise and fall together.

In Figure 2.2 the money supply curve appears as a vertical line indicating that it is determined by independent policy actions of a central banking institution. A given amount of nominal Hong Kong dollars is represented

Figure 2.1 Money Demand Functions

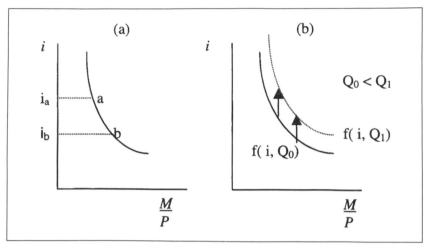

Figure 2.2 Shifts in Money Supply Functions

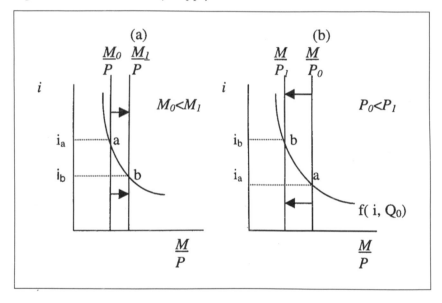

by M_0 in Part (a) of the figure. The price level, P, gives the ratio of M_0/P, and when the quantity of real money balances supplied equals the quantity demanded, the curves intersect at point a. Thus the interest rate is determined to be i_a.

If the nominal money supply increases to M_1, the curve shifts to the right and the interest rate falls to i_b. Thus the curve may shift right or left with changes in the money supply and when the price level remains unchanged.

In Part (b) of the figure the vertical line represents the supply of money for a given price level designated by P_0. Should the price level increase from P_0 to P_1, the supply curve shifts to the left. This is because the ratio M/P declines if the denominator P increases. The higher price level results in a higher interest rate level, as indicated by the move from point a to point b on the demand for money curve.

To summarize, the graphs show nearly all interrelations between all four of the variables in the equation $M/P = f(i, Q, X)$. And if variable X is specified, the demand curve would shift accordingly. For example, if X represents a substitute for money, then an increase in X would cause the demand for money to decline, that is, for the demand curve to shift to the left.

If X represented political stability and an unstable political situation were to develop, people would try to exchange their dollars for goods. The demand for money curve would shift to the left. But as people exercise their spending power, they might push up the price level so that the supply of real balances would decrease and the vertical supply curve would shift to the left. In this case the variable X may have an effect on both the supply and demand for money.

Although the curves as drawn cannot illustrate the complete interaction among all the variables, they do provide a frame of reference to use in analysing Hong Kong's monetary circumstances.

For example, a surplus in the balance of payments leads to an inflow of US dollars. Under the pegged exchange rate system the monetary authority stands by while people exchange their surplus US dollars for Hong Kong dollars. The nominal money supply increases. Interest rates fall and the economy booms. As prices begin to rise, the supply of real balances of money falls. The supply of money curve shifts to the left, placing upward pressure on interest rates. The result is that a rising price level in Hong Kong serves to act as the automatic adjustment force that offsets the domestic effects of a balance of payments surplus under the fixed exchange rate system. In contrast, if the exchange rate were free to fluctuate, the Hong Kong dollar would have risen in value, making imports more attractive to Hong Kong people and exports less attractive to foreigners. In such a case, the exchange rate would have acted to cushion the effects of the balance of payments surplus without causing domestic inflation.

As noted above, using monetary controls to manage inflation is effective only in the long run. It is less effective in the short run. Furthermore, the picture is complicated by the existence of international capital accounts. While the modern quantity theory of money does not contain all the answers to economic concerns, it does provide a framework for discussion and does suggest long-run implications of different monetary regimes.

Defining and Measuring Money in Hong Kong

Money is what people use to discharge debt in an exchange economy. This definition of money brings to mind the cash or currency in the hands of the public that is passed from hand to hand in the shops and markets. It is called currency in circulation in the United States. This means the total of currency issued by the Treasury and Federal Reserve Banks, but does not include currency held in vaults of the Treasury, the Federal Reserve, or any of the depository institutions such as commercial banks and thrift institutions. That is, vault cash is not 'in circulation' because it is not in the hands of the public and cannot be used to discharge debt unless it is withdrawn from the vault. In Hong Kong, the term currency in circulation refers to all of the legal tender notes and coins issued, including that in vaults. Only that part called 'legal tender notes and coins in the hands of the public' is included as part of the money supply. Not included are legal tender notes and coins held in banks and deposit-taking companies. So currency in the hands of the public, (C), is what is used to discharge debt and is a significant portion of the money supply in every country.

Another part of the money supply is in the form of demand deposits in banks or other depository institutions, (D), the ownership of which may be passed to a seller through cheque clearing, by electronic transfer using debit cards, or by other means.

Therefore the measure of money, (M), according to the definition above, is the sum of currency in circulation in the hands of the public and demand deposit balances held by the public in banks or other financial intermediaries. Thus M = C + D.

Table 2.1 shows measures of M as published in the Hong Kong Monetary Authority's *Monthly Statistical Bulletin* and available on the Internet.

In science it is important to define a thing first and then to take measure of it, otherwise you can't be sure what you are measuring. It is a concern, then, although a minor one, that there are three published measures of money in Hong Kong. The *Monthly Statistical Bulletin* refers to these measures as 'definitions' of money. The M1 measure is the sum of legal tender notes and coins held by the public plus customers' demand deposits placed with licensed banks. Money Supply 'definition 2', M2, refers to the sum of M1 plus customers' savings and time deposits with licensed banks, plus negotiable certificates of deposit (NCDs) issued by licensed banks held outside the banking sector. Definition M3 refers to the sum of M2 plus customer deposits with restricted licensed banks (RLBs) and deposit-taking companies, plus NCDs issued by these institutions held outside the banking sector. It is clear that M1 is the single and only measure of money that fits the definition of money—that which is used to discharge debt. The remaining two 'definitions' of money include time and savings deposits, and it is unlikely that anyone discharges debt using these deposits without changing them into money first.

Table 2.1   Currency Circulation and Money Supply Measures, End of January 2002 (HK$ million)

a) Currency in Circulation
   Legal tender notes and coins

Commercial Bank Issues:	113,405
Government Issue:	5,996
Total:	119,401
Authorized Institution Holdings:	14,075
Legal tender notes and coin in hands of public:	105,326

b) Money Supply
   Adjusted for foreign currency swap deposits

	HK$	FC	Total
M1	233,889	29,788	263,677
M2	1,966,372	1,502,296	3,468,668
M3	1,984,063	1,527,598	3,511,661

c) Components of the Money Supply (HK$ *in billions in this section*)*
   Hong Kong dollars only, adjusted for foreign currency swap deposits

Legal tender notes and coin in the hands of public	105.32
Demand deposits with licensed banks	128.563
M1	233.889
Savings deposits with licensed banks	605.855
Time deposits with licensed banks	1,066.67
NCDs issued by licensed banks & held by public	59.959
M2	1,966.3
Deposits with RLBs and DTCs	16.358
NCDs issued by RLBs & DTCs & held by public	1.332
M3	1,984.1

* The *Monthly Statistical Bulletin* carries additional tables. One shows components of foreign currencies. Another shows the combined total of Hong Kong dollar and Foreign Currency components. Others show breakdowns of amounts of different foreign currencies.

Technical Treatment of Foreign Currency Deposits

The monetary authorities maintain separate measures of Hong Kong dollars and foreign currency (FC) and add them together to measure M1. In this context the term 'foreign currency' does not refer to foreign coins and paper money. In the 1980s, Hong Kong had an ordinance that prohibited the circulation of foreign currencies. This ordinance was removed after the pegged exchange rate system became well established. There is no easy way to estimate the supply of foreign denominated coins and notes being used as money in Hong Kong, but the amount is probably very small. However, Hong Kong banks accept liabilities in foreign currency deposits and are active participants in the Asian-dollar markets. The amount of foreign currency bank deposits used in Hong Kong is probably large.

In Singapore, banking regulations require banks to establish an Asian

Currency Unit. It is a division of a bank created for the purpose of handling deposits in currencies other than Singapore dollars. Accounts in foreign currencies and those in Singapore dollars are kept in separate sets of books. Although no such restrictions exist in Hong Kong, banks can and do report the volume of foreign currency deposits alongside Hong Kong dollar deposits. So foreign currency deposits, as distinct from foreign currency cash, are readily observable as part of total deposit money and provide useful information. Foreign currency deposits are not part of Hong Kong's money supply, however; adding foreign currency is like adding apples to oranges.

One reason this would be misleading is that all of the foreign money held by people in Hong Kong is not included. Not only is there no measure of, say, US dollar currency held in private homes, but there is no measure of the ownership of deposits by residents of Hong Kong in foreign banks around the world.

A second reason why it would be misleading to add foreign currency deposits to those in Hong Kong dollars is that exchange rates change, so that the value of foreign currency changes although the number of units of it does not change. Of course, considering that US dollars make up the largest proportion of foreign currency, and considering the rigidity with which the authorities maintain the fixed rate of exchange with the US dollar, there is no significant variation in the exchange rate. Perhaps the money supply measures should include US dollar foreign currency as a separate category and not include foreign currency deposits denominated in other world currencies. The *Monthly Statistical Bulletin* shows large foreign currency positions of banks in UK sterling, Japanese yen, Canadian dollars, the euro, Swiss francs, and other currencies. One thing is clear: it is difficult for government officials to measure money in a financial centre like Hong Kong!

Adjusted for Foreign Currency Swaps

As mentioned in Chapter 1, banks offer contracts that let depositors give the bank Hong Kong dollars to be exchanged into US dollar deposits for a set period and then automatically re-exchanged into Hong Kong dollars at maturity. These are called 'fake US dollar deposits' since the depositor pays in and withdraws only Hong Kong dollars. The reader will note in Table 2.1 that the figures have been adjusted to include such 'US dollar swap deposits' in data for Hong Kong dollar deposits. In the measure of foreign currency deposits, the swap amount is excluded from the foreign currency component of the money supply.

In international foreign exchange markets, businesses that wish to hedge foreign exchange risk may want to buy US dollars and deposit them in the bank under a forward contract calling on the bank to buy the US dollars with HK dollars when the deposit matures. For analytical purposes these are Hong Kong dollar deposits, although in actuality they are US dollar time deposits.

The Monetary Base, Currency Issue, and Seigniorage Earned in Hong Kong

The monetary base, (B), of any country consists of those things issued and controlled by the government that are used as money—such as currency in the hands of the public, C—and those things that provide the basis for deposit money creation by banks—such as bank reserves, R. Thus B = C + R. Bank reserves consist of currency in bank vaults plus deposits held in central banks. Since a government can control what it issues, it can also control the growth of the money supply by controlling the monetary base. The supply of money, M, equals C plus D where D is some multiple of R under the fractional reserve banking system. Government provides currency through the minting and issue of coin, and the printing and issuing of notes. In Hong Kong the government regulates the printing of notes on behalf of the three note-issuing banks.

The result is that M = m B so that the amount of money is some multiple, m, of the base provided by government. Thus m = M/B = (C + D)/(C + R). Consumers choose to hold currency in some relation to deposits and banks choose to hold reserves in some proportion to deposit liabilities, and these can tell analysts the value of m. By knowing m and setting B the authorities can control M.

Data on the volume of base money in Hong Kong on 31 July 2001 appears in Table 2.2. The size of Hong Kong's monetary base was first published in November 1998.

Table 2.2   Monetary Base in Hong Kong

Hong Kong dollars (in billions)	29 Nov 2001	19 Dec 2001
Certificates of Indebtedness	102.48	103.85
Coins in Circulation	5.93	5.94
Aggregate Balance (of Banks)	0.13	0.33
Outstanding Exchange Fund Bills and Notes	116.03	116.20
Monetary Base	224.57	226.32

Source of data: Hong Kong Monetary Authority, *Quarterly Bulletin*, February 2002, p. 76.

Components of the Monetary Base

All components of the monetary base are liabilities on the Exchange Fund's balance sheet.

Certificates of Indebtedness (CIs) are an important item. They represent the deposits that note-issuing banks place with the Exchange Fund as backing for the issue of notes. In early days these notes were given out for gold or sterling deposits, but now they represent such items as highly liquid interest-earning securities that are denominated in US dollars, such as US Treasury bills.

Coins in Circulation are minted and issued by the Exchange Fund as the government's agent.

Aggregate Balance of Banks represents the clearing balances that banks hold with the Exchange Fund. This account has a recent history of change. Prior to 1988 the Hongkong and Shanghai Banking Corporation (HSBC) was the Management Bank of the Clearing House under arrangements made by the Hong Kong Association of Banks many years earlier. This meant that all clearing and settlement of clearing balances among banks in Hong Kong was carried on through accounts with the HSBC. In July 1988 the government introduced a new set of accounting arrangements under which the clearing house would be shifted to the Exchange Fund. For a time the regulations required the HSBC to hold an equivalent balance with the Fund and later all the individual accounts, including an account for the Hongkong Bank, were opened at the Fund. These now comprise the clearing balances of the banks and other depository institutions in Hong Kong (Yam, 1991; Scott, 1995, pp. 188–90).

After a report that was issued by the Exchange Fund in early 1994 recommended a system for real-time settlement of clearing accounts across the books of the Exchange Fund, the management began implementation of the plan. On 9 December 1996 the payments system shifted to one of real time gross settlement (Monetary Policy and Markets Department, 1997). Beginning in August 2000, the Exchange Fund in co-operation with the HSBC and others started work on a real time gross settlement system of US dollar transactions. This eliminated the need to assume settlement risk arising from two legs of a foreign exchange transaction existing in two time zones. The system was in place in December 2000 and represented a first in financial arrangements of this sort for Hong Kong (Monetary Policy and Markets Department, 2001).

Exchange Fund Bills and Notes. On 3 March 1990 the Exchange Fund conducted its first auction of Exchange Fund three-month bills. The amount auctioned was HK$300 million. The plan was to sell about the same amount each week to raise the total amount outstanding to around HK$4 billion. Next in line was the issue of six-month bills, and then one-year bills. In due course issues of notes maturing in two, three, five, seven, and ten years were undertaken. The amounts outstanding fluctuate, of course, but currently approximately HK$80 billion are bills and the remaining HK$40 billion are notes. Interest rates paid on these securities serve as benchmarks for other debt instruments denominated in Hong Kong dollars.

The Exchange Fund did not sell debt in order to raise funds on behalf of the government. Indeed, the government has nearly always run a tax revenue surplus and has only rarely borrowed funds by issuing government bonds. Instead, the Exchange Fund was interested in building up and supporting the development of an active money market—a market for short-term securities that would be a source of liquidity for banks and other businesses. Such markets are used in mature financial centres as a medium for carrying out exchanges that affect the volume of reserves of the banking system, which was the goal of the Exchange Fund.

Why are Exchange Fund bills and notes part of the monetary base? The reader may have noticed that the equations for the monetary base and the base multiplier, $M = m\,B$, and $m = M/B = (C + D)/(C + R)$, do not include a measure of the amount of Exchange Fund debt outstanding. Hong Kong has measured its base in a manner designed to accommodate the circumstances of the pegged exchange rate system. To accommodate the convertibility of HK dollars into US dollars, the monetary authority allows banks to trade exchange fund debt directly into aggregate balances of banks, which are bank reserves. Bank holdings of this debt are the equivalent of bank reserves. Further, any private business that holds exchange fund debt can sell it to obtain HK dollars, and then buy US dollars through the banking system. All of the exchange fund debt could be exchanged for US dollars under the convertibility arrangements, so this debt must have US dollar backing, in order to ensure that all HK dollars are backed by US dollars. All base money in Hong Kong is therefore backed by US dollar-denominated assets.

Government deposits with the Exchange Fund. One other very large and important liability on the Exchange Fund's balance sheet is 'placements by other HK Special Administrative Region government funds'. This liability item is not part of the monetary base, but it does represent surplus revenues that the Hong Kong government has collected from taxpayers and given to the Exchange Fund for it to invest in foreign currency denominated assets. Currently the Exchange Fund undertakes the responsibility for managing a roughly US$100 billion portfolio of investments on behalf of the people of Hong Kong. About US$30 billion of this backs the monetary base, and about $15 billion backs the currency issue and the monetary base.

Seigniorage Earned by the Exchange Fund in Hong Kong

Seigniorage is a form of taxation. Governments collect a tax indirectly because they have a monopoly over the minting of coins and printing of paper currency. In ancient times, when precious metals were used as money, the people in private exchanges had little way of knowing the purity of the metal. Governments took over the role of minting coins to verify and standardize their worth. Individuals could bring the metal to the mint and the government would charge a fee called *brassage* for turning bullion into coins. Later, when the mint mixed cheap metals with the precious metal and produced token, as opposed to full-bodied, coins, the value stamped on the face of the coin was much higher than the cost of the bullion and the minting of the coin. This difference in value is defined as seigniorage. It is sometimes called an inflation tax because as a government spends the newly printed money and purchases goods and services from the public, it takes goods and services but leaves more money than before in the hands of the public. The scarcity of goods remaining combined with the large money supply in circulation means that all prices rise. Through the indirect mechanism of inflation the government has diverted real goods and services away from public consumption and into tax coffers, thus the term 'inflation tax'.

There is a limit to the extent that governments can raise revenues through an inflation tax, because printing more and more money would soon make the money worthless. However, if the government buys productive assets when it spends the newly printed money, it can earn a steady stream of revenues from those assets. Such interest revenue also represents seigniorage. The money supply retains its value, and seigniorage steadily flows to the government.

In Hong Kong the flow of seigniorage to the government can be directly observed by a simple set of accounting entries, as follows:

Note-Issuing Bank Balance Sheet Items		Exchange Fund Balance Sheet Items	
Assets	*Liabilities*	*Assets*	*Liabilities*
Certificates of Indebtedness + 100(4)	Notes Payable +100(1)	Interest-Earning Assets +100(6)	Certificates of Indebtedness +100(5)
Interest-Earning Assets −100(3)	Mrs Wong's Deposit −100(2)		

Mrs Wong goes to a note-issuing bank and withdraws a HK$100 note from the ATM. The bank now has an outstanding note payable, represented by (1). The bank records a reduction in Mrs Wong's account by (2). Under banking regulations, the note-issuing bank must deposit interest-earning assets with the Exchange Fund. It takes a US Treasury bill worth HK$100 from its assets, as shown in (3), and takes those assets to the Exchange Fund, from which it receives certificates of indebtedness of 100, as shown in (4). The Exchange Fund records the issue of a certificate to the bank (5) and records the receipt of an interest-earning asset of 100 in (6).

The result of the regulation requiring note-issuing banks to hold certificates of indebtedness as reserves with the Exchange Fund is that the Exchange Fund has interest-earning assets equivalent to the amount of Hong Kong dollar notes in circulation. The Exchange Fund receives the interest that otherwise would be due to all of the holders of the issuing bank's outstanding debt in the form of circulating paper currency. The issuing bank does not receive interest on certificates of indebtedness, the public does not receive interest on the notes in circulation, but the Exchange Fund, representing the government, does receive interest. The interest earnings represent a tax on the public indirectly levied by the monopoly that the government holds over the issue of currency. A major reason that counterfeiting is against the law is to protect this source of government revenue.

Seigniorage Earned by Banks in Hong Kong

By granting banks a licence to create deposit money on the basis of fractional reserves, a government also gives banks rights to earn seigniorage on the deposit portion of the money supply. In return for the services banks provide to the public under tight supervision and regulation, the government shares its monopoly over the issue of money with banks. Banks then create deposit money when they make loans on which they earn interest. The earnings are seigniorage because the government does not require banks to maintain one hundred per cent non-interest-bearing reserves behind demand deposit money.

The bank-deposit portion of the money supply held by the public provides banks with seigniorage in the form of interest on loans. Some of this seigniorage is passed on to customers through interest paid on saving and time deposits, so it is more accurate to say that this seigniorage goes to banks and their customers.

Many economists argue that requiring banks to hold non-interest-bearing reserves is like levying a tax on banks, but from the point of view of government it is more like a means of reducing the amount of subsidy provided to the banking industry. The banking industry may be considered less a private business than an agent of government in carrying out the role of money creation and control. This essential role of banks causes some economists to argue that the best reserve requirement is 100 per cent.

Hong Kong's regulations do provide for 100 per cent reserves against outstanding issues of banknotes. That part of vault cash in the form of coins is held because of the needs of the banking business for transactions balances. No legal reserve requirement exists on coins. Hong Kong banks are, however, subject to a 'liquidity' reserve requirement of twenty-five per cent of deposit liabilities that must be held in the form of interest-bearing but highly liquid money market assets, such as Exchange Fund bills.

Historically, the banking industry in Hong Kong has enjoyed strong support from government. The earning of seigniorage by banks is indirect. It may or may not be justified by a need to maintain a sound payments system—a necessary ingredient of a prosperous exchange economy.

Operations of Central Banks and the Hong Kong Monetary Authority

Historical circumstances have guided each central bank to its own unique method of operation. However, most central banks carry out the following set of duties associated with the management of the banking system, the payments system, and the resulting macroeconomic conditions:

First, central banks are bankers to governments.

Second, central banks are bankers to commercial and other banks operating in the economy.

Third, central banks issue currency or hold backing for the issue of currency.

Fourth, central banks deal with international banks and foreign currency matters.

Fifth, central banks supervise commercial banks and other financial institutions.

Sixth, central banks play a role in the payments system, including cheque clearing.

Seventh, central banks help determine monetary policy with varying degrees of independence.

This list may be shorter or longer in individual countries, but it is characteristic.

The Hong Kong Monetary Authority carries out all of the above duties. It is Hong Kong's central bank. Consider each of the above in Hong Kong, and remember that the HKMA manages the Exchange Fund when considering the following:

First, in Hong Kong the government held accounts with the Hongkong and Shanghai Banking Corporation for many years. If the government had surpluses, it gave funds to the Exchange Fund for investment in foreign currencies. Today the Exchange Fund holds and manages about US$60 billion for the government over and above the amount it holds as backing for currency issue. For everyday transactions the government still has accounts with authorized institutions, but it also has a large account with the Exchange Fund.

Second, the Exchange Fund gained control over the volume of bank reserves by moving the clearing account balances of commercial banks from the HSBC to the Exchange Fund. The aggregate balance of the banking system is the aggregate of all the accounts of individual banks that hold their transactions reserves with the Exchange Fund. In 1998 the HKMA began a 'convertibility undertaking' that permitted all banks with clearing balances at the Exchange Fund to exchange clearing balances into US dollars by electronic transfer of funds through book entries at the HK$7.8 rate of exchange using discount window borrowing, if desired, on demand. This action was designed to strengthen the currency board operations by facilitating arbitrage through cashless transactions (see Tsang, 1998; Hong Kong Monetary Authority, 1998, pp. 38–9).

Third, the Exchange Fund issues certificates of indebtedness to the banks and then banks issue notes payable, giving the Exchange Fund control over the issue of paper notes.

Fourth, the HKMA approves applications on the part of foreign banking institutions to operate in Hong Kong.

Fifth, the HKMA has a Banking Supervision Department with an Executive Director.

Sixth, with the establishment of the real time gross settlement system, the HKMA has taken charge of the payments system.

Seventh, the HKMA has a Monetary Policy and Markets Department with an executive director.

It is therefore appropriate to say that the HKMA is Hong Kong's central bank. It also holds membership in the Bank for International Settlements in Basel, Switzerland—an institution known as a club of central bankers.

Monetary Tools of Control in Hong Kong

Open market operations are used by central banks as a direct means of controlling the volume of reserves of the banking system.

Since the Exchange Fund holds the Aggregate Balance of Banks and also issues Exchange Fund bills and notes, both accounts appear as liabilities on its balance sheet. It can enter the market for bills as either buyer or seller. If it sells bills, it collects money from the buyer through a cheque drawn on the buyer's bank. The result is an increase in the liability for outstanding bills and a decrease in the Aggregate Balance of Banks. This creates a shortage of funds in the Hong Kong interbank market and puts upward pressure on interest rates. If the Fund buys bills, it supplies funds to the interbank market. Therefore, through what can be called open market operations, it can influence credit market conditions using its portfolio of outstanding bills and notes as a slack variable. If it sells bills it drains reserves from the interbank funds market.

Changing discount window lending rates is an indirect method of influencing the volume of bank reserves and credit market conditions. Through the discount window, banks can borrow overnight funds from the Exchange Fund. The mechanism involves the sale and repurchase of eligible securities. There is a discount rate of interest applicable to the borrowing, called the Base Rate. This rate can be raised or lowered. If raised it discourages banks from borrowing more reserves, thus increasing the liquidity of the banking system. If lowered it encourages banks to take advantage of the availability of additional reserves, so indirectly the Exchange Fund can influence monetary conditions through discount window lending policies. There is also a 'liquidity adjustment facility window' through which banks can borrow funds on an intraday basis through repurchase agreements.

The Hong Kong Monetary Authority officials considered the introduction of reserve requirements in the form of legal ratios of reserves to deposit liabilities, but decided against introducing this form of control mechanism (Hong Kong Monetary Authority, 2001).

Central Banking and the Fixed Exchange Rate Systems

This chapter began with a discussion of the need for a stable monetary regime and a robust financial system to support a vibrant exchange economy. In 1983 the Hong Kong government chose to tie the Hong Kong dollar to the US dollar at a fixed rate of exchange. At the time, some economists recommended setting up a central bank to gain control over the money supply. The author proposed using existing Exchange Fund regulations to control the growth of the monetary base and leave the foreign exchange market free of regulations (Scott, 1984). But the assumed simplicity of the proposal to fix the exchange rate held sway.

There was strong objection to the establishment of a central bank as a solution to the rapidly depreciating value of the Hong Kong dollar in October 1983. The political circumstances of the time demanded expediency, and it would have taken too long to create a central bank. Twenty years on, however, Hong Kong has a central bank with only moderate independence from central government. This circumstance did not simply evolve: Joseph Yam purposefully created it, telling everyone what he wanted to do. The author recalls an impressive speech Mr Yam gave in or around 1990 to a small audience at the Chinese University of Hong Kong. His argument was that establishing monetary controls was necessary in order to defend the exchange rate system. Most memorable was the gentle and delightful metaphor he used at that time. He said that monetary policy was like an umbrella: one can open it for shelter from the rain, or one can use it as a weapon. Monetary policy can be used either to control money growth when needed or, through adjustments for conditions caused by the pegged exchange rate, to defend the peg.

So what has transpired? The Exchange Fund took over the clearing house, forcing banks to maintain accounts with the Fund itself. It issued bills and created a market for them in order to have a conduit for open market operations. It set up discount window facilities to ensure that the Fund could act as a lender of last resort if need be. All of these and other functions were placed under the auspices of the Hong Kong Monetary Authority.

These measures were taken with commendable transparency. At no time did most people stop and ask whether or not it would be desirable for Hong Kong to have a central bank. Nearly everyone agreed that each step was needed to defend the peg adequately. Having crossed the Rubicon by pegging the exchange rate, there was no turning back.

The irony is that the currency-board-style system was sold to the government and the public as a way to control money growth automatically without the need for a central bank, yet Mr Yam created a central bank in order to have powers to defend the pegged exchange rate!

With nearly all of the central banking controls in place, the HKMA has now established a research wing that examines questions of monetary regimes and other aspects of financial market developments. It also supports the recent opening of the Institute for Monetary Research. In his speech in November 2001 (Yam, 2001, p. 86) Mr Yam said:

> It is absolutely right that a policy that forms the keystone of our financial system should be open to scrutiny. The strong public and market confidence in our currency can only be sustained if the reasons for adopting the monetary policy we choose are properly understood, and if the limitations, and the merits and demerits of possible alternatives, are examined through informed and reasoned debate.

It is refreshing to read such encouraging words. In the author's opinion, this entire speech should be required reading in all economics courses offered in universities in Hong Kong. In it Mr Yam discusses the difficulties in the current Hong Kong economy, with falling prices and high unemployment rates. He acknowledges that the pegged exchange rate system adds to the current predicaments and prohibits the active use of monetary policy as a counter-cyclical tool. He also rightly suggests that the situation is one of adjustment and that conditions will change for the better over the long term. He then avers that adjustment costs are necessary in order to retain the benefits of a fixed exchange rate system.

The situation reminds the author of a class lecture in 1954 given by his mentor, Harvard Professor Gottfried Haberler, in which Professor Haberler discussed the problems with the gold standard. He said that it did many good things, but the automatic stabilization process in an economic downturn required falling prices and unemployment at home to such a large extent that it was simply 'unpalatable'. Similarly, the currency board in Argentina, established in 1991, at first did wonders for the economy. Inflation stopped and the economy boomed, but strong foreign investment led to inflated asset prices, and the economy's competitive position deteriorated. Then Brazil, Argentina's largest trading partner, devalued its currency, the real. Rising unemployment and sticky wages and prices led to banking problems and failing businesses, but dogged determination to retain its currency board system blinded the Argentinian government to the need to devalue in line with the devaluation of the Brazilian currency in order to maintain its trading status, and with it domestic economic stability. Foreign advisors, including Steve Hanke (2000, 2001), argued for resistance to any change in the peso peg to the dollar. He and other academics praised the peg, but the situation finally became totally unpalatable to the Argentine people and riots began in 2001. Argentina defaulted on its sovereign debt, much of which was denominated in US dollars, and catastrophe followed. By April 2002 the unemployment rate was twenty-five per cent and the Argentinian peso had fallen from a level of one to the US dollar to $0.30, or about seventy per cent. Even then the bottom was not yet in sight as renewed inflation began to appear.

The entire economic catastrophe could have been avoided if the rigid adherence to the pegged currency system had been instituted so that it was more flexible. Excessive price rigidity is one problem with pegged exchange rate systems, but the absence of a flexibility to respond to the changed status of the Brazilian real was the real cause of this particular disaster. Economists Ricardo Caballero and Rudiger Dornbusch (March 2002) now say that the only solution is for a group of foreign bankers to be put in charge of Argentina's banks and financial system.

It is fortunate that Hong Kong does not face Argentina's problem. Imagine what could happen to the Hong Kong economy if China decided to devalue the renminbi in relation to the US dollar. It would be difficult, but because of the foresight of Joseph Yam, there now exists a strong central bank in Hong Kong. A switch to a freely fluctuating exchange rate system would prevent a collapse of Hong Kong's economy. The Hong Kong Monetary Authority could easily maintain control over the monetary base and retain a viable monetary system similar to that of Switzerland, which has a small open economy with a hard currency and a freely fluctuating exchange rate system. While it does not have legally required reserves for its banking system, it does have effective tools of control over money and can exercise monetary policies when it needs them.

Mr Yam should be commended for building up central banking tools to defend the peg, which was a *fait accompli* when he entered the scene. Now Hong Kong has exceedingly valuable options. It can either keep the peg or not because it now deals from strength and need no longer fear speculative attacks.

Reputation and time consistency are becoming more and more important in economic theory and these can play a role in modelling the way a financial system works. Hong Kong has a reputation and it dominates any concerns with time inconsistency. For example, when Hong Kong changed to convertibility of bank deposits, it changed the convertibility rate from HK$7.75 to 7.80 in small, announced, transparent daily steps over a period of 500 days. This very slight devaluation of the HK dollar could be repeated any time that the HKMA chose to do so. Policy moves made with due deliberate and transparent gradual steps will eliminate the uncertainty that many commentators worry about. There is no reason why Hong Kong should not use its tools of monetary control for good purposes (see Latter, 2002).

Let us turn now to a small sample of research topics on questions relating to the best monetary regime for Hong Kong.

Samples of Theoretical and Empirical Research[1]

A huge body of literature exists on the question of exchange rate regimes. Each of the articles mentioned here has many citations of interest to the concerned reader. For example, the *Pacific Economic Review* devotes its October 1998 and June 1999 issues to special sections on Currency Boards and Exchange Rate Arrangements: Theories and Issues.

Carlos E. J. M. Zarazaga (1999) addresses two common objections to currency board regimes—that more flexible regimes are superior, and that currency boards are unsustainable. His mathematical model describes an economy in which interest groups compete for government subsidies but are unable to observe government spending. Such circumstances create inflationary pressures, and in some situations these can be offset by the transparency of currency board regimes. He cites articles by Barro, Dornbusch, Hanke, Schuler, and others in regard to the time-inconsistency problem arising from Argentina's history of experiences with currency boards. The model employs game theory which includes comparisons of Nash equilibria with Pareto-efficient payoffs. He concludes that currency boards can be more sustainable than suggested by time-inconsistency problems, but that the board is not powerful enough to guarantee a low inflation environment.

Reuven Glick of the Federal Reserve Bank of San Francisco's Center for Pacific Basin Monetary and Economic Studies provides readers with a concise, comprehensive, and readable review of the subject of exchange rate regimes. His 'Fixed or Floating: Is It Still Possible to Manage in the Middle?' (Glick, October 2000) examines data from many emerging economies. He concludes: 'for most emerging market economies of East Asia, exchange rate floating appears to be the most plausible policy option. Such a policy does not imply . . . no intervention in the foreign exchange market . . . nor does [it] imply no need to accumulate and hold foreign exchange reserves. . . . What matters is that policymakers not make any explicit or implicit policy commitments to keep the exchange rate within some range or crawling band for any extended periods of time.' Further, Glick and Hutchison (2000) conclude that capital controls are 'associated with higher probability of an exchange rate crisis' and probably are ineffective in protecting an economy from speculative attacks. Hong Kong's open economy, with an absence of capital controls, is testimony to the strength of a free-market economy.

Chan and Chen (1999) make the case for having the government write put options on the currency in situations in which it is under speculative attack and threatened with devaluation.

They argue persuasively that such action is better than raising interest rates. Since Hong Kong's peg makes it difficult to raise interest rates above those on US dollar deposits without triggering arbitrage activity, the suggestion is especially apropos for Hong Kong. Such options have been written up by the HKMA.

Cheng, Kwan, and Lui (1999, No. 128) examine the premium in the forward foreign exchange markets to establish a measure of the credibility of the pegged exchange rate system. They also discuss the possibility of using put options and structured notes in an alternative approach to defending the Hong Kong dollar (1999, No. 129).

Kwan, Lui, and Cheng (1999) look into the role of institutional arrangements in evaluating the credibility of the currency board in Hong Kong. They conclude that adherence to fixed rules provides greater credibility than existed when the HKMA relied on discretion during the Asian financial turmoil of 1998.

The interested reader is encouraged to note many interesting and relevant studies cited in these studies and in current journals (Lai, Ha, and Leung, 2002).

Summary and Conclusions

This chapter began with a brief discussion of money, its importance to an exchange economy, the Equation of Exchange, and the theory of the demand for money. Demand and supply curves for real balances of money indicate how interest rate levels determined in credit markets are influenced by money supply changes, among other variables. The discussion went on to describe money as defined and measured in Hong Kong. The certificates of indebtedness issued by the Exchange Fund to the three note-issuing commercial banks are unique forms of deposit placed with the Exchange Fund in exchange for interest-earning assets. The interest on these assets represents seigniorage earned by the government of Hong Kong as a result of its monopoly over the issue of paper currency and coins.

There was also a discussion of seigniorage earned by banks and bank depositors in Hong Kong through the difference in interest paid to depositors and interest received by banks from loans.

This discussion was followed by a description of the evolution of tools of control over the money supply in Hong Kong through the upgrading of the payments system and clearing accounts of banks in Hong Kong.

Also, it was noted that the Exchange Fund has borrowed funds through the issue of bills and notes and has essentially created by itself a world of short-term financial instruments. It did this with the purpose of developing its financial markets and now has these available to facilitate control over bank reserve positions by open market operations. It has developed discount window facilities for banks, which means that the HKMA has assumed provisional 'lender of last resort' powers. It can use these powers to bail out failing banks if it chooses to do so, and otherwise manage the aggregate liquidity of the banking system.

There was a brief evaluation of the HKMA as a central bank. These central banking powers now provide Hong Kong with valuable options to keep its linked exchange rate system if it likes, or to change to an alternative floating exchange rate system. Hong Kong has all of the necessary powerful central banking mechanisms available should it decide that there is a need to implement monetary policies and let the Hong Kong dollar float.

The chapter includes a brief section discussing a sample of relevant research studies.

A Concluding Viewpoint

In the past two decades, Donald Tsang, the former Financial Secretary, and Joseph Yam, as strategist for the development of Hong Kong's financial system, constructed an imposing, solid, and powerful Hong Kong Monetary Authority. They served Hong Kong well.

The author would like now to take the opportunity to lay out for the reader the economic principles he applies as the basis for opposition to Hong Kong pegging of the exchange rate.

The author believes that prices of all resources should be flexible. They can fulfil their function in the allocation of scarce resources effectively only if they are free to move and adjust to shocks of all sorts. Fixing goods prices will, in a short time, lead to shortages or gluts of individual goods. A fixed price that results in a shortage is not a true price, because some people pay black-market prices while others go without; the administered price is therefore not a 'true' price. When one price is fixed, it often leads to the fixing of other prices, say, for substitutes. After several prices are fixed, there will be a demand for the fixing of some factors of production. All of this leads to inefficient resource allocation. This describes the microeconomic situation, and it conforms to fundamental economic principles with which the profession agrees.

The same principles apply to the macroeconomic situation on a larger scale. In the macroeconomy there are essentially four types of price that need to be flexible. They are broad aggregates or indexes of prices reflecting macroeconomic conditions, and they should be kept flexible in order to act as cushions for the random but inevitable shocks that come to a market economy and so that economic resources can be allocated appropriately. They are interest rates, exchange rates, inflation rates, and wage rates.

First, fixing an exchange rate does not permit the prices of imported and exported goods to fluctuate in order to guide resource allocation. Second, when exchange rates are fixed and tied to the US dollar, then local interest rates must fall in line with those in the US in order to keep capital flows steady. If not, arbitrage will eliminate most of the difference. Thus, interest rate levels, like the exchange rate level, will fail to fluctuate appropriately to cushion the economy against changes in local economic conditions.

With no cushion from changing exchange rates or changing interest rate levels, the remaining general cushion is the inflation rate. Keeping exchange rates and interest rates fixed will generally result in a greater volatility in inflation rates. These will be observed mostly in non-traded goods such as property markets in the short run, but will affect traded goods in the long run. While risk and uncertainty about exchange rate movements is reduced under the pegged rate system, risk and uncertainty about inflation, wage rates, and interest rates are increased. Risk and uncertainty are not eliminated by fixing the exchange rate; they are simply shifted to other important macroeconomic variables. This view is in accord with empirical evidence.

Of course, after a period of inflation, governments will be asked to set higher wage rates or, in the case of Hong Kong, import cheap labour from China.

Fundamental economic principles dictate that fixed exchange rates will lead to fixed interest rates, to instability in property markets, inflation, and ultimately labour market problems. Regulations beget regulations. Fixed exchange rates will not provide real economic stability for any economy. They do a disservice because they give an illusion of stability. They obscure the pricing signals needed to guide resource allocation effectively.

In 1983 the fixed rate on the Hong Kong dollar was set too low. As a new American resident of Hong Kong at the time, the author estimated that a rate of HK$6 to the US dollar would have been appropriate. But the low rate of HK$7.8 to the US dollar meant that an export boom followed the pegging. In the meantime, the US economy was in an era of slowly declining interest rates, so as interest rates fell in both the US and Hong Kong there was steady inflation in Hong Kong. Wages rose, and a demand for cheaper labour led to government programmes to import workers. Interest rates on deposits were set at such a low rate that it meant negative real rates of six per cent or so. All of this actually happened in the wake of the pegging of the Hong Kong dollar and was predicted by fundamental economic principles.

Booming economies eventually stop booming. Not long after Hong Kong returned to China in 1997, the local economy experienced problems. These problems followed on the heels of difficulties in other Asian economies, and there was a bout of speculation against the Hong Kong dollar that the HKMA promptly analysed and quickly eliminated using its central bank powers. Declining property prices held the economy down; however, as this is written, in March 2002, modest economic problems continue to push the economy to the brink of recession.

Discussion Questions

1. Explain each of the terms in the Equation of Exchange.
2. Does money growth predict changes in the level of prices? What does the evidence show?
3. The modern Theory of the Demand for Money is based on a single equation. Explain each of its terms.
4. Draw and label free-hand graphs of the demand and supply for money. Describe how interest rate levels will change with an increase in the supply of real money balances.
5. Use similar graphs as in Question 4 to describe how an increase in Gross Domestic Product affects the level of interest rates.
6. Briefly describe how money is measured in Hong Kong. What are the special difficulties associated with measuring money in Hong Kong? Briefly explain.
7. What is a 'monetary base'? What are the components of the monetary base in Hong Kong?
8. Explain how the Exchange Fund collects seigniorage on the bank notes circulating in Hong Kong.
9. Do banks earn seigniorage from creating deposit money in Hong Kong? Explain.
10. What are the typical duties assigned to central banks around the world?
11. Explain the various tools of control over the money supply now in the possession of the Hong Kong Monetary Authority.

12. Discuss whether or not Hong Kong needs a central bank. What options does it provide for managers of Hong Kong's money supply? Explain.

Keywords

central banking, functions of
currency board
discount window lending
Equation of Exchange
fixed rate of exchange system
gold standard
Hong Kong Monetary Authority (HKMA)
inflation tax
liquidity adjustment facility
monetary base
money, definition of
pegged rate system
quantity theory of money
real time gross settlement (RTGS)
reputation
seigniorage, earned by banks in Hong Kong
time consistency
US dollar swap deposits

PART I

Financial Institutions and Intermediaries

3. The Banking System

HUGH THOMAS

Introduction

In Hong Kong, banking is important because it provides not only essential services to the local economy but also additional employment and income from exporting financial services to the region. Of the largest hundred banks in the world, eighty of them are represented in Hong Kong's banking sector. Table 3.1 provides evidence of the importance of the sector.

Table 3.1 The Importance of Banking and Finance to Hong Kong

Item	Hong Kong	USA
Balance on Services/GDP (%)	11%	1%
Labour Force in Finance (%)*	14%	5%
Stock Market Capitalization to GDP	3.7	1.8
Stock Market Capitalization in Finance (%)	29%	18%
Annual Clearing House Turnover per capita (US$)	1,854,243	1,503,073
Population Per Deposit Taking Financial Institution	27,092	29,335
Population Per Branch	4,533	3,936
Banking Assets Per Capita (US$)**	116,026	27,901
Banking Assets/GDP (ratio) **	5.21	0.80

* Includes banking, insurance, and real estate and other business services.
** Includes all Deposit Taking Companies
Sources of data: HKMA *Monthly Statistical Bulletin* Statistical Appendices (various issues); Hong Kong Financial Services Bureau; US Department of Commerce; US Federal Deposit Insurance Corporation; US Federal Reserve; OECD.

Hong Kong is an open economy with a negative balance of trade in goods that is more than offset by its positive balance of trade in services—making up eleven per cent of its gross domestic product (GDP). The export of financial services is a key part of the strong positive balance in services.[1] Finance and related services employ fourteen per cent of Hong Kong's labour force, almost three times the relative employment in finance in the US. The Hong Kong stock market is more than twice as important as the US stock market, in terms of capitalization relative to GDP. Financial institutions—dominated by banks[2]—make up twenty-nine per cent of the capitalization of the Hong Kong stock market, again substantially larger than the figure for the US. In terms of payments *per capita*, the number of persons per deposit-taking institution, and the number of persons per branch, Hong Kong is roughly on a par with the United States: the retail branch network offers about the same coverage in Hong Kong as it does in the US. But in terms of the size of banks' assets relative to the population and the GDP, banking is far more important to the Hong Kong economy than it is to the US economy. These facts reflect the importance of Hong Kong as a regional banking and financial centre.

When people say that Hong Kong is a regional banking and financial centre, they refer mainly to wholesale financial activities. Wholesale transactions, where the smallest transaction is, say, a million US dollars, naturally gravitate to international centres. These centres have educated and motivated financial workforces experienced in working together in environments conducive to providing financial services. Experience breeds experience, so international financial centres tend to become more concentrated through time thanks to advances in telecommunications. Not surprisingly, in a twenty-four-hour world consisting of roughly eight-hour working days, we find that the financial world is tri-polar, with three world financial centres that are more or less eight hours apart: London, New York, and Tokyo. These centres developed in part because they had the least to fear and the most to gain from international financial contact. As the financial capitals of the United Kingdom, the United States, and Japan respectively, they serviced the capital flows of the three largest successive capital exporters of the twentieth century. They achieved the critical mass of talent that still sustains their financial service exports.

For smaller or specialized transactions, as well as transactions needing closer customer contact, a second (regional) level of concentration has emerged. Regulatory constraints in neighbouring countries have often stimulated the growth of these regional centres, which can act as havens for capital that avoids taxation. Like Frankfurt, Luxembourg, Zurich, Bahrain, Bombay, Singapore, and recently Shanghai, Hong Kong is a regional financial centre. Hong Kong has competitive advantages over its geographically closest rivals—its legal heritage, accumulated expertise, and unfettered markets distinguish it from Shanghai, while its size, regional stability, and close links with China give it an edge over Singapore. Hong Kong also benefits from belonging to the region whose world financial capital, Tokyo, is mired in chronic recession exacerbated by a weak banking system (see Nakaso, 2001).

What Is Banking?

Banking in Hong Kong, as elsewhere in the world, gives the economy liquidity—the ability to exchange economic claims with minimal cost. When we lend money to non-financial corporations, we are conscious of lending, but when retail depositors lend money to a bank, they believe that they actually have 'money in the bank'. Banks' debts are defined as society's money—the most liquid asset that most members of society can hold. When we wish to make large payments using this money, we must access the payments system through banks. Because banking provides essential services—taking deposits, making payments, and a host of ancillary services—banking business is highly regulated. Regulation is most stringent at the retail level, where individuals have little choice and less ability to fully assess their choices; at the wholesale level, the disciplining of banking is left more effectively to the markets.

Banking is defined in law and regulated by the government. The banking law of Hong Kong is the Banking Ordinance, which is implemented by the Hong Kong Monetary Authority (HKMA), Hong Kong's central bank.[3] The Banking Ordinance defines 'banking business' as:

1. Receiving from the general public money on current, deposit, savings, or other similar account repayable on demand or within less than three months, and/or
2. Paying or collecting cheques drawn by or paid in by customers.

Although banks are lenders, lending does not define banking. Any company or person can lend, but only a bank can take deposits, clear cheques, and hold clearing balances with the central bank.[4]

In addition to providing these defined banking business services, banks lend. They also may manage financial assets for their customers and make markets in financial assets. In so doing, they are provide investment banking services—underwriting, issuing, and making markets, and advising companies as to how they should tap and invest in money and capital markets. Some banks also provide insurance. As insurers, they underwrite life and general risk insurance and sell insurance to the risk-averse. In executing these diverse roles, they frequently interact with government regulators as well as the HKMA in its role as banking regulator; insurance activities come into the ambit of the Commissioner of Insurance. Public securities must meet the requirements of the Securities and Futures Commission and, if they are listed on an exchange, of that particular exchange. Pension funds must meet the requirements of the Mandatory Provident Fund Authority.

These activities take different forms at wholesale and retail levels. Most individual depositors and lenders—you, me, most of the population, and small and medium-sized enterprises—function at the retail level.

Table 3.2 shows some of the services provided by banks. It is worth noting that the defined services of banking—the services shaded dark grey in Table 3.2—are not the only or even the majority of services performed by banks. The defined banking services may not be the most profitable, and they may not be the centre of focus of a particular banking manager wishing to maximize shareholder wealth.

In Hong Kong, companies can perform defined banking services and use the word 'bank' in their names only if they are registered by the HKMA as Authorized Institutions (AIs). There are three types of AI: banks, Restricted Licence Banks (RLBs), and Deposit Taking Companies (DTCs), although it is likely that in the near future DTCs and RLBs will be combined into a single type of restricted bank (see KPMG Barents (1998) and HKMA (1999)). Banks are allowed to perform all banking functions. In particular, they can take all deposits from retail customers. The activities of RLBs and DTCs are restricted to wholesale deposit-taking activities and, in the case

Table 3.2 Banking Services

Service	Retail	Wholesale
Payments	ATMs, cheque clearing, phone banking	Real time gross settlement
Deposit Taking	Cheque & savings A/C	Large corporates and governments
Lending	Credit cards, mortgages SME loans	Large corporates and governments
Asset management	Fund sales, custody	Fund management, pension management, custody
Market making	Retail brokerage	OTC trading, exchange member trading
Underswriting and placing of securities	N/A	Stocks, bonds, securitization
Advising	Financial planning	Merger and Acquisition advising
Insurance	Life, property, casuality	Large event risk, reinsurance

Decreasing need for regulatory oversight ▷

Note: ▉ Darker-shaded areas denote defined banking services
       ▉ Lighter-shaded area denotes traditional but not defined banking services

Table 3.3 Authorized Institution Restrictions by Type

	Banks	RLBs	DTCs
Minimum Deposit Amount	No restriction	HK$500,000	HK$100,000
Minimum Deposit Maturity	No restriction	No restriction	3 months
Minimum Share Capital of AI incorporated in Hong Kong	150 million	100 million	25 million
Minimum Assets of AI incorporated outside HK	US$16 billion	N/A	N/A
Minimum deposits of AI incorporated in Hong Kong	HK$3 billion	N/A	N/A
Minimum assets of AI incorporated in Hong Hong	HK$ 4 billion	N/A	N/A
Maximum Basel Capital Adequacy Ratio to be applied	12%	16%	16%
Registration Fee	474340	384270	384270

Source of data: Banking Ordinance; HKMA Monthly Statistical Bulletin Statistical Appendices (various issues).

of DTCs, deposits with terms of greater than three months. Even if a DTC wishes to repay a deposit before its three-month maturity, it is prevented from doing so.

Most DTCs and RLBs are owned by banks, either foreign or domestic. While there are no restrictions on the kinds of lending of the different types of AI, DTCs tend to focus on consumer finance, trade finance, and securities business, while RLBs tend to specialize in investment banking and merchant banking activities.[5] Table 3.3 details the restrictions of AIs by type, while Table 3.4 shows the changing numbers of AIs over the last decade.

As RLBs and DTCs are institutions catering more to wholesale banking activities, they are restricted in their ability to deal with retail customers and are subject to a lesser administrative burden by the HKMA.

In supervising the AIs, the HKMA requires various filings, and conducts both on- and off-site investigations generally in conformity with international standards of banking supervision. It also implements two statutory requirements: liquidity and solvency. As banks provide society with liquidity, it is natural that they themselves face liquidity risk with the average liquidity of their liabilities exceeding that of their assets. To be prudent, banks tend to keep levels of liquidity high to avoid losing money through forced sales of illiquid assets for a loss. In Hong Kong, they are legally required to hold as liquid assets not less than twenty-five per cent of qualifying liabilities (largely deposits).[6]

The solvency requirement is also statutory. Banks are required to maintain equity capital of not less than eight per cent of risk assets. This ratio and the definitions of 'equity capital' and 'risk assets' are consistent with the recommendations of the Basel Committee of the Bank for International Settlements (BIS). The BIS, a central bank for central banks, serves as a convenient forum for co-ordinating international financial regulatory policy. Neither the Basel Committee nor the BIS has the authority to impose its standards on Hong Kong or any other jurisdiction, yet the standards are agreed to through lengthy processes of transparent international consultation by the world's leading central bankers. The process is currently under way for a revised set of capital adequacy standards to be implemented by the end of 2006.

Most jurisdictions in the world believe that regulatory harmonization is essential for efficiency in the global financial system, so most countries implement these accords, albeit with some modifications. The HKMA, for example, additionally reserves the right to require banks and DTCs/RLBs to maintain at least twelve per cent and sixteen per cent capital respectively to risk assets.

Banks, Liquidity, and the Payments System

Banks are a necessary part of making all but the smallest payments, for which coins issued by the HKMA can be used. In Hong Kong, banks are

Table 3.4   Number and Types of Authorized Institutions

	Banks		Restricted Licence Banks		Deposit Taking Companies		
	Banks Incorporated in Hong Kong	Banks Incorporated outside Hong Kong	RLBs Incorporated in Hong Kong	RLBs Incorporated outside Hong Kong	DTCs Incorporated in Hong Kong	DTCs Incorporated outside Hong Kong	Total
1990	30	138	32	14	187	4	405
1991	30	133	31	22	155	4	375
1992	30	134	33	23	143	4	367
1993	32	140	33	24	139	3	371
1994	32	148	35	28	134	3	380
1995	31	154	37	26	129	3	380
1996	31	151	38	24	121	3	368
1997	31	149	39	27	113	2	361
1998	31	141	35	25	99	2	333
1999	31	125	33	25	71	0	285
2000	31	123	28	20	61	0	263
2001	29	119	28	20	55	0	251

critical to the money supply because they issue as liabilities (1) banknotes and (2) deposits. Banks further hold as the most liquid component of their assets high-power money.

Banknotes

Banknotes are issued by three commercial note-issuing banks—the Bank of China, the Hongkong and Shanghai Banking Corporation, and Standard Chartered Bank—and constitute non-interest-bearing liabilities of those banks. When these banks issue notes, they are required to submit US$100 for every HK$780 they issue to the HKMA for the account of the Exchange Fund. In return, the HKMA gives the issuing banks non-interest-bearing Exchange Fund Certificates of Indebtedness. The note-issuing banks hold these Certificates of Indebtedness as assets until they retire the banknotes, at which point they redeem their Certificates of Indebtedness, receiving from the HKMA US$100 per HK$780 notes issued.

This process accomplishes two goals: it ensures that Hong Kong dollar banknotes are fully backed by US dollars held by the Exchange Fund at the pegged rate of HK$7.8 per US$1.00, and it gives to note-issuing banks no unfair advantage of funding their assets with non-interest-bearing banknotes—although they receive 'free' advertising by having their names on the Hong Kong currency, and the benefit of such advertising more than offsets the cost of note issuance. The gains of seigniorage—the right to issue currency—accrue to the Hong Kong government through the Exchange Fund.

Table 3.5 Aggregate Balance Sheet of All Hong Kong AIs (as at end of January 2002) (HK$ billions)

ASSETS	Hong Kong Dollars	Foreign Currency	Total	LIABILITIES	Hong Kong Dollars	Foreign Currency	Total
Notes and coins	14	2	16	Amount due to AIs in Hong Kong	290	171	461
Amount due from AIs in Hong Kong	290	171	461	Amount due to banks abroad	155	1,312	1,467
Amount due from banks abroad	112	2,039	2,151	Deposits from customers	1,815	1,504	3,319
Loans and advances to customers	1,656	526	2,183	of which issued bank notes	113	0	113
Negotiable certificates of deposit held	90	41	131	Negotiable certificates of deposit outstanding	138	38	176
Acceptances and bills of exchange held	2	40	42	Other debt instruments outstanding	2	44	46
Floating rate notes and commercial paper held	45	218	263	Capital, reserves, and other liabilities	541	177	718
Government bills, notes, and bonds held	247	71	319				
of which Certificates of Indebtedness	113	0	113				
Other debt instruments held	100	221	321				
Investments in shareholdings	46	3	49				
Interest in land and buildings	64	1	65				
Other assets	115	74	188				
Total assets	2,780	3,407	6,187	Total liabilities	2,941	3,247	6,187

Source of data: HKMA *Monthly Statistical Bulletin* Statistical Appendices (various issues). Columns may not add up precisely due to rounding errors.

Table 3.5 shows that the note-issuing banks in January 2002 had a liability of HK$113 billion for banknotes outstanding. These banknotes outstanding are essentially non-interest-bearing deposits, against which the note-issuing banks held assets of HK$113 billion of Certificates of Indebtedness issued by the Exchange Fund. Table 3.6 shows how the Exchange Fund records those HK$113 billion Certificates of Indebtedness on its own balance sheet. The Certificates of Indebtedness are shown as non-interest-bearing debt.

Table 3.6   Exchange Fund Balance Sheet as at January 2002
(HK$ million)

ASSETS	
Foreign currency assets	882,299
Hong Kong dollar assets	109,243
Total assets	991,542
LIABILITIES	
Certificates of Indebtedness	113,405
Coins in circulation	5,744
Balance of banking system (clearing balances)	495
Exchange Fund Bills and Notes	115,967
Placements by banks and other financial institutions	40,458
Placements by other HKSAR government institutions	399,737
Placements by Hong Kong statutory bodies	4,975
Other liabilities	12,596
Total liabilities	693,377
Accumulated surplus	298,165

Source of data: HKMA *Monthly Statistical Bulletin* Statistical Appendices (various issues).

Bank Deposits

Most payments (by dollar amount) are not effected with coins or banknotes. Payments of large sums using coins or notes would be clumsy, inconvenient, and insecure. Large payments are effected by transferring ownership of deposits. Because of this, economists define bank deposits, together with banknotes and coins, as making up the external money supply.[7] In contrast, the internal money supply (also called the 'monetary base' or 'high power money') is the obligation of the central bank.

To make most payments, bank customers give orders to banks with whom they have deposits to debit those deposit accounts and credit the accounts of the payees. These orders can be in cheques, other drafts, or electronic instructions. If the accounts of both the payer and the payee are in the same bank, payment is simple: the bank debits the payer's account and credits the payee's. If the payer's and the payee's accounts are in two different banks, however, payment is made through the clearing and settlement system. In Hong Kong, the Exchange Fund is at the centre of the clearing and settlement system.

All banks in Hong Kong have settlement accounts directly with the Exchange Fund. These deposits that banks hold with the Exchange Fund are called 'clearing balances' and in aggregate they are known as the 'banking balance' or the 'balance of the banking system'. Just as bank deposits are liabilities of banks, so the banking balance is a liability of the Exchange Fund. Table 3.6 shows that at the end of January 2002 the banking balance stood at HK$495 million. Although banks' clearing accounts are the deposits of the Exchange Fund, it is Hong Kong Interbank Clearing Ltd—a company owned jointly by the HKMA and Hong Kong Association of Banks—that operates Hong Kong's clearing and settlement system. Hong Kong's Hong Kong dollar clearing and settlement system is composed of three subsystems, as summarized in Table 3.7.

Table 3.7   Hong Kong's Hong Kong Dollar Clearing and Settlement System

Name of Component	Securities clearing and settlement System	Electronic Debit System (EDS)	Clearing House Automated Transfer System (CHATS)
Input	Paper	Retail Electronic	Wholesale Electronic
Types of Transaction	Cheques, drafts, bills	Autopay, electronic clearing items generated by the securities clearing and settlement system, point-of-sale clearing and settlement system	Foreign exchange, payment for securities, banks obtaining clearing balances
Frequency of Clearing	Daily batch	Daily batch	Continuous
Reporting of balances to bank	Daily	Daily	Real time
Timing of Settlement relative to processing	Next day	Next Day	Simultaneous
Effect on balance with Exchange Fund	Net payments debited or credited	Net payments debited or credited	Gross payments debited or credited
Percentage of Transactions by Value	6%	6%	88%

High Power Money: Ultimate Liquidity

The previous section noted that the largest component of external money is the deposits held by non-banks with banks. In contrast, internal money— which is also known as the 'monetary base' and 'high power money'—is the set of assets of ultimate settlement in an economy. High power money includes coins and notes that are obligations of the currency-issuing government as well as clearing balances with the central bank. In Hong Kong, for a bank to make payment to another bank in the clearing system, it must have a positive clearing balance with the Exchange Fund of no less than the amount of the desired payment. If the paying bank does not have sufficient clearing balances, it can obtain them in three ways: (1) buy clearing balances with US dollars in the foreign exchange market; (2) borrow clearing balances from the Exchange Fund (banks borrow from the Exchange Fund by using Discount Window Sale and Repurchase Agreements, or repos); (3) borrow clearing balances from other banks in the Hong Kong interbank market (for an interest rate equal to the Hong Kong Interbank Offer Rate).

The Foreign Exchange Market

The foreign exchange market is a global over-the-counter market—a virtual market without a formal location made up of telephone and data linkages between buyers and sellers, most of whom are banks. Each market-making bank frequently updates quotes on information networks such as Reuters for prices at which they will buy (low) and sell (high) foreign exchange. Foreign exchange markets are highly liquid, so the difference between the buy and the sell prices are usually only a few hundredths of a per cent. In a purchase or sale of foreign exchange, a bank exchanges one currency for another. Payment is made through each currency's payments and settlement system, with settlement being in the appropriate currency's clearing balance.[8] For example, a bank requiring Hong Kong dollar clearing balances can sell US dollars to a second bank wishing to buy US dollars.

Most of the transactions in the foreign exchange markets take place between commercial banks, but some transactions involve central banks. The Hong Kong dollar is officially pegged to the US dollar at HK$7.8 per US$1. To effect the peg, the HKMA identifies a narrow target zone around HK$7.8 (e.g., 7.79 to 7.81). It lets the markets set their own Hong Kong dollar prices for US dollars within that narrow target range but intervenes when the market price strays outside the target zone. The HKMA buys US dollars when the value of the US dollar in Hong Kong dollar terms strays below that target zone, and sells US dollars when the US dollar strays above that target zone. When the HKMA buys US dollars, it pays for them with Exchange Fund clearing balances, increasing the amount of clearing balances in the system (i.e., increasing liquidity). When it sells US dollars, it receives Exchange Fund clearing balances. This is equivalent to the Exchange Fund 'buying back' its own debt. Figures 3.1a and 3.1b show the liquidity increasing and liquidity reducing operations of the HKMA in buying and selling US dollars against Hong Kong dollars.

Figure 3.1a Liquidity-increasing Effect of Purchase of US Dollars by the HKMA

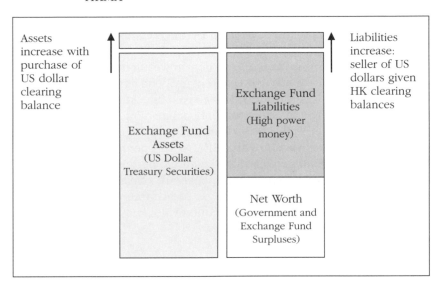

Figure 3.1b Liquidity-decreasing Effect of Sale of US Dollars by the HKMA

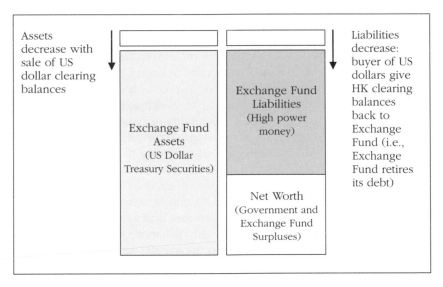

The Discount Window

Banks can obtain clearing balances by borrowing them from the Exchange Fund. They do so by using a Discount Window Sale and Repurchase

Agreement or Repo of Exchange Fund Bills (EFB) and Exchange Fund Notes (EFNs). The borrowing bank sells EFB or EFNs, with an agreement to buy back those EFBs and EFNs at a future time for a higher price. The difference between the price at which the security is sold and the price at which it is repurchased is the rate of interest. This interest rate is quoted by the HKMA as the Discount Window Base Rate. EFBs and EFNs, issued by the Exchange Fund and purchased by the bank as liquidity reserves securities, are the Hong Kong equivalent of Treasury Bills, Notes, and Bonds in the US. (Unlike the US Treasury, however, the HKMA does not issue its paper to raise funds for government spending; it issues EFBs and EFNs to provide a liquid riskless set of fixed-rate instruments for bank liquidity management and bond market benchmarking.) Banks keep their holdings of EFBs and EFNs in the Central Moneymakers Unit, a computerized depository run by the HKMA. This permits EFBs and EFNs to be repoed in real time for clearing balances. Because of this ability to convert EFBs and EFNs cheaply and quickly into clearing balances, they are also considered in Hong Kong to be part of the high-power money supply, the ultimate liquidity in the economy.

The Interbank Market

Banks borrow money in wholesale and retail deposit markets and invest that money by lending in various credit markets. They hope to earn a sufficient spread—after deducting expected loan losses and administrative costs—over their own cost of funds to provide attractive returns to equity holders. In lending, investing, and fulfilling other payments, banks' funding needs are seldom exactly met by the natural funding sources of their customer deposits plus long-term debt and equity. Either they have excess funds that they desire to sell (i.e., lend), or need to buy (i.e., borrow) to meet payments commitments. Banks borrow from and lend to one another in interbank markets. In the US onshore markets, the banks' buying and selling of 'good funds' or 'Fed Funds' (i.e., clearing balances within the Federal Reserve Bank system, the US central bank) from each other takes place in an over-the-counter interbank market that the Americans call the 'Fed Funds Market'. In Hong Kong, it is simply called the interbank market.

The Hong Kong interbank market, like the foreign exchange market, is an over-the-counter market. With a daily turnover of HK$174 billion (as at the end of 2000), the market provides a critical venue for redistributing Hong Kong dollar liquidity (Financial Services Bureau, 1999). Banks lend on an unsecured basis for periods ranging from one day (the overnight market) to in excess of one year. Banks active in the market will quote both the Hong Kong Interbank Offer Rate (HIBOR) and a lower Hong Kong Interbank Bid Rate (HIBID), with the difference between HIBOR and HIBID at any time being, say, one tenth of a per cent. HIBOR quotes are indicative, subject to the approval of the creditworthiness of the borrower. Settlement is made by crediting the Exchange Fund clearing account of the purchasing bank.

Traditional Banking Activities: Deposit Taking and Lending

Interest Rates

An interest rate is a price for borrowing money. Like any other price, it is affected by supply and demand. If there is, at a given interest rate, more money supplied to a given credit market than borrowed, the market experiences excess liquidity until either demand increases or the interest rate drops to the point where the market clears. Figure 3.2 shows the fluctuation of several key interest rates in Hong Kong since the last major reform of interest rate structure in late 1998.

As discussed above, banks can borrow funds directly from the public via deposits, from each other, via the interbank market, and from the government via Discount Window repos.

Figure 3.2 Monthly Average Interest Rates

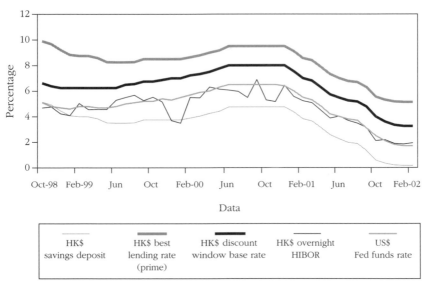

<table>
<tr><td>——</td><td>━━━</td><td>━━━</td><td>——</td><td>——</td></tr>
<tr><td>HK$
savings deposit</td><td>HK$ best
lending rate
(prime)</td><td>HK$ discount
window base rate</td><td>HK$ overnight
HIBOR</td><td>US$
Fed funds rate</td></tr>
</table>

Source of data: HKMA *Monthly Statistical Bulletin* Statistical Appendices (various issues).

Retail Deposits

Retail savings deposits form the cheapest source of funds for banks. In aggregate, the retail deposit base of banks is stable: retail customer withdrawals are generally offset by other retail customer deposits. So banks consider retail deposits to be core funding: stable and reliable. Retail depositors differentiate between banks largely based on the deposit rates and levels of service offered by those banks. In general, a retail depositor will not analyse the creditworthiness of the bank to which she lends her deposit money. If the bank fails, she will be less likely to have withdrawn her funds than the wholesale depositor who carried out a credit analysis of his bank, and she will lose more, relative to her wealth, than the wholesale depositor who diversified his investments. Recognizing this inequity, most developed countries have some form of retail deposit insurance.[9] Although implicit deposit insurance has characterized Hong Kong for many years in that the Hong Kong government has facilitated the rescue of failing banks in certain cases (see Beecham, 1996), in 2003 or early 2004 Hong Kong is scheduled to implement explicit deposit insurance for the first HK$100,000 of deposits (HKMA, 2000).

Traditionally, retail deposits are gathered from disbursed branch networks. The HKMA does not allow banks newly branching into Hong Kong to set up branches in more than one building, a policy that restricts their ability to compete in the retail market. In recent years, though, this condition has been relaxed by allowing a back-office operation and a regional headquarters to be sited in other buildings, as well as by exempting non-banking activities (such as advisory work) from the condition. The policy is also being eroded by competitive pressures, technology (such as Internet and phone banking), and bank consolidation.

Each bank sets its own retail savings deposit rate (and schedules of time-deposit rates) with reference to its funding needs, market rates of interest, and the rates of its competition.[10] As Figure 3.2 shows, HIBOR (the interbank rate) tends to fluctuate, occasionally dropping below the savings rate at times of high liquidity. During the 1997–8 Asian financial crisis, speculation against the Hong Kong dollar constrained liquidity so much that HIBOR at one point reached 260 per cent overnight. Since the reforms of September 1998, HIBOR has been far less volatile.

HIBOR and the Fed Funds Rate

If the Hong Kong dollar's peg to the US dollar were 100 per cent credible, US interest rates quoted at the same time for the same credit risk would equal HK interest rates. If rates differed, profit-seeking banks could simply borrow in the cheaper currency market and lend in the more expensive currency until the rates converged. But the peg is not one hundred per cent credible, so such profit-seeking is risky.

For the peg to be one hundred per cent credible, there could be no doubt in the minds of market participants that the Convertibility Undertaking would be honoured by the HKMA. The Convertibility Undertaking is the promise by the HKMA that it will convert Exchange Fund clearing balances and Certificates of Indebtedness at the rate of HK$7.8 per US dollar. If you look at the equation below, you can confirm that the HKMA has the ability to fully honour the Convertibility Undertaking. Note that:

$$\text{High power money} = \begin{array}{c} \text{Certificates of Indebtedness +} \\ \text{Coins in circulation +} \\ \text{Balance of banking system +} \\ \text{Exchange Fund Bills and Notes} \end{array} = \$235 \text{ billion}$$

That HK$235 billion obligation of the Exchange Fund commitments is just twenty-seven per cent of the total amount of foreign currency assets of the Exchange Fund. This calculation demonstrates that the peg *can* be fully and effectively defended today, if there is the will to defend it. The market generally believes that the Convertibility Undertaking will be maintained. The financial market stability induced by the 'certainty' of the peg strengthens the credibility of Hong Kong as an international financial centre. Yet there remains appreciable doubt concerning the peg. For example, what if the Hong Kong government decided that property owners facing negative assets in their mortgaged homes, who would benefit from inflation induced by devaluation of the Hong Kong dollar, were more important than the supporters of the current peg? Then the government would be tempted to devalue the Hong Kong dollar. Such doubts in the minds of investors and speculators allow Hong Kong interest rates to stray from US interest rates. As Figure 3.2 shows, the extent of that straying in the relatively calm atmosphere from late 1998 to the present is modest: overnight HIBOR has oscillated around the US dollar Fed Funds rate.

The Discount Window Base Rate

Like central banks in other jurisdictions, the HKMA acts as a lender of last resort,[11] supplying liquidity to solvent clearing banks against high quality securities. Prior to 1998, the HKMA supplied liquidity through the Liquidity Adjustment Facility. In September 1998, in response to currency speculators draining Hong Kong dollar liquidity to manipulate share prices, the HKMA implemented reforms both to restrict fluctuations of liquidity and strengthen the peg. The measures explicitly extended the Convertibility Undertaking to the banking balance, replaced the Liquidity Adjustment Facility with the Discount Window, removed restrictions on repeated borrowing at the Discount Window through EFN and EFB repos, undertook that new EFNs and EFBs would only be issued when Hong Kong experienced a net inflow of funds, and introduced higher discount rates for clearing banks repoing higher percentages of their EFNs and EFBs. The HMKA sets the Discount Window Base Rate at the higher of (1) the US dollar Fed Funds Target Rate (the rate announced by the Federal Reserve Board as its target for the Fed Funds) plus 1.5 per cent, and (2) the average of the five-day moving averages of (a) overnight HIBOR and (b) one-month HIBOR. As Figure 3.2 shows, this formula has allowed the Base Rate to float above commercial borrowing rates, so that a bank making use of the lender of last resort pays a penalty rate of interest.

Prime and HIBOR Loans

Banks lending Hong Kong dollars in Hong Kong set their lending rates with respect to two different interest rate bases: HIBOR and prime (also known as the 'best lending rate'). Corporate bank loans are frequently set at HIBOR plus a spread. This allows a bank to fund itself in the interbank market at HIBOR and enjoy the spread with no interest rate or funding risk, assuming the bank maintains its creditworthiness in the interbank markets.

As Figure 3.3 shows, the largest loan category on the balance sheets of Hong Kong banks is residential mortgage loans. Most of these loans, other consumer loans, and some corporate loans are priced relative to the prime. Unlike HIBOR, which is set by the supply and demand of banks in the wholesale markets, prime is set by each bank at its own discretion. But both 'prime' and the 'best lending rate' are misnomers. Banks are unable to enjoy the five per cent spread between the savings rate and prime, or even the approximately three per cent spread between HIBOR and prime. Especially in a slow economy such as that of the period 1998 to 2002, competition between banks for scarce creditworthy assets forced the interest rates of such good assets to be priced below prime. New retail mortgage loans, for example, are frequently priced at prime *minus* two per cent or more.

The Lending Portfolio of Hong Kong Banks

Figure 3.3 shows not only the importance of retail mortgage lending to domestic Hong Kong bank assets, but also that the dependence on retail mortgage loans is increasing. Moreover, when combined with loans financing buildings, construction, and property development, retail and wholesale property lending accounts for over fifty per cent of the exposures

Figure 3.3 AI Loans to Hong Kong Borrowers by Sector

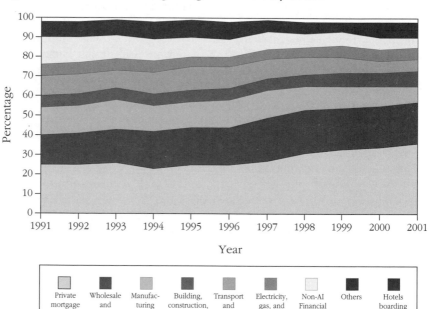

Source of data: HKMA *Monthly Statistical Bulletin* Statistical Appendices (various issues).

of Hong Kong domestic lending. Diversification reduces risk; yet for lenders in Hong Kong the opportunities for diversification are limited. Without diversification, small domestic AIs must hold more capital than they would need if they enjoyed diversification. Larger domestic AIs are pushed to seek diversification opportunities by expanding abroad. The HKMA has expressed concern about the exposure of its AIs to real estate, but it is unable to reduce that exposure without eroding bank profitability and putting further downward pressure on real estate prices.[12]

Hong Kong as an International Loan Booking Centre

One of the striking trends evident in Table 3.4 is the dramatic decline in the number of AIs in Hong Kong over the last decade. Whereas the numbers of banks and RLBs incorporated in Hong Kong have been roughly constant—declining by only about eight per cent—the number of DTCs has fallen by seventy per cent. Figure 3.4 shows that this decline is repeated in the foreign currency loans of Hong Kong. Whereas domestic loans have seen steady growth, plateauing in 1997 when the Asian financial crisis struck, foreign currency loans dropped from a peak of HK$2.5 trillion in 1995 by seventy-five per cent to just over HK$600 billion in 2002. This dramatic decline has been caused by banking consolidation and offshore loan reflux to onshore markets—especially among Japanese banks. While the dollar principal amount is large, the impact on the profitability of the Hong Kong banking sector is far more muted.

Figure 3.4 Total Loans Booked by Hong Kong AIs

Source of data: HKMA *Monthly Statistical Bulletin* Statistical Appendices (various issues).

Prior to the Asian financial crisis, fifty-six per cent of Hong Kong AIs' foreign claims were to Japan. These claims were largely lent back to Japanese companies in an exercise intended to avoid Japanese domestic loan regulation. In fact, Hong Kong served as a 'round-trip' offshore point for Japanese banks' domestic lending to Japanese corporations. Japanese onshore deregulation and an absolute decline in Japanese lending to domestic customers have resulted in the dramatic collapse (from a statistical point of view) of Hong Kong lending (McCauley and Mo, 1999).

Globalization of Traditional Banking Services

Traditional banking is an information business. Processing information about account balances, payments, securities, credit information, risk management, market making, and so on requires large and recurring investment costs in hardware, software, and training and involves strong economies of scale.

Previously, many countries jealously guarded national sovereignty by restricting the activities of non-national banks within their territories. In the 1990s, informed popular opinion the world over changed to embrace freer trade in financial services. Reflecting this change in attitude, the World Trade Organization (WTO)—the international organization that has set and policed the global rules of trade since 1995—turned its attention to trade in services, including, for the first time, banking and other financial services. Since the late 1990s, trade in financial services has been subject to the WTO principles of:

1. Non-discrimination. No member should apply more favourable rules to any other member than to all others. This 'most favoured nation' principle requires that each member receives the same treatment as the most favoured nation.
2. Transparency. Laws and regulations governing trade in services have to be precisely, clearly, and promptly published, and not subject to bureaucratic discretion.
3. National treatment. Members should apply to other member companies the same treatment applied to their own companies.

These three general principles, which are to be found in General Agreement on Tariffs and Trade (GATT) and WTO documents, represent medium-term objectives, not current reality. WTO accepts that members of trading blocs and bilateral treaties (e.g., European Union, NAFTA, and Mercosur) violate non-discrimination. The tendencies of governments the world over to help out their friends, ethnic groups, and political constituencies constantly militates against transparency. When countries deal with sensitive services such as banking, 'national treatment' frequently yields to 'national sovereignty'. The WTO addresses these conflicts by using a ratchet mechanism; WTO member countries explicitly catalogue their existing practices and undertake to liberalize restrictions according to a specific schedule. In no case is a member allowed to increase market protectionism. The end result will be a single world market in financial services, with differentiation based only on cultural and economic realities, not on regulatory barriers.

Smaller Hong Kong banks facing the challenge of globalization have little choice but to consolidate (Carse, 2001). Through consolidation they can achieve economies of scale in information processing and the scale to diversity, which is often denied to a small bank. China, for example, seems to present a natural venue for expansion. Notwithstanding the entry of China into the WTO in 2001 with a commitment to open its markets fully to foreign banking by 2007, the small Hong Kong bank is prevented from entering the huge market to the north. Chinese regulators require foreign banks branching into China to have assets of at least US$20 billion, a requirement that allows only the largest domestic bank,[13] Bank of East Asia, to branch into mainland China.

Non-Traditional Banking Services: Asset Management and Investment Banking

The outlook for non-traditional banking services is more positive than for traditional services.

Asset Management

Among the fastest growing services provided by banks is a non-banking service: asset management. Asset management has always been a part of financial intermediation, at least for the rich. Now, thanks to the information revolution and wealth accumulation, all active members of developed societies use asset management services. The proportion of institutional investor assets—assets of insurance companies, pension funds, trust funds, mutual funds, venture capital funds, and so forth—has increased from about 1.3 times to just under 2.0 times GDP in the US. In Hong Kong, the fund management industry—exclusive of insurance company assets and limited partnership vehicles such as venture capital funds—had grown to over two times GDP by 2001 year end (estimate based on Hong Kong Investment Funds Association reported investment funds aggregate of $311 billion). Hong Kong's asset management industry has enjoyed this growth because it not only serves its rapidly growing retail domestic fund management requirements, but it also serves as a regional asset management centre.

Fund Management

Funds (as the expression is used in 'fund management') are legally separate trusts and companies (often called 'special purpose entities') whose assets are financial securities (e.g. stocks, bonds, and money market instruments)

managed by professional fund managers. Typically, managed funds have
only one class of claimant—the fund investor. The funds do not have
fixed assets: they exist only on paper and in electronic records. The funds
do not have employees: they are managed by management companies
for a fee. Typically, fund management companies set up the funds. In
Hong Kong, the Hong Kong Investment Funds Association represents the
fund management industry. About a third of its members are banks or
subsidiaries of banks, while a sixth of its members are insurance company
subsidiaries. The rest are investment companies, investment banks, and
specialist asset management and fund management companies. Because
of the banks' customer access, however, and their ability to cross-sell
funds with other investment products (including deposits), banks are well
positioned to expand their position in fund management. Figure 3.5 shows
the assets under management of the members of the Hong Kong Investment
Fund Association as at 2001. The distribution of assets reflects the historical
dominance of equities in Hong Kong funds. It is likely, however, that
bond funds will increase their proportion in future as investors seek more
balanced portfolios.

Figure 3.5 Hong Kong Authorized Investment Funds and Unit Trusts

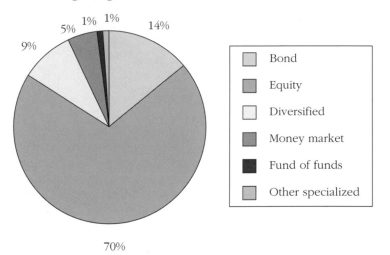

Source of data: Hong Kong Investment Funds Association website: http://www.hkifa.org.hk

Investment funds are increasingly attractive to Hong Kong retail investors
for three main reasons: (1) interest rates on deposits, as shown in Figure
3.2, have dropped to near zero levels; (2) recent investment losses
experienced by retail investors as a result of the Asian financial crisis and
the Internet bubble have dampened retail investors' enthusiasm for
managing portfolios themselves; and (3) the implementation of the
Mandatory Provident Fund (MPF, regulated by the Mandatory Provident
Fund Authority) has made available a rapidly growing pool of capital that
must be invested.

Of these three factors, the MPF is likely to have the greatest medium- and long-term impact. Initiated in 2000, the MPF requires all employees to place five per cent of their income (which employers match with another five per cent) into privately managed, approved retirement savings funds. In the first year of operation, over HK$33 billion was accumulated. This amount will grow rapidly over time to dominate the fund management industry in Hong Kong. Banks account for over forty per cent of Registered Intermediaries, the companies registered to deal with MPF Funds. As the scheme matures, MPF funds will account for an increasing share of the financial assets of Hong Kong, a share that will be managed in large measure by banks.

The MPF scheme typifies the extent to which financial services extend beyond traditional boundaries that separate banks from investment banks from insurance companies. The claims owned by investors in the funds are securities, so they are regulated by the Securities and Futures Commission. The majority of registered MPF intermediaries are insurance companies, who are regulated by the Commissioner of Insurance. Each MPF fund manager invests the fund's money in the type of instruments specified in the fund handbook (i.e., the fund prospectus). In terms of risk, the assets range from bank deposits through money market securities and bonds up to equities. All of these assets, with the exception of bank deposits, are securities ('publicly traded securities' in other jurisdictions).

Private equity, on the other hand, is an institutional investment category where the asset manager invests the money not in securities but in non-traded assets such as real estate, the debt and equity of private corporate buyouts, and partnership capital of venture capital. Hedge funds can also be included under the heading of 'private equity', but commercial banks are not active hedge fund managers. Venture capital is the only institutional source of capital for start-ups and early stage expansion firms, so its development is important to the stimulation of innovation and competition in the production of goods and services. Neither venture capital nor other forms of private equity are specifically regulated. Venture capitalists solicit investment from institutional investors. In the US, public and private pension funds supply about half of venture capital money, typically allocating two or three per cent of their portfolios to these high-risk, high-return investments. The money is pooled into limited partnerships, each of which is run by a general partner—the venture capitalist. The general partner invests the money in early-growth private firms, from which it hopes to earn high returns when the private firms realize their promise of growth and are either bought out by competitors or issue their shares publicly.

Venture capital was virtually unknown in Asia before the 1990s. Today, however, a pool of about US$86 billion (accumulated stock of funds) with an average annual flow of US$7–8 billion is available for Asia. The venture capital market in Asia outside of Japan is centred in Hong Kong. Hong Kong-based funds through the late 1990s obtained new capital commitments of about US$4 billion per year, although that fell to about US$1.6 billion in 2000–1 (*2001 Hong Kong Venture Capital Yearbook*).

Venture capital firms include not only firms specializing exclusively in venture capital, but also a variety of financial institutions, including investment and commercial banks.

Investment Banking

Investment banks underwrite, make markets in, and advise customers about securities. Because understanding and pricing securities involves the valuation of corporations, investment bankers skilled in valuation use their skills in advising corporations how to increase firm value through mergers, acquisitions, divestitures, spin-offs, and other corporate finance transactions grouped under the heading 'M&A' (mergers and acquisitions). Commercial banks traditionally intermediate between funds generators and funds users, and between risk generators and risk absorbers: they book the risks onto their own balance sheets and issue claims against themselves. Investment banks, on the other hand, disintermediate—they expel the financial institution that stands between the user and the owner of funds. Disintermediated securities issued by users of capital are held directly by the providers of capital, but markets in which securities are traded cannot function efficiently without specialist financial institutions providing market making, information, and analysis services. Investment bankers provide these services.

Between investment and wholesale commercial banking is the syndicated loan and the loan sales markets. In the syndicated loans market, underwriters commit to raise sums larger than single banks could comfortably book, and sell off participations to other financial institutions wishing to book the risk. Hong Kong is the regional centre for the syndicated loans market.

In Hong Kong, dealers must be registered with the Securities and Futures Commission, and if they deal in Hong Kong-listed stocks they must be members of the Hong Kong Stock Exchange. Banks may undertake investment banking.[14] In general, commercial banks do not excel at investment banking, although there are exceptions—JP Morgan Chase, Deutsche Bank, UBS, Credit Suisse, and Citigroup are largely commercial banks, but they have strong investment banking units. Investment banking is market-oriented, and its clientele is more global than commercial banks. It is concentrated at the wholesale end of financial services. Issuers of securities seek the most liquid markets into which to issue. Liquidity breeds liquidity. It is possible to predict with confidence that ultimately securities will trade in single global markets serviced by small numbers of large prestigious global investment banks offering the full range of investment banking services—the Bulge Bracket firms[15]—and large numbers of small firms offering specialist services—the boutiques. Hong Kong serves as the regional headquarters for several of the Bulge Bracket firms, whose equity analysts follow regional stocks and whose M&A specialists make corporate advisory pitches to companies throughout greater China.

Investment banking markets are highly cyclical: when markets are 'hot' the deals flow at a tremendous rate, requiring financial professionals to work extremely long hours but for high compensation based in large part on profit-sharing bonuses. When the deal flow dries up, investment banks, far more so than commercial banks, are ready to let their highly paid staff go until the next market boom. In Figure 3.4, the volatility of foreign currency lending from Hong Kong AIs reflects the volatility of the syndicated lending market. Figure 3.6 shows that other investment banking flows— new bond and equity issues, and M&A activity, which generates investment banking advisory fees—are even more volatile. An exceptionally busy year such as 2000 is sandwiched between years with a fraction of the activity. But, over time, investment banking activity is rising on average. It will continue to be centred in Hong Kong if Hong Kong provides the market with the critical mass of financial talent.

Figure 3.6 Hong Kong Investment Banking Indicators

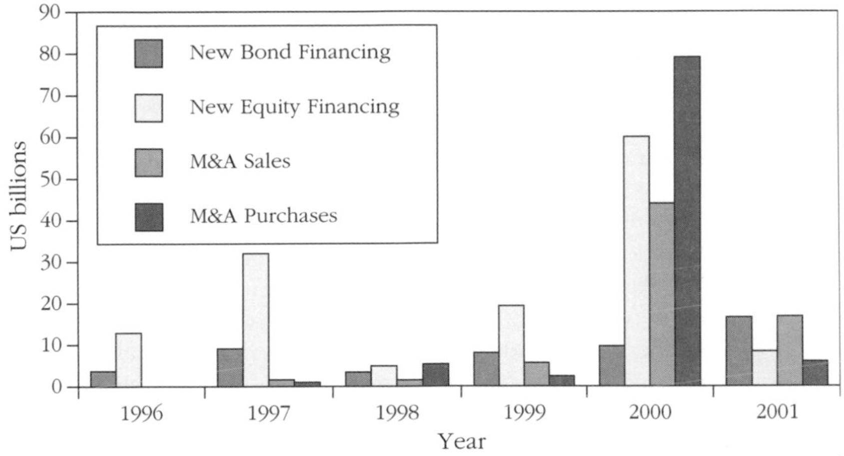

Source of data: Statistics section of the Hong Kong Securities and Futures Commission website: http://www.hksfc.org.hk

Summary

This chapter has discussed the nature of banking and its importance to the Hong Kong economy. Banks traditionally provide society with liquidity through taking deposits and transferring those deposits in the payments system. Hong Kong's banks carry out these roles in conjunction with the HKMA and the Exchange Fund that the HKMA manages. The chapter has specifically explained the banking market–foreign exchange market– domestic money market–government linkages that define Hong Kong's monetary and linked exchange rate systems. The differences between wholesale and retail banking have been discussed, and banking services versus other financial intermediary services provided by banks have been defined, with a brief explation of the regulatory structure of banking in Hong Kong. The globalization of the trade in financial services on the regulatory side through the BIS's Basel Committee on Banking and the regulation of trade in financial services through the WTO have had a direct impact on Hong Kong's banking evolution. In this evolution, non-traditional wholesale banking services—asset management, private equity (including venture capital), and investment banking—will continue to increase in importance.

Discussion Questions

1.   Discuss why each of the nine measures of the importance of banking to the US and the Hong Kong economies in Table 3.1 is a flawed measure.
2.   What services define banking and what services do banks perform in addition to defined banking services?
3.   Explain why the numbers of AIs in Hong Kong and the amount of foreign currency lending from Hong Kong have dropped in recent years.
4.   What is the purpose of Certificates of Indebtedness to AIs and the Exchange Fund?
5.   Describe how HKMA intervention in foreign exchange markets affects the high power money supply, bank liquidity, and interest rates in Hong Kong dollars.
6.   What is the significance of HIBOR to banking in Hong Kong?
7.   Describe the purpose and operation of the Discount Window.
8.   How does the World Trade Organization affect international banking?
9.   How does fund management differ from traditional banking and why is it growing faster than traditional banking?
10. Discuss how investment banks benefit from disintermediation.

Keywords

asset management
Basel Committee of the Bank for International Settlements
best lending rate
Bulge Bracket firms
Central Moneymakers Unit
Certificates of Indebtedness
clearing and settlement system
convertibility undertaking
deposit insurance
discount window base rate
disintermediation
exchange fund bills and notes

Fed Funds market
foreign exchange market
fund management
international loan booking centre
lender of last resort
liquid assets
mergers and acquisitions (M&A)
money supply (monetary base)
over-the-counter market
private equity
qualifying liabilities
repos
retail deposits
risk assets
seigniorage
settlement accounts
statutory liquidity ratio
syndicated loans
trade in services
venture capital

4. Fund Management and Mutual Funds

MATTHEW HARRISON AND QUEENIE YUK-PUI WU

Introduction

Hong Kong is recognized as the leading international fund management centre in Asia. Japan and Australia have bigger domestic markets, but Hong Kong has a larger offshore component. Because of Hong Kong's openness, the industry is dominated by international fund houses. The sector is in a growth phase at the time of writing, driven by the Mandatory Provident Fund (MPF) and increasing retail interest in pooled investment schemes.

This chapter describes the nature of fund management, and global trends in the fund management industry. It looks at the growth of fund management in Hong Kong and at current developments, including a focus on the operations of a typical international fund house. The regulation of fund managers and related intermediaries, such as trustees, is summarized, together with taxation and the regulation of the products. Finally, the chapter discusses Hong Kong's competitive position as a centre for fund management.

What is Fund Management?

'Fund management' is a loose term that is commonly applied to a wide range of activities. The activity of fund management is defined as the management of pooled monies provided by investors, with the objective of providing them with a return from the securities acquired with this pool over the medium to long term in accordance with a pre-set strategy. Key elements of fund management are therefore suggested to be:

1. A third-party relationship with the provider of money (i.e. the investing public).
2. A relatively wide customer base, so that small sums can be pooled and economies of scale achieved.
4. A high degree of discretion in the allocation of the monies provided.
5. A relatively wide scope in terms of permitted investment instruments.
6. Acceptance of a relatively high degree of risk—i.e. variability of return—on the part of the investor.
7. A long-term perspective, i.e. greater than one year.

Fund management under this definition would include some private banking activity, where the discretion and range of investment instruments is higher, but not where the bank merely finds the best deposit rate for the customer. It does not cover the treasury operations of banks or corporates where the objectives, scope, permitted investment instruments, time horizon, and customer base are typically much more limited.

This chapter concentrates on the activities of firms managing mutual funds or portfolios of investments for their clients. Self-managed investment, for example by life insurers, is also accorded some coverage.

Basic Principles of Portfolio Diversification

A mutual fund pools sums of money from investors, which are then invested in financial assets and managed by a professional investment company. Each mutual fund has its own investment objective, such as capital appreciation, high current income, or money market income. The basic Markowitz portfolio model derives the expected rate of return for portfolio of assets and a measure of expected risk (see Markowitz, 1952, 1959), which is the standard deviation of expected rate of return. Markowitz shows that the expected rate of return of a portfolio is the weighted average of the expected return for the individual investments in the portfolio. The standard deviation of a portfolio is a function not only of the standard deviations of the individual investments, but also of the covariance between the rates of return for all pairs of assets in the portfolio. Markowitz finds that risk reduction can only be achieved through combining securities that are not perfectly correlated: that is, their correlation coefficient is less than one. If two securities are perfectly correlated, then the returns of the two securities will go up and down in the same proportion and no diversification benefit can be achieved. Therefore, an optimum portfolio is a combination of investments, each having desirable individual risk-return characteristics that also fit together based on their correlation.

Evaluation of Portfolio Performance[1]

The major goal of portfolio management is to derive above-average returns for a given risk class and diversify the portfolio to eliminate unsystematic risk. Several techniques have been developed to evaluate equity portfolio in terms of both risk and return based on the capital asset pricing model (CAPM). The Treynor measure (Treynor, 1965) considers the excess returns earned per unit of systematic risk. The Sharpe measure (Sharpe, 1966) indicates the excess return per unit of total risk. Jensen (1968) evaluated performance in terms of the systematic risk involved. Following the work of Treynor, Sharpe, and Jensen, Fama (1972) suggested an evaluation model to further break down the portfolio performance. Portfolio managers can add value for their investors in one of two ways: selecting superior securities, or demonstrating superior market timing skills by allocating funds to different asset classes or market segments. Attribution analysis attempts to distinguish which of these factors is the source of the portfolio's overall performance. The total return of the portfolio manager's investment holdings can be compared to the return of a predetermined benchmark portfolio, breaking down the difference into an allocation effect and a selection effect. The various measures are outlined in Figure 4.1.

Figure 4.1 Measures of Portfolio Performance

TREYNOR MEASURE: $T_i = (R_i - R_f) / \beta_i$
Where
T_i : The slope of the portfolio possibility line
R_i : The average rate of return for portfolio i during a specified time period
R_f : The average rate of return on a risk-free investment during a specified time period
β_i: The risk variable beta measures systematic risk which tells the portfolio's co-movement with the market portfolio.

SHARPE MEASURE: $S_i = (R_i - R_f)/\sigma_i$
Where
S_i : Sharpe ratio of portfolio I
R_i : The average rate of return for portfolio i during a specified time period
R_f : The average rate of return on a risk-free investment during a specified time period
σ_i: The risk variable sigma measures the total risk, standard deviation, of the rate of return for portfolio i during the time period

JENSEN MEASURE: $R_j - R_f = \alpha_j + \beta_j (R_m - R_f) + \varepsilon_j$
Where
R_j : The average rate of return for portfolio j during a specified time period
R_f : The average rate of return on a risk-free investment during a specified time period
R_m : The average rate of return on a market portfolio during a specified time period
β_j: The systematic risk
ε_j : Random error term
α_j: The alpha value indicates whether the portfolio manager is superior or inferior in market timing and/or stock selection.

PERFORMANCE ATTRIBUTION ANALYSIS:
Allocation effect $= \Sigma_i [(w_{ai} - w_{pi}) \times (R_{pi} - R_p)]$
Selection effect $= \Sigma_i [w_{ai} \times (R_{ai} - R_{pi})]$
Where
w_{ai} , w_{pi}: The investment proportions given to the ith market segment (e.g. asset class, industry group) in the manager's actual portfolio and the benchmark portfolio, respectively
R_{ai} , R_{pi}: The investment returns to the ith market segment in the manager's actual portfolio and the benchmark portfolio, respectively
R_p : The total return to the benchmark portfolio.

Development of the Industry

Global Developments

As a relatively small open centre, the Hong Kong fund management industry is heavily influenced by global developments. This section introduces basic concepts of fund management and product developments which are global in nature.

A core fund management activity is managing collective investment schemes such as mutual funds or pension schemes, in which the savings of many individuals are pooled. The advantages of pooling, from the individual's point of view, are investment diversification, economies of scale in fees and charges, simpler administration (i.e. delegation of the administration to the fund manager), and the benefit of the fund manager's professional skill.

The first open-ended mutual funds for public investment were launched in the US in 1924. The sector grew over the following decades, fuelled particularly by the launch of money market funds in 1974, the creation of Individual Retirement Accounts (IRAs) in 1981, and the equity bull markets of the 1980s and 1990s. Assets held in US-based mutual funds rose from about US$1 trillion in 1990 to US$7 trillion in 2000, exceeding the level of bank deposits (which in June 2001 were US$4.3 trillion). Appendix 4.1 gives fuller details.

The mutual fund is a company, now often incorporated in a tax haven jurisdiction with flexible corporate regulation—Luxembourg, for example.[2] When investors buy a mutual fund they buy shares in the mutual fund company, these being created for them by the manager. The manager uses the money to purchase securities which are held in the name of the mutual fund company; thus investors are able to invest in a diversified portfolio of underlying securities for a small sum.

Typically, the mutual fund portfolio is valued daily for dealing at the valuation price. Depending on the nature of the fund, adjustments may be made for accrued interest and the manager's own fees. When investors sell their holdings, they give their shares back to the manager, who cancels them and pays them the attributable value of their shares. To make such repayment, he may sell a portion of the underlying securities. In practice the manager will keep a small proportion of the fund monies in cash to facilitate liquidations. Sometimes in a crisis the fund manager will cease to offer daily dealing and will require additional time to liquidate holdings in an orderly manner.

Mutual funds may be open-ended; in other words, the manager can create or cancel shares at will. A closed-end fund, known as an investment trust in the UK, is one where the number of shares is fixed at the outset. The life of the fund may also be fixed. The closed-end fund often trades at a discount to net asset value.

The penetration rate of mutual fund ownership is still very low in Asian countries compared with that in the US (Figure 4.2). In Hong Kong,

Figure 4.2 Penetration of Mutual Fund Ownership in Selected Countries

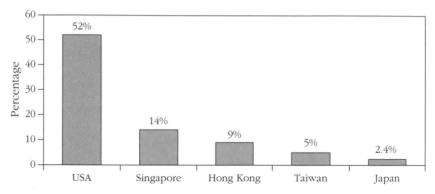

Note: Due to definition difference, the above figures are not strictly comparable
Sources of data: USA: Investment Company Institute website, '2001 Profile of Mutual Fund
　　　　　Shareholders' (http://www.ici.org/pdf/rpt_profile01.pdf).
　　　　　Singapore: CMG First State Investment website (http://www.cmgfirststate.
　　　　　com.sg/news/2001112100.html).
　　　　　Hong Kong: HKEx Retail Investor Survey 2001.
　　　　　Taiwan: Finance Asia website (http://www.financeasia.com/articles/
　　　　　BDAF788A-740C-11D4-8C110008C72B383C.cfm).
　　　　　Japan: JapanInc website (http://www.japaninc.net/mag/comp/2001/08/
　　　　　aug01_invest_sawakami.html).

Figure 4.3 Number of Funds Listed on Selected Global Exchanges

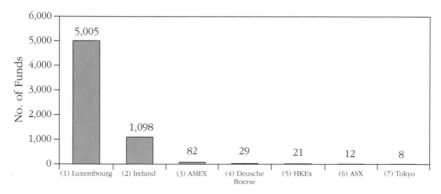

Note: Due to different definitions, the figures may not be strictly comparable
　　　1) No. of undertakings for collective investment as at June 2001
　　　2) As at 9 October 2001, figures included 984 investment companies funds, 112 unit
　　　trusts, and two limited partnership funds.
　　　3) Figures included 30 broad-based index ETFs, 29 sector index ETFs, and 23
　　　international index ETFs.
　　　4) Figures included 18 index funds and 11 actively managed funds currently traded in
　　　the XTF segment of Deutsche Boerse.
　　　5) Figures included 20 mutual funds/unit trusts and Tracker Fund.
　　　6) Figures included two classical ETFs, six hybrid ETFs, and four world link ETFs
　　　currently traded in the ETF segment of ASX.
　　　7) Figures included two Real Estate Investment Trusts and six ETFs.
Sources of data: The exchanges' respective websites, and email enquiries.

according to the Retail Investor Survey conducted in December 2001, nine per cent of the adult population invested (currently holding or had traded in the previous twelve months) in securities investment funds (excluding provident funds and Tracker Fund). In the US, as at May 2001, 93.3 million individuals, representing fifty-two per cent of all US households, owned mutual funds (Investment Company Institute, 2001).

Both closed- and open-ended funds are often listed on exchanges (Figure 4.3). Liquidity on the exchange is usually very low or non-existent; in the case of open-ended funds investors go directly to the manager and have new units created for them so there is no need for an exchange marketplace. Nonetheless, many institutional investors are bound by their mandates to invest only in listed securities, so a listing is often needed. Fund managers tend to list their vehicles on exchanges that provide the simplest and cheapest listing procedure, namely Luxembourg and, more recently, Dublin.

Traditional mutual funds offered to the public are governed by strict regulations and tend to adopt long-only investment strategies, i.e. they do not go short, and tend not to trade in derivatives such as options or futures. They mostly target a relative rate of return: that is, a return benchmarked against a market index. Consequently the returns on these funds tend to follow those of their benchmark. Moreover, it is difficult for the fund manager to outperform the benchmark, since in mature markets dominated by institutional investors, the fund managers essentially *are* the markets. Many investors became dissatisfied with paying the fund manager for average or even below-average performance, so in recent years there has been increasing focus on costs, i.e. on manager–expense ratios.

A parallel development has been the growing popularity of index funds. In these funds a lower fee is charged and the manager, typically a custodian bank, simply invests in the benchmark index. The manager's role here is more or less administrative, ensuring that the fund tracks the chosen index closely. In some mature markets, indexed assets under management may amount to a quarter or a third of the total.

A variant on the index fund is the exchange-traded fund (ETF) first introduced on the American Stock Exchange in 1993. Traditional mutual funds, including index funds, are dealt on daily basis at the day's end, so the pricing may not be transparent to investors. Only the fund manager can create or cancel shares in the fund. As noted above, in a crisis daily liquidity may not be available. In contrast, an ETF is traded on a stock exchange like any other security (Figure 4.4). Investors can buy and sell through their broker throughout the trading day at the prevailing market price. ETFs are open-ended funds, but new shares are created and existing ones cancelled on application to the ETF administrator from market makers (or, on the US exchanges, specialists). These market makers apply to create or cancel shares in the ETF when they see profit opportunity arising from discrepancies between the underlying net asset value of the ETF and its price. Such an arbitrage mechanism ensures that the ETF closely tracks its underlying index. ETFs have proved successful in the US markets, and have spread to a number of other markets around the world.

Figure 4.4 Number of ETFs Listed/Traded n Selected Exchanges (as at May 2002)

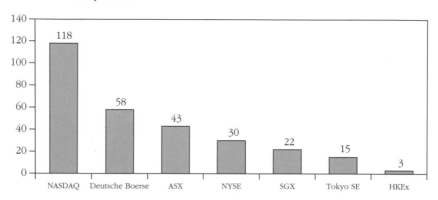

Source of data: Websites of the respective exchanges

Another alternative to the traditional long-only mutual fund is an alternative investment vehicle such as the hedge fund. Hedge funds target an absolute return, say fifteen per cent per annum, to be achieved on a steady basis year by year, and even month by month. They achieve this by adopting a wide range of investment strategies, including short selling and use of leverage and derivatives. While traditional fund houses make a virtue of their managers' independence, hedge fund managers invest in their own product and so have goals in common with their investors. In return for their efforts, hedge fund managers take a high level of remuneration, typically a fee of twenty per cent of gains achieved, in addition to a one per cent annual management fee based on assets.

Figure 4.5 CSFN/Tremont Hedge Fund Index Month by Month NAV Since Inception (January 1996 to June 2002)

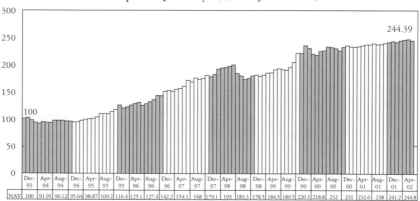

Source of data: https://www.hedgeindex.com/secure/analytics.cfm?sID=400

The first hedge fund was launched in 1949. In the 1980s and 1990s hedge funds grew in popularity. They are currently going through another expansion phase, following investor disillusionment with long-only strategies in the difficult equity markets of the last couple of years. There are over 4,000 hedge funds in the world, mostly domiciled in tax-haven jurisdictions, with capital before leverage of over US$500 billion. Most hedge fund managers are located in the US, where the major investors are. London and other European centres are growing in popularity, however, and there are a few hedge fund managers in Hong Kong and Singapore.

The net asset value (NAV) of the CSFB/Tremont Hedge Fund Index[3] as at the end of June is 244.39 (Figure 4.5), returning 144 per cent for the 102-month period since inception (1 January 1994 to 30 June 2002).

With the growth of the financial sector in the last two decades, and its globalization, fund management houses have themselves globalized and have grown to achieve economies of scale and meet the demands of their clients. Some houses have been acquired by financial conglomerates, while others have followed a more independent strategy.

Figure 4.6 Assets under Management in Selected Fund Management Centres

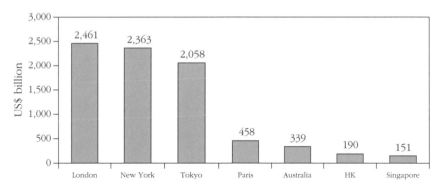

Note: Due to definition differences, the above figures are not strictly comparable.
Sources of data: SFC, *Hong Kong—Fund Management Activities Survey 2000*
                Singapore: 2000 Survey of the Singapore Asset Management
                Australia: Australian Bureau of Statistics
                London, New York, Tokyo, Paris: LSE website
                (www.londonstockexchange.com/international/sld003.asp)

While London is the leading global fund management centre, as shown in Figure 4.6, it should be noted that the US is the leading country for fund management: that is, cities other than New York, such as Boston and San Francisco, are also major centres. At present, Hong Kong is the second largest leading fund management centre in Asia after Japan, with total assets of US$190 billion. Total assets under the management of financial institutions in Singapore amounted to US$151 billion. The regional leader, Tokyo, has a total of US$2,058 billion.

Development in Hong Kong

Whereas the fund management industry in Western countries has been spurred by local investors, the growth of the industry in Hong Kong has been driven by overseas forces.

The industry came into existence in the late 1960s and early 1970s when merchant banks such as Jardine Fleming began their operations in Hong Kong. At that time, British companies were the key players (Table 4.1). The merchant banks set up their own investment arms mainly to manage retirement funds for their own groups but offering some unit trusts as well. At that time, unit trust investing was not popular among the general public, and expatriates were the target customers. The late 1970s saw the rise of the American asset management companies, and in the 1980s Japanese firms such as Nomura Asset Management and Daiwa SB Investment also established offices in Hong Kong. Wealth levels increased, leading to a demand for savings vehicles and social benefits such as insurance and retirement provision. In the mid-1980s, international investment consulting firms began to play a role, advising institutional investors on the selection of a manager.

Table 4.1   Entry of Foreign Asset Management Firms to Hong Kong

Established in HK in	Asset Management Company
1970	Jardine Fleming
1971	Schroders Investment Management
1972	Invesco Asia
1975	Baring Asset Management
1979	Citibank Global Asset Management
1981	Fidelity Investments Management (HK)
1981	Dao Heng Fund Management
1985	Global Asset Management (HK)
1988	Merrill Lynch Investment Managers
1988	Nomura Asset Management Hong Kong
1988	Daiwa SB Investments (HK)
1989	SHK Fund Management
1993	Value Partners
1994	AXA Investment Managers
1997	UBS Investment Funds Asia Pacific
1998	AIG Financial Advisor Services
1999	BOCI-Prudential Asset Management

Sources of data: Compiled from information on the Hong Kong Investment Funds Association (HKIFA) website and each company's individual website

The Hong Kong Unit Trust Association, now the Hong Kong Investment Funds Association, was established in 1986. It now has close to fifty members. The number of authorized unit trusts and mutual funds grew from 77 in December 1981 to 1,890 as at 31 March 2002. In 1981, there were only a handful of investment management firms operating in Hong Kong; now there are 97 groups comprising 203 companies. Twenty-seven of these claim to be regional headquarters. The sector is regarded by practitioners as healthy, with wide representation not only from the international houses but also players in the venture capital and hedge fund sectors. The fund management industry in Hong Kong is well supported by service providers such as international agency brokers, prime brokers, trustees and fund administrators, and lawyers and accountants. The penetration rate of mutual fund ownership in Hong Kong is on an increasing trend (Figure 4.7).

Figure 4.7 Penetration of Mutual Fund Ownership in Hong Kong

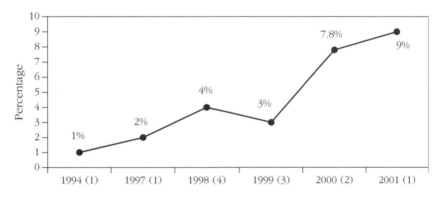

Sources of data: (1) HKEx Retail Investor Survey 2001, 1997, 1994
(2) HKIFA survey, press release on 6 September 2000
(3) SFC Retail Investor Survey 1999
(4) HK Trade & Industry Department (http://www.gov.hk/tid/online_pub/ hk_industry/service/fina.pdf)

Formerly, the global fund houses operated different families of funds. Under such a framework, the Hong Kong office might manage a Cayman-based fund family. Now, however, under pressure to cut costs, fund houses are concentrating on a single fund family which they market globally. Such a family will tend to be based in a European jurisdiction such as Dublin or Luxembourg, where it qualifies under the Undertaking for Collective Investment in Transferable Securities (UCITS)[4] regulations for the large European Union retail market. This trend has led to some hollowing-out of the fund management industry in Hong Kong. Local managers may no longer control the core product, and may do less of the actual management of the funds, their role focusing more on marketing and distribution.

A counter-trend to the above derives from a Hong Kong-based regulation that mandates a local product. The MPF rules require a locally designed fund, and they stipulate that thirty per cent of the assets must be denominated in Hong Kong dollars. A local product will also be required to comply with the Securities and Futures Commission's (SFC) guidelines for the approval of hedge funds (see page 90).

Generally, the MPF has been good for the fund management industry in Hong Kong. It provides new business for fund managers and their service providers directly, although there has been some switching from pre-existing Occupational Retirement Schemes Ordinance (ORSO) schemes. It has also indirectly raised the public's awareness of mutual funds, contributing to the increase in the penetration rate. However, since the introduction of the MPF coincided with a difficult period in equity markets, most funds have shown losses, leading to negative perceptions among the public.

Overall, practitioners comment that the fund management industry in Hong Kong is some years behind leading overseas centres.[5] Examples of this are the lack of publication of expense ratios, turnover ratios, and soft dollar payments. Conflict of interest in financial conglomerates is another issue. Investors are less sophisticated and so make lower demands.

Current Status of the Industry

Fund Management Activities

The SFC's Fund Management Activities Survey (FMAS) found that total assets under management (AUM) at the end of 2001 amounted to HK$1,484 billion (Figure 4.8). This comprised HK$668 billion (forty-five per cent) of assets managed in Hong Kong and HK$817 billion (fifty-five per cent) of assets sub-contracted or delegated to other offices or third parties overseas for management. The funds were mainly sourced from non-Hong Kong investors, amounting to HK$1,029 billion (sixty-nine per cent) (Figure 4.9). By fund type, institutional funds accounted for sixty-two per cent of the AUM, followed by pension funds (twenty-two per cent), SFC-authorized retail funds (eleven per cent), and private client funds (two per cent). Sixty-three per cent of the institutional funds were managed overseas (Figure 4.10).

Figure 4.8 Fund Management Activities Survey 2001 by SFC (as at December 2001) (in HK$ billion)

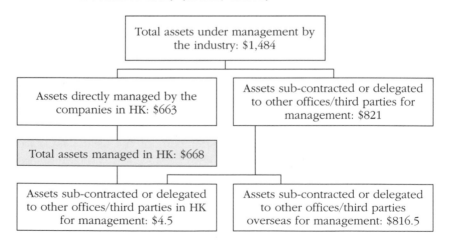

Figure 4.9 Assets Under Management by Fund Type and where the
Assets were Managed in 2001

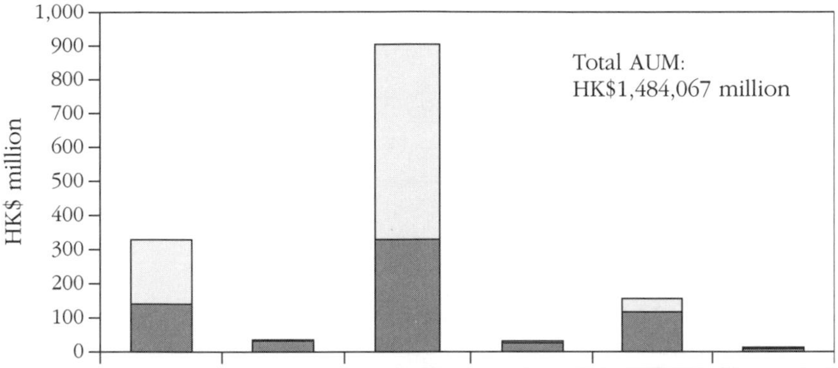

	Pension funds	MPF	Institutional funds	Private Clients' funds	SFC-authorized retail funds	Other funds
Managed overseas	188.50	3.30	573.90	5.70	39.20	3.60
Managed in HK	140.70	32.40	329.50	26.00	116.50	9.20

Total AUM:
HK$1,484,067 million

Figure 4.10 Total Assets Under Management by Fund Type in 2001

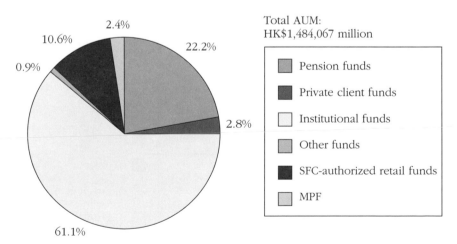

Total AUM:
HK$1,484,067 million

- Pension funds
- Private client funds
- Institutional funds
- Other funds
- SFC-authorized retail funds
- MPF

2.4%
10.6%
0.9%
22.2%
2.8%
61.1%

Source of data: SFC, *Fund Management Activities Survey 2001*

Figure 4.11 Number of SFC-authorized Funds by Origin (as at March 2002)

Total number of funds: 1,890

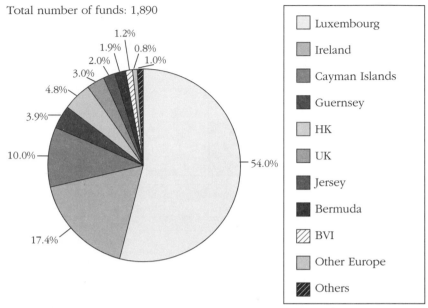

Source of data: SFC *Annual Report 2001–2002*

Figure 4.12 Net Asset Value of SFC-authorized Funds by Origin (as at December 2001)

Total NAV: US$285,210 million

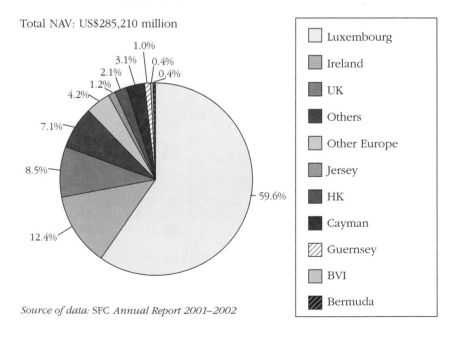

Source of data: SFC *Annual Report 2001–2002*

Authorized Funds

Funds totalling 1,890 in number were authorized by the SFC as at 31 March 2002 (Figure 4.14) (Table 4.2), these funds having an NAV of US$285 billion. Approximately ninety-five per cent of these funds are domiciled in offshore jurisdictions (Figure 4.11). There are 1,020 authorized funds of Luxembourg origin, which contributed sixty per cent of the total NAV of the fund industry, or US$170 billion. The Irish and UK funds contributed twelve and nine per cent of the total NAV respectively. Only ninety funds are domiciled in Hong Kong, accounting for two per cent of the total NAV (Figure 4.12).

Figure 4.14 Growth of SFC-authorized Funds

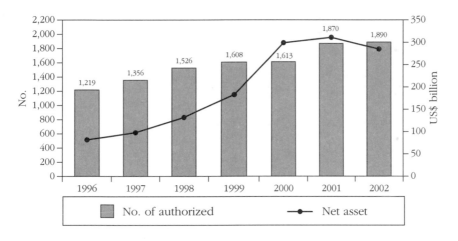

Source of data: SFC *Annual Report*, various issues

Table 4.2 Number of SFC-authorized Unit Trusts and Mutual Funds by Fund Type

Fund type	as at March 2002		as at March 2001		as at March 2000	
Equity	1,063	56.24%	1,118	59.80%	957	59.30%
Bond	290	15.34%	307	16.40%	277	17.20%
Umbrella structures	150	7.94%	140	7.50%	131	8.10%
Diversified	121	6.40%	128	6.80%	105	6.50%
Fund of funds	82	4.34%	77	4.10%	32	2.00%
Money market	61	3.23%	74	4.00%	90	5.60%
Other specialized*	81	4.29%	22	1.20%	14	0.90%
Index	38	2.01%	–	–	–	–
Warrant	4	0.21%	4	0.20%	7	0.40%
Total	1,890	100%	1,870	100%	1,613	100%

Note: * Futures and Options Funds, Guaranteed Funds, and Leveraged Funds
Sources of data: SFC *Annual Report* 1999–2000, 2000–2001, and 2001–2002

Standard equity funds and bond funds dominate the market, accounting for sixty-four and seventeen per cent of the total net asset value. Other specialized funds, such as index-tracking funds and guaranteed funds, are becoming more popular (Figure 4.13).

Figure 4.13   Net Asset Value of SFC-Authorized Unit Trusts and Mutual Funds by Fund Type (as at 31 December 2001)

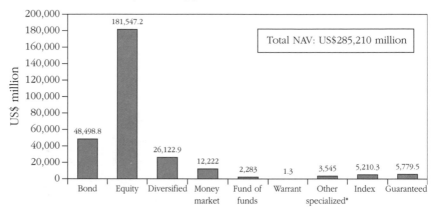

* Futures and options funds and leveraged funds

2001 Fund Sales

In 2001, as global equity markets experienced a bearish year, sales of funds of all types decreased except guaranteed funds, bond funds, and equity sector funds. Guaranteed funds ranked first in both gross and net sales, attracting gross inflows of US$3,809 million, or forty per cent of the industry total. Cash funds came second, attracting gross inflows of US$1,350 million and accounting for fourteen per cent of the industry total (Figure 4.15) (Table 4.3).

HKEx Listed Funds

Hong Kong Exchanges and Clearing Limited (HKEx) accepts the listing of funds. However, the number has declined over the years to eleven[6] (Figure 4.16), while at the same time overseas exchanges such as the Irish Stock Exchange have expanded. Dublin now lists more than 1,000 funds, including some from Hong Kong. In addition to the traditional mutual funds/unit trusts, Hong Kong Tracker Funds were listed on HKEx in 1999, and two Exchange Traded Funds— iShares MSCI Korea Index and iShares MSCI Taiwan index—were introduced to HKEx under a 'trading only' arrangement in 2001.

Retirement Funds and Mandatory Provident Funds

The Mandatory Provident Fund Schemes System came into full implementation on 1 December 2000. Unless exempted, all employees

Figure 4.15 Gross Sales by Type of Fund in 2001 and 2000

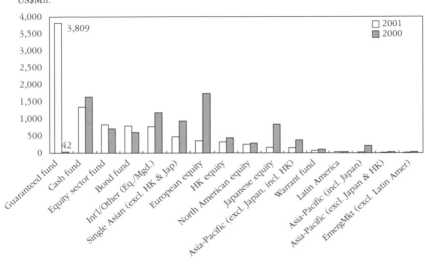

Table 4.3   2001 Sales by Mutual Fund Type

Gross sale by type of fund	2001 (in US$ million)	Gross sale as % of 2001 total
Guaranteed fund	3,809.0	40.2
Cash fund	1,350.2	14.3
Equity sector fund	836.3	8.8
Bond fund	792.4	8.4
Int'l/Others	778.3	8.2
Single Asian (excl. HK and Japan)	478.4	5.0
European equity	354.6	3.8
Hong Kong equity	320.3	3.4
North American equity	258.1	2.7
Japanese equity	166.4	1.8
Asia-Pacific (excl. Japan, incl. HK)	164.7	1.7
Warrant fund	72.2	0.8
Latin America	31.0	0.3
Asia-Pacific (incl. Japan)	28.3	0.3
Asia-Pacific (excl. Japan and HK)	16.4	0.2
Emerging market (excl. Latin America)	11.8	0.1
Total	9,468.4	100.0

Source: HKIFA website

Figure 4.16   No. of Unit Trusts/Mututal Funds Listed on HKEx (1990 to June 2002)

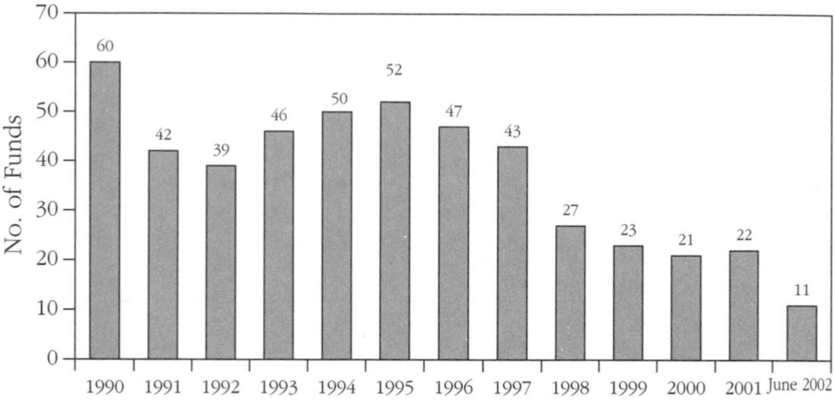

Source: Stock Exchange *Factbooks*—number of securities by type, Monthly Market Statistics

aged between eighteen and sixty-five, and self-employed persons under sixty-five, are required to participate as members of registered MPF schemes. As at 31 March 2002, there were twenty MPF trustees, 47 master trust schemes, 311 constituent funds, and 220 approved pooled investment funds. Approximately 88 per cent of the employers, 94 per cent of the employees, and 91 per cent of the self-employed covered by the MPF System had joined MPF schemes. Over 28,000 intermediaries had been registered. The net asset value of the approved constituent funds of MPF schemes amounted to HK$33,499 million. See Chapter 5 for more details on the MPF.

Major Investing Institutions

The Exchange Fund Managed by the Hong Kong Monetary Authority

The Exchange Fund was established in 1935. Since then, the Fund has held the backing to Hong Kong dollar note issues. In 1976, the assets backing coins issued and the foreign currency assets held in the government's General Revenue Account were also transferred to the Exchange Fund. On 1 November 1998, the assets of the Land Fund, amounting to HK$211 billion, were merged with the Exchange Fund and managed as part of its Investment Portfolio. As at 31 December 2001, the assets of the Exchange Fund totalled HK$981 billion.

The primary objective of the Exchange Fund is to safeguard the exchange value of the Hong Kong currency and maintain the stability and integrity of the monetary and financial systems of Hong Kong. The Hong Kong Monetary Authority (HKMA) is responsible for the active management of the fund's assets. The fund is held mainly in the form of marketable interest-bearing instruments and equities in certain foreign currencies. To meet the operational needs of the government, part of the Exchange Fund is also held in Hong Kong dollar-denominated securities. As at the end of December 2001, the official foreign currency reserve assets held by the Exchange Fund amounted to US$111 billion.

To meet the objectives of preserving capital, providing liquidity, maintaining financial and currency stability, and generating an adequate long-term return, the Exchange Fund is managed as two distinct portfolios: the Backing Portfolio and the Investment Portfolio. The Backing Portfolio was established to hold highly liquid US dollar-denominated interest-bearing securities to back fully the monetary base. The balance of the Exchange Fund assets that constitute the Investment Portfolio are invested in Organisation for Economic Co-operation and Development (OECD) bond and equity markets to preserve the value and long-term purchasing power of these assets.

The Exchange Fund Advisory Committee determines the long-term investment strategy, while the Reserves Management Department of the HKMA is responsible for the day-to-day management of the Exchange Fund. The Exchange Fund employs over forty external managers located in ten major financial centres to invest about forty per cent of its total assets (Hong Kong Monetary Authority, 2000).

In August 1998, the Hong Kong government acquired HK$158 billion of Hong Kong shares in its market intervention during the Asian financial crisis. Exchange Fund Investment Limited (EFIL) was established in October 1998 by the government to manage this portfolio and arrange its orderly disposal. In March 1999, the HKMA announced a five per cent allocation of the Exchange Fund to Hong Kong equities as a long-term investment; EFIL manages this portfolio too. EFIL is registered as an investment adviser.

To dispose of the equity portfolio (other than the long-term portion), the government chose to develop an ETF, the Tracker Fund of Hong Kong (TraHK). This was launched in November 1999 as the first step in the government's disposal programme. State Street Global Advisors Asia Ltd was appointed as both the fund manager and the trustee of TraHK.

Insurers
According to statistics for 2001 released by the Office of the Commissioner of Insurance, total gross premiums of the insurance industry amounted to HK$76.3 billion, representing 5.9 per cent of the Hong Kong gross domestic product. As at 28 February 2002, there were 202 authorized insurers in Hong Kong, of which 139 were general insurers, forty-five were long-term insurers, and the remaining eighteen were composite insurers.

Most of the insurance companies use their own asset management companies to invest the premiums received. As the product mix of the insurance companies varies greatly, the portfolio selection of the firms depends mainly on their liability structure. The assets of life insurance companies are usually segmented into two major portfolios: fixed-income and surplus. The primary requirement for life insurance companies is to earn a competitive return to fund well-defined liabilities. Investment strategy is geared toward 'spread management'—the difference between the return earned on investments and the return credited to policy or annuity holders. Duration-matching strategies are employed to meet liability requirements. Fixed-income instruments are the key investments to meet these long-term liabilities. The primary requirement of the surplus portfolio is to achieve higher returns through portfolio growth. Equity-related investments are used to achieve this objective.

Non-life insurance companies, such as those involved in health, property, and casualty, have a very different product mix from life insurance companies. The duration of their liabilities tends to be relatively short, and they are uncertain. Liquidity is therefore a very important consideration. The liquidity needs of a non-life company are dictated by its underwriting cycle. Maturity matching (duration modelling) is usually used to immunize the company's liabilities.

See Chapter 6 for a fuller discussion of insurance.

The Hong Kong Jockey Club

The Hong Kong Jockey Club is a large investing institution (with long-term investments of HK$6.8 billion in 2000) with a prominent place in the community. It is a conservative investor, and any new initiatives—such as its announcement in April 2000 of an investment of US$100 million in overseas-based hedge funds—are closely watched by the market.

Hedge Funds

At the time of writing, most hedge funds sold to Hong Kong investors are distributed on a private basis. In such cases, the fund does not need authorization. If a person (the hedge fund manager or a distributor) wishes to market the fund to public retail investors in Hong Kong, he or she must obtain authorization for the fund from the SFC. Presently, there is only one authorized hedge fund in Hong Kong, managed by the ED&F Man group. The SFC issued guidelines for the authorization of retail hedge funds in May 2002, and the first funds are expected to be authorized in the third quarter of the year.

According to the Eureka Asian Hedge Funds Directory 2002, it is estimated that twenty per cent of the managers of Asian hedge funds are located in Hong Kong (Figure 4.17). The two largest funds identified are headquartered in New York; they manage nearly a quarter of the assets of all the funds in the directory. Excluding these funds, on average, the US managers have assets under management in their Asian hedge funds of US$83 million. In comparison, UK managers, Hong Kong managers, and Australian managers manage on average US$65 million, US$40 million, and US$20 million respectively.

In terms of investment strategy, the majority of the managers follow some form of long/short equity style (Figure 4.18).

Figure 4.17   Estimated Geographic Spread of Asia-Pacific Hedge Fund
Managers (by number)

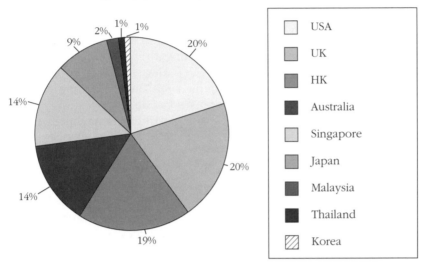

Source: Asian Hedge Fund Directory 2002, Eureka Hedge Advisors Pte Ltd.

Figure 4.18   Estimated Geographic Spread of Asia-Pacific Hedge Fund
Managers (by number)

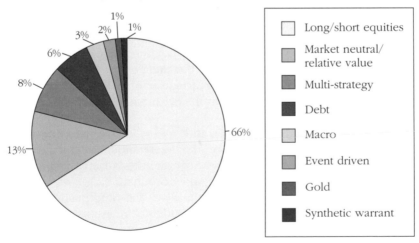

Source: Asian Hedge Fund Directory 2002, Eureka Hedge Advisors Pte Ltd.

Fund Management Operations

We will now describe the operations of an international fund manager in Hong Kong. Although perhaps not typical, given the diversity of the industry, the operations outlined may serve as an indication of the method of doing business. Specifics have been changed to protect the firm's identity.

International Fund Manager is the Hong Kong subsidiary of a European-based global firm which is also a major insurer. The Hong Kong subsidiary runs relatively independently. There is a global functional matrix, with the local functional heads reporting to a global functional head and also to the local country/office head. Like most of its peers in Hong Kong, International Fund Manager has a number of senior expatriate staff.

The Hong Kong office is responsible for investment in Asia with the exception of Japan but including Australia and New Zealand. The firm does not believe in carve-outs, so a European-sourced Asian equity fund would be managed by Hong Kong, and vice versa. The firm has a global dealing system such that an order for overseas stock entered in the Hong Kong office will be routed to the dealing desk of the appropriate local office for execution in the local market.

The firm also has a Singapore office; this manages Asian fixed income, although it reports to the Hong Kong office. The Singapore establishment was set up with a development grant from the Singapore government. Other incentives received include a fifty per cent subsidy for staff salaries, a two-year tax holiday, and a seventy per cent subsidy for overseas training. The Singapore office was also given mandates to manage government money.

The Hong Kong office targets the mass retail market, and also has institutional clients. With respect to the latter, where the mandate is less than US$100 million the firm will construct a portfolio out of its global fund family; that is, it will compile a fund of funds for the client rather than investing directly in the underlying stocks. The Hong Kong office operates with the guidance (say, eighty per cent of the allocation strategy) of the global strategy and research team in the head office in Europe, but will make tactical decisions (say, twenty per cent) around that guidance in Hong Kong. Consultants will advise the client on the strategy, including the benchmarks by which the performance of the portfolio is to be measured. Since the firm is also an insurer, it can provide such a consultancy service itself.

The Hong Kong office manages MPF funds. It earns about fifty basis points (i.e. 0.5 per cent per year on the assets under management), the bulk of the total fee going to the custodian because of the onerous administration involved in handling MPF accounts.

The firm is essentially a manufacturer—of the fund product—and a wholesaler. Although it has some retail outlets, it relies mainly on others to distribute its product. Although the firm competes with other local and international players in Hong Kong, each sells the other's products to their clients. So, for example, a major bank in Hong Kong will sell not only its own family of mutual funds, but also those of other providers. Clients demand a choice.

The manager outsources much of its back office operation to a trustee bank, one of the two major players in the Hong Kong market. The bank, which is a global operation, provides the following services: accounting and valuation of portfolios, transfer agency services, and the banking and custody of securities. By outsourcing these services, the fund manager is free to concentrate on the actual fund management and marketing.

International Fund Manager is watching the China market closely. It has insurance licences, and several thousand employees in China on the insurance side. However, the firm's philosophy is somewhat conservative, and it cannot contemplate a joint venture asset-management operation in China until the law is clear. A draft law on foreign joint venture asset-management companies was released in December 2001, which was encouraging. However, the law envisages initial thirty-three per cent foreign ownership, rising to forty-nine per cent in three years. The firm would prefer a wholly controlled operation.

Regulation

Authorization of Unit Trusts and Mutual Funds

The SFC authorizes unit trusts and mutual funds under Section 15 of the Securities Ordinance (now subsumed by the Securities and Futures Ordinance (SFO),[7] Part IV). The SFC's Committee on Unit Trusts considers authorization issues and administers the Code on Unit Trusts and Mutual Funds. Collective investment funds can be organized in Hong Kong either as unit trusts or as mutual funds, both open-ended and closed-end. Unit trusts and mutual funds must be authorized in order to be marketed to the public in Hong Kong. It is an offence to distribute a prospectus, explanatory memorandum, or any other advertising or marketing materials in relation to an unauthorized mutual fund to the public in Hong Kong. Unauthorized mutual funds, however, may be marketed to 'professional' investors 'whose business involves the acquisition, disposal or holding of securities, whether as principal or agent'. The non-statutory Code on Unit Trusts and Mutual Funds sets out the authorization criteria. Compliance with the code is voluntary, but compliance is a *de facto* condition of authorization. The SFC reviewed the Code in 1997 after consultation with the industry, and the third edition of the Code was published in December 1997.

An applicant for authorization of a fund must submit a completed form to the Investment Products Department of the SFC, accompanied by the fund's offering and constitutive documents, the fund's latest audited report and, if more recent, the latest unaudited report, the management company's latest audited report, the company profile, the trustee/custodian's latest audited report, the letter of consent to the appointment from the trustee/custodian, and the application fee. In addition, applicants for authorization of a fund not based in Hong Kong must supply a Hong Kong Representative Agreement undertaking. Applicants for authorization of a recognized jurisdiction fund must also supply evidence of the fund's authorized status in the jurisdiction. The basic requirements for authorization are as follows:

1. The management company must have appropriately qualified and experienced personnel with demonstrable track records in managing funds, and adequate internal controls.
2. The investment management operations of a fund management company or those of the investment adviser (where the latter has been delegated the investment management function) should be based in a jurisdiction with an inspection regime acceptable to the SFC.
3. The management company must have a minimum capitalization of HK$1 million.
4. The fund must have an independent trustee or custodian, who must have a minimum capitalization of HK$10 million and is responsible for the safekeeping of the fund's assets and supervision of the manager.
5. The fund must meet various operational requirements set out in the Code, such as a requirement for (at least) monthly dealing, requirements regarding net asset value calculations, and controls on transactions with connected persons.
6. The fund must meet various investment requirements set out in the Code, including diversification requirements, liquidity requirements, and limits on the use of derivatives.
7. The fund must provide detailed disclosures to enable investors to make informed decisions.
8. The fund must have a licensed representative in Hong Kong with whom the investor can deal.

Obtaining authorization from the SFC for a standard fund can take as little as twenty-one days.

The Marketing of Unit Trusts and Mutual Funds

The Protection of Investors Ordinance (now in the SFO, Part IV) regulates advertisements and offers of securities and investment arrangements to the public. It contains sanctions for the advertising or promotion of unauthorized investment products to the investing public in Hong Kong without prior authorization from the SFC. There are also sanctions for fraudulent inducement to persons to invest in securities or investment arrangements and statutory civil liability for fraudulent misrepresentation. The SFC monitors the print media in Hong Kong for offers to the public to invest in funds that are not authorized, and takes appropriate action to ensure that the provisions contained in relevant legislation are enforced and the interests of investors are protected.

Section 74 of the Securities Ordinance and Section 60A of the Commodities Trading Ordinance (now in the SFO, Part VII) prohibit soliciting investment by telephone or by visiting individuals at their place of residence or employment without first receiving an invitation from that person. 'Cold calling' individuals or companies in Hong Kong, whether in person or by telephone, is prohibited.

Regulations Governing Fund Managers, Fund Management Companies, and Trustees/Custodians

The SFC's regulatory ambit covers the investment management industry, through the regulation of intermediaries involved in dealing in securities or in giving investment advice, and through the regulation of the marketing of investment products to the investing public. Part VI of the Securities Ordinance and Part IV of the Commodities Trading Ordinance (now in the SFO, Part V) require those carrying on a business of dealing in securities or commodity futures contracts in Hong Kong, and those offering investment advice for remuneration, to be registered with the SFC as investment advisers, investment representatives, or dealer's representatives, depending on the functions they will perform. Fund management companies, which undertake a distribution function in Hong Kong or otherwise deal in securities or futures, have to be registered as dealers or declared as exempt dealers.

The SFC issued the Fund Manager Code of Conduct in late December 1997 after consultation with the industry. The Code highlights legislative and other requirements applicable to fund managers, consolidating references from pieces of legislation, codes, and guidelines.

In July 1999, the SFC issued a set of Guidelines for Review of Internal Controls and Systems of Trustees/Custodians. Trustees and custodians play an important role in the supervision of the activities of fund managers of collective investment schemes and pooled retirement funds. They are required either to be subject to regulatory supervision on an ongoing basis or to appoint an independent auditor to review periodically their internal controls and systems on terms of reference agreed with the SFC. The Guidelines provide guidance to trustees/custodians regarding compliance with the periodic internal control review requirement.

Regulations Governing Hedge Funds

Hedge funds not marketed to the general public do not have to be authorized by the SFC. In May 2002, the SFC released Hedge Funds Guidelines, setting out the regulatory requirements for the authorization of hedge funds that are offered to the public in Hong Kong. They will be incorporated into the Code on Unit Trusts and Mutual Funds. With the guidelines in place, the SFC expected that the Hong Kong public could start buying hedge funds by the third quarter of 2002.

The key features of the Hedge Funds Guidelines are summarized here:

(a) Market segmentation vs. full public offering
    Hedge funds with a capital guarantee feature   no limit
    Fund of hedge funds (FoHFs)   US$10,000
    Single hedge fund   US$50,000
(b) Entry requirements for management company
    (i)   *Single hedge fund manager.* Minimum US$100 million assets
          under management for the amount of assets that follow hedge
          fund strategies, plus five years' general experience in hedge
          funds strategies with at least two years' experience in the
          same strategy as the proposed hedge fund.
    (ii) *Fund of hedge funds manager.* Minimum US$100 million AUM
          for the amount of assets that follow hedge fund strategies,
          plus five years' general experience in hedge funds strategies
          with at least two years' experience as a FoHFs manager.
    (iii) *Managers of the underlying funds of FoHFs.* No AUM
          requirement, but at least two years' experience in the relevant
          investment strategies, provided, however, that up to ten per
          cent of the net asset value of a FoHFs may comprise underlying
          funds managed by investment personnel with less experience.
(c) Fund of Hedge Funds (FoHFs). The SFC:
    (i)   Places reliance on the FoHFs manager to perform suitable
          due diligence in the selection of the underlying hedge funds
          and fund managers. In this regard, the FoHFs manager must
          submit a plan to the SFC.
    (ii) Requires the FoHFs to invest in at least five underlying funds,
          with no more than thirty per cent of its total net asset value
          invested in any one underlying fund.
    (iii) Allows FoHFs to invest in non-SFC authorized funds, subject
          to additional requirements regarding the experience of the
          managers of the underlying funds.
    (iv) Requires the offering documents of FoHFs to insert additional
          risk disclosures.
    (v)   Requires the underlying funds to appoint independent
          trustees/custodians to perform the safekeeping function.
    (vi) Imposes rules against the retention of rebates and the double-
          charging of fees.
(d) Performance fees: The SFC requires 'high-on-high' calculation basis.
(e) Dealing: The SFC requires at least one regular dealing day per
    month. A ninety-day payout period is required.
(f) Valuation by the management company in accordance with
    generally accepted accounting principles and industry best practices.

Regulations Governing Pooled Retirement Funds and Mandatory Provident Fund Schemes

The Mandatory Provident Fund Authority (MPFA) is the statutory body
responsible for the regulation and supervision of the MPF system. The

MPFA has issued a Code of Conduct for MPF Intermediaries which gives guidance as to what would be expected of the intermediaries. The SFC is responsible for the approval of investment managers and authorization of disclosures in the offering documents, advertisements, and other materials marketing MPF products. The SFC has issued its own Code on MPF Products which sets out its authorization requirements for these products.

A list of the rules and regulations related to the fund management industry is given in Appendix 4.2.

Listing Rules Governing Funds Listed on HKEx

The Listing Rules identify three different categories of investment vehicle and provide procedures for the listing of each type of structure in Chapters 20 and 21. The qualifications for equity listing contained in Chapter 8 apply in general.

1. Authorized Funds. Chapter 20 of the Listing Rules sets out the requirements of the SEHK for the listing of the shares or units of funds authorized by the SFC. Authorization does not automatically ensure that a Listing will be granted, although it is a prerequisite for making an application under Chapter 20.
2. Investment Companies. Chapter 21 of the Listing Rules applies to listings by investment companies which include closed-ended funds and unauthorized mutual funds.
3. Restricted Marketing Investment Companies. Chapter 21 also applies to applications for listing by restricted marketing investment companies, the securities of which are not to be marketed to the public in Hong Kong. Although such funds cannot be offered to the public, they are allowed to be promoted to financial professionals or by way of private placement in Hong Kong.

The fund-listing rules are not tailored to meet the specific needs of funds; for example, most equity listing rules apply. The HKEx fund listing regime is therefore not considered attractive by practitioners, and most Hong Kong-managed funds are listed elsewhere; in Dublin or Luxembourg, for example.

Taxation of Fund Management

Pursuant to Section 14 of the Inland Revenue Ordinance, profits derived by unit trusts and mutual fund corporations are subject to profits tax if the company is carrying on a business and the profits are sourced in Hong Kong. There are some international fund management companies based in Hong Kong but operating in overseas markets and dealing with overseas clients. It is uncertain whether the profits arising from these cross-border activities are Hong Kong-sourced and thus subject to Hong Kong profits tax. Authorized unit trusts and mutual fund corporations are exempt from tax.

Previously, the Hong Kong Inland Revenue Department took no action on this issue. However, in 2002 it began issuing tax demand notes and enquiry letters to some fund management houses. Since the potential assessment to tax can cover back years and include gains enjoyed by investors who have long since left the fund, this could cause considerable difficulty for the fund manager. In the 2003/4 Budget, the Financial Secretary clarified that the tax exemption would be extended to unauthorized funds.

There is a very clear regime in Singapore. Earnings from offshore fund management activities enjoy a concessionary ten per cent rate of tax.

Hong Kong's Competitive Position

Hong Kong is the leading international fund management centre in Asia. Japan and Australia, although larger, have a mainly domestic focus. Hong Kong is well provided with suppliers to the fund industry, namely international brokerage houses, prime brokerage operations (for small fund operators such as hedge funds), trustees and fund administrators, accountants, and lawyers.

However, on a global scale Hong Kong is still relatively small in terms of AUM, and global trends are to some extent undercutting Hong Kong's role. For cost reasons, international fund management houses are concentrating on a single European-based fund family, thereby tending to reduce the role of the Hong Kong office. To some extent this development is offset by recent regulations that mandate a Hong Kong-based product, namely the MPF regulations and the SFC's guidelines for authorization of hedge funds. However, such developments are not without their drawbacks, and do not in themselves increase Hong Kong's attractiveness as a base for international fund management.

Hong Kong is not suitable as a jurisdiction for the incorporation of a fund. The Companies Ordinance is too complex, it does not allow readily expandable share capital, and stamp duty applies. Hong Kong fund managers had previously used the Cayman jurisdiction but, as noted above, this has fallen out of favour somewhat.

Hong Kong is missing out on the listing of funds. Although some 1,800 funds are authorized by the SFC (admittedly only a proportion of them are managed in Hong Kong), only some twenty-one are listed on HKEx.

Singapore has long been targeting itself as the leading offshore fund management centre in Asia. As at the end of 2002, it had 1,012 investment fund professionals. The assets under management totalled US$199 billion. To support this role, it has a concessionary tax regime, where profits from offshore fund management are taxed at ten per cent. There are subsidies for staff training and other incentives, and officials can promise fund managers locating in Singapore a tranche of the government's funds—for example, those controlled by the Central Provident Fund. The Singapore authorities have also made an effort to appear welcoming to fund managers in general, including hedge fund managers. Hong Kong does not present itself so well, and following the Asian financial crisis the tone of official statements regarding hedge funds was quite unwelcoming.

However, like Hong Kong, Singapore is not itself a suitable jurisdiction for incorporation of a mutual fund. The Companies Act is too complex, and it does not allow flexibility in changing share capital. Practitioners dealing with the Singapore authorities do not always find that the delivery matches the initial welcome. And, overall, tax relief and operating costs may be less important to fund managers than the overall economic, legal, and political infrastructure (see, for example, Ho and Wong, 1998).

Concluding Remarks

Hong Kong is the leading fund management centre in South-East Asia, with more than 200 firms managing some US$190 billion. International firms predominate.

Domestic retail interest in mutual funds has been slow to take off, but is growing. Spurred by MPF, some nine per cent of the adult population is invested in mutual funds. Funds totalling 1,890 in number are authorized by the SFC.

Cost pressures are forcing international fund management houses to concentrate on a single stable of funds, usually based in Europe. While HKEx lists just eleven funds, Dublin lists more than 1,000.

Although Hong Kong is basically attractive as a centre for fund management in the region, aspects of the policy framework need to be improved if Hong Kong is to maintain its position.

Discussion Questions

1. What distinguishes fund management from, say, the treasury function of a bank?
2. What are the advantages to the individual of investing in a pooled investment vehicle, such as a mutual fund, compared with investing on his own?
3. Why are mutual funds listed on exchanges?
4. Why is the use of 'passive' investment in index funds growing?
5. What are the differences between hedge funds and (traditional) mutual funds?
6. What are the main regulations applying in Hong Kong to the mutual fund, the fund manager, and the trustee?
7. Mutual fund penetration in Hong Kong is much lower than in the US. Why?

8. The vast majority of mutual funds authorized in Hong Kong are not domiciled in Hong Kong; instead they are incorporated in Luxembourg, Ireland, the Cayman Islands, and other such places. Why?
9. Singapore is competing with Hong Kong as a fund management centre. What are the respective competitive strengths of the two cities?
10. What are the growth factors for the fund management industry in Hong Kong? Are there any negatives?

Keywords

absolute return
authorization
closed-end fund
exchange-traded fund (ETF)
fund manager
hedge fund
listing
mutual fund
open-ended fund
relative return
trustee
unit trust

5. Retirement Schemes and the Mandatory Provident Fund

JASON YEH

Introduction

Established by legislation in 1995, the Mandatory Provident Fund (MPF) is a retirement protection system for the entire working population of Hong Kong. Except for certain exempt people[1] stipulated in the Mandatory Provident Fund Schemes Ordinance (MPF Ordinance), the MPF system covers all employees and self-employed people aged between eighteen and sixty-five. As a result, the majority of Hong Kong's workforce of 3.4 million people now enjoys some form of retirement protection since the implementation of the MPF system in December 2000.

Prior to the MPF scheme, the Occupational Retirement Schemes Ordinance (ORSO) was enacted in 1992 and brought into operation in October 1993. It regulates all voluntarily established private occupational retirement schemes operating in or from Hong Kong through a registration system. The objective of ORSO is not to mandate employers to provide retirement plans for employees, but to ensure that private schemes are properly administered and funded and to provide greater certainty that retirement benefits promised to employees will be paid when they fall due.

The introduction of the Mandatory Provident Fund system was prompted by Hong Kong's rapidly ageing population and the lack of a comprehensive system of retirement protection. According to the census of 2001, people aged sixty-five and over account for about 11.1 per cent of the population. This proportion is projected to increase to twenty per cent by 2029. Nevertheless, before the establishment of the MPF system only approximately one-third of the workforce had some form of retirement protection, and this was mainly covered by ORSO schemes and the Civil Service Pension Scheme, which is exclusively for civil servants and the staff of other government agencies. Prudence demanded that Hong Kong set up a formal system to help members of the workforce provide financial benefits for their retirement.

Contributions to Mandatory Provident Fund Schemes under the MPF Ordinance started on 1 December 2000. After one year of operation, the compliance rate reached a higher-than-expected figure of ninety-five per cent,[2] and the total MPF assets amounted to HK$33.5 billion at the end of November 2001, with a monthly contribution of about HK$2 billion, which was double the government's prediction of a HK$1 billion monthly contribution in the scheme's first year.

These accomplishments did not come about easily, but were the result of painstaking efforts and intense debate for over thirty years. As early as

1966, the Hong Kong Legislative Council (Legco) started the policy debate on public retirement plans. For a long time, though, proposals similar to that of Singapore's Central Provident Fund Scheme did not win majority support from Legco members. In fact, the Hong Kong government had not actively considered any form of public retirement plan until 1991, when it set up a Working Group on Retirement Protection. Before the MPF Schemes Ordinance was introduced and enacted in 1995, two alternative proposals were considered but later dropped for lack of public support (Lui, 1998). In 1998, the Ordinance was amended and supplemented by relevant subsidiary legislation, and meanwhile the Mandatory Provident Fund Schemes Authority was set up as a regulatory and supervisory body. Up to this point, the framework for the establishment of a system of privately managed, employment-based MPF schemes was finalized. This was a milestone in Hong Kong's history of retirement protection.

In addition to providing income for retirement, the compulsory retirement plans created by the MPF Ordinance are expected to have a great impact on the broader economy. Among the important effects to consider are those on national and private saving, capital formation and allocation, labour market incentives, financial markets, income redistribution, and the government's fiscal position. In countries where the pensions industry has a relatively long history, there is a rich body of economics and finance literature on such issues. Whether or not those conclusions either predicted by theoretical modelling or found by empirical research can be drawn to Hong Kong's context is yet to be explored and studied. The study of experiences from other systems will help us better understand the potential effects of our own.

The remaining sections of the chapter are organized as follows: the background section discusses the theoretical rationale for retirement plans in general and in Hong Kong in particular, then the main features of MPF are introduced by comparing its two counterparts, i.e. the ORSO schemes and the employment-based US 401(k) plans. The potential impacts of MPF on the general public, service providers, and the government are then discussed, and finally a brief conclusion is drawn.

Background

In a free-market economy, individuals are presumed to be able to make economic decisions for themselves. The choices between good x and good y, work and leisure, or risk and return are left to utility-maximizing consumers who know better than others their preferences and resource constraints. Obviously, people do not live just for one decision-making period, thus the choice between saving and consumption must also be factored into the rational individual's decision process. This issue is often described as a question of intertemporal allocation of resources, and economists have developed theoretical life-cycle models to tackle it (see, for instance, Modigliani and Brumberg, 1954; Ando and Modigliani, 1963). Consumers are hypothesized to maximize overall satisfaction, with their lifetime being the planning horizon, so as to determine work and saving patterns at different ages. As a result, people are net savers during their working life and turn into anti-savers after retirement. The life-cycle model which deals with only single individuals can be enhanced by allowing the family units to define the time horizons for borrowing, saving, and retiring. The models expand the economic agents of one generation to those of two or more generations and are therefore referred to as the overlapping generation model (see, for example, Samuelson, 1958; Diamond, 1965; Blanchard and Fisher, 1989).

However, if the choice between youthful consumption, savings, and retirement income needs are just like the choice between an apple and an orange, public intervention will not be justified. The decisions about retirement savings are indeed unique, as pointed out by Kotlikoff *et al.* (1982), in their irreversibility. As early as 1932, Pigou regarded 'economic myopia' as a rationale for state intervention in determining resource allocations over time. In the context of individual savings decisions for retirement, a common reason for the compulsory nature of government retirement programmes is paternalism: people are short-sighted and therefore cannot foresee their future needs; even if they can, they are not willing to sacrifice their current consumption to plan adequately for the future. The paternalistic argument is not plausible to many because of the ethical implication that people are ignorant and government knows best. Alternative approaches offer economic justifications by analysing several aspects of private-market imperfection, including informational inefficiencies, adverse selection, moral hazard, and free-rider problems (see, for instance, Fabel, 1994; Bodie and Davis, 2000).

Another interesting perspective is proposed by Posner (1995), who contends that the conventional economics assumption that a person is a single economic decision maker throughout his lifetime is problematic. He extends Strotz's (1955–6) argument and maintains that individuals can be modelled as a locus of competing multiple selves (simultaneous or successive). For example, an individual A at working age (A_w), especially at a young working age, is a different person from the same individual A at retirement age (A_r). Society should not allow A_w to condemn A_r to destitution by refusing to make any provision for the support of A_r who, retired, will not be able to support himself because of a lack of regular income from work. He sees an analogy between a compulsory pension system and societal prohibition of enforceable contracts of assisted suicide. Governments make pension systems mandatory so as to impose a limited fiduciary duty on the young self, A_w, who is a kind of trustee of A, the body that A_w and A_r successively dwell in.

An argument may still exist against compulsory retirement schemes in Hong Kong from a socio-economic standpoint. As the Chinese saying goes, the more children and grandchildren one has, the better the economic wellbeing of parents and grandparents. The Chinese, as the majority residents in Hong Kong, are famous for filial piety, and consequently many elderly citizens in our society actually receive financial support from their working children. Studies show that the level of co-residence of elderly parents with married children in East Asia is much higher than in the West (Logan and Bian, 1999; Milagros, 1995), which also indicates an intergenerational flow of wealth from the younger to the older generation (Clay and Haar, 1993). If support of the elderly is primarily a responsibility of families, then the public sector should restrict its role in this regard to the 'minimum intervention' philosophy that has long been upheld by the Hong Kong government. As a matter of fact, the government has maintained a long-lasting *laissez faire* position that poverty, infirmity, and natural disaster are personal matters, to be dealt with by the family system (MacPherson, 1993; Chow, 1994).

However, due to increasing urbanization and industrialization, changes in housing conditions, greater geographical mobility, decreasing fertility, shrinking family size, and longer post-retirement life expectancy, the traditional approach to old-age care and support has been weakened (Ng *et al.*, 2001). In the Hong Kong Census 2001, it was found that the size of the average household was only 3.1 people, a significant drop from the 4.2 revealed in the 1976 Census. What goes along with the fast-shrinking family is the striking speed of ageing. The median age of the population rose by fourteen years from twenty-two in 1970 to thirty-six in 2001. Hong Kong residents aged 65 or over, as indicated by the most recent census, represent 11.1 per cent of the territory's population, while in 1961, fewer than three per cent of Hong Kong residents had reached the age of 65. Comparing these statistics with other countries, only Japan has a higher share of elderly people amongst other rapidly ageing Asian societies such as Singapore, South Korea, Taiwan, and the People's Republic of China (Bartlett and Phillips, 1995). On the other hand, the fertility rate in Hong Kong is among the lowest of the world. The total fertility rate (TFR; the average number of children born to a woman during her lifetime) reached a level of 0.98 in 1998, followed by a historical nadir of 0.96 in 1999, going up slightly to 1.0 in 2000, due to the Chinese Dragon Year effect, but still far away from replacement level (the demographic level required for the population ultimately to stop growing or declining). The rate has fallen continuously over the past three decades from 3.3 in 1972 (Bartlett and Phillips, 1995) to present levels. Using the 1998 TFR and assuming zero net migration, a group of local statisticians (Yip *et al.*, 2001) estimated that the proportion of the population aged 65 or above would increase to forty-four per cent in 2048, suggesting an elderly support ratio of 1.1, down from the ratio of 6.5 in 2001. That is to say, while there are more than six people working to support an elderly dependant today, nearly half a century from now there will be just about one young person paying taxes to support an elderly dependant. In Hong Kong, ageing is accelerated by low fertility, with the estimated median age of the population turning 60.7 in 2048 under the worst-case scenario described by Yip *et al.* (2001). As such, the changing environment has resulted in an increasingly higher social expectation of an expanded government role in social security provision and structured retirement protection.

Several failed proposals in the early 1990s, including a Community Wide Retirement Protection System suggested by the government in 1992 and the Old-Age Pension Scheme (OPS) proposed in 1994, indicated the extensively different opinions among society as a whole. Lui (1998) provides an excellent chronological account of the events and debates between the government, legislative council, academia, and others. The OPS proposal, essentially a pay-as-you-go (PAYGO) system in which current workers pay the benefits of current retirees, was criticized severely because it might have reduced savings, capital accumulation, and economic growth, and because it was considered unsustainable in the face of long-term demographic shifts (Lui, 1998). The government abandoned OPS in early 1995 and alternatively proposed the MPF Ordinance, which was first passed in Legco on 27 July 1995. The subsequent administrative and legislative push was delayed partly because of the transfer of sovereignty in July 1997, but the newly formed Hong Kong Special Administrative Region (HKSAR) showed its support for the MPF Ordinance legislation. The Ordinance was amended in March 1998, and supplemented by subsidiary legislation in April 1998 and May 1999, promulgating detailed regulations on the standards and detailed requirements governing the operation of the MPF system and the exemption of people covered by certain schemes governed by ORSO, which was enacted in 1992 and brought into operation in October 1993. The MPF Ordinance, after a long wait, came into operation in December 2000.

The introduction of the MPF system completes the three-pillar structure of old-age retirement protection in Hong Kong, however imperfect it might be. Recommended by the World Bank (1994), the three pillars of old-age income security consist of:

1. A mandatory, publicly managed, tax-financed social safety net.
2. A mandatory, privately managed, fully funded contribution scheme.
3. Voluntary personal savings and insurance.

In Hong Kong, the first pillar is provided by a Comprehensive Social Security Assistance (CSSA) scheme, which, based on a means test, offers a safety net to those proven to be in need of financial assistance. Currently, the basic rate is HK$1,805 per month for those up to age 59 and HK$2,555 per month for those aged 60 and above. Statistics from the Social Welfare Department of the Hong Kong government reveal that 57 per cent of CSSA recipients are the elderly. In addition, an Old Age Allowance scheme was added to social security provision in Hong Kong in 1977. For those between the ages of 65 and 69, the Normal Old Age Allowance of HK$625 per month is paid on a means-tested basis. For those aged 70 and above, the Higher Old Age Allowance of HK$705 per month is paid without a means test. These payments are kept deliberately low and obviously do not provide substantial retirement protection. However, a government report indicates that the Old Age Allowance accounts for about 70 per cent of overall social welfare expenditure, and 77 per cent of total social welfare recipients (Hong Kong Government, 1998).

Complemented by government-provided social welfare programmes as the first pillar and individual savings as the third pillar, the implementation of ORSO and the MPF Ordinance concludes all three pillars for old-age retirement protection.[3]

Main Features

Under ORSO and the MPF Ordinance, employment-related retirement plans were created as the second source of retirement income. These plans differ from the government-sponsored first pillar in that the funding comes from employers and/or employees, while the latter are tax-financed. Saving through employment-related retirement plans differs from voluntary private savings in that they receive special tax treatment that generally makes them a preferred method of saving for retirement. Offsetting some of the tax benefits is the disadvantage that these plans are subject to numerous government regulations, chief among them being the restriction on using savings in these plans for other purposes prior to retirement.

Employment-based retirement schemes can be divided into two general categories: defined benefit (DB) schemes and defined contribution (DC) schemes. Under a DB scheme, the level of benefits is promised and predetermined according to a formula with reference to the employee's age, years of service, final average salary, and so forth, but the employer's contribution rates are not defined. To the contrary, a DC scheme is a scheme where the employer's and employee's contribution rates are defined, but the amount of benefits accrued is based on the accumulated contributions with investment earnings (or losses). Bodie *et al.* (1988) have provided a classic and insightful comparison of DB and DC plans, and discussed the possibilities of combining the best attributes of the two. Davis (1998) offers summary discussions of the underlying economic issues implied in various alternative pension systems. For example, regarding the effects on labour markets, DB plans are more likely than DC plans to reduce labour mobility, as transfers typically lead to losses of accrued rights. On the other hand, DB plans encourage loyalty and reduce the costs of labour turnover for employers. In other words, the DC plans can be much more valuable to workers who change jobs several times, because DC plan payouts depend on market returns rather than length of service, age, or salary at separation from the firm, as in a DB plan (Bassett *et al.*, 1998). As for the effects on capital markets, Davis (1998) points out that DC plans may be more cautiously invested than DB plans, given the direct risk to the individual participating members who are in control of investment decisions and bear the consequences.

Historically, the majority of employees covered by private retirement plans in the United States participate in DB plans. The benefits under DB plans are guaranteed in nominal terms and partially insured by the Pension Benefit Guaranty Corporation (PBGC), while a DC plan provides no guarantee as to the level of benefits that will ultimately accrue. In addition, assets under DC plans are not insured by PBGC (Bassett *et al.*, 1998; Papke, 1999).

However, over the past two decades the trend in retirement saving plans has been moving away from traditional employer-managed DB plans and towards DC plans that are largely managed and controlled by employees. Among the various DC plans, the rapid growth of the US 401(k) plans[4] is one of the most important reasons for the ongoing trend towards DC plans (Wang, 2002). The total assets invested under 401(k) plans grew from virtually nothing at the beginning of the 1980s to over US$1.83 trillion by 2000. There are more than 42 million active participants investing in over 327,000 plans (Employee Benefit Research Institute, 2001).

Similar to 401(k) plans, the MPF system is an employment-based system in which employers and employees contribute a certain percentage of the salaries to an individual retirement saving account that is largely controlled by employees. The main features of MPF will be discussed in the following sections, with a comparison of its similarities, and its differences, with ORSO and the US 401(k) plans.

MPF and ORSO

The Hong Kong ORSO scheme regulates retirement plans set up by an employer for employees which provide benefits to the employees in the form of pensions, allowances, gratuities, or other payments, payable on termination of service, death, or retirement. Before the implementation of MPF, about one-third of the Hong Kong working population was covered by ORSO schemes. As a consequence, it is worth highlighting the similarities and differences between the corresponding features of MPF and ORSO and the impact of the MPF Ordinance on existing and new employees.

Impacts of MPF on Existing and New Employees

Under the MPF legislation, an employer who already operates an ORSO Scheme can be exempted from MPF if the scheme satisfies several defined criteria. Therefore the employer will have to decide whether and to what extent he should, or can, continue that scheme, and the employee may choose between the existing ORSO and MPF. The options selected have different implications for the employees concerned.

Existing Employees Opting to Remain in MPF-Exempted ORSO Schemes

If the existing ORSO scheme is granted exemption, existing employees know that their existing and future benefits in the scheme will not be subject to the preservation requirements[5] found with MPF schemes. This

Table 5.1   A Comparison of Corresponding Features between MPF and ORSO Schemes

	MPF	*ORSO*
Type	• Always a DC Scheme	• May be a DC or a DB Scheme
Basis	• Mandatory	• Voluntary
Law	• Governed by Hong Kong law	• May be governed by a law outside Hong Kong
Trust	• Established under Trust • Trust must be approved	• May be established under Trust or Insurance • No need for trustee approval
Vesting	• Vesting 100 per cent immediately	• Employees can take away their contribution when they leave the company, while whether they can get the employer's contribution depends on the vesting scale which has been predetermined by the employers

Additional Provisions	• Other features:
	  - All employees aged between 18 and 65 to join
	  - Minimum contribution rate
	  - Benefits portable
	  - Benefits to be preserved
	  - Relevant income defined
	  - Minimum relevant income
	  - Maximum relevant income
	  - Minimum requirements for Trustee/Investment and Managers/Custodians
		• No equivalent provisions required

Tax Benefit	• The MPF contributions made by both employers and employees are tax-exempt	• The contributions made under ORSO DC plans by both employers and employees cannot enjoy any tax allowance
Investment Choice	• The employees can decide their own investment choices	• In the DC plans under ORSO, the investment choice may be at the discretion of employers. Some employers may allow their staff to decide the investment choices on their own

could be to an employee's immediate perceived advantage if he leaves the employer before retirement age, since he would then be entitled to receive the relevant termination of service benefit in cash at that time. Nevertheless, there could also be a disadvantage if an existing employee has benefits which are not fully vested under the existing ORSO scheme.

New Employees Opting to Join MPF-Exempted ORSO Schemes

A new employee opting to join an exempted ORSO scheme would be subject to the minimum MPF benefit rule (exemption criteria for the ORSO). That minimum benefit will be subject to MPF preservation and portability requirements, so it cannot be paid out until retirement or other eligible time. The minimum MPF benefit must be transferred to an MPF scheme upon change of employment. However, any accrued benefits above the minimum MPF benefit can be paid out on termination of service.

Existing Employees Opting to Join MPF Scheme

All accrued benefits under the ORSO scheme should remain in that scheme until the employee becomes entitled to receive them. Thus, for instance, such benefits are payable in cash upon termination of service. However, if the employer has obtained consent from the scheme member, they may do it otherwise.

MPF and US 401(k)

The 401(k) plans are the most common DC arrangement in the US. A 401(k) is a profit-sharing or stock bonus plan that contains a cash-or-deferred-arrangement (CODA). With a CODA, eligible employees have the option of having their employer make a contribution to a plan on their behalf, or of receiving an equivalent amount in cash. Plan contributions are excluded from employee income for the year they are made. The most prevalent CODA is a salary reduction agreement, with which eligible employees may elect to reduce their compensation and have the difference contributed to the plan by the employer. Employers often add a matched amount to the plan which depends on the amount contributed by the employees (Bassett et al., 1998). Prior to 1978, only employers could make pre-tax contributions to DC plans, but with the advent of the 401(k) plan, the ability to make pre-tax contributions was extended to plan participants (Papke, 1999). The 401(k) plan is a particularly flexible form of DC plan. Participants assume responsibility for the plan's investment performance and typically direct the management of their investment across a menu selected by their employer. Plan loads are allowed and plan assets are usually distributed to participants when leaving the sponsoring employer (Bassett et al., 1998).

With these understandings in mind, we now can move on to compare the features and characteristics of 401(k) and MPF, as tabulated below.

Table 5.2   A Comparison of the Features and Characteristics between US 401(K) and HK MPF

	US 401(k)	HK MPF
Potential problems of the traditional social security system and the resulting reasons for change	• The Old-Age, Survivors, and Disability Insurance programme (commonly known as Social Security), a PAYGO system, is going to crash in the next century on the demographic rocks of the Baby Boomers' retirements (Mastio, 1999). • A large fraction of US families reach retirement age with virtually no personal financial assets. For instance, the median level of all personal financial assets of families with heads aged 55–64 was only $8,300 in 1991; excluding Individual Retirement Accounts (IRAs) and 401(k) balances, the median was only $3,000. Nearly twenty per cent of families had no financial assets at all. Thus, it is important to encourage individual saving through retirement saving programmes (Poterba *et al.*, 1996).	• Before MPF, Hong Kong was already operating a Comprehensive Social Security Assistance (CSSA) Scheme, offering only basic social security to the needy. • Hong Kong's rapidly ageing population and the lack of a formal system of retirement protection is a threat that needs to be resolved. • Nevertheless, Hong Kong people already accept the notion that they should retain part of their salary as savings for the future. The hope is that the addition of MPF to CSSA and personal savings can complete the 'three pillars' concept for old age retirement protection.
Background	The 401(k) plan was introduced in 1978. At the end of 2000, nearly more than 42 million participants have amassed at least US$1.83 trillion in 401(k) accounts (EBRI, 2001).	The operation of MPF started in December 2000. Nearly 1.75 million relevant employees joined the MPF scheme, accumulating an aggregate net asset value of HK$33.5 billion at the end of November 2001 (MPFA, 2002).
Tax advantages and saving incentive	• Under the 401(k) plan, state and federal taxes on contributions and investment earnings are deferred until the assets are distributed or withdrawn (Bassett *et al.*, 1998). • Tax-deferred contribution implies that employee does not pay tax on the contributions until the money is withdrawn from the plan (usually at retirement). The	• Mandatory contributions by employees are tax-deductible, subject to the maximum contribution of HK$12,000 per year. • Mandatory contributions by employers are also tax deductible, but there is an annual limit. The maximum tax allowance equals fifteen per cent of total yearly emoluments of the employees. • Capital gains and dividends

Table 5.2 *(continued)*

	US 401(k)	*HK MPF*
	return on the contributions accrues tax-free and taxes are paid at withdrawal. That means the employee is in fact earning the before-tax rate of return then. The favourable tax treatment is the main incentive for people to save more through the plan (Papke, 1999). • Empirical evidence (e.g., Poterba *et al.*, 1996, 1998) has shown that 401(k) contributions are net addition to saving. • Elective deferrals are subject to an annual limit—US$10,500 for 2000 (indexed for inflation) (Rejda, 2001).	are not taxed in Hong Kong. • The tax rate system in Hong Kong is simpler and lower than that of the US. Per 1998/9 figures, the tax rate system in HK is as follows: *Taxable income(HK$) Tax Rate* First $35,000 2% Next $35,000 7% Next $35,000 12% Remaining 17% • Obviously, the tax advantage of MPF is relatively lower than that of the 401(k), because of the tighter limits and the lower tax rates. It could be even worse for low-income groups as most of them are already free from tax after deducting the basic allowances.
Effects of income level on participation	• Contribution rate is voluntary and it is around five to eight per cent across all income levels (Bassett *et al.*, 1998). • Low-income workers are less likely to be offered a 401(k) plan, less likely to participate given sponsorship, and contribute smaller fractions of their salary given participation. The main reasons are as follows (Bassett *et al.*, 1998): a. They face lower tax rates and therefore benefit less from tax-deferral. b. They are likely to be liquidity-constrained and therefore have better uses for their funds than retirement saving. c. They are more likely to be covered by social welfare programmes and accordingly have less incentive to save. • Since marginal tax rates increase with income, the distribution of tax benefits	• Workers with monthly income over HK$4,000 must contribute five per cent of their relevant income, regardless of the level of wages earned. • Those with high incomes may make voluntary contributions as a means to accumulate savings further. • The difference in tax benefit between high-income and low-income employees is less skewed compared with that of the 401(k).

Table 5.2 *(continued)*

	US 401(k)	*HK MPF*
	from 401(k) plan is skewed toward high-income workers (Bassett *et al.*, 1998).	
Employer's contribution	• Employer may make matching contribution (voluntary) in an amount equal to a certain percentage of employee's compensation contributed to the plan, up to a certain percentage of the worker's salary. Whereas employee contributions are immediately vested, employer contributions can be subject to vesting requirements. Reasons for this feature are: a. Nondiscrimination Rules b. Incentive c. Aligning compensation and productivity d. Taxes. The matching feature increases the administrative cost of the plan. • Employer match is tax-deferred (up to the limit) until the plan assets are distributed or withdrawn. This results in a large initial return on the employee's investment that supplements the tax advantages of 401(k) plans, and creates a greater incentive to participate and/or increase contribution (Bassett *et al.*, 1998). • Employers may terminate the election or reduce the deferral percentage at any time (Baum, 1997).	• Employers currently operating ORSO scheme should also operate an MPF scheme so that employees can choose which one to join. If operating both schemes, they will need to deal with two service providers and pay two sets of administrative fees. • Employer is mandated to contribute five per cent of the employee's relevant income. They can also make voluntary contributions for their staff. • Employer contributions are tax-deductible. Employers can enjoy this tax benefit and at the same time do something for the futures of their personnel. • Employer contributions can be used to offset Long Service Payment (LSP) and Severance Payment (SP), which can lessen the burden of employers when their staff retire or are laid off. • The employer compliance rate achieved eighty-eight percent at the end of November 2001 (MPFA, 2002).
Employee contribution	• Employees can elect (subject to limitation) to make tax-deferred contributions as a percentage of pretax earnings, in addition to the employer's tax-deferred contributions. There are a number of investment options ranging from money market and bond	• Employee contributions are tax-exempt. The maximum tax allowance for MPF is HK$12,000 per year, which is subject to the amount of employee contribution. • Basically, employees should contribute five per cent of their relevant income in each

Table 5.2 *(continued)*

	US 401(k)	*HK MPF*
	funds to individual stock (Mastio, 1999). • Employee participation in 401(k) plans typically is voluntary, and the level of employee contribution if they do participate is also voluntary. • Employees also typically have more discretion in how the funds of their 401(k) plans are invested compared with other DC plans (Harrington and Niehaus, 1999).	month. They can certainly choose to make voluntary contributions on their own. This contribution is not tax-deductible, but can be taken out at any time. • Employees have the right to decide their investment choices in accordance with their risk aversion. • The employee compliance rate achieved 94.6 per cent at the end of November 2001 (MPFA, 2002).
Ways to substitute the new plan for the old plan	• There are several firm-level channels where substitution could occur: a. firms may replace existing DB or DC plans with 401(k)s b. firms may keep existing plans but put all marginal resources and new employees into 401(k)s c. new firms may create 401(k)s when they would otherwise have created some other type of pension plan if 401(k)s did not exist (Papke, 1999).	• Companies operating an ORSO scheme can choose to distribute their resources to the newly set up MPF scheme. • However, if companies do not have existing ORSO scheme, MPF should be their only choice. • After MPF launch, thirty-five per cent of existing DC schemes consolidated into MPF. Some existing DB schemes became closed schemes and would be gradually phased out as members terminate (Chiu, 2001).
Management fee	• Most 401(k) plans are administered by financial intermediaries who charge for their services. The fee scale is approximately thirty-five basis points for bond portfolio and seventy basis points for equity portfolio. This is slightly less than the average shareholder costs of all no-load equity funds, which are approximately eighty-three basis points (Poterba *et al.*, 2000).	• According to different MPF service providers, the total amount of administrative fee, trustee fee, custodian fee, and investment manager fee ranges from about seventy-five to three hundred basis points, which is relatively high when compared with 401(k) plans.
Asset allocation and investment decision	• The analysis of 401(k) asset allocation shows that Americans are placing only between a third and forty-five	• According to MPF service providers, the choice of investment funds can be categorized into the following

Table 5.2 *(continued)*

	US 401(k)	HK MPF
Asset allocation and investment decision *(cont'd)*	per cent of their cash into equity fund. Another third of 401(k) funds goes into various lower-return, lower-risk categories like bond funds, guaranteed investment contracts, balanced funds, and money market funds. This seems a bit conservative, as less than half is allocated to equity. Low-income earners are far more conservative in their investment choices than are others, and far less knowledgeable overall. • Regarding the distribution of cash going into equity funds, Hewitt 401(k) index states that twenty-six per cent is in large-capitalization stock funds (funds that invest in companies valued at $5 billion or more), five per cent in mid-cap (between $1 billion and $5 billion), one per cent in small-cap ($1 billion and under) and three per cent in international funds. Although historical data has shown that medium-sized and small firms might have offered a better return, many people, perhaps for reasons peculiar to amateur investment psychology, still prefer large-capitalization stocks. • Even worse, 401(k) participants have a huge appetite for the stock of their own employers. Hewitt reports that twenty-eight per cent of balances are in stock of the participants' companies. Such a large concentration of retirement saving in a single stock is a mistake and introduces a large and unnecessary risk that can be diversified away. • The net problem is that too many 401(k) participants hold risky, unbalanced portfolios that might not provide the	two kinds: direct fund and fund-of-fund. • For direct funds, members can decide to invest their contribution in a specific fund included in the service provider's scheme. • For fund-of-fund, members have to understand their risk aversion. The investment funds provided by service providers generally include low-, medium-, and high-risk investment. In addition, MPFA requires that each service provider should operate a Capital Preservation Fund (CPF), which must be 100 per cent invested in HK dollar investments, and placed in short-term bank deposits or short-term debt securities. Therefore CPF is the safest type of investment choice in MPF scheme. Members can decide their choice of asset allocation in accordance with their risk aversion, and let their service provider's investment manager manage their portfolio. • The service providers will allow their members to switch their fund choices. The number of free-of-charge fund switching in each year is at the discretion of service providers. • At the end of November 2001, there were 300 approved MPF constituent funds, including 51 CPFs, ten Money Market Funds, 40 Guaranteed Funds, eight Bond Funds, 137 Balanced Funds, and 54 Equity Funds. The overall asset allocation of 300 funds showed 21 per cent in deposits and cash, 33 percent in debt securities, and 46 per cent in equities. (MPFA, 2002) • Investment decisions among

Table 5.2 *(continued)*

	US 401(k)	*HK MPF*
	growth needed to fund an adequate retirement (Mastio, 1999).	MPF participants are yet to be studied.
Withdrawal	• Distribution generally may be made only if the employee terminates employment, attains age 591/2, dies, becomes disabled, or (except for earnings) incurs hardship. • Employees can withdraw funds from their 401(k) plans prior to retirement under certain hardship conditions. For example, funds could be withdrawn to pay family medical expenses, to pay for college tuition, or to purchase a principal residence. A ten per cent exercise tax generally applies to hardship withdrawal before age 55. Hardship withdrawals, by definition, are intended to be used for immediate needs and so are not paid back (Baum, 1997). • Employees can also access the plan funds before retirement through a loan, to serve a hardship, or for any reason when leaving a job. The amount that can be borrowed is up to the lesser of (1) $50,000 or (2) the greater of (a) one-half of the employee's interest in the plan, or (b) $10,000. The loan from the plans must be paid back with interest and therefore are not permanent withdrawals (Bassett *et al.*, 1998). • This provides flexibility to the participant to meet expected or unexpected needs and allows even short-tenure employees to accumulate funds and consolidate them with a new employer's pension plan. However, there is also a risk that employees may use their 401(k) assets for current	• Members can only withdraw their accrued benefits if they meet one of the following specific circumstances: a. Reaches age 65. b. Reaches age 60 and makes a statutory declaration that the person has permanently ceased employment. c. Permanent departure from Hong Kong. (This reason can only be used once in a person's lifetime.) d. Death. e. Total incapacity (the member cannot carry out the same kind of work prior to the time of becoming totally incapacitated). f. Small balance account: total balance not exceeding HK$5,000, and the member has not worked and paid contributions for more than twelve months. • When employees leave their company, they can choose to: a. Retain their accrued benefits in the original MPF accounts and open a new MPF account in the new employer's service provider. b. Bring the accrued benefits out of the original MPF accounts and put them into the new MPF account. • According to the rules and regulations of the MPF scheme, members are not able to take out their accrued benefits for the following reasons: a. During hardship (Unemployment) b. Medical expenses c. Purchase of permanent residence d. Educational fees

Table 5.2 *(continued)*

	US 401(k)	HK MPF
Withdrawal *(cont'd)*	consumption at the expense of adequate future consumption (Bassett *et al.*, 1998; Baum, 1997). • Should the employee choose to roll over the distribution into a new employer plan, an IRA, or another qualified retirement arrangement, taxes and future gains on the plan assets remain tax deferred. When distributions are not rolled over, they are subject to taxation in the year received (Bassett *et al.*, 1998). • The flexibility afforded enhances the portability of 401(k) benefit. It reduces the risk, which is typical in DB plans, of forfeiting pension benefits as a result of job change. However, the flexibility associated with the 401(k) withdrawal options raises the possibility that 401(k) participants may draw down their account balance before retirement (Poterba *et al.*, 2000).	e. Early retirement (before age 60) f. Bankruptcy. • Members are also not allowed to borrow money from their accrued benefits. Therefore, it seems that the MPF rules and regulations are not flexible enough to help resolve existing hardship problems. Further review and evaluations of these policies are certainly encouraged.
The trend	• 401(k) plans are likely to play a central role in providing for the retirement income of future retirees. Younger workers are more likely to participate in 401(k) than are older workers, and younger firms are less likely to offer traditional DB plans than older firms. The net effect of these trends will be an important shift in the future composition of retirement incoming provision. Availability of 401(k) plan in small firms has been lower than in large firms (Bassett *et al.*, 1998).	• MPF is a compulsory scheme that each company should enact. The future living standards of Hong Kong residents can therefore be maintained at a certain level. • Companies currently operating both ORSO and MPF schemes will tend to let ORSO schemes fade out and concentrate on MPF. It will be more efficient and effective for them to handle only a single scheme and pay only one administrative fee.

Contrasting the Impact on Participants

Through comparison of various aspects of the US 401(k) and MPF schemes, we now better understand the main features of Hong Kong's MPF, as well as its similarities to and differences from the most noteworthy DC scheme in the US. As the 401(k) has already been operating for more than twenty years, it has been refined several times to suit general needs (EBRI, 2002). On the contrary, the MPF is new to Hong Kong and is still operating at its infant stage. People argue that there are still lots of opportunities for improvement, so it is worth contrasting the two schemes and highlighting what we can learn from the experience of 401(k) implementation.

Tax Advantage and Saving Incentive

One important aspect of saving through qualified pension plans is the favourable tax treatment. In the US, the 401(k) plan allows employees to defer the taxation of salary set aside to fund retirement benefits (up to an annual maximum of US$10,500 for 2000). Furthermore, earnings on assets are not taxed until they are received, so employees are in fact earning the before-tax rate of return. These special tax treatments are the main incentive for people to contribute savings to the pension plan. As mentioned earlier, some eligible employees in the US are even accepting lower wages in exchange for an employer match in order to capture the tax advantage. In Hong Kong, only the mandatory portion of the employee contribution (subject to a maximum HK$12,000 per year) is tax-deductible, and capital gains and dividends received from individual investment are not taxed in Hong Kong. Hence, the incentive for people to save/contribute more through the pension plan because of tax advantages is relatively limited when compared with its US counterpart. Another difference between the US and Hong Kong is tax rates. In the US, the tax rates are relatively high and are much more progressive. Consequently, the tax advantage to high-income employees is much greater than to their low-income counterparts, and the former group has a greater saving incentive (voluntary) through the pension plan. In Hong Kong, there is a simpler and significantly lower tax rate system. As mentioned, the saving incentive for employees is mainly governed by the liquidity constraint rather than the tax rate differential.

Empirical evidence has shown that 401(k) plans do work well to increase saving in the US (Poterba *et al.*, 1996, 1998). In Hong Kong, there is no doubt that the savings rate through the plan will increase because of its mandatory nature. However, whether this increasing MPF saving is offset by decreasing saving using other vehicles is yet to be studied. What is more, Engen *et al.* (1996) point out that the contributions to retirement saving plans are tax-deductible, thus reducing public saving (increasing the budget deficit) in the short run. The long-term impact on public saving is less obvious. Research must be done before we can address the issue from a Hong Kong perspective.

Flexibility of Saving Withdrawal

The withdrawal process of the 401(k) is much more flexible than that of the MPF. As an example, US citizens can withdraw money from their accrued benefits for reasons of hardship, medical expenses, purchase of permanent residence, educational expense, etc. The Central Provident Fund in Singapore has also gradually expanded from originally being a compulsory retirement saving system to a multi-purpose system. Withdrawals because of housing and medical reasons are allowed (Lui, 1998). The US 401(k) participants can even borrow money from these accrued benefits. However, people in Hong Kong are not allowed to take out their accrued benefits in their MPF accounts because of the above reasons. It is a controversial matter if people cannot take out their own savings in times of hardship, and the government should consider relaxing of this constraint and making the MPF more flexible, especially for the poor. Of course, there is also a risk of depleting savings before retirement, so there is a trade-off between costs and benefits that needs further evaluation.

Incentive to Workforce

Under 401(k), the employer may match the employee's contributions in order to promote a loyalty incentive as, because the matching contribution can be subject to vesting rules, employees are always willing to stay in the company in order to get the matching contributions. Productivity is therefore increased and turnover reduced. This kind of incentive is relatively limited under MPF, because the vesting of employer's contributions (mandatory portion) is 100 per cent immediate. People do not suffer under the plan if they switch jobs frequently.

Rules and Regulations

Now that the MPF has been in operation for a while, there are many areas in the rules and regulations that need refining. For instance, the existing retirement age is assumed to be 65. In fact, the labour participation rate for people aged 60 and above is so low that it is difficult for people to find a job above the age of 60. Although they may accumulate sufficient income in their MPF account for early retirement, they are not allowed to draw it out before the age of 65, which seems a debatable matter.[6] But on the other hand, under the MPF regulations, participants can withdraw money after reaching the age of 60 and making a statutory declaration that they have permanently ceased employment. This seems to violate the 'Fourth Pillar', or gradual retirement, concept that has been promoted in several Organisation for Economic Cooperation and Development (OECD) countries (Delsen and Reday-Mulvey, 1996). Under this concept, retirees are encouraged to continue working on a part-time basis with the option of a partial pension, so as to continue contributing to the economy, all the while facilitating personal end-of-career management. The mindset reflected in the MPF rules and regulations has not yet caught up with the 'Four-Pillar' philosophy from the standpoint of flexible or early retirement arrangements.

Overall, the general concept of the MPF is meaningful for all Hong Kong citizens. It allows people to become used to allocating a definite amount of their salaries to their MPF account so that they can maintain a certain standard of living after retirement. However, people must also equip themselves with an understanding of investments that helps them see their own risk attitude and know how to allocate their contributions into different types of investment tool. It is essential for citizens to understand that poor investment performance can cause their standard of living at an elderly age to deteriorate greatly. Understanding investment objectives and implementing them through MPF will lead to a more stable life when older.

General Impacts

The execution of the MPF began on 1 December 2000. It had and will continue to have various degrees of impact on different parties, namely the general public, employers, service providers, and the HKSAR government. We will now examine these influences and discuss several issues involved.

General Public

The general public includes all people living in Hong Kong. Apart from students and retirees, an adult can be an employee, a self-employed person, or an unemployed person.

Employees and Self-Employed People

For employees and self-employed people, the effective income, i.e. the monthly take-home amount of money, will be reduced because five per cent of their relevant income goes into their MPF account. Although the mandatory contribution can be treated as a portion of savings for their retirement, their immediate standard of living will be lowered if they face liquidity needs, i.e., if the forced saving could have been used for housing, medical, or educational consumption.

In addition, because employers have to allocate a greater portion of their capital to pay for their contribution, employees may be deprived of the fringe benefits to which they were entitled before, such as medical insurance and group life insurance. In this way, the amount of money paid to each employee by employers will be roughly the same as that paid before MPF is implemented. Consequently, the salary of employees may be reduced by their employers with a view to transferring the burden of MPF contributions from employers to employees themselves.

Apart from viewing MPF as an employee benefit, employees should also bear the sole responsibility of making sound investment decisions. People need to equip themselves with knowledge of investment products, and conduct a risk analysis on those investment tools. This is because they have to make use of their contribution to invest in different kinds of unit trust with different levels of risk. They should understand their risk preference and their ability to encounter loss on their investment. They should also know how to allocate their accrued benefits to different unit trusts so that they can get the best return at their preferred risk level. The data indicate that, one year after its inauguration, the majority of MPF equity funds and more than half of balanced funds recorded an investment loss of between ten and twenty per cent (Yiu, 2001b). The volatile nature of equities markets makes this a particularly important issue for people who are close to retirement age and thus have a shorter investment horizon.

Unemployed and Non-Employed People

If the unemployed want to return to the job market, they may have to prepare themselves to receive lower wages because the burden of the employer's MPF contribution may be imposed on them. Moreover, job seekers now face greater than ever competition as capital movement makes the cross-border substitution of labour usage both possible and common. Hong Kong's unemployment rate hit a historical high of seven per cent in April 2002, suggesting that an increasing number of citizens are not able to prepare for their income needs in retirement, due to the nature of the employer-based MPF system.

Concern has also been raised regarding non-employed persons, notably women who voluntarily leave the labour market to become full-time housekeepers after marriage and childbearing. Whether or not they participate in the labour market again will not change the fact that their interrupted career has reduced their lifetime working income, as well as the MPF balances in their accounts. Studies suggest that women's lower lifetime income and disrupted work histories make the current MPF scheme inadequate for them to meet retirement security needs (Lee, 2001).

If the unemployed and the non-employed cannot rely on themselves (and employers) for retirement protection then social security—the CSSA and the Old Age Allowance—will become the safety net of last resort. An alternative proposal was brought forward to allow for public contributions on behalf of the unemployed, full-time mothers, and so on at the minimum wage (Ho, 1997). This fine-tuning will enhance the facets of the MPF system, but debates may arise about whether the government should use the tax revenue of the current generation or that of the next to fund the retirement protection of the unemployed and non-employed of the current generation.

The Poor

MPF is not a risk-pooling tool and it is not designed for social redistribution purposes. It means that retirees will not share the current contribution of the workforce and that people save for their own retirement. In this way, poor people in Hong Kong will not benefit from this scheme, because their low wages will allow them to contribute only a small amount of money into their own MPF account. Currently, two hundred thousand low-paid workers earning less than HK$4,000 a month are exempted from making any MPF contribution (Yiu, 2001b), so the amount of their accrued benefits will obviously not be enough for them to rely on these 'savings' after they have retired. Besides, five per cent of a poor person's monthly salary may be critical to their daily living expenses. If they have to contribute by putting five per cent of their salary into their MPF account, they cannot improve their present standard of living. The poor tend to have lower elasticity of intertemporal substitution, and the current MPF design may cause their overall lifetime welfare to deteriorate, rather than improve. We need empirical research in this regard.

Employers

The implementation of the MPF has added to Hong Kong employers' liabilities for Long Service Payment (LSP), Severance Payment (SP), tax reduction, probation period, and contribution period. As the employer's MPF contribution can be used to offset the LSP and SP, if employees are entitled to these, employers can actually consider their MPF contribution as regular savings which can be accumulated to pay for LSP and SP. It can also lead to a lower burden on the employers, because the actual amount that they need to take out of company funds to contribute to LSP and SP will be smaller than before.

In addition, the maximum tax allowance on the employer's contribution is fifteen per cent of the total annual salary of all employees of the company. As a result, if employers think of paying employees a voluntary contribution on top of the five per cent mandatory contribution in order to retain and attract talented employees, the tax allowance may make them feel that it is worth doing so.

The probation period of a new employee is normally three months. Since employers need to make a contribution for employees who have worked for the company for more than sixty days (around two months), they may consider changing the length of the probation period from three months to two so as to meet the MPF regulations.

The salary payment period may be different for different types of job in Hong Kong. Staff working in an office usually receive their salary once a month, workers in a factory may be paid twice a month, and casual employees working on a construction site or in restaurant may be paid on a weekly or even a daily basis. Employers need to evaluate the costs and benefits of meeting the MPF requirements and changing their payroll cycle.

As the cost of employing staff will become greater because of the employer's MPF contributions, employers may consider saving costs by paying lower wages, increasing working hours without overtime compensation, and even reducing employee benefits. In this way, the total profit earned by the company will not be greatly affected, enabling the company to maintain its present operation. Some employers, though, may feel that the burden of MPF is so overwhelming that they would prefer to close down or move their businesses. If so, redundancies will become unavoidable, and a large number of people will join the ranks of the unemployed. This is one potential adverse impact brought about by the implementation of MPF. Whether the MPF system actually causes a higher unemployment rate is, to some extent, an empirical matter that certainly deserves investigating.

Since MPF implementation, employers have probably had to adjust their methods of calculating the relevant income of each employee. As relevant income includes all cash payment except housing and medical allowances, employers may try to restructure the composition of the relevant income of employees in order to reduce the effect on the total profits of the company. Further, employers have to store remittance statements for seven years, and the monthly payment records for six months. Employers must therefore keep all of these documents in good condition so as to cope with the regulatory requirements of MPFA inspectors.

Service Providers

There are several types of MPF service provider, namely banks, insurance companies, and securities firms. As at 30 November 2001, the MPFA registered a total of 29,683 MPF intermediaries, fifty-five per cent of them whose primary sponsoring corporations are insurance firms, forty-two per cent banking companies, and three per cent securities firms (MPFA, 2002). They provide customers with not only MPF services, but also banking, insurance, or investment product services. Before MPF implementation, these service providers prepared for customer service (after-sales) support, marketing strategy, and corresponding activities, and also provided training for front-line staff, in order to compete for market share.

With an injection of as much as HK$30 billion a year, the launch of MPF has definitely boosted the fund management industry in Hong Kong. The competition has been intense among market players. Around twenty trustees and forty service providers were in the race at the beginning, but both numbers are declining as consolidation continues. To excel in the MPF market, companies need a broad clientele base of small and medium enterprises (SMEs), because the majority of Hong Kong breadwinners work for SMEs with around one to five hundred staff. Certainly, a successful MPF market player also needs a strong sales team with qualified and well-trained MPF intermediaries who observe the Code of Conduct and provide the most up-to-date information to customers. Cross-selling opportunities also offer incentives for alliances (e.g., AIA-JF, an alliance between American International Assurance and Jardine Fleming) and mergers and acquisitions (e.g., HSBC acquiring Pacific Century's MPF business) as consumers demand one-stop services for their various financial needs.

Compared to the service providers' primary businesses in insurance, retail banking, or asset management, profit margins in the MPF market are generally thin, therefore demanding a substantial critical mass to sustain a viable operation. People in the industry have usually referred to a five per cent market share as the cut-off point for survival. Since MPF implementation, keen competition and a price war has worsened the outlook for profitability. Providers are commonly poised for years of red ink before breaking even; pessimists suggest ten years. While MPF trustees and service providers do their utmost to expand their business coverage so as to strengthen relationships with their customers and maintain market status, more cross-selling marketing and mergers and acquisitions activity is expected.

Government

As the average age of the Hong Kong citizen increases, the HKSAR government has to find some way of solving the problems of the aged and lessen the pressures they bring. The objective of the HKSAR government in implementing MPF is mainly to transfer from itself to the general public the heavy burden of financial assistance (Comprehensive Social Security Assistance) to an ageing population. The government body handling this project is the Mandatory Provident Fund Scheme Authority (MPFA).

As a new department, the MPFA has done a successful job, judging by the high compliance ratio and relatively few incidents of fraud. But it is also widely recognized that the rules governing MPF would need modifications to meet the needs of a changing society. The US 401(k) market has been so successful because several amendments have been made over the years. The regulator should work closely with representatives from employees, employers, and service providers on a regular basis to fine-tune the rules and regulatory frameworks. Currently, the existence of the Retirement Schemes Industry Group (RSIG), formed in May 2001 and consisting of the Hong Kong Federation of Insurers, the Hong Kong Investment Funds Association, and the Hong Kong Trustees Association, provides a communicative bridge between the government and the industry. Among various stated objectives, RSIG hopes to:

> (i) provide an effective forum for the government and relevant authorities to conduct industry consultation on policy issues and proposed legislative amendments; (ii) work closely with legislators to develop new legislation to ensure that a sound and robust retirement fund platform is provided for all the people of Hong Kong; (iii) obtain consensus of opinions across associations and respond rapidly to the government on issues affecting the retirement fund industry (Hong Kong Federation of Insurers, 2001).

This cross-industry group has played an essential role in the MPF Schemes Operation Review Committee set up by the MPFA in August 2001, which recently proposed amendments to MPF legislation that was expected to be processed in the Legislative Council in the second quarter of 2002.

To cover any employee who might suffer losses as a result of misfeasance or illegal conduct by the trustee or any party in the administration and management of a registered MPF plan, Section 17 of the MPF Schemes Ordinance requires the MPFA to set up a Compensation Fund. The government will initially inject a sum of HK$600 million into the Fund. The Fund will then accumulate money from levies on asset values of registered schemes at a rate of 0.03 per cent. Noticeably, there was no compensation fund established or prepared for any default in voluntary retirement schemes established under ORSO.

Lastly, the recent industrial trend towards the convergence of financial services companies has brought challenges to regulators. For example, the regulatory role of ORSO was taken by the MPFA from the Office of the Commissioner of Insurance (OCI), the government department that regulates insurance companies. Insurance companies, however, are offering MPF plans, and many insurance agents have registered with the MPFA to sell MPF products. The growing popularity of bancassurance[7] and investment-linked insurance products inevitably involves the participation of the Hong Kong Monetary Authority, which regulates banking activity, and the Securities and Futures Commission, which regulates the investment fund industry. The consolidation among regulators may generate synergy and simplify the regulatory framework. At a minimum level, the merger of OCI (with ninety staff) and the MPFA (which has 260 staff) could be recommended, as is the case in Australia, where there is a single body which regulates both the pensions and insurance businesses (Yiu, 2001a).

Conclusion

The introduction of the Mandatory Provident Fund System is a milestone for Hong Kong. It provides Hong Kong with the missing component of comprehensive retirement protection along the lines of the World Bank's 'three-pillar' approach, which calls for (1) a mandatory, privately managed, fully funded contribution scheme, (2) a publicly managed, tax-financed social safety net for the old, and (3) voluntary personal savings and insurance. Notwithstanding the teething problems we have seen so far and further anticipate, the MPF system does bring Hong Kong one step further towards providing retirement protection for Hong Kong's workforce. The annual injection of HK$30 billion is positive for the development of the local capital markets. Many issues, including the effects of the MPF on savings, unemployment, the labour market, capital markets, (implied) wealth redistribution, and so on, are still to be explored. When the system matures, we would hope to see more research conducted in order to enhance our understanding of those effects. Only with solid and robust scholarly findings can we objectively evaluate what the creation of MPF has brought to Hong Kong.

Discussion Questions

1. The main issue for pension funding, according to Professor Alan Waler of Sheffield University, UK, is not population ageing *per se* but the way it relates to changes in birth rates, the structure of employment, and the practice of retirement. Do you agree? Disagree? Does this assertion hold in the Hong Kong context?
2. The World Bank (1994) suggested the three-pillar structure of old-age income security. What are the three pillars? Do you think the implementation of the MPF system completes the three-pillar structure of old-age retirement protection in Hong Kong? If not, what is missing?
3. Briefly discuss the differences of defined-benefit (DB) and defined-contribution (DC) retirement plans. What are their respective advantages and disadvantages? What category does MPF belong to? Does MPF share the generic advantages and disadvantages of that type of retirement plan?
4. Conventional economics theory assumes a person to be a single economic decision maker throughout his or her lifetime; Posner (1995), on the other hand, argues that an individual could be modelled as a locus of competing selves in which a person at working age may have different objectives from the same person at retirement age. Do you agree or disagree? Why? Ask your parents, relatives, or friends who have already retired which theory better describes them.
5. Conduct an interview with a company or organization that operates both ORSO and MPF Schemes. Which scheme is preferred by their new employees? Why?
6. There are similarities as well as differences between the US 401(k) plans and Hong Kong's MPF plans. Briefly discuss them.
7. On 12 July 2002, Hong Kong lawmakers voted to raise the minimum salary threshold for the five per cent MPF contribution by $1,000 to $5,000. It was estimated that about 57,000 low-income earners who earn between $4,000 and $5,000 would be exempted from MPF. Will the affected parties be better off as a result of this policy change for the time being? How about at retirement?
8. According to a survey conducted by Watson Wyatt Consulting Company, the top three players in the MPF market are HSBC, Manulife, and AIA, who represent twenty-three per cent, fourteen per cent, and ten per cent of market share respectively. Visit the Hong Kong Office of the Commissioner of Insurance (OCI) web site and look for market concentration of life and non-life insurance business in Hong Kong. What are the factors that make the differences in market concentration between the MPF and insurance markets?

9. In your opinion, should MPFA merge with the OCI? Why or why not?
10. Is MPF neutral towards income redistribution? Would MPF increase, decrease, or have no effect on Hong Kong's savings rate?

Keywords

Comprehensive Social Security Assistance
defined benefit
defined contribution
life-cycle model
Mandatory Provident Fund Schemes Authority
Occupational Retirement Schemes Ordinance
Pension Benefit Guaranty Corporation
US 401(k) plans

6. The Insurance Industry

Jason Yeh

Introduction

The term 'risk management' gained wide currency in the 1960s and 1970s amongst those interested in exploring broader options for managing insurable risk or 'pure risk' (Doherty, 2000). Apart from loss prevention and loss control, insurance is an essential aspect of risk management and presumably the dominant form of commercial risk transfer. Traditionally, insurance has focused on pure risk such as premature death, illness, property damage, liability, and related insurable risks that offer only a chance of downside loss but no upside gain. In contrast to pure risk, 'speculative risk' refers to those price and credit risks where the possibility of gain, as well as loss, exists. Speculative risks are usually excluded in insurance products, but are dealt with in financial derivatives, such as futures and options, which became popular in the 1980s and 1990s. Around the turn of the century, organizations increasingly began to recognize the benefits of managing all risks simultaneously, both through particular products and through management within the organization itself. Along with increasing risk awareness, the traditional distinctions between types of risk have become blurred, as have the lines between the business products that manage risk. The landscape of the insurance industry is therefore changing, promoted by several factors including the rapid growth of derivatives markets, incessant global mergers and acquisitions activities, and the increasing integration of financial services institutions.

As the financial marketplaces of the world undergo rapid change, insurance firms worldwide are facing greater challenges as well as opportunities. Globalization, liberalization, consolidation, and the information technology revolution, among other factors, are creating a marketplace unimaginable just a decade ago. The insurance industry in Hong Kong, being an essential division of the territory's energetic financial sector, has also gone through various dramatic changes throughout the 1990s and into the new millennium. One chapter of the first edition of *The Hong Kong Financial System* (Wong, 1991) described and discussed Hong Kong's insurance industry before 1990. This chapter will take up where it left off, characterizing the changes and issues that have emerged since then.

Several features of development can be characterized, including the continuous growth of the markets, the sophistication of the marketplace, the establishment and maturation of the regulatory framework, and the improvement in training and education. The Office of the Commissioner of Insurance (OCI), the regulatory body set up for the administration of the Insurance Companies Ordinance (Chapter 41 of the laws of Hong

Kong), the central piece of insurance legislation, was established in June 1990 to enhance the sound development of the insurance industry in the territory. In June 1995, the regulatory framework for insurance intermediaries, i.e. insurance agents and brokers, was first introduced. The Hong Kong Mortgage Corporation, founded in March 1997 and a wholly owned Hong Kong Special Administrative Region (SAR) government corporation through the Exchange Fund, created the mortgage insurance and reinsurance business in March 1999. At the beginning of 2000, the Insurance Intermediaries Quality Assurance Scheme was imposed to offer uniform standards with a minimum qualification for insurance agents and brokers. On 1 December 2001, the Mandatory Provident Fund Scheme (MPF) came into effect, changing the landscape of the working population's retirement protection system and providing the industry with challenges and opportunities. Besides the marketing efforts for the MPF, the emergence and increasing popularity of investment-linked products created a need for more knowledgeable and professional insurance practitioners. Universities in the SAR started to offer undergraduate programmes in actuarial science, risk management and insurance, pension management, and so on. Insurance education offered at the higher diploma level not only supplies the industry with well-trained professionals with a broader scope, it also improves societal perceptions of insurance by providing potential employees with a high level of professionalism and business integrity.

Since the handover in mid-1997, Hong Kong has integrated into China's economy more closely than before. China's insurance sector, although it remains rather underdeveloped, experienced double-digit growth per annum during the 1990s. The Hong Kong and mainland Chinese insurance markets are expected to see a higher level of integration since China's acceptance into the World Trade Organisation (WTO) in 2001. There is no space here to delineate the development of the Chinese insurance industry, but the integration will doubtlessly bring challenges and opportunities to Hong Kong's insurance industry.

The growth of the Hong Kong insurance markets continued to outperform the growth of gross domestic product (GDP) over the past decade, thereby resulting in a steady increase in the insurance penetration ratio, which is defined as gross premiums divided by GDP. In 2000, the most current comparable figure indicated that the ratio in Hong Kong was 4.86 per cent, still far behind the average ratio of industrialized countries,[1] which was 9.08 per cent. In the same year, Hong Kong had an insurance density, defined as gross premiums per capita, of US$1,162, less than half of the industrialized countries' average of US$2,384. The statistics revealed by market comparisons point on one hand to a tremendous growth potential ahead; on the other, they indicate that much more needs to be done for Hong Kong to become a comprehensive financial centre in the region.

A further breakdown of the market statistics shows that Hong Kong is particularly underinsured in terms of general (non-life) insurance compared to the global average. In 2000, the Hong Kong insurance penetration for non-life business was 1.12 per cent, not only far below the world average of 2.96 per cent, but also lower than the Asian average of 1.76 per cent. While the OCI is actively promoting Hong Kong as a regional insurance centre, it is apparent that more proactive measures have to be taken to achieve this goal. The Insurance Authority has been developing captive insurance and reinsurance business potential in Hong Kong, which should boost the incomparably weak general insurance business sector.

The structure of this chapter is as follows. First, a brief theoretical background of insurance is provided. Next, an overview of the Hong Kong insurance markets is given. The insurance regulatory framework in Hong Kong is then examined, and several industry trends and issues will be discussed and explored. Special attention will be paid to the Hong Kong government's effort to promote the reinsurance and captive insurance centre. Finally, there is a discussion of the Hong Kong insurance industry's prospects and outlook.

Insurance: The Brief Micro Foundation and Macro Comparisons

Theories of insurance are treated in the context of choice under uncertainty in microeconomics texts, such as Varian (1992), Kreps (1990), and Mas-Colell *et al.* (1995). Risk-averse individuals rationally demand insurance when facing uncertainty of loss. Under the maximization of expected utility paradigm, people will buy full insurance if the insurance contract is actuarially fair (premiums charged precisely equal to the expected loss). If not, consumers will only partially insure against the unexpected loss and choose to bear some of the risk. A good result relies on assumptions of homogeneous risk and fortuitous loss. When the risks of consumers are heterogeneous, adverse selection occurs. People with higher risk tend to buy more insurance, whereas the low-risk group tends to self-insure. If insurance is compulsory and premiums do not reflect the level of riskiness, cross-subsidization will arise. If on the other hand the loss is not fortuitous, i.e. consumers can influence the probability or severity of loss, then problems of moral hazard will be unavoidable. Consequently, less-informed insurers will suffer adversely under asymmetrical information. Theoretical and empirical work has been done to study such phenomena, contributing to and expanding the field of economics of insurance. A substantial amount of literature on market signalling, revelation principle, and mechanism design (such as optimal contract, deductibles, coinsurance, and indemnity limit) exists which addresses the above situations.

There will be no disagreement that the demand for insurance (or a broader sense of economic security) comes after the basic human needs of food, clothing, and shelter, suggesting a positive relationship between an individual's wealth and insurance purchase. However, the marginal utility of insurance consumption may decrease with income, as do other normal goods. One luxurious dinner may buy a high level of satisfaction if affordable, but even if ten were affordable, nobody would try to consume ten dinners in a single evening. Insurance demand theory under the expected utility paradigm suggests that the purchase of insurance depends on a number of factors including income, wealth, price of insurance, risk aversion, and probability of loss. For example, in examining the optimal amount of insurance purchase, Mossin's (1968) theoretical model shows that an individual's deductible level is positively related to wealth, assuming decreasing risk aversion.[2] Feldstein (1972) suggests that the net effect of income on the demand for insurance is indeterminate. High-income earners are more willing to retain risks which will, in turn, decrease the level of insurance consumption. On the other hand, when a person's income increases, the demand for insurance might also increase because of the increased tax benefit under progressive tax structure and the increased usage of health service. Empirically, Manning *et al.* (1987) have shown that the probability of use of medical services increases with income.

At a macro level, empirical studies on international insurance demand found a positive relationship between demand for insurance and national income (e.g. Beenstock *et al.*, 1986; Browne and Kim, 1993; Browne *et al.*, 2000). An interesting model was developed by Swiss Re Economic Research & Consulting (1996) to explain cross-country insurance demand patterns. The so-called S-curve depicts the relationship between economic development (GDP per capita) and insurance market development (based on insurance penetration, i.e. premiums per GDP) and reveals that insurance spending rises particularly fast where GDP per capita levels are in the region of US$1,000 to US$10,000. These countries show a steep line in the mid-range of S-curve, indicating that insurance expenditures grow significantly faster than income. Outside the range, for countries of lower and higher income levels, the income elasticity of insurance demand is closer to one, reflecting a much flatter line in the S-curve.

Other than income, one important factor in evaluating cross-country insurance demand is the extent to which it is needed. A socialist nation, for example, would need less insurance than a capitalist nation because the socialist society provides protection against many losses. In most industrialized nations, for instance, health insurance and/or health care is available through the government. Similarly, a nation with extensive social programmes would have a lower need for insurance because people would receive income protection from the government. Institutional variations, macroeconomic conditions, and demographic determinants are all important in explaining the different levels of international insurance consumption.

In her paper discussing the emerging insurance markets in Asia, Chu (2001) specifically stratified Asian insurance markets into three levels: fully mature, transitional, and incipient. She considers Japan the only fully mature market, as it accounts for over seventy-five per cent of the insurance premiums in Asia. Hong Kong, together with South Korea, Taiwan, and Singapore, can be classified as transitional markets, where the demand

Figure 6.1 The Insurance S-Curve

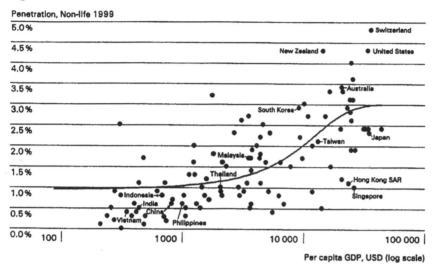

Source: Courtesy Swiss Re Economic Research & Consulting. *Sigma* No. 4/2001

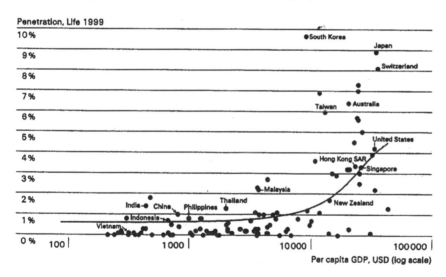

Note: The S-scurve shows the statistical relationship between insurance penetration and economic development (represented by per capita GDP). The curve is estimated using panel data from more than 60 countries.
Source: Courtesy Swiss Re Economic Research & Consulting. *Sigma* No. 4/2001

for insurance grows substantially faster than wealth. The two major incipient markets identified are China and India, which are also the world's two most populated countries. Table 6.1 shows the comparison of insurance density and insurance penetration in eight insurance markets, as well as the comparable Organisation for Economic Cooperation and Development (OECD) and world insurance statistics.

Table 6.1   Comparison of Insurance Density and Insurance Penetration (2000)

	(1) Insurance Premiums (US$M)	(2) Yr-to-Yr Growth (%)	(3) Population (Million)	(4) Insurance Density (US$)	(5) GDP (US$M)	(6) Insurance Penetration (%)
USA	865,327	4.8	274.5	3,152.1	9,873,000	8.76
Japan	504,005	0.6	126.8	3,973.3	4,616,000	10.92
South Korea	58,348	10.4	47.3	1,234.1	447,000	13.05
Taiwan	22,790	9.6	22.1	1,030.0	308,000	7.39
Hong Kong	7,898	17.2	6.8	1,162.0	163,000	4.86
Singapore	3,965	7.4	4.0	966.3	93,000	4.21
PR China	19,278	14.1	1,265.8	15.2	1,080,000	1.79
India	9,933	16.6	999.1	9.9	428,000	2.32
OECD	2,292,755	6.4	1,128.2	2,032.1	25,674,000	8.93
World	2,443,673	6.6	6,035.0	404.9	31,161,000	7.84

Note: 1. (2) Year-to-year change is inflation-adjusted
        2. (4) Insurance Density = (1) Insurance Premiums / (3) Population
        3. (6) Insurance Penetration = (1) Insurance Premiums / (5) GDP
        4. The USA and Japan are the two giant players in the insurance industry, accounting for 35.4 and 20.6 per cent of global insurance market share respectively. The two countries together make up 56 per cent of the market. The other 142 economies have the remaining 44 per cent.
        5. OECD figures are from 29 member countries, whose insurance premium volumes account for 93.8 per cent of world market.
Source: Swiss Re (2001)

Overview of the Markets (Size and Market Structure)

The insurance marketplace in Hong Kong has recorded remarkable growth since the 1980s. As Table 6.2 shows, while Hong Kong GDP grew six-fold from HK$192 billion in 1982 to HK$1.26 trillion in 1999, the insurance gross premium expanded twelve times from HK$4.7 billion to HK$58.6 billion during the same period. The robust growth momentum, which outpaces the overall economy, has shown the receptive attitude to insurance products among an increasingly affluent population and the gradually mature corporate risk management culture. However, despite this strong growth, Hong Kong's insurance industry is far from saturation point. Judging from the most recent data on insurance density and penetration, Hong Kong is only slightly above one-half of the OECD average. In 2000, a typical Hong Kong citizen spent US$1,162 on insurance products, representing 4.86 per cent of GDP, compared to the OECD average of US$2,032 per head and 8.93 per cent of GDP, as revealed in Table 6.1. With a reference to the per capita GDP comparison, Hong Kong's US$23,970 is even somewhat higher than the OECD average of US$22,756 in the same year. The contrast suggests that the insurance industry in Hong Kong is still lagging behind and has a lot of catching up to do.

Table 6.2   Gross Domestic Product, Gross Premiums, and Penetration
              Ratio (1982–2000)

Year	GDP (HK$M)	Gross Premium (HK$M)	Penetration Ratio (%)
1982	192,488	4,771	2.48%
1983	212,673	6,254	2.94%
1984	256,493	7,535	2.94%
1985	271,655	8,760	3.22%
1986	312,561	10,658	3.41%
1987	384,488	12,145	3.16%
1988	455,022	13,585	2.99%
1989	523,861	15,819	3.02%
1990	582,549	18,975	3.26%
1991	668,512	23,083	3.45%
1992	779,336	28,021	3.60%
1993	897,463	33,986	3.79%
1994	1,010,885	41,086	4.06%
1995	1,077,145	44,040	4.09%
1996	1,191,890	46,730	3.92%
1997	1,323,862	51,173	3.87%
1998	1,259,306	55,595	4.41%
1999	1,226,983	58,622	4.78%
2000*	1,266,653	63,873	5.04%

Note: * Figures are subject to revision later as more data become available.
Sources of data: Census and Statistics Department, Hong Kong, *Estimates of Gross Domestic Product*, March 2002.
        Census and Statistics Department, Hong Kong, *Survey of Storage, Communication, Financing, Insurance & Business Services*, 1982–2002.

A breakdown of statistics across the line of general (non-life) versus long-term (life) insurance business indicates that the latter is stronger than the former. The strength of the long-term business defeated the economic recession during the 1997 Asian financial crisis and continued to grow, while the general insurance business grew approximately in line with the overall economy and recorded negative numbers of growth in the second half of the 1990s. Looking at it from an international perspective, Hong Kong's general insurance business is located far below the global non-life S-curve, suggesting underinsurance in general business. As regards the long-term insurance business, it is in fact located slightly above the global life S-curve. Yip (1994) and Yu (1997) provide arguments that partially explain the phenomenon. They maintain that the demand for life insurance and its use as a savings tool in personal financial portfolios is likely to increase as the standard of living improves, while the demand for general insurance is largely driven by general business activities rather than standard of living. Other explanations may lie in Hong Kong's demographic condition and natural environment. A gradually ageing Hong Kong society needs more life insurance products (many of which contain a savings component) for retirement provision, thereby continuously expanding the life insurance sector. Conversely, the limits on car ownership and natural catastrophe exposure have restricted non-life insurance business growth (Swiss Re, 2001).

General Insurance Business

Looking at it from the supply side, the general insurance sector can be characterized as highly fragmented and over-competitive. Of the 204 authorized insurers as at 31 December 2001, 140 were direct non-life insurers, compared to 45 direct life insurers.[3] The top five non-life insurers accounted for only 23 per cent of market premium in 2000, compared to 57 per cent of life insurance concentration ratio (OCI, 2001a).[4] In addition to fierce price competition, insurers further suffer from rising legal costs and court awards in the liability lines of business. The sector recorded an underwriting loss of HK$872.3 million in 2000, the fourth consecutive year of seeing underwriting results in negative territory, as shown in Table 6.3.

Breaking the numbers down, the Employees' Compensation (EC) and Motor Vehicle business contributed most significantly to the poor performance of the non-life sector, with underwriting losses of HK$1,059.6 million and HK$407.2 million respectively.[5] The year 2000 was not a particular unlucky time for these two categories of business; rather, EC

Table 6.3   Overall Performance of General Insurance Business (1996–2000)

	1996 (HK$M)	1997 (HK$M)	1998 (HK$M)	1999 (HK$M)	2000 (HK$M)
Gross Premiums	18,508.1	19,483.2	17,930.5	16,531.6	17,872.1
Net Premiums	12,033.2	12,634.7	12,221.1	11,127.6	12,199.8
Technical Reserves	14,890.2	16,494.4	16,681.3	17,506.0	18,244.1
Underwriting Results:					
Earned Premiums	12,415.2	12,473.2	12,294.3	11,466.5	11,698.6
Underwriting Expenses	5,148.2	5,522.3	5,458.9	5,105.8	5,077.0
Net Claims Incurred[1]	6,666.7	7,009.4	7,539.5	7,739.4	7,493.9
Underwriting Profit/(Loss)	600.3	(58.5)	(704.1)	(1,378.7)	(872.3)
	%	%	%	%	%
Growth of Gross Premiums	−7.9	5.3	−8.0	−7.8	8.1
Retention Ratio	65.0	64.8	68.2	67.3	68.3
Commissions Payable Ratio	25.5	25.6	26.7	25.5	24.0
Net Claims Incurred Ratio	53.7	56.2	61.3	67.5	64.1
Underwriting Margin[2]	4.8	−0.5	−5.7	−12.0	−7.5
Technical Reserves Ratio[3]	123.7	130.5	136.5	157.3	149.5

Note: 1. Sum of Commissions Payable, Management Expenses, and Unexpired Risks Adjustment.
     2. Underwriting Profit/(Loss) expressed as a percentage of Earned Premiums.
     3. Technical Reserves expressed as a percentage of Net Premiums.
Source of data: Office of the Commissioner of Insurance, Hong Kong, *Annual Report*, 2001(a).

insurance had been making consecutive losses over the previous decade, while motor vehicle insurance recorded losses in seven out of the previous ten years, as shown in Figure 6.2. This continuous loss-making has made EC business unsustainable in Hong Kong, and it is widely acknowledged that action is urgently needed to maintain the survival of the whole industry. From the regulator's standpoint, the transparency of EC insurance business and adequacy of technical reserves are the main areas that attract the attention of the OCI. From the insurers' perspective, a substantial upward adjustment of premiums seems unavoidable in order to reflect the true cost of operation and maintain solvency. Since EC is compulsory in Hong Kong, rising premiums will cause already skyrocketing business operating costs to rise further. Particularly during the current economic downturn and historically high unemployment rate, employees as a group will ultimately shoulder the burden of this problem.

Figure 6.2 Underwriting Profit/Loss of Motor & Employees' Compensation Business

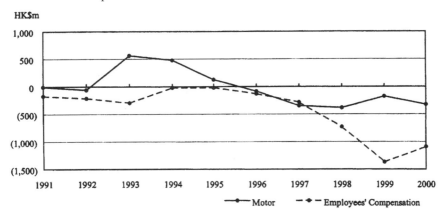

Source: Courtesy The Hong Kong Federation of Insurers

The author believes that the problem lies in the structural defect of Hong Kong's EC system. Currently, an injured worker is entitled to statutory as well as common law benefits, leading to a huge financial burden to the system. A cross-country study offered in a joint report by an actuarial consulting firm and a law firm (Trowbridge Consulting and Deacons, 2000) indicated that, besides Hong Kong, only the UK provides both statutory benefits and unrestricted access to common law. Although the statutory benefits provided in the UK are much lower, the report suggests that the UK scheme is experiencing some of the cost pressures evident in Hong Kong, albeit not yet to the same extent.

Harrington and Niehaus (1999) have criticized a system that incorporates both employer strict liability and tort benefits,[6] because it creates an excessive safety incentive (additional safety that would not be worth the costs), excessive compensation (such as damages for pain and suffering that could not be objectively measured), and the highest administrative/ dispute resolution costs. The substantial uncertainty (as opposed to certainty under the arrangement of mandatory EC benefits without tort liability rights) will probably result in lower wages and less employment. The author agrees with the argument made by Harrington and Niehaus that employees would want insurance (risk sharing and risk transfer) for economic losses resulting from a work-related injury, but not insurance for non-monetary losses (pain and suffering). Therefore, a system with mandatory EC benefits as the exclusive source of remedy will best meet the interests of employees and employers both in the short run and in the long run. Raising premiums or requiring stricter reserves and solvency standards will only prolong the problem; thus the author believes that the only solution is an overhaul of the Employees' Compensation Ordinance.

Long-Term Insurance Business

As stated above, Hong Kong's long-term insurance business had a robust growth momentum for two decades, even during the Asian financial crisis. Despite continuous double-digit expansion, the market is believed to be still far from saturation. Table 6.4 shows the number of policies and premiums by breakdown across types of life insurance business. The data imply there are sixty-nine life policies per hundred Hong Kong citizens, a number that is still significantly lower than that of other mature markets, where it is common for a person to own more than one life insurance policy. Table 6.4 also indicates that a source of strong growth contributing to the long-term insurance business is investment-linked policies. Although still a small component in the individual line, linked products have gained substantially in popularity. Linked products are whole-life insurance policies with an investment component that is controlled to some extent by policyholders themselves. For the five years from 1996 to 2000, the growth rate was tremendous, at an average of around twenty per cent both in terms of number of policies and premiums, compared to the lower growth rate of about ten per cent from ordinary non-linked policies. One possible explanation is attributed to the lower rate of return on the savings component and the lack of transparency of the cash value accumulation of traditional products. Amid keen competition pressure from mutual funds, commercial banks, and other financial institutions, insurers are using linked products offering higher returns in order to win customers.

Non-linked life insurance products can be further divided into four categories: whole life, endowment, term, and others. Term insurance, the purest form of life insurance, provides temporary death protection and has no savings component. Whole life and endowment are cash-value life insurance policies that bundle premature death protection and long-term savings. Endowment policies are no longer sold in the US, but are still popular in Asia, including Hong Kong. The premiums of such policies are expensive, with extremely high costs per unit of insurance, but they guarantee a payout (of the face amount) after a specified period, usually twenty or

Table 6.4 Long Term Insurance Business (1996–2000)

NUMBER OF POLICIES					
Types of Insurance	1996	1997	1998	1999	2000
Individual Life Non-linked	3,032,419 9.8%	3,321,914 9.5%	3,630,879 9.3%	4,043,138 11.4%	4,319,680 6.8%
Individual Life Linked	93,908 23.0%	122,773 30.7%	150,322 22.4%	202,612 34.8%	285,700 41.0%
Individual Life Subtotal	3,126,327 10.2%	3,444,687 10.2%	3,781,201 9.8%	4,245,750 12.3%	4,605,380 8.5%
Group Life	10,487 13.9%	11,864 13.1%	12,147 2.4%	13,295 9.5%	14,335 7.8%
Retirement Scheme	13,549 10.5%	12,940 9.1%	13,825 6.8%	13,886 0.4%	17,527 26.2%
Others	9,599 3.5%	10,955 14.1%	12,420 13.4%	35,980 189.7%	88,152 145.0%
Total	3,159,962 10.2%	3,480,446 10.1%	3,819,593 9.7%	4,308,911 12.8%	4,725,394 9.7%
OFFICE PREMIUMS					
Types of Insurance	(HK$M)	(HK$M)	(HK$M)	(HK$M)	(HK$M)
Individual Life Non-linked	17,176.1 16.3%	20,096.3 17.0%	22,761.1 13.3%	26,313.5 15.6%	29,767.4 13.1%
Individual Life Linked	2,439.7 34.8%	2,915.5 19.5%	3,621.5 24.2%	4,714.7 30.2%	5,845.4 24.0%
Subtotal	19,615.8 18.3%	23,011.8 17.3%	26,382.6 14.6%	31,028.2 17.6%	35,612.8 14.8%
Group Life	794.5 18.0%	954.5 20.1%	966.9 1.3%	1,015.0 5.0%	1,094.0 7.8%
Retirement Scheme	7,248.3 13.8%	8,453.9 16.6%	8,747.9 3.5%	8,933.4 2.1%	8,801.8 −1.5%
Others	106.7 8.9%	105.1 −1.5%	152.9 45.5%	320.4 109.5%	1,006.5 214.1%
Total	27,765.3 17.0%	32,525.3 17.1%	36,250.3 11.5%	41,297.0 13.9%	46,515.1 12.6%

Note: Figures in percentages denote percentage changes over the previous year.
Source of data: Office of the Commissioner of Insurance, Hong Kong, *Annual Report,* 2000 and 2001(a).

thirty years, if the insured person survives the period. The policy usually generates insufficient death protection, but the notion of getting money back, whether alive or not, attracted 13.1 per cent of premium volume of total individual life insurance (business in force) in 2000.

Out of the 4.6 million individual life policies in force in 2000, term life insurance only accounted for eight per cent, representing 9.1 per cent of total sums assured, as shown in Table 6.5. The respective figures in the US are far greater. Roughly one quarter of life insurance policies sold there are term life, representing nearly a half of the total face amount of coverage. Yu (1997) provides a probable explanation for this sharp contrast. He believes that the popularity of term insurance in the US is due to the availability of retirement pension plans. Americans who wish to participate in long-term savings plans will do so via pension funds, leaving life insurance mostly for risk protection in the form of term insurance. Looking ahead in Hong Kong, since the introduction of the Mandatory Provident Fund (MPF), which enforced participation in long-term savings schemes and came into effect in December 2000, the author expects that an increasing popularity of term insurance will be seen in the near future. The fact that term insurance has taken up 17.3 per cent of *new* individual life business in terms of number of policies in 2000, as revealed in Table 6.5, seems to be in line with this view.

Table 6.5   Term Insurance: Percentage of Individual Life Business (1996–2000)

			IN FORCE BUSINESS		
	1996	1997	1998	1999	2000
Number of Policies	6.8%	7.1%	7.3%	7.6%	8.0%
Office Premiums	1.9%	2.0%	2.0%	1.8%	1.7%
Sum Assured	7.5%	8.6%	8.8%	9.0%	9.1%
			NEW BUSINESS		
	1996	1997	1998	1999	2000
Number of Policies	13.4%	12.8%	13.2%	12.5%	17.3%
Office Premiums	3.7%	3.4%	3.7%	2.7%	2.6%
Sum Assured	N/A	N/A	N/A	N/A	N/A

Source: Calculated from data from the Office of the Commissioner of Insurance, Hong Kong, *Annual Report,* 2001(a).

The implementation of the MPF scheme in December 2000 has provided a boost to long-term pension business, with the statistics partly factored into Table 6.4. Discussions on issues related to MPF can be found elsewhere in this book, so duplication will be avoided here. One issue that is relevant, though, is the method of payout. As the MPF system evolves and more participants reach the payout phase, the issue of large amounts of lump sum payments to senior citizens will be of concern. According to current regulations, MPF plans give a lump-sum benefit rather than an income in the form of an annuity on retirement. The outlay of money may create problems of outliving assets. Senior citizens in advanced countries typically use annuity products to finance part of their retirement income. An annuity can be defined as a periodic payment that continues for a fixed period or for the duration of a designated life or lives (Rejda, 2001). In contrast to life insurance, which offers protection against premature death, an annuity provides a shield against the risk of longevity. Holloway and Basu (2001) explain why the annuity market in the Asia-Pacific region is underdeveloped. Among the reasons are the lack of awareness of the risk of longevity and fiscal incentive, plus the requirement for more advanced training for the distributors of annuity products.

The level of sophistication of consumers and intermediaries will need to be raised if progress is to be made in the annuity market in Hong Kong. The data have shown a certain improvement already. As seen in Table 6.4, the 'Others' category recorded a remarkable growth rate of more than 100 per cent in the two consecutive years of 1999 and 2000, both in terms of number of policies and premium volume. The growth driver came mostly from annuity products. The OCI's 2001 annual report noted a significant increase in the annuity business: the number of annuity policies increased from 1,960 in 1998 to 28,957 in 2000, representing approximately a fourteen-fold increase. The premium volumes also increased more than eleven times to HK$532 million during the same period. In the future, as the marketplace becomes increasingly mature and those now middle-aged MPF participants gradually move into the payout phase, the annuity market will also expect to boom, thereby propelling another growth dynamic for Hong Kong's insurance industry.

The Regulatory Framework

The Hong Kong government has been famous for its *laissez faire* attitude toward regulation of the economy. Prior to 1983, when the Insurance Companies Ordinance (ICO) came into operation, there was no comprehensive system of control. Only companies carrying on life, fire, marine, or motor vehicle insurance were subject to regulation. The enactment of ICO also led to an upgrade of the small Insurance Registry within the Commercial Division of the Registrar General's Department to an independent Insurance Division. Wong (1991) gives a brief account of early development of legislation and supervision governing the insurance industry in Hong Kong. The regulator initially focused only on capital and solvency requirements, and relied on self-regulating bodies for regulatory issues dealing with intermediaries. Tighter supervisory attention forced out some insurers that were undercapitalized. During the period from June 1983 to May 1990, the number of insurers fell from 305 to 272. After the birth of the OCI in 1990, the market underwent continuous consolidation through both mergers and acquisitions and the transfer of business as the number of authorized insurers further dropped to 204 at the end of 2001. However, this is still the highest number among the major Asian markets.

In recognition of the growing importance of the insurance industry, the Insurance Division was further upgraded to a separate office for regulation of the industry. Since the OCI came into being, insurance regulation has become more sophisticated and comprehensive, although the fundamental free-market philosophy has remained intact. For example, policy approval is not required before launching a new product, and insurance companies are free to determine the premium rates for their products to whatever the market will bear.

The OCI soon faced challenges after its establishment on 8 June 1990. Between June 1990 and December 1991, the effectiveness of the regulatory framework was tested on several occasions. During that period, the OCI put four general business insurers into compulsory liquidation, and another insurer was wound up by a creditor. It was natural that in succeeding years the OCI devoted much of its effort to laying a solid foundation for the regulatory regime so as to protect policyholders. Important regulatory measures introduced during this period included the requirement for general business insurers to maintain assets to meet their liabilities in Hong Kong,[7] regulation on the valuation of assets of general business insurers,[8] determination of liabilities of long-term business insurers,[9] and a self-regulatory framework for insurance intermediaries.[10] The monitory framework displayed its effectiveness in 2001 when the bankruptcy of Australia's third biggest insurance group, HIH, triggered the insolvency of four subsidiary insurers in Hong Kong. The liquidation process was smooth due to the prompt regulatory actions taken by the OCI.[11]

In the second half of the 1990s, the OCI focused more on the promotion of Hong Kong's status as an international insurance centre, as well as on market transparency and the professionalism of insurance practitioners. This included the introduction of regulatory concessions to captive insurers, tax concessions to reinsurers, the publication of individual insurer's statistics, and the launch of the Insurance Intermediaries Quality Assurance Scheme (IIQAS). The IIQAS, proposed in 1998 and coming into effect in January 2000, is probably the most significant regulatory move towards enhancing the quality of insurance intermediaries and the public's overall image of the industry. The Scheme requires all insurance agents and brokers to satisfy the Qualifying Examination requirements before they are allowed to sell insurance products to customers. According to the OCI, the pass rate remained steady at around fifty per cent one year after of the launch of the examinations. As the two-year transitional period expired on 31 December 2001, many unqualified intermediaries left the industry. Meanwhile, statistics show a growing percentage of agents and brokers with university degrees, which it is believed will improve further the important role of the insurance industry in Hong Kong.

Another aspect of the IIQAS is the Continuing Professional Development (CPD) Programme. All insurance intermediaries were asked to comply with the requirements of the CPD Programme upon its implementation in January 2002 as a condition for renewal of their registration or authorization. The CPD Programme contains ten core credits and twenty non-core credits which can be earned through participating in activities such as seminars, conferences, training courses relating to insurance legislation and regulatory aspects of insurance practice (core), and other insurance, risk management, finance, and business fields approved by the OCI-appointed Hong Kong Council for Academic Accreditation. While it is yet to be tested for its real effects, it is the regulator's hope that the CPD requirements (of earning ninety credit points every three years) will ensure that agents and brokers keep pace with the increasing sophistication of insurance products and their regulation. In a paper presented at the 6th Asia-Pacific Risk and Insurance Association Annual Conference held in Shanghai, Lui (2002) examined the structure of the IIQAS (including CPD), analysed a survey result that revealed industry practitioners' attitudes towards IIQAS, and studied the implications of an effective CPD programme.

In addition to the role of quality control for the insurance industry, the OCI has also been actively promoting captive and reinsurance business in Hong Kong. In 1996, the government set up a Working Group on Reinsurance and Captive Insurance, which proposed that regulatory concessions, including reduced minimum capital and solvency margins, be introduced for captive insurers and tax incentives for reinsurers. These regulatory concessions were subsequently introduced in May 1997 by the Insurance Companies (Amendment) Ordinance 1997. A concessionary tax rate equal to fifty per cent of the profit tax was also provided, by an amendment in April 1998 to the Inland Revenue Ordinance, to professional reinsurers in respect of their offshore business income. The results of these efforts will be discussed next.

Reinsurance and Captive Insurance Centre?

Reinsurance and captive insurance are the insurance lines that require the greatest expertise and professional knowledge. Therefore, the developmental status of these two lines of business connotes the level of maturity of the insurance industry. The earliest government effort on the promotion of Hong Kong's status as an international reinsurance and captive insurance centre, as mentioned above, took place in 1996 when a Working Group was established. The result, however, was far from satisfactory.

Reinsurance

As the self-explanatory term suggests, reinsurance provides protection for primary insurers. The functions of reinsurance include enhancing capacity, providing stability, providing catastrophe protection, providing underwriting expertise, and assisting with withdrawal from a territory or a line of business. With reinsurance, the depth and scope of insurance operation can be enhanced. Hong Kong has been promoting itself as a reinsurance centre since the mid-1990s. There were about twenty-six authorized professional reinsurers in Hong Kong, compared with forty-five in Singapore, at the end of 2000. Singapore has positioned itself as a regional reinsurance centre for Asia, and has achieved some level of success judging by the number of reinsurers in operation and also from the strong growth of the reinsurance business in the Lion City. Statistics indicate that in Singapore, reinsurance premiums in the Singapore Insurance Fund (SIF), which represents the primary domestic sector, grew 9.3 per cent in 2000, while the premiums in the Offshore Insurance Fund (OIF), which represents non-domestic business, grew 33.1 per cent in the same year. Also in 2000, professional reinsurers in Hong Kong posted total gross premiums of HK$1,530 million, a modest 3.2 per cent increase, reversing the downward trend since 1996. The modest increase in 2000, however, was not able to reach the peak of HK$2,873 million in 1995, representing a decrease of nearly fifty per cent between 1995 and 2000.

Accompanying the shrinking business for professional reinsurers was gloomy profitability. From 1996 to 2000, professional reinsurers in Hong Kong recorded underwriting profits/(losses) of 78, (278), (165), (173), and 71 million Hong Kong dollars. Even though Hong Kong has a simple and concessionary tax system, a transparent and well-defined legal system, a well-developed banking system, and the free foreign exchange to promote itself as a reinsurance centre, the perceived saturated operating environment and unfavourable underwriting results have made the promotion of reinsurance unsatisfactory.

On a worldwide scale, around seventy-five per cent of reinsurance business is generated in the mature markets of North America and Western Europe. By contrast, the share of global reinsurance business in the emerging markets is just about sixteen per cent (Swiss Re, 1998). Despite this, the emerging markets tend to show a stronger demand for reinsurance, due to the lower capitalization of insurers and the higher weight of industrial risks in their portfolios. Hong Kong's efforts to strengthen its status as a reinsurance centre is likely to receive a boost now that China has been accepted into the WTO. The author believes there is a great prospect for the further development of the reinsurance markets in Hong Kong, as it will be necessary to cover the businesses that will flood the market as China opens up its domestic market further. Certainly, as summarized by Pope (2000), besides regulatory and geographical factors, the generic characteristics of ideal reinsurance centres also rest on marketplace/infrastructure and economic factors. Issues such as the size of the local primary insurance market, the availability of sufficiently high-quality human capital, the stability of the marketplace, and the general health of the overall economy are also vital determinants of whether or not the reinsurance business in Hong Kong can be strengthened.

Captive Insurance

The concept of captive insurance dates back to the early 1950s. Since then, the number of captives in the world has grown to over 4,400. Nearly half of the captive insurers are domiciled in Bermuda and the Cayman Islands. While the scope of operation of a captive may differ from another depending on the purposes for which it is formed, it is legally defined in Hong Kong under the Insurance Companies Ordinance as an insurer that is formed by its parent company to underwrite exclusively the insurance business of the parent or group companies or their associated companies.

Several reasons are outlined for firms to form a captive subsidiary in order to insure against the parent's multi-dimensional risks. These include: reduced insurance costs, direct access to the reinsurance market, insurance of hard-to-place risks, better risk management, increased cash flow, and centralized insurance management. In the 1990s, the increasing corporate demand for approaches to integrated risk management called for the rapid growth of captive insurance operations. In a promotional pamphlet issued by the OCI (2001b), ten reasons for setting up a captive in Hong Kong are delineated: 'sound regulatory framework, government support, simple and low taxation, free flow of funds, excellent banking services provided by banks of international status, accessibility to the reinsurance market, high-quality accounting and legal services, advanced telecommunications facilities, social and political stability, and proximity to the huge market of China'. To provide further incentives for multinational conglomerates to establish their captive insurers in Hong Kong, several regulatory concessions were put in place with the enactment of the Insurance Companies (Amendment) Ordinance 1997, as outlined in Table 6.6.

Despite recent efforts, the number of captive insurers domiciled in Hong Kong is a meagre two, compared to the fifty-two operating in Singapore. The Lion City was ahead of Hong Kong by three years in promoting the captive business, but a brief comparison of the two as captive domiciles, as listed in Table 6.7, does not pinpoint a clear answer to the huge difference between Hong Kong and Singapore in the promotion of captive business. Communications with practitioners have led the author to summarize three key points: tax (the tax rate in Hong Kong is sixteen per cent compared with Singapore's ten per cent); infrastructure (Singapore has a solid captive services infrastructure while Hong Kong is less experienced); and government attitude.

Singapore has been renowned for its proactive policy formation. The Singaporean government aims at developing Singapore into the single world-class financial centre in Asia, and the insurance industry is an integral part of this vision. The Monetary Authority of Singapore (MAS) has shown its strong commitment towards contributing to Singapore's development as a regional insurance hub and an international financial centre. The government has clearly stated its attractive policies for captives and demonstrated its effort in their promotion. The MAS forms the Financial Centre Advisory Group and International Advisory Panel to obtain feedback

Table 6.6   Highlights of Regulatory Concessions for Captives

	General Business Insurer	Captive Insurer
Minimum Capital Requirement	HK$10 million	HK$2 million
Solvency Margin	The greatest of (a) generally 20% of the relevant premium income; or premium (b) generally 20% of the relevant claims outstanding; or (c) HK$10 million	The greatest of (a) generally 5% of the relevant income; or (b) generally 5% of the relevant claims outstanding; or (c) HK$2 million
Requirement for Assets in Hong Kong	To maintain assets in Hong Kong of an amount not less than 80% of its Hong Kong liabilities plus solvency margin	Exempted
Valuation Regulation	Assets and liabilities to be valued on statutory basis as prescribed by Valuation Regulation	Assets and liabilities to be valued on the basis of Generally Accepted Accounting Principles

In addition, a captive is also exempted from the requirements to demonstrate to the Insurance Authority before authorization that:
(1) it has undertaken a feasibility study in respect of its proposed operation in or from Hong Kong;
(2) it would not engage in a 'fronting' operation;
(3) it would be managed and operated independently of its group.

Source: Hong Kong An Ideal Domicile for Captives (Office of the Commissioner of Insurance, 2001(b)), also available online at http://www.info.gov.hk/oci/ideal/index07.htm, last accessed September 2002.

and views from the financial industries, including the insurance industry. The regulatory body reviews its approach to the insurance industry continuously to liberalize the restrictions and allow more new entrants. It has adopted an open admission policy for reinsurers and captive insurers, and there is no fixed limit on the number of new entrants. In order to be competitive with other successful domiciles and increase the number of captive insurers, MAS reduces the paid-up capital requirement for captive insurers to S$400,000 and also reduces the tax rate to ten per cent from the ordinary 24.5 per cent. Plus, it has given captive insurers blanket approval to write certain non in-house risks. Such dedicated commitment and extensive efforts have reaped promising results in that the Lion City has successfully developed into the captive insurance hub in Asia within a few years. With a view towards continuously enhancing Singapore's position as the leading Asian captive domicile, the MAS has promised that the open policy on admission to captive insurance will remain intact and that it will continue to modify regulatory flexibility to further enhance its existing strengths.

Table 6.7   Captive Domicile Comparisons between Hong Kong and
Singapore

	Hong Kong	Singapore
Capitalization	HK$2 million	S$400,000
Registration and Incorporation Expenses	Standard	S$500,000 annual
Investment Restrictions	None	No specific requirement, but prudence in investment is expected
Tax issues	Corporate tax is 16%. No capital gains tax and value-added tax. Dividend and income are not subject to tax.	Corporate tax rate is 24.5%, but insurers, including captives, may apply for a concessionary tax rate of 10% in respect of non-Singaporean businesses.
Applicable Act	Insurance Companies Ordinance 1997	Insurance Act 1994
Supervisory Body	Office of the Commissioner of Insurance	Monetary Authority of Singapore
Reserve and Underwriting Requirements	The greatest of (d) generally 5% of the relevant premium income; or (e) generally 5% of the relevant claims outstanding; or (f) HK$2 million	Solvency requirements; surplus of assets over liabilities of S$400,000
Number of Captive Insurers	2	52

Sources of data: Office of the Commissioner of Insurance, Hong Kong, and Monetary Authority of Singapore.

To catch up with Singapore's achievements, Hong Kong needs to re-evaluate its strategy and take more proactive steps towards overcoming its disadvantageous position while simultaneously utilizing existing opportunities. Being the gateway to China, Hong Kong should be attractive to Chinese enterprises as a captive domicile.[12] Although until now the insurance industry in China has been under-developed and companies have yet to reach an awareness of their need for insurance and reinsurance, the author believes that China's entry into the WTO will accelerate the process, as greater competitive pressure will push corporations to adopt a risk-management framework that complies with international standards. Therefore, it is expected that many captive business opportunities will come Hong Kong's way in the near term. After China's insurance market is fully liberalized, numerous insurers and reinsurers will be attracted to this market of 1.2 billion people. Meanwhile, new companies will be set up and the existing ones will expand their business scope as the economy continues to grow. All of these companies are the potential targets for forming their own captives. By then, if Hong Kong could successfully improve in aspects which include: (1) maintaining a competitive tax rate for captive insurers; (2) adopting more favourable policies and proactive government actions to create incentives and attract business; (3) continuing to maintain and strengthen good business relationships with Mainland companies; and (4) preparing more qualified human resources for the industry by investing in insurance education and promoting the insurance and actuary professions, it will be best positioned to become a captive insurance centre for state-owned enterprises and multinational corporations in China. This will also increase Hong Kong's overall competitiveness over its counterparts in the region and allow it to become the captive hub in Asia.

Trends and Drivers around the Century

Several factors that emerged in the 1990s will continue to evolve and play even more critical roles in shaping the insurance industry in Hong Kong. The convergence of the financial services sector created innovative distribution channels and composite products that have lowered costs, boosted revenues, and improved profit margins. Financial groups have been developing bancassurance (such as the HSBC group, BOC group, and other strategic alliances between banks and insurers) and beginning to distribute insurance products in the widespread banking network. Since the announcement of the MPF scheme, there has been a flurry of activity, with commercial banks and insurance companies teaming up for a share of the pension fund market. The inevitable development in the future is a deeper bancassurance penetration that is projected by *Asia Insurance Review* to more than double its current share of 12.5 per cent of the insurance market by 2010 (Koh, 2001).

The convergence also blurred the traditional boundaries of insurance and financial products. Examples are abundant—such as investment-linked life insurance that bundles risk protection and asset appreciation, and the insurance-linked bonds and derivatives that specify the pay-off of securities contingent upon insurance events. As previously discussed, investment-linked products have been a key driver of growth in today's life insurance market in Hong Kong. Also emerging recently, but not yet making a significant impact, are alternative risk transfer (ART) products. These are capital market innovations in the (particularly non-life) insurance industry that transfer underwriting risk to the capital markets with the effect of increasing insurance (and reinsurance) capacity. Amongst them, catastrophe (CAT) bonds are one major product pioneered by Hannover Re in 1994, to the tune of US$85 million. Since then, the issuance of CAT bonds has recorded robust growth worldwide, but the majority of the reported transactions occurred in North America and Europe, with only a few taking place in Japan. Certainly, Hong Kong is a blessed land with relatively few natural catastrophes. Nonetheless, as a part of China in which catastrophe damage is frequent and substantial and the insurance market is yet in its infancy, Hong Kong should use its strengths in the human resources and capital markets to develop its proactive role in the market evolution for insurance-linked securities in China in the foreseeable future.

The birth of the New Economy also has an impact on the insurance industry. Advances in information technology have not only provided the sales force with cutting-edge tools such as laptop computers, wireless application protocol (WAP) phones, and personal digital assistants (PDAs) to boost productivity and maintain customer relationship management,[13] they have also created a whole new Internet distribution channel that has prompted an energetic online insurance market. In March 2001, the Office of the Commissioner of Insurance conducted a survey on the use of the Internet for insurance activities and found that 94 authorized insurers and 85 authorized insurance brokers were providing insurance services over 112 and 94 websites respectively. The survey also revealed that household, personal accident, and travel insurance are the three most popular online insurance products offered (OCI, 2001a), which is reasonable because of the short-term and relatively uncomplicated nature of these products. The online marketplace will continue to become important as rising consumer sophistication demands quicker, cheaper, more timely, and more accessible insurance services. A recent study in the US (Brown and Goolsbee, 2000) found that the Internet has reduced search costs and made life insurance markets more competitive. The results suggest that the growth of the Internet has increased consumer surplus in insurance purchases by an amount of US$115–215 million a year, and perhaps more in the future. The paper provides empirical evidence that the online insurance market, albeit still fledgling, will be a promising focus for further development.

Another driver of growth is the China factor. Since the People's Republic of China formally became a World Trade Organization member, its insurance market will gradually open up until all official restrictions are removed (after five years). The Chinese government, however, maintains a strict asset test, which has made nearly all local insurers in Hong Kong unqualified for obtaining licences to operate on the Mainland. While it is unclear whether Hong Kong insurers will eventually be treated more favourably, there are still many local insurers who have set up representative offices in China in the hope that asset and other restrictions will be lifted. Hong Kong companies can also provide expert support for Chinese companies, such as training Chinese personnel in Hong Kong, sending staff to work in China as part of their own training and development, and providing the know-how for product innovation. The human resources flow to the less developed but highly expertise-hungry Chinese companies may create upward promotion opportunities to some extent, as can be seen in the case of Taiwan, where some high-level actuaries, IT professionals, and sales managers were reportedly head-hunted by China, freeing high-level positions in the nearly saturated Taiwanese human resources market.

Conclusion

Insurance has been one of the fastest growing industries in Hong Kong since the 1980s, notwithstanding the Asian financial crisis of 1997, which somewhat restricted the growth driver of the general insurance business. Amid a historically high unemployment rate of 7.1 per cent at the time of writing (April 2002), insurance recruitment appears to be the only bright spot. A trend of rising insurance awareness, increasing customer sophistication, and the popularity of investment-linked insurance products is expected to continue, further boosting the life insurance sector. MPF participants gradually entering the payout phase, accompanied by increasing life expectancy, will also be a driver of strong demand for annuities products. The importance of market transparency and the quality of insurance intermediaries cannot be overstated for swift and healthy growth, particularly when financial innovations blur insurance products (for risk protection) with financial products (for asset appreciation). To meet this challenge, the OCI has been working towards improving the professionalism of the insurance market as well as maintaining an efficient and transparent regulatory framework. These efforts have seen a return in terms of improving public perception of the insurance industry and life insurance agents in particular.

The general insurance business, however, still suffers from the near-term uncertain outlook of the overall economy. In the employees' compensation insurance line, the dual (statutory plus unlimited tort) compensation system creates adverse incentives for the workplace-injured and has led to underwriting losses for ten consecutive years. The rising cost pressure will inevitably be transferred to the insured companies and employees, to the degree that the premiums will no longer be bearable. An overhaul of the relevant legislation seems unavoidable. Reform is also needed for another continuous loss-making line: the motor insurance business. Because of its compulsory nature, some distortion has been presented, as people who cannot obtain insurance coverage use others' names to meet the insurance requirement. Some kind of 'residual market' mechanisms—such as assigned risk pool, whereby motor insurers are required to participate so as to split the premiums and underwriting results for high-risk drivers who otherwise cannot get coverage proportionally according to market share—are worth considering.

It is always a dilemma for government regulators whether to adopt a *laissez faire* attitude or a proactive position. The author is not capable of answering the fundamental question raised by Yu (1997), 'Are there sufficient reasons to believe that insurance supervision in Hong Kong should be elevated to a tool for economic policy?' But the regulatory and tax concessions for reinsurance and captive insurance business in the late 1990s signalled a move away from the traditional *laissez faire* role. The same sentiment could be found in January 2000, when the OCI set up a Policy and Development Division, hoping to enhance Hong Kong's status as a major international insurance centre. However, the determination to adopt a proactive role still needs to be strengthened. Hong Kong lags far behind Singapore in both reinsurance and captive insurance operations. It is believed that the difference in the level of government support is one of the main causes.

The shifts in distribution channels have created opportunities for insurers to improve cost efficiencies and improve their bottom line. Both bancassurance and online insurance marketing will grow significantly over the next few years. This does not mean that the quality of agents can be ignored. The OCI has emphasized the importance of boosting the standards of insurance intermediaries so as to protect policyholders' interests. The pre-registration examination, as well as continuing professional development education, will help to meet this goal. The use of mobile equipment, such as PDAs, will enable agents to serve their clients in a prompt and accurate manner, thanks to the latest advances in information technology.

Insurance education is probably the most important infrastructure for sound growth in the future. Insurance itself is an integrated discipline that combines knowledge of business, economics, mathematics, finance, and law. Whether we are in need of quality insurance intermediaries for long-term insurance, improving underwriting results for general insurance, or the better development of reinsurance and captive insurance, what is necessary is professional talent. Compared with other countries in the region, Hong Kong lacks university-level insurance and risk management programmes that provide specialist insurance training as well as comprehensive business education. It is astonishing that the majority of tertiary insurance professionals and high-level managers receive their college education overseas. The human capital investment is—and it sounds almost like a cliché—the key to the triumph of today's knowledge-based, services-oriented economy. Obviously, today's insurance activities are far broader than just sales and thus require better-quality practitioners. To excel in an increasingly complicated and competitive insurance operations environment, Hong Kong needs more formal university education on insurance and related fields. The traditional vocational training and apprenticeship approach will not do.

Discussion Questions

1. The S-curve looks at the relationship between per capita GDP and insurance penetration across countries. However, besides income, there are other macroeconomic and demographic determinants on the demand for insurance. Provide a couple of examples and discuss their effects.
2. In 2000, the ratio of global life and non-life insurance premium volume was 62 to 38, while in Hong Kong the ratio was 77 and 23. Can you offer explanations as to why Hong Kong has a relatively small portion of non-life insurance business, compared to the global average?
3. Why is term life insurance so insignificant in Hong Kong?
4. What are the linked products? Why they are becoming increasingly popular today?
5. What should the government do to 'save' employees' compensation insurance in Hong Kong? Is there any reason that the business should not be compulsory?
6. From what you or your family members have observed, what is the general public's perception on insurance intermediaries before and after the IIQAS?
7. According to a survey of insurance professionals conducted by Lui (2002), seventy-two per cent of respondents indicate their agreement with the IIQAS, but only twenty-one per cent agree with CPD. Why? What kind of design is essential to make the CPD programme effective?
8. Are there sufficient reasons to believe that insurance supervision in Hong Kong should be elevated to a tool for economic policy? Specifically, do you agree that tax and regulatory concessions should be made to boost reinsurance and captive insurance business in Hong Kong?
9. Some predict that the Internet economy will eventually lead to 'disintermediation', where traditional agents and brokers will become obsolete, to be replaced by the Internet as the primary direct distribution channel between insurers and end-customers. Some contend that it is just a myth. What do you think?

Keywords

annuity
captive insurance, alternative risk transfer
catastrophe (CAT) bonds
Insurance Companies Ordinance
insurance density
Insurance Intermediaries Quality Assurance Scheme (IIQAS)
insurance penetration
investment-linked policies
Office of the Commissioner of Insurance (OCI)
S-curve

PART II

Financial Markets

7. Money Markets and Short-Term Interest Rates

ROBERT HANEY SCOTT

Classification schemes are widely used in science and other fields to understand and communicate more effectively. Thus in finance there are money markets and capital markets. There are also primary markets and secondary markets, debt markets and equity markets, stock markets and bond markets, and each of these broad classes may be broken down into many overlapping sectors. There is a rich variety of financial instruments available to borrowers and lenders, just as there is a rich menu of delightful dishes in a good restaurant.

This chapter is about money markets. These markets are huge—the dollar volume of transactions in them far surpasses the dollar volume of transactions in stock and bond markets, and even in markets for consumer goods. In some classifications the term money markets includes the literal market formed by trades in world currencies, known as the foreign exchange market. Daily trading in this market exceeds two trillion dollars. (The foreign exchange market in Hong Kong is the subject of Chapter 8.)

The money market is a market for short-term funds. An arbitrary dividing line is frequently drawn between money and capital markets. Money market securities have one year or less to maturity; one year is also the typical basis for interest rate calculations. Hence we refer to the 'annual interest rate'. We multiply a monthly interest rate by twelve in order to convert it to an equivalent annual rate. For example, if your credit card specifies the rate of interest as one per cent per month, this is said to equal an annual rate of twelve per cent. Quarterly rates are multiplied by four to arrive at estimates of the equivalent annual rate, and so forth.

Securities traded in capital markets have more than one year to maturity. Thus a three-month Exchange Fund bill is classified as a money market security and a ten-year bond is classified as a capital market security. Shares of stock traded on stock exchanges never mature and they are, of course, also classified as capital market securities.

News media report on stock and bond markets routinely, so the public is well aware of capital market developments. Money markets, on the other hand, operate largely out of sight, and the general public is far less aware of the size and importance of money markets.

Types of Money Market Instrument

Many types of money market exist in different countries around the world. Many of these are directly attached to the banking system. Bank loans themselves comprise one type of money market instrument, and in Hong

Kong they are, in the aggregate, more important in the financing of business enterprise than other money and capital markets. However, different types of money and capital market instruments serve different purposes in the operation of a financial system.

In a money market an individual or business firm is often said to 'purchase money'— that is, they borrow money for temporary use and repay it later. For this use of money they pay interest, so interest is the price paid for the use of money. Interest is also called the price of credit or the cost of borrowing. Borrowers pay the price of credit, and lenders receive a return called interest.

A partial list of money market instruments is:

1. Certificates of Deposit
2. Negotiable Certificates of Deposit
3. Interbank Loans
4. Commercial Bank Loans
5. Commercial Paper
6. Repurchase Agreements
7. Exchange Fund Bills
8. Bankers' Acceptances

Many general textbooks also list euro markets as a unique type of investment. However, Hong Kong banks have long held deposits denominated in foreign currencies, and they make loans and issue certificates in currencies other than Hong Kong dollars. There is nothing especially unique about the euro market to Hong Kong financial institutions.

Variations exist on all of the above categories, which means that individual borrowers and lenders have the ability to make contracts with each other with all the variety of terms and conditions that satisfy the needs of both borrower and lender. And when types of money market instrument become uniform and widely traded, it is common practice for government to intervene in money markets to ensure that fiduciary and prudential responsibilities are enforced on market participants.

Savings, Time, and Certificates of Deposit

Nearly everyone in Hong Kong is familiar with one type of money market: the market for time deposits in banks. Every bank lobby displays the rate of interest paid by that bank for a variety of maturities of time deposit. Depositors are encouraged to hold funds in savings accounts that do not mature, or in time deposits with various maturities. Certificates of time deposit may be printed on a piece of paper that reads 'This is to certify that depositor, Mrs Wong, has HK$1,000 on deposit in this bank, and this deposit will mature in six months', or words to that effect. Retail certificates of deposit may be set to mature within one year, or may be set for maturities of one to three years or more. By our classification, the certificates that mature in more than one year could be considered capital market instruments for certain analytical purposes. One can see that any classification scheme based on an arbitrarily selected time period such as one year will have some fuzziness. Thus, the user of data may find it suitable to include the two-year retail certificate of deposit as a money market security.

Negotiable Certificates of Deposit (NCDs or CDs)

Each individual banker knows that a good way to grow is to attract more funds in the form of deposits. Of course, banks can grow with long-term funds obtained by the issue of subordinated bonds—subordinated to deposit liabilities. They can also issue more capital stock and accumulate surpluses out of earnings. But the basic source of funds for banks is deposits of various types.

The market for NCDs emerged in the US in the 1970s. Monetary conditions had gradually tightened and City Bank wanted a way to attract more deposits, so it created a new type of deposit, the negotiable certificate of deposit. Certificates are not generally negotiable: a typical depositor needs to take the certificate to the bank in order to get his money, but managers at City Bank decided to print a standard deposit certificate worth $100,000 dated to mature for a certain number of months.

Appropriate legal arrangements were made for these NCDs to be negotiable—that is, transferable to another party by signature. Then City Bank arranged for these uniform NCDs to be sold over-the-counter by brokers and dealers to investors, and these soon became a successful type of money market instrument that is now used by large banks all over the world.

There is a large secondary market for this special type of deposit. Any investor with $100,000 can ask a broker to buy one with a specific maturity date. Many small country banks now obtain funds by calling brokers and asking them to issue NCDs, so there is large supply flowing to the market. There is also a large demand partly fuelled by a regulation relating to bank deposit insurance in the US. The Bank Insurance Fund of the Federal Deposit Insurance Corporation in the US provides coverage of up to $100,000 per individual deposit in case of bank failure, so a person who wants a one million dollar insured short-term investment will often hire a broker to place ten $100,000 amounts in NCDs in ten different banks and in this way the full million becomes insured.

NCDs were first created in Hong Kong in the late 1970s and were issued by Deposit Taking Companies (DTCs) after the Ordinance establishing DTCs was passed in 1976. One problem at the time was that, under the Interest Rate Agreement, the Hong Kong Association of Banks set interest rates to be paid on deposits of one year or less, so NCDs issued by DTCs had to mature in a time period greater than one year in order to circumvent this restriction. The final stage of deregulation and abandonment of the Interest Rate Agreement occurred in July 2001, so this restriction no longer applies to authorized institutions in Hong Kong.

However, many issues of certificates of deposit are made for up to seven years and come under the heading of capital market instruments.

Table 7.1 indicates that a total of nearly HK$200 billion of NCDs was outstanding in July 2000. About thirty billion of these were denominated in foreign currencies, while the remaining 170 billion were in Hong Kong dollars. About forty per cent of the Hong Kong dollar NCDs, or nearly seventy billion, were held by the public, while the remaining hundred billion were held by the authorized institutions that issued the NCDs in the first place. That is, banks not only issue NCDs but they also invest in the NCDs issued by other authorized institutions. Banks may accept deposits but do not always have loans to make use of the funds, so to keep their assets in interest-earning form they buy the NCDs issued by other banks. All of this sets the stage for active trading in NCDs.

Table 7.1   NCDs Outstanding in Hong Kong at End of May 2000 (HK$ million)

	Authorized Institutions	*Held by Public*	*Percentage Held by Public*
HK$	168,308	67,926	40.3%
Foreign Currency	39,701	17,580	57.3%
Total	199,009	85,406	42.9%

Source of data: Hong Kong Monetary Authority, *Monthly Statistical Bulletin,* July 2000; Tables 3.3, 3.4.

Floating Rate Deposits

Some issues of certificates of deposit carry provisions for the interest rate to be adjusted periodically to bring it in line with some general index of interest rate levels. Usually the interest rate paid changes when there is a change in the Hong Kong Interbank Offered Rate (HIBOR). This will be discussed in the section on the interbank funds market below.

Short-Term Bank Loans and Floating Rate Notes

Deposits and NCDs are bank liabilities, not assets. When issuing these securities, banks are borrowing funds from the public. Some bank assets may be the NCDs of other banks and are also money market instruments. Another form of bank asset—bank loans—is also a money market instrument. These are created when banks lend money to consumers and businesses.

Bank loans are very important sources of funds used to finance business expansion by small entrepreneurs. These are not often traded in a secondary market, so they may be left out of discussions of money markets as such. However, short-term bank loans should be considered as an important money market instrument because they play such a large role in developing economies. They certainly played a principal role in the development of Hong Kong's economy.

Interest on Bank Loans

The borrowing customer will sign an IOU to the bank, i.e. a promise to pay the bank a certain sum of money at a future date. The bank then discounts this future sum to present value and gives the discounted sum to the borrower. The IOU may call for repayment to the bank of $100 one year from the date of signing, but the bank gives the customer only $90 today. This is the discounted value when the interest charged is $10. The discount rate is said to be ten per cent, but the simple interest of $10 on a loan of $90 is one-ninth or $11, so the effective interest rate on this loan is eleven per cent instead of ten per cent. Thus, interest rates on discounted loans are often understated because interest is charged in advance (up front) rather than at the end of the period. Bank loans based on promises to pay are called 'notes' and are often quoted at discount rates rather than in terms of simple interest rates.

Floating Rate Notes

This type of note is now very popular in Hong Kong. It was first issued by the Mass Transit Railway Corporation in 1986. The interest rate paid on these notes is adjusted periodically according to changes in the Hong Kong Interbank Offered Rate (HIBOR).

Commercial Paper (CP)

The Mass Transit Railway Corporation was the first to issue commercial paper in Hong Kong in 1977. It was not until 1984 that the government agreed to let businesses collect short-term funds directly from investors. Banks had argued that the issue of commercial paper was the equivalent of the 'taking of deposits', and this was, of course, the market reserved for banks alone. In the intervening years issuers had to obtain permission from the government. However, many financial institutions operate as dealers in commercial paper and often underwrite the issue of CP by businesses. Dealers typically charge fees of 0.125 per cent of an issue as commission. Issues of CP may be underwritten fully or sold on a 'best effort' basis. A managing dealer may form a syndicate of financial institutions to help underwrite, market, and distribute the issue of CP for a firm when the issue is large.

Revolving Underwriting Facilities (RUF)

Dealers often establish a revolving underwriting facility for firms in order to enable them to tap the CP market for funds as needs arise. Dealers agree to bid for any issues of CP that the firm wishes to sell under agreements that establish a time period of, say, three years, and that are subject to limits on the total amount of CP issues outstanding. This gives a firm the opportunity to acquire liquid funds as needed and enables it to avoid issuing long-term debt just to cover short-term liquidity requirements. Furthermore, borrowing directly from investors may be less expensive than acquiring funds through traditional bank loans. In most cases, however, issues of CP need to be backed by a bank-issued line of credit. By lending its own credit standing to the firm through a line of credit, the bank earns fee income, so banks themselves may prefer to help the firm with the issue of CP and earn fee income rather than take on the additional risk associated with issuing loans to the firm directly.

In Chapter 3, Table 3.5 with data on the aggregate balance sheet of Authorized Institutions in Hong Kong provides both Hong Kong dollar and Foreign Currency figures on the volume of money market instruments they held at the beginning of 2002. It shows loans and advances to customers. These two assets are generally not tradable in a secondary market, but in recent years in the US, banks have often sold their loans. The table also shows the volume of NCDs held as assets and the volume held as liabilities, as well as the volume of floating rate notes and commercial paper held as assets. A huge volume of assets is held in deposits in foreign banks denominated in foreign currencies.

Two other very large money markets exist in Hong Kong. One is the market for the issue of bills by the Exchange Fund. These bills were briefly described in Chapter 2. The other closely related market is the interbank funds market.

Exchange Fund Bills and the Interbank Market

A brief description of the market of Exchange Fund Bills (EFB) may be found in Table 7.2. It shows amounts of bills in maturity categories, yields on these securities, and turnover measures that indicate the extent of trading in these money market instruments.

Table 7.2   Outstanding Amounts, Yields, and Turnover of Exchange Fund Bills (HK$ million)

Maturity Class	91-day	182-day	364-day	Total
Amount at End of June 2000	44,708	16,900	8,450	70,058
Yields at End of June 2000	6.26%	6.51%	6.66%	
Average Daily Turnover Amount during June 2000	16,054	1,014	1,039	18,107

Source of data: Hong Kong Monetary Authority, *Monthly Statistical Bulletin,* July 2000; Tables 4.1, 4.2, 4.3.

Amounts of bills outstanding at the end of June 2000 are shown for various maturity ranges. There was the amount of HK$44.708 billion outstanding that would mature within ninety-one days, or three months.

Figures are also shown for six- and twelve-month maturities outstanding. (Source tables also provide data on outstanding Exchange Fund notes for two, three, five, seven, and ten years.)

To see how active the market is for this most liquid of securities, note that the average daily amount of 91-day bills traded during the thirty days of June was HK$16 billion. This indicates that about one-third of all 91-day bills was traded every day. Average yields on these securities at the end of June 2000 were 6.36 per cent per annum. Short-term interest rates were quite high at that time because of tight monetary policy in the US. During 2001, interest rates in the US were reduced eleven times from over 5 per cent to 1.75 per cent. Rates on Hong Kong's Exchange Fund Bills fell by similar amounts, and in line with the policy of the Hong Kong Monetary Authority (HKMA), the rate remains about 1.5 per cent above the rate in the US.

A Note on Interest-Yield Calculations on Exchange Fund Bills

The Exchange Fund auctions bills in minimum amounts of HK$500,000 or multiples thereof. Tenders are made through recognized dealers and must be submitted by 10:30am on the day of tender, which is announced in advance. Settlement is made on the first business day following the tender. Titles and records are maintained by the HKMA. Trading in the bills is done by Market Makers, who quote bid and offer yields during the normal hours of 9:00am to noon and 2:00 to 4:00pm during market days.

Tenders are made on a bid–yield basis. The amount of payment required for the bills, or price, P, is calculated by the following formula in which F is the face value, D is the actual number of days to maturity, and Y is the annual percentage yield bid:

$$P = F / (1 + (D/365)(Y/100))$$

For example, say Y = 8.00 per year rounded to two decimal places. Thus the far right term after dividing by 100 will be .0800. The number of days in a 13-week bill is usually 91 days. So 91/365 is .2493. Multiply this by .0800 and add 1 to get 1.0199, the reciprocal of which is .9805. Multiply this by F, or HK$500,000, to arrive at HK$490,250, which is P, or the price the investor must pay for the bill. The difference between F and P is HK$9,750. This amount is what the investor will receive in interest when his loan of HK$490,250 to the Exchange Fund is repaid with interest at maturity. So the rate of return or yield on the amount invested was 1.99 per cent, which may be rounded up to two per cent for the quarter year, or eight per cent for the year. (For complete information on the rules in Hong Kong see Hong Kong Monetary Authority (1998)).

If readers take a look at textbooks on the money markets (Scott, W. 1999; Scott, R. 1995; Stigum, 1983; Fabozzi and Modigliani, 2003), they will find discussions of the way in which US Treasury bills are sold at auction on a bank discount basis.

The yield on a bank discount basis is: $Y_d = ((F - P)/F)\, 360/D$. The Y in this formula needs to be multiplied by 100 to state the yield in percentage terms. Traditionally, banks have long based loan quotations on a 360-day year. This keeps the calculations simpler. With the computer revolution, investors now find it easy to make more complicated and more accurate yield calculations.

The bank discount basis differs in two ways. First, the 360-day year introduces a departure from an accurate effective annual yield measure. Second, using the discount formula bases the yield on the full face value as the amount invested rather than on the price paid for the bill as the full amount invested. This also introduces a bias away from the true effective interest yield on an investment. To report a bond equivalent yield needed for accurate comparisons among different investments, the formula would read:

$$Y \text{ in } \% = ((F - P)/P)\, 365/D \times 100.$$

The interest return as stated on a discount basis understates the true effective interest yield, and this is the same formula, with terms rearranged, that is used by the Exchange Fund. So in comparing returns on US Treasury bills at auctions with returns on EF Bills at auctions, one should understand that the Treasury bill rate as quoted understates the actual yield by several basis points. Dealer quotation sheets will report different yields to take account of this inconsistency in yield calculations. Other money market instruments may base calculations on a discount basis too. Watch out for this.

The Aggregate Balance of Hong Kong Banks and the Interbank Market for Funds

Exchange Fund Bills were introduced in Chapter 2 as a principal item in Hong Kong's monetary base. Another element of the monetary base is the aggregate balance of Hong Kong banks. All Exchange Fund (EF) debt issues, both bills and notes (EFBN), are, of course, liabilities of the fund. A bank's balance held with the EF is like a bank deposit that can be withdrawn on demand. It can also be converted into US dollars at a fixed rate under Hong Kong's currency board arrangements. Banks can also use their balances to buy Exchange Fund Bills. When banks sell EFBN to the fund they receive payment in the form of an increase in their balance with the fund.

Banks in Hong Kong clear their cheques with each other through their balance held with the EF. For example, if you deposit a cheque in your account that was drawn on the account of another bank, your bank will send the cheque to the EF, and it will increase your bank's balance and reduce the balance of the other bank on which the cheque was drawn. This is the way cheques are cleared through the banking system. The aggregate balance in this exchange does not change, because the funds were simply moved from one bank to the other. Under real time gross settlement, interbank clearing operates continuously during the day.

Banks need to maintain a balance in their clearing account at all times. Most of the time, funds flowing into a bank's balance will be roughly equal to funds flowing out. Bank managers cannot always count on having a sufficient balance to accommodate a net outflow of funds, though, so sufficient funds will be kept in the bank's balance with the EF at all times.

The Interbank Market

If a bank's balance with the EF becomes unusually low, its managers can borrow funds directly from other banks. It will enter the network of communications between banks and offer to purchase the funds of other banks. A bank willing to supply funds will respond with an offer to lend funds overnight or for a few days to the requesting bank in return for interest. To see the volume of interbank liabilities that can be traded among banks, and a measure of the volume of transactions in the interbank market, please refer to Table 7.3.

Table 7.3   Hong Kong Interbank Liabilities and Transactions
                (HK$ million)

As at End of May 2000

Interbank Liabilities Payable on Demand	Repayable within 3 months			Repayable Later than 3 months			Total
(HK$)	(Foreign Currency)	(HK$)	(Foreign Currency)	(HK$)	(Foreign Currency)		
25,743	18,780	299,725	120,662	30,123	15,161	570,193	

Transactions During April 2000

With Hong Kong Institutions			With Banks outside Hong Kong		
Placement Borrowing	Swaps	Total	Placement Borrowing	Swaps	Total
44,528	50,423	94,951	45,012	56,131	101,143

Source of data: Hong Kong Monetary Authority, *Monthly Statistical Bulletin*, July 2000; Tables 3.1, 3.2.

Hong Kong Interbank Offered Rate (HIBOR)

The interbank offered rate is the rate of interest paid to the bank offering to supply funds to other banks. That is the rate your bank must pay to borrow funds. A large volume of funds changes hands each day in this market, which only banks and other authorized institutions enter. The interbank offered rate fluctuates throughout the day.

HIBOR is something slightly different: it is the middle closing rate quoted by the Standard Chartered Bank each day at the end of trading. It is the interbank offered rate determined at a set time each day, a reference rate for floating rate notes and deposits. A business may borrow funds from a bank and agree to pay two per cent above HIBOR. The contract may provide for the interest rate to be adjusted every three months. If so, three months later the rate will be lowered or raised in line with the rate determined on that future date by the Standard Chartered Bank. Thus, HIBOR becomes the reference rate for floating rate deposits and notes.

A brief set of values recorded for HIBOR interest rates appears in Table 7.4. Rates on overnight borrowings were 5.25 per cent per annum at the end of June 2000. Rates on twelve-month borrowings were set at seven per cent per annum, and rates on other intermediate term borrowings were set within this range, indicating a gradual rise in the HIBOR yield curve at that date.

Table 7.4   Hong Kong Dollar Interbank Offered Rates End of June 2000 (per cent per annum)

Overnight	1-week	1-month	3-month	6-month	9-month	12-month
5.25	5.75	6.13	6.38	6.69	6.75	7.00

Source of data: Hong Kong Monetary Authority, *Monthly Statistical Bulletin,* July 2000; Table 5.3.1. Daily and daily average figures for the month are also available in Tables 5.3.2 and 5.3.3.

It is useful to note that rates of interest on Exchange Fund Bills closely follow those interest rates in the interbank market for funds. At the end of June 2000 the rate of 3-month bills was 6.21. It was 6.35 on 6-month bills, and 6.53 on 12-month bills. Thus, on that date the spreads between rates indicate that bills yielded seventeen, thirty-four, and forty-seven basis points less, respectively, than interbank loans. This spread indicates that interbank lending is very slightly more risky than lending to the Exchange Fund, and therefore carries a slightly higher interest return. From a bank's point of view, Exchange Fund Bills and interbank funds are nearly perfect substitutes for each other—but the bills are totally risk-free financial instruments for investments denominated in HK dollars, so they sell at a price that is slightly higher, and a return slightly lower, than the return on interbank borrowings.

Interest Rate Benchmarks and Risk Factors on Securities

Spreads between interest rates on different types of securities are largely determined by various risk factors. Several types of risk exist, and different securities are subject to different risks. There is the risk of inflation, reinvestment risk, maturity risk, liquidity risk, default risk, among others. Two of these are relevant here.

First, consider the well-understood default risk. Borrowers may not be able or willing to repay a debt, or they may fail to pay interest on the debt. Any violation of the covenant of the debt instrument is a violation of the terms of the agreement on the part of the borrower, and the security is said to be 'in default'. The risk of default is simply the risk that the borrower will not repay the creditor. All Exchange Fund debt in the form of bills and notes is free of the risk of default. This is because the terms of the covenant require repayment in amounts of Hong Kong dollars, and the HKMA has the ability to issue Hong Kong dollar accounts to banks in exchange for EF debt instruments. Therefore, it is never in a position to default on interest payments or the principal at maturity of bills and notes that it has issued. It has the ability to create the money needed to repay its debt. A security that is free of default risk can fetch a higher price than one burdened by default risk, so the default-free security carries a lower interest rate and lenders willingly hold it knowing that their wealth in the form of EF Bills or notes is free of default risk.

Second, consider liquidity risk (or capital risk, or maturity risk). These names all have a common important element. A security is highly liquid if it can be easily liquidated—that is, exchanged for money easily. 'Easily' means without trouble or without incurring expense. Transactions costs in terms of time, effort, or money are very low on highly liquid securities.

But some highly liquid assets in this sense, such as ten-year Exchange Fund notes, are still risky because the value of the note fluctuates with market interest rates. There is uncertainty about what price the note will bring when it is exchanged for cash. The value of the note goes up or down over the holding period, so it has what may be called capital risk—a risk of a change in capital value over time. The longer the term to maturity of a note or bond, the greater the security's capital risk. For this reason it is common to view securities with long-dated maturities as more risky than short-dated securities, and long-dated securities are therefore expected to carry higher interest rates than short-term securities. These higher interest rates include a base interest rate plus a term premium—a premium because the term to maturity is longer. The short-term three-month Exchange Fund bill has such a short term to maturity that it fluctuates in value only by very small amounts before maturity, and is thus considered to be the ultimate 'risk-free' security. It is completely free of default risk and has only a minute amount of maturity risk.

Benchmarks

Because of Exchange Fund Bills' risk-free status, their interest rate yields are used as a basis for evaluating rates of return required on privately issued securities. Banks selling NCDs will estimate the interest cost of raising funds by estimating that they may have to pay half a per cent more than the rate on the same maturity of EF bill. It is important that a good market exists for default-free securities so that benchmarks will be available for financial institutions, corporations, and other security issuers.

Clearing Services in Hong Kong's Money and Debt Markets

In Hong Kong, a Central Money Markets Unit (CMU) service is operated by the HKMA. It provides custodial services for debt instruments and acts as a clearing agent for trading in securities denominated for the most part in Hong Kong dollars issued by private companies. It does not act as a clearing agent for trading in Exchange Fund Bills or other government-issued securities by authorized banking institutions, since the Exchange Fund itself is the clearing agent for its own issues and for bank reserves. However, the CMU plays a facilitating role in the development of private debt markets in Hong Kong, such as the market for commercial paper (see Chapter 9; also Jiang, 2002.)

From Table 7.5 it appears that in July 2000 there were 206 members of the CMU, and that these members issued a total of 1,003 securities. These debt issues include commercial paper as well as notes and bonds issued in Hong Kong dollars, and a relatively small amount denominated in foreign currencies. Daily average turnover was quite small, which fits with the custodial function provided by the CMU. It is not a trading institution, but a custodial and clearing institution.

Table 7.5   Central Money Market Unit (CMU) Institutions and Debt Issues

End of period figures: June 2000

Number of CMU Members	Number of Debt Issues in Service	Outstanding Amount of Debt Issues in HK$million	Outstanding Amount of Debt Issues Foreign Currency HK$million	Average Daily Turnover
206	1,003	213,175	6,884	408

Source of data: Hong Kong Monetary Authority, *Monthly Statistical Bulletin,* July 2000; Table 4.5

The Role of Interbank Markets and Exchange Fund Debt in Monetary Policy

The Hong Kong Monetary Authority's *Annual Report 2001* provides a succinct description of the way it achieves the goal of monetary policy, which is a stable external value in terms of the US dollar. Here is the statement (p. 35):

> Under the currency board arrangements, the exchange rate remains stable, while interest rates adjust to changes in the demand for Hong Kong dollars. Specifically, when there is a decrease in the demand for Hong Kong dollar assets, and the market exchange rate weakens [say from HK$7.80 to 7.85 per US$], the HKMA stands ready to purchase

Hong Kong dollars from banks [supply US dollars to banks] at $7.80 (provided they have sufficient clearing balances to settle the transactions). The Aggregate Balance (as part of the Monetary Base) will fall [when banks pay HK dollars for US dollars]. Interest rates then rise [as banks compete for scarce Hong Kong dollar balances in the inter-bank market], creating the monetary conditions conducive to inflows of funds to maintain exchange rate stability [that is, investors are encouraged to supply US dollars for Hong Kong dollars in order to receive higher interest returns].

From this statement it is clear that the interbank money market is the conduit through which the HKMA carries out the equivalent of open market operations in the US. The US uses government securities markets to affect the volume of bank reserves. In Hong Kong, the HKMA uses its supply of US dollars to affect the volume of banks reserves. Any time a central bank sells anything—government securities, foreign currencies, or anything else—the volume of reserves available to banks will be reduced and interbank interest rates will rise. Higher interest rates relative to interest rates abroad will encourage an inflow of foreign currency, and capital inflows will help raise the value of the local currency relative to foreign currencies. Efficient money markets permit this outcome with very small changes in asset values and with little disruption of monetary system fundamentals. (See Chapter 8 on the foreign exchange markets in Hong Kong for a complementary description of this process.)

Sale–Repurchase Agreements (RPs or Repos)

An agreement to sell a security today for a certain sum of money, and at the same time agree to buy it back tomorrow at a slightly higher price, is a repurchase agreement. The seller of the security is borrowing funds and providing the security being 'sold' as if it were collateral for the loan. The buyer of the security is lending funds to the seller, usually overnight, and 'owns' the security for one day. The lender then sells it back to the original owner the following day at a predetermined price that is slightly higher than the original selling price. The difference between the original selling price and the resale price represents a return to the lender of funds, and a cost of borrowing to the borrower of funds.

Repurchase contracts have proven to be very useful to dealers in securities. A dealer holds an inventory of securities, which must be financed in some fashion. Typically a dealer will have a large loan from a bank that is used to buy an inventory of securities to have available for sale to customers, but often the dealer will sell some securities and simultaneously arrange to buy them back the next day so that he will have an inventory available to customers then. In this fashion he 'borrows' money to finance his holding of an inventory of securities. Typically, a person borrows money and signs a promise to repay; this promise, or IOU, becomes a security. In the case of repos the same result is accomplished without an IOU. In place of an IOU is a promise to repurchase the security and give the money back to the lender tomorrow. Thus sales–repurchase contracts become an instrument for borrowing and lending funds, and are included in our list of money market instruments.

Repurchase agreements are used by central banks in carrying out the open market operations needed to supply reserves or withdraw from banks. The Exchange Fund uses them with Exchange Fund Bills as the underlying security. To reduce the aggregate balance of banks, the EF can sell bills to a dealer, and when it wishes to reduce the aggregate balance temporarily for only a few days, it may sell securities under a repurchase contract. If it wishes to increase rather than reduce the aggregate balance for a short period, it can enter a reverse-repurchase agreement; that is, it buys EF Bills from a dealer or a bank under an agreement to sell them back in a few days. Without having to change the title of ownership to the security in question, the parties can effectively borrow and lend money to each other through simultaneous contracts (see Stigum (1983), Chapter 12).

The author first encountered a repurchase contract many years ago in the case of a bank and its relation with a customer. Company A was accumulating cash that it would use on Monday to meet its payroll. It wanted to earn interest on funds over the weekend rather than leaving the funds in its current account without earning interest. It could go to a securities dealer, buy securities, and sell them back on Monday morning, and earn interest over the weekend. Could Company A's banker assist the company in handling this without transactions costs? The solution the banker came up with was to sell to the depositor some government bonds that the bank owned under a repurchase contract. On Monday the bank bought the securities back and gave the depositor back his deposit with interest in the form of a higher price. Regulations did not allow the bank to pay interest on a business deposit account; the repo contract allowed it to get around this restriction. Under the contract the securities did not actually change ownership—all that the legal work required was that there be a contract created to that effect. Possession of the government securities did not have to be transferred and then transferred back again. A contract was created and a contract expired, and that took care of the borrowing and lending at interest.

It is possible to think of interest being paid as due to the lender because he holds the interest-earning security for a day. He should receive the one-day's interest that accrues to the owner of the security. Although the security that is the subject of the transaction, and that may be viewed as collateral for some purposes, advances toward maturity and may be accruing interest as the days go by, this interest accumulation is not explicitly considered by the parties to the contract. The return to the lender is simply found in the difference between the sale price and the repurchase price. The percentage yield is this difference as a proportion of the sale price. The effective interest rate paid on interbank repurchase contracts is lower than the interbank rate itself, because the risk of default is even less than the default risk on bank debt itself because of the implied collateral involved in the contract. There is no similar collateral generally available on interbank loans.

Bankers' Acceptances

Students of international trade and finance will already have encountered bank letters of credit, under which a bank customer is given a letter in which the bank indicates that it guarantees obligations assumed by the customer. For example, the customer may be an importer who travels abroad and negotiates a contract to purchase goods. The customer shows the supplier the letter of credit. When the supplier puts the goods on board the ship, he goes to his own bank with the letter of credit. The supplier writes an 'order to pay' to the customer's bank, citing the terms of the letter of credit. The local bank sends the pay order to the customer's bank, and the bank may stamp the pay order 'accepted' and send it back to the foreign bank and supplier. The order to pay is post-dated: it may take a month for the goods to arrive, so the acceptance will be for one month hence. The customer's bank has guaranteed payment on that date by the acceptance, so this piece of paper, called a banker's acceptance, is a promise by the bank to make the payment. The piece of paper may be held by the supplier, or the supplier may want to sell it to his bank. His bank will discount the face value of the acceptance and earn interest, holding the acceptance as an asset until maturity. Many banks in Hong Kong hold numerous bankers' acceptances. If a bank needs funds it may decide to sell a block of acceptances in the money markets to dealers such as those who deal in corporate commercial paper, or to other banks.

Banks in Hong Kong may also provide letters of credit for Hong Kong importers and create bankers' acceptances on the basis of those letters. Also, banks may hold their own acceptances as well as the acceptances created by other banks.

Summary

Money markets are huge in terms of dollar volume and volume of trading. They are arbitrarily defined to be in securities with a year or less to maturity. They are characteristic of well-developed financial institutions, such as those that exist in Hong Kong, but they are not as well known to the general public as are the stock markets because there is not as much media attention given to them.

Important types of money market instrument are certificates of deposits, bank short-term loans to businesses, commercial paper, interbank loans, Exchange Fund Bills, sales–repurchase contracts, and bankers' acceptances.

It wasn't many years ago that commercial banks obtained funds largely from depositors, but since the advent of NCDs in the 1970s, banks can simply sell these deposits through brokers and dealers in the securities markets. They no longer have to attract deposits from customers walking through their doors.

A large volume of lending in Hong Kong is based on floating, as opposed to fixed, rates of interest. Floating rates are often referred to as adjustable rates. Floating rates are indexed, and according to terms of the contract will be changed in line with changes occurring in the interbank funds market at the rate of interest referred to as HIBOR, the Hong Kong Interbank Offered Rate.

Corporations and other businesses may issue commercial paper in Hong Kong. Terms to maturity do not usually exceed 270 days, although terms and conditions are structured for each issue, as each may depart from uniformity in many ways. There is not a large and active market for commercial paper because most issues are placed by underwriters and held to maturity. However, there is some trading in CP, and there is a structure to handle trading called the Central Money Market Unit.

The HKMA created the benchmark money market and debt market instruments when it issued a range of Exchange Fund Bills and Notes with maturities of up to ten years. This market is used by the Exchange Fund in the management of the aggregate balance of banks. It needs to monitor the balance for the purpose of seeing that money market conditions, as indicated by short-term interest rates on Hong Kong dollar securities, are consistent with the rate of exchange between the Hong Kong dollar and the US dollar.

Interest rates on EF Bills are set in auctions, and yield quotations are equivalent to the theoretically correct bond equivalent yield. In other countries, yields on similar securities may be quoted on a discount basis, which gives a yield that is lower than that calculated on a bond equivalent basis.

Bankers' acceptances are an old type of financial instrument. They are used in international and inter-regional trade where participants are under different legal jurisdictions.

Sales–repurchase contracts are a recent invention of financial institutions and a new type of security. However, they are widely used by those who do huge volumes of borrowing and lending.

Discussion Questions

1. Distinguish between liquidity risk, default risk, and capital (maturity) risk.
2. What is the importance of benchmark securities? What are the benchmark securities traded in Hong Kong?
3. What are the functions of the Central Money Markets Unit in Hong Kong?
4. You wish to bid for a newly announced issue of six-month bills to be auctioned by the Exchange Fund next Wednesday. Do you bid a

price, or do you bid a yield? Explain the process and the formula you use to determine the price you must pay if your bid is accepted.

5. Briefly explain the role of the Exchange Fund in influencing the aggregate balance of banks.

6. Explain how NCDs are different from everyday certificates of deposit. Give an example of each.

7. Discuss what HIBOR is, how it is determined, and what role it plays in finance.

8. Describe how one can borrow and lend money for short-term use by entering into a sales–repurchase contract.

9. Explain how a bank manager might find it beneficial to enter a sales–repurchase contract.

10. Are bankers' acceptances a useful money market instrument? Explain.

Keywords

bankers' acceptances
Central Money Markets Unit (CMU)
certificates of deposit
commercial bank loans
commercial paper
effective interest yield
Exchange Fund Bills
floating rate notes
Hong Kong Interbank Offered Rate (HIBOR)
interbank loans
interbank market
interest rate benchmarks
negotiable certificates of deposit
repurchase agreements
revolving underwriting facilities (RUF)

8.   The Foreign Exchange Market

KEITH LAM

Introduction

The market in which international currencies are traded is called the foreign exchange market. It is important for an international financial centre and a highly export-oriented economy such as Hong Kong to have an efficient foreign exchange market.

In fact, Hong Kong's foreign exchange market is widely regarded as one of the most efficient markets in Asia. As at April 2001, according to a survey carried out by the Bank for International Settlements, the global (after adjustment) average daily turnover was US$1,200 billion, or US$1,618 billion before adjusting for reporting errors.[1] The top ten exchange markets at the same date were the United Kingdom (US$504 billion, 31.1 per cent of $1,618 billion), the United States (15.7 per cent), Japan (9.1 per cent), Singapore (6.2 per cent), Germany (5.4 per cent), Switzerland (4.4 per cent), Hong Kong (4.1 per cent), Australia (3.2 per cent), France (3 per cent), and Canada (2.6 per cent). Hong Kong was therefore ranked seventh in the world, with an average daily turnover of US$67 billion, 4.1 per cent before adjustment of total turnover, and third in Asia after Japan (third in the world and first in Asia) and Singapore (fourth in the world and second in Asia). Hong Kong also has a well-developed interbank market with an average daily turnover of US$49.699 billion.[2]

This chapter discusses the important concepts behind the foreign exchange market. We will focus our attention on the balance of payments, its impact on the exchange rate, interest rate parity, purchasing power parity, and the theory of efficient market hypothesis (EMH) on the foreign exchange market.

Balance of Payments

The balance of payments account is a set of accounts that keeps track of detailed records of transactions between residents and non-residents of an economy. The transactions are recorded in two groups of accounts: the current account, and the capital and financial account. The current account measures the flow of real resources through an economy's net exports of goods and services. It includes exports and imports of goods and services, income receivable and payable abroad, and current transfers from and to abroad. The capital and financial account shows the difference between sales of assets to foreigners and purchases of assets from abroad. The capital account measures external transactions in capital transfers, transfers of ownership of a fixed asset or forgiveness of a liability, and non-produced and non-financial assets (patents and copyrights, for example). The financial account shows how an economy's external transactions are financed. The transactions are recorded in the following accounts: direct investment, portfolio investment, financial derivatives, other investment, and reserve assets.

Balance of Payments Accounts

The balance of payments accounts follow a double-entry accounting system. Every transaction is entered into the account twice, once as a credit and once as a debit. A transaction resulting in a payment to non-residents is entered into the account as a debit and is represented by a negative (–) symbol. By the same token, a transaction resulting in a receipt from non-residents is entered into the account as a credit and is represented by a positive (+) symbol. Under the double-entry system, a debit entry must be accompanied by a credit entry. Therefore, in principle, the sum of the credit and debit entries in the balance of payments accounts is zero: in other words, the sum of the current account balance and the capital and financial account balance should be zero. Changes in the current account must be financed by the changes in the capital and financial account. Changes in the current account may have two causes: visible and invisible trade deficits or surpluses, or an imbalance between flows of investment income. The current account deficit must be financed either by selling foreign exchange assets or increasing foreign liability. However, in practice, discrepancies between the entries may occur because the data are collected from different sources, so a special account, net errors and omissions, is set up to correct the imbalance in the balance of payments accounts caused by errors in measurement, inaccuracy, and omission.

For example, if a resident exports goods to a non-resident and receives foreign currency payments, the transactions will be credited to goods exported and debited to a financial claim on the non-resident. The credit entry (a '+' symbol) into the goods exported account represents the transaction resulting in a receipt of foreign currency from a non-resident, while the debit entry (a '–' symbol) represents the obligation of the resident to deliver the goods to the non-resident according to the transaction.

A current account deficit simply means that the economy is saving less than it is investing and is drawing on the resources of foreign economies. A short-term current account deficit may not be bad for an economy: it depends on the economic condition of the economy at that time. However, some economists will raise concerns about huge and persistent current account deficits, seeing them as an unhealthy sign. Their arguments are as follows: since the deficit has to be financed by either selling foreign assets or borrowing foreign assets, the amount of foreign assets will be reduced or foreign debts will be increased. Fewer foreign assets will decrease interest income and more foreign debts will increase interest expenses in the future, which will be reflected later in the current account. This will cause an even higher future current account deficit.

Continuing increases in current account deficits and high levels of foreign-owned debt are routinely viewed as bad for an economy, but some economists see such views as narrow and ill-advised. They point out that these views tend to reflect only private interests and/or political interests of what are called rent-seeking constituents. They seldom reflect the interests of people in free and open economies such as Hong Kong.

For example, over the past few decades the US has had huge current account deficits and foreigners have invested equally large sums of capital in the US, giving it a surplus on its capital account. This has been going on for years, and some observers say that in the future the interest paid to foreigners will be so large that the US will have to declare bankruptcy. However, the investments represent the best outlook for increased returns. They are believed to have a positive net present value, and these beliefs are based on business judgements that on average turn out to be largely correct. The interest on this investment should be paid out of positive cash flows from the projects that the investment supports, so future returns to foreign holders of securities should be available from future cash flows and should cause no difficulties. Indeed, just the opposite is the case, as both borrower and lender benefit.

It should also be recognized that the balance of payments is an accounting statement about a large number of completely interdependently determined values. If a consumer chooses to buy a car from Japan there will be more foreign currency in the hands of a Japanese person, who can use it either to buy clothing made in Hong Kong or to buy an Exchange Fund bill. Restricting imports of cars will not, in general, reduce the size of a current account deficit or an imbalance between current and capital accounts.

The economic problems that arise out of imbalance in payments aggregates usually stem from attempts by private interests to gain from government protection or support. Current account deficits and capital account surpluses that arise from the free choices of consumers and investors at market-determined prices simply reflect the aggregate of individual preferences and indicate efficient economic outcomes.

Balance of Payments Accounts in Hong Kong

There is no complete set of balance of payments accounts published before 1997, the year that Hong Kong reverted to China and became a Special Administrative Region (SAR). On 23 April 1999, the Hong Kong SAR government published its first set of complete balance of payments accounts for 1997 (Table 8.1). Various types of external transaction statistics had been recorded before 1997, and the consolidation of these data and other statistics enabled the compilation of a complete set of balance of payments accounts. It is important for Hong Kong to publish its own set of balance of payments accounts for two reasons: (1) it provides financial data in compliance with international standards to the international financial community, and (2) it provides more financial information for the analysis and assessment of the macroeconomic performance and external transactions of Hong Kong, an export-oriented economy and a major world financial centre.

Table 8.1 Hong Kong's Balance of Payments Account (1997–2001) (HK$ million)

	1997	1998	1999	2000	2001
Current Account	–47,681	30,238	89,088	69,471	93,338
(% of GDP)	(–3.6%)	(2.4%)	(7.3%)	(5.5%)	(7.4%)
Capital and Financial Account	47,681	–31,514	–83,374	–57,863	–85,717
(% of GDP)	(3.6%)	(–2.5%)	(–6.8%)	(–4.6%)	(–6.8%)
Net Errors and Omissions	N/A	1,276	–5,714	–11,609	–7,621
(% of GDP)	(N/A)	(0.1%)	(–0.5%)	(–0.9%)	(–0.6%)
Overall Balance of Payments	95,087	–52,581	77,867	78,321	36,530
(% of GDP)	(7.2%)	(–4.2%)	(6.3%)	(6.2%)	(2.9%)
Net Inflow/(Outflow) of non-reserve assets*	142,768	–84,095	–5,507	20,458	–49,187
Reserve Assets (net change)**	–95,087	52,581	–77,867	–78,321	–36,530

* Positive (negative) values represent net inflow (outflow) of assets
** Negative (positive) values represent increase (decrease) in foreign currency assets
Source: The Hong Kong Census and Statistics Department

There are four components in the current account: goods, services, income, and current transfers. The goods account consists of exports and imports accounts. Exports are goods that residents sell to non-residents (recorded as credits and '+'), while imports are goods that residents purchase from non-residents (recorded as debits and '–'). The services account covers services (financial, business service, etc) provided by residents to non-residents (credits) or *vice versa* (debits). The income account covers income earned (international interest, dividends, etc) by residents from non-residents (credits) or *vice versa* (debits). Current transfers is an offsetting entry required in the balance of payments account when resources are provided, without any economic value being received in return, by non-residents to residents (credits) and *vice versa* (debits).

There are six components in the capital and financial account. These are: capital transfers, direct investment, portfolio investment, financial derivatives, other investment, and reserve assets. Capital transfer is a transfer of ownership of a fixed asset or forgiveness of a liability. Direct investment is international investment where residents invest in another economy. According to the international standard,[3] an initial as well as an incremental investment in equity of companies with more than ten per cent ownership is considered as direct investment. The portfolio investment component covers transactions in equity and debt securities, except those related to direct investment and reserve assets. Financial derivatives are financial instruments that are linked to a specific financial instrument or indicator or commodity, and through which specific financial risks can be traded in financial markets in their own right. Other investments include all financial transactions not covered by the above components and reserve assets, for example, trade credits, loans, and currency and deposits are classified as other investment. Reserve assets constitute foreign currency assets managed by the Hong Kong Monetary Authority (HKMA). They include monetary gold, foreign currency assets, and other claims. The foreign currency assets consist of bank deposits, foreign government securities, bonds and notes, money market instruments, financial derivatives, and equity securities.[4]

In 1997 (Table 8.2), the current account showed a net deficit (credit) representing a net financial capital inflow of non-reserve assets of $47.681 billion, which is 3.6 per cent of the estimated gross domestic product (GDP) of the year. The current account deficit was the net effect of a visible trade deficit of $133.925 billion, an invisible trade surplus of $88.236 billion, a net inflow of factor incomes of $10.475 billion, and a net outflow of current transfers of $12.467 billion for the year. The net increase of $95.087 billion in the overall balance of payments represented a net increase in reserve assets, which were foreign exchange assets managed by the HKMA. Therefore, in 1997, Hong Kong had a net financial capital inflow of non-reserve assets of $142.768 billion, the sum of $47.681 and $95.087 billion, from the rest of the world.

The current account balance turned from net deficit to net surplus after 1997. The net non-reserve assets also changed from inflow to outflow at the same time. Visible trade deficits remained for the entire period from 1997 to 2001, but imports were substantially cut after the Asian financial crisis, which reduced the visible trade deficit significantly. For instance, the cut in imports lowered the visible trade deficit from 1997's $133.925 to 1998's $60.667 billion. However, the combined net visible and invisible trades are in surplus. The combined net trade surplus is due to a sustained improvement in invisible trade surplus, a continued net inflow of external factor income, and a continued net outflow of current transfers. Except for the year 2000, the non-reserve assets also changed from net inflow to net outflow for the period 1998 to 2001. However, other than in 1998, the reserve assets—foreign exchange assets managed by the HKMA—increased during the period. Generally speaking, this evidence indicates that Hong Kong's financial position was stable and did not deteriorate much between 1997—the time of the handover of Hong Kong's sovereignty to China and the Asian financial crisis—and 2001.

Factors Affecting Balance of Payments Accounts

There are many factors affecting an economy's balance of payments accounts. The most influential factors on the current account are domestic inflation, domestic income, exchange rates, and government restrictions. For capital and financial accounts, the most important influence is the intervention of governments.

Table 8.2   Hong Kong's Balance of Payments Account (Figures as percentage of GDP in parentheses) (HK$ million)

	1997	1998	1999	2000	2001
A) CURRENT ACCOUNT: SUB-ACCOUNT COMPONENTS					
Current Account	−47,681	30,238	89,088	69,471	93,338
	(−3.6%)	(2.4%)	(7.3%)	(5.5%)	(7.4%)
Goods	−133,925	−60,667	−24,501	−63,832	−64,970
	(−10.1%)	(−4.8%)	(−2.0%)	(−5.0%)	(−5.1%)
Services	88,236	74,507	90,755	124,548	135,282
	(6.7%)	(5.9%)	(7.4%)	(9.8%)	(10.7%)
Income	10,475	28,762	34,777	21,768	36,137
	(0.8%)	(2.3%)	(2.8%)	(1.7%)	(2.9%)
Current transfers	−12,467	−12,364	−11,943	−13,013	−13,110
	(−0.9%)	(−1.0%)	(−1.0%)	(−1.0%)	(−1.0%)
B) CAPITAL AND FINANCIAL ACCOUNT: SUB-ACCOUNT COMPONENTS					
Capital and Financial Account	47,681	−31,514	−83,374	−57,863	−85,717
	(3.6%)	(−2.5%)	(−6.8%)	(−4.6%)	(−6.8%)
Capital Transfers	N/A	−18,445	−13,812	−12,044	−9,059
	(N/A)	(1.5%)	(−1.1%)	(−1.0%)	(−0.6%)
Direct Investment	N/A	−17,016	40,737	19,767	108,036
	(N/A)	(−1.4%)	(3.3%)	(1.6%)	(8.6%)
Portfolio Investment (+ : surplus, − : deficit)	N/A	171,052	256,812	190,782	−309,317
	(N/A)	(13.6%)	(20.9%)	(15.1%)	(−24.5%)
Financial Derivatives	N/A	25,374	78,999	1,871	39,141
	(N/A)	(2.0%)	(6.4%)	(0.1%)	(3.1%)
Other Investment (+ : surplus, − : deficit)	N/A	−245,059	−368,243	−179,917	122,013
	(N/A)	(−19.5%)	(−30.0%)	(−14.2%)	(9.7%)
Reserve Assets	−95,087	52,581	−77,867	−78,321	−36,621
	(−7.2%)	(4.2%)	(−6.3%)	(−6.2%)	(−2.9%)

Source of data: The Hong Kong Census and Statistics Department

If an economy's inflation is relatively higher than that of another economy, its current account balance will generally decrease. This is because with higher inflation the price of local goods becomes more expensive than in other economies, and the price of imported goods becomes cheaper. Residents will consume more of the cheaper imported goods, so domestic imports will increase and exports will decrease.

If an economy's disposable domestic income increases more than that of another economy, its current account balance will generally decrease. This is because when income increases, domestic residents will consume more goods, including imported goods. Higher domestic income will translate into the increase in demand for foreign goods.

If an economy's exchange rate appreciates against another economy, its current account balance will generally decrease. This is because export goods will be more expensive than before for foreign consumers, and they will consume less. As a result, the demand from the foreign economy will decrease. However, at the same time, the demand for foreign goods from domestic residents will increase because the imported goods are now cheaper than before. So there is an inverse relationship between the exchange rate and the current account.

In order to reduce the amount of goods imported from abroad, local governments can choose to impose tariffs or quotas on foreign goods. Imposing tariffs or taxes on foreign goods will increase their prices to domestic residents and thus reduce the domestic demand for these foreign goods. The effect of imposing quotas is to limit the amount of goods imported from abroad. It may not affect the price of the goods, but will limit the amount that domestic residents can consume. This of course decreases the amount of imports in the current account. The local government can also provide production subsidies to domestic industries. The impact of production subsidies is to decrease the costs of domestic goods, which will make import goods less attractive. The intention is to encourage domestic residents to consume more of the cheaper domestic goods and less of the expensive import goods. This also decreases the amount of imports in the current account.

For capital and financial accounts, the local government can always control the flow of capital in and out of the economy. For example, a government can impose a special tax on income earned by domestic residents from the purchase of foreign securities. This will increase the capital account initially, but it may discourage domestic investors from investing abroad and eventually decrease the capital outflow in the capital account. Also, other economies may retaliate by imposing a similar tax on their domestic residents. The final outcome may be an overall reduction in foreign investment, which will lead to a decrease rather than an increase in the capital account.

The exchange rate between two economies is determined by the demand and supply of the currencies. Since the balance of payments accounts record the economy's currency demand and supply activities, the economy's exchange rate can therefore be explained by the change of the balance of payments accounts. This approach to explaining the exchange rate determination process is called the balance of payments approach.[5] For example, a transaction involving the importing of goods and services (or purchasing foreign assets) from abroad will be recorded in the debit side of the current account (or capital and financial account) of the Hong Kong balance of payments accounts. The transaction involves a payment of foreign currency and, thus, increases the demand for foreign currency, whereas a transaction involving the export of goods and services (or selling of financial assets) to another economy will be recorded in the credit side of the current account (or capital and financial account) of the balance of payments accounts. The transaction involves a receipt of foreign currency and, therefore, increases the supply of foreign currency. The process of determining the exchange rate is described next.

Exchange Rate Determination

The exchange rate between two currencies represents the relative price of the goods of one economy to those of another. It is important to the residents of economies that engage in international trade because it affects their costs and benefits. The major factors that determine the exchange rate are relative money supplies, real incomes, inflation rates, and the interest rates of the local and foreign economies.

In this section, we will discuss three concepts: the determination of the exchange rate with the balance of payments (the BOP approach), the Hong Kong exchange rate system, and the arbitrage mechanism of the exchange rate system in Hong Kong.

Exchange Rate Determination and BOP

Under a floating exchange rate system, the exchange rate is solely determined by the interaction between supply and demand of the two currencies. These demand and supply forces affecting local and foreign currencies are summarized in the transactions recorded in the balance of payments accounts.

Foreign currency demand arises from transactions that require payments to foreign residents in foreign currency. The import of goods and services, the payment of income earned by non-residents, and the remittances of non-residents to their home countries are all transactions recorded in the current account and represent uses of foreign currencies. The purchase of foreign securities and investments in foreign countries are transactions recorded in the capital and financial accounts. These transactions, which also give rise to a demand for foreign currency, are listed on the debit side of the Hong Kong balance of payments accounts and also represent users of foreign currency.

The supply of foreign currency stems from transactions that receive foreign currency from foreign residents. Transactions from the current account such as the export of goods and services, the receipt of income earned by local residents abroad, and the receipt of local residents' remittances from foreign countries are transactions recorded in the current account. The sale of foreign securities and investments in a local economy by non-residents are transactions recorded in the capital and financial account. These transactions, which give rise to supplies of foreign currencies, are listed on the credit side of the Hong Kong balance of payments accounts.

The exchange rate of the two economies will be determined at the point of equilibrium between the demand and supply of foreign currencies. See

Figure 8.1 for an illustration of how this works. The vertical (y) axis is the exchange rate denoted by the Hong Kong dollar to the US dollar (HK$/US$). The horizontal (x) axis is the quantity of US dollars in the market (foreign currency). The curve DD, the demand curve for foreign exchange, is downward sloping because a higher exchange rate will cause the prices of the goods and services imported or financial services purchased to be more expensive to domestic residents. If all else remains unchanged, higher prices will reduce the domestic demand for imported goods or foreign financial services. As an example, suppose that the exchange rate is HK$7.5/US$1 (7.5 hereafter). The price of an imported US$10 good is HK$75 in Hong Kong. If the Hong Kong dollar depreciates and the exchange rate increases to 8.0, the price for the same US$10 good should now be HK$80, which is HK$5 more expensive than before. Hong Kong residents will now buy fewer imported goods; when the Hong Kong dollar depreciates against the US dollar and the exchange rate increases, the demand for US goods and services will be lower, and the demand for US dollars will be lower too. The situation will be reversed when Hong Kong dollar appreciates against the US dollar. The quantity of US dollars demanded will be higher when the exchange rate becomes lower. Therefore the foreign exchange demand curve DD is downward sloping.

The foreign exchange supply curve SS is upward sloping. A higher exchange rate will cause Hong Kong's exports to be cheaper to foreign buyers than before. US buyers will buy more and Hong Kong will receive more US dollars. The supply of US dollars will thus increase with the higher exchange rate. When the exchange rate is at 7.5, a HK$75 export

Figure 8.1 The Determination of Foreign Exchange Rate in the Balance of Payments Approach

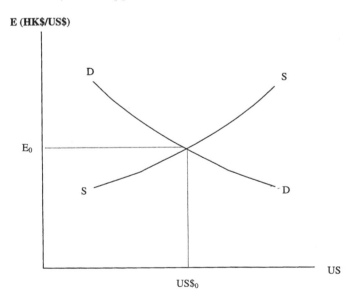

good will sell at US$10 to US residents. If the Hong Kong dollar depreciates and the exchange rate increases to 8.0, the goods will sell at US$9.375 in the US, making the goods US$0.625 cheaper than before. The result will be more purchases from US residents, Hong Kong will receive more US dollars, and the supply of US dollars will increase. Therefore, the relationship between the exchange rate and the supply of US dollars is positive. This means that the supply curve SS should be upward sloping.

The equilibrium exchange rate E_0 is determined by the intersection of the demand and supply curves, where demand equals the supply of US currency. However, changes in exchange rates may be caused by factors such as a change in domestic prices, real income, and tastes. The demand for imported goods and services can be changed by a rapid increase of domestic real income of Hong Kong. The change in demand of imports will cause the demand curve DD to shift rightward to a new demand curve D'D' (Figure 8.2). In other words, with increased real income, Hong Kong residents will buy more imported goods at the exchange rate E_0. Demand for US dollars will therefore increase from $US\$_0$ to $US\$_0^1$. The new equilibrium exchange rate will change from E_0 to E_1, representing a depreciation of the Hong Kong dollar. It is important to emphasize that the increase in foreign currency demand ($US\$_0^1$) is not due to the decrease in exchange rate along the demand curve DD. If it were caused by a decrease in the exchange rate, the change would slide along the curve to P rather than shifting to D'D'.

By the same token, changes in prices, real income, and tastes in the US may cause the supply curve SS to shift to S'S' (Figure 8.3). If relatively higher inflation occurs in the US than in Hong Kong, the prices of goods

Figure 8.2 The Effect of an Increase in Demand for Foreign Currency

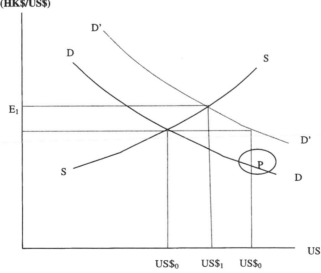

Figure 8.3 The Effect of an Increase in Supply of Foreign Currency

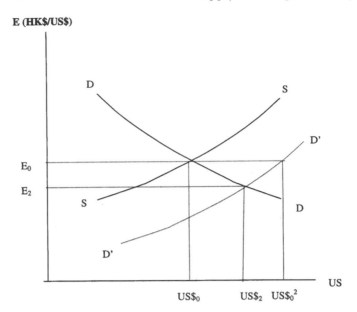

imported from Hong Kong will be relatively cheaper. This encourages US residents to buy more of Hong Kong's exports and will eventually cause an increase in the supply of US dollars. This will shift the supply curve SS outward to S'S'. With a higher supply of US dollars (US$$_0^2$), the US currency will depreciate or the Hong Kong dollar will appreciate. The new equilibrium exchange rate will change from E_0 to E_2. It is useful to note that demand and supply curves for US currency are mirror images of demand and supply curves for the Hong Kong dollar. The demand curve for the US dollar by Hong Kong residents contains the same information as the supply curve of the Hong Kong dollar available to US residents. Similarly, the supply curve of the US dollar to Hong Kong residents contains the same information as the demand curve for the Hong Kong dollar by US residents.

The Hong Kong Exchange Rate System

From 1944 to 1971, most countries around the world adopted a fixed exchange rate system. After the Bretton Woods (New Hampshire, USA, 1944) conference, exchange rates were either held constant or allowed to fluctuate narrowly around a parity level. At the same time, the International Monetary Fund (IMF) was established to maintain the exchange rates. The IMF was given the power to instruct central banks to intervene in foreign exchange markets through buying and selling currencies. This fixed exchange rate system required the US to maintain a reserve of gold and other nations to maintain a reserve of US dollars. However, due to the continuous balance of trade deficits in the US and the oil crisis in the early 1970s, many countries worried about the ability of the US to change its currency into gold at the official price.[6] They started selling US dollars, finally causing the fixed exchange rate system to collapse in 1971. The floating exchange rate system was adopted after this date. Under the freely floating exchange rate system, exchange rates are determined only by market forces. Most countries' central banks regularly intervene to set the exchange rates, however. This managed floating (or dirty float) exchange rate system lies somewhere between the freely floating and fixed exchange rate systems. Some countries also use the linked (or pegging) exchange rate system for their currencies. This pegs the exchange rate of a currency with another currency at some fixed value. For example, the Hong Kong dollar is pegged to the US dollar at a rate of HK$7.80 to US$1.

From 1863 to 1935, Hong Kong used the silver dollar as its currency. During this period, the silver standard became the basis of its monetary system. The silver standard was changed to a link with the pound sterling after a world silver crisis. From December 1935 to July 1972, Hong Kong belonged to the sterling area and adopted a pegged exchange rate system[7] in which the Hong Kong dollar was pegged to the pound sterling at a rate of HK$16 to £1 (until 20 November 1967) and HK$14.55 to £1 (after 20 November 1967). At the same time, an exchange control system was also implemented to prevent reserves from draining from the sterling area. Due to exchange controls, trading in the foreign exchange market was inactive, but in July 1972 Britain decided to float the pound sterling because of heavy devaluation pressure. To avoid a loss in the value of Hong Kong reserves, which were mainly in pounds sterling, the Hong Kong government decided to shift its peg to the US dollar. The pegged rate was HK$5.65 to US$1 at first, changing to HK$5.085 to US$1 after February 1973. The exchange control system was also removed. On 26 November 1974, the Hong Kong government stopped pegging the Hong Kong dollar to the US dollar because the local currency was under severe attack and the Hong Kong dollar floated freely between 26 November 1974 and 17 October 1983. The foreign exchange market started to take off in 1978 when the government lifted the restriction on foreign banks entering Hong Kong. Subsequently, foreign exchange trading was boosted by the influx of foreign banks. In September 1982, a crisis of confidence emerged following the visit of Mrs Thatcher, the then British Prime Minister, to Beijing to discuss Hong Kong's post-1997 future. This crisis triggered a collapse in the colony's property, stock, financial, and foreign exchange markets. The Hang Seng Index (a major stock index in Hong Kong) fell thirty-three per cent from 1035.33 in August 1982 to 690 on 4 October 1983. Banks suffered huge losses. Financial institutions began tightening their credit lines to banks and, in turn, their financial situation worsened. Hong Kong residents began to worry about the stability of the financial system and rushed to banks to convert their money to foreign currencies. On 24 September 1983, the exchange rate with the US dollar reached a record high of HK$9.60 to US$1, a fifty-seven per cent depreciation from

6.10 at the end of August 1982 and a drop of thirteen per cent in just two days. The interest rate was increased from twelve to sixteen per cent during the period, but it could not stop the outflow of capital. In order to cope with the capital outflow and stabilize the exchange rate, the Hong Kong government announced on 15 October 1983 that it would peg the Hong Kong dollar to the US dollar once more at a fixed rate of HK$7.80 to US$1. The new linked exchange rate system allowed the exchange rate to fluctuate narrowly around the 7.80 rate.

The current linked exchange rate system in Hong Kong is a currency board system, which requires both the stock and flows of the monetary base to be fully backed by foreign reserves. Banknotes are issued by banks authorized by the HKMA. Currently there are three authorized note-issuing banks (NIBs) in Hong Kong: HSBC, Standard Chartered Bank, and Bank of China. When these banks issue notes, they are required to pay an equal amount of US dollars at the rate of 7.80 to the HKMA for the account of the Exchange Fund[8] to purchase Certificates of Indebtedness (CIs). The notes are therefore fully backed by US dollars. If NIBs want to reduce note circulation, they simply redeem the CIs from the Exchange Fund.[9] With the CIs, the Exchange Fund agrees to provide and redeem the notes from the NIBs at the 7.80 rate.[10] Under the arrangement, the NIBs also agree to provide notes to, and accept notes from, other non-NIBs at the same 7.80 rate. Therefore, an interbank market for the Hong Kong dollar notes at a fixed price now exists.

The Adjustment Process

Under a linked exchange rate system, interest rates and the money supply should adjust automatically through the balance of payments account without government intervention.[11] The adjustment process is illustrated in Figure 8.4. Suppose there is an increase in trade surplus and this induces the inflow of US dollars. The supply curve SS shifts outward to S'S', causing the exchange rate to fall below the lower parity level (E_1). With more US dollars on hand, NIBs can now issue more Hong Kong notes. The Hong Kong money supply increases, the interest rate drops, and eventually domestic prices will rise. Hong Kong people will consume more foreign goods, thereby increasing imports.[12] The result is to shift the demand curve DD outward to D'D'. Eventually the trade surplus reduces until the demand and supply of currency reach equilibrium again. The new equilibrium exchange rate (E_0') now falls back within the parity range.

If there is an increase in trade deficit, the adjusting process will be reversed. An increase in imports will increase the demand for US dollars and shift the demand curve DD to D'D'. The new exchange rate is at E_2 and is well above the upper parity level. The NIBs will issue fewer notes to or redeem notes from the market. With the lower Hong Kong money supply, the domestic price decreases and the interest rate increases. Hong Kong people will consume fewer imported goods and export more domestic goods. Imports will be lower than before and the demand curve will shift back to

Figure 8.4 The Arbitrage Process

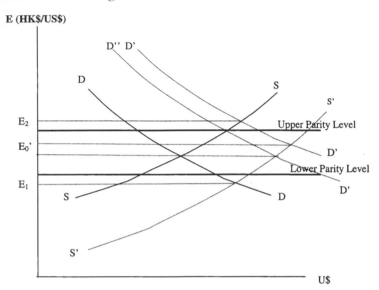

D"D". At the same time, the supply curve will shift out to S'S'. Imports will decrease and exports will increase, and the trade deficit will reduce until the new equilibrium exchange rate is reached (E_0").

The movement of the exchange rate after October 1983 is summarized in Table 8.3. We can see that, except for 17 October 1983 and 7 July 1984,[13] the exchange rate fluctuated within a narrow range over the nineteen years from October 1983 to April 2002. For most of the time, especially in the 1990s, the exchange rates remained slightly below the 7.80 level, and the variations were mostly less than one per cent of 7.80. The figures suggest that the exchange rate has been rather stable since the implementation of the linked exchange rate system on 17 October 1983. In fact, it survived the October 1987 world stock market crash, the events of 4 June 1989, the August 1990 Gulf crisis, the 1992 Exchange rate mechanism turmoil in Europe, the January 1995 Mexican crisis, and the 1997–8 Asian currency turmoil. However, despite the advantage of stabilizing the economy, there are costs for Hong Kong in using a linked exchange rate system.

Potential Costs of the Adjustment Process

One of the costs of the linked exchange rate system is to force the interest rate to assume a more passive role as an instrument of monetary policy. If the US increases interest rates but Hong Kong does not follow, funds will flow from Hong Kong to the US. With more funds leaving Hong Kong, the money supply will decrease and interest rates in Hong Kong will eventually increase. Hong Kong's interest rate must therefore follow the

Table 8.3   History of HK/US Exchange Rate

Dates	Close HK/US	Low	High	High/Low difference	% of low from 7.8	% of close from 7.8
17 Oct 1983	8.000	N/A	N/A	N/A	N/A	2.5641%
End of 1983	7.790	7.790	7.812	−0.2816%	−0.1282%	−0.1282%
7 July 1984	7.900	N/A	N/A	N/A	N/A	1.2821%
End of 1984	7.833	7.789	7.850	−0.7771%	−0.1410%	0.4231%
End of 1985	7.811	7.750	7.811	−0.7809%	−0.6410%	0.1410%
End of 1986	7.795	7.784	7.814	−0.3839%	−0.2051%	−0.0641%
15 Dec 1987	7.751	N/A	N/A	N/A	N/A	−0.6282%
End of 1987	7.760	7.760	7.809	−0.6275%	−0.5128%	−0.5128%
End of 1988	7.808	7.790	7.816	−0.3327%	−0.1282%	0.1026%
End of 1989	7.807	7.775	7.814	−0.4991%	−0.3205%	0.0897%
End of 1990	7.801	7.760	7.811	−0.6529%	−0.5128%	0.0128%
End of 1991	7.781	7.735	7.796	−0.7825%	−0.8333%	−0.2436%
End of 1992	7.741	7.723	7.762	−0.5024%	−0.9872%	−0.7564%
End of 1993	7.726	7.762	7.756	0.0774%	−0.4872%	−0.9487%
End of 1994	7.738	7.727	7.738	−0.1422%	−0.9359%	−0.7949%
End of 1995	7.732	7.732	7.742	−0.1292%	−0.8718%	−0.8718%
End of 1996	7.736	7.731	7.740	−0.1163%	−0.8846%	−0.8205%
End of 1997	7.746	7.732	7.751	−0.2451%	−0.8718%	−0.6923%
End of 1998	7.746	7.732	7.749	−0.2194%	−0.8718%	−0.6923%
End of 1999	7.771	7.746	7.771	−0.3217%	−0.6923%	−0.3718%
End of 2000	7.796	7.781	7.799	−0.2308%	−0.2436%	−0.0513%
End of 2001	7.797	7.797	7.800	−0.0385%	−0.0385%	−0.0385%
30 Apr 2002	7.799	7.799	7.800	−0.0128%	−0.0128%	−0.0128%

All figures are in end-of-year exchange rate values

movement of the US interest rate, losing its active and independent role in the monetary policy. Whenever the US decides to increase (or decrease) interest rates, Hong Kong's interest rate has to follow suit, causing the Hong Kong economy to become more US-dependent. However, since Hong Kong and the US may face very different economic conditions, the loss of the function of the interest rate in the monetary policy may induce problems in the Hong Kong economy. For instance, if the US increases interest rates to cool down an overheated economy, Hong Kong must also increase its rates even if it is facing an adverse economic situation and needs low interest rates to stimulate economic recovery. Hong Kong people have to suffer from this mismatched high interest rate policy.

Another cost is the internal cost. Price adjustment to sharp external currency depreciation will be slower than a rapid change in the exchange rate. A slow process may sometimes be painful. After the 1998 Asian financial crisis, there was a slowdown in the world economy. Many countries devalued their currencies and/or decreased their interest rates sharply to stimulate their economies and exports. Hong Kong could not do so too because of the linked exchange rate system. Instead, Hong Kong had to cut the price of domestic goods by decreasing costs such as labour costs and property prices. Cutting labour costs meant redundancies and reduced wages for workers, resulting in increases in the unemployment rate and a reduction in disposable incomes. The unemployment rate surged substantially to a record high of 7.1 per cent for the February to April 2002 quarter, causing a number of social problems. Wage cuts caused conflicts between employees and employers, including between civil servants and the Hong Kong government, and the fall in incomes, together with the slowdown in the world economy, also brought property prices down: a fall in value of sixty per cent since 1998 has created a lot of negative asset owners, adding further to existing social problems. Problems such as these, decreases in asset prices, and a reduction in self-confidence are the consequences of a painful adjustment in nominal prices and wages caused by the linked exchange rate system. The costs of keeping a stable exchange rate after 1998 have been huge.

The Arbitrage Process

The pegged exchange rate arrangement fixes the exchange rate at the interbank level but allows it to float at the open market, or retail, level. In the foreign exchange market, the exchange rate is still determined by the market supply and demand of the currency. If the rate deviates from 7.80, market arbitrage forces will move the exchange rate back to the equilibrium rate. But arbitration activities are only allowed in the interbank market, not in the open exchange rate market.

Suppose that the market exchange rate is 7.90 instead of 7.80. A non-NIB can convert its Hong Kong dollar deposits (say HK$780 million) into US dollars for US$100 million (at 7.80) with a NIB. The non-NIB can then sell the US$100 million dollars in the open market for HK$790 million (at 7.90). The bank makes a profit of HK$10 million through this arbitrage activity. The NIB can work through the same process with the Exchange Fund by converting the CIs (the same as Hong Kong dollar deposits) to US dollars with the Exchange Fund and selling the US dollars on the market and making a profit. The banks sell US dollars and buy Hong Kong dollars in the foreign exchange market, which increases the supply of US dollars and the demand for Hong Kong dollars, and exerts an upward pressure on Hong Kong dollars. When the NIBs redeem CIs from the Exchange Fund, the effect is to reduce note circulation in the market. With less money in the market, interest rates will rise until they are high enough to attract foreign investments. With higher capital flowing into Hong Kong, the demand for Hong Kong dollars increases. The overall effect is to push up the exchange rate of Hong Kong dollars until it goes back to 7.80.

If the exchange rate is 7.70 instead of 7.80, the arbitrage activities will be reversed. The non-NIB will convert US dollar deposits (say US$100 million) to Hong Kong dollars (HK$780 million) at a fixed rate (7.80) with a NIB and exchange the Hong Kong dollars for US dollars (US$101.30 million) at the market rate (7.70). The non-NIB will make a profit of US$1.30 million in the arbitration. By the same token, the NIBs go through the same arbitration process with the Exchange Fund. The result is a decrease in the supply of Hong Kong dollars and an increase in the demand for them, which will push the exchange rate back to 7.80, the equilibrium rate.

In reality, the market exchange rate will not be exactly the same as the official 7.80 rate. There are three factors contributing to the deviation. First, arbitrage opportunities are not open to all foreign exchange market participants, only to banks in the interbank market. Other participants in the open market, such as corporations and individuals, are prohibited from accessing the arbitration process. Second, the arbitration ability of banks is restricted because, by law, banks need to keep certain cash ratio requirements, so they cannot convert all Hong Kong notes to US dollars even if they spot arbitrage opportunities. Third, only banknotes, not deposits, can be converted at 7.80 in the interbank market. US dollar deposits can be converted to Hong Kong dollar banknotes, but US dollar deposits cannot be converted to Hong Kong dollar banknotes and *vice versa*. With such limitations on the arbitration process, it is not surprising that the market exchange rate is slightly different from the official 7.80 exchange rate.

The arbitration adjustment process holds when the economic situation is normal. It may not be held when there is worry about the future of the economy, such as at the time of the Asian financial crisis. Then, Hong Kong dollars faced a huge selling force and were under high devaluation pressure, forcing the Hong Kong government to intervene in the foreign exchange market to buy up Hong Kong dollars and sell US dollars. At the same time, to keep the economy stable, the government also intervened in the stock market by buying up more than HK$100 billion of stock listed on the Hong Kong Stock Exchange.

Interest Rate Parity

The exchange rate of two economies is in equilibrium when rates of return generated from the deposits of the two economies are the same. The condition that the expected rates of return on deposits of the two economies are equal when measured in the same currency is called interest rate parity. With interest rate parity, Hong Kong's interest rate has to follow the movement of the US interest rate, otherwise the rate of return in the US will be higher (lower) than in Hong Kong and funds will flow out of (into) Hong Kong. It will then exert devaluation (appreciation) pressure on the Hong Kong dollar and cause the exchange rate to deviate from the 7.80 level.

To illustrate interest rate parity, let us assume that the nominal annual interest rate in Hong Kong (R_{HK}) is two per cent, and the nominal annual US interest rate (R_{US}) is five per cent, i.e. the US nominal annual interest rate is three per cent higher than Hong Kong's. The current spot market exchange rate (E_0) is 8.0155 and the expected future spot exchange rate in one year (E_1) is 7.7750. That is, the market expects the Hong Kong dollar to appreciate by three per cent in one year $(= (8.0155 - 7.7750)/8.0155)$. The three per cent appreciation in the Hong Kong dollar will offset the three per cent deposit interest rate difference between Hong Kong and the US.

These assumptions imply that the rates of return in Hong Kong and the US will be the same no matter where the investors choose to invest. If Hong Kong investors invest HK$1 million in Hong Kong deposits, they will receive HK$1.02 million after one year: a two per cent return. If they choose to invest in US deposits instead, they need to convert Hong Kong dollars to US dollars at the current spot market exchange rate of 8.0155 (E_0) for US$124,758.28. After one year, they receive US$130,996.19 from their five per cent US deposits. When they convert the US dollars back to Hong Kong dollars at the expected future spot exchange rate of 7.7750 (E_1), they will eventually receive HK$1.02 million. The net rate of return from investing in the US is two per cent: five per cent from US deposits less three per cent loss in the exchange rate change due to the appreciation of Hong Kong dollars.

The investment processes in both Hong Kong and the US are summarized in Figure 8.5. It shows that investors may drop directly down to gain a two per cent return. Alternatively, they can circle in a clockwise pattern, selling Hong Kong dollars for US dollars, investing US dollars at a five per cent return, then repurchasing Hong Kong dollars at the forward exchange rate to end up with a two per cent return. Investors end up at the same spot on the diagram.

The general formula for the relationship between interest rates and the exchange rate over n periods is as follows:

$$(1 + R_{HK})^n = (1 + R_{US})^n \times (1 + (E_1 - E_0)/E_0)^n$$

Taking the nth root of both sides and expanding the right-hand side of the equation gives:

$$1 + R_{HK} = 1 + R_{US} + (E_1 - E_0)/E_0 + (R_{US}) \times (E_1 - E_0)/E_0$$

Figure 8.5 The Investment Processes in Hong Kong and the US

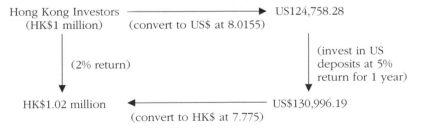

Hong Kong Investors   US124,758.28
(HK$1 million)   (convert to US$ at 8.0155)

(2% return)   (invest in US deposits at 5% return for 1 year)

HK$1.02 million   US$130,996.19
(convert to HK$ at 7.775)

Assuming R_{US} and $(E_1 - E_0)/E_0$ are small compared to 1, the last term on the right-hand side of the equation will be very small, and we have the following approximation of the equation:

$$R_{HK} = R_{US} + (E_1 - E_0)/E_0 \qquad\qquad (Equation\ 8.1)$$

If the interest rate in the US increases to six per cent but the rate in Hong Kong does not change, funds will flow to the US to take advantage of the higher interest income. These investments will come from both Hong Kong and US investors. For example, Hong Kong investors can borrow one million Hong Kong dollars at two per cent interest from a financial institution—assuming that lending and borrowing rates are the same. They then convert the money into US dollars at 8.0155, receiving US$124,758.28. They invest the money in the six per cent US deposits and receive US$132,243.77 after one year. They then convert the US dollars back to Hong Kong dollars at 7.7750 and receive HK$1,028,195.30. They will make HK$8,195.30 after paying the $20,000 (two per cent) interest expense for their one million dollar loan. This does not require investors to invest any money out of their own pockets: it is a zero-investment profit-making arbitrage activity. US investors can go through the same arbitrage process by borrowing Hong Kong dollars and investing in US deposits; they will also make a net profit of HK$8,195.30. The results are that money will flow from Hong Kong to the US, with an increased demand for US dollars and an increase in Hong Kong dollars supply. To keep the linked exchange rate intact, Hong Kong needs to increase its interest rate in order to restore the imbalance between the demand and supply of Hong Kong and US dollars. These activities will eventually force the interest rate in Hong Kong to increase.

The investment gain is shown in Figure 8.6:

Figure 8.6 Investment Gain

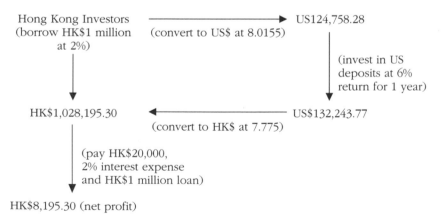

There are opportunities to gain if either $R_{HK} > R_{US} + (E_1 - E_0)/E_0$ or $R_{HK} < R_{US} + (E_1 - E_0)/E_0$. In the previous example, we assumed that the investors were speculating on what they expect the future spot exchange rate to be, and the expected future spot exchange rate in one year turns out to be correct. However, in reality, this expected future spot exchange rate might not come out as expected, so the investment may not be risk-free. In order to hedge their positions, investors can choose to hedge their arbitrage activity using the one-year forward exchange rate (F_0) in the market. The one-year forward exchange rate represents the spot exchange rate expected to prevail after one year: the forward contract's value date. The relationship in equation (8.1) is now replaced by the following equation:

$$R_{HK} = R_{US} + (F_0 - E_0)/E_0 \qquad\qquad (Equation\ 8.2)$$

Covered Interest Rate Parity

This relationship is called covered interest rate parity, whereas the relationship in equation (8.1) is sometimes referred to as non-covered interest rate parity. The second term on the left-hand side of Equation 8.2, $(F_0 - E_0)/E_0$, is called the forward premium on Hong Kong dollars against US dollars, or the forward discount on US dollars against Hong Kong dollars. Therefore, we can say that under covered interest rate parity the interest rate on Hong Kong deposits equals the interest rate on US deposits plus the forward premium on Hong Kong dollars against US dollars.

From Equation 8.1 and 8.2, we can see that they are the same when E_1 equals F_0. In fact, on average, they are the same. If investors are risk-neutral and prefer more wealth to less, they will not enter into forward contracts if the forward rate is different from the expected future spot exchange rate. If the one-year forward rate (7.7750) is greater than the one-year future spot exchange rate (7.7700), no-one will enter into a forward contract to sell Hong Kong dollars. They will wait and sell them after their value rises relative to the US dollar. If the forward rate (7.7750) is less than the future spot exchange rate (7.7780), no-one will enter into a forward contract to buy Hong Kong dollars; they will wait and buy them later. These activities will force the forward rate and the future spot exchange rate to converge, so the forward rate is widely regarded as an unbiased predictor of the future spot rate. This is called the unbiased forward rate hypothesis. The hypothesis may not hold true if there is the presence of significant transaction costs and if the risk attitude of investors is not risk-neutral. For example, if investors are risk-averse, they may buy or sell forward contracts even if the expected forward rates are different from the future spot rates. This is because expected future spot rates are uncertain, and investors will require a rate of return difference to compensate for the risk they take on future spot rates.

If the covered interest rate parity deviates from equilibrium, arbitrage activities will be the same as before—the only difference being to replace the forward exchange rate with the future spot exchange rate. In this case, the equilibrium condition will be restored quickly. Since arbitrage is risk-free, the arbitrage opportunity is sometimes regarded as a money machine. Investors will try to borrow as much money as possible to engage in arbitrage, and this will generate a large market force even with a small group of investors. Such a force can restore the equilibrium in a very short period of time.

If we rearrange Equation 8.2, we can derive the formula for the forward rate as follows:

$$F_o = E_0(1 + R_{HK})/(1 + R_{US}) \qquad \textit{(Equation 8.3)}$$

With a known forward rate, importers and exporters can hedge their foreign currency exposures. For example, a Hong Kong importer imports goods from the UK and has to pay in pounds sterling after thirty days. Instead of worrying about the Hong Kong dollar/sterling exchange rate thirty days in the future, the importer can enter into a thirty-day forward contract to buy pounds. With the forward contract, his pound position is known and hedged and the cost of the import goods is also known to him. He could, however, also solve the problem in a more complicated way. First, he borrows Hong Kong dollars from his bank. He sells the dollars right away for pounds at the spot exchange rate and puts the money into a thirty-day sterling deposit. Next he uses the proceeds of the deposit to pay the UK supplier, and uses the realized proceeds of his Hong Kong sales to repay his Hong Kong dollar loan. If covered interest rate parity holds, the result will be the same as hedging with a forward contract.

There is strong evidence that covered interest rate parity holds for different foreign currency deposits issued within a single financial centre. If the deposits being compared are located in different countries, deviation from parity may occur because of possible government restrictions on the free movement of funds across countries. Political risks may also cause parity conditions to be violated.

Purchasing Power Parity

The theory of purchasing power parity (PPP) explains the movements between the exchange rates and price levels of two countries. It states that the exchange rate between the currency of two countries is equal to the ratio of the price levels of the two countries. The price level of a country, which is the price of a referent basket of goods and services, reflects the purchasing power of the country's currency.

In order to understand PPP, we need first to discuss the concept of the law of one price. The law of one price states that, in competitive markets, which are free of transaction costs and barriers to trade, identical goods sold in different countries must sell for the same price when they are expressed in the same currency. For example, a good that sells for US$10 in the US must sell for HK$78 if the exchange rate is 7.80. The price of the good sold in the US, if expressed in Hong Kong dollars, is HK$78 (= US$10 x HK$7.80/US$), the same price as in Hong Kong.

If the exchange rate were 7.75, Hong Kong importers and US exporters would have an incentive to buy the goods in the US and ship them to Hong Kong: without transportation costs and trade barriers, the goods sell more cheaply, at HK$77.5 (= HK$7.75/US$ x US$10), in Hong Kong than in the US. People who buy in one market and sell in another market are known as commodity arbitrageurs. This arbitrage action will push the price up in Hong Kong and down in the US until the prices in the two locations are equal. If the exchange rate is 7.85, the price in the US is cheaper than in Hong Kong. Commodity arbitrageurs do the reverse, buying the goods in Hong Kong and shipping them to the US for sale. Prices in the US will go up and those in Hong Kong will come down until they are equal.

The theory of the law of one price can be expressed in the following formula:

$$P^i_{HK} = E_0 \times P^i_{US} \qquad\qquad (Equation\ 8.4)$$

Where P^i_{HK} is the price of good i in Hong Kong;
P^i_{US} is the price of good i in the US;
E_0 is the spot exchange rate between Hong Kong and the US

If we rearrange Equation 8.4, the exchange rate can be expressed as the ratio of good i's price between Hong Kong and the US. The relationship is shown below:

$$E_0 = P^i_{HK} / P^i_{US} \qquad\qquad (Equation\ 8.5)$$

Absolute PPP

The law of one price theory is for individual goods—such as good i—whereas the PPP theory is for the general price level, a basket of selected goods in a country. Assuming that a single basket of goods accurately measures the purchasing power of money in both Hong Kong and the US, PPP theory can be expressed as follows:

$$P_{HK} = E_0 \times P_{US} \qquad\qquad (Equation\ 8.6)$$

Where: P_{HK} is the price of a referent basket of goods in Hong Kong;
P_{US} is the price of the same referent basket of goods in the US

This PPP relationship is sometimes referred to as absolute PPP. The right-hand side of Equation 8.6 measures the purchasing power of a Hong Kong dollar when exchanged for a US dollar and spent in the US. Absolute PPP holds when, at the prevailing exchange rate, domestic purchasing power is the same as foreign purchasing power. From Equation 8.6, we can also see that PPP predicts that a fall in domestic purchasing power (an increase in domestic price level or increase in the right-hand side of Equation 8.6) will result in a proportional depreciation in domestic currency (an increase in E_0). By the same token, an increase in domestic purchasing power will cause a proportional appreciation in domestic currency.

If we rearrange Equation 8.6, the exchange rate can be expressed as follows:

$$E_0 = P_{HK}/ P_{US} \qquad\qquad \textit{(Equation 8.7)}$$

The absolute PPP predicts that the exchange rate is expressed as the ratio of price level of a basket of goods in Hong Kong and the US. For example, with a basket of goods worth HK$78 in Hong Kong and US$10 in the US, PPP predicts that the exchange rate should be 7.80. If the price in Hong Kong increases to $78.50 while that in the US remains intact, the exchange rate will change to 7.85, causing a depreciation in the Hong Kong dollar.

As stated before, there is a difference between the law of one price and PPP. The law of one price applies to individual goods, whereas PPP applies to a referent basket of goods. If the law of one price holds for every individual good in the basket, PPP holds automatically as long as the baskets in two countries are the same. Even if the law of one price does not hold for individual goods, PPP may still hold—when the law of one price does not hold and the goods sold in Hong Kong are more expensive than those sold in the US, the demand for goods in Hong Kong falls but the demand for goods in the US rises. This change of demand will push the exchange rate down (i.e. the Hong Kong dollar depreciates) as well as the general price level of the goods in Hong Kong, which results in the restoration of the PPP condition. The adjustment will be in the opposite direction if the goods sold in Hong Kong are cheaper than those in the US. The demand for goods in Hong Kong will increase, pushing up the value of the Hong Kong dollar (i.e. it appreciates), and restore the PPP relationship. Economic forces in the market will therefore ensure that PPP holds across countries even if the law of one price does not hold for individual goods.

Relative PPP

Absolute PPP offers a very simple explanation of exchange rate and commodity prices. However, different baskets of goods are commonly used in the price indexes of different countries to reflect the preferences of the countries, so it is difficult to test the validity of absolute PPP. An alternative and more useful form of PPP, relative PPP, is advocated. Relative PPP states that the percentage change in the exchange rate between two currencies over any period equals the difference between the percentage changes in the countries' price levels. Absolute PPP shows the relationship between price and exchange rate levels, while relative PPP depicts the relationship between price and exchange rate changes. It asserts that the price levels and exchange rates will change in a way that preserves the ratio of the two countries' purchasing power. There are two ways of deriving relative PPP: short-term and long-term PPP relationships. The short-term PPP relationship is derived as follows. If absolute PPP (Equation 8.7) holds, the following also holds at the end of one year:

$$P_{HK}(1 + I_{HK,t}) = E_0[1 + (E_{0,t} - E_{0,t-1})/E_{0,t-1}]P_{US}(1 + I_{US,t}) \quad \text{(Equation 8.8a)}$$

where $E_{0,t}$ is the spot exchange rate between Hong Kong and the US at time t; $E_{0,t-1}$ is the spot exchange rate between Hong Kong and the US at time t-1; $I_{HK,t}$ is the inflation rate in Hong Kong, which is the percentage change in Hong Kong price level $[(P_{HK,t} - P_{HK,t-1})/ P_{HK,t-1}]$; $I_{US,t}$ is the inflation rate in the US, which is the percentage change in the US price level $[(P_{US,t} - P_{US,t-1})/ P_{US,t-1}]$.

The left-hand side of the equation is the price level in Hong Kong after one year (t), which is the price level now (t-1) multiplied by one plus the Hong Kong annual rate of inflation. By the same token, the right-hand side of the equation is the price level in the US after one year. Dividing Equation 8.8a by Equation 8.7 yields:

$$1 + I_{HK,t} = [1 + (E_{0,t} - E_{0,t-1})/E_{0,t-1}](1 + I_{US,t}) \quad \text{(Equation 8.8b)}$$

Rearranging Equation 8.8b, we have the following equation:

$$(E_{0,t} - E_{0,t-1})/E_{0,t-1} = (I_{HK,t} - I_{US,t})/(1 + I_{US,t}) \quad \text{(Equation 8.8c)}$$

Equation 8.8c is the relative form PPP. It says that the change in exchange rate equals the inflation rate difference between two countries divided by one plus the inflation in the foreign country. For example, if inflation in Hong Kong is two per cent and that in the US is five per cent, the exchange rate should fall at a rate of 2.86 per cent. The calculation is as follows:

$$(E_{0,t} - E_{0,t-1})/E_{0,t-1} = (2\% - 5\%)/(1 + 5\%) = -0.0286 \text{ or } -2.86\%$$

If both inflation rates are small, the denominator on the right-hand side of Equation 8.8c, $(1 + I_{US,t})$, is close to one. We can rewrite Equation 8.8c in the following approximate form:

$$(E_{0,t} - E_{0,t-1})/E_{0,t-1} = I_{HK,t} - I_{US,t} \quad \text{(Equation 8.8d)}$$

The approximate form of relative PPP states that the change in the exchange rate is equal to the difference of inflation rates between local and foreign countries. With the same example above, the exchange rate should fall by three per cent (= 5% – 2%), which is pretty close to the value (–2.86 per cent) computed from the exact formula.

We can also derive the long-term relative PPP relationship using the arbitrage behaviour of speculators in the markets. If we ignore risk and the markets are efficient, the expected returns on buying and holding the same commodities in Hong Kong and the US should be the same. The expected return in Hong Kong is represented by the annual expected price difference between two periods, which is the Hong Kong expected annual inflation rate ($I^e_{HK,t}$), whereas the expected returns for the same commodities in the US in terms of Hong Kong dollars is the sum of the expected annual inflation rate in the US and the expected annual change in the exchange rate [$I^e_{US,t} + E[(E_{0,t} - E_{0,t-1})/E_{0,t-1}]$]. If the markets are efficient, market arbitration forces will push the two returns towards convergence. Therefore, we can set the return in Hong Kong as equal to the return in the US and arrive at Equation 8.8e below:

$$E[(E_{0,t} - E_{0,t-1})/E_{0,t-1}] = I^e_{HK,t} - I^e_{US,t} \qquad \textit{(Equation 8.8e)}$$

Equation 8.8e is the relative form of PPP written in terms of expected rates of change. If expectations were rational, we would expect the long-term expected values on average to equal realized rates of change. Therefore, Equation 8.8e should be able to explain the long-term relative PPP condition, while Equation 8.8d is the approximate form for relative PPP when US (foreign) inflation is moderate and should explain the short-term relative PPP condition. If PPP holds in its relative form (Equation 8.8d), we would be able to explain short-run changes in exchange rates from short-run differences in inflation rates.

The difficulty with using absolute PPP is that countries have to compute indexes according to an internationally standardized basket of goods. The advantage of using relative PPP is that, even if countries use different baskets of goods, relative PPP still holds. Relative PPP also holds even if the absolute PPP condition deviates from equilibrium. As long as the factors causing the deviations are stable over time, percentage changes in prices still approximate percentage changes in exchange rates.

Empirical Evidence

Empirical evidence on the law of one price suggests that the relationship does not hold for individual goods. Goods that are very similar to each other sell at widely different prices in different countries. Empirical findings on absolute PPP indicate that the theory also does not hold. The prices of identical baskets of goods differ substantially across countries when measured in a single currency.

Astonishingly, relative PPP empirical results also perform poorly. Studies largely confirm that relative PPP held up rather well before the 1970s, when exchange rates were fixed within narrow margins through the intervention of central banks, but deviations from relative PPP occurred after this, when exchange rates were allowed to be market-determined. Since it takes time for prices to respond to changes, it is expected that the short-term violation in PPP is stronger than the long-term violation. Empirical studies support this prediction. Over the long term, relative PPP seems to hold most of the time. However, in general, different versions of PPP do not seem to hold well empirically.

The negative empirical results on the law of one price, absolute PPP, and relative PPP can be caused by trade barriers and non-tradables, departures from free competition, and different inflation measurements. One of the assumptions of the law of one price is that there are no transaction costs and trade barriers, but in reality transaction costs, such as transport costs and trade barriers, do exist. These restrictions may be high enough to cause the deviation of the law of one price and PPP. Sometimes transportation costs may be so large that they cause some goods never to be traded internationally. These goods are called non-tradables. A haircut is a typical example of a non-tradable—it would be too expensive for a US resident to fly to Hong Kong to have a haircut, so haircut services will only be provided to Hong Kong residents. Non-tradables are primarily services and the output of a construction industry, such as haircuts, medical treatment, housing, and so on. These non-tradables, with prices affected only by domestic demand and supply, will cause the law of one price and PPP to deviate from their equilibrium condition except in the very long run.

When market imperfection occurs together with trade barriers and transaction costs, the deviation from the law of one price and PPP strengthens further. If there are monopolistic or oligopolistic practices in the market, the goods can be sold for different prices in different markets. This price discrimination will further weaken the relationship between prices and exchange rates. Different countries measure their price levels differently. The Japanese may consume more sushi and, therefore, put more weight on sushi in their goods basket, while the Italian government may put more weight on olive oil in their goods basket. The components in the goods basket will be different across countries. This difference in the components of the goods basket will cause violations in both absolute and relative PPP.

Another difficulty of finding empirical support for PPP may be due to statistical problems. Most empirical tests are based on the estimation of the following regression equation:

$$(E_{0,t} - E_{0,t-1})/E_{0,t-1} = b_0 + b_1(I_{HK,t} - I_{US,t}) + m$$

If PPP holds, b_0 should be close to zero and b_1 should be close to one. The error terms, m, should be very small, and on average zero. We normally encounter two problems with this kind of regression. First, the error in measurement arises in the inflation differential term $(I_{HK,t} - I_{US,t})$. If the inflation differential is poorly measured because of the problem of different baskets in each country, the regression coefficients would be biased toward zero. We could find b_1 smaller than 1 even if the true b_1 is exactly 1. Second is the causality relationship between the dependant variable and the independent variable. If the causality relationship goes from inflation to exchange rates and *vice versa*, there is a need to run the regression using simultaneous equation methods. Failure to do so will cause the estimated coefficients to be biased towards zero. For PPP, causation goes both ways and the estimated b_1 is thus biased towards zero.

Since the summer of 1986, the *Economist* magazine has conducted an extensive survey on the prices of Big Mac hamburgers at McDonald's restaurants throughout the world. Since the Big Mac is sold in different countries with very little change in recipe, the comparison of hamburger prices can serve as a 'light-hearted guide' to PPP. In their first survey in 1986, they found that the price of a Big Mac in New York was 50 per cent higher than in Australia and 64 per cent higher than in Hong Kong. But in Tokyo, a Big Mac cost 50 per cent more than in New York. Only in Britain and Ireland was the price of a Big Mac close to that of New York. In April 1992, the survey showed that only the prices of the burgers in two countries, Canada and Ireland, were close to New York. Hong Kong and Australia were 91 per cent and 13 per cent cheaper than in New York respectively, while China was 89 per cent cheaper and Russia 273 per cent cheaper. In April 2002, Hong Kong was 42 per cent cheaper, whereas Australia was 35 per cent cheaper than in New York. Japan, China, and Russia were 19 per cent, 49 per cent, and 50 per cent cheaper than in the US respectively. There were only a few countries (Euro areas, Peru, Israel, and Mexico) where prices were close to the US. The survey results show that, over the past sixteen years, hamburger prices are in no way close to PPP. There are many reasons, such as costs and government regulations, for this PPP violation. The costs, including transportation costs, the cost of ground meat and buns, workers' wages, rent, and electricity, may also vary considerably across countries, causing PPP to depart from its equilibrium.

The Fisher Condition

With some additional derivation, we can combine the interest rate parity and relative PPP conditions to derive the Fisher condition. Assume that P^e_{HK} and P^e_{US} are the prices expected in Hong Kong and the US one year from now. The expected percentage changes in inflation rate, I^e_ts, are:

$$I^e_{HK,t} = (P^e_{HK} - P_{HK})/P_{HK} \qquad \textit{(Equation 8.9a)}$$

And $$I^e_{US,t} = (P^e_{US} - P_{US})/P_{US} \qquad \textit{(Equation 8.9b)}$$

If the relative PPP holds, the expected percentage change in the inflation rate will be the same as the actual percentage change in the inflation rate. So we can replace I^e_ts in equation (8.9a) and (8.9b) for the I_ts from Equation 8.8e. We get:

$$(E_{0,t} - E_{0,t-1})/E_{0,t-1} = I^e_{HK,t} - I^e_{US,t} \qquad \textit{(Equation 8.10)}$$

We can rewrite Equation 8.1 as follows:

$$R_{HK} = R_{US} + (E_{0,t} - E_{0,t-1})/E_0 \qquad \text{(Equation 8.11)}$$

Substituting Equation 8.10 into 8.11 we get,

$$R_{HK} = R_{US} + I^e_{HK,t} - I^e_{US,t}$$

$$R_{HK} - R_{US} = I^e_{HK,t} - I^e_{US,t} \qquad \text{(Equation 8.12)}$$

Equation 8.12 is the Fisher-open condition, which states that the expected inflation difference between two countries is exactly offset by the interest rate difference. Since it is in expected value, the relationship is a long-run relationship. For example, if Hong Kong's expected inflation rate is expected to increase by five per cent more than the US, its interest rate will increase by five per cent more than that of the US. The increase in the interest rate in Hong Kong is offset by the same magnitude increase in inflation rate, leaving the real interest rate in Hong Kong unchanged.

The conventional Fisher condition, or Fisher equation, involves only one country. It was first advocated by Irving Fisher and states that the nominal interest rate (R_{HK} or R_{US}) of a country equals the expected real interest rate (r_{HK} or r_{US}) plus the expected rate of inflation ($I^e_{HK,t}$ or $I^e_{US,t}$) of that country, assuming that the expected real interest rate is constant over time. The conventional Fisher condition is shown as follows:

$$R_{HK} = r_{HK} + I^e_{HK,t} \qquad \text{(Equation 8.13a)}$$

or
$$R_{US} = r_{US} + I^e_{US,t} \qquad \text{(Equation 8.13b)}$$

The Fisher-open condition can be further extended to include the movement of the real exchange rate. The real exchange rate is the net exchange rate when inflation is deducted from the (nominal) exchange rate. The real exchange rate, E^r_0, is defined as follows:

$$E^r_0 = E_0 - I_{HK} \qquad \text{(Equation 8.14)}$$

Alternatively, we can define the real exchange rate as follows:

$$E^r_0 = (E_0 \times P_{US})/P_{HK} \qquad \text{(Equation 8.15)}$$

Therefore, from Equation 8.14, we know that the change in the real exchange rate is the difference between the nominal exchange rate and inflation. We can express the equation as follows:

$$(E^r_{0,t} - E^r_{0,t-1})/E^r_{0,t-1} = (E_{0,t} - E_{0,t-1})/E_{0,t-1} - (I^e_{HK,t} - I^e_{US,t}) \qquad \text{(Equation 8.26)}$$

After substituting Equation 8.11 into Equation 8.16, we have

$$R_{HK} - R_{US} = (E^r_{0,t} - E^r_{0,t-1})/E^r_{0,t-1} + I^e_{HK,t} - I^e_{US,t} \qquad (Equation\ 8.17)$$

Equation 8.17 tells us that the expected changes in the nominal interest rates between two countries is equal to the sum of two components: the expected changes in the real exchange rate and the expected changes in inflation. If Hong Kong's inflation rate is expected to increase by five per cent more than that of the US, its interest rate may not increase by five per cent more than that of the US. If we expected the real exchange rate of the Hong Kong dollar to appreciate by one per cent, the expected increase in the nominal interest rate is six per cent, which is the sum of the five per cent expected inflation rate increase plus the one per cent real exchange rate increase. If relative PPP prevails, the real exchange rate should be stable over time and $E^r_{0,t}$ must be equal to $E^r_{0,t-1}$. The first term on the right-hand side of Equation 8.17 will be zero and drop out of the equation. Equation 8.17 will then be reduced to Equation 8.12.

Since each of the three parity conditions—interest rate parity, purchasing power parity, and the Fisher-open condition—can be derived from the other two, any one condition must be correct if the other two are correct. If we believe that interest rate parity holds, we are implicitly assuming that PPP holds also. The relationships between the three parity conditions are demonstrated in Figure 8.7:

Figure 8.7 The Relationship between Interest Rate Parity, Purchasing Power Parity, and the Fisher-open Condition

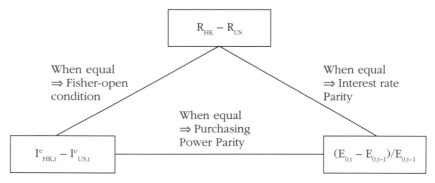

Efficient Market Hypothesis (EMH)

The underlying assumption for interest rate parity, PPP, and the Fisher condition to hold is that the foreign exchange markets are efficient. In this section, Efficient Market Hypothesis (EMH) and empirical findings on EMH are discussed.

Fama (1991; p. 1575) states that the EMH is 'the simple statement that security prices fully reflect all available information'. In an early paper (1970), he points out that the primary role of the capital market is to allocate the ownership of the economy's capital stock. An efficient capital market is a market in which prices provide accurate signals for the efficient allocation of resources. In other words, the capital market is efficient when asset prices always 'fully reflect' available information in a speedy fashion.

The types of information to be fully reflected include past price information, publicly available information, and all available information, including inside or private information. In his seminal 1970 paper, Fama classifies the EMH into three forms according to the types of information to be reflected. They are: weak-form, semi-strong form, and strong-form market efficiency.

The weak-form market efficiency hypothesis states that today's prices fully reflect all information contained in historical asset prices. That means we cannot find any pattern in prices, or prices have no 'memory'. The hypothesis is concerned with the forecasting power of past returns. This implies that, if the market is weak-form efficient, no investor can earn excess risk-adjusted returns by developing trading rules based on historical price or return information. However, investors may still be able to make excess risk-adjusted returns by utilizing publicly available information or insider information.

The semi-strong form market efficiency hypothesis says that prices fully reflect all publicly available information. Thus, if the market is semi-strong efficient, no investor could earn excess returns using publicly available information such as annual reports, dividend announcements, dividend policies, fund-raising activities, and any other information relevant to the valuation of the asset. Only investors who have access to insider information could trade and earn excess returns based on the specific information they acquired.

The strong-form market efficiency hypothesis states that prices fully reflect all information whether it is private information, inside information, or publicly available information. That is, all information, whether publicly available or not, is reflected in prices. No investor could earn excess returns using any type of information.

There are basically two approaches in testing the efficiency of the foreign exchange market: fundamental analysis and technical analysis. We will discuss these two approaches in the following sections.

Fundamental Analysis

Fundamental analysts use basic factors to predict the future path of a currency. The basic factors include inflation rate differentials, interest rate differentials, forward premiums, relative growth rates of money supply, the state of current accounts, the balance of payments positions, and central bank behaviour. If the predicted values deviate insignificantly from the actual values, the market is efficient. Since most of the factors are publicly available, they are public information. Thus, the efficiency tests are semi-strong form efficiency tests.

Traditional studies (Meese and Rogoff (1988); Diebold and Nason (1990)) find that monetary fundamentals can predict short-term movement in US dollar exchange rates. However, several authors (Mark (1995); Chinn and Meese (1995); Chen and Mark (1996)) have recently documented evidence of monetary fundamentals to predict long-horizon exchange rate changes but are unable to verify the short-run exchange rate prediction. Mark and Sul (2001) conducted a test for the long-run relationship between exchange rates and monetary fundamentals for nineteen countries. They found that monetary fundamentals are able to forecast future exchange rate returns. The empirical results on fundamental analysis are mixed in the US.

If the market is efficient, there should be a significant linear relationship between interest rate differentials and basic factors. There is a growing body of literature on the linear relationship between macroeconomic basic factors and interest rate differentials for European countries. However, the picture obtained from the results is disappointing. Many of the explanatory variables have no significant effect on interest rate differentials, and several coefficients have the wrong sign. The results suggest that the foreign exchange markets in Europe are not efficient in semi-strong form, but a recent study by Bernhardsen (2000) found that, for nine European countries relative to Germany, the relationship between interest rate differentials and macroeconomic variables is significant and the coefficients are estimated with the predicted signs using twelve-month interest rate differentials. The macroeconomic variables are the rate of unemployment, the real income growth differential, relative labour costs, the inflation differential, the current account, and the public deficit. This suggests that the European foreign exchange markets may be semi-strong form efficient and are able to reflect public information speedily.

Another fundamental analysis test on market efficiency is to test the ability of forward foreign exchange rates to predict changes in future spot rates. If the market is efficient, the unbiased forward rate hypothesis— which states that the forward rates are unbiased predictors of future spot rates—should be correct. Studies in the US have obtained mixed results. Authors such as Hansen and Hodrick (1980), Bilson (1981), Froot and Thaler (1990), and MacDonald and Taylor (1991) have rejected the unbiased forward rate hypothesis, but other researchers such as Kohlhagen (1978), Levich (1979), and Chiang (1988) have found evidence in favour of the unbiased forward rate hypothesis. There are also substantial tests on whether the forward rate contains a risk premium, which implies that the forward rate equals the future spot rate plus a risk premium. This is merely a re-specification of the simple unbiased forward rate hypothesis. The empirical evidence is mixed with little conclusive consensus. Some studies fail to identify the existence of such a premium, while others do find evidence consistent with the existence of a premium.

Technical Analysis

Technical analysts use past rates or trading volumes to derive patterns or charts to predict exchange rate movements. Those who use this technique believe either that the basic factors of exchange rates are irrelevant or that they are too complicated to understand. They believe that market information is revealed in the charts of historical data that can be used to forecast. Since it uses historical prices, technical analysis testing is weak-form efficient. If extra profits can be made using technical tools, the exchange rate market is said to be weak-form inefficient.

The most commonly used technical tool is a simple moving average (SMA) of exchange rates. An SMA curve can be constructed by summing the data for a specific period (e.g. ten days) and taking the average. This is called the n-day moving average. If the moving average is twenty days or below, it is regarded as a short-term moving average; if it is between twenty and fifty days, it is a medium-term moving average; if it is greater than fifty days, it is a long-term moving average. The rule is that if the short-term moving average breaks the medium or long-term moving average from below, it sends out a buying signal, because when the short-term moving average breaks from below the market must be rising. It is expected that the market will keep on rising for a while, so it is time to buy at the beginning of the rising market trend. A selling signal emerges when the short-term moving average breaks the medium or long-term moving average from above. It signals that the market is falling.

Other than the SMA, the channel (CH) and filter rules are also widely employed to test market efficiency. The CH rule is similar to the SMA rule in identifying the trend in the price series. An upward (downward) trend is identified when the current foreign exchange price is equal or greater (less) than the maximum (minimum) of prices over the period of prespecified length. A long (short) position is taken when the exchange rate breaks the maximum (minimum) barrier. The filter rule generates a buy (sell) signal when the price rises above (falls below) the most recent local minimum (maximum) by a predetermined amount. A local minimum (maximum) is taken to be a point where the two prices on either side of it are both greater (less) than the price at that point.

Researchers such as Allen and Taylor (1989) and Frankel and Froot (1990) find that trading rules are commonly used in the foreign exchange markets. The empirical results are mixed, with some studies showing that spot exchange rates provide some evidence to support technical trading rules in developed countries. Some of the empirical tests and results of the three trading rules—the SMA, the CH, and the filter rule—are presented below.

Sweeney (1986) used filter rules on ten currencies and found that profits persisted into the early 1980s. Schulmeister (1988) tested the filter rule and other models, and provided profitable results in US/deutschmark rates net of transaction costs. Dooley and Shafer (1983) reported profitable results using the filter rule strategy on nine currencies, and the profits remained for small filters even after transaction costs. Sweeney (1988) found superior profits under the filter rules for ten currencies. Levich and Thomas (1993) tested filter and moving average rules on five currency futures and found that these trading strategies are profitable. Lee *et al.* (2001) studied the efficiency of the foreign exchange markets of thirteen Latin American countries, finding that the SMA rules were profitable for four currencies: the Brazilian real, the Mexican peso, the Peruvian new sol, and the Venezuelan bolivar. They further found that CH rules were profitable for the Brazilian real, the Mexican peso, and the Venezuelan bolivar. Taylor (1994) also found that CH rules were profitable on currency futures in the US. However, Raj (2000) studied two currency futures—the Japanese yen and the deutschmark—traded on the Singapore International Monetary Exchange and found that both SMA and CH rules could not generate significant profits after transaction costs. Lee and Mathur (1996) applied the SMA rule in six European spot cross-rates and found that only two cross-rates—Japanese yen/deutschmark and Japanese yen/Swiss franc—were marginally profitable. Martin (2001) studied the profitability of SMA in twelve developing countries and found that profit opportunities could result from applying SMA to the spot foreign exchange markets of developing country currencies. He concluded that the vast majority of the countries he examined generated statistically significant out-of-sample profitable returns.

In addition to foreign exchange markets, mixed empirical results on the testing of the EMH were also found in the equity markets.[14] In fact, the research continues on the question of market efficiency in money and capital markets. There are also fundamental questions being raised by some observers about the validity of the empirical analysis—a discussion that is presented in the endnotes.[15]

Discussion Questions

1.   From the discussion of the balance of payments, we know that to reduce a current account deficit a country must increase its private saving, reduce domestic investment, or cut its government budget deficit. In the 1980s, many people recommended that the US impose restrictions on imports from Japan and other countries to reduce its current account deficit. Do you agree that import restrictions would necessarily reduce a US current account deficit?

2.   Explain how each of the following transactions generates two entries, a credit and a debit, in the Hong Kong balance of payments accounts, and describe how each entry would be classified:

     a) A Hong Kong resident buys a share of US stock, paying by writing a cheque on an account with a Hong Kong bank.

     b) A tourist from Phoenix, US buys a meal at a restaurant in Hong Kong paying with a VISA credit card.

  c) A British-owned company in Hong Kong uses local earnings to buy stocks in Hong Kong.

3. Can you think of reasons why a government might be concerned about a large current account deficit or surplus? Why might a government be concerned about its balance of payments?

4. In Hong Kong a sandwich costs HK$10, and a hot dog costs US$1 in the US. At an exchange rate of HK$7.80 per US$, what is the price of a sandwich in terms of hot dogs? All else being equal, how does this relative price change if the Hong Kong dollar appreciates to HK$7.50 per US$1? Compared with the initial situation, has a hot dog become more or less expensive relative to a sandwich?

5. Suppose the Hong Kong dollar interest rate and the pound sterling interest rate are the same: five per cent per year. What is the relationship between the current equilibrium HK$/£ exchange rate and its expected future level? Suppose the expected future HK$/£ exchange rate, HK$1.20 per pound, remains constant as Britain's interest rate rises to eight per cent per year. If the Hong Kong interest rate also remains constant, what is the new equilibrium HK$/£ exchange rate?

6. Traders in the market suddenly learn that the interest rate on Hong Kong dollars will decline in the near future. What is the effect on the HK$/US$ exchange rate, assuming current interest rates on Hong Kong and US dollar deposits do not change?

7. Discuss the adjustment process for the linked exchange rate system in Hong Kong.

8. What are the potential costs of the linked exchange rate system?

9. How can you arbitrage if the HK$/US$ exchange rate deviates from the equilibrium rate of 7.80?

10. What is interest rate parity?

11. What is purchasing power parity? Discuss absolute and relative PPP.

12. What is the Fisher condition?

13. Discuss the relationships between interest rate parity, purchasing power parity, and the Fisher condition.

14. What is the unbiased forward rate hypothesis?

15. Discuss the three forms of the market efficiency hypothesis. How are these hypotheses related to the market information?

16. Describe and distinguish the difference between fundamental and technical analysis. Are these analyses consistent with the efficient market hypothesis?

Keywords

arbitrage
balance of payments (BOP)
Certificates of Indebtedness (CIs)
current transfers

capital and financial account
channel (CH) rule
equilibrium exchange rate
efficient market hypothesis (EMH)
exchange rate determination process
filter rule
Fisher equation, Fisher condition
forward exchange rate
fundamental analysis
interest rate parity
law of one price
linked exchange rate system
managed floating (or dirty float) exchange rate system
non-reserve assets
non-tradables
pegged exchanged rate system
portfolio investment
purchasing power parity (PPP)
reserve assets
risk-adjusted return
semi-strong form market efficiency
simple moving average (SMA) rule
unbiased forward rate hypothesis

9. The Debt Market

PAUL S. L. YIP

Introduction

One major economic role of the financial system is to channel funds from agents with surplus funds to agents with shortages of funds. This channelling of funds will substantially augment economic efficiency because the agents who save are frequently not the same agents who have profitable investment opportunities. The pooling of funds can remove the financial barrier of huge but profitable projects, such as the building of railways or container ports, or the setting up of airline or telecommunications companies. Without the financial system, it is hard to imagine financing through individual savings alone could have enabled the world economy to develop to the current modern stage. With the financial system, corporations and individuals with good investment opportunities can concentrate on and become specialized in finding, planning, and implementing investment projects, while individuals and corporations with surplus funds can also easily diversify their investment risk. It is well recognized that the gains from specialization and diversification are enormous. Such a channelling of funds will also allow both parties to share the benefit of these efficiency gains.

Broadly speaking, this financing channel can be divided into indirect finance and direct finance. That is, the borrower can obtain funds by either: (1) Borrowing from a financial intermediary, such as a bank; or (2) Issuing financial instruments, such as equities or bonds, in the financial markets.

In Chapters 3 to 6, we looked at the various types of financial intermediary and their contributions to economic efficiency and growth. In this chapter and in Chapter 10, we will discuss the second financing channel. In this second channel, a corporation with good investment opportunities can raise funds from the financial markets in two ways. The most common way in Hong Kong is by issuing equities, such as common stock, which are claims to share the net income and assets of the firm. The second method is to issue a debt instrument such as a bond, which is a contractual agreement by the borrower to pay the holders of the instrument specified amounts (interest and principal payments) at regular intervals until a specified date (the maturity date), when a final payment is made.

Each of the ways has its own advantages and disadvantages to the issuers and holders of the financial instruments. From the point of view of the issuers, the advantage of issuing debt instruments is that there is no need for the corporation to share the profit with the debt holders; the disadvantage is that the specified interest and principal payments must be made in order to avoid filing for bankruptcy. Thus there will be more risk (of gain or loss) for the corporation in issuing debt instruments instead of equities. This ordering of risk is exactly opposite for holders of the financial instruments: equities could allow them to share higher returns where the firm performs well, but it could also make the equities worthless if the firm's performance is extremely bad. On the other hand, the holding of a debt instrument will give them the specified interest and principal payment as long as the company is not undergoing bankruptcy proceedings.[1] The relative advantages will also depend on the tax and other government policies. For example, in the US, there is an incentive to use debt because the interest can be expensed and dividends are taxed twice.

In the first section of this chapter, the common types of debt instrument in Hong Kong will be described. The next section discusses the theoretical reasons for promoting debt market development in Hong Kong. We will then investigate the relative size and development trend of Hong Kong's debt market. The final section draws some conclusions.

Types of Debt Instrument

Debt instruments can be divided into short-term debt instruments (maturity of one year or less) and long-term debt instruments (maturity of more than one year). Short-term debt instruments are usually more widely traded than longer-term debt instruments and so tend to be more liquid. In addition, short-term debt instruments have smaller fluctuations in price than do long-term.[2] As a result, corporations and banks actively use this market to earn interest on surplus funds that they expect to have only temporarily (see Chapter 7 for more on short-term debts). Long-term debt instruments are often held by financial intermediaries such as insurance companies and pension funds, which have little uncertainty about the amount of funds they will have in the future.

Following are details of the common types of debt instrument available in Hong Kong.

Negotiable Certificate of Deposit (NCD)

A certificate of deposit (CD) is a debt instrument issued by a bank to depositors that pays interest of a given amount and at maturity pays back the original purchase price. Unlike the usual saving and time deposits offered by retail banks, the denomination of a CD is large and the interest rate is usually higher. 'Negotiable' means that the CDs could be resold in the secondary market. In the past, CDs were not negotiable, but since the launch of the first negotiable CD in the US in 1961, negotiable CDs have become more popular because the greater flexibility to their holders mean a lower interest rate cost for the issuers. By now, virtually all CDs are negotiable. NCDs are an extremely important source of funds for commercial banks. The Hong Kong dollar NCD market is reasonably well-developed, with an outstanding amount of HK$134.9 billion at the end 2001 and a turnover of HK$34.9 billion in the secondary market in 2001.

Commercial Paper (CP)

Commercial Paper is a short-term debt instrument issued by large corporations and banks.

Exchange Fund Bills and Notes (EFBNs)

Exchange Fund Bills are short-term instruments issued by the Exchange Fund in 91-, 182-, and 364-day maturities. Exchange Fund Notes are a long-term debt with a maturity of up to ten years. One of the justifications used by the Hong Kong Monetary Authority (HKMA) for the issuance of EFBNs is to establish a benchmark yield curve. The outstanding amount of Exchange Fund Bills (HK$72.4 billion at end 2001) is larger than that of Exchange Fund Notes (HK$41.4 billion at end 2001). The gap in the average daily turnover between the two is even greater (HK$18.7 billion for the former, and only HK$2.5 billion for the latter in 2001).

Corporate Bonds

These are long-term bonds issued by corporations with strong credit ratings. The typical corporate bond pays the holder an interest payment at regular intervals and pays off the face value when the bond matures. Some corporate bonds, known as convertible bonds, have the additional feature of allowing the holder to convert them into a specified number of shares of stock at any time up to the maturity date. The possibility of capital gain (in the case of a rise in share price) has increased their attractiveness to prospective purchasers, which will in turn allow the corporation to offer the bonds at lower interest costs.

Mortgage-Backed Securities (MBS)

These are securities backed by a standardized pool of mortgage loans. Banks and the Hong Kong Mortgage Corporation (HKMC) are the issuers of these debt instruments. One of the aims of these instruments is to reduce the maturity mismatch of banks' assets and liabilities. In this setting, a representative bank will wrap its mortgage loans of similar characteristics (e.g. a property less than ten years old, with an average mortgage rate of prime +0.5 per cent, 160 months of mortgage instalments remaining, and an outstanding loan-to-valuation ratio of 55 per cent) into a standardized pool and sell it to the HKMC,[3] who will issue bonds that give their holders the right of claims on the income and asset value of this pool of mortgage loans. With the money received from the sales/securitization of the loans, the bank can then offer more mortgage loans and repeat the above securitization process. The only limit to this process is the required percentage of loans to be retained to cover any unexpected loss; the remaining risk is then underwritten by international insurance companies of high ratings. For example, if the required retaining ratio is five per cent, a capital of HK$1 billion will allow the HKMC (or the bank) to make or securitize HK$20 billion mortgage loans. In the whole process, both the bank and the HKMC are acting as agents providing services (and receiving servicing income) between the mortgager and the holders of the MBS. They do not own the loans, nor are they exposed to the default risk. Thus a bigger role for the MBS in the mortgage market will reduce the banking industry's risk of a maturity mismatch between its assets (mortgage loans with long maturity) and liabilities (deposits with short maturity). On the other hand, pension funds, insurance companies, and individuals preferring higher returns (and possibly a higher risk) than the deposit rate will be interested in purchasing an MBS.

Benefits for Promoting the Domestic Debt Market Development in Hong Kong

The major source of external financing for Hong Kong corporates' operations and investments are bank financing and equities financing.[4] One major reason for developing a sizeable and active domestic debt market in Hong Kong is to provide an effective alternative source of financing. As noted by Greenspan (2000), such alternative source of financing could mitigate adverse consequences on real economic activity brought about by credit disruptions associated with bank crises. Examples of these are the Latin American debt crisis of the 1980s and the real estate crisis of 1990 in the US. During these periods, the US banking sector suffered large losses that drastically reduced its capital base and severely curtailed its ability to lend. Fortunately, the relatively developed bonds market in the US has allowed US corporates to substitute some of the loss of bank financing by bond financing (see Figure 9.1b in the next section). Without such a substitution, the US economy could have been more badly impaired by the two crises.

The existence of an active bond market could also reduce the likelihood that a crisis will happen. During the stock market corrections of the early 2000s in the US, there were occasions where funds withdrawn from the US stock market were invested in the US bonds market. Had there been no such alternative market for the US dollar, a significant portion of the withdrawn funds could have been invested outside the US, which could in turn have caused a substantial change in the US exchange rate and in US economic activities. In fact, some economists have argued that, had there been a well-developed bond market in Asia, the impact of the Asian financial crisis could have been less severe. The existence of a developed domestic debt market could reduce the private sector's reliance on external debt, which could imply substantial exchange rate risk.

The development of a domestic debt market could also reduce the problem of maturity mismatch inherent in the banking industry, and domestic debt market development will create employment opportunities and contribute to Hong Kong's gross domestic product (GDP). It would also enhance Hong Kong's status as a regional and international financial centre. Finally, the existence of a well-established and active domestic debt market could lay the foundation for future expansion opportunities into other related areas such as the RMB bond market and interest-rate derivatives market, both of which could represent a substantial contribution to Hong Kong's economy and status as a financial centre.

Existing Size and Development Trends of Hong Kong's Domestic Debts Market

In this section, we will focus on two measures of Hong Kong's domestic debt market. The first one is the existing size, which is measured by the outstanding amount of domestic debt. This measure will indicate how much the current corporate operations are financed by the domestic debt market. The second measure is the new funds raised per annum, which is measured by the change in the outstanding amount of debt between consecutive year-ends.[5] Unlike the first measure, this is a measure more related to growth (i.e. the extent to which new funds are raised to finance investments by firms).

The Corporate Bonds Market

The first market to be discussed is the (non-financial) corporate bonds market, as this is the main source of benefits discussed in the previous section. Let us first look at the US corporate bonds market as a benchmark for subsequent discussions. Figure 9.1a shows that the size of the US corporate bonds market, as measured by the outstanding amount of corporate bonds, is large when compared with the outstanding amount of commercial bank loans to US corporates.

The difference between the two is even greater in terms of new funds raised. As indicated in Figure 9.1b, the US bond market has become an even more important (and more stable) source of funding for US corporate growth. Thus, both measures have indicated that the US corporate bonds market is a more important source of finance for US corporates than bank-loan financing.

This is, however, not the case in many other economies, including that of Hong Kong. In terms of existing size, the outstanding amount of domestic corporate bonds at the end of 2001 was HK$38.8 billion (US$5 billion). While the figure is not particularly small in absolute amounts, it is very small when compared with Hong Kong's GDP, outstanding amount of bank loans, and stock market size. For example, the figure is only five per cent of the estimated outstanding amount of bank loans to Hong Kong corporates for domestic use[6] at end 2001, suggesting a minor role for the domestic corporate bonds market in financing Hong Kong corporates' business operations. The figure is also small when compared with the

Figure 9.1a US Corporate Financing: Outstanding Amount of Bonds and Commercial Bank Loans (US$ billion)

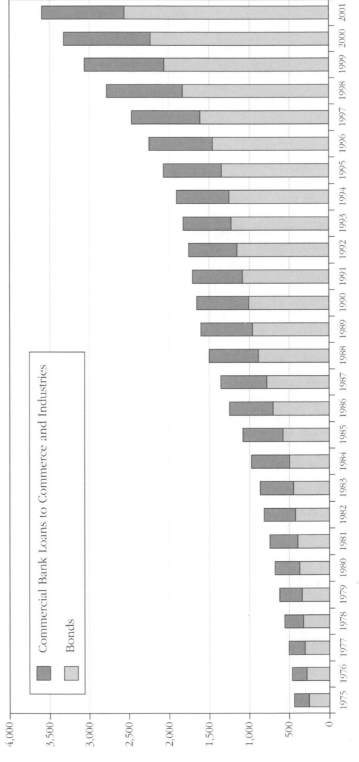

Source of data: Bank of International Settlement; Jiang *et al.* (2001).

Figure 9.1b US Corporate Financing: New Funds Raised from Bond Market and the Commercial Banking System (US$ billion)

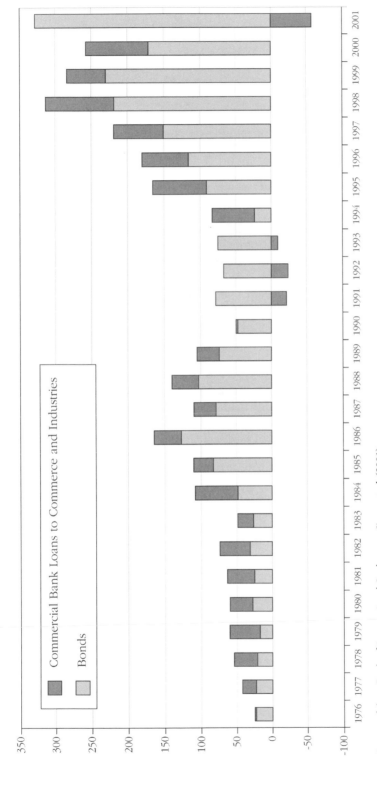

Source of data: Bank of International Settlement; Jiang *et al.* (2001).

stock market capitalization or the cumulative amount of funds raised from Hong Kong's stock market over the past ten years.[7]

Table 9.1   Relative Size of the Corporate Bond Market, Bank Loans to HK Corporates, and Stock Market (HK$ billion, end 2001)

Corporate Bond (Outstanding amount)	Bank loans (Outstanding amount)	(Capitalization)	Stock Market (Funds raised over last 10 yrs)
38.8	762	3,885	1,330

Source: Bank of International Settlement; HKMA's *Monthly Statistical Bulletin*; Hong Kong Stock Exchange.

In fact, the figure is also smaller than the outstanding amount of corporate bonds in the international bond market (HK$57 billion at end 2001). That is, Hong Kong corporate business operations are usually financed by bank loans and equity issues. Even if some of them do sometimes decide to resort to bond financing, a significant portion of it is from the international rather than the domestic bonds market. Thus, in terms of existing size, Hong Kong's domestic corporate bond market has not yet played an important role in the Hong Kong economy.

The relative insignificance of the domestic corporate bonds market persists even in terms of new funds raised. Table 9.2 shows the level of new funds raised by Hong Kong corporates in the domestic bonds market, in the international bonds market, and from bank financing (for domestic use). For purposes of comparison, the amount of funds raised from the Hong Kong stock market is also included.

Table 9.2   New Funds Raised (HK$ billion)

	94	95	96	97	98	99	00	01
Domestic corporate bonds market	−1.6	14.0	0.0	4.7	8.6	3.1	7.0	0.1
International corporate bonds market	19.5	−1.6	3.1	5.5	1.6	10.1	5.5	−7.0
Bank loans to corporate for domestic use	138.7	56.8	111.4	165.0	−50.6	−93.3	37.3	−49.8
Stock Market (including H-shares)	52	39	100	248	38	148	451	59

Source: Bank of International Settlement; HKMA's *Monthly Statistical Bulletin*; Hong Kong Stock Exchange.

As we can see, the new funds raised from the domestic corporate bonds market are negligible when compared with those of bank financing (and the stock market). During the post-crisis period, the amount of new funds raised from bank financing was negative in 1998, 1999, and 2001, suggesting that the amount of outstanding loans available to corporates actually declined during these years (i.e. there was a liquidity crunch). Unlike the US, the contraction here was not matched by a rise in net corporate bond issues of comparable magnitude. The domestic corporate bonds market in Hong Kong is therefore still far from the target of being a meaningful alternative financing channel as discussed earlier. Nevertheless, the crunch in bank loans during the post-crisis period did induce some corporates to source part of their financing from the domestic (and international) bonds market. That is, the liquidity crunch did stimulate some development in the corporate bonds market, although the extent of the stimulation was extremely small.

Other Domestic Debts Markets

In addition to the corporate bonds market, Figure 9.2 shows that there are other types of domestic debt that are somewhat more developed.

Debts Issued by Financial Institutions (FIs)

The debts issued by the FIs, mainly in the form of NCDs, form the biggest component of Hong Kong's domestic debt instruments. FIs usually use this market to finance part of their loans. During the three years preceding the Asian financial crisis, the market grew at an impressive rate of thirty-nine per cent per annum, pushing the outstanding amount of this debt to a peak of US$24.7 billion (HK$193 billion) at the end of 1997. Thereafter, the fall in the outstanding amount of bank loans induced the FIs to reduce the issuance of this type of debt, implying that growth or development here had been negative in recent years. Nevertheless, as the market is still the largest and most developed category, if the economy ever recovers in the future, growth here could be the major contributor of growth to the overall domestic debts market.

The Exchange Fund Bills and Notes (EFBNs) Market

The EFBN market is the second largest category of the overall market, with an outstanding amount of HK$113.75 billion at end 2001. Before the Asian financial crisis, growth here was substantial, with a big jump in late 1996. There was, however, a decline followed by relatively little change during the crisis period; thereafter, it experienced moderate growth from 1999. On the whole, growth in this market is reasonably fast because of the HKMA's intention to promote the domestic debt market development through the establishment of a benchmark yield curve up to ten years.

Nevertheless, the costs and benefits of this effort have not so far been well discussed, and it is perhaps a good idea to raise some questions here. We have seen that there could be some real benefits for the corporates in issuing bonds (to finance their investments) and the FIs in issuing NCDs (to finance their loans). The expected interest differentials are also likely to be in favour of the issuers. These are, however, not necessarily

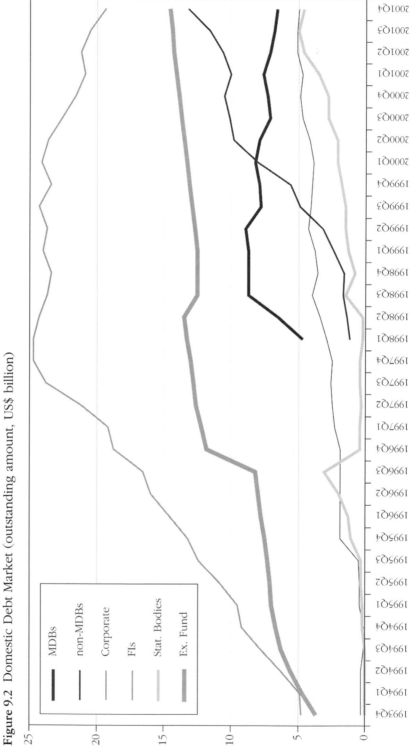

Figure 9.2 Domestic Debt Market (outstanding amount, US$ billion)

the case for the issuance of the EFBNs. First, the HKMA is likely to use the proceeds to purchase US government debts. Thus the cost (or profit) of maintaining the outstanding amount of EFBNs is the interest rate differential between the EFBNs and the US government debts. For example, if the average interest rate gap is twenty-five basis points in favour of the US government debts, an outstanding amount of HK$113.75 billion EFBNs will mean an interest maintenance cost of HK$284 million per annum— not to mention the issuing and other administrative costs.

Let us now have a look at the potential benefits. In the US and many European economies, government debt is a way of financing budget deficits. The existence of a large pool of government debt also allows the corresponding central bank to fine-tune the economy through monetary policy. The contribution could be substantial if the central bank can use the monetary policy to avoid a recession. These types of benefit are, however, not valid for Hong Kong, as the Hong Kong government usually runs a budget surplus. Even when it runs a deficit, as has been the case in recent years, it will not issue debt to finance the budget deficit. Next, under the currency board system, the HKMA is supposed to refrain from any money-market intervention, letting the market decide the quantity of money in the economy. The only benefit for maintaining an EFBN of this size is, as the HKMA highlights, to promote domestic debt market development through the establishment of a benchmark yield curve. Unfortunately, as we have seen, the level of domestic corporate bond market development is still extremely low. It is also not clear whether its development will be promising in the future and, if so, how much of it will be generated from the benchmark yield curve so established. Thus the contribution of a developed EFBNs market is at best yet to be seen. Unless there is evidence that the EFBNs were issued with a profit, it is at least a sensible question to ask whether the current amount of outstanding EFBNs is optimal or not.

Debts Issued by Statutory Bodies

Statutory bodies such as the Hong Kong Mortgage Corporation (HKMC), the Kowloon–Canton Railway Corporation (KCRC), the Mass Transit Railway Corporation (MTRC) Limited, and the Airport Authority (AA) also issue debts to finance their businesses and infrastructural constructions. With the exception of a very brief period in 1995/6, the total amount of outstanding debt was relatively small until recent years. However, with the setting up of the HKMC in March 1997 and the subsequent gradual increase in debt issues,[8] the total amount of outstanding debts issued by the statutory bodies has begun to exhibit a more impressive growth. By the end of 2001, the outstanding amount of debts in this category was comparable to the corporate bond market.

Before October 2001, all of the debts issued by these bodies were meant for institutional investors such as banks, insurance companies, funds, etc. Retail investors did not have a chance to subscribe to these debts.

Two possible reasons for this are the higher issuing costs for retail bonds and the absence of a developed secondary market for retail bonds. However, bond market development will be hindered without sufficient participation by retail investors. In October 2001, the HKMC launched its first retail bonds with three major retailing banks (the HSBC, Hang Seng Bank, and Doa Heng Bank) acting as placing agents. Thereafter, the MTRC and the AA made their first retail bonds, with the HKMC making two more issues, in the first half of 2002. The number of placing banks was also increased. Because of (1) the much bigger customer network brought in by these retailing banks; (2) the low deposit rate and the deflation of 2002 which made the three to five per cent bond yield[9] particularly attractive; and (3) the listing of the bonds on the stock exchange so that retail investors could sell (and buy) the bonds in this secondary market when deemed necessary, the retail bond issues have received a solid and growing response. For example, in the MTRC issue of May 2002, nine major retailing banks acted as the placing agent and the total bond issue was reported to exceed HK$5.6 billion. In addition to individual investors, many non-profit-making local organizations such as churches and neighbourhood organizations were active subscribers. The average amount of individual subscription was reported to be around HK$280,000 to HK$300,000, while the subscription by local organizations could reach as much as HK$500,000 to HK$600,000 Hong Kong dollars.

With the growing popularity of retail bonds issued by these statutory bodies, growth in this market is likely to be promising as long as bank deposit rates remain relatively low. Nevertheless, it should be noted that this is still at an early stage, and whether there will be a sufficiently liquid secondary market is yet to be seen. More importantly, there are not yet similar retail bond issues in the corporate bonds market. One possible reason for this is the corporates have a lower credit rating (and hence a higher risk premium) than the statutory bodies. For example, with the relatively low credit rating, Chinese companies listed in Hong Kong (e.g. H-share or red chip companies) may find it cheaper to source their funds through syndicated loans instead of retail bond issues. In fact, debt issuance promotion for lower credit rating corporates is unlikely to be promising in the near future. Perhaps the sector worth trying is that of the top blue chip companies, but whether or not this could be successful is yet to be seen.

Before proceeding to the next section, it is perhaps necessary to distinguish the HKMC from other statutory bodies. For the latter, the potential amount of debt issue would be limited by the amount of infrastructural projects in the future. On the other hand, the theoretical upper bound for HKMC debt issuance would be much greater mainly because there are enormous amounts of property loans that could be securitized. This does not necessarily mean that development along this line is particularly easy or promising. One main reason is that many major banks still see mortgage loans as one of their core businesses. Selling the loans to the HKMC would reduce their risk (of maturity mismatch) as well as the huge interest income associated with the risk premium over the service charge (for bridging the needs between the mortgager and the HKMC). In fact, it is this risk premium over the service charge that discourages major banks from selling their mortgage portfolio to the HKMC. There is also a tendency for the banks to sell the less desirable loans within the standardized package. For example, Table 9.3 shows that the HKMC's share of outstanding mortgage loans in the New Territories surged substantially from 56.1 per cent to 62.6 per cent between May 2001 and May 2002. This could mean the banks are more inclined to sell their New Territories mortgage loans, which have been more vulnerable to the recent fall in property prices and competition from China. Meanwhile, although there was little variation in the loan to valuation (LTV) ratio at origination, there was a sharp rise in the estimated current LTV ratio from 89.6 per cent to 103.1 per cent between May 2001 and May 2002.

Of course, the sharp rise of the latter could be due to a general asset deflation as well as the government's policy of helping home owners with negative asset value. However, it could also reflect the fact that banks are only interested in selling their more risky loans to the HKMC. Thus, proper procedures to ensure that these extra risks are mostly covered by the insurance companies are essential. Last but not least, despite the HKMC's effort to purchase mortgage loans from the banks, the total amount of portfolio held by the HKMC is still negligible when compared with the whole mortgage market. Its ability to reduce the banks' risk of maturity mismatch could be much lower than it was originally planned to achieve, although it is beginning to provide an alternative investment instrument to retail investors.

Debts Issued by Multilateral Development Banks (MDBs)

As shown in Figure 9.2, debt issued by MDBs is another important source of debt supply in Hong Kong. The outstanding amount reached a peak of US$8.7 billion in 1998. However, following the HKMA's advice for MDBs not to raise Hong Kong dollar debt instruments with a maturity shorter than three years, the outstanding amount has since then exhibited a gradual decline. Barring any drastic changes, the trend will continue as long as the HKMA finds this advice necessary. One reason for the HKMA's advice is to avoid speculators from using the debt issuance to pre-fund themselves with Hong Kong dollars for subsequent speculation. For example, when a MDB issues a two-year Hong Kong dollar bond, they might want to convert the Hong Kong dollar proceeds into US dollars and at the same time hedge their exchange risk by buying Hong Kong dollar two-year forward. Effectively, this swap activity (selling Hong Kong dollar spot and buying Hong Kong dollar forward) would mean an offer of Hong Kong dollar loans for two years to the market. Speculators can then borrow this supply of Hong Kong dollars for two years, commence their speculation, and then unwind their position within this two-year period.

Table 9.3 District Distribution of Outstanding Balance and Loan to Valuation (LTV) Ratio of the HKMC Portfolio

	5/01	6/01	7/01	8/01	9/01	10/01	11/01	12/01	1/02	2/02	3/02	4/02	5/02
Outstanding Bal.													
• HK (%)	25.3	24.7	25.1	24.7	21.4	21.4	21.4	21.4	21.2	19.3	18.6	18.6	18.6
• Kowloon (%)	18.7	18.6	18.5	18.6	18.5	18.5	18.5	18.5	18.5	18.8	18.8	18.8	18.8
• NT (%)	56.1	56.7	56.4	56.7	60.1	60.1	60.1	60.1	60.3	61.9	62.6	62.6	62.6
LTV ratio at origination (%)	63.2	63.4	63.6	63.7	63.5	63.8	63.9	63.9	63.9	63.9	64.8	64.8	64.9
Estimated Current LTV ratio (%)	89.6	90.3	90.3	91.3	93.3	95.6	96.4	96.4	96.6	95.8	102.5	103.2	103.1

Source of data: Hong Kong Mortgage Corporation.

Debts Issued by non-MDB Overseas Borrowers

In addition to the MDBs, non-MDB overseas borrowers also raise their funds from Hong Kong. As we can see, the size of the market is relatively large, and growth is promising. Recently, there have also been signs of diversification in the issuer base, from Australian and European borrowers to Taiwanese borrowers. Nevertheless, readers are reminded that the speculative vulnerability problem for MDBs mentioned above should also apply here.

Conclusion

Developing Hong Kong's debt market could provide an alternative source of financing for corporates, statutory bodies, and financial institutions. It could also provide an alternative investment instrument to investors and increase economic efficiency. Meanwhile, this alternative source of financing could mitigate adverse real economic consequences brought about by credit disruptions associated with bank crises. The existence of an active debt market will reduce the likelihood that a crisis could happen, and debt (especially the MBS) development could reduce the maturity mismatch inherent in the banking industry. Other than these factors, domestic debt market development will create employment, contribute to Hong Kong's GDP, strengthen Hong Kong's role as a regional and international financial centre, and lay the foundation for future expansion opportunities, such as the RMB bond market. Successful bond market development in Hong Kong will also benefit the region. At the early stage, it would allow companies (investors) in the region to source (invest) their funds from (in) Hong Kong's bond market. Once more and more companies and investors in the region have grown used to the culture of raising funds or investing in the bond market, it would reduce the hurdle of bond market development in other financial centres in the region. There could also be a strong demonstration effect. For example, in the cases of Singapore and Hong Kong, when one attempted some years ago to stimulate bond market development through the issuance of retailing bonds by the statutory companies, the other was quick to implement a similar strategy in its own economy.

Having said that, bond market development—especially the corporate bond market—is far from able to achieve the role stated above. Funds from the corporate bond market are still negligible when compared to those raised through the stock market or borrowed from banks. The recent success in retail bonds issued by statutory bodies is an encouraging breakthrough, but whether there could be a similar development in the future for the blue chip companies is yet to be seen. In terms of potential market size, mortgage-backed securities issued by the HKMC are far greater in number than those of other statutory bodies. In practice, however, this is constrained by the banks' reluctance to sell their core businesses to the

HKMC. In fact, there are signs that the increase in the HKMC's portfolio was only achieved with a lower asset quality. Thus, proper procedures to ensure these extra risks are mostly covered by the insurance companies are essential. Finally, despite the HKMC's effort to increase its portfolio, its market share is still negligible when compared with the whole mortgage market.

Discussion Questions

1. Why is the development of a financial system crucial to the development of a modern economy?
2. What is direct finance, and what is indirect finance?
3. What are the relative advantages and disadvantages for a corporate to finance their investment through the issuance of bonds and shares? What are the relative advantages to the investors?
4. What is a negotiable certificate of deposit? What are the benefits to the issuers and the buyers of making the certificate negotiable?
5. If you have some money to finance your retirement, should you use the money to buy long-term bonds or short-term bonds? Why?
6. What is a convertible bond? What are the advantages and disadvantages for a company to issue a bond that is convertible?
7. What is a mortgage-backed security? What are the benefits to the economy in the government's promotion of mortgage securitization?
8. What does a bank earn by securitizing its mortgage loans? What does it get in exchange for the loss of risk premium income? If the bank's risk is lower, who will take the risk?
9. What are the benefits of promoting domestic debt market development in Hong Kong? How much has it achieved so far?
10. Discuss the costs and benefits for the HKMA in issuing Exchange Fund Bills and Notes.
11. Why did the retail bond issues in the first half of 2002 turned out to be relatively successful? What other promotion strategy do you recommend?
12. During the financial crisis, why did the HKMA advise the MDBs not to issue bonds with maturities shorter than three years?

Keywords

bond market development
corporate bond
direct finance
Exchange Fund Bills
Exchange Fund Notes
indirect finance
long-term debt

mortgage-backed securities
negotiable certificate of deposit
retail bond
short-term debt

10. The Stock Market I: The New Issue Market

KIE ANN WONG AND MD. HAMID UDDIN

Introduction

A key component of the financial system is its capital market. A distinct section of the capital market is the stock market. This is the market for companies that want to raise equity capital, and for investors who want to invest in equities. The stock market consists of both primary and secondary markets. The primary market is also known as the new issue market, and the secondary market is known as the stock trading market. In the new issue market, public companies bring their offerings to sell new shares to investors, followed by the listing of stocks on stock exchanges. When trading of stock starts, investors are able to adjust their investment portfolio through their market transactions. An important element of the capital market is that the new issue and trading markets are interlinked. The offer to sell new shares to the public would not attract the interest of investors if newly issued stocks were not to be listed for trading on the stock exchange.

This chapter is about the new issue market; the following chapter discusses the stock trading market in Hong Kong. A number of concerns regarding the new issue market expressed by different interest groups—such as companies, investors, regulators, and intermediaries—are discussed in this chapter. The main issues include the economic functions of a new issue market, rules and requirements of new issues, procedures of new stock listing on the Hong Kong exchange (Hong Kong Exchanges and Clearing Limited (HKEx), formerly known as the Stock Exchange of Hong Kong (SEHK)), pricing theories of initial public offerings (IPO), and performance of newly listed stocks in the trading market.

Economic Functions of the New Issue Market

Raising Capital Funds

When a government authority issues a corporate charter, shares of ownership are divided among members of the founding group. As long as only a small number of owners hold shares, the company is called a private company. When the number of people who hold shares exceeds fifty, it can no longer be called a private company. A company is said to be 'going public' when it makes a public offering of shares and hundreds of individuals buy shares. The main role of a new issue market is to provide a market for the firms that are going public to raise additional funds. If going public is relatively easy and inexpensive, this will generally help to reduce the cost of equity financing of a firm. Funds are mainly raised for new capital expansion of the firm, as the majority of initial public offerings (IPOs) involve the offering of new shares to the public. However, a portion of the new funds raised may also go to existing holders of shares who are entrepreneurs, venture capitalists, or governments, because IPOs often include an offer to buy or replace existing shares. However, in Hong Kong, most of the funds raised by the private enterprises through the public offer of shares are for the purpose of the capital expansion of their firms.

Table 10.1   Funds Raised by the Firms from the New Issue Market in Hong Kong During the Period 1994–2001

Year	Number of IPOs	Funds Raised (HK$)
1994	52	16,732,240,000
1995	26	8,084,858,847
1996	49	31,215,773,776
1997	82	81,653,619,796
1998	32	6,386,424,900
1999	31	15,557,186,759
2000	43	117,214,490,742
2001	31	20,580,297,120
Total	346	297,424,891,940

Source: Data collected and compiled from the HKEx website

Table 10.1 shows that HKEx-listed firms raised nearly HK$300 billion from the market over the period 1994 to 2001. That is, the firms going public in Hong Kong raised an average of HK$37 billion per year, which is nearly five per cent of the gross domestic product (GDP). The table shows that a total of forty-three firms raised about HK$117 billion from the market in 2000 alone, eighty-two firms raised HK$82 billion in 1997, and forty-nine raised HK$31 billion in 1996. The very high growth of funds raised from the market in 2000 was due to buoyant economic activities during the period when Hong Kong's real GDP growth rate was recorded as 10.5 per cent. The surge in fund-raising activities by a growing number of firms in recent years showed the economic significance of an organized new issue market in Hong Kong.

Diversification of Ownerships, Risk Sharing, and Control

Many unlisted private firms in Hong Kong are closely held by groups of family members and friends. This is because the development of the Hong Kong economy is historically linked to the progress of family businesses in the region. As the businesses grow larger, the sharing of risk becomes necessary. The easiest way to share risk is to take in new business partners with relevant expertise. A dilemma that existing members often face is how to strike a balance between the bringing in of new partners while retaining control over the firm. A firm that is going public can effectively diffuse the outside shareholdings by issuing new shares to a diverse group of small investors (Brennan and Frank, 1997). However, the firm may need to include one or two directors from the diverse groups of outsider investors. It is generally found that the public equity component of Asian companies is not high; for example, the average public shareholding in Malaysian companies is only about twenty-five per cent (Uddin, 2001). In Hong Kong, a set of Listing Rules require firms that are going public to have at least twenty-five and sometimes fifty per cent of the total market capital in the hands of public investors.

Access to the Capital Market

If a firm remains privately held by family members and friends, it does not have access to the capital market. The firm therefore becomes heavily dependent on the support of banks and financial institutions for its additional funding needs. If the firm is burdened with heavy debts, the cost of financial distress will increase and it cannot concentrate on tapping its business opportunities. Once the firm goes public and is listed on the stock exchange, it has access to the capital market for subsequent fund-raising through seasoned new issues. In Hong Kong, most of the seasoned issues are made through private share placements with institutional investors—investment banks and fund managers, for example. However, if the issuing firm does not want to dilute the present ownership and control, the offer of share sales can be made to the existing shareholders through a rights offering. What method a listed firm would use to raise new capital depends on the time and cost involved with each method. The important aspect here is that a publicly held firm enjoys the privilege of accessing the large pool of liquid capital when a need arises, whereas a privately held company does not have easy access to capital markets.

Access to the Debt Market

Going public provides not only future access to the equity market, but also to the debt market. Obtaining a listing on the stock exchange greatly enhances the credit-worthiness of the firm, and often attracts a high credit rating. Upon listing, the company is evaluated by market analysts and rating agencies. Although having a listing status for a company is not compulsory for obtaining a credit rating, it increases the possibility of receiving a good credit rating from the agencies, and this will be critical to raising debt capital from the market at low cost. This is because a listed company has already passed through a set of stringent rules and requirements for obtaining the listing on an exchange and gaining access to the capital market. Listing reduces the reliance on financing from banks and other financial institutions. It is a common feature of most capital markets, including Hong Kong's, that corporate bonds are typically issued by listed firms. This is not surprising, because a lender may be less interested in buying bonds issued by private firms, even though they may have an agency credit rating. In fact, the rating agencies are unlikely to provide a good ranking of the bonds issued by unlisted firms, as much of the information about these companies is not disclosed to the public.

Exit Door for Venture Capitalists and Government

Hong Kong is the largest venture capital (VC) centre in Asia, with 111 VC funds currently outstanding. It has the second-largest concentration of venture capital professionals (439) in the region, managing thirty-two per cent of the total seed capital pool in the South-East Asian region. Despite the economic and financial crisis in Asia, total funds under the management of Hong Kong venture capital firms grew by fifty per cent to HK$112.38 billion at the end of 1998, which is sixteen per cent higher than that of Japan and more than double that of Singapore. It has to be noted that Hong Kong is largely an administrative hub serving the region. Over ninety per cent of the venture funds in Hong Kong were sourced from overseas and disbursed to overseas companies. An immediate question is whether the organized new issue market contributes to the success of the VC industry in Hong Kong.

VC firms are specialized institutions that take risk by providing seed funding to potential start-up ventures. An organized new issue market in Hong Kong provides an exit route for the venture capitalists when new ventures take root in the market. Therefore, the new issue market has an important role in promoting entrepreneurship in Hong Kong, as the venture capitalists or original entrepreneurs may recover their seed money in the start-up firms more easily by selling shares to the public when the venture firms have grown up.

The new issue market has an additional role in some countries, such as China, Malaysia, Singapore, Indonesia, Thailand, the Philippines, India, and Bangladesh, where governments have privatized many state-owned enterprises. The two Chinese stock exchanges (Shanghai and Shenzhen) were started in the early nineties, with equity stocks issued mostly by state-owned enterprises. Therefore, like venture capitalists, governments also use organized new issue markets as an exit route from the burden of doing business.

Providing Market Liquidity

Shares held by the public are most likely to turn over once the stock is listed on the stock exchange. Shares held by directors or original owners rarely contribute to the secondary market liquidity. There are two reasons for this: pre-listing stockholders would like to retain their managerial control, and regulatory restrictions are generally imposed on pre-listing shareholders to liquidate their shareholdings in the company in the first twelve months after listing the stock (Listing Rule 10.07). This restriction is to protect the interests of public investors who purchase shares through offers. Like other stock markets, HKEx promotes an open and liquid secondary market. The listing rule prescribes a minimum percentage of shareholdings by the public[1] at all times. It is suggested that a company aspiring to a listing on HKEx must have minimum expected initial market capitalization of HK$100 million, of which HK$50 million must be held by the public. The minimum initial capitalization of the public offer increases to HK$75 million if the initial market capital of the company is expected to be greater than HK$300 million. This promotes a greater shareholder spread for large companies. Also, in global offerings, a sufficient portion must be offered to Hong Kong investors. Therefore, the new issue market—through which public interest in a listed company is ensured—plays a very significant role in increasing the liquidity of the secondary market.

Growth of the Capital Market

It was mentioned that both the new issue and secondary markets are interlinked and interdependent. While a new issue market will not develop without an organized secondary market, the growth of the secondary market also owes much to IPO activities. The market capitalization of the secondary market increases due partly to the growth of the value of existing stocks and partly to additional value added by the newly listed stocks. Table 10.2 shows that IPO activities increased significantly during the 1990s. A total of forty-eight IPOs listed in 1991, comprising nearly fourteen per cent of the total listed stocks on HKEx. IPO activities in Hong Kong were markedly higher during the period 1991 to 1997 than in the earlier and later periods of the decade. Out of 757 listed stocks, 373 listed during this seven-year period.

Many factors contributed to the rise in the IPO market during this period: bullish stock market conditions, high growth in the Hong Kong economy, and an influx of mainland Chinese investments. The slowdown of IPO activity in the late 1990s was partly due to the Asian financial crisis, which affected the real economy. However, the market was temporarily up in 2000, with forty-three new listings, and again slowed down in 2001 due to the global economic recession. The aggregate market capitalization of HKEx also reflects a similar trend in that the total market capitalization increased significantly during the same period when IPO activities were markedly higher than in the other periods. This is perhaps not too surprising, because both the new issue market and secondary market are linked in many ways.

A rising stock market is generally considered good both for companies going public, which can raise capital, and for investors, who are interested in new issues. Investors would demand a low required rate of return in the up-market compared to that in the down-market (Loughran and Ritter, 1993). Hence, issuers could sell new shares at a higher price during the hot market period. Investors also benefit from issues listed during the hot market periods, as IPO investors receive a much higher initial return during hot market periods compared to that of cold periods. In Malaysia, investors

Table 10.2   New Listings and Market Capitalizations in the HKEx 1980–2001

Year	Total number of listed stocks	Total market capitalization of all stocks (HK$ million)	Number of IPO listings	IPO listing as percentage of total stocks
1980	262	209,752	5	1.91
1981	269	232,331	12	4.46
1982	273	131,640	2	0.73
1983	277	142,093	4	1.44
1984	278	184,642	8	2.88
1985	279	269,511	4	1.43
1986	253	419,281	5	1.98
1987	276	419,612	15	5.43
1988	304	580,378	19	6.25
1989	298	605,010	5	1.68
1990	299	650,410	13	4.35
1991	357	949,172	48	13.45
1992	413	1332,184	54	13.08
1993	477	2,975,379	62	13.00
1994	529	2,085,182	52	9.83
1995	542	2,348,310	26	4.80
1996	583	3,475,965	49	8.40
1997	666	3,202,630	82	12.31
1998	688	2,661,713	32	4.65
1999	705	4,727,527	31	4.40
2000	737	4,7951,50	43	5.83
2001	757	3,885,342	31	4.10

Note: Data compiled from various issues of the HKEx *Fact Books* from 1986 to 2001. This table represents only the equity stocks listed on the Cash Market–Main Board section of the HKEx; the stocks listed with Cash Market–Growth Enterprise Market section are not included due to its short history.

earned an average of 167 per cent initial return from IPO stocks listed in hot market periods compared to an average of twelve per cent initial return during cold market periods (Uddin, 2001).

In addition to a substantial growth in IPO listings on the HKEx Main Board, a remarkable increase in the listing of emerging companies on the Growth Enterprise Market (GEM), a market for emerging companies operated by HKEx, is observed. GEM is popularly known as a 'buyer beware' market for informed investors, as start-up companies with growth potentials are normally listed on the GEM. The listing requirements are less stringent: there is no past profit requirement, twenty-four months of business history is sufficient, and the underwriting of issue is not compulsory. In the three-and-a-half years since its inception in 1999, a total of 132 companies obtained listing on the GEM and raised about HK$22,476 million from the market. An important feature of GEM listing is that most companies obtain a listing through the offer for placing, because only informed investors are interested in buying GEM stocks as there is limited public demand. Of the HK$22,476 million raised, a total of HK$20,410 million was raised through private placement with the institutional investors, and the rest through offer for subscriptions and offer for sales (information collated from the GEM website).

Characteristics of Companies Going Public

Domicile Features

Generally, companies domiciled and incorporated in Hong Kong raise their equity capital from this market. These companies could have their business in Hong Kong or elsewhere. A group of local companies whose major business interests and assets are in mainland China are known as 'red chip' stocks. These are popular in the Hong Kong market.

In recent years, it has also been observed that some companies have relocated their incorporation from Hong Kong to Bermuda, the Cayman Islands, and the Cook Islands while keeping their business interests and fixed assets in Hong Kong. One such company is Jardine Matheson, which changed its incorporation from Hong Kong to Bermuda in 1984. Many other companies followed suit in the late 1980s and early 1990s. This could have been due to the fear of potential changes in the corporate laws and regulations after the return of Hong Kong to Chinese sovereignty in 1997.

As well as a trend in the shift of domicile for Hong Kong companies that have raised capital from the market, there is another trend to be observed. Many China-incorporated companies have raised equity capital from the Hong Kong market by issuing shares to Hong Kong investors and obtaining a listing with HKEx. These shares are popularly known as H-shares. Although these H-shares are listed on HKEx, the control of the companies remains in the hands of the original Chinese entities. The issue of H-shares is offered under Chinese law, but HKEx accepts the listing of H-shares provided that the company meets the basic listing criteria set by HKEx.

An important feature of this type of offering by Mainland companies is that existing company shares are not listed on HKEx; only the component of the issue that is offered to Hong Kong investors is listed and traded in Hong Kong. Tsingtao Breweries was the first China-incorporated company to raise capital in Hong Kong and list H-shares on HKEx. Although both red chip and H-share issues have business interests in mainland China, they differ in their location of incorporation. Red chip companies are incorporated outside mainland China—mostly in Hong Kong—while H-share companies are incorporated in mainland China.

Global Offerings

As the Hong Kong new issue market matures, it is gradually becoming integrated with the global capital market. When the offer of H-shares by

China-incorporated companies to Hong Kong investors was implemented in 1993, local companies also engaged to offer shares to both the local and global markets. The global offer typically involves placing a portion of the total issue with selected overseas institutional investors. A distinct feature of global offerings is that a book-building approach is used to price the offer. Since the prices of these offers are fixed shortly before exchange listing, after taking into consideration investor demand through roadshow and other information gathering, the pricing risk for the underwriters is much less than that of purely local offers. The stocks of global offerings are mainly listed on HKEx, although a secondary listing on a foreign market is also possible. Typically, the size of a global offer is much larger than that of a purely local offer. It often appears that the public shareholding requirement of at least twenty-five per cent of the total outstanding shares is not necessarily maintained with companies making global offers (Listing Rule 8.08).

Rules and Requirements of New Issue and Stock Listing

The basic requirements for companies aspiring to float their shares on the market are determined by the Securities and Futures Commission (SFC), while HKEx implements the rules. The basic requirements are set out in Chapter 8 of the Rules Governing the Listing of Securities. A summary of the updated main requirements of listing is provided below:

Rule 8.02:   The issuing company must be duly incorporated in any place under its laws.

Rule 8.03:   If the issuing company is incorporated in Hong Kong it must be a public limited company within the meaning of Section 29 of the Companies Ordinance.

Rule 8.04:   Both the issuer and its business must be suitable for listing, in the opinion of the HKEx.

Rule 8.05:   The issuer, or its group, must have three years' track record, with a minimum profit of HK$20 million attributable to its shareholders in the most recent year, and not less than HK$30 million in the two preceding years—except for the natural resources companies, newly formed project companies, or for exceptional circumstances.

Rule 8.06:   The latest financial period must not be ended more than six months before the listing document (prospectus).

Rule 8.07:   HKEx must be satisfied that there is a sufficient market for the listed stocks, meaning that there is enough public interest in the business of the issuer.

Rules 8.08–09: The listing applicant must have, or attain through new issue, at least a certain percentage of shares in public hands. This minimum public interest component varies with the expected total market capitalization of the company to be listed. An applicant with the minimum market capitalization of HK$100 million must have at least fifty per cent shares in public hands. However, for larger companies with expected market capitalization above HK$200 million, at least twenty-five per cent of the issued shares must be in public hands. This rule ensures sufficient shares to be traded on the market, particularly the shares of small companies. This rule also requires an adequate spread of shareholders. Shares must be held by a minimum of 100 holders.

Rule 8.10:   If the listing company has controlling shareholders (holding at least thirty-five per cent of total shares), the other businesses of the controlling shareholders should not compete with the businesses of the listing company.

Rule 8.11:   The issuers will not issue non-voting 'B' shares.

Rule 8.12:   The issuing company must have adequate management presence in Hong Kong with at least two executive directors who reside in Hong Kong.

Rules 8.13–14: The listing securities must be issued according to the law of the place where the company is incorporated, and these securities must be freely transferable.

Rules 8.15–16: The issuer must have an approved share registrar in Hong Kong, who will ordinarily be a resident of Hong Kong with requisite qualifications to act as the secretary of the issuing company.

Rules 8.17–19: If the issuer offers options, warrants or similar rights with the equity offers, then the issuer must comply with both the requirements for equity stocks listing and that for listing of the other tradable securities. In each class of security, the listing must be sought for the total number of securities becoming outstanding after the flotation.

Rule 8.20:   The issuer must have not changed its financial year-end during the latest financial period of twelve months immediately prior to the date of prospectus.

Of the above Listing Rules, some are subjective in nature. For example, the issuer and its business must be suitable for listing (Rule 8.04). This suggests that the decision as to whether or not an issue will be listed lies solely with HKEx. However, an applicant can appeal to the Listing Appeal Committee to review a rejection of its application for listing, if the issuer satisfies other listing requirements. The stock must have adequate public interest and market demand for obtaining listing approval (Rule 8.07), but it may be difficult to assess the market demand long before the stock listing.

Although the Listing Rules are generally applicable to all applicants, exceptions are made for infrastructure project (IP) companies. An IP company is one that involves developing physical facilities for the delivery of public goods and services mainly in Hong Kong, under the long-term mandate of the government. HKEx considers the listing application of IP companies which do not meet the general three-year profit requirement (Rule 8.05), provided that they directly implement the specific projects and do not engage in any business other than that mandated in the contract.

The general Listing Rules also apply to overseas issuers, with some additional requirements. In general, issuing companies incorporated in Bermuda, the Cayman Islands, and the Cook Islands may list with HKEx subject to additional rules in Chapter 19. The important additional requirement for overseas issuers is that their companies must be incorporated in a jurisdiction where the standard of shareholder protection and incorporation requirements are at least equivalent to those in Hong Kong (Rule 19.05.01). Overseas companies aspiring to listing on HKEx must offer shares to investors in Hong Kong (Rule 19.05.05) and must have an approved share registrar in Hong Kong with approved qualifications (Rule 19.05.02–03).

In addition to the general Listing Rules and additional requirements for overseas issuers, a set of additional rules is introduced for companies incorporated in mainland China but seeking a HKEx Main Board listing. This is because existing Chinese mainland laws are not based on the common law system, and in many respects these laws do not match those in Hong Kong. To obtain a listing on HKEx, a China-incorporated company must ensure that (1) the company is duly incorporated in China as a joint stock company, (2) HKEx has adequate communication with the relevant securities authority in China regarding the listing of H-shares, (3) the Mainland laws and the company's Articles of Association must adequately protect the interests of the holders of H-shares issued to Hong Kong investors, and (4) the company must present its annual accounts in accordance with Hong Kong or international standards.

Procedures of New Listing

General Procedure

The detailed procedures of new listing with HKEx are set out in Chapter 9 of the Rules Governing the Listing of Securities. The procedures for new listing in Hong Kong are described briefly in this section. A sponsor[2] of the listing applicant prepares the application for stock listing and lodges it with the Listing Division of HKEx with all supporting documents. The sponsor is responsible for dealing with HKEx with regard to information provided in the application (Rules 3.03–04 and 9.02). The listing application does not come to HKEx suddenly; rather it comes through a process of discussion between the sponsor and HKEx. An advance booking of the listing application, along with a draft timetable of share flotation and the required initial listing fee, is made at least forty working days before the printing and submission of the final prospectus to the Listing Division (Rule 9.03). The advance application booking provides enough time for the applicant to submit all of the necessary documents during the period, while HKEx also has enough time to review them. HKEx may refuse advance booking if there are too many applications in a certain period (Rule 9.04). After advance booking for final application lodgement, the sponsor must submit the draft prospectus, memorandum and articles of associations, and accountant's reports twenty-one days before printing and issuing the prospectus to both HKEx and the SFC. Other supporting documents, such as the subscription form and the issuer's declaration about its other business, must be submitted fourteen working days before printing the prospectus (Rule 9.12).

The Listing Division of HKEx reviews the application and related documents and issues a recommendation to the Listing Committee, which will finally approve the listing application. If the Listing Committee confirms the issue and has no further comments, the listing document or final prospectus and other publicity materials will be submitted to HKEx. These materials can also be circulated to the public, in compliance with the statutory requirements, after confirming them with HKEx (Rules 9.07–08). Trading of the security will only start when all the formalities are completed and a listing approval is finally granted; there will be no trade after the submission of the listing application to HKEx until listing is finally granted (Rule 9.09).

Appeal Mechanism

If the Listing Division of HKEx rejects the listing application, the applicant can appeal to the Listing Committee. If the Listing Committee also rejects the application, the applicant has the right to apply for further review of the rejection. The decision of the Listing Committee on the review is binding. However, if the rejection was due to any subjective reason— such as the Listing Committee deeming that the issuer or its business is not suitable for HKEx listing—then the applicant can appeal to the Listing Appeals Committee, whose decision will be final.

Procedure for Overseas Issuers

The general listing procedure and the appeal mechanism described above also apply—with some modifications and additional requirements as mentioned in Rules 19.06–10—to the overseas issuers seeking a listing of their securities with HKEx. Importantly, HKEx may require overseas issuers to disclose additional information considered necessary in their particular cases. The listing document must include a summary of the constitutive documents and the relevant regulatory provisions of the place in which the overseas company is incorporated or established, which may affect shareholder rights and directors' powers.

Methods of New Issues

To obtain a listing with HKEx, a new issue can be floated by a variety of methods, as specified in Chapter 7 of the Rules Governing the Listing of Securities. These include (1) offer for subscription, (2) offer for sale, (3) placing of shares, (4) introduction, (5) rights issue, (6) capitalization, (7) consideration, (8) exchange of securities, and (9) exercising the options.

Local new issues are floated mostly through an offer for subscription, offer for sales, or a combination of an offer for subscription and sales. An offer for subscription involves the issuance of new shares to the public. The funds collected through the offer for subscriptions go to the company's account. As additional new shares are issued in the offer for subscriptions, the equity base of the company is enlarged and the shareholdings of the existing owners are diluted after stock issue. The offer for sale, on the other hand, involves the issuance of no new shares. Instead, a portion of the existing shares are sold through public offers. The total proceeds of the sales are transferred to the vendors or existing shareholders without any funds passing to the company. The total outstanding shares do not change due to the offer for sale, but the shareholdings of the existing owners are diluted after the offer.

Although the offer for subscription differs from the offer for sale in terms of the issuance of new shares and use of the funds raised, these two types of offer are commonly known as the primary public offer of shares. A primary public offer must be underwritten by an underwriter (or a syndicate of underwriters). A prospectus must be issued and published in the newspapers, containing all of the details about the company and its offer of shares. It must be ensured that shares are allocated to the applicants in an orderly manner, meaning that every investor who applies at the same price for the same number of shares must receive equal consideration.

Among other methods, the listing by introduction involves no public offer of shares. Instead, HKEx listing and trading for the securities already in issue are sought if the company is able to show that its minimum shareholding spread is sufficient to ensure adequate trading activity in the market. The introduction is normally appropriate for seeking a secondary listing in another stock exchange, or for seeking the relisting of a reorganized public company. The placement of shares involves receiving subscriptions by an issuer from the selected individuals or institutions. HKEx may refuse the listing of a new issue solely by the placement of shares if there is a significant public demand for the stock to be listed. Therefore, the placement of shares is normally evident in global offerings where a part of the offer is placed with certain individuals or institutions and the remaining part of the offer is sold through a public offer.

The rights and open offers are made to the existing shareholders by a listed firm when it needs to raise additional equity capital from the market. In a rights offer, the existing shareholders are given proportionate rights to buy the new shares of their own company. In an open offer, however, the existing shareholders receive a right to apply for any number of new shares from the offer. Rights offers are common in Hong Kong, but open offers are rarely used. In a capitalization issue, a proportional allotment of new shares is given to existing shareholders and credited as fully paid by making adjustments with the shareholders' reserve or retained earnings. In a consideration issue, new shares are offered in connection with a takeover of or merger with another company. Sometimes, the listing of a particular security is also allowed by exchanging the new security for the currently listed security. This kind of security listing is not common, but it is sometimes necessary due to a major restructuring of the company's capital structure.

Pricing of New Issues

It is important to an economy that the new issue market operates efficiently so that issuers can raise equity capital with the lowest possible cost. If the new issue market is efficient, little initial underpricing or overpricing of the issue would occur when the stock is traded on HKEx. In reality, however, the most difficult task for the issuer or underwriter is to estimate the fair value of the issue and fix an appropriate price. There are many factors that make the pricing of a new issue difficult. Issuers or underwriters set a price for an offer with ex-ante uncertainty about its fair value, as the fair value of a new issue will only be known when the stock is traded on HKEx. However, they might attempt to reduce the ex-ante uncertainty by undertaking roadshow and pre-selling activities and by fixing an offer price shortly before the stock listing.

Despite pre-selling and information-gathering activities that try to assess the fair value of an offer, it is routinely found across the markets that the new issue price is set at a significant discount from the market value revealed on the listing day. Therefore, investors generally receive a significant initial return on the listing day, which is known as the initial underpricing of new issue. The findings reported in Table 10.3 show that the underpricing of a new issue is a common phenomenon across different markets, including that of Hong Kong, although the extent of average underpricing varies from market to market. Researchers have developed numerous theories to explain IPO price behaviour and underpricing.

Theories of New Issue Pricing

Why is the offer price normally fixed with a discount, or why is the new issue underpriced? The main explanation for underpricing is based on information asymmetry among the IPO parties: investors, issuers, and underwriters. This leads to the development of the winner's curse, signalling, and price delegation theories. Researchers have also identified the issues of a firm's ownership dispersion and secondary market liquidity as other possible reasons for new issue underpricing. IPO underpricing has also been examined in the context of certain market characteristics, which are mostly found in the US. The main IPO pricing theories will be briefly discussed below, followed by an analysis of their relevance in the context of the new issue market in Hong Kong.

Table 10.3   Level of Underpricing of Initial Public Offers (IPOs) in Different Markets over Different Time Periods

	Sources	Sample	Time Period	Average Initial Underpricing (%)
USA	Ibbotson (1975)	120	1960–9	11.40
	Ibbotson and Jaffe (1975)	2,560	1960–70	16.83
	Ritter (1984)	5,162	1960–82	18.80
	Aggarwal and Rivoli (1990)	1,598	1977–87	10.67
	Ritter (1991)	1,526	1975–84	16.40
	Lougrhan and Ritter (2002)	3,025	1990–8	14.07
UK	Davis and Yeomans (1976)	174	1965–71	8.50
	Buckland et al. (1981)	297	1965–75	9.60
	Levis (1993)	712	1980–8	14.30
Australia	Finn and Higham (1988)	93	1966–78	29.20
	How and Low (1993)	523	1970–89	16.05
	Lee et al. (1996a)	266	1976–89	11.86
	Allen and Patrick (1996)	161	1974–84	20.40
Japan	Hamao et al. (2000)	456	1989–95	15.70
	Beckman et al. (2001)	216	1980–98	31.50
Hong Kong	Dawson and Hiraki (1985)	31	1979–84	10.90
	Dawson (1987)	21	1978–83	13.80
	McGuinness (1992)	80	1980–90	17.60
China	Mok and Hui (1997)	101	1990–3	289.20
	Wong and Xie (2001)	200	1992–6	217.61
Malaysia	Wong and Chiang (1986)	16	1975–84	104.45
	Dawson (1987)	21	1978–83	166.60
	Paudyal et al. (1998)	77	1984–95	52.50
	Wong and Uddin (2002)	493	1989–98	96.58
Singapore	Koh and Walter (1989)	66	1973–87	34.70
	Saunders and Lim (1990)	17	1987–8	45.40
	Lee et al. (1996a)	132	1973–92	30.00

Note: The initial raw underpricing is typically determined with reference to the initial return an investor receives, which is measured as $[(P_t - P_o)/P_o] \times 100$, where P_t is the closing market price of IPO stock on the listing day and P_o is the offer price. However, the initial underpricing results reported in the table are mostly adjusted for the market movements during the period between the issue subscription and stock listing.

Information Asymmetry Theories

The information asymmetry theories are based on the differences in information about the issue value among the parties involved in the issuance process. The parties are the issuer, underwriter, and investors. These theories assume that any one party might have superior information in a given market structure, which may be useful for valuation of the offer. An optimal underpricing in equilibrium is needed to mitigate problems arising from the asymmetry of information on the issue value.

Investors' Information and Winner's Curse Problem

If some investors are assumed to be better informed about the market value of an IPO, Rock (1986) argues that the uninformed investors face the winner's curse problem. This is because they stand a greater chance of being allocated more shares in the overpriced issues rather than the underpriced ones, whereas informed investors could avoid the overpriced issues. If a new issue market depends on the continued participation of uninformed investors—since the informed demand may be insufficient to take up the whole issue—discounting the offer price is needed to compensate the uninformed investors for their losses. However, the Rock model cannot explain why an individual issuer should necessarily underprice the offer to support the continued participation of uninformed investors in the other issues, particularly when the listing of a company is a one-time event.

Rock's model shows that if we adjust for the allocation rationing, the IPO initial return reduces to a risk-less rate of return, which is just enough to compensate the uninformed investors for losses from the adverse selection of IPOs while providing a normal return to the informed investors for information production. Although this has not yet been tested in the US market, Koh and Walter (1989), Lee *et al.* (1996a), Keloharju (1993a), and Levis (1990) provide direct evidence from Singapore, Finland, and the UK that supports the model. However, studies by McGuinness (1993) and Cheung *et al.* (1993) using Hong Kong data do not seem to support strongly the Rock theory of new issue underpricing, although the findings have some empirical value. McGuinness found that after adjustments for the winners' curse (rating factor) and the trade settlement mechanism, significant returns (between 2.85 per cent and 8.22 per cent) from random share applications are attainable for relatively large applications.

Beatty and Ritter (1986) improved Rock's model by showing that the level of underpricing is positively related to ex-ante uncertainty of the issue value, as the problem of winner's curse is aggravated if uncertainty is high. This positive relationship has been shown overwhelmingly across the markets (Beatty and Ritter (1986), Ritter (1984), Miller and Reilly (1987), James and Wier (1990), Slovin and Young (1990), and Ritter (1991) in the US; Wasserfallen and Wittleder (1994) and Ljungqvist (1997) in Germany; Clarkson and Merkley (1994) in Canada; Finn and Higham (1988) in Australia; and Wong and Xie (2001) in China).

The winner's curse model also implies that the choice of an underwriter could reduce the asymmetry of information between informed and uninformed investors. Since the problem of the winner's curse imposes the cost of underpricing on the issuers to float their company, they could have incentives to reduce the asymmetry of information between the two groups of investors by choosing a more reputable underwriter, so the underpricing may be related to the reputation of the underwriter. Using US data, McDonald and Fisher (1972), Logue (1973), Neuberger and Hammond (1974), Neuberger and LaChapelle (1983), and Block and Stanley (1980) found that prestigious investment bankers are less likely to underprice their IPOs. Johnson and Miller (1988) and Carter and Manaster (1990) later found that prestigious underwriters avoid risky new issues. These earlier findings indirectly support the winner's curse model in the US market. Studies using non-US data, however, provided mixed evidence about the underwriter-reputation effect on underpricing. For example, Jenkinson (1990) and McGuinness (1992) found no significant relationship between the reputation of the underwriter and the initial underpricing of IPOs in the UK and Hong Kong respectively, while Kim *et al.* (1993) found a significant relationship in Korea.

Issuer's Information and Signalling Theory
The signalling model of underpricing is based on the assumption that insiders know their firm better than outsiders do. If the informed party (issuer) wants to disseminate the information to the market effectively, they must signal it through action (Spence, 1974). Leland and Pyle (1977) first showed that the issuer's fractional holding of the firm's equity signals the expected future cash flows of the firm. They argued that issuers are presumably risk-averse. The issuers of high-quality firms hence retain a high percentage of shares for sale in a seasoned offer, when the value of the firm is revealed. Based on the above premises, Grinblatt and Hwang (1989), Allen and Faulhaber (1989), and Welch (1989) formalized the IPO signalling model.

Grinblatt and Hwang (1989) showed that if the issuer knows the mean value of the future cash flows of the firm but investors know only the approximate distribution of cash flows, the issuer could credibly convey the information by issuing a fraction of total shares at a discounted price. The remaining shares could be disposed of at the market price later so that the issuer's wealth is maximized. Allen and Faulhaber (1989) added that only good firms could credibly and cost-effectively signal their quality by underpricing the offer and ensuring a successful seasoned offering at a later stage when the quality of the issue is revealed from its performance. Welch (1989) went further, saying that the marginal underpricing cost of high-quality firms is lower than that of low-quality firms, as they incur imitating costs. The additional cost and chance of being detected as a low-quality firm would force the issuer to reveal the issue quality before making the offer. Therefore, only high-quality firms can benefit from underpricing the initial offer, as the seasoned offer could be made at a higher price if the market value of the firm is revealed. The underlying economics and motivations of the signalling model focused on issuer wealth maximization. The model produces empirical implications involving the secondary issue of shares, insider retention of shares, announcement of secondary issues, operating performance of the firms after IPO listing, and IPO ex-ante uncertainty.

The signalling theory implies a positive relationship between underpricing and secondary offerings. The evidence on this is not, however, consistent across the markets. For example, Michaely and Shaw (1992) and James (1992) found that underpricing did not significantly vary between secondary issuing and non-secondary issuing firms in the US, and the probability of a secondary issue of shares was not significantly related to the degree of underpricing (Garfinkel, 1993). In the non-US markets, Jenkinson (1990) found no significant positive relationship between underpricing and secondary offers in the UK, while McGuinness (1992), Keloharju (1993b), and Hameed and Lim (1998)[3] found a significant positive relationship between underpricing and secondary offers in Hong Kong, Finland, and Singapore respectively.

The signalling theory suggests a positive relationship between the degree of underpricing and insider retention of shares. However, the evidence is not consistent with this hypothesis (Michaely and Shaw (1994) and Keasey and Short (1997)). If more shares in an underpriced offer are retained by insiders, a positive relationship between underpricing and the after-market insider sale of shares is expected. Jegadeesh *et al.* (1993) and Keloharju (1993b) provide weak evidence supporting the hypothesis in the US and Finland, while studies by Michaely and Shaw (1994), Garfinkel (1993), and Levis (1995) found no evidence to support the hypothesis.

Some researchers hypothesize that the market should be less surprised by the announcement of secondary issues by newly listed firms if investors truly received a signal of initial underpricing. The studies using US data, however, provide mixed evidence. For example, Jegadeesh *et al.* (1993) and Slovin *et al.* (1994) found a significant positive relationship between the initial underpricing and stock return of the secondary issue announcement day, while Michaely and Shaw (1994) and Garfinkel (1993) found no significant relationship. Although US evidence on this hypothesis is mixed, non-US evidence is yet to be made available.

If the signalling theory suggests that only high-quality firms could signal by underpricing their new issues, firms with high initial underpricing should have a better operating performance in the after-market period than those with low initial underpricing. The empirical evidence does not support this hypothesis, however. For example, Hansen and Crutchley (1990), Jain and Kini (1994), Loughran and Ritter (1997), and Mikkelson *et al.* (1997) found a significant decline in the operating performance of newly listed companies (gross turnover, net profits, and return on assets) in the after-market period.

Although most empirical evidence does not support the signalling theory of underpricing, we cannot yet discard it as invalid. This is because the signalling theory has a link with Beatty and Ritter's (1986) proposition regarding the relationship between underpricing and the ex-ante uncertainty of new issue, which is strongly supported by empirical evidence. If ex-ante uncertainty is high, it could be difficult for high-quality firms to effectively signal quality, so the low-quality firms could more easily mimic high-quality firms.

Investment Banker's Information and Price Delegation Theory

The winner's curse and signalling models were built on the assumption of information asymmetry between the buyers and sellers of shares in the new issue. However, an investment banker, being the underwriter of the issue, is directly involved in the pricing of a new issue. Investment bankers develop expertise in offer pricing, as they are frequently involved in the flotation of new issues. It has therefore been assumed that they have better information on the market demand of a new issue. Appointing an investment banker as underwriter to set an offer price and manage the flotation of shares creates an agency relationship between the issuer (principal) and the banker (agent). In this principal–agent framework, the principal has bargaining power in providing compensation but cannot control the agent's behaviour with respect to marketing the IPO. On the other hand, the agent has useful information, unavailable to the principal, on the market demand of the new issue. This creates a moral hazard situation, because the banker's efforts in the marketing and distribution of the shares are not sufficiently observable.

Based on the principal–agent relationship between the issuer and the investment banker, Baron and Holmström (1980) and Baron (1979, 1982) developed the price delegation theory. They argued that the decision on pricing is delegated to the investment banker so that the offer price could be fixed with better information on the market demand. The issuer needs to offer a package for the banker, involving underwriting commissions on sales proceeds and professional fees as well as the freedom of decision on the pricing of the offer. The banker would then determine his own efforts and fix the offer price based on the best information available on the market demand. The underpricing of new issues helps reduce the risk of failure and the cost of moral hazard arising from the possibility that the issuers might not put much effort into selling the issue. If the pricing decision is delegated to the bankers, they would optimally underprice an issue, which benefits both the issuers and the bankers.

If IPO underpricing by the bankers was due to the moral hazard problem in the agency relationship, the degree of underpricing would be much lower for a new issue underwritten by the issuing firm itself. This is because the agency problem would not arise as there is no conflict of interest between issuer and underwriter. However, evidence from Muscarella and Vetsuypens (1989) does not support this hypothesis in the US. If the moral hazard problem arises due to the level of the distribution and selling efforts of the bankers, large offers would require more underpricing. This is because large offers need greater distribution and selling efforts than small offers. Michaely and Shaw (1994) found only weak evidence to support this hypothesis. Although the above direct evidence does not strongly support the price delegation theory, it has a link with the well-supported proposition of the positive relationship between underpricing and ex-ante uncertainty. This is because the underwriter would bear more risk if ex-ante uncertainty of the issue is high.

Ownership Structure Theories

For a company, going public is normally a step towards separation of ownership and control of the firm, which leads to agency problems between management and owners (Jensen and Meckling, 1976). The agency problem may arise between the managing and non-managing shareholders with respect to the managerial control of the firm. The managing shareholders may want to maintain their control over the firm even after going public in order to retain their personal benefits as well as avoid the possibility of takeover by the new shareholders (Harris and Raviv (1989), Zingales (1994), and Grossman and Hart (1980)).

Theory of Reduced Monitoring by Dispersed Ownership
Brennan and Frank (1997) argued that IPO underpricing is one way to reduce the risk of losing managerial control. An underpriced issue will typically be oversubscribed, allowing the founding owners or directors to allocate shares in such a manner as to achieve a dispersed ownership structure after flotation. When the ownership of outside investors is widely dispersed, a small investor could have less incentive to monitor the activities of management. The founding owners or directors are therefore able to entrench their control over the firm. If the ownership is widely diffused, it would be more difficult to assemble a large block of shares in the secondary trading. Hence, control over the firm can be retained over a longer term (Shleifer and Vishny, 1986). This theory is fairly well supported by evidence from the UK, Sweden, and the US respectively from Brennan and Frank (1997), Holmén and Högfeldt (2000), and Smart and Zutter (2000).

Other Motivations for Dispersed Ownership
Researchers have explored other motivations for achieving a dispersed ownership via underpricing. Booth and Chua (1996) argued that a broad and dispersed ownership improves secondary market liquidity, which is important for the issuers. A liquid secondary market is important for the correct valuation of shares, because market risks may not be estimated correctly in an illiquid market (Dimson (1979); Scholes and William (1977)). Booth and Chua also showed that the issuer encourages investors to procure more information about the new issue. The offer is therefore oversubscribed, which helps achieve a dispersed ownership structure for the firm. The issuer underprices a public offer in equilibrium because it compensates the investors for incurring the cost of information. Booth and Chua found that the cost of achieving ownership dispersion was higher for best-effort issues than for firm-commitment issues, as investors need to incur higher information costs for best-effort issues. Zingales (1995) argued that founding owners might want a dispersed ownership structure to extract more premiums from potential after-market buyers, because

the allocation of a small number of shares to each of the diverse investors would create a free-ride opportunity for insiders to sell more shares at a higher price in the secondary market. This hypothesis is yet to be tested in any market.

Initial Underpricing in the Hong Kong Market

From the above discussion, it appears that underpricing of public offers of shares is still a puzzling research issue. Researchers have progressed to the point where they understand the reasons for money being given away to new shareholders in the company through setting the offer price at a discount. The evidence reported from different countries does not yet unequivocally support these theories, but it is generally recognized that issuers and underwriters face varying degrees of uncertainty regarding the fair value of new shares to be floated. Until the after-market trading of shares starts, it is hard for them to assess the market value of new stocks, so issuers and underwriters need to fix the offer price with some discount to avoid the risk of overpricing and failure.

Earlier studies (Dawson and Hiraki (1985); Dawson (1987); McGuinness (1992)) found that IPO investors in Hong Kong received about eleven to eighteen per cent of initial returns after adjusting for the market return. This suggests that issuers in the Hong Kong new-issue market, like other markets, face some degree of ex-ante uncertainty about new issue valuation. McGuinness (1992) found that IPO initial return (underpricing) in Hong Kong is positively correlated with the daily fluctuations (standard deviation) of the newly listed stock returns over the first month after listing. This finding provides direct evidence of issuer ex-ante uncertainty in Hong Kong. It suggests that if the intrinsic value of the issuing firm is hard to assess, the market cannot settle on a fair price quickly after the new shares are listed. It has also been found that the valuation of a new issue and initial underpricing are affected by the state of the market around the time that the offer price is determined (Dawson and Hiraki (1985); McGuinness (1992)).

The limited evidence shows that Hong Kong issuers face ex-ante uncertainty with respect to fixing an offer price that may require them to provide discounts by setting the price conservatively. However, it is not known whether the discount was indeed due to reasons suggested by the theories of IPO initial underpricing, as discussed above, or to other characteristics of the Hong Kong new-issue market. It has recently been found that Hong Kong IPOs tend to underforecast their profits (Cheng and Firth, 2000), which could lead them to fix a lower offer price.

IPO After-Market Performance

The IPO theories discussed above are based on an implicit assumption that the new-issue market is efficient and the stock is correctly priced on the first trading day. Therefore, according to equilibrium asset pricing theories, IPO stocks would perform more or less neutrally in the after-market period. However, the evidence reported in Table 10.4 generates scepticism about this assumption. It has been found that IPO stocks generally underperform the market or other benchmarks in many different markets, including Hong Kong's. The exceptions are Malaysia and Korea, where IPOs outperformed the market benchmark over the long run after exchange listing.

Table 10.4   IPO After-Market Performance (Cumulative Abnormal Returns) in Different Markets

	Study	Sample Period	Sample Size	Window period (Years)	Return (%)
Australia	Lee *et al.* (1996)	1976–89	266	3	–51.0
Brazil	Aggarwal *et al.* (1993)	1980–90	62	3	–47.0
Chile	Aggarwal *et al.* (1993)	1982–90	28	3	–23.7
China	Wong and Xie (2001)	1992–8	200	1.5	+16.5
Finland	Keloharju (1993)	1984–89	79	3	–21.1
Germany	Ljungqvist (1996)	1970–90	145	3	–12.1
Hong Kong	McGuinness (1993)	1980–90	72	2	–18.3
Hong Kong	Dawson (1987)	1978–83	21	1	–9.3
Japan	Cai and Wei (1996)	1971–90	172	3	–27.0
Korea	Kim *et al.* (1995)	1985–8	99	3	+91.6
Malaysia	Wong and Uddin (2002)	1989–98	493	3	+44.0
Malaysia	Dawson (1987)	1978–83	21	1	+18.2
Singapore	Hin and Mahmood (1993)	1976–84	45	3	–9.2
Sweden	Loughran *et al.* (1994)	1980–90	162	3	+1.2
USA	Loughran and Ritter (1995)	1970–90	4753	5	–30.0
USA	Ritter (1991)	1975–84	1526	3	–29.1
UK	Levis (1993)	1980–8	712	3	–8.1

Note: The returns are generally adjusted for the market returns over the same period. Methods of return computation may vary from study to study.

The consistent long-run underperformance of IPO stocks in many markets raises questions about the validity of the efficient market hypothesis with respect to the pricing of newly listed stocks. This anomaly has attracted the interest of researchers. Miller (1977) suggested that different investors might have different opinions about the prospects of an issuing firm, but a small group of investors is always over-optimistic about its future cash flows. He argued that the initial market price is affected by the behaviour of over-optimistic small investors, which results in a high initial return on the first trading day upon listing. As more information about newly listed stock becomes available over the long run, investor over-optimism diminishes and the divergence of opinions converges to a fair value of the stock. Hence, most IPO stocks underperform the market benchmark over the long run. Miller's conjecture has not yet been directly tested in any market, possibly because researchers have not found any appropriate proxy for the divergence of opinions and could not measure the arrival of information in the market after listing. However, the evidence of declining operating performance of IPO firms during the post-listing period indicates that investors are unable to anticipate the future operating performance of the company before applying for IPO shares (Jain and Kini (1994); Pagano *et al.* (1998); Loughran and Ritter (1997)). This evidence seems to provide indirect support for Miller's conjecture.

Another explanation of the anomaly is linked to the market overreaction hypothesis developed by De Bond and Thaler (1985, 1987, and 1989). If the market overreacts to a new listing on the exchange, it may lead to mispricing of the newly listed stocks on the first day. Aggarwal and Rivoli (1990) argued that there are mean-reverting fads in the IPO market.[4] Investors are over-optimistic about the prospects of the newly listed firms and could then bid up the initial market price beyond its value. When the over-optimism diminishes after a few weeks, the market price will revert to its correct level. High initial underpricing could therefore result from the temporary overvaluation[5] of newly listed stock.

McGuinness (1993) and Dawson (1987) show that newly listed stocks in Hong Kong do underperform the market benchmark, which is largely consistent with the large body of international evidence on the long run performance of IPO stocks. McGuinness (1993) also found that there was a strong positive correlation between the post-listing performance of Hong Kong IPOs and the capital commitment by the pre-listing owners measured as a percentage of the equity that the pre-listing owners commit to retain for the first six months of listing. Once the capital commitment period elapses, the initial owners are able to liquidate their shareholdings and a reversal in the positive correlation is noted thereafter. For the post-listing period of between 180 to 250 trading days, the correlation is strongly negative, suggesting that newly listed stocks with larger capital commitments perform poorly in the longer run.

Discussion Questions

1. How does a new-issue market contribute to an economy? Explain your answer in the context of the Hong Kong economy.
2. How does a new-issue market link to the secondary trading market?
3. Describe characteristics of the IPOs listed in the Hong Kong market. Elaborate your answer by discussing red chip, H-share, and global offerings.
4. Discuss the major requirements of listings on the Hong Kong exchange.
5. What are the rules regarding the minimum public interest in IPO firms?
6. Briefly describe the IPO listing procedure in Hong Kong. How do the offer for subscription and the offer for sale differ from each other? What impacts do they have on the outstanding share capital of a firm?

7. Explain why issuers and/or underwriters are not able to fix an offer price close to the market value of the offer revealed on the listing day.
8. What are the main theories of IPO underpricing? Briefly explain the information asymmetry theories of underpricing.
9. Do you consider the IPO long-run underperformance to be consistent with the efficient market hypothesis? Elaborate your answer.
10. Discuss empirical evidence of IPO initial underpricing and long-run performance in the Hong Kong market.

Keywords

capital market
general listing procedure
global offerings
initial public offerings (IPO)
IPO After-Market Performance
market liquidity
new-issue market
primary market
Risk Sharing and Control
Rules and Requirements of New Listing
venture capitalists

11. The Stock Market II: The Trading Market

KIE ANN WONG AND MD. HAMID UDDIN

Introduction

A stock market comprises a new-issue (primary) market and a trading (secondary) market. A new-issue market is a market where corporations sell new issues of their stocks to initial buyers to raise funds for their expenditures and investments. Here, investment banks or underwriters usually facilitate the initial sale of a stock by providing a guarantee of its total issue proceeds before selling to the public. A trading market consists of the stock exchange and brokerage firms that facilitate the trading of stocks which have been previously issued in the new-issue market.

However, the issuer acquires new funds only when its shares are first sold in the new-issue market. The trading market does not raise any new funds: it merely redistributes the ownership of stocks that were made in the new-issue market. When an individual buys a stock in the trading market, the seller of the stock receives the money, not the issuer of the stock. The rest of this chapter will describe the economic functions of the trading market and the development, the rules and regulations, the trading and settlement systems, and the characteristics of Hong Kong's equity market. We will also discuss the stock market indices, concepts of risk and returns, asset pricing models, market efficiency, and anomalies in the Hong Kong context as well as internationalization of the Hong Kong exchange.

Economic Functions of the Trading Market

Although no new funds are raised from the trading market, it performs several important functions that benefit not only the issuer but also the investors. First, the interactions of numerous buyers and sellers in the trading market produce signals in the form of prices that indicate the value of securities as perceived by the market as a whole. Such information helps issuers better assess how well they are using the funds acquired from earlier new issue market activities and how much value the market attaches to a firm's stock. It also indicates the likely response of investors to new offerings.

Second, it reduces the cost of capital for the issuers and the cost of transactions for the investors. Searching costs for potential counterparties (buyers or sellers) are reduced as the trading market brings together many interested parties and provides a matching service for the bid and ask orders. The price of a traded stock also affects the amount of funds that can be raised in the new issue market if the issuer intends to make another issue of the stock. This is because buyers of the new issue will only be willing to pay the issuer a price that they think the stock will command in the trading market. That is, the issuers need to make the terms attractive in the new issue market relative to the existing traded stocks to induce the purchase of new issues. Hence, the higher the stock's price in the trading market, the higher the offer price the issuing firm can command in the new issue market. This will increase the amount of capital it can raise and thus lower its cost of capital.

Third, because the trading market provides a mechanism for investors to sell and buy securities, it creates liquidity for the securities. Investors would not like their funds to be tied up in securities they purchase; neither do they want to be prevented from buying an existing security. If there is no liquidity, the owners of a firm's stocks may have to hold them until the company is liquidated. Therefore, unless investors are confident that they can convert their stocks to cash when they wish to, they would most likely be reluctant to purchase the stocks in the first place, or they would demand a very high rate of return as compensation for the expected illiquidity in their stocks. With a trading market, individuals and institutions have the flexibility to allocate and reallocate their investment portfolios at any time by paying a small amount of transaction costs. The increased liquidity makes investors willing to accept a lower rate of return.

A Brief History of the Hong Kong Exchange

Before 1986

In 1891, Hong Kong's first formal stock exchange, The Association of Stockbrokers in Hong Kong, was formed. It was later renamed The Hong Kong Stock Exchange in 1914. A second stock exchange, The Hong Kong Stockbrokers' Association, was incorporated in 1921. The two exchanges then merged to form The Hong Kong Stock Exchange Ltd in 1947, re-establishing stock exchange activities after World War II.

However, capital funding using equity was insignificant. From 1957 to 1967, only fifty to seventy companies were listed, and less than twenty-five of them were being actively traded. The uncertainty over Hong Kong's political future affected investor confidence in Hong Kong, resulting in the small number of listed firms and the inactive trading of the counters.

In 1969, reassurances from China about Hong Kong's future increased the level of investor confidence and the stock market boomed. In the same year, the Far East Exchange was opened. Another two exchanges, the Kam Ngan Stock Exchange and the Kowloon Stock Exchange, were opened in 1971 and 1972 respectively. By 1972, the presence of the four exchanges hastened the development of Hong Kong's stock market, and soon the community at large was investing in stocks.

The stock market crash of 1973 and the oil crisis in 1974 led to the enactment of the Hong Kong government's first significant securities legislation: the Securities Ordinance and the Protection of Investors Ordinance. The Commissioner for Securities and the Securities Commission were also established to regulate and oversee the four exchanges. The need to strengthen market regulation and unify the four exchanges prompted the incorporation of the Stock Exchange of Hong Kong (SEHK) Limited in 1986.

Since 1986

On 27 March 1986, the four exchanges ceased business operations and the SEHK commenced trading through a computer-assisted system on 2 April. The SEHK is a limited company with the exclusive rights to establish, operate, and maintain a stock market. It is owned by its member brokers who must at least hold one A-share, which confers membership and trade privileges.

After the market crash in 1987, the Securities Review Committee chaired by Ian Hay-Davison conducted an evaluation of the Hong Kong stock market. It was found that the settlement system was inadequate and the listing procedures were abused. The management was incompetent, allowing an inside group to operate the stock exchange as a private club rather than a public entity for the benefit of stakeholders. Together with the Davison report, a list of changes and reforms was also provided to bring the Hong Kong stock market up to international standards.

Both the Securities Commission and the Office of the Commissioner for Securities were merged in 1989 to form the Securities and Futures Commission (SFC). Consisting of ten members, it acts as a security watchdog, enforces regulations, propagates new legislation, and supervises the exchange, the dealers, and the clearing houses. A point to note here is that the SFC does not impose too much regulation, since a tightly regulated financial market is unattractive to investors.

Another change was the restructuring of the SEHK Council to reflect more accurately the interests of the market participants. In 1991, the number and composition of council members were both changed. The current council has thirty-one members, up from the twenty-two of the 1988 original council. It comprises individual, corporate, and independent members instead of the individual members of the 1988 council.

As part of the reforms stated in the 1999 Financial Budget, the SEHK and the Hong Kong Futures Exchange Limited demutualized. Together with the Hong Kong Securities Clearing Company Limited, they became wholly owned subsidiaries of Hong Kong Exchanges and Clearing Limited, known as HKEx. In March 2000, the merger was completed and HKEx went public on 27 June by way of introduction.

Rules and Regulations of Equity Trading

The Securities and Futures Commission (SFC) and HKEx regulate equity trading in Hong Kong. The SFC is an autonomous entity supported by the securities market and it became the main regulator of exchange participants on 6 March 2000, when the regulatory functions underwent rationalization. However, the power to elect the chairman and directors for the SFC lies with the Hong Kong government. The SFC aims to ensure a transparent and efficient securities market by laying down legislation and codes. It oversees the exchange, the clearing houses, and all other non-exchange members in the market.

On 6 March 2000, The Stock Exchange of Hong Kong (SEHK), Hong Kong Futures Exchange Limited (HKFE), and Hong Kong Securities Clearing Company Limited (HKSCC) merged and became wholly owned subsidiaries of a single holding company, HKEx. HKEx is recognized by the SFC as the operator of the SEHK and is endowed with the power to set rules to manage its clearing houses and members. The following sections discuss some of the legislation, codes, and rules relevant to equity trading in Hong Kong as well as possible penalties for offenders.

Ordinances

The Securities and Futures Commission Ordinance (SFCO) defines the powers and purposes of the SFC. The SFC was established with the aim of promoting and developing the securities and futures markets in Hong Kong to meet international standards. It is responsible for overseeing the operations of HKEx, HKEx's subsidiaries (SEHK, HKFE, and HKSCC), and financial market intermediaries. Market integrity is of utmost importance, and the SFC has the power to set laws and codes to control the activities of the securities and futures markets and protect investors.

The Protection of Investors Ordinance protects investors against fraud and misrepresentation when making investments in securities or other properties. It also applies when investors are approached by people claiming to be investment advisers but who are actually not registered under the Securities Ordinance. Offenders in the former case are subject to a fine of HK$1 million and imprisonment for seven years. Offenders in the latter case can be fined HK$10,000. Offenders are also obliged to compensate investors for any monetary losses.

An insider dealer under the Securities (Insider Dealing) Ordinance (SIDO) is defined as any entity that possesses and uses asymmetric information to trade securities in order to earn monetary gains or avoid losses. Situations deemed appropriate and not considered to be insider dealing are defined in Section 10 of the SIDO. SIDO aims to ensure a level playing field on the securities market.

The Insider Dealing Tribunal deals with people found guilty of insider trading. Offenders are banned from participating in any management activities of companies specified by the Tribunal. They are also liable to a penalty of an amount not exceeding three times the profit made or loss avoided. In addition, a penalty up to the amount of profit made or loss avoided has to be paid to the government. If the guilty party is a registered person in the securities market or an exchange member, their registration may be withheld or rendered void.

The purpose of the Securities (Disclosure of Interests) Ordinance (SDIO) is to promote transparency in the market by ensuring that material information with regard to shareholdings is available to all investors. SDIO was set in September 1991 and applies to all companies listed on the SEHK. Under the SDIO, a shareholder has to disclose his interest in a company if he possesses more than a ten per cent interest in the company. As for any director or chief executive of a SEHK-listed company, the disclosure of interest in the companies has to be made regardless of the amount. The interests of spouses and children are also subject to disclosure even if they are not directors of the company.

Certain sales tactics by dealers are forbidden under the Securities Ordinance (SO). For instance, Section 74 of the SO states that dealers are not allowed to initiate calls to potential clients[1] to induce them to trade securities. Section 76 forbids dealers to carry out options or forward trading. This means that a dealer is not allowed to offer a person an option to trade with SEHK-listed securities. He is also forbidden to carry out transactions that will be completed after T+1, the day after the transaction (changed to T+2 since June 1992). Exceptions are made for some stock borrowing and lending transactions and stock options trading at SEHK specified by the SFC. Section 80 prohibits uncovered or naked short sales, i.e. the short seller does not ensure that he will be able to fulfil delivery of stocks to his buyer upon settlement.

Sections 82 to 97 of the SO detail the requirements for accounts maintenance and the appointment of auditors. Dealers are required to keep accounting data for at least six years. The dealer has to be able to verify transactions and show his financial position in a true and unbiased manner.

In general, any form of fraud related to securities trading is intolerable under the SO. Any person found to have influenced others to trade securities by misstatement is committing an offence. Any person who actually attempts to create a false market or tries to present a false impression of an active market for SEHK-listed stocks is also guilty under the SO. Offenders can be fined or sentenced to jail.

The enactment of the new composite Securities and Futures Ordinance (SFO) on 13 March 2002 marks the beginning of a new regulatory framework, which has integrated all the existing security-related ordinances mentioned above and expanded into the SFO. It is believed that the new ordinance is on a par with internationally accepted regulatory practices. Since then, the SFC has been busy with drafting subsidiary legislation and changing procedures and processes to fit the requirements of the SFO. More details on the SFO are provided in Chapters 15 and 16.

Statutory Provisions and Subsidiary Legislation Administered by SFC

The Financial Resources Rules (FRR) are set to ensure the healthy financial position of securities and futures dealers and advisers. The liquid capital of corporate dealers has to be kept at a minimum level of HK$3 million or five per cent of total liabilities, whichever is greater. Individual dealers have to keep a minimum liquid capital of HK$500,000 or five per cent of total capital, whichever is greater. Assets and liabilities are defined by the FRR, and appropriate adjustments are also specified. Investment advisers simply need to ensure that their net tangible assets do not fall below zero.

A contract note must be issued for every securities transaction carried out in Hong Kong. Dealers must complete the contract note by T+1. The information required includes the dates of the transaction, the settlement and issuance of the contract note, the name of the dealer and client (if applicable), the amount of commission payable and tax (if any), the quantity and description of the security, and the transaction price. The dealer also has to specify whether he is representing a client as an agent or dealing for himself. Dealers and investment advisers are also required to declare the amount of interest they hold in any securities recommended in any written medium by themselves.

Rules and Regulations Set by HKEx

HKEx promulgates the Listing Rules, which control the listing of new firms, and the Code of Best Practices for listed firms to follow to enhance accountability and transparency. HKEx also sets rules to monitor the activities of its Clearing Houses and Exchange members to ensure a transparent, fair, and efficient market. Although it is self-regulatory, proposed rules are pending until approved by the SFC.

SEHK imposes financial and accounting requirements on its members and other rules to manage its operating activities. SEHK trading rules specify permissible spreads and quotations (both opening and subsequent quotations) for each security. The Automatic Order Matching and Execution System (AMS) ensures that trades are carried out strictly on a price/time priority. The clearing and settlement of trades are taken care of under the Central Clearing and Settlement System (CCASS).

The Professional Conduct Regulations set the minimum standard of conduct expected of exchange members during securities trading. The main purpose is to uphold market integrity and ensure client interests and assets, which are always given top priority. Members are to be honest and fair at all times and must be adequately equipped with both the financial and operational resources to perform their duties well. Members should also try to avoid any conflict of interest and the misrepresentation of information which will affect client investment decisions. Members should also gather sufficient information (such as financial position, existing portfolio, and risk-tolerance level) about their clients before giving suitable investment advice, and then make sure that they disclose enough information about the transactions that their clients have entered into.

Trading System and Mechanism

Types of Order

The most frequent type of order is a market order, which means that the investor is willing to buy or sell a stock at the best current market price. Investors placing a market buy (sell) order indicate that they accept the immediate execution of the transaction at the lowest (highest) market price that is available.

Another type of order is a limit order, whereby investors specify the buy or sell price. This is used when investors indicate the highest buying or lowest selling price that they are willing to accept. For instance, the trade will be executed immediately if the ask price in the market is equal to or below the price ceiling specified by the buying investor. Any remaining quantity will be matched against the next highest ask price below or equal to his stated limit price.

A variation of the limit order is an enhanced limit order (ELO). The main difference is that an ELO has the advantage of matching up to two price queues at a time. Take, for example, an ELO to buy 100,000 shares at HK$100, and the best ask quote is HK$99 for 60,000 shares followed by the next best price at HK$100 for 60,000 shares. The ELO will be matched first with HK$99, followed by HK$100. Thus the trade will be executed with 60,000 shares at HK$99 first, and the remaining 40,000 shares of the ELO at HK$100. If there is any unfilled quantity at the second best price, it will be stored in the system as a normal limit order at the original input price of HK$100.

A special limit order (SLO) is similar to a market order, but it allows the matching of up to two price queues. Consider the example of an SLO to buy 100,000 shares at HK$100. Assume the prevailing market ask quote is HK$97, followed by HK$98, HK$99, HK$100, and HK$101 on the queue, and the volume is 40,000 shares at each quote. The SLO will be matched first with the best price (i.e. the prevailing price), followed by the next best price of HK$98. Thus the SLO will be executed with 40,000 shares at HK$97 and 40,000 shares at HK$98. The remaining unfilled 20,000 shares will be cancelled and not stored in the system

Another two types of order, at-auction orders and at-auction limit orders, are exclusively for pre-opening sessions. An at-auction order is equivalent to a market order without a specified price, while an at-auction limit order is a limit order with a specified price. An at-auction order has priority over an at-auction limit order, but will be cancelled once unfilled after order matching during the pre-opening session. On the other hand, if the input price of an unfilled at-auction limit order deviates less than nine times from the prevailing nominal price, the order will be entered as a limit order at the input price to be matched when the morning continuous trading session begins.

Investors can use certain types of orders to prevent missing out on profit opportunities or to limit their losses. For instance, a stop order can be placed to purchase a stock only when the price has risen to a specified price level. An investor who expects the price increase to be sustained once it has gone over the specified level will place a stop order in anticipation of capital gains. An extension of stop order is a stop-limit order to buy. The order to purchase a stock will be executed once the price reaches a certain stop level but on the condition that the purchase price must be below a specified maximum price.

Conversely, an investor who expects a stock price to continue dropping once it has fallen to a certain level will place a stop-loss order. This means that the sale will be executed once the price level has fallen to the specified price level in order to limit the amount of losses. The corresponding extension is a stop-limit order to sell. This means an order to sell the stock if the price has fallen to a certain stop-loss level provided that the selling price is above a specified minimum price that the investor is willing to accept.

Stock Trading Mechanism

Since January 1996, SEHK has been using an automated trading system known as the Automated Order Matching and Execution System (AMS). Prior to this, trading was done manually through SEHK's internal terminals on the exchange floor. Subsequently, AMS replaced this system as the increasing trading volume proved to be too much for the latter to handle. Each A-share held by a member broker (evidence of membership and trading rights) permits him to keep one AMS terminal on the trading floor and a second AMS terminal at his principal office. The AMS system was later upgraded to the Third Generation Automatic Order Matching and Execution System (AMS/3) in October 2000. New trading facilities, quotation rules, and order types (such as ELO and SLO) were introduced.

The AMS/3 trading system comprises four trading channels: Trading Terminal, Multi-Workstation System (MWS), Broker Supplied System (BSS), and Order Routing System (ORS). Exchange members are allowed to choose their preferred trading channel, but each trading right (A-share) is entitled to one trading channel only. The ORS was introduced on 23 February 2001, and this enables investors to place orders electronically over the Internet, by mobile phone, and through other electronic channels. The ORS automatically directs the orders to an Exchange Participant for approval and submits to the AMS/3 for matching and execution. Only Exchange Participants using MWS and BSS can receive orders through the ORS.

Quotation rules that impose limits to the opening quotations and subsequent quotations during the day were revised. The first bid (ask) order has to be higher (lower) than or equal to the previous closing price minus (plus) eight spreads, instead of four spreads before revision. The intra-day orders are governed by another set of quotation rules, but they should not be made at a price that deviates nine times or more from the nominal price. In addition, to avoid extreme volatility in trading prices, each security is allocated a spread indicating the price increment that is allowed to be quoted and transacted. This spread is an increasing function of the stock's market price and ranges from HK$0.001 to HK$2.50. Table 11.1 shows the spread schedule.

Table 11.1   Spreads

	Stock Price			1 Spread
From	HK$ 0.01	to	HK$ 0.25	HK$ 0.001
Over	0.25	to	0.50	0.005
Over	0.50	to	2.00	0.010
Over	2.00	to	5.00	0.025
Over	5.00	to	30.00	0.050
Over	30.00	to	50.00	0.100
Over	50.00	to	100.00	0.250
Over	100.00	to	200.00	0.500
Over	200.00	to	1,000.00	1.000
Over	1,000.00	to	9,995.00	2.500

Stock trading is mostly automated, which means that the orders entered are automatically matched and transacted at the best prices available. In the case of orders having the same quote for the same stock, the order that is entered earlier will be executed first. Orders entered into the trading system are liable up to the quantity of stocks entered. In a case where only part of the quantity entered can find a match for the desired price, this part of the order will be executed first. The remaining unfulfilled quantity will wait for the next match but still maintain its position in the queue until the end of the trading day or until the entire order is executed or cancelled. To avoid the unfair hogging of queue positions, brokers are only allowed to cancel or decrease, but not increase, their order size.

Short Selling

Short selling at HKEx was introduced in 1994 under the regulation of Section 80 of the Securities Ordinance and the Rules of the Exchange. This was first introduced under a pilot programme where only seventeen securities, known as designated securities, were allowed to be short sold and the number of designated securities was adjusted every quarter. The short selling described below refers to non-market-maker short sales unless otherwise specified.

One rule is that a short selling order must only be entered during the continuous trading session and can only be done for designated securities.

However, the tick rule stipulates that a short sale must not be done below the best prevailing price. Short selling by market makers is exempted from the tick rule.

In addition, to protect the buyer, the short seller, and the market, short sellers must make arrangements to ensure that they will be able to fulfil delivery of the stocks upon settlement. A securities borrowing and lending (SBL) market provides a medium for such arrangements to be made. In an SBL market, a short seller can first borrow the obligatory quantity of stocks from a stock lender for delivery to his buyer by the settlement date. The buyer will then secure ownership of the stocks.

To protect the stock lender from counterparty risk, the borrower has to provide collateral, which must be easily realizable (such as the proceeds from the sale to the buyer). The collateral must be at all times not less than 105 per cent of the market value of the borrowed securities, which will be marked to market at least daily. According to the SBL agreement, the short seller has to return the borrowed stocks within twelve months or as and when demanded by the lender. In 1994, the Stamp Duty Ordinance (SDO) exempted transactions under a SBL agreement from tax, provided that the borrowed stocks are used for certain purposes defined in the SDO and the borrower returns the stock within twelve months.

Settlement Mechanism

Prior to June 1992, trade settlements involved the physical transfer of share certificates to the buying broker, who would in turn issue cheque payments to the selling broker. Settlements had to be done for every transaction and were due one day after the trade (i.e. T+1). This system is inefficient and the T+1 settlement date does not allow the brokers enough time to fulfil the obligations of their trades. This system became obsolete when SEHK introduced the Central Clearing and Settlement System in June 1992.

CCASS is a computerized clearing and settlement system for stocks listed on HKEx. The Hong Kong Securities Clearing Company Ltd (HKSCC), a non-profit company, runs this system. HKSCC was established in 1992 by its six members: the SEHK, the Bank of China, the Hang Seng Bank, the Standard Chartered Bank, the Bank of East Asia, and the Hongkong and Shanghai Banking Corporation.

The participants in CCASS include brokers, clearing agencies, custodians, stock lenders, and stock pledgees. CCASS provides depository and nominee services for its participants. The participants can deposit their share certificates in the CCASS depository and shares will be credited or debited electronically to their stock accounts upon settlements. These deposited share certificates will be registered in HKSCC's nominee name. The HKSCC's nominee will thus retain the rights to claim any share dividends and also other privileges such as voting rights and warrant conversions.

Trades recorded in the SEHK computer system are directed to the HKSCC computer system, where HKSCC will use either the Continuous Net Settlement (CNS) or the Isolated Trade Settlement (ITS) method to process the trades for settlement. Settlement is due on the second day after the transaction (i.e. T+2).

Continuous Net Settlement

Instead of having to process every single transaction for settlement, the buy and sell transactions for each stock for each broker are cancelled against each other to obtain a net buy/sell quantity. HKSCC will then act as the settlement counterparty to the brokers. Daily statements declaring the amount due from/to the brokers are issue to them after 6.00pm on the trading day (T). A net clearing statement will be issued after 2.00pm on T+1 so that brokers have enough time to arrange for settlements on T+2.

Isolated Trade Settlement

Under the Isolated Trade Settlement system (ITS), settlement obligations are processed by electronic transfer of shares (money) between the transacting brokers' stock (bank) accounts. By default, settlements are done through CNS unless otherwise requested by both transacting parties to use ITS. As HKSCC is the settlement counterparty under CNS, it is exposed to counterparty risks. Thus a trade may be settled through ITS, if the risk associated with the trade is deemed to be too high by HKSCC.

CCASS's Settlement Instruction (SI) system provides settlement facilities for other transactions, such as stock borrowing and lending and portfolio activity; for example, transactions between a broker and a unit trust use the SI system for settlement. Parties involved include both the buying and selling brokers as well as a trustee (usually a bank) appointed by the unit trust to take care of stocks and money settlements. The buying broker and the trustee will enter SIs[2] into the CCASS computer system, where they will be matched and settled on T+2.

CCASS Risk Management

By becoming the settlement counterparty under the CNS system and providing the depository service, HKSCC exposes itself to various counterparty risks such as credit risk and liquidity risk. HKSCC therefore has to guard itself against such risk through various risk-management measures.

For example, potential participants have to furnish evidence to convince HKSCC of their financial position and other abilities necessary to fulfil their role as participants in CCASS before HKSCC approves their admission. Deposited share certificates are recorded and checked for authenticity, and participants are accountable for any defective certificates uncovered. In addition, a minimum sum of HK$200 million contributed by the participants as insurance is retained as a guarantee fund to help HKSCC to fulfil its obligation as settlement counterparty. To guard against broker defaults, HKSCC employs a measure called 'securities-on-hold' before the buying broker confirms payment. This enables HKSCC to sell the stocks and pay to the selling broker in case of buying broker defaults.

Stock Market Indices

A stock market's daily performance can be assessed by its market index on the day. A stock market index measures the price level in the stock market on a particular day relative to a pre-determined base date. Comparing the index values at two different dates gives a summary performance of the stock market between the two dates. Some indices are computed using all the stocks traded on the exchange, while some use only a selected sample. Stock market indices are often used as benchmarks by money managers for evaluating portfolio performance, or predicting future market movements in technical analysis. They are also commonly used as a proxy for the market portfolio when computing the systematic (market) risk of a stock using the capital asset pricing model (CAPM).

The major stock market indices in Hong Kong are the Hang Seng Index, Hang Seng Composite Index Series, the Morgan Stanley Capital International Hong Kong Index, and the All-Ordinaries Index. However, some other sub-indices have also been developed since the 1990s as the Hong Kong stock market has grown and internationalized.

The Hang Seng Index

The Hang Seng Index (HSI) is a value-weighted index computed using a sample of thirty-three stocks, which account for about eighty per cent of the total market capitalization as at the end of 2001. The original base day was 31 July 1964, with the base-day index fixed at 100. However, to provide a common benchmark for the four sub-indices introduced in 1985, the base day was changed to 13 January 1984, and the new base day index was set to that day's closing HSI value of 975.47. Table 11.2 shows the turnover, market capitalization, and P/E ratios of the thirty-three constituent stocks.

To be eligible for inclusion in the HSI, a company must first be listed on HKEx for at least two years. Second, its total market equity[3] of all listed ordinary shares and turnover volume[4] must be among the top ninety per cent of the listed companies on HKEx. Last, its principal operation must be based in Hong Kong. Eligible companies are then selected based on their past and present earnings and financial positions and management quality. The prospects of the companies as well as the industry that they are in are also taken into consideration. The stocks in the HSI are classified into four sectors (Finance, Properties, Utilities, and Commercial and Industrial) and a sub-index is computed for each sector.

Table 11.2   Turnover, Market Capitalization, and P/E Ratios of HSI
              Stocks (end of 2001)

Rank	Company	Turnover (HK$mil)	% of Equity Total	Market Capitalization (HK$mil)	% of Equity Total	P/E Ratio (times)
1	HSBC Holdings	171,877.47	9.44	853,564.06	21.97	15.41
2	China Mobile	164,772.00	9.05	510,718.37	13.14	23.26
3	Hutchison	122,514.83	6.73	320,818.65	8.26	9.40
4	Cheung Kong	89,830.94	4.93	187,609.31	4.83	9.62
5	Hang Seng Bank	44,613.95	2.45	163,940.51	4.22	16.37
6	SHK PPT	62,041.37	3.41	151,257.16	3.89	18.16
7	China Unicom	64,067.69	3.52	107,955.77	2.78	31.65
8	CLP Holdings	25,091.83	1.38	72,801.43	1.87	12.88
9	HK Electric	23,267.58	1.28	61,893.59	1.59	11.07
10	Henderson Land	29,625.87	1.63	60,619.33	1.56	13.80
11	CNOOC	23,344.51	1.28	60,374.12	1.55	4.79
12	MTR Corporation	17,491.39	0.96	51,559.09	1.33	12.58
13	HK & China Gas	14,891.72	0.82	50,096.39	1.29	17.32
14	PCCW	46,550.43	2.56	48,747.67	1.25	–
15	Wharf Holdings	14,649.77	0.80	46,605.91	1.20	18.79
16	Swire Pacific 'A'	22,050.40	1.21	39,954.76	1.03	16.96
17	Citi Pacific	24,200.96	1.33	37,992.69	0.98	11.15
18	Cathay Pac Air	13,335.95	0.73	33,298.18	0.86	6.74
19	Johnson Elec H	15,250.78	0.84	30,125.07	0.78	26.55
20	Legend Hold	27,785.22	1.53	29,904.06	0.77	34.48
21	CKI Holdings	4,564.40	0.25	27,388.65	0.70	8.48
22	Li & Fung	16,618.01	0.91	25,187.03	0.65	27.17
23	Bank of E. Asia	15,377.61	0.84	24,080.04	0.62	12.61
24	Amoy Properties	6,483.30	0.36	23,259.14	0.60	16.82
25	Henderson Inv	4,193.62	0.23	17,044.83	0.44	8.62
26	TVB	7,864.32	0.43	14,804.40	0.38	19.12
27	China Resources	18,271.24	1.00	14,712.79	0.38	8.75
28	New World Dev	17,673.97	0.97	14,511.14	0.37	68.00
29	Wheelock	3,806.82	0.21	13,508.85	0.35	26.14
30	Shanghai Ind H	7,781.49	0.43	12,840.70	0.33	11.24
31	Sino Land	6,225.79	0.34	11,907.36	0.31	23.08
32	Hang Lung Dev	4,009.99	0.22	9,129.43	0.23	12.26
33	Hysan Dev	3,252.41	0.18	8,095.73	0.21	9.54
	Total	1,133,377.64	62.24	3,136,306.20	80.72	
	Equity total	1,821,114.84	100.00	3,885,342.08	100.00	

Source of data: HKEx *Fact Book 2001*

The Hang Seng Composite Index Series

Since the late 1990s, there have been a rising number of Chinese-incorporated companies listed on HKEx, which led to the introduction of the Hang Seng Composite Index Series on 3 October 2001. The Hang Seng Composite Index Series comprises two distinct groups: the geographical series (Hang Seng Hong Kong Composite Index, and Hang Seng Mainland Composite Index) and the industry series (Oil and

Resources, Industrial Goods, Consumer Goods, Services, Utilities, Financials, Properties and Construction, Information Technology, and Conglomerates). These specific indices provide a more accurate picture of the performance of specific groups of companies. The Hang Seng Composite Index Series aims to cover ninety-five per cent of the market capitalization of stocks listed on the Main Board of HKEx, and there are currently 200 constituent stocks.

To be eligible for inclusion in the Hang Seng Hong Kong Composite Index, a company must derive the majority of its sales revenue from Hong Kong or places outside mainland China. There are three sub-indices under this index. Among the constituent stocks in the Hang Seng Hong Kong Composite Index, stocks are ranked according to their market capitalization. The top fifteen stocks by market capitalization form the Hang Seng HK LargeCap Index, stocks ranked sixteenth to fiftieth form the Hang Seng HK Mid-Cap Index, and those ranked fifty-first and below form the Hang Seng HK SmallCap Index.

To be eligible for inclusion in the Hang Seng Mainland China Composite Index, a company has to derive at least fifty per cent of its sales revenue from mainland China. The two sub-indices under this index are the Hang Seng China-Affiliated Corporations Index (HSCCI) and the Hang Seng China Enterprises Index (HSCEI). The HSCCI was introduced on 16 June 1997 to monitor the performance of red chips. The original base day was 4 January 1993, with the index value set at 1,000. The base day was later reset at 3 January 2000, with the base value set to 2000. To be included in the HSCCI, the company must not be incorporated in China but must be at least thirty-five per cent owned by Chinese enterprises or authorities for a minimum of twelve months. The number of red chips rose from fifty-nine at the end of 1997 to sixty-eight at the end of 2001. Only twenty-seven out of the sixty-eight red chips are included in the HSCCI, but they are quite representative of the red chips in general.

The HSCEI is a value-weighted index introduced in August 1994. It is intended to measure the performance of the H-shares listed on HKEx. The base day is 3 January 2000, with the base value set to 2000. The number of H-shares increased from thirty-nine in 1997 to fifty in 2000. At the end of 2000, only twenty-five out of the fifty H-shares were included in the HSCEI. However, these twenty-five stocks accounted for 2.21 per cent of the total market capitalization, while the entire fifty H-shares accounted for 2.57 per cent. Therefore, the HSCEI is considered to be very representative of the H-shares.

Morgan Stanley Capital International Hong Kong Index

It is not possible to compare the performance of different stock markets using their local market indices, as the selection criteria and computation methods may differ. To facilitate such comparisons, Morgan Stanley Capital International (MSCI) devised a MSCI index for each of the markets using a standardized approach.

The MSCI Hong Kong Index aims at better representing the local market and minimizing the effects from foreign markets. Thus, investment funds and companies with cross-ownership are minimized or excluded to avoid double counting. It is a value-weighted index. Although it includes more stocks than the HSI, it has a smaller market capitalization and is also sensitive to price changes in fewer stocks than the HSI.

The All-Ordinaries Index

The All-Ordinaries Index (AOI) includes all the stocks traded in HKEx,[5] so it reflects the Hong Kong market performance better than the HSI. Even though some stocks that have very thin trading are included in the AOI, it is not a serious problem as they only account for a small proportion of the total market capitalization. The AOI commenced on 2 January 1989 and is a value-weighted index. Its value was set at 1,000 on its base day, 2 April 1986. The constituents can be classified into seven sectors: Finance, Utilities, Properties, Consolidated Enterprises, Industrials, Hotels, and Others. Each has its own sectoral index. Table 11.3 shows the number of constituent stocks and the weighting of each sector in the AOI as at end of 2001. The AOI is computed as follows:

$$\text{Current AOI} = \frac{\text{Current Aggregate Market Value of AOI Constituents}}{\text{* Adjusted previous Minute's Aggregate Market Value}} \times \text{Previous Minute's AOI}$$

* The aggregate market value will be adjusted for capital changes and stock additions and deletions.

Table 11.3   The Number of Constituent Stocks and the Weighing of Each Sector in AOI as at End of 2001

Sector	Aggregate Market Value (HK$mil)	Weighting (%)	Number of stocks
Finance	1,142,376	29.40	52
Utilities	265,601	6.84	11
Properties	576,601	14.84	97
Consolidated Enterprises	1,435,118	36.94	236
Industrials	431,069	11.10	325
Hotels	27,974	0.72	14
Miscellaneous	6,363	0.16	8
	3,885,103	100.00	743

Source of data: HKEx *Fact Book 2001*

Growth Enterprises Index

The Growth Enterprise Market (GEM) began operations on 15 November 1999 as a secondary board to the Main Board, to provide capital formation facilities for growth companies that are usually not qualified to list on the Main Board. As of the end of 2001, 111 companies were listed on the GEM with a total market value of HK$61.0 billion, and the daily average turnover value during the year was HK$162 million. The number of GEM stocks rose to 127 as at the end of April 2002, and market value increased to HK$70.0 billion. The Growth Enterprise Index (GEI) is a value-weighted index designed to measure the overall performance of the Growth Enterprise Market. All of the GEM stocks are included in the GEI, which is updated every sixty seconds. The base date is on 17 March 2000, with the base value set to 1000. The GEI is calculated in a similar way to the AOI.

Hang Seng London Reference Index

As of 11 June 2001, twenty-nine of the thirty-three stocks in the HSI are traded on the London Stock Exchange (LSE). The daily performance of the HSI after the Hong Kong market has closed can be estimated by the performance of these twenty-nine stocks on the LSE using the Hang Seng London Reference Index (HSLRI). The HSLRI represents about ninety-five per cent of the market capitalization of HSI and about sixty-five per cent of the total market capitalization of the Hong Kong stock market. The HSLRI is computed using the following formula:

$$\text{Current HSLRI} = \frac{\text{Current Aggregate Market Value of HSLRI stocks}}{\text{HK Closing Market Value of HSLRI stocks}} \times \frac{\text{HK Closing}}{\text{HSI}}$$

Hang Seng Asia Index

The Hang Seng Asia Index (HSAI) commenced on 6 May 1996 and involves stock indices of eight Asia stock markets, namely Hong Kong (Hang Seng), Indonesia (JSX Composite), South Korea (Korea Composite), Malaysia (KLSE Composite), The Philippines (PSE Composite), Singapore (All-Sing Equities), Thailand (SET), and Taiwan (TSE Capitalization Weighted). All eight market indices are value-weighted and they represent more than eighty per cent of the total market capitalization of the stock exchanges they represent. The HSAI is in turn a value-weighted index of these eight indices.

Characteristics of the Hong Kong Equity Market

As of the end of December 2001, Hong Kong had a total market capitalization (Main Board and GEM) of HK$3,946.3 billion, making it the tenth largest stock exchange in the world and the second in Asia after

Japan. The Main Board had a listing of 756 companies and 1,075 securities by December 2001. The average daily turnover value of the Main Board and GEM during the year was HK$8.1 billion. Table 11.4 shows the various types of securities listed on HKEx.

Table 11.4 Number of Securities by Type Listed on HKEx as at December 2001

Type	Number Listed
Ordinary shares	757
Preference shares	5
Warrants	96
Equity warrants	74
Derivative warrants	22
Unit trusts/Mutual funds	22
Debt Securities	195

Source of data: HKEx *Fact Book 2001*

Ordinary and Preference Shares

From Table 11.4, we can see that the largest number of securities listed on HKEx is ordinary shares. They also account for most of the market's turnover. A company that is going public usually raises funds by issuing ordinary shares. Preference shares are not common on HKEx; they are not popular, as they pay fixed dividends and investors are more attracted by capital gains than dividend income.

Table 11.3 shows the breakdown of market capitalization for each sector in Hong Kong. The Consolidated Enterprises and Finance sectors account for more than one half of the total market capitalization, with about thirty-seven per cent and twenty-nine per cent respectively.

Table 11.5 The Ten Leading Firms in Stock Market Capitalization as at December 2001

Company	Market Capitalization (HK$mil)	Percentage of Total Market Capitalization
HSBC Holdings Plc	853,564.06	21.97
China Mobile (Hong Kong) Ltd	510,718.37	13.14
Hutchison Whampoa Ltd	320,818.65	6.26
Cheung Kong (Holdings) Ltd	187,609.31	4.83
Hang Seng Bank Ltd	163,940.51	4.22
Sun Hung Kai Properties Ltd	151,257.16	3.89
China Unicom Ltd	107,955.77	2.78
CLP Holdings Ltd	72,801.43	1.87
Hongkong Electric Holdings Ltd	61,893.59	1.59
Henderson Land Development Co Ltd	60,619.33	1.56
Total	2,491,178.18	62.11

Source of data: HKEx *Fact Book 2001*

The ten leading companies in stock market capitalization are presented in Table 11.5. The Hongkong and Shanghai Banking Corporation (HSBC) Holdings alone makes up 21.97 per cent of the total market capitalization. The ten firms have a total market capitalization of 62.11 per cent, suggesting that Hong Kong's stock market is top heavy. Unlike Hong Kong, the ten leading firms on the London Stock Exchange capture only fourteen per cent of the total market capitalization.

During the 1980s, much of the capital raised by locally listed companies was actually invested in factories in China. In fact, some of the IPO prospectuses emphasized Chinese investment as their objective. The stocks of such companies whose assets or earnings have significant Chinese exposure are known as China concept stocks.

Companies with Chinese entities as the controlling shareholders but which are incorporated and listed in Hong Kong are called red chips, and they are powerful and diversified conglomerates. An example of these companies is CITIC Pacific, which has been on the Hang Seng Index since 1992.

Recently, Hong Kong's stock market has allowed mainland Chinese firms to be directly listed on HKEx without having to set up a local holding company. The stocks of these companies are known as H-shares, and unlike the red chips, these firms usually specialize in a single business activity. Tsingtao Brewery Co Ltd was the first Chinese-incorporated firm to obtain a primary listing on the Main Board in 1993.

Table 11.6 shows the market capitalization of China-related stocks on HKEx from 1997 to 2001. The percentages of red chip stocks and H-shares have been on the increase since 1997. This signifies HKEx's role as a gateway to China, and thus it is becoming China's primary source of fund-raising.

Table 11.6   Market Capitalization of Red Chip Stocks and H-shares from 1997 to 2001

| | Red chip stocks | | H-shares | |
Year	Market Capitalization (HK$mil)	Percentage of Total Equity	Market Capitalization (HK$mil)	Percentage of Total Equity
1997	472,970.42	14.77	48,622.01	1.52
1998	334,966.21	12.58	33,532.66	1.26
1999	956,942.33	20.24	41,888.78	0.89
2000	1,203,551.95	25.10	85,139.58	1.78
2001	908,854.82	23.39	99,813.09	2.57

Source of data: HKEx *Fact Book 2001*

Warrants

A warrant on a stock gives the holder the right, not the obligation, to buy a specified number of shares at a specified exercise price within a specified time period. In Hong Kong, the exercise period is within one to five years. There are two types of warrant: equity and derivative. A company issuing the underlying stocks issues equity warrants. A third party, usually a financial institution (often a merchant bank), issues derivative warrants which can be on a stock, market index, or a basket of equities, currencies, or commodities. Both the equity and derivative warrants follow the American style, in which they can be exercised at any time prior to expiration.

Table 11.7 shows the number of equity and derivative warrants listed on the exchange from 1997 to 2001. In the late 1990s and 2000, warrants trading played a significant role in the total market turnover. However, there was a sharp decrease in the market value of warrants in 2001 from HK$16,004 million to HK$ 2,900 million.

Table 11.7 Warrant Issues on the HKEx from 1997 to 2001

Year	Number of Equity Warrants	Number of Derivative Warrants	Total Number of Warrants	Total Market Value of Warrants (HK$mil)
1997	187	346	533	16,391.82
1998	129	142	271	14,169.78
1999	100	92	192	19,809.27
2000	89	202	291	16,003.79
2001	74	22	96	2,900.86

Source of data: HKEx *Fact Book 2001*

Derivative warrants often flood the market in times of rising stock prices, as in 1997 and 2000. The changes in market conditions and investor sentiment appear to be far more marked in warrants than in many of the underlying cash market products. Recently, the derivative warrants have usually been short-term in nature. For example, there were 189 newly listed derivative warrants in 2001. However, the total number of derivative warrants outstanding by the end of the year was only twenty-two. With a few exceptions, all of the newly listed derivative warrants expired in the same year. In fact, all of the 189 issues were listed in the first half of 2001. This is partly due to the uncertainty created by the fact that the SFC had worked with HKEx to revise the rules for the listing of derivative warrants and review warrants applications.

Derivative warrants issues have been extended beyond individual stocks to baskets of stocks or equity indices in addition to containing exotic features. They are treated as 'sub-index options' and traded actively among other derivatives. Such warrants have certain advantages against single stock instruments, as they provide investors and fund managers with market or sector exposure at low investment costs. Moreover, the issuers of constituent stocks are companies from different industries, resulting in relatively lower total volatility due to diversification. It is believed that the derivative warrant market has a good future once the SFC and HKEx settle the revised rules for listing derivative warrants.

Investor Profile

The results of the Cash Market Transaction Survey 2000/2001 are shown in Table 11.8. The local individual and institutional investors remained as major market participants, comprising fifty-five per cent of the total market trading volume, which is a decrease from the sixty-seven per cent of the previous year. There was an increase in overseas participation from thirty per cent to forty-one per cent, especially from institutional investors.

In December 2001, the stock exchange conducted a survey on retail investor participation and reported that a typical Hong Kong retail stock investor was a forty-two-year-old professional or manager, with upper secondary or above education, and with a monthly personal income of about HK$18,750. Similar to the findings of the 1999 and 2000 surveys, retail investors made a median number of three transactions, which cost HK$30,000 each, within the previous twelve months.

Table 11.8   Distribution of Market Trading Volume by Investor Type from 1998 to 2001

	Percentage by Investor Type		
	1998/1999	*1999/2000*	*2000/2001*
Brokers' principal trading	5	3	4
Local individual investors	45	49	36
Local institutional investors	18	18	19
Overseas individual investors	1	2	3
Overseas institutional investors	30	28	38

Source of data: HKEx *Fact Book 2001*

Concepts of Risk and Return

An asset is priced according to its perceived risk level, and there exists a positive relationship between the expected return of the asset and its level of risk. That is, the higher the expected return, the riskier the stock. Therefore, investors face a trade-off: they must be prepared to take on a greater amount of risk if higher expected returns are desired, and they will achieve lower returns if they insist on a lower amount of risk. Thus, we should observe that no stock stochastically dominates any other, as arbitrageurs would eliminate these irregularities if they were to be found.

Measuring Risk

The total risk of an asset is measured by the volatility in its future returns. Volatility or dispersion from its mean can be in the form of variance, semivariance, standard deviation, range, or mean absolute deviation.

Variance and standard deviation are the proper measures of a security's total risk, since they meet the assumptions for a normal distribution.

One point to note is that the asset's return is in ex-ante form, whereas the standard deviation is in ex-post form. Though the nature of the two variables differs, Black *et al.* (1972) showed that ex-ante returns could be transformed into ex-post returns by working through the market model. Similarly, Poterba and Summers (1986) showed that current volatility changes had little impact on the forecast volatility over short periods. This implies that the ex-post standard deviation can be transformed into ex-ante form, given that the forecasts of volatility based on historical measures are stable and unbiased.

The total risk of an asset comprises two components: systematic and unsystematic risk. Unsystematic risk, also known as diversifiable risk, can be reduced or eliminated when two or more stocks are combined into a portfolio. Therefore, investors are not compensated for bearing unsystematic risk, as it can be diversified away. On the other hand, systematic risk cannot be diversified away. The price of the asset is determined by its level of systematic risk, which is measured by beta. Therefore, the appropriate measure of an asset's risk is beta—the covariance between the asset and the market portfolio.

Capital Asset Pricing Model

The capital asset pricing model was developed by Sharpe (1963, 1964), Lintner (1965), and Black (1972). While many empirical studies have been done to test the model, Roll's (1977) critique stated that an exact linear relationship between the expected return and beta exists 'if and only if' the market portfolio lies on the mean-variance efficient frontier. Since it is impossible to define a truly efficient market portfolio, this means that the CAPM cannot be empirically tested. Nonetheless, the CAPM is still used as an important pricing model for securities.

The CAPM is an equilibrium model, with the following assumptions:

1. The market is perfect: that is, there are no market imperfections such as taxes, regulations, or restrictions on short selling.
2. The market is frictionless, and information is simultaneously available to all investors at no cost.
3. Investors are price takers and have homogeneous expectations about the normal distribution of asset returns.
4. Investors can borrow or lend unlimited amounts at a known risk-free rate.
5. Investors are risk-averse and maximize the expected utility of their end-of-period wealth.
6. The quantities of assets are fixed, and all assets are marketable and perfectly divisible.

The expected return for stock i is given by the following CAPM equation:

$$E(R_i) = R_f + \beta_i [E(R_m) - R_f]$$

where $E(R_i)$ is the expected return on stock i, R_f is the risk-free rate, $E(R_m)$ is the expected return on the market portfolio, and $\beta_i [=\dfrac{\sigma(R_i, R_m)}{\sigma^2(R_m)}]$ is the beta of stock i and measures the co-movement of stock i with the market portfolio.

As β_i increases, the stock's risk premium $\beta_i [E(R_m) - R_f]$ also increases. This is consistent with the notion that investors are compensated for bearing systematic risk. The first property of the CAPM is that, in equilibrium, every security is priced such that its risk-adjusted return lies on the Security Market Line (SML). Assets that lie above the SML are underpriced, whereas those below the SML are overpriced. However, the actions of the arbitrageurs bring the assets' returns back to their equilibrium levels, suggesting that investors will not persistently find an underpriced or overpriced asset. The second property states that when securities are combined into portfolios, the measure of risk for individual securities is linearly additive. This means that the beta of the portfolio is the weighted average of the betas of individual securities.

The beta of the market is one and the beta of a risk-free asset is zero, as it is uncorrelated to the market portfolio. A stock with a beta greater than one means that it is riskier than the market index. It would outperform the index in a bullish market and would underperform in a bearish market. In Hong Kong, it was found that betas of listed companies in the property sector ranged from 0.5 to 0.8. Such stocks are more attractive when the market is down, since they fare better than the market index.

The CAPM can be applied in the corporate world to determine the acceptability of investment projects. First, the level of systematic risk, the beta of the project, has to be estimated. The project's expected return is then derived using the CAPM equation. A comparison between the expected return and the required return of the project allows a decision to be made. If the expected return is greater than the required return (the cost of capital for the project), the project is accepted, but rejected if the reverse is true.

Market Model

Prior to the CAPM, Sharpe (1963) developed the market model, which illustrates a simplified relationship between the stock and market returns. The return on security j is given as:

$$R_j = a_j + b_j * R_m + \varepsilon_j$$

where R_j is the return on security j, R_m is the return on the market portfolio, a_j and b_j are constants, and $\varepsilon_j \sim N(0, \sigma_\varepsilon^2)$. The market model is similar to the CAPM when we equate $b_j = \beta_i$ and $a_j = R_f(1 - \beta_i)$. In fact, the market model and CAPM are the same when $\beta_i = 1$ and $a_j = 0$.

Arbitrage Pricing Theory

Lintner (1969) found that the existence of heterogeneous expectations of investors did not critically affect the results of the CAPM. However, since investors have different information about the distribution of future returns, they would hold different market portfolios. Thus, the market portfolio might not be efficient and empirical tests of the model are not possible.

Developed by Ross (1976), the arbitrage pricing theory (APT) provides an alternative pricing model to CAPM. It is an equilibrium asset pricing model and assumes that the return on any asset is a linear function of k common factors that affect the asset's returns and is shown as:

$$R_i = E(R_i) + b_{i1}F_1 + \dots + b_{ik}F_k + \varepsilon_i$$

where R_i is the return on asset i, $E(R_i)$ is the expected return on asset i, b_{ik} is the sensitivity of asset i's returns to the kth factor, F_k is the mean zero kth factor common to the return of all assets under consideration, and ε_i is the zero mean noise term for asset i.

CAPM is a special case of APT when the market return is assumed to be the single relevant factor. A comparison between APT and CAPM reveals that APT is more robust than CAPM. First, APT makes no assumptions about the empirical distribution of asset returns. Second, a market portfolio is not required in APT, whereas an efficient market portfolio is necessary in CAPM. Last, APT measures the asset's equilibrium returns based on many factors, and thus it accounts for the returns that are not captured by beta.

Extensions of CAPM

CAPM is closely related to the concept of Efficient Market Hypothesis (EMH), which states that current market prices should reflect fully all available information. Deviations from market efficiency are termed as market anomalies; this will be discussed below. A point to note here is that the testing of CAPM is a joint hypothesis with the validity of EMH, leading to inconclusive results for the tests.

Fama and French (1992) believed that the size of the firm and the book-to-market (BTM) ratio could explain the cross-sectional returns, which were not captured by beta. Fama and French (1996) found that the firm size, BTM ratio, and beta explained most of the pricing anomalies and concluded that the single index CAPM is not sufficient. The results are consistent with APT, where two or more factors are used to explain the asset's returns.

Chan (1997) tested the CAPM in the Hong Kong stock market from 1984 to 1991. The results rejected the validity of CAPM, as they revealed that small firms with smaller betas earned much higher returns than the

CAPM predicted. This contradicts the intuition that small firms are riskier and thus have larger betas. This suggests that beta may not be a useful variable for explaining stock returns.

Chui and Wei (1998) reported that the average excess returns (portfolio returns minus risk-free rate) are positively related to BTM ratio, and negatively related to firm size. Regardless of the use of beta in univariate or multivariate analysis, a 'flat' relation between the market beta and stock return was always found. Similarly, Ho *et al.* (2000) found that beta does not describe the cross-sectional average returns at all, refuting the positive relation between beta and return as given in the CAPM equation. In the same study, a marginally significant firm-size effect was found in Hong Kong, where larger firms, due to their diversified activities, tend to have lower risk and therefore lower returns. There also exists a significantly positive relation between BTM and average return.

In Wong *et al.* (2002), the BTM ratio and beta were significantly positive, explaining the cross-sectional returns in the Hong Kong market for the period 1989 to 1997. The firm size was only significant in a quadratic model with an adjusted beta value, and was found to be insignificant in most of the linear models while holding BTM ratio and beta constant.

Based on the research done on the Hong Kong market, there seems to be an indication that the beta has failed to account significantly for the average stock returns. The BTM ratio is an important explanatory variable for stock returns, while the evidence on the firm-size effect is mixed.

Market Efficiency

Fama (1970, 1976) identified three forms of market efficiency: weak, semi-strong, and strong. The market is said to be weakly efficient when stock prices reflect relevant historical price information. Technical analysts try to make use of the weak-form efficiency by detecting patterns from past price movements and trading on possible opportunity windows. They believe that the past price history will be repeated in the future. The semi-strong-form efficiency requires the market to be efficient with respect to historical price information as well as publicly available information. In the strong-form efficient market, stock prices incorporate both public and private information. As such, no profits could be made from insider trading.

Chan and Fong (1996) examined the Hong Kong stock market's reactions to the buy, sell, and hold recommendations made by investment analysts of the *Hong Kong Economic Journal*, a local Chinese financial newspaper. Their results showed that the Hong Kong stock market was efficient during the one-year period examined. Fung (1999) found the existence of stock price overreaction in Hong Kong from 1980 to 1993, where the loser portfolios on average outperformed the winner portfolios by 9.9 per cent one year after the formation period, suggesting the inefficiency of the stock market. It seems that the evidence on the efficiency of the Hong Kong market is mixed. We will further illustrate this in the next section.

Market Anomalies

Turn-of-the-Year/January Effect

The turn-of-the-year effect, also known as the January effect, refers to the situation in which an abnormally high return is experienced in January over other months. It is reported that January outperforms non-January months after factoring in transaction costs. This was first documented in the US stock market by Rozeff and Kinney (1976). Gultekin and Gultekin (1983) extended it to international markets and found the existence of the January effect in twelve of the thirteen countries they examined.

To avoid being taxed on capital gains, investors sell stocks which have declined in value in December so as to incur short-term capital loss in order to reduce capital gains tax. Stock prices are therefore low because of this selling in December, returning to their equilibrium levels in January, leading in turn to the turn-of-the-year effect. This was supported by Reinganum (1983), Roll (1983), and Constantinides (1984). However, the argument of this 'tax-loss selling hypothesis' is weakened by Gultekin and Gultekin (1983) and Draper and Paudyal (1997). They found high January returns also in countries with fiscal year-ends that do not coincide with calendar year-ends. Lakonishok and Smidt (1988) also found that high January returns existed in the US before the introduction of the income tax system. These results have made the tax-loss selling hypothesis less convincing.

Ritter and Chopra (1989) offered another explanation for the January effect. They proposed that the portfolio rebalancing at the turn of the year—for the purpose of window dressing—causes the January effect. As they are evaluated on a calendar-year basis, the fund managers might rebalance their portfolios after evaluation to include more risky (higher return) stocks in January. Thus, the inflow of money into the stock market might contribute to the January effect.

Being aware of the January effect, investors can arbitrage by buying in December and selling in January. Chen (1989) found that after adjusting for transaction costs, investors in Hong Kong could earn an excess return of about six per cent by trading on this effect. Ho (1990), Cheung *et al.* (1994), and Agrawal and Tandon (1994) also found that the January effect was prevalent in the Hong Kong market. The returns in January are significantly large and positive compared to the returns in the non-January months. This is consistent with the findings in other stock markets.

In contrast to the findings by Keim (1983), Chui and Wei (1998) found that in Hong Kong it was the large firms, not the small firms, which experienced higher returns in January. They proposed that it was due to the composition of the market participants. During the sample period, foreign institutional investors were the major players in the Hong Kong stock market. This group of investors focused on the blue chips, which are usually large-firm stocks. So the buying pressure in large stocks in January leads to large firms recording higher returns in January.

Since there is no capital gains tax in Hong Kong and the tax year-end is in March, the tax-loss selling hypothesis should not be applied as an explanation of the January effect. Chen (1989), Ho (1990), Cheung *et al.* (1994), and Agrawal and Tandon (1994) confirmed that January returns were higher than April returns. One argument is that the bonus pay at calendar year-end leads to higher buying pressure in January than in other months. The higher stock return in January could be caused by the buying pressure, which might lead to inflated stock prices.

Turn-of-the-Month/Intra-Month Effect

Ariel (1987) found that stock returns were generally higher on average during the first half of the month. This is known as the turn-of-the-month effect, which illustrates the concentration of higher than average returns around the first few days of each month. Consistent with Ariel's findings, Lakonishok and Smidt (1988) revealed that positive returns from the first half of each month were concentrated in the four-day period, from the last trading day of a month to the third trading day of the following month in the US market.

Extending the work of Ariel (1987) to other markets, Wong (1995) found that the intra-month effect was not significant in the Hong Kong stock market. Similarly, Agrawal and Tandon (1994) also found little evidence supporting the presence of the turn-of-the-month effect in Hong Kong. Wong and Ho (1997) showed that the intra-month effect did occur in Hong Kong during the period 1985 to 1989. However, this turn-of-the-month effect diminished and became insignificant after 1989.

Day-of-the-Week/Weekend Effect

Seasonality has been found in daily stock returns, indicating that the probability distributions of daily returns vary significantly from day to day. This day-of-the-week effect refers to the phenomenon where Monday's return is negative and Friday's return is typically higher than that of other weekdays. This effect was documented by Cross (1973), French (1980), and Gibbons and Hess (1981) in the US market. Agrawal and Tandon (1994) extended the analysis to international markets and found that thirteen out of the eighteen countries examined had negative returns on Monday, twelve had negative returns on Tuesday, and most of them had large and positive returns on Friday.

Rogalski (1984) suggested that the information released at weekends is primarily negative. Investors might short-sell just prior to the Friday close, when stock prices are high. They also close out their positions at the following Monday open in anticipation of lower stock prices due to the negative information being disseminated over the weekend.

Ho (1990), Lee *et al.* (1990), Wong *et al.* (1992), and Ho and Cheung (1994), using Hong Kong data prior to 1990, found that the returns on Monday were negative but not significant. The returns on Tuesday and Thursday were positive and insignificant, and the returns on Wednesday and most of the returns on Friday were significantly positive. The findings seem to support the presence of the weekend effect in Hong Kong. However, any gains earned by trading on this weekend effect would most likely be offset by the transaction costs incurred. McGuinness (1997) found that the average daily return was negative after taking into account the round-trip transaction costs. At the same time, he found, using data from 1994 to 1996, that the returns on Monday and Friday were negative but not significant. The returns on the other weekdays were positive, but only the Tuesday return was significant. The difference could be due to the change in the settlement period.

The settlement period for stock trading in Hong Kong was changed from T+1 to T+2 in 1992. Using the T+1 period before 1992, investors had to make payment within one business day after the transaction. If an investor bought stock on a Friday, he would be given two extra days of credit; but he would not sell stock on a Friday, as he would receive payment only on Monday. This increased the buying pressure on Fridays and the selling pressure on Mondays (and possibly also Tuesdays), causing a strong weekend effect. The change in the settlement period to T+2 implies that by buying stock on Thursdays the investor will be given three extra days of credit, so the buying pressure is increased on Thursdays, leading to higher Thursday returns. McGuinness (1997) showed that the average return on Thursday (0.16 per cent) was higher than that on Friday (–0.01 per cent) under the current T+2 system. This illustrates the weakening of the weekend effect.

Holiday Effect

The holiday effect means that the average daily stock return is higher on the day before a holiday than those on the remaining days of the year. The studies by Roll (1983), Keim (1983), Lakonishok and Smidt (1984), and Ariel (1990) demonstrated support for this effect in the US market. Cadsby and Ratner (1992) and Kim and Park (1994) also provided evidence for the holiday effect in Australia, Canada, Japan, and the UK. It is suggested that investors tend to close out their short positions before a holiday, as they are worried that adverse news could be released when the market is closed during the holiday period.

Mok (1990) conducted a study on the Hong Kong stock market and found that there was an increase in stock prices on the eve of the Lunar New Year for all sixteen years of data. In the recent work of Cervera and Keim (1999), the mean return on a pre-holiday day was higher (0.42 per cent) than the mean return on other days (0.07 per cent), but the difference was insignificant. Therefore, the support for the holiday effect is somewhat weak in Hong Kong.

Earnings-Yield Effect

The earnings-yield effect implies that high earnings-yield stocks (value stocks) tend to have higher average returns than low earnings-yield stocks (growth stocks). This was found by Basu (1977), who reported a positive relationship between earnings-yield and the average risk-adjusted return of stocks. The findings by Reinganum (1981) also support the earnings-yield effect in the US market, but Ho *et al.* (2000) found that the earnings-yield effect was not significant in Hong Kong during the period 1980 to 1994.

Overall, there is not much evidence on the turn-of-the-month, earnings-yield, and holiday effects available for the Hong Kong stock market. As for the January and weekend effects, they are significant. However, the weekend effect has been diminishing since the change in the settlement period from T+1 to T+2. It is not likely that the day-of-the-week effect can be used to earn abnormal returns, because of transaction costs.

Internationalization of HKEx

The reforms and regulations implemented in 1987 and 1999 have set HKEx on its path to becoming an international market. The move to bring HKEx to international standards has developed the market infrastructure by promoting transparency, disclosure, and efficiency. The established trading, clearing, and settlement systems also increase international participation as overseas investors have greater confidence in the Hong Kong market. The SFC creates a level playing field by providing investors equal access to pertinent information. In addition, the principle of *caveat emptor*—'let the buyer beware', where investors are responsible for their own actions—is in place.

HKEx has been negotiating a series of possible trades among various stock exchanges. It has arranged for the trading of global securities in Hong Kong under the NASDAQ Amex Pilot Programme. This allows Hong Kong investors to trade on a small number of established securities listed on NASDAQ. Other agreements include the strategic initiative with the Sydney Futures Exchange to explore the development of a range of new derivatives trading and clearing services for the Asia exchange-traded and over-the-counter marketplaces. There are also discussions with the New York Stock Exchange (NYSE) on a possible link between NYSE, HKEx, and the Toronto Stock Exchange in the Global Equity Market partnership. All of these moves suggest that HKEx is moving towards the internationalization of its exchange services.

Table 11.9 provides a comparison of the market statistics of various regional and international stock exchanges. There are two striking differences between the regional and international markets: the number of listed firms and the market capitalization. The number of listed firms in each regional stock exchange is less than 800, compared to more than 2,000 listed companies in each international market. The market capitalization of the regional stock exchanges ranges from US$36.59 billion for Thailand to US$498.20 billion for Hong Kong. In contrast, the market capitalization of international exchanges ranges from US$2,579.99 billion for London to US$11,442.38 billion for New York.

Table 11.9 Comparison of Market Statistics of Various Regional and International Stock Exchanges, 2001

Market	Number of listed firms	Market Capitalization* (US$ billion)	Annual Turnover* (US$ billion)	Ratio of Turnover to Market Cap.*	P/E Ratio	Dividend Yield (%)	Trading Methods	Trading Hours	Trading Hours per Day	Trading Days	Delivery Period
Hong Kong	867	506.07	238.14	0.47	12.18	2.92	AMS/3	10.00–12.30; 14.30–16.00	4	Mon – Fri	T+2
Malaysia	807	118.98	21.03	0.18	65.36	2.52	SCORE	9.00–12.30; 14.30–17.00	6	Mon – Fri	T+3
Singapore	492	117.34	68.80	0.59	16.75	2.62	CLOB	9.30–12.30; 14.00–17.00	6	Mon – Fri	T+3
South Korea	688	194.47	380.51	1.96	29.30	1.70	SMATS	9.30–11.30; 13.00–15.00	4	Mon – Fri	T+2
Taiwan	586	292.62	544.17	1.86	41.57	4.85	CATS	9.00–13.30	4.5	Mon – Fri	T+2
Thailand	385	35.95	31.03	0.86	4.92	2.06	ASSET	10.00–12.30; 14.30–16.30	4.5	Mon – Fri	T+3
London	2,332	2,164.72	1,877.17	0.86	20.29	2.59	SETS	8.00–16.30	8.5	Mon – Fri	T+3
New York	2,400	11,026.59	9,601.65	0.87	25.2	1.24	Super Dot	9.30–16.00	7.5	Mon – Fri	T+3
Shanghai (A-Shares)	636	326.48	240.93	0.74	37.6	0.98	STAQ	9.00–11.30; 13.00–1500	4.5	Mon – Fri	T+3
Tokyo	2,141	2,264.53	1,656.32	0.73	61.40	1.30	CORES	9.00–11.00; 12.30–15.00	4.5	Mon – Fri	T+3

* The values for market capitalization, annual turnover, and ratio of turnover to market capitalization are based on listed shares of domestic companies only. The values for the P/E ratio and dividend yield of New York Stock Exchange are based on the year 2000.

Sources of data: Fact Books and official web pages of the various exchanges and World Federation of Exchanges.

Among the regional markets, Taiwan has the highest annual trading volume of US$532.25 billion, South Korea is in close second place with US$516.77 billion, and Thailand has the lowest with US$35.92 billion. The high trading volumes also translate into high turnover-to-market-capitalization ratios for Taiwan (1.80) and South Korea (3.34). The relatively low transaction costs in both Taiwan and South Korea might account for the relatively higher trading volume in these two markets.

The price-earnings (P/E) ratio of the regional markets ranges from a low 4.92 in Thailand to a high 41.57 in Taiwan, while the Tokyo Stock Exchange has the highest P/E ratio of 170.80 among the ten markets examined. The dividend yield in the regional markets does vary quite a lot: it ranges from 2.06 per cent to 4.61 per cent.

All of the regional exchanges trade from Monday to Friday. The daily trading hours range from fours hours in Hong Kong to six in Singapore and Malaysia. The opening and closing hours of the various exchanges with respect to those of the Tokyo and New York stock exchanges are shown in Table 11.10. Considering all of the exchanges, we can conclude that the stock market does not close, as different markets are linked together, trading twenty-four hours a day worldwide. Regardless of the timing, there is a continuous international transmission of information from one market to another; when the Singapore Exchange closes, the London Stock Exchange opens for trading, and *vice versa*.

Table 11.10 Opening and closing hours of selected stock exchanges

US Eastern Standard Time	*Opening and Closing Hours of Stock Exchanges*
7.00pm	Tokyo stock exchange opens
7.30pm	South Korea stock exchange opens
8.00pm	Taiwan stock exchange opens
8.30pm	Kuala Lumpur and Singapore stock exchanges open
9.00pm	Hong Kong exchange opens
10.30pm	Thailand stock exchange opens
11.00pm	Taiwan stock exchange closes
1.00am	Tokyo and South Korea stock exchanges close
2.55am	Hong Kong exchange closes
4.00am	London stock exchange opens; Kuala Lumpur and Singapore exchanges close
4.30pm	Thailand stock exchange closes
9.30am	New York stock exchange opens
11.00am	London stock exchange closes
4.00pm	New York stock exchange closes

Source of data: Fact Books and official web pages of the various exchanges

Discussion Questions

1. What are the major economic functions of a stock-trading market? Elaborate your answer by referring to its roles for the companies, the investors, and the economy.
2. Briefly discuss the major rules and regulations of stocks trading in Hong Kong's market.
3. Discuss the trading mechanism in the Hong Kong exchange. Elaborate your answer, highlighting the market order system and different types of limit order system.
4. How are the stock transactions settled in Hong Kong? Distinguish between the Continuous Net Settlement (CNS) and the Isolated Trade Settlement (ITS) systems.
5. Explain how the short-selling of shares is managed in the Hong Kong exchange. How is the risk of share lenders protected?
6. What is the role of the stock market index in asset pricing? What are the different indices available for stocks traded on the Hong Kong exchange? Distinguish between the Hang Seng Index and the Hang Seng Composite Index Series.
7. Briefly describe the historical developments of Hong Kong Exchanges and Clearing Limited (HKEx).
8. Explain the CAPM, APT, and market efficiency theories. How are the CAPM and market efficiency theories interrelated? Discuss the empirical evidence on the tests of CAPM in Hong Kong.
9. What are the different types of market anomaly? Provide an analysis of the evidence of market anomalies in the Hong Kong stock market.
10. Provide a comparative analysis of the regional and international markets.

Keywords

All-Ordinaries Index
arbitrage pricing theory
automated order matching and execution system (AMS)
beta
capital asset pricing model (CAPM)
Central Clearing and Settlement System (CCASS)
Continuous Net Settlement
day-of-the-week/weekend effect
earnings-yield effect
economic functions of trading market
equity trading rules
Growth Enterprises Index
H-shares
holiday effect

12. The Financial Futures, Options, and Swap Markets

R. Terpstra and Worapot Ongkrutaraksa

Introduction

Derivative financial instruments can be quite bewildering, particularly in terms of the terminology used to describe their characteristics. In the simplest terms, derivative instruments are contracts that create opportunities for investors to transfer or exchange specified cash flows at particular points of time in the future. Most importantly, the behaviour of these specified cash flows is derived from their reference to underlying commodities, including individual securities and financial indices, which are traded in cash markets.

The growth in the trading of derivative instruments has been dramatic in all major securities markets throughout the world, and Hong Kong is no exception. In fact the trading of options, warrants, and futures consistently accounts for a substantial portion of the total value of the transactions on the Hong Kong Exchange. Complementing these traded derivatives is an over-the-counter (OTC) market where both options and swaps are popular products. As a result, Hong Kong has become one of the largest and most active derivatives markets in the Pacific Rim.

This chapter will provide an overview of the derivative instruments that are popular in Hong Kong together with a description of how these instruments influence the manner in which people manage their investments. It begins with a discussion of the characteristics and functions of futures contracts together with a review of some useful trading strategies. This will be followed by a similar review of financial options (i.e., options on common stock and common stock indexes) and a discussion of the similarities and differences between futures and options. The chapter will conclude with a description of interest rate swaps and the development of a swap market in Hong Kong.

Characteristics of Financial Futures Contracts

One of the most popular derivatives in Hong Kong is the Hang Seng Index (HSI) Futures Contract and its close cousin, the Mini HSI Futures Contract. As such they represent an agreement to buy or sell the HSI on a specific date in the future at the future or settlement price. Every transaction involves a buyer and seller, where the buyer is said to be in a long position and the seller a short position.

The very essence of a futures agreement means the positions are set up without an initial transfer of funds between the buyer and seller. This makes the futures price quite unlike the price of most other financial instruments. A stock price, for instance, is what an investor pays for a share of stock and the right to receive dividends and resell the stock; and a bond price is what an investor is willing to pay for the right to receive future interest and principal payments. A futures price is neither of these. A futures contract is an agreement to trade at a future date at the futures or settlement price. One does not 'buy' the contract by paying the 'future price'. The futures contract merely stipulates that the parties promise to transact at that price in the future.

A 'good faith' security deposit, referred to as margin, must be paid when opening a futures position. This deposit is very small relative to the value of the contract and thus allows for considerable leverage. The margin is held by a clearing house and is to ensure that the buyer/seller can complete the contract at expiration.

The clearing house is an agent or subsidiary of the futures exchange and is unique to exchange-based transactions in contrast with over-the-counter transactions. The most important role of the clearing house is to serve as counterparty to every transaction. In other words, once the buyers and sellers settle on a transaction price, the clearing house will act as a buyer to every seller and a seller to every buyer.

Another role of the clearing house is to determine the settlement price at the end of each trading day. This price is based upon the closing bid–ask prices or last transacted price. If the settlement price is higher than the previous day's settlement price, the difference is credited to the margin accounts of those holding long positions and charged to the margin accounts of those holding short positions. If the settlement price is lower than the previous day, the difference is credited to those holding short positions and charged to those holding long positions. This is called the daily settlement or 'marking-to-market'. It is intended to monitor the financial integrity of the parties to the contract on a daily basis. While this is a significant factor in the maintenance of trust in the context of exchange-based trading, it has little or no impact on the futures prices.

Each account must maintain a minimum margin. If the daily settlement results in a deficiency in the margin account, additional funds must be deposited or the broker must close out the contract by selling (or, for short positions, buying) it back in the market. Excess margin can be withdrawn or left to meet future margin calls.

The Futures Market Participants

Traditionally, futures markets have served the needs of four user groups: those who want information about future prices of assets or indexes; those who want to speculate; those who want to transfer risk by hedging; and those who engage in arbitrage.

The first group consists of market-watchers who look to the futures markets for unbiased information about what will happen to the spot price in the future. For example, the HSI Futures Contract is viewed as a popular barometer of market sentiment in Hong Kong. A strong premium on HSI Futures over the spot index is thought to bode well for the future performance of the cash market, while a discount on the futures may trigger selling. Unfortunately the accuracy of futures prices as predictors of future spot prices is somewhat disappointing as there is a tendency for such forecasts to have large errors. However, the forecasts seem to be as good as any other; and they are inexpensive as they are readily available from futures exchanges.

Speculators make up another important user group, particularly in Hong Kong. In fact, annual surveys conducted by the Hong Kong Futures Exchange, and more recently by the Hong Kong Exchange, have found that 'pure traders', or speculators, account for about three-quarters of the futures transactions. Speculators enter the futures market in search of profit by increasing their risk exposure. For example, if you buy a stock index futures contract it is as if you are betting that the Hang Seng Index will rise. If it does rise, you can make a profit, but if it falls, you will lose. As a speculator, you are taking risks. Alternatively, if instead of buying you decide to sell a stock index futures contract *and* you don't own any of the stocks in the index, then again you are speculating by taking on risk in search of profit. You do not have any pre-existing risk exposure because you do not own any of the index stocks. Thus, the profit you might earn is viewed as compensation for risk taking. Whether or not you belong to this group and are pursuing a speculative motive, however, depends upon your current investments. If you buy contracts but are not short the underlying commodity, or if you sell contracts but do not own or plan to purchase the underlying commodity in the future, you are a speculator.

Speculators are sometimes classified by the length of time they plan to hold a position. The shortest period would range from a few seconds to a few minutes, and traders in this category are called scalpers. Normally they do not expect to make much profit on each trade, but they trade frequently. Since they are almost certain to be members of the Exchange, their transactions costs are very low. Another category is day traders who profit from price movements that take place over the course of one trading day and will not maintain their position overnight. The majority of speculators are either scalpers or day traders. Those who hold their positions overnight are called position traders. While there are no statistics available to indicate the trading volume of these three categories of trader in Hong Kong, the behaviour of the open interest does shed some light on the magnitude of position trades. Open interest is simply the number of outstanding or 'unliquidated' contracts for both long and short positions. Since daily changes in the total open interest typically account for less than fifteen per cent of the daily volume of transactions, it suggests that trades by scalpers and day traders greatly outnumber those of position traders.

The third user group, the hedger, tries to reduce risk by entering the futures market with a pre-existing position or in anticipation of establishing a position sometime in the future. This group accounts for between ten and twenty per cent of the futures transactions in Hong Kong. Referring back to the previous example of someone who sold a stock index futures contract, if he owned the index stocks he would be hedging. No matter which way the index moved, he would have offsetting gains and losses. Hedgers may wish to buy or sell futures contracts, depending upon the nature of their pre-existing or anticipated position.

Hedging is often viewed as a form of insurance, with the premiums paid to the speculators who bear the risk the hedgers are trying to avoid. In some instances, however, no speculators are needed as long as the long and short hedgers balance each other's positions. Thus, hedgers as a group need speculators to assume the risk whenever there is a mismatch between long and short hedgers. This does not mean that speculators are not performing a useful service unless there is a mismatch. Any activity by hedgers or speculators brings liquidity to the market and makes it easier and less costly for all participants to trade.

The fourth user group consists of the arbitrageurs, or those who seek to profit from divergence between the prices of the futures and their underlying assets. Since mispricing conditions are necessary for prompting transactions by this group, the volume arbitrage transactions tend to be quite volatile. In Hong Kong, arbitrageurs occasionally account for a substantial portion of futures transactions while, on average, the percentage of the annual futures transactions by this group has been between ten and fifteen per cent. To see how the process might work, consider the investment strategy involving arbitrage between the cash market and the Hang Seng Index Futures contract depicted in Table 12.1. Arbitrage opportunities arise when the equilibrium or theoretical futures price differs from the actual futures price. As you can see, the underlying asset—the HSI in this example—plays a crucial role in establishing the theoretical price of the futures contract. In fact, for financial index futures, the theoretical price will be same as the value of the underlying index when the risk-free rate of interest equals the dividend yield on the index.

To simplify the arithmetic, the futures contract we are pricing will not expire for one year—normally contracts are not available that far out. Under the assumed conditions, the theoretical price of the futures contract is $11,000(1 + 0.05 - 0.03)^{365/365}$ or $11,220, while its actual price is $11,500, or a difference of $280 or basis points. Since the price of the futures contract exceeds its theoretical value, it is 'overpriced' relative to the cash market and the proper investment strategy is to sell or short the futures and simultaneously establish a long position for an equal amount in the index portfolio.

This position is held until the futures contract expires and the position is unwound. The fact that the settlement price of the futures contract must equal the cash price of the index portfolio at expiration, i.e. $F_{expiration} = I_{expiration}$, means this arbitrage strategy will always yield a gain that equals the mispricing of the futures contract at the time the position is established.

It should be emphasized that the outcome described in this example does not depend on the assumption about the level of the index in the

Table 12.1   Arbitrage in the Hang Seng Index Futures

ASSUMPTIONS
1. There are no transactions costs or taxes.
2. Interest rates and dividends for the period under consideration are known with certainty.
3. Margin deposits earn interest at the risk-free rate.
4. Initial market setting:
    - Quoted price for Hang Seng Index Futures contract at time t is $11,500
    - Spot price of the Hang Seng Index at time t is $11,000
    - Annual Dividend yield on the Hang Seng Index is 3%
    - One-year risk-free rate of interest is 5%
    - The Hang Seng Futures contract will expire in one year
5. The theoretical price for a futures contract can be expressed as:

$$F^e_{(t,T)} = I_t (1 + r - d)^{T/365}$$

where:

$F^e_{(t,T)}$ = the equilibrium, theoretical, or arbitrage-free futures price at time
     t for a contract that expires in T days.
I_t = the underlying stock index at time t.
d = the annual dividend yield on the index.
R = the annual risk-free rate of interest.

ARBITRAGE STRATEGY

Stock Market	Futures Market

t = 0 • Borrow $11,000 at 5% and
        • Purchase a $11,000 portfolio
          of index stocks
	t = 0 • Sell a one-year futures
	          contract for $11,500

t = 365 • Receive dividends of $330
          or $11,000 (.03)
        • Sell the portfolio of index
          stocks for $11,500 for a
          total cash inflow of $11,830
        • Repay debt of $11,550 or
          (1.05) $11,000
	t = 365 • Buy a one-year futures
	           contract for $11,500

PAYOFF
Net cash flow or gain from the strategy = $11,830 – $11,550 or $280 per contract

---

cash market at expiration of the futures contract. The level of the index at expiration simply does not matter. If it had gone up in our example, the additional gain from the sale of the portfolio would be offset by the loss on the futures position. That is why the existence of arbitrage opportunities produces the seeds for 'risk-free' gains. The prospect of these gains, in turn, motivates arbitrageurs to transact in a manner that will eliminate the mispricing in the market.

Seldom do the various futures contracts traded in Hong Kong sell at their theoretical prices. This does not necessarily mean that unexploited arbitrage opportunities exist in Hong Kong, as there may be departures from the previously cited assumption of the pricing model. When various transactions costs are considered, theoretical prices may diverge from actual prices without producing arbitrage opportunities. In addition, another departure from the assumptions used in the example involves the margin that traders must put up against outstanding contracts. In Hong Kong at present, members of the Exchange can use Exchange Fund bills to meet the margin requirement, but clients must put up cash.

Another explanation for the existence of unexploited arbitrage opportunities is the manner in which the expiration settlement price for equity futures is established in Hong Kong. Rather than using the value of the underlying asset at the close of trading as employed in the example, the Hong Kong Exchange uses the average of the quotations for the underlying asset taken at five-minute intervals during the last day of trading. This means that F will not equal I at expiration.

Types and Specifications of Financial Futures Products in Hong Kong

Despite the fact that a number of new types of financial futures products have been introduced in Hong Kong in recent years, the product of choice since its inception in 1986 is clearly the HSI Futures contract. The various products available, as of January 2002, are summarized in Table 12.2.

Table 12.2   Exchange-Traded Financial Futures Contracts in Hong Kong

Contract	Date Introduced	Trading Volume (Expressed as percentage of total number of futures contracts traded in 2000)
HSI Futures	May 1986	89.7%
Mini HSI Futures	October 2000	2.7
MSCI China Free Index Futures	May 2001	Not traded in 2000
Stock Futures	March 1985	Nil
International Stock Futures	October 2001	Not traded in 2000
Rolling Forex:		
Japanese Yen	November 1995	Nil
British Pound	September 1996	Nil
Euro	April 1999	Nil
1-Month HIBOR* Futures	October 1998	0.3
3-Month HIBOR* Futures	September 1997	7.3

* Hong Kong Interbank Offered Rate

Over the years, a number of other products have come and gone, such as the HSI Sub-Indices Futures, the Hang Seng 100 Futures, and the Red

Chip Index Futures, and it seems that the GBP Rolling Forex contracts may be destined to incur the same fate.

As you can see, trading in the HSI Futures contract accounted for nearly ninety per cent of the total transactions in futures contracts for 2000, while there was virtually no trading in stock futures or Rolling Forex contracts. The recently introduced Mini HSI Futures contract has proved to be quite popular as well. In only three months of trading it accounted for 2.7 per cent of the total futures contracts traded for the entire year. Both of the HSI Futures contracts are particularly popular with local retail investors, who accounted for fifty per cent of the HSI Futures and eighty-eight per cent of the Mini HSI Futures transactions in 2000. The three-month HIBOR Futures was the most actively traded interest rate futures, and is clearly preferred by institutional investors, who were responsible for seventy-nine per cent of the transactions in 2000.

The contract specifications for the HSI Futures, the Mini HSI Futures, and the three-month HIBOR Futures contracts are presented in Table 12.3. As revealed in the table, the Mini HSI is nothing more than a scaled-down version of the HSI Futures. The only differences between the contracts are the contract size, minimum fluctuation, and margin requirements, with the Mini HSI Futures having smaller values for all three of these features.

The settlement prices for both of the index futures are established by the clearing house at the close of each trading day. For all but the last trading day, the settlement prices for each quoted month are calculated as follows:

1. If the last trade was less than or equal to the closing bid price, the settlement is the bid price at close. For example, if the bid is 11,490, the ask 11,500, and the last trade was at 11,485, the settlement price is set at 11,490.
2. If the last trade was greater than or equal to the closing ask price, the settlement is the ask price at the close. Using the bid–ask prices of the previous example, if the price of the last trade was 11,505, the settlement would be set at 11,500.
3. If the last trade was between the closing bid–ask prices, the settlement is the price of the last trade. For example, if the last trade was at 11,495 while the closing bid–ask were 11,490–11,500, the settlement price would be 11,495.
4. If there has been no trading in the quoted month, the settlement price is set equal to the mid-point of the closing bid–ask spread.
5. If there has been no trading nor any bids or offers in the quoted month, the settlement price will be set by the clearing house.

As mentioned previously, the final settlement price is set quite differently. HSI quotes are taken every five minutes during the last day of trading, and the final settlement is set equal to the average of these quotes, rounded down to the nearest whole number. As a result, the futures prices and spot prices converge on the final day of trading, but only in terms of an average price as opposed to a particular closing price.

Table 12.3 Contract Specifications of Selected Futures Products

Specification	Hang Seng Index Futures	Mini Hang Seng Index Futures	3-Month HIBOR Futures
Contract Size	The Hang Seng Index Futures times HK$50	The Hang Seng Index Futures times HK$10	HK$1,000,000
Quotation	Index Points	Index Points	100 minus the 3-mth HIBOR Rate
Minimum Fluctuation	One Index Point (HK$50)	One Index Point (HK$10)	One Basis Point (HK$25)
Delivery or Trading Months	Spot month, the next calendar month and the next two calendar quarters (Mar, Jun, Sep, and Dec)	Spot month, the next Spot month, the next calendar month and the next two calendar and quarterly months quarters (Mar, Jun, Sep, and Dec)	Two calendar months (Mar, Jun, Sep, and Dec) up to two years ahead
Trading Hours Hong Kong Time	Two trading sessions: 9.15am – 12.30pm; 2.00pm – 4.15pm Except last trading day. 9.45am – 12.30pm; 2.30pm – 4.00pm	Two trading sessions: 9.15am – 12.30pm; 2.00pm – 4.15pm Except last trading day. 9.45am – 12.30pm; 2.30pm – 4.00pm	Two trading sessions: 8.30am – 12.00 noon; 1.30pm – 5.00pm Except last trading day. One trading session: 8.30am – 11.00am
Last Trading Day	The business day preceding the last business day of the month	The business day preceding the last business day of the month	Two business before the third Wednesday of contract month
Settlement Day	The first business day after the last trading day	The first business day after the last trading day	The third Wednesday of the contract month
Settlement Price	An average of quotations for the HSI taken at five-minute intervals during the last trading day, rounded down to the nearest whole number	An average of quotations for the HSI taken at five-minute intervals during the last trading day, rounded down to the nearest whole number	100 minus the 3-mth HKAB interest settlement rate at 11:15 am on the last trading, rounded up to the nearest 0.01 of a percentage point, times HK$2,500
Settlement Method	Cash	Cash	Cash
Initial Margin	HK$44,250 (subject to change)	HK$8,850 (subject to change)	HK$1,200 (subject to change)
Maintenance Margin	HK$35,400 (subject to change)	HK$7,080 (subject to change)	HK$960 (subject to change)

Table 12.4 shows the settlement prices for the HSI Futures as they were reported in the *South China Morning Post* for the trading day 28 December 2001. The settlement price for the spot month HSI Futures contract was 11,387, and at HK$50 per index point represented a contract value of HK$569,350. Given the seventeen-point increase over the previous day's settlement of 11,370, the one-day increase in the contract value was HK$850. In the cash market, the HSI closed at 11,431.59 on 28 December 2001, a 72.09 increase over the previous day. Thus, the December HSI Futures sold at a discount to the cash market.

Table 12.4   Quotations for Hang Seng Stock Index Futures (For the Trading Day 28 December 2001)

Contract Month	Daily		Settlement		Lifetime		Volume	Open Interest	Change in Open Interest
	High	Low	Price	Change	High	Low			
Dec-01	11,388	11,301	11,387	+17	13,885	8,940	1,711	6,603	−4,706
Jan-02	11,471	11,344	11,459	+39	11,990	11,071	7,855	31,484	+5,780
Mar-02	11,413	11,290	11,402	+49	11,870	8,851	08	86	67
Jun-02	11,393	11,317	11,371	+87	11,865	10,405	30	490	+10

Source: South China Morning Post, 29 December 2001

For those who held long positions in the December contract from the previous day, their one-day gain was HK$850 per contract. Since contracts are marked to market at the close of each trading day, participants with long positions were credited with the gain. Meanwhile, those who were short lost HK$850 and had their accounts debited with the loss. Also, since the initial margin requirement in December 2001 was HK$44,250 per contract, the one-day profit of HK$850 for those with long positions translated into a one-day rate of return of 1.92 per cent.

The futures contracts on the three-month Hong Kong Interbank Offered Rate (HIBOR), like the HSI Futures, have standardized specification in size, maturity months, and minimum fluctuation. They are quoted in terms of an index that is measured by subtracting the interest rate from 100.00. For example, if the HIBOR is 3.5 per cent, the index becomes 96.5. Thus the daily quotes for HIBOR Futures vary inversely with interest rate expectations, and for each basis point increase (decrease) in expected interest rates, the quote for the HIBOR Futures index will decline (increase) by 0.01 per cent.

Table 12.5 shows the settlement prices for the three-month HIBOR Futures for the trading day 28 December 2001, as reported in the *South China Morning Post*. As indicated in the table, the settlement price for the spot month contract was 98.3, an increase of 0.03 from the previous day's settlement price. At HK$25 per basis point, the value of the contract was HK$245,750, and investors who held long positions from the previous day earned HK$75 per contract. Also, given that the calculation of the settlement price involves subtracting the future HIBOR three-month rate from 100, a settlement price of 98.3 equates to a three-month HIBOR Futures rate of 1.7 per cent.

Table 12.5   Quotations for the Three-month HIBOR Futures Contracts (for the Trading Day 28 December 2001)

Contract Month	Daily		Settlement		Lifetime		Volume	Open Interest	Change in Open Interest
	High	Low	Price	Change	High	Low			
Jan 02	98.00	98.00	98.03	+0.03	98.21	97.69	50	800	–
Feb 02	–	–	98.03	+0.03	98.00	97.90	–	15	–
Mar 02	97.90	97.90	97.95	+0.08	98.19	94.20	1	26,307	–
Jun 02	–	–	97.37	+0.08	97.75	93.03	–	22,117	–
Sep 02	–	–	96.55	+0.12	97.23	93.15	–	4,840	–
Dec 02	–	–	95.85	+0.13	96.55	94.57	–	3,350	–
Mar 03	–	–	95.15	+0.15	96.16	95.03	–	650	–
Jun 03	–	–	94.60	+0.13	96.13	94.80	–	600	–

Source of data: South China Morning Post, 29 December 2001

Since the prices of interest rate futures contracts vary with changes in interest rates, the increase in the settlement price might be viewed as an indication that traders were revising interest rate expectations downward. In addition, given that the spot rate for the three-month HIBOR at the close of trading on 28 December was 2.03 per cent, the 1.7 per cent rate implicit in the settlement price suggested that the anticipated trend in the three-month HIBOR rate until the contract expired on 16 January was downward.

An examination of the lifetime high and low settlement prices for the eight contracts listed in Table 12.5 reveals a mixed pattern of volatility. The differences in the highs and lows for the January and February contracts are very low, less than 100 basis points, while the variation in the June 2002 contract was 472 basis points. As will be discussed later, interest rate volatility is a major factor in shaping the attractiveness of interest rate derivatives.

Financial Futures Trading Strategies

A wide range of strategies is possible with financial futures. Basically all of the strategies seek to exploit, modify, or eliminate the risk exposure associated with the fluctuations in the value of the underlying financial instrument.

For those who want to exploit the risk of the stock market, for example, stock index futures contracts are very effective instruments. One of the most basic speculative strategies is to use stock index futures to profit from anticipated market movements. If a trader is bullish about the market and anticipates a major rally, he could simply buy a futures contract and hope for a price rise on the contract when the rally occurs. The high gearing and relatively low transactions cost make this an attractive strategy when compared to the alternative of taking a position in the index stocks in the cash market.

Stock index futures also permit investors to change their exposure to the underlying cash market much more quickly than by transacting in each of the underlying stocks. For example, a fund manager wishing to increase her exposure to Hong Kong stocks can do so quickly by buying HSI Futures contacts. If she wishes to hold the underlying stocks for the long term, she may roll the contracts over or buy the underlying stocks and unwind her futures position. Similarly, selling HSI Futures contracts can quickly reduce a portfolio's exposure to the HSI stocks.

While speculators do not play a major role in the HIBOR Futures market, nonetheless it is also an instrument that can be effective for exploiting opinions about the future course of interest rates. For example, if an investor thinks that interest rates have declined too far and are likely to rise, he can sell a HIBOR Futures contract. If interest rates do rise, the HIBOR Futures prices will fall and the investor will make a profit by buying the futures at a lower price to close out his position.

Financial futures markets also offer a means to hedge the risk of unexpected changes in the price of the underlying financial instrument. As such, hedging involves the transfer of price risk from hedgers to speculators and represents one of the major economic functions of futures markets.

Hedging with futures involves locking in a value for an investor's portfolio of stocks or loans. A hedge is simply the purchase (sale) of a futures market position as a temporary substitute for the purchase (sale) of the investor's portfolio in the cash market. If the prices of the stocks or loans that make up the portfolio move together with futures prices, any loss realized by the hedger in one position will be offset by a profit on the other position. When the profits and losses are equal, the hedge is called a perfect hedge.

In practice, hedging is not that simple. A perfect hedge can only be obtained when the cash market prices of the securities in the portfolio that is being hedged move identically with the prices of futures contracts used to hedge the portfolio. The difference between the cash and futures price is called the basis. The basis can be positive or negative and the chance of changes in the basis is called basis risk. The quotations for the HSI Futures in Table12.4 can be used to illustrate the basis for this product. The December contract's settlement price of 11,387 was forty-five points below the HSI closing value of 11,432. Also, as previously noted, the method used to determine the final settlement price for the HSI Futures does not guarantee convergence between the cash and futures prices and therefore creates basis risk. Thus, perfect hedges are seldom possible and hedging reduces risk to the extent that the basis risk is smaller than the price risk of the portfolio being hedged, as illustrated in Figure 12.1.

There are two basic types of hedge transaction: the short or selling hedge, and the long or buying hedge. A short hedge is used to protect

Figure 12.1 Return Distribution for Assets Hedged by Selling Futures

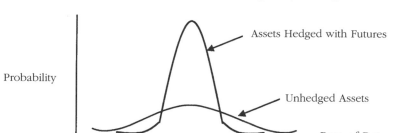

against the possibility of a price decline in the future cash value of a portfolio of index stocks or HIBOR loans. To execute a short hedge, the hedger sells futures to fix the future cash price and transfer the price risk of owning the portfolio to the buyer of the futures—for example, an investor who anticipates a general decline in the stock market but is reluctant to liquidate the portfolio of stocks he is holding. Selling stock index futures will compensate for the loss on his portfolio if the stock market declines as anticipated. This is also referred to as a cash hedge since it involves the hedge of an existing position in the cash market.

In contrast, a long hedge is undertaken to protect against changes in the price to be paid for the purchase of a portfolio of stocks or loans in the cash market at some time in the future. In a long hedge, the hedger buys futures contacts. For example, a fund manager who receives investment funds on a regular basis anticipates a 'bull' market in the next three weeks before the additional funds are received. By buying index futures he can lock in the current prices for the index stocks. When the additional funds are received, he can buy the index stocks in the cash market and use the profit from his long hedge to cover the appreciation in the stocks' values. In other words, he can effectively buy the index stocks in the cash market at prices that prevailed three weeks ago. This is also referred to as an anticipatory hedge, since the cash position that is being hedged has not been taken but is expected to be taken in the future.

Hedges may also be referred to as direct or cross hedges. When a futures contract is available in the financial instrument owned, a direct hedge may be established. When a futures contract is not available for the financial instrument to be hedged, a cross hedge may be constructed with a futures contract on another closely correlated index or instrument.

Characteristics of Exchange-Traded Financial Options Contracts

An option is defined as 'the exercise of the power of choice'. Consistent with this definition, an option contract provides the buyer the right, but not the obligation, to complete a transaction in a particular commodity, at a particular price, at some time in the future. Option contracts are similar to futures contracts in terms of their ability to provide the holder of the contract with a mechanism to lock in a future price for the underlying commodity. Unlike futures, however, the holder of the option can exercise the power of choice by deciding whether or not he wants to exercise his right to buy or sell the underlying commodity.

Options, like many other derivative products, trade either through organized exchanges or privately on over-the-counter markets. One of the advantages of exchange-traded derivatives is the significant reduction in credit or counterparty risk. As mentioned in the section on futures, this occurs because of the presence of the clearing house acting as a buyer to every seller and a seller to every buyer. The clearing house also guarantees the availability of funds to ensure performance of the contracts. In contrast, investors in OTC derivatives do not have recourse to such protection and must depend upon the creditworthiness of the counterparty. Another advantage of exchange-traded derivatives is the existence of a liquid market for trading the derivatives prior to expiration. In OTC markets, such opportunities do not generally exist and most parties to OTC derivatives must take their positions all the way through to settlement or expiration. Offsetting the advantages of exchange-traded derivatives is the standardization of the product in contrast with the ability to custom design the product's terms in the OTC.

The Language of Options

The parties to an options contract are commonly referred to as the holder or buyer and the writer or seller. The position of a holder is referred to as a long position and that of a writer as a short position. While the holders have no obligations to exercise their rights, writers are required to honour the contracts if the holders choose to exercise—regardless of how disadvantageous this may be to the writers. When writing options, the writers incur the risk of having to forego profits or suffer out-of-pocket losses. In return they receive a payment from the holders that is referred to as a premium. Thus, the price at which the option trades is commonly referred to as the option's premium, and it is the limit to the holder's exposure to the option contract.

There are two types of option: a call and a put. A contract that provides its holder with the right to buy the underlying asset is called a call option, while a contract that provides the right to sell is called a put option.

Every option contract has four defining elements: underlying asset, exercise or strike price, quantity, and exercise period. Every option is issued on an underlying asset. For options on financial instruments there is a wide range of products that can play this role, including a common stock, a stock index, a futures contract, a bond, or a currency. In Hong Kong, exchange-traded options are available on a variety of individual stocks as well as the Hang Seng Index. Table 12.6 provides a description of the exchange-traded options in Hong Kong.

Table 12.6   Specifications of Exchange Traded Options in Hong Kong

Specifications	Stock Options	HSI Options
Option Types	Puts and calls	Puts and calls
Contract Size	One board lot of the underlying shares	Index multiplied by HK$50
Contracted Value	Option premium times the contract size	Option premium times HK$50
Contract Months	Spot, the next two calendar months, and the next two quarter months	Short-dated options: Spot month, the next two calendar months, and the last months of the next three quarters Long-dated options: the next two months of June and December
Payout Protection Adjustments	In the event of a rights issue, bonus shares, unusually large dividend etc., the strike price and contract size will be adjusted to hold constant, as far as possible, the value of the option position	None
Option Premium	Quoted in HK$0.01	Quoted in whole index points
Exercise Style	American: options can be exercised at any time up to 5.30pm on any business day and including the last trading day	European: options may be exercised at expiration
Settlement on Exercise	Physical delivery of underlying shares	Cash settlement
Expiry Day	Business day immediately preceding the last business day of the contract month	Business day immediately preceding the last business day of the contract month
Assignment Method	Random	Not applicable
Official Settlement Price	Not applicable	Average of the quotations of the Hang Seng Index taken at five-minute intervals during the expiry day, rounded down to the nearest whole number

Specifications	Stock Options		HSI Options
Strike Prices	Share Price of Underlying Stock (HK$) up to $2 $2 to $5 $5 to $10 $10 to $20 $20 to $50 $50 to $200 $200 to $300 $300 to $500	Strike Price (HK$) $0.10 $0.20 $0.50 $1.00 $2.00 $5.00 $10.00 $20.00	For short-dated contracts, strike prices are set as follows: • At intervals of 50 index points at strike prices below 2,000 index points; • At intervals of 100 index points at strike prices • At or above 2,000 index points but below 8,000 index points; and • At intervals of 200 index points at strike prices • At or above 8,000 index points. For long-dated contracts: strike prices are set at approximately 5% above, at, and approximately 5% below the previous day's closing price of the HSI at the time of the options introduction for trading, rounded down to the nearest multiple of: • 50 index points with the strike prices below 2,000 index points; • 100 index points with the strike prices at or above 2,000 index points but below 8,000 index points; and • 200 index points with the strike prices at or above 8,000 index points.

The strike price, also known as the exercise price, is the price at which the underlying asset will be delivered if the option is exercised. A call option whose strike price is below the market price of the underlying asset is referred to as an in-the-money option. Such an option allows the call holder to buy the underlying asset for less than the current market price. A call whose strike price is above the underlying market price is said to be out-of-the-money. Conversely, a put whose strike price is above the underlying price is in-the-money. This means the put holder can sell the asset for more than the current market price. A put whose strike price is below the current market price is out-of-the-money. Only in-the-money options are likely to be exercised by their holders since they can buy or sell directly in the market at a better price. If an option's strike price is very close to the market price of the underlying asset, the option is said to be at-the-money.

There are two types of exercise: the American style and the European style. An American-style option can be exercised any time from its issuance up to its expiration. A European style can only be exercised at expiration. Since the American style offers more flexibility to its holders in terms of exercise, it can command a slight premium over its equivalent European-style option. All of the exchange-traded options in Hong Kong are American-style.

An option contract also specifies the quantity of the underlying asset that the option holder has the right to buy or sell. For exchange-traded stock options in Hong Kong, the number of shares represented by an option contract, or contract size, is equal to one board lot of the underlying stock. For HSI options, the contracts are cash settled-contracts of difference, which means there is no physical delivery if the HSI option is exercised. The notational quantity of the HSI option contract is HK$50 per index point.

The exercise period limits the life of an options contract. After the exercise period, the option can no longer be traded or exercised. The common exercise period for exchanged traded options is between one and nine months. In Hong Kong the length of the exercise period consists of the nearest three months and the next two quarterly months. It may come as a surprise to discover that most stock options expire unexercised. When an option is exercised, the exchange must select the short open position against which to exercise. This is done on a random basis and those chosen must deliver (in the case of a call option writer) or buy the underlying stock (in the case of a put option writer).

Another important feature of stock options is the so-called payout-protection rule. This is intended to protect investors in stock options from the possible adverse effects of capitalization changes associated with the stocks that underlie the options. For example, capitalization changes that result in the creation of shareholders' entitlements such as rights issues, stock splits, bonus shares, and unusually large dividends can have a significant effect on the price of the stock as soon as the entitlement passes. When the entitlement passes—the ex-day—the value of the shareholder's total portfolio will not change. The same is not true for the option holder, unless an appropriate adjustment is made to the terms of the option contract. Without a change to the exercise price and/or contract size, the adjustment to the share price in response to the capitalization change will arbitrarily and unfairly affect the value of the option position. A payout protection rule therefore ensures that the fair value of the option contracts is maintained after the ex-day has passed. For ordinary cash dividends that are not unusually large, however, no adjustment will be made and there will be some effect on the value of the option.

Pricing Stock Options

The price at which an option trades, or the premium, is ultimately determined by market forces. But there are certain factors that reliably shape the market's view of the option's value. Let us start with the simplest case: the terminal value or worth of an option when it expires, or the option's intrinsic value. For example, consider a call option with a $30 exercise price on a stock. At expiration, the option will either be worthless or equal to the difference between the option's exercise price or strike price and the market value of the underlying stock. In other words, if the stock price is at or below $30 at the expiration date, the call option will be worthless; if the stock price is above $30, the intrinsic value of a call will be equal to the stock price minus $30. This relationship is illustrated in Figure 12.2.

Figure 12.2 Terminal Value of a Call Option at Expiration

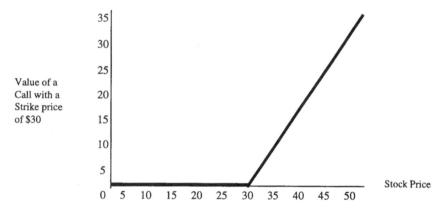

In the more difficult case—the interim value or worth of an option that has not yet reached its expiration date—it is necessary to view valuation in terms of 'upper' and 'lower' boundaries or limits. The lower limit of the value of a call option is the intrinsic value depicted in Figure 12.2. The upper limit is the market value of the underlying stock as illustrated by the 45-degree line emanating from the origin in Figure 12.3. It simply reflects the obvious fact that a rational investor would never pay more for an option than what it would cost to buy the underlying stock. Most of the time, however, the value of a call option before expiration will fall between the upper and lower limits, as shown by the curved, upward-sloping dashed line in Figure 12.3. This curve begins at zero, where the upper and lower limits meet, and rises gradually and becomes parallel to the lower limit. Thus the value of a call option increases as the stock price increases and is worthless when the stock price is worthless. Furthermore, when the stock price substantially exceeds the exercise price, the option's value approaches the stock price less the present value of the exercise price. The reasoning is that once the call option is 'deep-in-the-money', the probability that the stock price will fall below the exercise price before the option expires approaches zero, and exercise becomes a virtual certainty. It also means that the holder of the option effectively owns the stock and does not need to pay for it—by paying the exercise price—until later, when the option is exercised. This characteristic is sometimes referred to as the 'instalment credit' feature of call options and is one of the determinants of an option's so-called time value or the difference between the value of an option and its intrinsic value. In addition to interest rates and time to expiration, the time value of an option (i.e., the height of the dashed line in Figure 12.3) is influenced by the likelihood of substantial movements of the underlying stock price. In fact, stock price variability is one of the most important determinants of the time value of options and thus option prices. An option on a stock whose price is not expected to vary will not be worth very much unless the instalment credit feature is very attractive, i.e. interest rates are very high and the time to expiration is very long. On the other hand, an option on a stock whose price may half or double is valuable. Furthermore, a call option on a stock that has a high degree of expected price volatility *and* a long time to expiration would be more valuable than one that is about to expire. Finally, the dividend payout policy of a firm affects the time value of call options. A high dividend payout policy normally equates to a lower rate of capital gain or price appreciation for the firm's stock. It also decreases the potential payoff from a call option and thereby lowers its value.

Figure 12.3 Interim Value of a Call Option Prior to Expiration

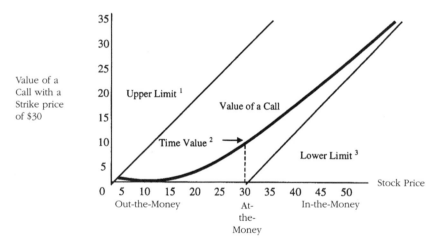

[1] Market value of the underlying stock
[2] Value of the call minus the intrinsic value
[3] Intrinsic value of the call option

Table 12.7 summarizes the influence of the six factors that have been discussed for both call and put options. As can be seen, values of put options respond to changes in three of the six factors—underlying stock price, interest rates, and dividend payout—in a manner that is opposite to the behaviour of call options. Since the buyer of a put acquires the right to sell a stock at the stated exercise price, one would expect the value of a put to increase in response to a declining stock price or increased dividend payout. The inverse relationship between the value of a put and changes in interest rates is not quite so obvious. The reasoning here is that the proceeds from a put occur in the future, if and when the put option is exercised. Since the present value of those proceeds is inversely related to interest rates, the value of the put is also inversely related. The time to expiration is the real surprise. There are actually two contrary effects. First, greater time to expiration tends to increase put values by widening the dispersion of possible future stock prices. Second, greater time to expiration, like higher interest rates, tends to decrease put values by lowering the proceeds from exercising the put. At lower stock prices relative to the exercise price, the latter effect dominates, since the increased dispersion has relatively little influence on put values. However, for put options that are well out-of-the-money, the opposite occurs and the first effect dominates.

Table 12.7 Factors Influencing Option Values

	Effect of an Increase of the Determining Factor on the value of	
Factors	*Call Options*	*Put Options*
Current Stock Price	Increase	Decrease
Exercise Price	Decrease	Increase
Time to expiration	Increase	Increase/Decrease*
Stock Price Volatility	Increase	Increase
Interest Rates	Increase	Decrease
Dividend Payout	Decrease	Increase

* Increase for well-out-of-the-money and decrease for near or at-the-money puts

Financial Options Trading Strategies

There is virtually no limit to the variety of payoff patterns that can be achieved by investing in calls and puts with various strike prices, either separately or in combination with each other or other securities. What matters most is the investor's motivation together with the expectations the investor would like to exploit. The following are examples of the more popular strategies.

Strategy Buying puts with an existing long position in underlying asset (covered position).

Motivation Desire to hedge or limit risk.

Expectation Bearish, overall market or specific stock to experience some downside variability.

For this strategy, an investor can limit the downside risk of an existing long position in an individual stock or a market portfolio by buying put options on the individual stock or market index. If the individual stock or market index subsequently declines, investors who employ this strategy can limit their downside losses by exercising their right to sell at the strike price. Thus investors maintain an exposure to upward movements but limit their exposure to downward movements to the strike price. The price of this form of 'insurance' is the put premium.

Strategy	Buying puts without an existing long position in underlying asset (naked position).
Motivation	Desire to speculate when the price of underlying asset falls.
Expectation	Bearish, overall market or specific stock is likely to experience downward movement.

An investor who is bearish about the prospects of an individual stock or market index can exploit her expectation by buying puts. The investor will incur a profit if the stock price or market index drops below the breakeven point, which equals the strike price minus the put premium. If the investor's expectations turn out to be incorrect and the individual stock or market index rises, the loss is limited to the put premium.

Strategy	Buying calls.
Motivation	Desire to speculate with a leverage effect or create an anticipatory hedge.
Expectation	Bullish, overall market or specific stock is likely to experience upward movement.

Investors who are bullish about the prospects of an individual stock or market index can exploit their expectation by buying calls. The investor will incur a profit if the stock price or market index rises above the breakeven point, which equals the strike price plus the call premium. Given the 'instalment credit' characteristic of a call option, this strategy provides investors with a leverage effect if their expectations prove to be correct. If the investor's expectations prove to be incorrect and the individual stock or market index drops, the loss is limited to the call premium. This strategy is also useful as an anticipatory hedge. This occurs when investors who only have enough money to pay the call premium but are going to have sufficient funds to purchase stocks at a later date and 'lock in' a price—the strike price—in anticipation of establishing a long position at a later date.

Strategy	Writing or selling calls without an existing long position.
Motivation	Desire to speculate.
Expectation	Bearish, overall market or specific stock is likely to decline.

Investors who sell calls without existing long positions profit from the receipt of the option premium as long as the market or individual stock does not rise above the strike price. If the investors' expectations prove to be incorrect, the potential loss is the difference between the level of the market index or price of the individual stock and the strike price less the call premium. Alternatively, investors employing this strategy can buy back the call to close their position and reduce further losses if their expectations fail to materialize.

Strategy   Writing or selling calls on an existing long position.
Motivation   Desire to enhance income.
Expectation   Stagnant to bearish, overall market or specific stock is likely to move sideways or decline.

This strategy is somewhat similar to the previous one, except that the investors have an existing long position in the market index or specific stock that underlies the option being sold. As a result, if the investors' expectation is correct, they can enhance the income from their long position by selling calls and receiving the premiums. If their expectations do not materialize, the losses incurred by this strategy are the same as in the previous strategy except that the losses will be 'opportunity losses', given their pre-existing long position.

Strategy   Buying a call and a put on the same market index or stock at the same strike price.
Motivation   Desire to speculate.
Expectation   Volatile market, overall market or specific stock is likely to move up or down.

This strategy is useful when an investor thinks the market or a specific stock is likely to encounter a big move, but he is not sure whether the move will be up or down. Thus the investor does not need to predict the direction of the price movement, only its magnitude. Referred to as a 'straddle', the profit from this strategy is measured by the extent to which the stock is 'in-the-money' by rising or falling, less the sum of the premiums paid for the put and call. Given the need to pay for both a put and call option, the strategy requires large price rises or falls in order to be profitable.

Characteristics of Interest Rate Swap Contracts and Forward Rate Agreements

Interest rate swap contracts are similar to financial futures contracts. By definition, an interest rate swap contract is an OTC agreement by which two parties known as counterparties agree to exchange their periodic cash flows derived from interest receipts or payments over the life of the swap contract. The amount of the interest payments exchanged is based upon the principal amount of the underlying debt instrument, called the notional amount. However, the only amount exchanged between the parties is the netted interest payment, not the notional amount. In a typical interest rate swap transaction, the first party, called a swap buyer, agrees to pay fixed interest payments to, and in turn receive floating interest payments from, the second party at pre-specified future dates. The second party, called a swap seller, agrees to make the floating-rate interest rate payments that vary with certain short-term reference rates such as Treasury-bill rate, prime rate, HIBOR, or London interbank offered rate (LIBOR) in exchange for the fixed-rate interest payments from the first party.

The gain and loss from buying and selling an interest rate swap will fluctuate with market interest rates, as shown in Table 12.8 below. When interest rates rise after the counterparties have entered the contract, the swap buyer will gain while the swap seller will lose; as interest rates fall, the swap buyer will lose while the swap seller will gain.

Table 12.8 Gain-and-Loss Profile of Swap Parties

Party	Interest Rates Rise	Interest Rates Fall
Swap Buyer	Gains	Loses
Swap Seller	Loses	Gains

The reason for this is that an interest rate swap contract allows the swap buyer to lock in the interest cost he is expected to pay no matter which direction the market interest rates move in the future. The swap seller, on the other hand, will be affected, as his interest receipts or payments are tied with the movements of the market interest rates. If he expects to receive interest income, then the rise in interest rates would certainly benefit him. However, the same interest rate increase would hurt this swap seller if he expects to make the interest payments.

Pricing Interest Rate Swap Contracts and Forward Rate Agreements

To understand the pricing mechanics for an interest rate swap, one could use the insights gained from the knowledge of futures contracts discussed earlier. The interest rate swap contract is related to its short-term counterpart, called a forward rate agreement (FRA). A forward rate agreement is an over-the-counter equivalent of the exchange-traded futures contract in which the parties agree that a certain interest rate will apply to a certain principal during a specified future period of time. The FRA can also be seen as a special case of the interest rate swap, in which there is only one settlement date.

There are conventions in a typical FRA worth defining; these include the contract date, settlement date, contract rate, reference rate, settlement rate, and notional amount. The parties to an FRA agree on the contract date (T_1) to buy and sell funds on the settlement date (T_2) in the future. The contract rate (R_k) is the fixed interest rate specified in the FRA at which the buyer of the FRA agrees to pay for funds and the seller of the FRA agrees to receive for investing funds. The reference rate (R_1) is the floating interest rate used in the FRA. The settlement rate (R_2) is the value of the reference rate at the FRA's settlement date, or future reference rate. The amount from which the interest payments are to be calculated under the FRA is called the notional principal (N). As in an interest rate swap contract, this amount is not exchanged between the two parties.

On T_1, the FRA buyer agrees to pay R_k—in other words, to buy N at the settlement date at R_k. The FRA seller agrees to receive R_k—or, equivalently, to sell N at the settlement date at R_k. If, on T_2, R_2 is greater than R_k, the FRA buyer will gain because he can borrow N at a below-market rate. If R_2 is less than R_k, this will benefit the FRA seller, who can lend N at an above-market rate. If R_2 is the same as R_k, neither party will benefit.

On T_2, one party must compensate the party that benefits from the difference between R_2 and R_k. The FRA buyer will receive compensation if the former is greater than the latter. Similarly, the FRA seller receives compensation if the former is lower than the latter.

The compensation amount is calculated as follows:

Compensation = Interest payment difference / $[1 + R_2$ x (Days to contract period / 360)]

where: Interest payment difference = $|R_2 - R_k|$ x N x (Days to contract period / 360)

It is important, however, to note that the amount that must be exchanged at T_2 is not the interest payment difference, but rather the present value (PV) of the interest payment difference. The discounting method used to derive the PV is the continuous discounted cash flow (DCF) method.[1]

The value of the FRA or of the interest rate swap can be found by taking the present value of these two sets of interest flow:

Swap Value = $[N e^{R_k (T_2 - T_1)} e^{-R_2 T_2}] - [N e^{-R_1 T_1}]$

where: $[N e^{R_k (T_2 - T_1)} e^{-R_2 T_2}]$ = PV of the interest flow to be received on T_2

$-[N e^{-R_1 T_1}]$ = PV of the interest flow to be paid on T_1

$R_k = (R_2 T_2 - R_1 T_2) / (T_2 - T_1)$

Interpretation of Interest Rate Swap Position

There are two ways to interpret an interest rate swap position: first as a portfolio of FRAs or interest rate futures contracts (IRFs), and second as a package of cash flows resulting from buying (or investment in) short-term, and selling (or being financed by) long-term, instruments in the spot market as opposed to the futures market.

Interest Rate Swap as a Portfolio of Futures Market Transactions

It is important to note first the difference between FRA and IRF. For the FRA, the unit of analysis is an 'interest rate'. In contrast, the unit of analysis for the IRF is a 'market value' of the underlying asset, such as a price of a fixed-income instrument. Since the FRA and the IRF have different units of analysis, Table 12.9 shows how the changes in the market interest rates can affect the payoffs to the buyers and sellers of both FRA and IRF.

Table 12.9   Swap as a Portfolio of FRAs and of IRFs

	Settlement Rate Rises		Settlement Rate Falls	
Party	FRA	IRF	FRA	IRF
Buyer of	Gains	Loses	Loses	Gains
Seller of	Loses	Gains	Gains	Loses

Using the conventions defined above, the buyer of FRA gains if R_2 rises above R_k and loses if R_2 falls below R_k. Taking a long position in a portfolio of FRAs yields identical results as those shown in Table 12.18, since the FRA buyer assumes the position of the swap buyer, while the FRA seller takes the same position as the swap seller.

Considering the long position in an IRF portfolio, the buyer of IRF loses if R_2 rises above R_k and gains if R_2 falls below R_k. Comparing the gain and loss with those of the interest rate swap party in Table 12.8, the gain-and-loss profiles are complete opposites. This is because the movement of the interest rates has an 'inverse' relationship with the movement in the market value of the fixed-income instrument. As a result, the IRF buyer would assume the same position as the swap seller, whereas the IRF seller would take a similar position to the swap buyer.

The pricing of an interest rate swap will depend on the price of a package of FRA with the same settlement dates and in which the underlying rate for the FRA is the same reference rate. Using interest rate swaps proves to be more beneficial than trading FRA or IRF alone because interest rate swaps can accommodate longer maturity with one contract, which effectively saves transaction costs for both parties. Moreover, the liquidity of the interest rate swap markets has grown rapidly since inception in 1981.

Interest Rate Swap as a Portfolio of Spot Market Transactions

An interest rate swap contract can also be seen as a net cash-flow position resulting from a combination of an investment in a floating-rate instrument (i.e., a long position in money market securities) and a financing of such an investment using a fixed-rate instrument (i.e., a short position in fixed-income securities), which effectively generates the equivalent cash-flow payoffs. Considering the financing side of this transaction, the combination calls for fixed-rate interest payments. For this fixed-rate payer, the transactions involve buying a floating-rate instrument and issuing a fixed-rate obligation. For the floating-rate payer, the transactions would be equivalent to buying a fixed-rate bond and financing that bond purchase with a floating-rate loan.

Equivalently, a fixed-rate payer can be viewed as being a swap buyer who desires to lock in his future interest payment. Assume that the floating-rate investment is based on the six-month LIBOR and the fixed-rate semi-annual obligation is based on the ten per cent annual interest rate, Table 12.10 below illustrates how the package of investment in short-term securities financed by long-term borrowing can be arranged for the fixed-rate payer to yield the same net cash-flow position as that of the swap buyer.

Table 12.10 Swap as a Portfolio of Short-Term Investment and Long-term Financing

Period	Floating-Rate Investment	Fixed-Rate Borrowing	Net Cash Flow
0	− $100	+ $100	$0
1	+(LIBOR$_1$/2) x 100	− 5	+(LIBOR$_1$/2) x 100 − 5
2	+(LIBOR$_2$/2) x 100	− 5	+(LIBOR$_2$/2) x 100 − 5
3	+(LIBOR$_3$/2) x 100	− 5	+(LIBOR$_3$/2) x 100 − 5
4	+(LIBOR$_4$/2) x 100	− 5	+(LIBOR$_4$/2) x 100 − 5
5	+(LIBOR$_5$/2) x 100	− 5	+(LIBOR$_5$/2) x 100 − 5
6	+(LIBOR$_6$/2) x 100	− 5	+(LIBOR$_6$/2) x 100 − 5
7	+(LIBOR$_7$/2) x 100	− 5	+(LIBOR$_7$/2) x 100 − 5
8	+(LIBOR$_8$/2) x 100	− 5	+(LIBOR$_8$/2) x 100 − 5
9	+(LIBOR$_9$/2) x 100	− 5	+(LIBOR$_9$/2) x 100 − 5
10	+(LIBOR$_{10}$/2) x 100 + 100	− 105	+(LIBOR$_{10}$/2) x 100 − 5

When some dynamics in the market interest rate are put into the picture, an increase in LIBOR would increase the net cash flow of this portfolio, whereas a decrease in LIBOR would reduce the portfolio's net cash flow. This is similar to the gain-and-loss profiles of the FRA buyer and the buyer of an interest rate swap. The opposite effects on the net cash flow are true if the investment is based on the fixed interest rate and the borrowing on the floating rate. In this situation, the gain-and-loss profiles from holding such a portfolio are akin to those of the FRA seller and of the seller of an interest rate swap.

The Market for Interest Rate Swaps in Hong Kong

The interest rate swap market in Hong Kong is inextricably connected to the US interest rate swap market because of the Hong Kong dollar's peg to the US dollar, along with the interest rate parity that stems from such a close tie between the two currencies. Since its inception in the early 1980s, the interest rate swap market in Hong Kong has experienced constant development, adding a greater breadth of variety and depth of sophistication for the market participants. Until the mid-1990s, long-term interest rate swap contracts were still thinly traded. Shortly afterwards, they became more ubiquitous, even before the first ten-year fixed income instruments issued by the Hong Kong Exchange Fund (HKEF) in late 1996.

In order to fully appreciate the interest rate swap market in Hong Kong, we should be able to identify who the important market participants are, along with their motives to use swaps and to gain some perspective on the chronological development of the market itself.

Swap Market Participants and Their Motives

There are two types of market participant in the swap market: the natural floating-rate payers who want to swap for fixed-rate payments and become swap buyers, and the natural fixed-rate payers wanting to pay floating rates, thereby becoming swap sellers. Along with their natural cash-flow positions, both types of market participant have different motives in buying or selling swaps. The first kind of motive for swap counterparties is to hedge their interest rate risk. As market interest rates rise, the natural floating-rate payers would want to buy swaps in order to reduce their rising interest payments. When the market interest rates start to fall, the natural fixed-rate payers would seek to sell swaps so that their fixed-rate obligations are lightened. Most hedging-motivated participants are firms and financial institutions that are attempting to lower their financing costs as well as optimizing their asset and liability portfolios.

The second kind of swap motive is for arbitraging the interest rates between two markets. Such an arbitrage opportunity is possible when interest-rate spread exists in yield curves between two different currencies. For example, an arbitrageur would initially borrow from the low-yield US dollar market and then swap the interest payments with a counterparty who has invested in the high-yield Hong Kong dollar market for a certain swap transaction fee. The net result is that the arbitrageur effectively utilizes the swap arrangement as a vehicle to mobilize a cheaper US dollar fund in order to tap a higher-yield Hong Kong dollar investment opportunity without having to convert the underlying US dollar principal into a Hong Kong dollar one. However, the arbitrage opportunity will quickly disappear whenever the swap transaction fee exceeds the profit from arbitrage or the yield-curve spread between the two currencies diminishes.

As the market interest rates began declining in the early 1980s, banks operating in Hong Kong were more interested in selling interest rate swaps (i.e., receiving a fixed rate and paying a floating rate) to profit from lower floating-rate obligations. From 1987 onwards, however, the market interest rates began to rise, causing shrinkage in banks' interest margins. At the same time, the interest rate swap market in Hong Kong began to lose its attractiveness and momentum. Without the swap-selling counterparty to which their interest-rate risk could be shifted, Hong Kong-based banks continued to suffer deteriorating profitability and started to look for other means of hedging their interest-rate exposure.

Historically, an important swap buyer in Hong Kong has been the Mass Transit Railway Corporation (MTRC). From 1976 until the end of the 1980s, the MTRC was a leading buyer of interest rate swaps due to its natural position as a floating-rate payer. By the mid-1990s, the firm embarked on an infrastructure project to build new subway lines linking its existing systems with the new Chep Lap Kok International Airport on Lantau Island. In order to finance this mega-project, the MTRC began to buy long-term swaps to change its floating-rate interest payments into fixed-rate ones. This coincided with the preference of many banks to sell their swaps in order to become the counterparty to MTRC.

It was quite fortunate for Hong Kong that after the introduction of HKEF debt securities in 1990, an interest-rate hedging instrument had emerged and been available in the organized market in which the HKEF itself also acted as a swap counterparty. Practically, the HKEF entered the swap market whenever they issued bonds and simultaneously swapped their fixed-rate obligations to floating-rate ones.

During the early to mid-1980s, however, the banks were willing to take the fixed long position under Hong Kong dollar interest rate swaps as interest rates began to fall, while gradually profiting from paying the lower floating rates. The big players since the start of the Hong Kong dollar swap market had been major American banks such as Bankers Trust, J. P. Morgan, and CitiGroup, as well as the Hongkong and Shanghai Banking Corporation (HSBC). The book runners on local floating-rate debt instruments were underwriting the instruments, entering the swap contracts—which converted the issuer's obligations to a fixed rate—and then keeping the fixed long positions on their own books.

Swap Market Development in Hong Kong

As interest rates rose in both the US and Hong Kong credit markets in 1987, the banks receiving fixed rates and paying higher floating rates were adversely affected by the asset-liability positions they had taken. A year later, the Hong Kong swap market began to lose its attractiveness; yet its resilience was demonstrated when the market made a rebound in the early 1990s. First, there were ever increasing numbers of receivers of fixed-rate Hong Kong dollars in the market; with growing levels of sophistication, traditional Hong Kong investors such as the Hong Kong Jockey Club and the Schools Fund were more ready to receive fixed-rate interest flows. Second, the development of private banking had brought to the market large private clients with a greater appetite for different instruments, creating a larger pool of fixed-rate receivers. Third, arbitrage opportunities between the US and the Hong Kong dollar yield curves had revived the banks' interest in the swap market.

Based on the third factor alone, most investors were interested in the fact that there was a steady spread between the US and the Hong Kong dollar yield curves, which tracked each other, with the Hong Kong dollar traditionally showing a steeper and higher curve (with usually about a thirty to forty basis-point difference between the two yield curves). This gave investors an arbitrage opportunity by receiving the higher fixed-rate Hong Kong dollar and paying fixed-rate US dollars on a swap or on the underlying obligation and capturing the spread. By the early 1990s, this arbitrage opportunity was being pursued by most banks as well as other market participants. In effect, the spreads between the two yield curves forcibly became narrower until the arbitrage positions were no longer attractive.

Soon afterwards the Hong Kong swap market was revitalized with the help of the HKEF's fixed-rate Hong Kong dollar bond market. From 1989, foreign fixed-income issuers such as the World Bank and other players began to issue bonds in fixed-rate Hong Kong dollars and then swap their obligations into floating- or fixed-rate US dollars. The fixed-rate bank issuers of negotiable certificates of deposit (NCD) also re-entered the market at this time, having had no issuing opportunities after the death of the swap market in 1988. For these intermediaries, they were eagerly interested in swapping their fixed-rate NCDs to floating-rate Hong Kong dollar obligations.

However, the Hong Kong dollar swap market was unstable, engendering and enticing many speculative transactions in the early 1990s. The market began to stabilize and mature over 1995–6 as transactions gained in volume and frequency. The maturing of the market meant that there would be fewer speculative positioning and arbitrage opportunities for active participants, which led to a shrinking number of international market players from the large group of the early 1990s that had included many European, Japanese, and American firms. By 1996, the Hong Kong swap market became an exclusive arena for banks that would claim the sophistication required to generate profits in such a mature climate: these included major American institutions and some European banks, such as the Union Bank of Switzerland (UBS) and HSBC. Most of the local banks entered the market as clients of these major financial institutions. The active participants are those who quote prices on swaps and hedge their positions through the active management of their own swap books rather than by taking a matching position.

In summary, the current Hong Kong swap market can be seen as a relatively active market, with a wide range of local and global market participants, and prices quoted by the organized HKEF and large financial institutions. Conventional Hong Kong dollar swap transactions are arranged on a matching basis between those financial institutions. As a result of the increased volume and frequency in swap transactions, financial institutions set up off-balance-sheet (OBS) accounts to net their transactions without matching all individual payers and receivers. However, local corporate clients have been conservative in their use of derivative interest-rate products in spite of the depth of the Hong Kong dollar swap market, which allows a wide range of interest rate swap products to be arranged where demand arises.

Interest Rate Swap Arrangement Strategies

Between any two counterparties, the typical arrangements for an interest-rate swap involve the periodic exchange of a fixed stream of interest flows for a variable stream of interest flows for one party, and *vice versa* for the other party to the swap contract. The interest flows that are exchanged can be either the cash inflow or the cash outflow. With respect to the swap arrangement strategies, there are two broad objectives. The first is for the swap counterparties to lock in their net interest margins (NIMs) as a result of asset and liability duration matching. The duration swap arrangement pertaining to the first objective is discussed in detail in the following sub-section. The second objective is concerned only with the liability side of the balance sheet, in that both swap counterparties attempt to minimize their costs of financing based on the comparative advantage argument. Under this second objective, two strategies can be implemented: quality swap and basis swap.

Strategy 1: Locking in the Net Interest Margin through Duration Swap Transactions

One of the more frequently arranged interest rate swaps among banks and other financial institutions is a duration swap as the need for it arises from duration matching between the institution's asset and liability portfolios. For the purposes of asset-liability management (ALM), banks whose average asset portfolio duration is greater than the average liability portfolio duration—the positive duration gap—would want to swap out their fixed-rate interest income for floating-rate cash inflow so that the expected rise in market interest rates, which directly affects bank funding costs, would have a lower negative impact on their NIMs. However, if the market interest rates were to fall instead of rise, the positive-duration gap institutions would not be so interested in selling their fixed-rate interest income, simply because they still enjoy the falling costs of funding.

On the other hand, financial institutions, such as insurance companies, whose average asset portfolio duration is less than the average liability portfolio duration—the negative duration gap—would prefer swap arrangements that provide them with fixed-rate interest income when market interest rates are expected to fall, as they tend to decrease the company's NIMs. When the market interest rates actually rise instead of falling, negative-duration gap institutions should not swap, as rising interest rates would naturally increase their NIMs.

In order for duration swaps to be successfully arranged, both counterparties should have not only the opposite duration gaps but also different expectations in terms of future interest rate movement. The following scenario and tables help illustrate how duration swap is set up and arranged by a third-party duration matchmaker.

Duration Swap Scenario

1. Two institutions have duration mismatch in their asset and liability portfolios and wish to lock in their NIMs from undesirable movements of market interest rates.
2. First-party institution has a positive-duration gap with a cash inflow from long-duration asset portfolio (i.e., fixed rate) and a cash outflow for short-duration liability portfolio (i.e., floating rate). It is afraid of an unexpected increase in short-term interest rates because such an increase will hurt its target NIM.
3. Second-party institution has a negative-duration gap with a cash inflow from short-duration asset portfolio (i.e., floating rate) and a cash outflow for long-duration liability portfolio (i.e., fixed rate). It fears an unexpected decrease in short-term interest rates because such a decrease will reduce its target NIM.
4. Third-party institution intervenes to arrange interest-rate swaps for both institutions.

Table 12.11 provides the input variables for both swap counterparties in terms of interest rates underlying their asset and liability portfolios as well as their desirable NIMs. Table 12.12 includes additional inputs to short-term floating rates in which the first party must pay 140 basis points on top of its HIBOR payment of 4.6 per cent, whereas the second party will receive 150 basis points in addition to its LIBOR receipt of three per cent. Both parties' current NIMs and duration gaps are then calculated accordingly. The pre-swap NIM of the first party was two per cent, whereas that of the second party was –0.5 per cent.

Table 12.11 Asset-Liability Portfolios and Target NIMs

Swap Party	Short-Term Rate Portfolio	Swap Party	Long-Term Rate Portfolio	Swap Party	Target NIM
1st Party pays	HIBOR 4.60%	1st Party gets	Lending Rate 8.00%	1st Party	3.00%
2nd Party gets	LIBOR 3.00%	2nd Party pays	Deposit Rate 5.00%	2nd Party	2.50%

Table 12.12 Swap Parties' Duration Gaps

Swap Party	Cash Inflow	Cash Outflow	Pre-Swap NIM	Duration Gap
1st Party	8.00% + 0.00% = 8.00%	4.60% + 1.40% = 6.00%	2.00%	Positive Gap
2nd Party	3.00% + 1.50% = 3.50%	5.00% + 0.00% = 5.00%	–0.50%	Negative Gap

With the target NIMs of 3 per cent and 2.5 per cent for the first and the second party, which are provided as the inputs in Table 12.11, the third-party swap arranger has proposed in Table 12.13 that the first party makes a fixed-rate interest payment of the 8 per cent it originally received from the swap arranger in exchange for the receipt of HIBOR plus 4.4 per cent, while the second party pays LIBOR plus 1.5 per cent to, and receives 7.5 per cent fixed interest cash flow from, the swap arranger.

Table 12.13 Swap Arranger's Proposition

Swap Party	Floating Rate	Fixed Rate
1st Party	Gets HIBOR + 4.40% from swap arranger	Pays 8.00% to swap arranger
2nd Party	Pays LIBOR + 1.50% to swap arranger	Gets **7.50%** from swap arranger

In Table 12.14, both swap counterparties would be able to realize their target NIMs after they have adopted the swap deal proposed by the third-party swap arranger. It clearly follows that the first party's fixed-rate interest receipt from its asset portfolio and payment to the swap arranger cancel each other out, while the floating-rate interest payment to its liability portfolio is less than the floating-rate interest income from the swap arranger, leaving it with a post-swap NIM of 3 per cent no matter which direction the market interest rates take. The same logic applies to the second party, who receives the locked-in, post-swap NIM of 2.5 per cent.[2]

Table 12.14 Duration Swap Outcomes

Swap Party	Receipts		Payments		Post-Swap NIM
	Short-Term Rate	Long-Term Rate	Short-Term Rate	Long-Term Rate	
1st Party	HIBOR + 4.40%	8.00%	HIBOR + 1.40%	8.00%	3.00%
2nd Party	LIBOR + 1.50%	**7.50%**	LIBOR + 1.50%	5.00%	2.50%

Strategy 2: Lowering the Cost of Funding through Quality Swap Transactions

The second swap arrangement strategy involves the exchange of interest payments between the two counterparties based upon the comparative advantage argument with the objective of minimizing the overall costs of financing their liabilities. Assume that both parties can borrow funds from both the money market and the capital market, but the credit ratings, which indicate the quality of a borrower's creditworthiness, of the two parties differ. Assume further that the first party has a higher credit rating, whereby it can borrow in both money and capital markets more cheaply than the second party. In this instance, the first party is said to have an absolute advantage in borrowing.

However, when interest-rate spreads between the two parties are calculated based on their ability to borrow in both credit markets, the quality differences, or quality spreads, emerge. This means that an arbitrage opportunity exists between the two markets for loanable funds. It also implies that the second party possesses a comparative advantage in borrowing from one market and a comparative disadvantage in the other. The wider the difference in quality spreads, the greater the arbitrage opportunity to be exploited and shared between the potential swap counterparties. To illustrate, the scenario and the four tables below describe how the strategy for arranging a quality swap can be implemented with pre-negotiated swap gain-sharing ratio.

Quality Swap Scenario

1. The credit markets for short-term floating rates (i.e., money market) and long-term fixed rates (i.e., capital market) are segmented, in which interest-rate arbitrage can exist.
2. Two institutions are able to access both interest-rate markets and wish to minimize the overall costs of funding their liabilities.
3. The first party has a higher credit rating, thereby giving it an absolute advantage, which enables it to borrow from both the money market and the capital market more cheaply than the second party.
4. The second party has a lower credit rating, thereby giving it a comparative advantage in one of the two markets, which enables it to borrow from either market more cheaply than the first party, where its quality spread is smaller.
5. The swap can be arranged between the two counterparties to share the gain from interest-rate arbitrage based on negotiated gain-sharing ratio.
6. The third party can intervene to arrange the swap for both counterparties with pre-specified compensation, which can be obtained from the gain from swap.

Table 12.15 specifies the required inputs for the two counterparties to swap with or without the third-party swap arranger. The quality spread derived from the money-market borrowing is 1.5 per cent, whereas the one derived from the capital-market borrowing is 0.75 per cent. The swap gain shown in Table 12.16, which is the difference between the floating-rate spread and the fixed-rate spread, is 0.75 per cent, with the comparative advantages lying in the floating-rate borrowing for the first party and in the fixed-rate borrowing for the second party.

With a third-party swap arranger requiring a 10 per cent share from the realizable swap gain, the swap counterparties are left with 90 per cent to share between them. Assuming that the first party agrees to receive 20 per cent of the swap gain and the remaining 70 per cent belongs to the second party, the swap gain of 0.75 per cent would be distributed accordingly. The resultant negotiated swap gain turns out to be 0.15 per

Table 12.15 Swap Parties' Costs of Borrowing

Swap Party	Money Market	Capital Market	Negotiated Gain-Sharing Ratio	
			Swap Parties	Swap Arranger
1st Party	HIBOR + 0.75%	7.00%	20%	10%
2nd Party	HIBOR + 2.25%	7.75%	70%	
Quality Spread	1.50%	0.75%	90%	10%

Table 12.16 Swap Parties' Comparative Positions

Swap Party	Comparative Advantage	Comparative Disadvantage	Swap Saving	Shared Saving
1st Party	In the money market	In the capital market	1.50%	**0.15%**
2nd Party	In the capital market	In the money market	0.75%	**0.53%**
			0.75%	0.68%

cent (i.e., 0.75 per cent total gain times 20 per cent gain share) for the first party and 0.53 per cent (i.e., 0.75 per cent total gain times 70 per cent gain share) for the second party.

As the comparative advantage for the first party lies in floating-rate borrowing, it should have borrowed from the money market while letting the second party borrow from the capital market. While the first party paid the floating-rate interest of HIBOR plus 0.75 per cent to the market, it also expected to receive another 0.15 per cent share of swap gain from the second party. The second party, on the other hand, would pay fixed-rate interest of 7.75 per cent to the market and claim its share of swap gain of 0.53 per cent from the first party. The swap parties' transactions are laid out in Table 12.17.

The post-swap borrowing costs, as a result, are shown in Table 12.18, in that the first party would finally pay a fixed interest rate of 6.85 per cent while the second party would pay HIBOR plus 1.73 per cent. With the swap gain factored in, the first party could pay 0.15 per cent less than it could have paid to the market without a swap, and the second party could enjoy a substantial reduction in its floating-rate borrowing cost of 0.53 per cent. At the same time, the swap arranger would pocket 0.075

Table 12.17 Swap Parties' Transactions

Swap Party	Payments to the Markets		Swapping with Counterparty	
	Floating Rate	Fixed Rate	Floating Rate	Fixed Rate
1st Party	HIBOR + 0.75%	–	Gets HIBOR + 0.75%	Pays 6.85%
2nd Party	–	7.75%	Pays HIBOR + 1.73%	Gets 7.75%

Table 12.18 Quality Swap Outcomes

Swap Party	Post-Swap Borrowing Cost	
	Floating Rate	*Fixed Rate*
1st Party	–	6.85%
2nd Party	HIBOR + 1.73%	–

per cent (0.75 per cent swap gain times 10 per cent gain share) whenever such a swap deal was successful. However, the swap gain shared between counterparties could be higher if they eliminate the intervention by the third-party swap arranger.

Strategy 3: Minimizing the Cost of Borrowing through Basis Swap Transactions

Basis swap involves an exchange of interest payments that are tied either to the same index with different maturities or to different indexes with the same maturity. The combination of both features, where spreads between two indices and two maturities exist, is also possible. For the first two cases, a basis swap can be treated like a quality swap in the sense that there are arbitrage opportunities to exploit from the segmentations between two different index groups and between two maturities. With respect to the combination case, which is illustrated below, both basis spread and maturity spread are used to calculate the swap gain to be shared between the two counterparties.

Basis Swap Scenario

1. The markets for the first floating rate (e.g., three-month) tied to one index (e.g., HIBOR) and the second floating rate (e.g., six-month) tied to another index (e.g., LIBOR) are segmented, in which interest-rate arbitrage can exist.
2. Two parties have access to both interest-rate markets and wish to minimize their costs of borrowing.
3. Basis spread arises from the difference between the interest rates that each party can borrow from each index.
4. Maturity spread arises from rate difference of the same index that both parties can borrow at different maturities.
5. Basis swap can be arranged to share the gain from interest-rate arbitrage based on derived gain-sharing ratio.

The costs of borrowing of both swap counterparties are pre-specified in Table 12.19, with basis and maturity spreads being calculated at both margins resulting in a joint spread—swap gain—of 0.50 per cent. Using a comparative advantage argument based on the basis spread, the first party should pay the six-month HIBOR and the second party the six-month

LIBOR to their respective markets. In Table 12.20, the difference between basis gain and maturity gain is 2 per cent for the first party, while that of the second party is 1 per cent. When the differences between the basis saving and the maturity saving of both counterparties are combined— which is equal to 3 per cent—the saving-sharing ratio can then be derived. The first party will be entitled to a two-thirds share, with the remaining one-third share belonging to the second party. Thus the swap gain of 0.50 per cent can be divided between the two parties, leading to a 0.333 per cent cost-saving for the first party and a cost saving of 0.167 per cent for the second party.

Table 12.19 Swap Parties' Costs of Borrowing

Swap Party	3-month Floating Rate	6-month Floating Rate	Maturity Spread
1st Party	HIBOR + 1.00%	HIBOR + 2.75%	1.75%
2nd Party	LIBOR + 1.25%	LIBOR + 3.50%	2.25%
Basis Spread	0.25%	0.75%	0.50%

Table 12.20 Swap Parties' Gain Sharing

Swap Party	Basis Saving	Maturity Saving	Difference	Sharing Ratio	Shared Saving
1st Party pays 6-month HIBOR to market	0.25%	2.25%	2.00%	66.67%	0.333%
2nd Party pays 3-month LIBOR to market	0.75%	1.75%	1.00%	33.33%	0.167%
	0.50%	0.50%	3.00%	100.00%	0.50%

In Table 12.21, a swap arrangement follows suit after the cost saving to be shared between the two parties has been established. To the markets, the first party pays six-month HIBOR plus 2.75 per cent, while the second party pays three-month LIBOR plus 1.25 per cent. To each other, both counterparties swap their interest payments, which, in conjunction with the payments to the markets, results in post-swap borrowing costs of three-month HIBOR plus 0.67 per cent to the first party and six-month LIBOR plus 3.33 per cent to the second party, as shown in Table 12.22.

Conclusion

In today's often volatile global financial markets, individual and institutional investors alike have been increasingly concerned with controlling and managing the risk exposures of their internationally diversified portfolios

Table 12.21 Swap Parties' Transactions

Swap Party	Payments to the Markets		Swapping with Counterparty	
1st Party	–	6-mth HIBOR + 2.75%	Pays 3-mth HIBOR + 0.667%	Gets 6-mth HIBOR + 2.750%
2nd Party	3-mth LIBOR + 1.25%	–	Gets 3-mth LIBOR + 1.250%	Pays 6-mth LIBOR + 3.333%

Table 12.22 Basis Swap Outcomes

Swap Party	Post-Swap Borrowing Cost
1st Party	3-month HIBOR + 0.667%
2nd Party	6-month LIBOR + 3.333%

rather than improving portfolio-return performance. The search for efficient methods and cost-effective instruments to help these investors manage various financial risks has become prominent in finance study and practice over the last three decades. The methods of hedging and insurance have long been used by commodity traders and merchants to reduce or eliminate their risks, yet the costs incurred to manage those risks, especially for traded securities, were prohibitively high as the markets for risk sharing had not been well established. Thanks to continuing developments in both organized and over-the-counter derivatives markets for futures, options, and swap contracts around the world, all investors are now able to participate in this exciting around-the-clock trading to hedge and/or speculate their portfolio positions at relatively lower transaction costs than in the past, despite certain market frictions and differing market microstructures in some geographical areas.

For Hong Kong, the markets for derivative instruments have generally been highly developed relative to the rest of the Asia-Pacific countries in terms of product variety, maturity dates, and trading volume. Major participants are globally based and competitively active, leading to the relentless introduction of new and more sophisticated instruments tailor-designed by financial institutions, corporate borrowers, and organized markets to meet the rising demands of various investor groups. On the one hand, those who wish to hedge the variability in the market value of their local stock portfolios usually enter into and consequently trade stock index futures contracts in the HSI and Mini HSI Futures Markets. Short hedgers sell index futures to protect the value of their underlying portfolios in the event of price decline, while long hedgers buy index futures to lock in the price to be paid for the formation of their portfolios. On the other hand, those who wish to hedge unfavourable risks of price and return volatility in their underlying portfolios while profiting from the favourable movements in prices and returns could opt to hold appropriate types of financial options. Buyers and sellers of options in Hong Kong can trade their calls and puts for both individual stocks and stock index using a variety of trading strategies based on their investment motives and market expectations. For institutional players in Hong Kong, many OTC markets exist to accommodate the exchanges of their customized contracts, such as currency forwards, FRAs, interest rate swaps, and more exotic options that have become increasingly essential for risk management despite the higher transaction costs and counterparty risks than those found in the organized markets.

Needless to say, the fast-paced development of global derivatives markets in general has undoubtedly benefited financial market participants on various fronts. Nonetheless, those benefits must be weighed against the potential operational risks involved in the uses of these derivative instruments and contracts. Risk dimensions other than counterparty and operational risks include model risks that stem from the design and engineering of those derivative products themselves. All of these new-breed, higher-level risk exposures are the ongoing research issues that confront both the academic and professional worlds of finance that we currently live in and experience.

Discussion Questions

1. Distinguish between a speculator and a hedger.
2. What is 'counterparty risk' and why is it important?
3. Suppose the Hang Seng Index October contract is currently trading for 9,200 and it has forty days remaining until expiration. The current value of the Hang Seng Index in the cash market is 9,050. If the expected dividend yield is four per cent and the risk-free rate of interest is six per cent, is it possible to profit from arbitrage? If so, describe the process. Ignore transaction costs, and assume the cash market can be purchased at 9,050 and October contracts can be bought or sold at 9,200.
4. What is the meaning of 'marked-to-market' and what is its purpose?
5. What is the necessary condition for a fixed-for-floating interest rate swap to be possible?
6. Miss To expects to receive a large New Year bonus next month and would like to invest in stocks, believing that the current stock market prices are extremely attractive while at the same time realizing that the Chinese New Year may change this situation. Discuss how Miss To might use stock index futures to capture the expected price appreciation in the stock market.
7. You expect a very volatile market over the next two months but are not at all certain about the direction in which the market will move. How can you use stock index options to exploit this expected market volatility?

8. The Hang Seng Index was at 9,800 in early September 2002. At the same time, futures contracts on the index with a settlement date of October 2002 were trading at 9,900. If you purchased one futures contract and the index closed at 9,990 on the settlement date, what was your gain or loss, ignoring transaction costs?

9. Provide an intuitive explanation of why put premiums tend to drop when interest rates rise.

10. Comment on the following statement: 'A covered call writer can only profit if the underlying share price does not rise.'

Keywords

arbitrage
basis spread
counterparty risk
derivative instruments
duration gap
exercise or strike price
financial futures contracts
forward rate agreements
hedge
interest rate swaps
marking-to-market
options
over-the-counter market
quality spread
settlement

13. The Gold and Commodities Markets

David Y. K. Chan

Introduction

The Chinese Gold and Silver Exchange Society

The Chinese Gold and Silver Exchange Society was formed in 1910. Gold, silver, and foreign currencies have been traded at different times throughout the nine decades of its operation. Members of this Society are very active and dominate the physical gold trade of South-East Asia.

The Society began informally, with people engaging in gold and silver coin trading among themselves. Trading was then done under the counter, with a handshake between the two parties involved.

It is not known how many members were in the Society during World War I as all records were lost during the turmoil of the war. On the advice of the Hong Kong government's Secretary for Chinese Affairs, Mr E. R. Halifax, the Society applied for registration as The Chinese Gold and Silver Exchange Society in 1918, and a series of by-laws were drawn up. Re-registration of members at that time showed more than 200 members.

Business flourished, reaching its zenith in 1934 when US President Franklin Roosevelt replaced the tariff system by fixing the price of a gold coin, weighing 0.89 taels (32.89 grams), at US$20. To avoid losses in foreign exchange fluctuations, big firms in Hong Kong booked gold coins at the Society in advance against their trading in US dollars in anticipation of future settlement.

The Society was closed during the Japanese occupation of Hong Kong in 1941, but business resumed immediately after the conclusion of the Pacific War. Foreign currencies and gold continued to be traded side by side until 1962, when the Society encountered difficulties in the physical deliveries of foreign currencies and trading had to be dropped. Business has since been done only in gold bars.

At present, the affairs of the Society are run by the Executive and Supervisory Committees of twenty-one members elected at the Members' General Meeting, held on 15 June every other year.

The Hong Kong Futures Exchange Limited

Futures trading has a long history, but its origin is unknown. It is believed that the early futures market developed from deals of tangible agricultural products. In the early nineteenth century, producers, manufacturers, and consumers had already started making agreements on future deliveries. Following the development of international trading, the establishment of futures markets became popular as they provided a place for hedgers to deal in order to avoid losses brought about by adverse price movements.

In 1976, the Hong Kong Legislative Council passed the Commodities Trading Ordinance after three years of intense study by the government and commodity experts, and paved the way for the establishment of a commodity exchange. It was on 17 December 1976 that the Hong Kong Commodity Exchange was incorporated.

The first futures contract traded was cotton, in May 1977. This was followed by sugar futures in November 1977, soya bean futures in November 1979, and gold futures in August 1980. The proposal for a Hang Seng Index Futures contract gained government approval and trading started on 6 May 1986. While the Hang Seng Index Futures market is covered in Chapter 11, this chapter concentrates on the commodity futures market.

In order to expand its membership and introduce new contracts of different natures, the Hong Kong Commodity Exchange Limited began to reorganize its structure in mid-1984. It has since changed its name to The Hong Kong Futures Exchange Limited. On 6 March 2000, The Hong Kong Futures Exchange Limited, The Stock Exchange of Hong Kong Limited, and Hong Kong Securities Clearing Company Limited merged under a single holding company, Hong Kong Exchanges and Clearing Limited (HKEx), in order to increase competitiveness and meet the challenges of an increasingly globalized market.

The Chinese Gold and Silver Exchange Society

The Nature of the Market

The Society has a limited membership of 189.[1] It is a principals market, and the Exchange Society acts as a monitor. Dealings are based on spot gold with undated delivery. A daily premium/discount rate establishes the carrying charges for either the buyer or seller of gold. Transactions are made through open outcry as well as privately between members. As a rule, balances between members are settled on a daily basis before the market is closed, based on the morning and afternoon settlement prices.

The Society is self-governing and no default has ever marked it in its history of operation. A variable safeguard rule is in effect, which limits the gain or loss of each open position from the previous day's close.

Membership

The 192 members are all corporate members with unlimited liability. According to the Constitution of the Society, no new members can be accepted unless the existing membership drops to below 150. Therefore, interested parties can only gain membership through a transfer from an existing member if both parties agree. To apply to the Society for a change of membership, the applicant must secure recommendations from two members, drawn from the Executive and Supervisory committees. The Society will first examine the applicant's qualifications, then put up a notice for ten days to allow for objections. The matter will be put to a vote by the committee and the applicant will be admitted and the change of the firm's name on the Society register will be granted.

Each member may have four floor traders and four messengers. No person is allowed to enter the trading hall except those aforementioned. The Society has ruled that members who were admitted into the Society after 1 April 1979 can be represented with only three floor traders and three messengers.

Trading Methods

The trading hall of the Chinese Gold and Silver Exchange Society is packed with gold traders. Whether the price of gold is up, down, or stable, that the bidding is hectic is evident by the shouts and cries among traders on the floor.

The method of trading is like playing 'catch' for a fortune. Verbal quotations and hand signs are used to illustrate gold prices, and the first trader to touch a seller's body wins the deal. This explains the phenomenon that all the traders on the floor are men. We call it the 'Open Outcry System'; it is fascinating to strangers to gold trading and is the reason why women do not become traders, although there is no particular legislation in the Constitution of the Society which prohibits this. This trading method, although it appears old-fashioned and even somewhat obsolete, has existed ever since the days when the Society was still in its embryonic stage. Time has proven that the system is sound and reliable.

Gold Fixing

The fixing prices are determined twice a day, based on the approximate market price (correct to the nearest HK$5) at 11.30am and 4.00pm during weekdays and at 10.30am on Saturday. These prices are used by member brokers to settle their accounts. An example will illustrate this: Broker A has a long buying position of 100 taels against Broker B's short selling position at HK$4,000. If the price fixing is HK$4,010, Broker A will receive Hong Kong dollars from Broker B.

Through this mechanism, the brokers do not build up big unsettled payments between themselves, and the healthy condition of the local market is therefore maintained.

The Daily Premium/Discount Rate

The Daily Premium/Discount Rate is variable and is determined at 11.00am from Monday to Friday and at 10.00am on Saturday by the relative demand for physical gold. This daily rate quoted is based on ten taels of gold, and by rule cannot exceed 2.1 per cent of contract value on a monthly basis.

By accepting or paying this rate a buyer or seller of gold in the Hong Kong Market can defer delivery of gold indefinitely. Thus, the Hong Kong gold contract is actually a futures contract with an undated delivery.

Tael bars can be physically transacted every day at 11.00am, when the daily premium/discount rate is established.

Determination of Interest

Interest is determined once a day at 11.00am Monday to Friday and 10.00am on a Saturday. Interest can be positive, negative, or even.

Positive interest arises when the demand for physical gold is greater than its supply. Buyers who cannot get hold of gold are awarded 'interest', which is paid by sellers who cannot make physical delivery.

Negative interest arises when the supply of physical gold is greater than demand for it. Sellers flood the market with gold but cannot find buyers for it. As a result, sellers who do not get sale proceeds have to be awarded 'interest', which is paid by buyers who do not have sufficient cash to pay the entire amount to sellers.

When we say today's interest is positive fifty cents, we mean that those who have a long position to carry forward to the next day receive from the seller fifty Hong Kong cents per ten taels of gold per day.

Particulars of the Market

The trading hours of the market are as follows:

Monday to Friday:	9.00am to 12.30pm
	2.30pm to 4.30pm
Saturday:	9.30am to 12.00 noon

Settlement Price:

Monday to Friday:	11.00am, 4.00pm
Saturday:	11.00am

Unit of Trade

A contract lot is 100 taels of 99 per cent fine (pure) gold made up of twenty bars of five taels of gold with approved brand names and assay marks. One tael of Hong Kong gold is equivalent to 1.20377 troy ounces of 99.99 per cent pure gold.

An example will make this clear. A trader went long in five lots of Hong Kong gold at a price of, say, HK$3,570 per tael on 15 July 1989. Let us assume the interest factor to be a negative HK$17 per ten taels of gold on the day of purchase.

1. On the Day of Purchase. Assuming an original margin of, say, ten per cent, the trader would have to furnish a sum of ten per cent of HK$(3,570 x 5 x 100), that is, HK$178,500. In addition, he would have to pay a commission of HK$50 per lot.

Total Commission Payable = HK$50 x 5
= HK$250
Total Amount Payable on 15 July 1989 = HK$(178,500 + 250)
= HK$178,750

The amount of HK$178,750 would be credited to the trader's account with the broker. Furthermore, as the interest factor was negative (that is, the longs had to pay interest to the shorts), on 15 July 1989 an interest amount would be debited to the trader's account.

The Negative Interest Amount = HK$17 x 10 x 5
= HK$850

2. One Day after the Purchase if the Price Rose. If the price rose to, say, HK$3,600 per tael on 16 July 1989 and the interest factor became a positive HK$10 per ten taels of gold, the following entries would be made to the trader's account:

Excess Equity (Excluding Interest)
HK$(3,600 − 3,570) x 5 x 100 = HK$15,000

As the interest factor was positive (that is, the shorts had to pay interest to the longs), interest would be credited to the trader's account.

The Positive Interest Amount = HK$10 x 10 x 5
= HK$500

On 16 July, the trader could actually withdraw an amount equal to HK$15,000 + HK$500 − HK$850; that is, HK$14,650.

3. One Day after the Purchase if the Price Fell. If the price fell to, say, HK$3,500 per tael on 16 July 1989 and the interest factor remained the same as above, the trader would have to pay a maintenance margin:

Maintenance Margin = HK$(3,750–3,500) x 500
= HK$35,000

The interest factor remained the same, that is, HK$500 credit. On 16 July, the trader would have to pay in an amount equal to HK$35,000 + HK$850 − HK$500; that is, HK$35,350.

Factors Affecting the Gold Market

Before we examine the Hong Kong gold market performance of 1988, we should consider the factors affecting gold prices. Some factors have gained worldwide attention, and they are regarded as the leading reasons for the change of gold prices. Each of them has a different degree of influence on price fluctuation.

Demand and supply: gold trading is under a free-market system in which the price is simply influenced by the 'invisible hand' of the market. If there is an increase in demand, the price of gold will be bid up, while an increase in supply will pull down the market price. Another factor in the volatility of gold prices is speculation. Speculators tend to buy when inflation is expected to increase and sell when it is expected to decrease. Therefore, in a time of high inflation, gold prices will rise due to the increasing demand for gold.

Political instability in the world contributes to the increasing demand for gold. Investments are liquidated into the gold market, which is seen as a 'store of value' asset.

Official holding of gold leads to instability of the demand for gold. Private and official reserves are large relative to current production— official holdings alone are probably about thirty-five times larger than current production. As a result, the gold market is quite different from that of most other commodities, as only slight changes in expectation concerning adjustments in stock levels can have profound effects on the speculative demand for bullion.

A Review of Hong Kong's Gold Market in 1988

To illustrate how some factors affect the market, major movements during 1988 are briefly reviewed here. In the first month of 1988, the price of gold was quoted at around HK$4,450, slightly down from its closing level in December 1987. The most substantial decrease in price came in the second month of that year, when gold dropped almost HK$500 to close at HK$3,994 in February. Thereafter, gold traded in the range of HK$4,000 to HK$4,300 for the following four months. Starting in mid-June, gold prices continuously dropped from HK$4,322 to the year's lowest level of HK$3,702 in late September. After this wave, there was a major technical rebound of HK$300, almost 50 per cent of the previous downward wave from HK$4,322 to HK$3,702.

In January 1988, gold prices moved sharply downwards. They could not breach the psychologically important level of HK$4,525, which was strong resistance when compared with the previous Double Top of HK$4,850 in January 1980 and HK$4,750 in September 1983 (see Figure 13.1a; for the closing prices between the 1980s and the mid-1990s, see Figure 13.1b; and for the yearly tael gold prices between 1990 and 2001, see Figure 13.1c). Fundamentally, this movement was due to a smaller-than-expected United States trade deficit of US$13.20 billion for November 1987, which put gold on a technically bearish track. The market was influenced by the US dollar's volatility and also by easier crude oil value.

Gold prices dropped steadily during February 1988. This was due to the news of gold selling by the Soviet Union. This bearish trend was

Figure 13.1a   Hong Kong Gold Monthly Price Chart — High, Low, Closing (2 January 1974 to 31 December 1988)

Source of data: Hong Kong Economic Journal, 1989 (in Chinese). Trans. David Y. K. Chan.

Figure 13.1b   Hong Kong Gold Monthly Price Chart — Closing (August 1980 to 31 August 1995)

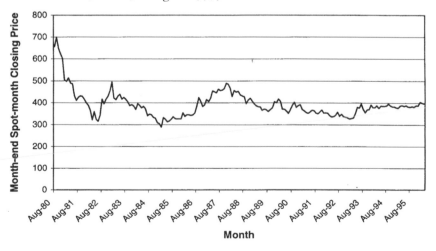

Figure 13.1c   Hong Kong Tael Gold Yearly Price Chart, 1990–2001

Year	Open	High	Low	Close
1990	3743	3915	3228	3624
1991	3630	3802	3176	3289
1992	3296	3322	3050	3078
1993	3078	3769	3018	3592
1994	3596	3662	3410	3533
1995	3532	3650	3438	3569
1996	3567	3839	3393	3409
1997	3398	3400	2612	2670
1998	2666	2890	2498	2652
1999	2655	3016	2335	2692
2000	2675	2908	2457	2537
2001	2538	2742	2377	2572

Source: Courtesy of The Chinese Gold and Silver Exchange Society

influenced by weak petroleum prices and heavy selling of gold by producers, including Australia and South Africa.

In March 1988, gold prices rose dramatically to a high of HK$4,258 from HK$3,994. Technically, it was a major correction of more than 50 per cent of the previous downward wave. In fact, this trend was supported by a fall in the US dollar and by the inflationary implications of a jump in crude oil prices. The political instability of tension between Panama and the United States also contributed to the positive sentiment.

In April and May 1988, a lack of substantial news caused gold to fluctuate around HK$4,162 and HK$4,288. Many investors kept out of the market as it seemed to have no clear direction. Gold prices became firmer because of the coincidence of the clashes between the United States and Iran and growing selling pressure.

But in June the price of gold renewed its downward trend, although it failed to break the HK$4,000 level. This trend was supported by the expectation of inflationary pressure in the United States and the backing of commodities prices. The continuing US dollar appreciation and decreasing oil prices also contributed to the downward trend.

In early July, buying pressure from the profit takers caused gold to rally. Afterwards, prices continued to drop and tried to break the supporting level of HK$4,000. This downfall was due to the sharp rise of the US dollar after the report of a smaller-than-expected US May trade deficit, and the possibility of an end to the Iran–Iraq conflict.

Gold prices consolidated within the narrow range of HK$4,069 to HK$3,992 due to a lack of substantial news in August. Usually there is either a continuation of decline or a reversal after a consolidation. In this case it was a continuation, with the year's lowest price at HK$3,702 in September. The downturn in the price of crude oil made gold vulnerable to selling in the market. Moreover, the continuing appreciation of the US dollar reinforced the downward trend of the gold market.

From October until early December, prices moved continuously upward. This was mainly due to the depreciation of the US dollar, caused by the US presidential election. Reduction of the trade deficit, which is a long-standing problem in the United States, was one of the election promises made by President Bush. He won the election, not keeping the US dollar too strong in order to stimulate domestic exports and maintain a good trade deficit figure.

The major trend for the year was therefore upwards, but for most of the year gold traded in a fairly broad and constant range—when compared with previous years—of between HK$4,525 and HK$3,702. If the US economy could continue to improve and the country's debt decreased, then gold might fall through the HK$3,531 or US$380 level in the following year.

The Hong Kong Futures Exchange Limited

The Structure of the Exchange

The Hong Kong Futures Exchange Limited is managed by a twelve-member Board of Directors. The chairman and three vice-chairmen have executive functions, and they are vested with specific powers to cope with contingencies in the market. As a whole, the Board formulates rules and regulations and sets the policies of the Exchange. In addition, it has the power to appoint members to the various committees of the Exchange, as well as the power to discipline members.

The commodity futures markets of the Exchange are grouped under different divisions according to the nature of the markets. Currently, there are four market divisions: Agricultural Products, Metals, Indices, and Currency and Interest Rates. Each market division has its individual characteristics and practices.

The exchange is supported by four staff departments: the Audit and Surveillance Unit, the Training Unit, the Market Section, and the Membership Section. The Audit and Surveillance Unit supervises members' financial positions in order to protect the financial integrity of the market. The Training Unit undertakes training programmes for members and the general public through seminars and courses. The Market Section is responsible for the orderly conduct of the market, while the Membership Section is responsible for the registration and administration of membership. In the case of queries, members are encouraged to approach the Membership Section for clarification of the Exchange rules as well as other regulatory matters.

Membership of the Exchange

Members of the Exchange can be divided into three categories. They are either Full Members, Market Members, or Trade Affiliated Members. Full Members must be either individuals ordinarily resident in Hong Kong or limited companies incorporated in Hong Kong. They must hold at least one Ordinary Share (of HK$100,000 par value) in the capital of the Exchange. Full Members are entitled to trade on the floor in all market divisions upon application. They must contribute to the Compensation Fund as shareholders of the Exchange. Full Members should have had capital or paid-up capital of not less than HK$2,000,000 in December 2001.

Market Members must also be individuals ordinarily resident in Hong Kong, or limited companies incorporated in Hong Kong. They must hold at least one Standard Share (of HK$25,000 par value) in the capital of the Exchange. They are entitled to the right of trading in one market division only. They may be granted the right to trade in other market divisions by special approval of the Board. As shareholders of the Exchange, they must also contribute to the Compensation Fund. Market Members should have had capital or paid-up capital of not less than HK$1,000,000 in December 2001.

Overseas companies can apply as Trade Affiliated Members. Such members will not be granted the right to trade in any market. Therefore, all of their trading orders are placed through a Full Member or a Market Member. Since they are not shareholders of the Exchange, they are not required to contribute to the Compensation Fund.

The Trading Systems of the Futures Exchange

All trading at the Hong Kong Futures Exchange is centralized in a marketplace, where facilities such as booths, trading rings, price quotation boards, and audio and visual devices are installed.

Futures markets are traded under various systems. The soya bean market is traded under the One Price Group Trading System. This system is popular in Japanese futures markets, with its special feature of using hand signals to indicate the quantities of buy and sell orders. Trading is carried out by members' floor representatives standing around a trading ring under the control of a chairman. Trading is not continuous but is held in separate sessions. All business in one session for one month of delivery is recorded at one price.

The gold market is traded under the Open Outcry System. The tempo of this system is quicker than the other two methods of trading. It is known as the 'double auction method', with declining offers meeting rising bids until an acceptable price is reached. This method is popular in Chicago, New York, and London and is extensively used in these centres. The sugar market uses both the Group Trading and the Open Outcry systems.

The Board Trading System is used for the Hang Seng Index Futures. This is a system which is similar to that of the Hong Kong stockmarket, whereby members actually write their bids and offers on a trading board located in the front of the trading area.

In the past, there were five products traded in the Exchange. These were cotton, gold (see Figure 13.2 and Table 13.1), soya beans (see Figure 13.3 and Table 13.2), sugar (see Figure 13.4 and Table 13.3), and the Hang Seng Index Futures. However, due to insufficient demand, the futures markets of cotton, soya beans, and sugar have closed and have not been reopened. The futures markets now remaining are gold and the Hang Seng Index Futures (see Chapter 12). Since the commodity futures markets were closed in Hong Kong, the buying and selling of commodity futures contracts can take place outside Hong Kong, such as in the Minneapolis Grain Exchange (MGEX), which offers futures and options contracts on agricultural and non-agricultural products.

Figure 13.2 Trading Volume for Futures Contracts in Gold

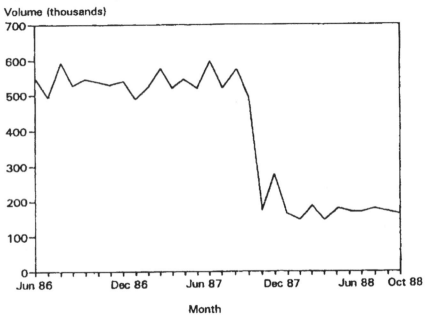

Table 13.1   Gold Futures Contract Specifications

Standard Grade:	Refined gold of not less than 995 fineness
Trading Units:	100 oz. fine gold
Tenderable Grades:	Bars of 100 oz., 50 oz., and 1 kg.
Delivery Point:	Hong Kong
Price Quotation:	United States currency
Min. Fluctuations:	10 cents per oz.
Trading Months:	Even months, spot month, and the following two months
Trading Method:	Open Outcry
Original Margin:	US$1,500
Daily Limits:	US$40**

Notes: * No limit is imposed on the spot month.
          + Market is closed for thirty minutes and reopened without limit on price movement.

Figure 13.3 Trading Volume for Futures Contracts in Soya Beans

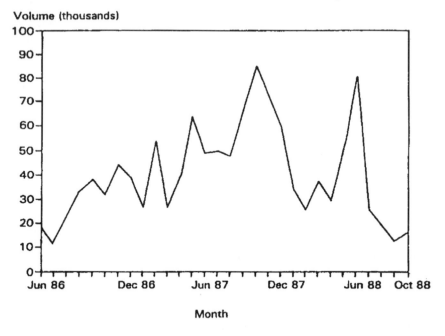

Table 13.2 Soya Bean Futures Contract Specifications

Standard Grade:	Unselected China yellow soya beans
Trading Units:	100 bags of 80 kg each
Tenderable Grades:	US IOM soya beans
Delivery Point:	Tokyo or Kanagawa, Japan
Price Quotation:	Hong Kong currency
Min. Fluctuations:	Ten cents per bag
Trading Months:	Each consecutive month up to six months ahead
Trading Hours:	09.50, 10.50
	12.50, 14.50
Trading Method:	Group Trading
Original Margin:	HK$7,500
Daily Limits:	Nil

Figure 13.4 Trading Volume for Futures Contracts in Sugar

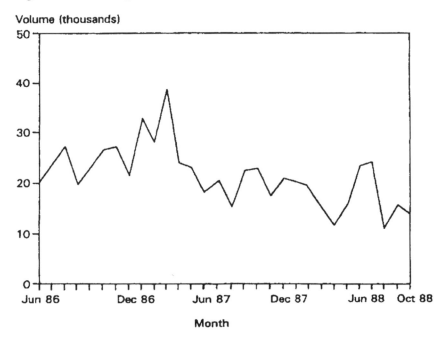

Table 13.3 Sugar Futures Contract Specifications

Standard Grade:	Raw cane sugar of 96 polarization
Trading Units:	50 long tons (112,000 lbs.)
Tenderable Grades:	Growth of S-E Asian countries
Delivery Point:	FOB, S-E Asian countries
Price Quotation:	United States currency
Min. Fluctuations:	1/100 cents per lb.
Trading Months:	January, March, May, July, September, October
Trading Hours:	10.30–1200
	14.25–18.00
Trading Method:	Group and Open Outcry
Original Margin:	US$1,350
Daily Limits:	US one cents**

Notes: * No limit is imposed on the spot month.
        * Market is closed for thirty minutes and reopened without limit on price movement.

The Hong Kong Futures Exchange Limited issues reports daily and weekly to provide information about all transactions made in the market. This information is also disseminated to the public through Reuters and other media channels.

A newsletter is published every month, giving a monthly review together with graphs and statistics of the market.

The Financial Integrity of Futures Markets

The financial integrity of futures markets is protected by the Guarantee System and the Compensation Fund. In Hong Kong, the International Commodity Clearing House (ICCH) acts as the manager of the Hong Kong Commodities Guarantee Corporation and handles day-to-day affairs. The Guarantee Corporation, owned by a consortium of banks, guarantees the due fulfilment of contracts. The corporation calls each day for original margin and variation margin when prices move adversely. This has a disciplinary effect upon clearing members and is a major component for maintaining the financial integrity of the futures markets.

Private investors are protected by a Compensation Fund. This is used for compensating for losses incurred by the improper conduct of any member of the Exchange. Every member of the Exchange is required to make an initial contribution of HK$50,000 to the Compensation Fund, which is administered by the government. A flat-rate levy is collected from members for each contract traded on the Exchange. An investor who has a legitimate complaint against a member may bring it to the attention of the Exchange. The complaint will be investigated, and the member advised as to whether or not the party should receive compensation.

The Exchange sets the rules and regulations that lay the framework for floor trading and brokerage practices. All traders have to apply for membership before they can trade on the Exchange floor.

A Review of Commodity Futures Markets

The futures markets in Hong Kong were extremely volatile in 1986 and 1988. The soya bean market was obviously experiencing an upward trend from mid-1986 to late 1987, with its highest trading volume in October 1987 (see Figure 13.3). Then prices became firmer. The trend was partly attributable to the fall in both the Japanese and Chicago markets and partly to the weak US dollar. After October 1987, the trading volume steadily dropped during the following four months. This was because of the poor crop in eastern Europe and the short supply of soya bean oil in India. The trading interest largely concentrated in the December 1987 and April 1988 deliveries. Another rally occurred in July 1988 with strong prices, sparked by the continued forecast of dry weather in the major Midwest growing areas in the US.

In the sugar market, prices dropped steadily, leading to a increasing demand for sugar from early May 1986 onwards. Trading volume then steadily increased, to 38,850 lots in March 1987 (see Figure 13.4). It was believed that the market had over-reacted to the Soviet nuclear accident at Chernobyl in April 1986, and the consequent uncertainty over the extent of damage to Soviet crops pushed prices lower in the second half of the year. In April 1987, buying orders made prices firmer and market sentiment gained support from reports made by Cuba that sugar cane production in that country was running some 8,000,000 tons behind estimates. Under a firmer price market, the trading volume dropped rapidly during the following three months. Thereafter, due to different market sentiments that made market prices firmer, the trading volume was consolidated at a lower level, forming a downward movement of the market in terms of trading volume.

The Loco-London Gold Market

History

The success of the Hong Kong gold markets has given rise to opportunities for investors, brokers, and overseas bullion dealers to trade, hedge, or arbitrage gold in Hong Kong with local bullion dealers and each other. The London bullion dealers have established offices in Hong Kong and have created a market in gold, creating, in effect, basic London vaults parallel to the Hong Kong gold markets.

The Loco-London gold market was established in Hong Kong in the mid-1970s and has been operating effectively. It is the largest London gold trading centre for Asia, and the daily turnover at the end of 1997 was estimated to be US$190 million, or about seven times the daily turnover of the Chinese Gold and Silver Exchange Society. For the clearing statistics of the London Gold Market, see Figures 13.5a, 13.5b, and 13.5c.

The Nature of the Loco-London Gold Market

The Loco-London gold market is basically an extension of the London gold market into Hong Kong and other major gold market time zones. Transactions are based on spot market prices, with settlement within two business days of the transaction. However, the extension of settlement dates can easily be arranged with the payment of a daily interest factor. Delivery of gold takes place in London and payment is in US dollars in New York (see Figure 13.6). Most transactions are made via telex or telephone between dealers.

In Hong Kong, the Loco-London gold market is an alternative market running parallel to the Hong Kong gold market, and it has become important because business can be transacted on international terms. The arbitrage between these markets is so frequent that both markets express a fair market value for gold, as determined by both local and international dealers.

Arbitrage between the Loco-London gold market and the Chinese Gold and Silver Exchange has been active at times, primarily due to the

Figure 13.5a   The Daily Turnover of Gold of the Loco-London Gold
Market, 1997–2002

| London Bullion Market Clearing Turnover (Daily Averages) | | | | | | | | | | | |
| *Ounces Transferred (millions)* | | | | | | *Value (US $Billions)* | | | | | |
Month	*1997*	*1998*	*1999*	*2000*	*2001*	*2002*	*1997*	*1998*	*1999*	*2000*	*2001*	*2002*
January	37.2	37.5	28.9	22.2	19.7	16.3	13.2	10.8	8.3	6.3	5.2	4.5
February	40.3	37.0	26.7	30.0	24.2	20.1	14.0	11.0	7.7	9.0	6.3	5.9
March	36.3	38.5	28.5	24.2	28.7	17.4	12.8	11.4	8.1	6.9	7.5	5.1
April	32.1	34.5	25.2	25.2	25.1		11.1	10.6	7.1	7.1	6.5	
May	32.4	32.5	32.6	25.5	28.7		11.1	9.7	9.0	7.0	7.8	
June	32.2	35.0	30.5	28.2	20.5		11.0	10.2	8.0	8.0	5.5	
July	37.0	30.0	34.7	20.5	16.1		12.0	8.8	8.9	5.8	4.3	
August	33.2	28.6	36.4	19.8	19.9		10.7	8.1	9.3	5.4	5.4	
September	34.3	34.0	37.1	21.1	19.5		11.1	9.8	9.8	5.8	5.5	
October	42.0	35.8	37.2	18.9	16.7		13.6	10.6	11.5	5.1	4.7	
November	40.8	27.5	25.3	18.6	18.0		12.5	8.1	7.4	4.9	4.9	
December	43.7	30.4	28.5	23.6	20.4		12.6	8.9	8.1	6.4	5.6	

Source: Courtesy of The London Bullion Market Association

Figure 13.5b   The Daily Turnover (in Ounces) of Gold of the Loco-
London Gold Market, 1996–2002

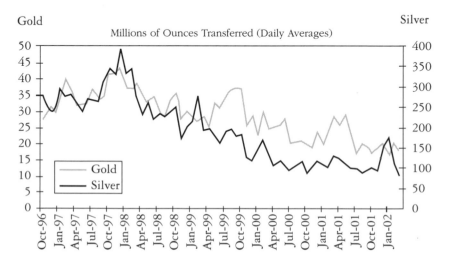

Source: Courtesy of The London Bullion Market Association

Figure 13.5c The Daily Turnover (in Dollars) of Gold of the Loco-London Gold Market, 1996–2002

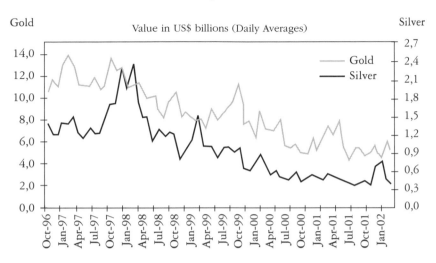

Source: Courtesy of The London Bullion Market Association

Figure 13.6 The Loco-London Gold Market, 1988

Source of data: Hong Kong Economic Journal, 1989 (in Chinese), Trans. David Y. K. Chan.

differences in size of the weight contracted (troy ounces versus taels), the quality of the gold, and the currency (US dollars versus Hong Kong dollars). However, since the Hong Kong dollar was pegged to the US dollar in 1983, arbitrage possibilities have been less attractive.

The Relationship between the Loco-London and the Hong Kong Gold Markets

By understanding the relationship between the Hong Kong and Loco-London gold markets, investors can exercise arbitrage between the two.

Since one tael equals 1.2033 ounces, to convert one tael of 99 per cent pure gold to ounces of 100 per cent pure gold, the factor we use is 1.1913 (1.2033 x 99/100). We then come to two variables: the Hong Kong dollar/US dollar exchange rate (TT) and the market price of Hong Kong gold. For example:

HK$4,000
TT = US$1.00 = HK$7.80
The equivalent of Hong Kong gold in US dollars per fine ounce:

Hong Kong gold market price   =   4,000
TT factor   =   7.8 x 1.1913
                                                         =   US$430.47

	Purity of Gold (Per Cent)	Unit of Trade	Currency (Per Unit)
Hong Kong gold	99	Tael	HK dollar
Loco-London	100	Ounce	US dollar

Gold Fixing

Gold fixing is done twice a day in London. At the start of fixing, the chairman of the Chinese Gold and Silver Exchange Society suggests a price midway between bid and offer of the pre-fix price. The five London gold dealers then indicate their net buying, selling, or nil interest at that price, together with the number of bars they want to trade. If the buying interest matches the offers, the gold is fixed. If not, the chairman changes the suggested price, obtains figures from the five dealers again, and fixes the price at which a balance is reached. According to London Gold Market Rules, no commission is paid by sellers at fixings. Buyers are charged a commission of thirty US cents per ounce on the fixing price. However, most clients here enjoy concessionary rates for deals done at the fixings.

	London Standard Time	Hong Kong Time	London Summer Time	Hong Kong Time
Morning Fixing	10.30am	6.30pm	10.30am	5.30pm
Afternoon fixing	3.00pm	11.00pm	3.00pm	10.00pm

Summary

Various gold markets are situated in different parts of the world, and each operates during different time periods on a worldwide basis (see Table 13.4).

Table 13.4   Round-the-Clock Trading Hours for Gold

Hong Kong Time		
Summer	Winter	
	07.30	Australia Open
	08.30	Tokyo Open
	09.30	Hong Kong Open
	12.30	Hong Kong Morning Open
	14.30	Hong Kong Afternoon Open
15.30	16.30	London Open
	16.30	Hong Kong Afternoon Close
17.30	18.30	London Morning Fixing
20.20	21.20	New York Comex Open
22.00	23.00	London Afternoon Fixing
02.30	03.30	New York Comex Close
02.30	05.30	United States West Coast

The three major gold markets—New York, London, and Hong Kong—operate on a continuous basis in that one opens just before the close of the preceding one (see Figure 13.7). This arrangement enables gold traders to reduce their risk.

Hong Kong is one of the largest gold trading centres in the world, ranked after New York and London. It was further enhanced when the government lifted restrictions on gold imports in January 1974.

Activity at the Chinese Gold and Silver Exchange Society appears chaotic: there is a lot of shouting, pushing, and general physical contact. This is, however, the traditional way of transacting business at the Gold Exchange. Therefore, Reuters and other sophisticated facilities that report gold trading information are able only to collect statistics and other data, not the tangible, palpable information evident or visible in the interaction and contact between traders on the floors.

Figure 13.7
Round-the-Clock Trading
among the Three Largest Gold
Markets

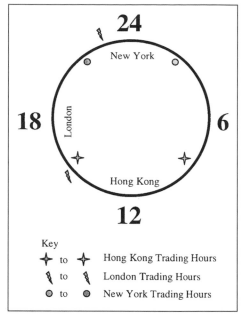

The trading traditions of Hong Kong gold and the Society members' esteem have always been highly regarded. In fact, it is because of the members' rigorous self-discipline and integrity that the exchange's trading system has been functioning well, without a hitch, since 1910. The virtue of trustworthiness among members has indeed become the most valuable asset for those involved in gold trading.

For centuries the London market has been considered the gold capital of the world. This market has been used increasingly by producers, industrial consumers, and dealers. In recent years the number of trading firms, investors, and speculators using this market has grown substantially. Consequently, the volume of transactions processed in this market has reached new heights. Today, London gold market prices serve as benchmarks for private gold dealings throughout the world.

All authorized banks in the United Kingdom may deal in gold, but activity is concentrated in the hands of the five members of the London Gold Market: Société Générale;[2] Deutsche Bank AG;[3] HSBC Bank USA, London Branch;[4] N. M. Rothschild & Sons;[5] and The Bank of Nova Scotia– Scotia-Mocatta.[6] All five members of the London Market have operating subsidiaries in Hong Kong.

The gold market in New York has been usually called the COMEX gold market. The daily volume of transactions in the COMEX (now a division of the New York Mercantile Exchange (NYMEX)) is large, surpassing any other gold futures market in the world. All economic or political decisions announced during market hours tend to increase its market activity significantly. Over the years, the COMEX gold market has established itself as a market leader in setting gold prices within the North American time zone. Even though the physical transactions in COMEX are a fraction of those in other major gold centres, futures prices on this market are carefully monitored by gold traders throughout the world.

Since the closure of the commodity futures market in Hong Kong, those futures can be traded in the other markets, such as the Chicago Mercantile Exchange, the New York Mercantile Exchange, and the Minneapolis Grain Exchange (MGEX), all in the US. In the Minneapolis Grain Exchange, the commodity futures that can be traded include spring wheat (see Figure 13.8) and cottonseed. Commodity index futures of soya beans (see Figure 13.9) and corn (see Figure 13.10) can also be traded in MGEX. The commodity contract specifications of spring wheat and cottonseed are shown in Table 13.5.

Figure 13.8 Spring Wheat Futures Price, 1999–2001

Source: Courtesy of Minneapolis Grain Exchange

Figure 13.9   National Soya Bean Index Figures, 1997–2001

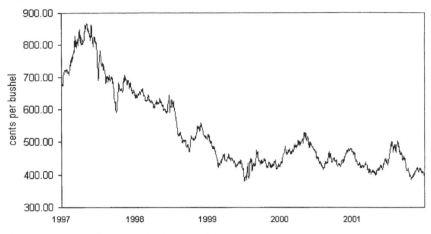

Source: Courtesy of Minneapolis Grain Exchange

Figure 13.10   National Corn Index Figures, 1997–2001

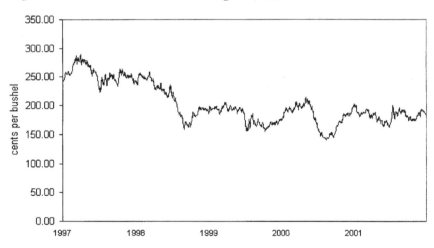

Source: Courtesy of Minneapolis Grain Exchange

Table 13.5   Contract Specifications of Spring Wheat and Cottonseed

	Spring Wheat	*Cottonseed*
Trading Hours	9.30am–1.15am (Central Time)	9.15am–1.00am (Central Time)
Contract Unit	5,000 bushels	120 tons (2000 pounds each ton)
Ticker Symbol	MW	CS
Delivery Months	March, May, July, September, and December	January, March, May, August, and November
Daily Price Limits	$.30 per bushel or $1,500 per contract	Ten US dollars ($10.00) per ton
Minimum Price Fluctuation	1/4 cent per bushel or $12.50 per contract	Ten US cents ($0.10) per ton
Speculative Position Limits	Spot month: 600 contracts Single month: 3000 contracts All months: 4000 contracts	1000 contracts net long or short in all months 400 contracts in any month as of the day preceding First Notice Day
Deliverable Grades	No. 2 or better Northern Spring Wheat with a protein content of 13.5% or higher, with 13% protein deliverable at a discount	Cottonseed with a basis grade of 90 or better as defined in Chapter II of the National Cottonseed Products Association's 1999–2000 Trading Rules at par. Cottonseed below 90 basis grade is deliverable at a 1.0 percent of settlement price discount per whole basis point down to a minimum of 85 basis grade. Buyer and seller may mutually agree to modify or change the par delivery grade on the contract.
Delivery Points	Elevators located in Minneapolis/St. Paul, Red Wing and Duluth/Superior	Memphis, Tennessee (Settlement Location)

Source: Data Courtesy of Minneapolis Grain Exchange

Discussion Questions

1. What are the major factors affecting the Hong Kong Gold Market? Discuss.
2. It is said that gold will turn into copper in ten years. Do you agree? Why or why not?
3. Explain the trading systems of the Hong Kong Futures Exchange Ltd.
4. The volume of commodity futures trading of The Hong Kong Futures Exchange Ltd began to diminish after 1988. What are the reasons underlying this?
5. Explain the historical development of the Loco-London Gold Market.
6. What are the characteristics of the daily premium/discount rate? Discuss.
7. Describe the gold fixing process of the gold market in London.
8. In terms of gold price calculations:
    a. How do we calculate the equivalent of Hong Kong gold in US dollars per fine ounce?
    b. If the market price of Hong Kong gold is HK$3,000, what is the equivalent of Hong Kong gold in US dollars per fine ounce?

Keywords

daily premium/discount rate
determination of interest
gold fixing
The Chinese Gold and Silver Exchange Society
The Hong Kong Futures Exchange Ltd
unit of trade

14. The Mortgage Market

David Y. K. Chan, C. K. Wong, and Camay K. M. Chan

Introduction

A mortgage is a loan guaranteed with the collateral of property, where the borrower has an obligation to make a predetermined series of payments. If the borrower fails to make the payments, the lender has the right to liquidate the property to repay the loan.

In Hong Kong, most mortgage loans are conventional mortgages, meaning that the lenders make the loans based on the borrowers' creditworthiness and the collateral. Lenders can also take out mortgage insurance to ensure that the borrowers pay back the loans. An example of this is the Hong Kong Mortgage Corporation's Mortgage Insurance Programme (MIP), which is discussed below.

The properties that can be mortgaged in Hong Kong can be categorized as either residential or commercial. The demand for housing in Hong Kong is great because of the scarcity of land and the large population. This high demand, together with the limited supply, makes housing costs high. Residential mortgages play an important role in the local mortgage market.

Risks Associated with Mortgage Lending

The originator of mortgage loans bears a certain level of risk. Generally speaking, the risks associated with mortgage lending relate to default, liquidity, interest rates, and prepayment.

Default risk is the risk of the borrower not meeting the contracted payments. The measurement of the default risk is called the conditioned default rate, which is the probability of a mortgage loan defaulting in a particular year.

Liquidity risk is the risk associated with the liquidation of the mortgage loan and can be measured through the bid–ask spread in an active secondary market. In Hong Kong, there was no secondary mortgage market before the establishment of the Hong Kong Mortgage Corporation (HKMC). The liquidity risk faced by the mortgage originators in Hong Kong is the price spread of the originators cashing out their position when the borrowers default.

With regard to interest rate risk, a mortgage loan is a debt instrument which is usually long-term and therefore affected by interest rate changes. The price of the loan will move in the opposite direction to the movement of the risk-free rate.

Lastly, the prepayment risk is the risk of borrowers prepaying loans, which they may have the right to do, either totally or partially. This creates the problem of uncertain cash flow and variable loan duration.

Overview of the Hong Kong Mortgage Market

Since the late 1980s, the real estate market has been active and speculative for two reasons. First, the Hong Kong government has been unable effectively to cool down the speculative activities of the property market. Second, the growth of the economy and a high inflation rate has led to an appreciation in asset value. The high inflation rate is directly related to the low interest rate environment which existed before the Asian financial crisis. As the Hong Kong dollar is pegged to the US dollar, the Hong Kong government's monetary policy (e.g. the interest rate) must follow that of the US. However, the economic cycles of Hong Kong and the US do not usually proceed at the same pace, so the Hong Kong government cannot utilize monetary policy effectively.

The speculative property market drives the growth of mortgage lending, with property-related lending becoming increasingly important to financial institutions. From 1980 to 1995, the share of residential mortgage loans in the total domestic loan portfolio rose from 9.9 per cent to 22.1 per cent. According to the Hong Kong Monetary Authority (HKMA), in the first quarter in 2002 the proportion was about 34 per cent. In mid-2003, private property mortgage loans comprised 35 per cent of local bank loans (*Ming Pao*, 2003).

From the statistics of new loans approved, the demand for mortgages increased between the early 1990s and its peak in 1997. Over time, the 'bubble economy' burst, property prices fell sharply, and real estate market participants suffered from the lack of property liquidity. Most properties became negative equity and the number of new loans approved gradually decreased (see Figure 14.1).

Figure 14.1 Monthly New Loans Approved

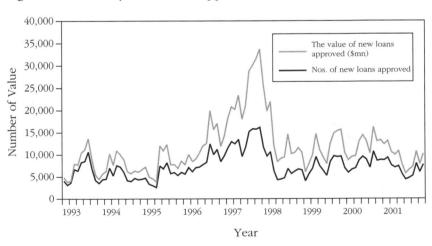

Source: Courtesy of HKMA

As mentioned already, mortgage lending is critically important business for banks due to the huge demand for housing in Hong Kong. The Hong Kong mortgage lending market was an oligopoly before the interest rate agreement, which allowed the leading banks of the past to dominate, was released. Because mortgage lending must be backed up by an enormous deposit base, a strong balance sheet, under-utilized funds, and high operating efficiency, the large banks such as HSBC, Hang Seng Bank, Bank of China Group, and Standard Chartered have an advantage over the smaller banks in terms of economies of scale and better resource allocation. After the interest rate agreement changed, price competition between financial institutions was more vigorous and the mortgage market became freely competitive.

Competition

Prior to 1996, competition in the mortgage market was not focused on direct price competition. Price competition is detrimental to bank profits, so banks competed by product differentiation. The HKMA issued guidelines to banks stating that the ceiling on the loan-to-valuation ratio of the residential mortgage should be 70 per cent, so banks fine-tuned their respective mortgage-lending policy offerings to the public.

Until early 1996, the price war in the residential mortgage rate was mild and short-term. Historically, the standard mortgage rate was determined by adding certain basis points above the Prime Rate, which was a benchmark for mortgage lending. Before 1996, the standard mortgage rate offered by local banks ranged from 1.25 per cent to 1.75 per cent above Prime.

After price competition in residential mortgage lending began in 1996, the mortgage rate was reduced from above the Prime Rate to below it. The changes in the Prime Rate from 1996 to 2002 are summarized in Figure 14.2. This shows that the Prime Rate did not decrease sharply before 2001, suggesting that the reduction in the mortgage rate is mainly due to the vigorous price competition of 2001.

Statistics show that most mortgage rates of new approved loans in 1998 were at Prime Rate (or best lending rate (BLR)) plus 1 per cent (see Table 14.1).

Table 14.1   Distribution of new mortgage loans in March 1998

At BLR*	0.40%
more than BLR to BLR+0.25%	5.40%
more than BLR+0.25% to BLR+0.5%	0.70%
more than BLR+0.5% to BLR+0.75%	6.40%
more than BLR+0.75% to BLR+1%	12.40%
more than BLR+1%	64.40%
Others	10.30%

* BLR: Best Lending Rate
Source: Courtesy of HKMA

Figure 14.2   The Change in the Hong Kong Prime Rate 1996–2001

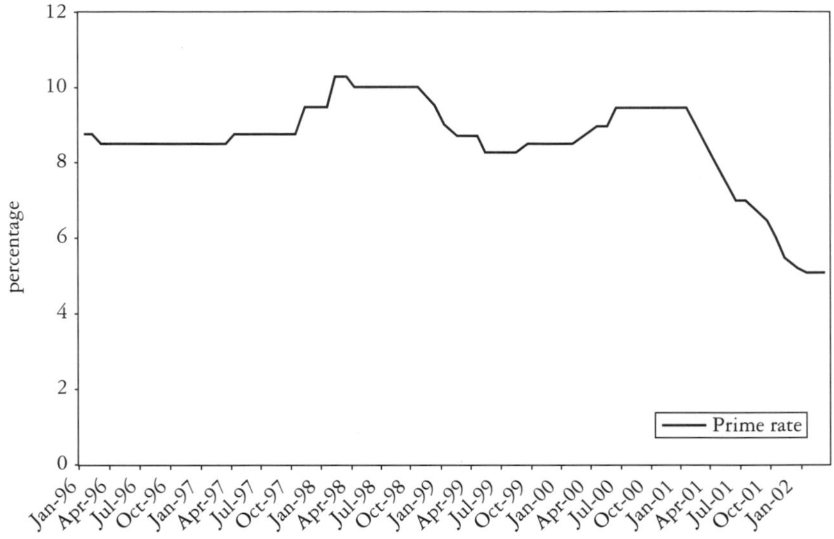

Source: Courtesy of HKMA

At the beginning of 1999, the price war continued, but the competition shifted from trying to obtain market share in the primary or secondary markets to the refinancing market. The main reason for this change was the bearish property market, which reduced the demand for new loans but whose rate reduction enticed property owners to refinance their existing loans to reduce their interest burden. To encourage customers to refinance their mortgage loans, the banks offered attractive prices (low mortgage rates). Most of the new mortgage loans were approved at Best Lending Rate (about 62.6 per cent) or Best Lending Rate plus 0.25 per cent. The figures are shown in Table 14.2

Table 14.2   Distribution of new mortgage loans in March 1999

At BLR	62.60%
more than BLR to BLR+0.25%	22.20%
more than BLR+0.25% to BLR+0.5%	5.30%
more than BLR+0.5% to BLR+0.75%	2.20%
more than BLR+0.75% to BLR+1%	0.70%
more than BLR+1%	2.00%
Others	5.00%

Source: Courtesy of HKMA

Competition in the refinancing market continued until the second half of 2000. Statistics show that in April 2000 46.4 per cent of new loans were in the refinancing market, whereas the primary market had only 19 per cent and the secondary market 34.6 per cent. The high proportion in the refinancing market was maintained until June 2000, when the figures for the refinancing, primary, and secondary markets were 50 per cent, 15 per cent, and 34.3 per cent respectively. This time, the mortgage rate continued to fall and most of the new loans approved were below or at the Best Lending rate.

Table 14.3 Distribution of new mortgage loans in March 2000

Below BLR	65.10%
At BLR	30.90%
more than BLR to BLR+0.25%	0.60%
more than BLR+0.25% to BLR+0.5%	0.20%
more than BLR+0.5% to BLR+0.75%	0.10%
more than BLR+0.75% to BLR+1%	0.10%
more than BLR+1%	0.10%
Others	3.00%

Source: Courtesy of HKMA

Since the last quarter of 2000, the US Federal Reserve has reduced the interest rate ten-fold and the standard mortgage rate has decreased further (see Table 14.4).

Table 14.4 Distribution of new mortgage loans in March 2001

Below BLR	91.10%
At BLR	4.60%
more than BLR to BLR+0.25%	0.10%
more than BLR+0.25% to BLR+0.5%	0.00%
more than BLR+0.5% to BLR+0.75%	0.00%
more than BLR+0.75% to BLR+1%	0.10%
more than BLR+1%	0.20%
Others	4%

Source: Courtesy of HKMA

A little under 50 per cent (45.9 per cent) of mortgage loans were approved at less than the Best Lending rate minus 2.25 per cent. The continuous reduction in mortgage rates in these years may lead to consideration of the suitability of the Prime Rate as the benchmark for future mortgage lending rates.

Securitization

Securitization is a financial development trend in financial markets all over the world. It means packaging together the pool of individual loans or receivables and distributing them to investors in the form of bonds or notes.

The securities that are the underlying assets are mortgage loans called mortgage-backed securities (MBS). The predominant type of MBS is the mortgage pass-through security. It is created by one or more mortgage holders from a collection of mortgages, and shares in the pool are sold. The cash flow from the collateral pool is 'passed through' to the security holder as monthly payments of principal, interest, and prepayments. Usually the mortgages are packaged into pools by agencies. The agencies can be owned by the government or other private financial institutions.

Benefits of Securitization

The Financial Market

Securitization enhances the stability of financial markets in the long run because Hong Kong's funding source depends mainly on deposits and interbank borrowings. The prudent banks will prefer floating rate mortgage lending to reduce the interest risk, but mortgagees will prefer fixed interest rate terms because they prevent their exposure to interest rate fluctuation, which directly affects repayments.

The feasibility of banks supplying fixed rate mortgages will be a function of the supply of fixed-rate borrowing. HKMC tries to tap long-term savings and turn these funds into fixed rate mortgage loans, which it encourages (and assists) the banks to provide. If fixed-interest borrowing becomes more readily available and popular, the degree of insulation from interest rate fluctuation will increase for the economy as a whole. The interest rate risk will have shifted from the mortgagees to MBS holders, who are usually institutional investors able to bear interest risk. This helps to improve financial stability.

The Financial Institutions (The Originators): Selling Assets

The liquidity risk due to a mismatch of the maturities of assets and liabilities of the originators can be reduced. They usually lend long-term money at fixed rates financed in the short-term market. The originators can decrease part of the long-term mortgage pool and achieve immediate cash inflow through securitization.

Securitization can enhance the proportion of banks' non-interest income. It generates a stable income, as the originators can obtain servicing fees for managing the pool of mortgages. The originators can also finance new mortgages without depending solely on the increase in the deposit base, because securitization enables diversification of source of funding.

Securitization provides liquidity for originators. The banks can obtain extra funding to increase lending business or for other financial needs. Also, securitization of assets can be used to remove any internal or external constraints that might apply to the originator's balance sheet with regard to both lending and borrowing. The originator can carry out further profitable lending business without breaching the limits, and can also achieve better portfolio management as the risk can be passed to the note holder by securitization.

The Investors

Due to the complexity and uncertainty of the MBS, the yield is higher than other securities of comparable quality. Also, excluding early prepayment, retail investors can obtain a regular monthly income.

Liquidity is important for portfolio management. The MBS market is very active and liquid, and the variety of MBS available enable investors to choose those that best suit their portfolio and needs.

Consumers

If the demand for mortgage funds continues to increase, the mortgage interest rate will also increase due to an insufficient supply of funds. Securitization can increase the funding sources of the existing banking system, which helps to lessen the mortgage interest rate.

Securitization of Mortgages in the US

The system of securitization in the US is the most representative in the world, and the Hong Kong system was modelled on it. In the US, three main government agencies provide mortgage-backed securities: the Government National Mortgage Association (Ginnie Mae), the Federal Home Loan Mortgage Corporation (Freddie Mac), and the Federal National Mortgage Association (Fannie Mae). The securities they provide are called agencies pass-through.

The agencies usually guarantee the payment of the MBS in one of the following two forms: first, the timely payment (when due) of both interest and principal, and second, the timely payment (when due) of interest with the payment of the principal only passing to the investor when it is collected.

Some private financial institutions also issue mortgage pass-through securities called private-label pass-through securities. The formation process of these securities is similar to that of those issued by government agencies. However, they must be registered with the Securities and Exchange Commission and rated by the nationally recognized rating companies.

As the securitization of the mortgages in the US was developed many years ago, there is now a large variety of mortgage-backed securities besides the mortgage pass-through—for example, collateralized mortgage obligations (CMO) and stripped mortgage-backed securities—all of which have different payment structures.

Securitization of Mortgages in Hong Kong

Before the Establishment of HKMC

Before the establishment of the Hong Kong Mortgage Corporation, the MBS in Hong Kong were issued by private companies. MBS in Hong

Kong began in 1994 when the property market was bullish, with issues from four companies: Bank of America (Asia), Citibank Hong Kong, Cheung Kong Holdings Ltd, and Standard Chartered Bank. All of the issues were one-off, as there was at that time no well-organized secondary market presence. Except for the issue from Cheung Kong Holdings, which was partially priced against Prime, they were priced against the Hong Kong Interbank Offered Rate (HIBOR).

Hong Kong Mortgage Corporation (HKMC)

Background

Stability of the Banking Sector
Before the establishment of the HKMC, the mortgage financing supply in Hong Kong came mainly from the banking sector. As most of the mortgage loans are on floating rate terms and the bulk of authorized institutions' funds are also on floating rate terms, these institutions are not exposed to any substantial interest rate risk, apart from basis risk; they are, however, subject to other funding risks.

First, the funding source of these institutions comes mainly from customer deposits and short-term interbank borrowings. As a result, the maturity of their funding is less than three months on average. However, the mean actual contractual life of mortgage loans was 15.2 years as at September 1994, and 18.4 years as at September 1997, although the actual mortgage life could be shorter because of prepayment. The mismatch between that and the funding makes them subject to the maturity mismatch risk.

Second, as mortgage loans cannot be converted into liquid funds without a secondary mortgage market, the authorized institutions are also exposed to liquidity risk. In the case of default in particular, the institutions usually require a long time to liquidate the underlying property of a mortgage loan.

Lastly, a high concentration of loans in mortgage lending endangers the banking sector by increasing the risk on the institutions, because the fluctuation of the property market can affect the collateral value significantly.

Fund Supply for Mortgages
Apart from increasing the stability of the banking sector, the fund supply for mortgages is another reason for the establishment of the Hong Kong Mortgage Corporation and the development of securitization. According to the HKMC's 1995 proposal, the projected amount to meet the demand for residential loans would increase from $347.9 billion to around $1,970 billion by 2005 (or $871 billion at 1995 prices). The projected increase in supply in mortgage lending would only be $1,183 billion in 2005 ($523 billion at 1995 prices). There would be a potential gap of $788 billion (or $348 billion at 1995 prices). Although the above figures were only estimates,

with demographic changes such as the increase in population and the emergence of a middle-class income group, the demand for mortgage loans was seen definitely as rising. To meet this huge potential demand, the development of securitization seemed to be a way of increasing the short-term mortgage fund supply.

Function of HKMC

As mentioned above, the reasons for establishing the Hong Kong Mortgage Corporation were to enhance the stability of the banking sector by providing a reliable source of liquidity through the securitization process and the development of a secondary mortgage loans market. Its establishment has another important role, though, which is to promote the development of a debt securities market. The introduction of the MBS market in Hong Kong also encourages the development of the Hong Kong bond market. It can help financial institutions achieve better risk management, as their mortgage pools can be securitized and related risks shifted to the holders of MBS. It also increases the range of financial instruments available to portfolio managers, and allows them to formulate diversified and efficient portfolios.

HKMC's Beginnings

The incorporation of the HKMC in March 1997 marked an important milestone in the development of the residential mortgage market and mortgage-backed securities in Hong Kong. Because of insufficient initial funding, from 1998 the HKMC issued debt securities and then used the net proceeds to purchase mortgage loans from authorized institutions. Payments were made to securities holders each month. The monthly cash flow for debt securities was less than the monthly cash flow of the underlying mortgages by an amount equal to servicing and other fees. The other fees included those charged by the HKMC for guaranteeing the issue.

The HKMC formally commenced operations in October 1997 as scheduled. Marking this occasion was the signing of the Master Sale and Purchase Agreement and the Master Mortgage Servicing/Servicers by eight banks on 20 October 1997. The first block of mortgage purchases followed suit. The HKMC purchased a total of HK$650 million loans from four Approved Sellers in November 1997.

HKMC's Mortgage Business

The business model of the HKMC is issuing debt to purchase mortgage loans from approved financial institutions and then packing the loans to form mortgage-backed securities and issuing them to investors. As a result, the core products of the HKMC can be divided into three categories: debt issuance programmes, mortgage purchase programmes, and mortgage-backed securities. The income sources of the Hong Kong Mortgage Corporation are mainly the interest margin between the funding sources (debt issuance business) and the lending business (MBS or fixed rate mortgage), and the premium from the Mortgage Insurance Programme.

Mortgage Purchase Programmes

Generally, the HKMC purchases mortgage loans pools from Approved Seller/Servicers for its own portfolio according to a set of criteria for different products. Some of them are:

1. Loan size
2. Maximum loan-to-value ratio (at time of origination)
3. Maximum debt-to-income ratio (at time of origination)
4. Minimum seasoning
5. Maximum original term to maturity
6. Remaining term to maturity
7. Maximum sum of 'original term' and 'age of property' at origination
8. Occupancy status

The loans will then be serviced by these lenders on behalf of the HKMC for a servicing fee. Besides issuing unsecured debt to fund mortgage purchases for its own retained portfolio, the HKMC also packages mortgage loans from its own portfolio and from the approved institutions into mortgage-backed securities. There are two main purchase programmes for different mortgages: floating rate mortgages (Prime-based) and HIBOR-based mortgages.

Floating Rate Mortgages

The HKMC purchases Prime-based floating rate mortgages from its approved sellers at a gross mortgage rate, which will be adjusted according to the market rate. To qualify for sale to the HKMC, the mortgage loan must be fully amortized and must fulfil other mortgage purchasing criteria (both core and product-type), as seen in Table 14.5.

At the discretion of the HKMC, floating rate mortgages offered for sale may be subject to an additional requirement of current loan-to-value valuation.

HIBOR-based Mortgages

As mentioned earlier, the Prime Rate is the benchmark for mortgage loan rates in Hong Kong, and most mortgage loan rates are originated based on the Prime Rate, including floating rate mortgage products. Beginning in May 1999, the HKMC included floating rate mortgage products based on HIBOR as eligible mortgages under its mortgage purchase programme. The interest rate can be fixed on a daily, monthly, quarterly, and semi-annual basis, and the interest cost can be computed on a daily or monthly basis.

HIBOR is volatile. To guard against potential fluctuations, the gross mortgage rate of HIBOR-based mortgages has been placed with a rate

Table 14.5 HKMC Floating Rate Mortgage Purchasing Criteria

Purchasing Criteria	HKMC Floating Rate Mortgage Purchasing Criteria
(a) Loan Size Outstanding Principal Balance (at time of mortgage sale)	Maximum : HK$5.0 million Minimum : HK$3.0 million
Maximum original loan size (at time of origination)	HK$8.0 million
(b) Maximum Loan-to-Value ratio (at time of origination)	70%
(c) Maximum Debt-to-Income ratio (at time of origination)	50% (for general and insured mortgage) 60% (with additional requirements)
(d) Minimum Seasoning	Nil
(e) Maximum original term to maturity	30 years
(f) Remaining term to maturity	Maximum: 30 years Minimum: 3 years
(g) Maximum sum of 'original term' and 'age of property' at origination	50 years
(h) Occupancy status	Owner-occupied only

Source: Courtesy of HKMA

cap and a rate floor. The level of the cap and floor will be negotiated between the seller and the HKMC. The core and product-type purchasing criteria will also be applied to these mortgage loans.

Debt Issuance Programmes

The mortgage purchase programme is financed by the Debt Issuance Programme (DIP) of the HKMC. The HKMC established its debt issuance platform by launching the HK$20 billion Note Issuance Programme (NIP) and the HK$20 billion DIP in January and June 1998 respectively.

In 1999 the HKMC facilitated the growth and development of the mortgage-backed and debt securities markets in Hong Kong. The HKD Note Issuance Programme and its seven outstanding issues totalling HK$3.5 billion were listed on the Stock Exchange of Hong Kong in October 1999. For retail investors, the non-competitive bidding method was introduced. To attract those retail investors, the minimum denomination was reduced to HK$50,000 per transaction. The eighth issue of HK$500 million under the NIP was also favourably received. This not only provided a convenient platform for the Hong Kong public to invest in high quality fixed-income securities, but also broadened the investor base of the HKMC.

At the end of May 2003, the total outstanding debt securities under the two debt issuance programmes was HK$32.8 billion. With its good credit rating, and its market-friendly and investor-driven approaches, the HKMC's debt securities were well received by financial institutions and institutional investors. However, those retail bonds which listed on the Exchange have suffered from a liquidity problem.

New Market-Making System of Retail Bonds

Since November 2001, the HKMC has used a new system to issue its retail bonds, as listing on the Hong Kong Exchange cannot provide an active secondary market because of a thin trading volume. Instead of public listing, the new debts were issued through placing. Investors could apply for the bonds through the authorized banks. There were three placing banks in the initial public offering (IPO) in November 2001: Dao Heng Bank, HSBC, and Hang Seng Bank. In total 1,660 applications were received with a total amount of HK$ 651 million. Another five banks joined the programme in February 2002: Bank of China (Hong Kong), Bank of Communications Hong Kong Branch, CITIC KA Wah Bank, Standard Chartered Bank, and Wing Lung Bank. Over 3,490 investors submitted applications, with a total amount of HK$1,371 million.

As well as their IPO responsibilities, the authorized banks also act as the market makers in the secondary market. The banks provide the bid and ask price for the retail bonds until the expiration of the issue. To enhance the ability of placing banks to quote offer prices, the amount to be held in reserve for tapping by the banks to meet the demand of retail investors in the secondary market is 30 per cent of the total issue amount. The banks are committed to quote firm offer prices until the reserve amount is exhausted, and they will continue to do so on a best-efforts basis afterwards. Using this market-making mechanism, investors can buy and sell the retail bonds through the banks at the bid and ask prices of that day. However, the trading cost varies between banks.

Mortgage-backed Securities

The MBS programme started in October 1999. The target customers of the MBS are professional investors, and no retail MBS have been issued up to this date. However, private investors may still have the opportunity to purchase the securities through some banks.

The HKMC's Mortgage-backed Securitisation Programme uses a back-to-back structure. After buying mortgages from the bank, the HKMC will pass the mortgages to a bankruptcy-remote special purpose company (SPC). The SPC will then issue MBS to the bank with the HKMC's guarantee for the timely payment of principal and interest. Since the launch of the Guaranteed Mortgage-backed Securitisation Programme in October 1999, the SPC has arranged four issues with several banks, with an aggregate issue amount of HK$2.8 billion.

The 'swap and hold' structure allows the banks to retain the income stream less the guarantee fee, with the option to offload the MBS to professional investors. The HKMC's guarantee fee for the timely payment of scheduled principal and interest will substantially reduce the credit risk of the mortgage loans and hence the need for the bank to make provisions. Moreover, the MBS will carry a lower risk-weighting of 20 per cent compared with 50 per cent for mortgages in the determination of capital adequacy ratio, thereby resulting in savings in capital cost to the bank. For the HKMC, this programme not only opens a new line of business, it also paves the way for more complicated MBS products to be issued in the future.

The aim of the Guaranteed MBS programme is to provide an efficient way of developing a secondary market for the mortgages held by the bank through a standardized structure which is under the guarantee of

Figure 14.3 Structure of the 'Swap and Hold' Transaction

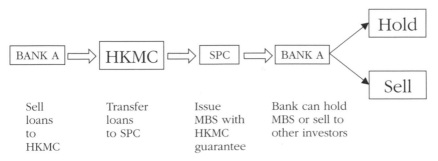

| Sell loans to HKMC | Transfer loans to SPC | Issue MBS with HKMC guarantee | Bank can hold MBS or sell to other investors |

Source: Courtesy of HKMA

Figure 14.4 Pass-through of Coupon

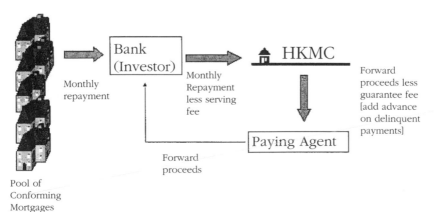

Source: Courtesy of HKMA

the HKMC as well as the Hong Kong government. As the HKMC is wholly owned by the Exchange Fund, MBS are therefore guaranteed by the Hong Kong government, increasing investor confidence in them. Further, with the objective of being a regular issuer, the HKMC's MBS programme, with its standardization of structure and documentation, will serve to create greater liquidity and support the development of a more active secondary mortgage market in Hong Kong.

Other Business

Other than its core businesses, the HKMC also provides different products according to different market environments. The aim of these programmes is to meet the needs of home buyers and stabilize the property market in the wake of the Asian financial crisis.

The Fixed Adjustable Rate Mortgage (FARM) Pilot Scheme

As a result of high interest rates, the Fixed Adjustable Rate Mortgage Pilot Scheme was launched in March 1998 to give an option to home buyers for mortgage financing at a fixed rate for three years. Following favourable market reception, the HKMC started to offer fixed rate mortgages as one of its standard products in August 1998. The HKMC further expanded the FARM product by adding one- and two-year fixed terms in June 1999.

The FARMs begin with a gross mortgage rate which is fixed and determined by the HKMC. At the end of the respective fixed periods (one to three years), the borrower can choose either to refix the mortgage rate for another fixed term at the then prevailing fixed rate specified by the HKMC, or to convert to a floating rate mortgage. The rate of the FARM programme is a function of the cost of the HKMC.

The eight participating banks in the FARM scheme are Bank of East Asia, Chase Manhattan Bank, Chekiang First Bank, Dao Heng Bank, First Pacific Bank, Hang Seng Bank, Hong Kong Bank, and Standard Chartered Bank.

The Mortgage Insurance Programme (MIP)

The Hong Kong government reduced the loan-to-value (LTV) ratio to suppress speculative activities in the property market, cutting the ratio from 90 per cent to 70 per cent. However, the property market became bearish after the Asian financial crisis and there was a huge demand for a reduction in the entry costs of house buyers with a view to stimulating the property market. The Hong Kong government had simultaneously to resolve the need for stimulating the property market and stabilizing the banking system. The high LTV ratio exposed the financial institutions to additional risks, such as default risk, which can be high in a bearish property market. After further evaluation, the Hong Kong government did not relax the regulation of the LTV ratio immediately; instead the HKMC provided another programme to respond to the need for lower entry costs into the property market.

Table 14.6   HKMC Fixed Rate Mortgage Purchasing Criteria

Purchasing Criteria	HKMC Fixed Rate Mortgage Purchasing Criteria
(a) Loan Size Outstanding Principal Balance (at time of mortgage sale) Maximum original loan size (at time of origination)	HK$4.0 million
(b) Maximum Loan-to-Value ratio (at time of origination)	70%
(c) Maximum Debt-to-Income ratio (at time of origination)	50% (for general and insured mortgage) 60% (with additional requirements)
(d) Minimum Seasoning	Nil
(e) Maximum original term to maturity	30 years
(f) Remaining term to maturity	N.A.
(g) Maximum sum of 'original term' and 'age of property' at origination	50 years
(h) Occupancy status	Owner-occupied only

Source: Courtesy of HKMA

Figure 14.5 The Mortgage Insurance Programme

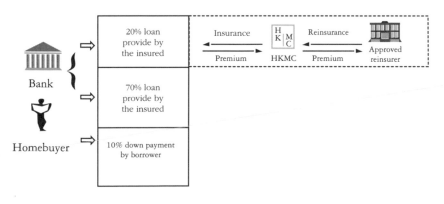

Source of data: Courtesy of HKMA

The Mortgage Insurance Programme provides a way to reduce homebuyers' deposits (entry costs) without increasing the risk exposure of the financial institutions. Under the MIP, the HKMC provides insurance cover at a fee to the insured for an amount of up to twenty per cent of the property value, which allows the insured to lend up to ninety per cent loan-to-value ratio. The HKMC hedges the position by taking out reinsurance with the approved reinsurers.

Experience from other markets demonstrates that mortgage loans with a higher LTV ratio carry a higher risk of borrower default. It is important that the additional credit risk will be mitigated by more prudent underwriting criteria and be adequately reflected in the insurance premium.

For a mortgage loan of HK$1.5 million with a repayment period of twenty years, the insurance premiums under the single payment and annual payment methods are as follows:

Table 14.7   Insurance Premium of MIP

Product Type	Loan-to Valuation	Insurance Premium					
		Single Payment Method		Annual Payment Method			
				Initial Year		Until OPB drops to 70% LTV ratio	
		% of Loan amount	$	% of loan amount	$	% of loan amount	$
Floating Rate Mortgage	Up to 80%	1.40	21,000	0.70	10,500	0.24	3,600
	Up to 85%	2.15	32,250	0.90	13,500	0.45	6,750
	Up to 90%	**2.98**	**44,700**	**1.28**	**19,200**	**0.63**	**9,450**

Source: Courtesy of HKMA

On 1 March 2001, the Board of Directors of the HKMC approved an expansion of MIP to include equitable mortgage loans secured on residential properties under construction. The HKMC stated that the introduction of the equitable mortgage product would be in two phases. The first phase was launched on 27 April 2001; it covers equitable mortgage loans with LTV ratios of up to eighty-five per cent. The second phase was launched on 18 July 2001 and covers equitable mortgage loans with LTV ratios of up to ninety per cent. The same insurance premium as for standard mortgage loans is charged on equitable mortgage loans.

The HKMC announced an expansion to increase the loan ceiling for mortgages covered under the programme from HK$5 million to HK$8 million. This expansion, which was launched on 5 November 2001, initially covered mortgage loans for completed properties with an LTV ratio of up to eighty-five per cent.

Table 14.8   Approved Sellers/Servicers as at July 2003 (for updates, see the HKMA website)

ABN AMRO Bank N.V.	Hang Seng Credit Limited
AIG Finance (Hong Kong) Limited	Hang Seng Finance Limited
American Express Bank Limited	The Hong Kong Housing Authority
Asia Commercial Bank Limited	Hong Kong Housing Society
Bank of America (Asia) Limited	The Hongkong and Shanghai Banking
Bank of China (Hong Kong) Limited	Corporation Limited
Bank of Communications	Inchroy Credit Corporation Limited
The Bank of East Asia, Limited	Industrial and Commercial Bank of China
Brilliant Oscar Limited*	(Asia) Limited
Canadian Eastern Finance, Limited	International Bank of Asia Limited
Chekiang First Bank Limited	Liu Chong Hing Bank Limited
Chiyu Banking Corporation Limited	Nanyang Commercial Bank, Limited
Citibank, N.A.	ORIX Asia Limited
CITIC Ka Wah Bank Limited	ORIX Finance Services (Hong Kong) Ltd**
Dah Sing Bank, Limited	Pacific Finance (Hong Kong) Limited
DBS Bank (Hong Kong) Limited	Shanghai Commercial Bank Limited
Fortis Bank Asia HK	Standard Chartered Bank
GE Capital (Hong Kong) Limited	Wing Hang Bank, Limited
Hang Seng Bank Limited	Wing Lung Bank, Limited

* Approved as Servicer Only; ** Approved as Seller Only
Source: Courtesy of HKMA

The Future of the Mortgage Market in Hong Kong

Benchmark of Mortgage Loans

Due to price competition, the mortgage rate has dropped significantly and the Prime Rate may no longer be an adequate benchmark for the mortgage rate. One of the alternatives is the one-month HIBOR. However, we should notice that the one-month HIBOR is much more volatile than the Prime Rate.

Future Role of Banks in Mortgage Lending

Residential mortgages accounted for about thirty-four per cent of total loans in Hong Kong Kong in the first quarter of 2002, and thirty-five per cent as at July 2003. As a result, residential and related lending is significant to the earnings of the banking sector. This is unhealthy and risky in the long run because any downturn in the residential property sector may lead to a banking crisis.

The development of mortgage-backed securities could change the role of the banks in mortgage lending by transforming them from the final lenders of mortgage loans to the financial intermediaries of the MBS issue. A bank can enjoy a servicing fee without bearing the significant credit risk of the pool of mortgages. The importance of the mortgage lending business for bankers does not limit it to being the main income source, but extends it to act as the beginning of a long-term customer relationship wherein banks can offer services such as credit card lending, personal loans, and some retail investment services.

Future Development of HKMC

We expect that the Hong Kong Mortgage Corporation will provide an increasing number of products to investors. To broaden its funding source, the HKMC may launch multi-currency MBS and Medium Term Note programmes in the future. We also expect that mortgage-backed securities will be developed further.

Conclusion

The ultimate effect of the securitization of mortgage loans is intended to be a significant reduction in the risk exposure of the banks so that the Hong Kong economy is less affected by the booms and busts of the residential property market. However, this effect has yet to be fully felt as banks are still heavily dependent on mortgage lending as their main profit generator. Another effect for banks is that the service fee will become a main source of income in the administration of MBS. If banks can increase the mortgage pool and obtain greater service fees through securitization, they can still be profitable even when interest rates are reduced. It is therefore reasonable to project that competition in the mortgage market will continue for some time, and that the mortgage rate will remain steady or increase slightly according to the interest cycle in the US. In contrast, however, the property market seems to have reached its lowest point. The high level of competition in the mortgage market will cool down, and the demand for mortgage loans will increase. The securitization of mortgage loans provides flexibility to the banks in the usage of funds.

The HKMC has driven the development of mortgage-backed securities in Hong Kong, stabilized the banking sector, and hastened the development of the debt market in Hong Kong. So far, it has been quite successful, especially with regard to the development of the debt market. The low-interest environment has provided a good opportunity for the sale of retail bonds, as the bonds under the new system usually have a higher yield and better potential for capital gain. The HKMC's agreement with the banks has provided a better distribution network and market-making mechanism for the retail bonds. The latest IPOs have been quite successful. The debt market and the mortgage-backed securities market will continue to develop in this direction.

Discussion Questions

1. What are the characteristics of the Hong Kong mortgage market?
2. Discuss the benefits of the securitization of mortgage loans.

3. What are the major businesses of the Hong Kong Mortgage Corporation?
4. Discuss the risks involved in mortgage lending.
5. Explain the differences between the two main purchase programmes offered by the Hong Kong Mortgage Corporation.
6. Describe Hong Kong's Mortgage-backed Securitisation (MBS) Programme.
7. What are the likely future developments and prospects of the mortgage market in Hong Kong?
8. Elaborate on the Mortgage Insurance Programme (MIP) in Hong Kong. Explain its purposes.

Keywords

default risk
interest rate risk
liquidity risk
mortgage
mortgage-backed securities (MBS)
prepayment risk
securitization

PART III

Issues and Policies

15. Corporate Governance and Disclosures

Simon S. M. Ho

Introduction

It is commonly agreed that the 1997 Asian financial crisis was mainly the result of structural weaknesses—i.e. a lack of effective corporate governance and transparency—in many of Asia's financial markets and institutions (Choi, 1998). Misinvestment, overborrowing, and low-quality disclosures were blamed on the absence of proper checks and balances to monitor Asia's tycoons. Many banks were controlled by owner–managers, and the boards of directors played limited roles in much connected lending. Growth was more important than returns and liquidity, and risk management was usually poor. In fact, there was a tendency for the less transparent markets in the region (such as Thailand, Malaysia, Japan, and Indonesia) to be subject to more volatile shocks than the more transparent markets (such as Hong Kong, Taiwan, and Singapore) (Ho, 2000). Analysts agree that the reason for the relatively smaller effect of the crisis on Hong Kong's businesses was the territory's established corporate governance regime. Thus, a solution to restore international investors' confidence in the Asian corporate sector and attract more capital inflow has been to strengthen its corporate governance and disclosure. Over the last several years, most East Asian economies have been actively reviewing and improving their corporate governance and transparency. However, only a few have made substantial progress.

The recent collapse of the Enron Corporation in the US and similar incidents have underscored the critical importance of structural reforms in the governance of large companies and financial institutions. These will undoubtedly result in stricter economic, financial, and accounting regulations for capital markets around the world. While the problems to be dealt with have a US focus, the Hong Kong market, banks, companies, and regulators will draw their own conclusions on how to prevent such incidents because Hong Kong often looks upon US financial regulatory frameworks as models to be emulated. In any case, improving corporate governance practices should be an ongoing process rather than an *ad hoc* reaction to sudden events or failures. This chapter systematically surveys the key concepts, current practice, effectiveness, core problems, and future prospects of corporate governance in Hong Kong.

The Concept of Corporate Governance

According to Monks and Minow (2001), a corporation is 'a mechanism established to allow different parties to contribute capital, expertise and labour, for the maximum benefits of all of them'. This independent entity relates to a wide variety of 'stakeholders', 'participants', or 'constituents' including its shareholders, directors, managers, employees, customers, creditors, suppliers, market intermediaries, auditors, regulators, and the government, as well as members of the community. The first three are known as primary stakeholders or participants.

The Organisation for Economic Co-operation and Development (OECD) (1998) defines corporate governance (CG) as 'the system by which business corporations are directed and controlled'. In a narrow sense, it is the relationship between various primary participants in determining the directions and performance of corporations. In a broader sense, it delineates the rights and responsibilities of each primary stakeholder and the design of institutions and mechanisms that induce or control board directors and management to serve best the interests of shareholders and other stakeholders of a company (see Figure 15.1). Many of these other stakeholders also play a role in monitoring the behaviour of the board/management.

Figure 15.1 Stakeholders Influencing the Corporate Governance of a Company

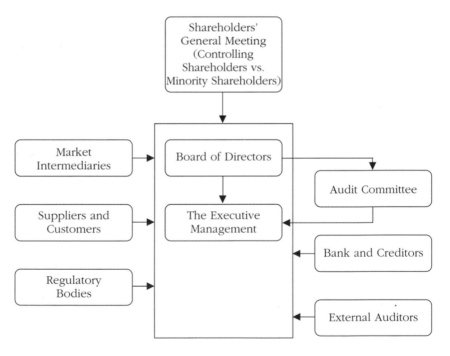

The part of any organization that has the most control over governance is the board of directors, and the board is the 'soul' of a company—the foundation of all business decisions and the origin of corporate culture of the whole entity. The essence of corporate governance includes discipline, independence, fairness, transparency, responsibility, accountability, and social awareness (Gill, 2002).

Our knowledge of corporate governance is largely derived from the agency theory that was developed in the West. Governance problems in the West often originate from the problem of the separation of ownership and control within a business organization, which gives rise to information asymmetry and agency costs (Fama and Jensen, 1983a and 1983b). Therefore, the actions of executives need to be properly monitored, and incentive schemes should be used as a means of aligning managerial and shareholder interests (Jensen and Meckling, 1976; Fama, 1980; Fama and Jensen, 1983a and 1983b). In the US, conflicts of interest exist mainly between the board, the management, and the shareholders (institutional and individual). However, in East Asian markets with concentrated ownership by controlling families, unchecked insider or connected party transactions are frequent and the main conflict is between the board/management (dominated by controlling shareholders) and minority shareholders. Therefore, the protection of the rights of minority shareholders is one of the key concerns in East Asian countries.

There are four layers of CG or sources of forces shaping a company's CG: (1) individual ethics and corporate cultures, (2) internal control and incentive mechanisms, (3) external monitoring mechanisms, and (4) law and regulations. Professional and ethical market players, self-disciplined firms with effective governance mechanisms, a sound regulatory framework, and informed and active investors are the necessary conditions of a successful capital market.

For a market to be efficient and effective, all stakeholders or participants must play their respective roles diligently and support each other with integrity. High ethical values can reduce costs to achieve a high corporate governance standard and make it more sustainable. This relies on companies setting ethical guidelines and good communication channels with all levels of staff so that the same corporate values are attained by every member of the organization. Corporate culture does begin with the personal values of the top management.

Good corporate governance also implies the need for an interrelated network of monitoring and incentive mechanisms set up by a company to ensure the accountability of the board/management to shareholders and other stakeholders. Besides being classified as monitoring versus incentive mechanisms, the governance mechanisms of modern corporations can be broadly classified as internal or external. Common internal governance mechanisms include the functions of ownership structure, the shareholders' general meeting, the composition of the board of directors and its committees, the separation of role of the board chairman from that of the chief executive officer (CEO), independent directors, board–management interaction, financial reporting and disclosure policies, internal auditing, and other internal codes, rules, and procedures. External control mechanisms are concerned with guidelines and standards prescribed by regulators, managerial monitoring by creditors, large institutional shareholders, external auditors, the stock market, the financial analysts, the executive labour market, the market for corporate control, and individual shareholders.

The amount of laws and regulations that a country needs depends to some extent on individual ethical standards and corporate cultures, as well as the effectiveness of existing governance mechanisms. However, it must be noted that no matter how comprehensive and strict is a legal system, it cannot avoid all inappropriate, unethical, and illegal practices. Hill (1999) argues that no one single mechanism is a governance panacea and suggests that 'it is desirable to have a system of overlapping checks and balances'. Further, it is the substance and not the form of good corporate governance that will enhance the performance of individual companies.

Does Corporate Governance Really Matter?

The President of the World Bank, James Wolfensohn, has equated the importance of corporate governance with that of the governance of countries. It is believed that with better corporate governance, firms can reduce agency costs and inefficiencies arising from conflicts of interest between controlling owners, management, and minority shareholders; become more competitive in global markets; and fulfil their social responsibilities. It is via the corporate governance system that the broad objectives of the company are determined, the means of reaching these objectives are agreed upon and performance is evaluated (OECD, 1998), and inflows of capital and returns on capital are ensured (Shleifer and Vishny, 1997). The OECD Principles of Corporate Governance (1999) emphasize that good corporate governance is important in building market confidence and encouraging more stable, long-term international investment flows. It is generally agreed that effective corporate governance does contribute positively to the development of financial markets.

Empirical evidence has shown that firms which practise good corporate governance enjoy lower costs of capital and higher share values. Improvements in corporate governance, according to McKinsey, can raise the value of companies anywhere, but for American and British firms the likely benefit is less than twenty per cent, whereas for Indonesian and Thai companies it is closer to thirty per cent (*The Economist*, 2001). The investment bank CLSA's research findings show that corporate governance pays when investing in emerging markets, and that there is a strong correlation between higher corporate governance rankings and superior financial return indicators (e.g. ROCE and EVA), higher valuations, and medium-term share price out-performance (see Gill, 2002). Low corporate governance companies are high investment risks, and markets and stocks with poor corporate governance are punished.[1]

Therefore, both McKinsey and the CLSA provide sound testimony as to the increasing importance of corporate governance. Other research has also suggested robust correlations between corporate governance and key financial indicators. These findings should provide the necessary impetus for regulators and companies to implement more measures to enhance the standard of corporate governance. Most investment managers believe that companies with better governance have better growth prospects, are less vulnerable to market downturns, and have lower costs of borrowing (Chow, 2002). Recent research on corporate governance by Standard and Poor's indicates that investors are willing to pay a premium for shares in well-governed companies.

Although good governance may not guarantee better performance in a company, there is empirical evidence that bad corporate governance is a good early warning of deeper trouble. In the 1990s, takeovers, corporate collapses, scandals, and the emergence of institutional investor activism in the West have all led to a serious assessment of how companies should be directed and governed in the future. Both the United States and Europe have also had their share of questionable management behaviour, leading to the loss of billions of dollars and even re-auditing and indictment in some cases. These cases include Enron, WorldCom, Xerox, Tyco, and Sunbeam in the US, and Morgan Grenfell, Cable & Wireless, Guardian IT, and Elan Corp in Europe. These are but a few of the more recent cases that highlight the increasing importance of effective corporate governance.

The issues transcend national boundaries. Although the West has been the home of the bulk of recent corporate controversy, certainly Hong Kong and other East Asian economies are not innocent. Recent corporate oversight or misgovernance cases in Asia include Barings and Asia Pulp & Paper in Singapore, Daiwa Bank and Sumitomo Corporation in Japan, and Peregrine Investment, Shun Shing Group, Guangnan Group, Kit Wai International, and Euro-Asia Agriculture in Hong Kong. For instance, in Hong Kong, Peregrine Investment had virtually no practice of corporate governance before its collapse in 1998 under the weight of a huge loan to an Indonesian taxi company. The Guangnan collapse also revealed how some red chip firms abuse corporate assets and manipulate their accounting records. The Kit Wai and Euro-Asia Agriculture scandals revealed how the controlling shareholders, the board, and all initial public offering (IPO) intermediaries did not fulfil their fiduciary duties. These incidents also suggest that there are shortcomings in the local legal and regulatory frameworks and their enforcement. Not only have many of these incidents hindered financial market development, but they have also substantially reduced investors' confidence in the market.

The Standard and Core Problems of Corporate Governance

Good corporate governance is certainly important to Hong Kong. From the perspective of globalization, it is the way that firms in Hong Kong are able to compete with well-governed overseas companies. As an international financial centre, corporate governance is vital to building this infrastructure and creating financial stability. Because of its unique regulatory framework (relatively few and loose regulations and weak legal protection for investors) and ownership structure (most listed firms are controlled by a single individual or a family), corporate governance in Hong Kong-listed companies continues to attract much international debate and interest.

The Hong Kong government has realized that good corporate governance is necessary to improve corporate competitiveness and attract international capital. Former Financial Secretary Donald Tsang said in his budget speech in 1999 that high corporate standards were the hallmark of a first-class financial centre. According to Tsang, 'our aim is to establish Hong Kong as a paragon of corporate governance, ensuring that those investments in Hong Kong are afforded the best protection and that our listed companies are managed with excellence, complying with the highest international standards including those related to risk management and disclosure of information'. In his 2000 budget he tasked the Standing Committee on Company Law Reform (SCCLR) with conducting an overall review of corporate governance, particularly relating to proposed changes to the Companies Ordinance. Corporate governance reforms then took place through accelerated legal reforms, the enforcement of rules and regulations, industry awareness and training, school and public education, and market forces.

The standard of corporate governance can be determined at a corporate level or at country level, and it is natural that they are interrelated. The corporate governance system of a country and its standard is determined by a number of interrelated factors including its political beliefs, culture, legal system, accounting systems, transparency, ownership structures, market environments, level of economic development, and ethical standards (see Table 15.1). Most countries in East Asia are still a long way from conforming to the international rules of business, possibly with the exceptions of Singapore and Hong Kong. These two economies benefit from a colonial legacy of common law institutions, relatively strong judiciaries, good ethical standards, and low corruption. According to a survey by the Political and Economic Risk Consultancy in early 2002, among ten East Asian countries Hong Kong was ranked second in terms of the quality of corporate governance and transparency, ranked just after Singapore in both indicators (*The Economist*, 2001; *Ming Pao*, 12 June 2002) (see Table 15.2). In April 2003, CLSA placed Singapore, Hong Kong, and India as the top three countries in their annual Asian CG ranking exercise (CLSA, 2003).

While many Asian countries made significant improvements in their CG scores in 2002, Hong Kong's score was unchanged from the previous year. This was attributed to a number of setbacks, including the Boto and the Pacific Century Cyberworks (PCCW) incidents (see below), to be explained later. At the corporate level, several blue chip Hong Kong companies were selected by *Euromoney* in 2002 as the best companies in Asia. Three Hong Kong companies were also ranked by CLSA as being among the best thirty CG Asian companies in 2003, and the top-ranked company was HSBC Holdings. (Singapore and India also had three companies each.) CLSA said that while Asian CG standards were improving, they still had a long way to go (*South China Morning Post*, 2003).

The Managing Director of the International Monetary Fund (IMF) said in 2001 that Hong Kong was the standard setter for corporate governance and transparency in Asia. According to Standard and Poor's, Hong Kong is a leader in the domain of corporate governance in Asia. However, like Singapore, there is still a general perception despite these rankings that corporate governance matters in Hong Kong are not as well regulated as in other major financial centres, such as London and New York.[2] In particular, although the corporate governance of banks is relatively good by regional standards, there were weaknesses in the performance of the boards of directors of a few local banks during the Asian crisis (Carse, 2002).

At country level, there is a good regulatory foundation of corporate governance in Hong Kong. Standard and Poor's (see Dallas, 2002) had five positive observations for Hong Kong as a whole: a stable common law legal system and independent judiciary, active advocacy of improved corporate governance by regulators, international accounting standards, good overall standards on a global basis and a trend of improvement, and leadership in Asia. Other strengths of the Hong Kong investment infrastructure include being the freest economy in the world and a relatively low level of corruption. The overall infrastructural environment is conducive to achieving international governance standards. However, in Asia in general and Hong Kong in particular, Standard and Poor's also observed several governance weaknesses, such as family ownership being the norm, a high level of legal compliance—but with form being of more significance than substance, and the limited independence of directors. At the corporate level, there are still a number of corporate governance problems and deficiencies in Hong Kong. According to Jamie Allen (2002), the Secretary-General of the Asian Corporate Governance Association, while Hong Kong may have the best corporate standards in greater China, it actually contains few companies that practise world-class corporate governance.

The core problems or unique concerns of corporate governance in Hong Kong can be summarized as follows:

1. Seventy-five per cent of listed companies are domiciled outside of Hong Kong and are not subject to some relevant local laws.
2. High ownership concentration and low free floats of shares.
3. The manipulations of controlling shareholders via insider or connected party transactions.
4. The lack of truly independent board directors.
5. The lack of corporate transparency, particularly on connected party transactions and directors' remunerations.
6. The low quality of many listed firms which have recorded net losses and very low stock prices across several years.

Table 15.1 Profile of East-Asian Economies

	% of Firms Controlled by Families[2]	Total Voluntary Disclosure Index[1]	Transparency of Business Environment[4]	IAS Adoption[3]	Accounting System[5]	Legal System	Legal Protection Minority Shareholders (0-6)[6]	Treatment of Minorities[7]	Confucian Culture	Corruption Perceptions Index (1-10)[8]	Capitalization as % GNP
Hong Kong	0.70	0.2	3.58	2	AA	Common	5	84.2	Y	7.70	208
Taiwan	0.59	0.17	6.55	2	AA	Code	3	34.0	Y	5.60	73
Singapore	0.50	0.15	4.55	1	AA	Common	4	100.0	Y	9.10	172
Philippines	N/A	0.16	6.29	2	AA	Mixed	3	35.0	N	3.60	78
Thailand	0.74	0.14	7.29	2	CE	Code	2	N/A	N	3.20	89
Indonesia	0.78	0.14	8.00	1	CE	Code	2	N/A	N	1.70	36
Malaysia	0.77	0.14	6.50	1	AA	Common	4	N/A	Mixed	5.10	275
S. Korea	0.79	N/A	8.50	3	CE	Code	2	33.3	Y	3.80	43
Japan	0.09	N/A	7.13	2	CE	Code	4	N/A	Y	6.00	76
PRC	N/A	N/A	8.63	2	Mixed	Code	N/A	N/A	Y	3.40	5
US	0.20	0.45	1.93	3	AA	Common	5	N/A	N	7.50	N/A
UK	0.00	N/A	N/A	3	AA	Common	5	N/A	N	8.60	N/A

Note: 1. Williams and Tower, 1998
2. La Porta *et al.*, 1999; Fan and Wong, 1999
3. Guan and Lau, 1999, 1 = Wholly on largely adopted IAS as domestic standards, 2 = used IAS to formulate some domestic standards, 3 = did not adopt IAS
4. Political and Economic International Advisory Board (1999), 0=Best, 10=Worst
5. AA = Anglo-American, CE = Continental European
6. La Porta *et al.*, 1998 (0=lowest, 6=highest)
7. Gill, 2002
8. Transparency International, 1999 (1=most corruptions, 10=least corruptions)

Table 15.2   Ranking of Corporate Governance in Asia

Country	2003	2002	2001
Singapore	1	1	2
Hong Kong	**2**	**2**	**3**
Japan	N/A	3	6
Philippines	9	4	9
Taiwan	4	5	4
South Korea	5	6	7
Malaysia	6	7	1
India	3	8	5
Vietnam	N/A	9	12
Thailand	7	10	9
China	8	11	10
Indonesia	10	12	11

Note: The ranking for 2001 and 2002 was conducted by the Political and Economic Risk
    Consultancy, and the 2003 ranking was conducted by CLSA.
Source of data: Ming Pao, 12 June 2002; *SCMP,* 6 May 2003.

7. Weak legal protection for minority investors and a relative lack of
   shareholder activism.
8. Weak enforcement of rules and the lack of a super-regulatory body
   with full investigative powers.
9. Insufficient legal status of listing and CG-related regulations.

Although a number of measures have been adopted to improve the
CG standard, Hong Kong still has a long way to go. One major goal of
improving corporate governance in Hong Kong is to reduce abuses and
inefficiencies that are due to conflicts between controlling owner–directors
and outside investors using various rules, standards, and mechanisms.
The protection of minority shareholders has become the focal point of
international investors. Effective CG in Hong Kong must incorporate a
critical approach which covers all of these aspects that are required to
enhance shareholder protection.

The more unique and critical issues of corporate governance in Hong
Kong are divided into the following eight areas for discussion: the legal
and regulatory framework, conflicts between owner–directors and minority
shareholders, directors' duties and board practices, the setting of accounting
disclosure standards, auditor independence and accountability, market
intermediaries and analysts, shareholder empowerment and activism, and
convergence and the globalization of corporate governance.

The Legal and Regulatory Framework

When other foundation sources and means are not sufficient to maintain
the market equilibrium, more laws and regulations are needed to ensure

minimum fairness and market efficiency. Regulatory bodies establish and implement rules and regulations, monitor compliance, and take part in enforcement activities. They monitor company shareholders, boards of directors, accountants, auditors, investment analysts, and the financial market and institutions. Rules and regulations are always needed to ensure that participants strike the right balance between self-interest and the interest of the majority public. It is generally agreed that sound legal regulation and enforcement are key pillars upon which good corporate governance is built. An ideal regulatory framework should be preventive, protecting the interests of the majority public, and have clarity, transparency, and market orientation. Unlike the comprehensive and stringent regulatory system in the US, the Hong Kong government prefers a more market-oriented self-regulated system to reduce compliance and transaction costs. Hong Kong's legislative regime is comparable to many major jurisdictions in the world, although it is always a case of playing catch-up because the world is also changing very quickly. Further, there has been a recent increase in regulatory commitment and a growing emphasis on compliance. Particularly after the Enron incident, stricter rules and regulations relating to CG have been implemented worldwide. Some people argue that in Asian countries in which relationship-based capitalism (i.e. back doors, corruption, and connections) is the norm, more laws are necessary to safeguard CG.

Regulatory requirements relating to CG rules are covered by a variety of sources in Hong Kong and administered by different authorities. As Hong Kong was a British colony before July 1997, its legal and financial reporting system is largely influenced by British practices. Statutory rules on corporate governance in Hong Kong are stipulated by the Hong Kong Companies Ordinance (with Cap 32 being a primary statute that applies only to Hong Kong companies) under the continuous revision of the Companies Registry and the SCCLR, and the new composite Securities and Futures Ordinance (SFO) enforced by the Securities and Futures Commission (SFC).

Non-statutory rules and standards include the Code on Takeovers and Mergers and Share Repurchase (the 'Takeover Code') enforced by the SFC; Listing Rules, Listing Agreements, and the Codes of Best Practice that are promulgated by the Stock Exchange of Hong Kong Ltd (SEHK), a subsidiary of Hong Kong Exchanges and Clearing Limited (HKEx);[4] and the Statements of Standard Accounting Practice (SSAPs) and Statements of Auditing Standards as issued by the Hong Kong Society of Accountants (HKSA).

Banks and authorized deposit-taking financial institutions are exempt dealers and are further regulated by the relevant Hong Kong Monetary Authority (HKMA) governance and disclosure rules, including their securities trading business. Recently, bank regulations worldwide have stressed the role of directors and senior management in ensuring that banks are prudently managed, and the role of disclosure and market discipline in promoting the accountability of directors/management (Carse, 2002). The HKMA issued a guideline on corporate governance for locally incorporated authorized institutions in May 2000. It stipulates that the board of banks should have a minimum of three independent directors, and that there should be a separation of the board chairman from the CEO.

Under the Companies Ordinance, directors and senior management are subject to criminal and civil liability in cases of misconduct. The relevant offences include fraudulent trading and other breaches in relation to insolvent companies. The SCCLR proposal on the Hong Kong Companies Ordinance aims to empower shareholders and to encourage them to stop 'voting with their feet'. As mentioned earlier, due to attractive tax incentives and less restrictive corporate control rules in countries such as Bermuda and the Cayman Islands, over seventy-five per cent of listed firms in Hong Kong are domiciled or incorporated outside Hong Kong. These companies are not principally governed by the Hong Kong Companies Ordinance, but rather by the corporate laws of their home jurisdictions. This would cause the individual shareholders of different listed firms to be subject to different levels of legal protection. The lack of legal parity may lead some companies to change their domiciles in order to enjoy the greatest level of unchecked powers at the expense of minority shareholders. To ensure fairness and a high consistency of corporate governance standards, some market experts have suggested revising the local laws and rules so that they override those of the listed companies' home jurisdictions.

While the Companies Ordinance covers all companies incorporated in Hong Kong, the responsibility for regulating the conduct of listed companies (both locally and overseas incorporated) falls on HKEx, which is in turn supervised by the SFC. As the statutory securities regulator, the SFC is expected to ensure that investors have enough information to assess the difference in disclosure risks, enhance allocational efficiency, prevent fraudulent offerings and manipulative practices, and restrain opportunistic behaviour by directors and controlling shareholders.

Until recently, besides the Companies Ordinance, several statutes regulated the activities of Hong Kong listed companies—and in particular their directors—which is essential for sound corporate governance (Anonymous, 2001). The Securities (Disclosure of Interests) Ordinance (Cap 396) (SDIO) obliged directors, together with their spouses and children, and substantial shareholders of listed companies—i.e. those who hold more than ten per cent (to be revised to five per cent in the new SFO) of the company's voting share capital—to disclose to the stock exchange and the company their shares in the company or any associated companies, as well as any additional acquisition or disposal of their interests. The Securities (Insider Dealing) Ordinance (Cap 395) prohibited directors or other people connected with the company (widely defined as including a director, employee, substantial shareholder, or anyone who occupies a position that may reasonably be expected to offer them access to relevant information) from using price-sensitive information when dealing in or procuring the company's shares. In a case of suspected insider dealing, the SFC could refer the case to the Insider Dealing Tribunal, which can disqualify the defaulting director. These two securities ordinances, together with eight others, have been incorporated into the new composite SFO.

The Takeover Code regulates takeovers and mergers of public companies to protect shareholders' interests as a whole. To afford fair treatment for minority shareholders who are affected by a takeover, the Takeover Code sets standards to which offeror and offeree companies must comply. For example, any person who acquires more than thirty per cent of the shares of a company is obliged to make an offer to all voting shareholders of the offeree company, and privatization requires approval by a majority of the shareholders who vote with ninety per cent of the shares. Additionally, an independent financial advisor must provide an opinion that the proposal is fair and reasonable. With the Takeover Code, all shareholders of the same class are treated similarly. Recently, the SFC has conducted an overview of the Code to bring it into line with international standards.

In Hong Kong, the first formal corporate governance initiative took place in 1992, when the SEHK created a Corporate Governance Project to raise awareness of such issues. The governance regime in respect of listed companies is set out in HKEx's Listing Rules. In fact, the Listing Rules had already covered some important elements of good corporate governance (such as seeking independent minority shareholders' approval for connected transactions and recognizing the importance of directors' fiduciary duties) in the late 1980s, even before the term 'corporate governance' became popular in the mid-1990s.

The Listing Rules prescribe the timely disclosure requirements for notifiable transactions and connected transactions. In terms of notifiable transactions, details of significant acquisitions or dispositions of assets have to be disclosed when the value of the transaction relative to the value of the issued share capital of the company exceeds a specified percentage. The company has the obligation to keep the market informed of all sensitive information. Should the stock exchange and the SFC be aware of any price-sensitive information that may have an effect on the market, the stock exchange may use its powers to suspend trading in the shares of the company until such information enters the public domain. Connected transactions between a listed company or its subsidiary and a connected person (including a director, chief executive, or substantial shareholder of the company or its subsidiaries, or an associate of any of these) are subject to disclosure to the stock exchange and shareholder approval in the general meeting while interested parties are prevented from voting. An opinion of an independent expert is required as to whether the transaction is fair and reasonable as far as the shareholders of the company are concerned. These connected transaction requirements are significant in the context of the predominance of family ownership and the control of listed companies.

Since 1993, the Listing Rules have also required all listed firms to appoint at least two independent directors. In 1998, the SEHK issued the 'Market

Consultation Policy Paper on Financial Disclosure' which further improved the quality of financial reporting by ensuring timely and relevant reporting of listing companies. As an integral part of the Listing Rules, in 1993 HKEx also introduced a Code of Best Practice for firms to follow. The Code seeks to increase the accountability of directors and enhance transparency. As guidelines for directors of listed companies, the Code provides for the following:

1. Full board meetings to be held at least every six months with adequate notice.
2. Full minutes of meetings to be kept and to be open for inspection.
3. Full disclosure of directors' fees and dues payable to independent non-executive directors in the annual report and accounts.
4. Non-executive directors (NED) to be appointed for specific terms, and all appointments to be noted in the annual report and accounts.
5. A full board meeting to be held for matters that involve conflicts of interest for substantial shareholders and director resignations, and the removal of independent NEDs to be explained to the stock exchange.
6. The establishment of an audit committee consisting of a minimum of three NEDs (a majority of them should be independent).

Although compliance with the Code is voluntary, listed companies are required to disclose in their interim and annual reports whether they have so complied, and if not, the areas of and reasons for non-compliance. In the case of audit committees, firms have to report the establishment, or the reasons for non-establishment, for accounting periods beginning 1 January 1999.

Several professional bodies have also introduced corporate governance and disclosure guidelines beyond their professional standards. Following the model of the UK Cadbury Report, in 1993 the HKSA formed a Corporate Governance Working Group (which was subsequently renamed the Corporate Governance Committee). The HKSA has issued the following reports on corporate governance: Improving Corporate Governance Practices, 1995; A Survey of Family-Controlled Companies and Audit Committees, 1996; A Guide for the Formation of an Audit Committee, 1997; A Guide for Directors' Business Review in the Annual Report, 1998; Directors' Remuneration—Recommendations for Enhanced Transparency and Accountability, 1999; and Corporate Governance Disclosure Practice in Annual Reports, 2001. The HKSA prescribed a number of recommended practices for listed firms. These practices included the introduction of independent non-executive directors; the separation of CEO and board chairman positions; increased disclosure of directors' interests and connected transactions; the introduction of two new board committees to be composed mainly of non-executive directors (an audit committee and a remuneration committee); and the limitation of family members on the board to no more than fifty per cent. The key recommendations in the general statement of corporate governance include a statement of corporate governance, directors' remuneration, directors' responsibilities in relation to the preparation of financial statements, the work of the audit committee, and non-audit fees that are paid to audit firms. The HKSA guidelines on the audit committee have been formally adopted by HKEx in the form of additional Listing Rules or by inclusion in the Stock Exchange's Code of Best Practice. Other professional bodies, such as the Hong Kong Institute of Company Secretaries (HKICS) and the Hong Kong Institute of Directors, have also developed guidelines for their members to follow.

Recent Regulatory Reforms

In order to improve CG and market quality, there have been a number of recent market and legal reforms in Hong Kong. Under a new ordinance, the SEHK, the Hong Kong Futures Exchange, and the Hong Kong Securities Clearing Company Ltd (HKSCC) were merged to become a single listed holding company—HKEx—in March 2000. While this change forced HKEx to become more publicly accountable and subject to market forces and transparency requirements, there are also some potential conflicts of interest. HKEx is the primary regulator of the companies listed on the SEHK as well as the primary regulator of SEHK participants with respect to trading matters. Many people suggest it would be best if HKEx's listing and regulatory functions were assumed by the SFC.

Other legal reforms include the revision of the Companies Ordinance, the enactment of the SFO, and the continuous revisions of the Listing Rules. While the existing Companies Ordinance provides restrictions and disclosure requirements that are central to sound corporate governance, in many respects it falls short of a satisfactory standard. Recognizing this, and with a view to bringing the Companies Ordinance and Hong Kong's existing corporate governance regime more into line with the international trend, the Financial Services Bureau and the SCCLR put forward sixty-two recommendations in July 2001 for public consultation. These recommendations, to be legislated in different stages over three years, cover directors' duties and responsibilities, shareholders' rights, and corporate reporting. The key recommendations include abolishing corporate directors; making a director vicariously liable for the acts and omissions of his alternates; reducing the threshold for circulating shareholders' proposals from the existing 5 per cent to 2.5 per cent of the voting rights; giving every shareholder the personal right to sue to enforce the terms of a company's memorandum and articles of association; and allowing Hong Kong-incorporated listed companies to issue summary financial statements in place of full accounts. These recommendations, noted for their progressiveness, have been generally well received by different sectors in Hong Kong, although critics have voiced the concern that the recommendations are not sufficiently far-reaching. In particular, since the Companies Ordinance is not enforced by the SFC, it is more difficult for the SFC to regulate listed companies in Hong Kong.

With the similar objective of providing a regulatory regime that is on a par with international standards, and in view of local needs, the SFO, which was enacted in March 2002 and became effective in April 2003, is seen as another significant step in the direction of sound corporate governance in Hong Kong. As a consolidation of existing laws governing the securities and futures markets currently spread over some ten statutes and parts of the Companies Ordinance, the SFO is expected to enhance the SFC's investigatory powers, prevent fraudulent behaviour, increase the channels of adopting criminal prosecutions, and strengthen market efficiency. Amongst the new measures that will improve corporate governance, one is the promotion of the timely and accurate disclosure of price-sensitive information by lowering the initial shareholding disclosure threshold for persons other than directors and chief executives from ten per cent to five per cent, and shortening the disclosure notification period from five to three business days. This proposed amendment is comparable to regulations in the US, Australia, Japan, and Singapore.

The new SFO also allows individual investors a statutory right to ask for loss compensation via civil procedures against company directors and management who release false and misleading information. As a matter of right, they can also claim compensation against those proven guilty by the courts or by the newly formed Market Misconduct Tribunal (MMT) without the need to seek redress under the common law. This will also reduce the onus of proof on the part of the victim. However, since the government wishes to keep regulations flexible enough both to suit Hong Kong's unique circumstance and avoid rigid laws that might prove inefficient for business, some long-standing issues have not been handled in the new SFO—for example, means such as class action and proof of burden on the defendant. Detailed discussions of specific SFO rules can be found in the next chapter.

HKEx released its Consultation Paper on Proposed Amendments to the Listing Rules Relating to Corporate Governance Issues in January 2002 (HKEx, 2002). The paper promoted level-playing-field disclosure via the HKEx Price-sensitive Information Guide issued previously. It also suggested more frequent disclosure of profit warnings and more restrictions on rights issues; voting by poll for connected transactions and transactions requiring controlling or interested shareholders to abstain from voting; the introduction of 'total assets tests'; increasing the required number of independent non-executive directors from two to three; directors' contracts and remuneration; the requirement of quarterly reporting; and a revision of the Code of Best Practice. However, there were certain areas on which diverse views were expressed. After one year of open consultation, HKEx published its Consultation Conclusions on the proposals in January 2003. Unfortunately, only some of the proposed changes in the Consultation Paper were finally adopted, to be implemented to the Listing Rules or the Code of Best Practice by the middle of 2003. Major proposals not accepted included restrictions on the number of refreshments of the general mandate, quarterly reporting, and the disclosure of individual directors' pay by name. HKEx claimed that they had to drop some of these proposals in order to strike a proper balance between the protection of shareholder rights on the one hand and commercial practicality on the other.

The HKEx Code of Best Practice will also be revised to contain two tiers of recommendations. The first tier will contain minimum standards of board practices, and the second will be the recommended good practices serving as guidelines for issuers' reference. The revised Listing Rules require issuers to include a report on corporate governance practice in their annual reports, and to provide details of any deviation from the minimum standards set out in the Code of Best Practice.

Most of these current change proposals on rules and regulations will certainly advance board practice, increase the transparency of issuers, and improve the protection of shareholders' rights. However, given the vested interests of the different stakeholders and the complicated relationship between big family business groups and the government, plus other core problems discussed earlier, all regulatory reforms so far have been slow as well as conducted in a piecemeal manner. Many critical proposals were dropped after a long lobbying process by the big market players. Since the Enron incident, many people in Hong Kong believe that the recommendations as proposed in the Companies Ordinance, the new SFO, and the HKEx consultation papers are far from sufficient.

Enforcement of Rules

After several revisions in the past two decades, the regulatory structure of Hong Kong still has a number of weaknesses which need continuous improvement. According to the 'Report of Security Review Committee' in 1987, Hong Kong has adopted the so-called 'three-tier' market regulatory system: the government, the Securities and Futures Commission, and the stock exchange. The government is the overall policy maker, facilitator, and regulator of regulators, the SFC enforces the new SFO and the Takeover Code and is the statutory regulator of listed companies, and HKEx is the non-statutory frontline regulator of listed companies and enforcer of the Listing Rules. However, there are some grey areas and the division of responsibilities is not particularly clear in certain areas. Communication between the three bodies is sometimes good and sometimes insufficient. When incidents occur, they often blame each other. Although there were reviews of the structure during the legislative process of the new SFO, no change was made. After the 'penny stock' incident and certain Chinese private enterprises scandals in 2002, the loopholes in the existing regulatory structure were further exposed to the public.

SEHK/HKEx

The profit-making HKEx has been criticized for allowing low-quality firms to list on its two boards for reasons of revenue and a lack of full-time experienced professional staff to assess listing applications. The Listing Rules set out the obligations of listed companies and attempt to address those areas not covered by corporate and securities laws in order to provide basic shareholder protection. It should be noted that the Listing Rules (and the Code of Best Practice) are non-statutory regulations and only form a contract between the stock exchange and the issuer and each director of the issuer wherein the parties are bound. The merit of non-legal rules and guidelines is that they can avoid the lengthy legislative process involved when HKEx wishes to revise the Listing Rules to reflect the latest market changes. When a firm violates the rules, or when HKEx does not enforce the rules diligently, shareholders cannot sue the firm or the stock exchange as they are not party to the contract.

The sanctions that are imposed by HKEx for breaches (the sanctions being private reprimand, public censure, or a public announcement that a particular director is not suitable for retention in office) emphasize self-regulation through public and peer pressure rather than stringent regulation and disciplinary action. Nevertheless, in a case of a severe breach of the rules, the stock exchange can cancel or suspend the listing of the defaulting company. However, delisting has so far not been used as a disciplinary tool, as this measure penalizes innocent outside shareholders (leaving them with no exit) more than the issuers and their management. Sometimes these problem companies wish to be delisted in any case.

There has been public criticism that, as a front-line regulator of listed firms, HKEx's regulatory abilities are too weak and its enforcement record is too lenient. The record of leniency may be due partly to the fact that there are entrenched conflicts of interest in that HKEx serves both as a profit-making listed company and the front-line regulatory body of listed companies, and it seeks part of its revenues from companies that list and trade with it. The more companies listed and the more share-trading transactions that go on, the greater the revenue for HKEx. Naturally, the Listing Division does not want to be a tough gatekeeper on listing applications, nor a super-cop for violators. Another possible reason is that although HKEx may have the will to enforce the rules, it does not have enough experienced professionals who know the market operations sufficiently well to enforce the rules effectively.

It is also commonly admitted that the non-legal status of the Listing Rules reduces their effectiveness. The Pacific Century Cyberworks incident mentioned earlier was a good example. This company drew negative attention in the CLSA 2003 report on Asian CG, which saw its CG score fall more than that of any other Hong Kong company. The giant Hong Kong telecommunications firm made a botched attempted in early February 2003 to take over Britain's Cable & Wireless, and then offered different statements to exchange officials in two jurisdictions—a move that prompted a huge outcry and a sharp fall in its share price. PCCW finally received a warning from HKEx only in mid-2003, indicating that the firm had violated the Listing Rules. In the long run, some people believe certain rules that are related to disclosures and substantial transactions should become statutes. By giving part or all of the Listing Rules legal status, directors who are at fault can be sued through both criminal and civil channels.

Only a substantial personal liability will serve as an effective deterrent to future misconduct. However, under pressure from giant investment banks and other parties with vested interests, the Legal Department of the Hong Kong government agreed not to convert part of the Listing Rules into law. Whether non-statutory rules or codes can effectively regulate corporate behaviour seems a major issue worthy of continuous review.

The SFC

To maintain an appropriate level of regulation and a fair, open, and reliable market is the most difficult target that a regulatory body can wish to achieve. The SFC insists on a 'disclosure-based' regulatory framework to avoid over-regulation. Except for commercial secrets, the SFC encourages all firms to increase transparency by more voluntary disclosures.

Although there are occasional voices to be heard saying that the SFC over-regulates and abuses its power, the more common impression is that it does not enforce its own rules diligently, and that it lacks the power and will to tackle big market players. There also appears to be an apparent reluctance on the part of the judiciary to impose tough punitive measures or sanctions against wrongdoers as provided for by law. Examples that best illustrate this leniency are the cases involving Hwa Tay Thai Holdings Ltd, South East Asia Wood Ltd, and Sino-i.com. The controlling shareholder (and the former executive chairman) of Hwa Tay Thai Holdings Ltd, Mr Wong Chong San, disposed of more than 330 million shares in the company in 1999 via personal holdings and the Flying Elephant, a company that he controlled. This represented a total of some sixteen per cent of its issued capital, and Mr Wong carried out the disposal without the requisite disclosure under the former Securities (Disclosure of Interests) Ordinance. He was, however, fined only HK$18,000 for the offence. The sum, which was derisory, cast substantial doubt on the willingness of the judiciary to impose strict sanctions in accordance with the provisions of the applicable ordinances. This and other similar decisions send out the wrong message to the marketplace, and may impede the establishment of a level playing field (Low, 2002). This kind of enforcement shows that violators are treated leniently and cannot therefore serve as an effective deterrent to others considering abusing their positions. Some fund managers expressed the view that the SFC should become tougher on board directors and fine them personally if they behave in a way that is not in their shareholders' best interests; companies will become cleaner if directors are taken to court once in a while.

However, some senior SFC officials deny that they are unable or unwilling to curb market abuses. In a speech given in May 2001, SFC Chairman Andrew Sheng indicated that since 1998, eight insider-dealing actions had been referred to the Insider Dealing Tribunal (IDT). The SFC claimed it had one of the most successful prosecution records in the world with regard to insider dealing. In its 2002 annual report, there were 391 new cases under investigation (twenty-five per cent more than in 2001), although only two were referred to the police Commercial Crime

Investigation Bureau, and only thirty-seven people were successfully prosecuted in that year. The SFC Chairman explained that the recent drop in the number of successful prosecutions was due to the SFC's focus on serious market misconduct in 2002. In early 2003, nine listed firms were being investigated by the SFC.

The new SFO allows the SFC to choose between criminal, civil, or both channels to handle market misconduct cases. The IDT has also been expanded into the new Market Misconduct Tribunal to facilitate the process of civil claims. The MMT is empowered to impose fines of up to HK$10 million, or ten years' imprisonment. However, whether this new set-up will increase the determination of the SFC to impose more appropriate penalties is not yet known.

In view of the Enron and the Euro-Asia Agriculture incidents, it is believed by many that more bold and radical steps are needed to further protect public investors. Some suggestions involve expanding the investigative power of the SFC, and strengthening measures for combating market misconduct by introducing class action suits and shifting the burden of proof to those who are carrying out the alleged misconduct. In the US, the Securities and Exchange Commission (SEC) is the single regulatory body that oversees almost all security-law-related corporate governance issues. Under the protection of the US Constitution and the Security Exchange Act, the SEC has almost unrestricted investigative powers to administer oaths and affirmations and to issue subpoenas nationwide against any person who is a critical element in the investigation of suspected misconduct cases (Lang, 2002). The SEC is also empowered to compel attendance, take evidence, and require the production of any documents or records which it deems relevant to its inquiry. If a person refuses to comply with a subpoena, the SEC can apply to the federal district court to enforce it. Similar arrangements are seen in the UK and Canada, but in Hong Kong the rules relating to corporate governance are rather dispersed, and are enforced by different bodies—the Companies Registry, Financial Services and the Treasury Bureau, HKEx, the SFC, the HKMA, the Independent Commisssion Against Corruption (ICAC), the HKSA, and the Hong Kong Police's Commercial Crime Investigation Bureau. Before the introduction of the new SFO, their investigative powers were not entirely clear.

The new SFO expressly gives the SFC the power to inquire into the circumstance and instructions relating to accounting entries. It also empowers the SFC to verify such findings with other sources not previously available to them. Such sources include the papers of the auditors, suppliers, customers, and even the banks of the listed company. However, there are still concerns about the degree of power afforded to the SFC when conducting such investigations. Since the new SFO still does not allow the SFC to regulate the banks' securities business, many people believe that the SFC can only act as a second-class regulator. As the SFC does not have a mandate from the government to impose bolder changes in legislation and law enforcement, it is very hard for it to change itself into a single super-governance body with full powers of investigation and prosecution.

HKEx has expressed openly the view that the SFC intervenes too much in its listing operations, and the co-operation between them in policy development is also not particularly satisfactory. To improve the quality of newly listed companies, the SFC launched the 'dual filing' scheme in mid-2003 under the new SFO. This new scheme requires all companies applying for listing to submit all prospectuses and other mandatory disclosures to both HKEx and the SFC. While the SFC will not investigate individual applications on its own initiative, it could use its veto to reject any applications where misleading information is found in the submitted materials. However, some market players believe that this mechanism will cause more duplication of effort and hence conflicts.

In late July 2002, the government unveiled a number of delisting proposals, the details of which were released by HKEx in a subsequent consultation paper. The paper suggested the delisting of firms that had suffered losses for several years, or those with insufficient assets. About 350 firms trading below fifty Hong Kong cents might have needed to consolidate their shares, as HKEx planned to remove penny stocks. But when the proposal was announced, the market overreacted and numerous small investors dumped their penny stocks in a single day, with a loss of HK$5,800 million of capitalization. The government, the SFC, and HKEx officials apologized for the unexpected incident, and an independent inquiry was conducted into the matter. Due to market pressure and the sentiments of public investors, there is a high possibility that the proposal on delisting penny stocks will finally be dropped.

Both HKEx and the SFC feel that the role of the government in their operations is unclear. In theory, the government, as an overall policy maker, should strike a balance between public and private interests. In practice, the government's participation or intervention in actual market and regulatory activities is excessive and hampers the independence of the SFC and HKEx. The 'penny stock' and 'waiving minimal brokerage fee' incidents are typical examples of such interventions. Under the SFC, the Chief Executive of the Hong Kong Special Administrative Region can give non-public orders to the SFC or even request a suspension of market trading. When the SFC wishes to apply certain powers under the SFO, they need the prior consent of the Financial Secretary. In the US and the UK, the government is not allowed to instruct its regulatory bodies, and the Hong Kong government has indicated that it would like to reduce its participation in SFC and HKEx affairs in the future.

Even though Hong Kong may not want to move to a statutory regime like that of the US, we need at least to streamline the existing regulatory structure and processes to avoid duplication and delays in the regulatory response to corporate misconduct. Currently, there are grey areas in the division of regulatory duties between the government, the SFC, and HKEx, and further clarification is needed to avoid potential conflicts. To achieve this and to improve further the quality of listed firms, many have argued that HKEx should hand over its listing and regulatory functions to the SFC. In the wake of the penny stock incident, the relationship between the government, the SFC, and HKEx was under substantial review in late 2002 by a team of three experts appointed by the Financial Secretary.

The Expert Group Report

After three months of studies and public consultations, The Expert Group to Review the Operation of the Securities and Futures Market Regulatory Structure submitted its report to the government in late March 2003. The report was perceived by many market participants as thoughtful, decisive, and certainly far-reaching, although there were some worries about the future possibility of over-regulation. Following the UK and Australian models, the report called the existing structure 'fundamentally flawed', and the central recommendation was that HKEx should drop its regulation business, including the listing function. It was the group's view that HKEx could not exist both to make a profit and regulate in the public interest, no matter how many control mechanisms had been installed.

In order to avoid a conflict of interest, to divide areas of responsibilities clearly, and to enhance market quality, the report called for the SFC to establish the Hong Kong Listing Authority (HKLA), which would take over the regulatory role from the existing Listing Division of HKEx. Furthermore, it recommended that the Listing Rules be given statutory backing without going through any legislative process. It would become a legal offence to violate the Listing Rules, and it would also allow for prosecution with more meaningful fines. Also, the enforcement of the Listing Rules would be conducted by full-time experienced professionals of the HKLA, including the approval of listing applications. A Listing Panel would be set up under the HKLA to handle listing decision appeals and serve as an advisory body to the SFC in revising the Listing Rules. In case of further appeals, there would be judicial reviews by the courts. The Listing Panel would include a greater number of investor representatives than does the current issuers-dominated Listing Committee under HKEx (currently there is only one fund manager on the twenty-five-member Committee). Since the new SFO already contains the necessary legal framework, no new legislation would be needed to set up the HKLA. The report also recommends that government consider putting some Companies Ordinance rules under the SFO and allowing the SFC to enforce them.

On the day (21 March 2003) of the release of the report, the Financial Secretary endorsed the report and committed the government to implementing its recommendations as soon as possible. HKEx responded the same day with a statement that 'it is disappointed with the conclusions and recommendations', but it promised to co-operate with the government and the SFC on the implementation of the recommendations as public policy. However, after further inside deliberation over the following four days, HKEx submitted a letter to the Financial Secretary expressing thirteen reasons against the proposals and demanding a public consultation before making a final decision. Under this pressure from HKEx and a few other big market players, the Financial Secretary suddenly announced that, in view of the controversial nature of the proposals and their far-reaching implications, the proposals would be postponed for twelve to eighteen months to allow for further public consultation before a final decision was made. The matter has unfortunately become a political battle, and it is viewed by many people as a power struggle between the SFC and HKEx.

It is generally believed that although HKEx has built a 'Great Wall of China' separating its listing activities from other businesses and many other internal control mechanisms, as long as it continues to control the nominations of the Listing Committee members, the resources of the Listing Division, and the senior staff of the Listing Division sharing the group's net income as bonuses, the inherent agency problem and potential conflicts of interest are inevitable. Further, although the quality of newly listed firms is often outside the control of HKEx, enhancing market quality via the proposed changes is a valid point. According to the philosophy and the track record of the SFC, the possibility of over-regulating is remote. Although it may increase the cost of listing applications in the short run due to tighter listing procedures, in the longer run this would raise the overall quality of the market and thus transaction volume.

Although the main Expert Group report recommendation is correct in its direction and is feasible, it is not the only option. For reasons of history, the conflicting interests of different stakeholders, the legal and ethical responsibilities towards HKEx shareholders, the unclear extra monitoring costs to be incurred, and the political sensitivity of the issues, the author suggested to the government a compromise resolution for consideration. A new Listing Authority can be set up that is solely owned by HKEx or co-owned by HKEx and the government. All council members of this new entity must be appointed by the government with the consent of the Legislative Council. All staff and businesses of this new entity will be totally separate from HKEx, and all senior staff will be paid a fixed salary. The budget of the new entity will be approved by its independent council. Full-time staff with extensive market experience will handle and approve listing applications. A Listing Panel will also be set up, with substantial representation by investors, and it will handle decision appeals and give advice to the SFC for revising the Listing Rules. Further, there is a doubt as to whether it is feasible to give all Listing Rules legal status without changing them into statutes or going through the legislative process. A more effective approach is to convert some of the important disclosure requirements under the Listing Rules and the Takeover Code to statutes. In the future, such important requirements under the Companies Ordinance should also be enforced by the SFC.

It is believed that this counter-proposal will be more acceptable to the government than the HKEx proposal; in any case, the final decision should be based on public interest and the future competitiveness of the market.

Besides reforming the listing function, other regulatory measures must be implemented as soon as possible in order to improve the quality of the market. Amongst other measures, these include the tighter supervision of market intermediaries, greater legal protection for investors via derivative and class actions, freezing the shareholding of controlling shareholders for at least twelve months after IPO, and restricting the number of genuine outside shareholders to, say, not less than 300.

Class Actions and Burden of Proof

Unlike Hong Kong, the US legal system enables victim investors to sue over market misconduct through class action and contingency fee arrangements. Currently, given the high level of expense and difficulty involved in civil claims, it is almost impossible for an individual investor in Hong Kong to sue a suspected market player. Therefore, a certain kind of class action seems necessary to provide the minimum basic protection for public minority investors. However, the SFC Chairman put forward the view that, under Hong Kong's legal system, which is similar to that of British common law, if the plaintiff loses, he or she has to pay the defendant's legal fees, and legal fees are high in Hong Kong. Further, if all of the assets of the implicated firm have already been expropriated, merely winning a case would not help the victim gain monetary compensation. Class action suits also imply that any compensation after wining a case would be shared between the plaintiff and his or her lawyers, and some people think this will lead to a litigious society. Regarding the burden of proof, in the Blue Bill of the SFO, it was proposed to put the burden of proof on the defendant. However, under pressure from big market players, the White Bill shifted this burden of proof back to the prosecutors. In the US, once the SEC initiates a hearing, the defendant has the burden of effectively rebutting the prosecutor's case. Most SEC cases are finally settled by civil suits, not by litigation (Lang, 2002).

In the past, many regulators and market players in Hong Kong opposed the introduction of class action and the burden of proof on the defendant, but in view of the consequences of the Enron incident, it is clear that such proposals are worthy of serious consideration. While Hong Kong has not adopted such measures, imposing additional criminal penalties on top of civil liability for false or misleading statements is important. In addition, the SFC should launch formal public consultations on the introduction of these two measures rather than picking up selective comments at random.

Owner–Directors and Conflicts with Minority Shareholders

Ownership structure is always the foundation of corporate governance mechanisms. On the basis of ownership structure and other governance attributes, the four most common generic corporate governance models can be identified: the US/UK Market Model, the Germany/Japan Main Bank Model, the East Asia Family Control Model, and the State Control Model.

The major characteristics of the US/UK market model include widely diffused and actively traded ownership, the separation of owners and managers, arm's length business activities (i.e., by parties who do not know each other), an active and liquid stock market, tight regulation and strict disclosure requirements, better minor shareholder protection, and an active and competitive corporate control market. In the US, many corporate boards are actually controlled by powerful management, and highly dispersed ownership leads to the opportunistic behaviour of managers. Sometimes an outside blockholder or a low level of managerial ownership would motivate executives to maximize firm value. On the other hand, the major characteristics of the Germany/Japan Main Bank Model include more concentrated ownership, cross-holding and external monitoring by banks and financial institutions, a two-tier board structure, mainly bank-centred debt financing, more collective decisions, lower reliance on public disclosures and legal protection for investors, and an inactive corporate control market. At a country level, Hong Kong adopts the US/UK model to some extent, as its legal and accounting systems are similar to the British model and its market regulatory framework to the American model. At the corporate level, the Family Control Model is dominant.

In the 1980s, many of the debates on corporate governance focused on the merit of the two major corporate governance systems: US/UK versus Germany/Japan. The family control model has not garnered any attention over the last thirty years in the Western literature. In contrast to the assumption of Berle and Means (1933) that all large companies will mature to an ultimate structure that will be characterized by the separation of ownership and control, recent evidence suggests that concentrated ownership by an individual or a family exists in many countries, particularly in those of East Asia (Shleifer and Vishny (1997), Ho (2000), Claessons *et al.* (2000), Roe (2000)). According to La Porta *et al.* (1999), Claessons *et al.* (2000), and Fan and Wong (1999), over seventy per cent of the listed firms in East Asian countries (except Japan) have a dominant shareholder that is usually a family (see also Table 15.3).

The first report of the HKSA's Corporate Governance Working Group (CGWG) confirmed that over seventy per cent of Hong Kong listed companies were majority controlled by a family or an individual (Hong Kong Society of Accountants, 1996). The ten wealthiest families in Hong Kong owned over forty-seven per cent of the total market capitalization of the SEHK in 2000. Fifty-three percent of all listed companies had one shareholder or one family group of shareholders that owned fifty per cent or more of the entire issued capital (Hong Kong Society of Accountants, 1997). The average shareholdings of the board of directors were 43.5 per cent of the total shares on the SEHK (Hong Kong Society of Accountants, 1997). In over eighty-five per cent of listed firms, board directors owned at least one third of all shares (Ho, Lam, and Sami, 2002). The HSBC is apparently one of the very few firms that is traded on HKEx with no majority controlling interest by one group. Together, these controlling shareholders or families represent the most powerful groups in Hong

Table 15.3 Percentage of Widely Held Firms among Twenty Largest Public Firms

Country	Percentage
Austria	5
Belgium	5
Hong Kong	10
Italy	20
Norway	25
Sweden	25
Netherlands	30
Finland	35
Denmark	40
Germany	50
Canada	60
Switzerland	60
France	60
Australia	65
United States	80
Japan	90
United Kingdom	100

Source of data: Roe, Mark J. (2000), 'Political Foundations for Separation Ownership From Control', *Stanford Law Review.*

Kong, their interests sometimes further promoted by political connections. The government has been often criticized for being too close to powerful vested business interests, and for not disentangling itself from such interests—the CyberPort Project is a good example of this.

Most of these controlling families secure their control via a complicated ownership structure (such as pyramid cross-shareholding, or interlocking directorships), and a large separation of voting from cash flow rights (Claessons *et al.*, 2000). A pyramid allows the controlling families to exercise a great deal of control for very little ownership. It works in the following manner: a family owns fifty-one per cent of company A, which owns fifty-one per cent of company B, which owns fifty-one per cent of company C, which owns twenty-five per cent of company D. Hence the family controls twenty-five per cent of company D, but its ownership stake is only 3.3 per cent: fifty-one per cent of fifty-one per cent of fifty-one per cent of twenty-five per cent. To enhance a family's control, other companies that own shares are mainly its own affiliated companies or private investment companies associated with controlling family members. Many families develop a business from its inception, and even when the company is growing bigger or has been publicly listed, the founding family still wishes to retain its tight control. In recognition of this situation, the SEHK only requires that twenty-five per cent or more of the issued shares of listed companies be held by unconnected persons.

In general, Hong Kong-listed firms are owned and managed through blood and marriage ties. Many of these family members also actively participate in the daily operations of their firms by appointing themselves or trusted relatives and colleagues as senior executives or board directors. Ho and Wong (2001b) found that the average percentage of family members sitting on boards was 32.1 per cent. In the case of family control of a company's board, the potential for a family patriarch to influence decisions is particularly strong. It is also assumed that every family owns and votes collectively.

Although some people perceive family businesses as old-fashioned and slow to grow due to their relationship-based business networks, research shows that family-controlled companies are at least as successful as widely held multinational companies (see, for example, Lang and Young (2001); Ho and Lam (2003)). Because of the close attention that is paid to the front-line business, family-controlled companies can always make efficient decisions. In Hong Kong, Li Ka-shing has blended some elements of international best practice with Chinese culture, though he still makes use of pyramid structures to maximize family control with minimal capital. Currently, there is a lack of empirical evidence about whether companies with a greater number of directorships and senior management posts in the hands of the controlling family perform more successfully. Nevertheless, as Andrew Sheng, Chairman of the SFC, once noted, every successful business started as a family business.

However, there are inherent conflicts between the controlling and minority shareholders of firms due to the high incentives for controlling shareholders to extract private benefits through their control in connected party transactions. According to CLSA, one case in 2002 affecting the corporate governance (CG) score for Hong Kong involved plastic-tree-maker Boto Holdings (now renamed IMI Global), which proposed disposing of its core business for less than its share price to a company that would be seventy per cent owned by a US company and thirty per cent by the Boto chairman's son. The company revised the structure of the deal in such a way as to allow the controlling shareholders a vote on the deal, which then passed.

Through connected party transactions between affiliated companies controlled by a family, owners can effectively transfer wealth from one company to another by selling assets at lower-than-market prices. With pyramid and cross-shareholding structures, insiders can gain wealth by setting unfair terms for intra-group sales of goods and services and the transfer of assets and controlling stakes, at the expense of minority shareholders. One possible way of expropriation is that the listed company at the base of the pyramid sells its shares to the public and then passes the proceeds up the pyramid via numerous internal transactions. In return, less profitable assets are passed down the pyramid. Another example is that the holding firm receives very low-interest loans from associated companies or takes on high-risk projects jointly with its associated company.

Other common forms of misbehaviour among controlling shareholders in Hong Kong include directing corporate resources to themselves, the dilution of existing shareholders' holdings by share placement with outsiders or issuing shares to insiders, seeking outside loans that are secured through the assets of associated listed companies, the payment of excessive executive compensation despite poor firm performance, and unfair dividend policies. Regarding share placement, it is unfortunate that the current SEHK Listing Rules do not adequately deal with this, as companies are allowed to issue new shares equal to up to twenty per cent of existing issued shares capital, as long as they obtain a 'general mandate' resolution from a shareholders' meeting. This resolution requires a mere simple majority which, given the low rate of blocked resolutions in Hong Kong, has caused great concern. This mandate can last through to the next annual general meeting, at which point the mandate is likely to be renewed. Further, a company can immediately convene a general meeting to obtain a new general mandate upon using up the twenty per cent limit. The HKEx CG Consultation Paper does not change this twenty per cent limit practice or restrict the number of times in a year; it only restricts the placement price, which could not be at more than a twenty per cent discount. It is also disappointing that the Consultation Paper does not restrict only minority shareholders to voting on share placement.

Regarding unfair dividend policies, in early 2000 the South China Group announced that it would distribute dividends in the form of shares in its unlisted subsidiaries. Small investors then faced the risk of finding no way of selling these shares. However, this kind of practice does not violate the Listing Rules and does not need approval from the shareholders' general meeting. Taking another example, in late April 2000 David Webb, an independent market critic, published an article the day before the release of the iSteelAsia.com prospectus. iSteelAsia.com was a steel exchange portal that was a spin-off from the listed Van Shung Chong Holdings (VSC). Webb revealed that the VSC chairman, his mother, and two others effectively bought more than eighteen per cent of iSteelAsia shares from VSC at a fraction of the IPO price without seeking the approval of independent shareholders.

Outside independent directors who are nominated and elected by controlling shareholders are hardly independent and are unlikely to protect the interests of minority shareholders. While market-based systems require transparency as a guarantee of protection, relationship-based systems (*guanxi*) are designed to be non-transparent to avoid external monitoring and the threat of competition. This may be why boardrooms in Hong Kong are often viewed by international investors as preserving opacity and being little more than rubber-stamp authorities that exist simply to approve the wishes of the controlling shareholders. Other people equate investing in a family-held conglomerate in Asia with going to a casino. Claessens *et al.* (2000) also found evidence that the expropriation of minorities and higher control rights were associated with lower market valuations (see also Claessens *et al.* (1999), Claessens *et al.* (2000), Lang and Young (2001)). In fact, family ownership may not be the root problem. In western Europe family control is just as common as in Asia, but Europe has largely avoided the inherent problems of disclosure and dividend policies in East Asia (Lang, 2002). Lang argued that this is probably because the European community has a more stringent and effective regulatory environment.

Theoretically, to reduce the possibilities of managerial expropriation of firm assets, administrative means can be employed so that management is more separate from controlling shareholders. However, this may also destroy the free-market spirit and many merits of traditional family business practice, such as more cohesive management teams and more efficient decision making. To protect minority shareholders further, it is suggested by some experts that the minimum proportion of issued shares held by the public should be increased from twenty-five per cent (for firms with a market capitalization of less than HK$4,000 million) to forty or fifty per cent, depending on the size of the market capitalization. This would also help to raise the size of the free floats of most listed firms in Hong Kong to a more international standard. Regarding the share placement problem, one solution is to place stricter restrictions on such practices by revising the Listing Rules. Limits need to be imposed on the number of shares that can be placed over a period of time, as opposed to allowing companies to roll over mandates every time a general shareholder meeting is called. Countries such as the US and Singapore have already imposed such restrictions to prevent abuses by controlling shareholders. Until the laws are changed in Hong Kong, some investor activists urge all minority shareholders to vote against such a general mandate as a standard policy.

Other regulations of shareholding structure (most notably the family-controlled cross-holdings) need to be considered and dealt with carefully. Currently some subsidiaries of a group make use of their shareholding in their parent company as collateral for huge borrowings from banks. They further use such funds for trading their parent company's stocks and other risky investments. Currently, there are no rules directly governing or restricting cross-shareholding in Hong Kong. The government may consider restricting the highest percentage of cross-shareholding or the voting rights of cross-shareholdings in parent companies. In terms of financial reporting, to avoid off-balance-sheet liabilities, group members with cross-shareholdings should be required to prepare consolidated financial statements regardless of their business nature.

Moreover, the Listing Rules should be revised to limit the percentage of family members on corporate boards to fifty per cent, and small investors only should be allowed to elect independent non-executive directors and external auditors. The role of some traditional corporate governance mechanisms in family-owned companies requires further research, as the economic incentives for managers and owners of family-owned companies are expected to be different. Other suggestions for protecting minority shareholders will be discussed in later sections, but it is believed that the most effective measure would be to change the corporate culture of many family-controlled businesses.

Directors' Duties and Board Practices

The focus of many international guidelines on corporate governance is the role of the board of directors in ensuring sound corporate governance practices. The part of any organization that has the greatest control over governance is the board of directors, because it is the board's core responsibility to be accountable.

In the US, recent high-profile corporate scandals indicate that many directors' acts are not for the benefits of the company, but originate from a desire for personal benefit. In fact, this could happen in any country regardless of how strict its regulatory framework is. Establishing good director and board practices is intrinsic to ensuring that directors and their boards act responsibly in the governance of their companies, and that working outwards they are accountable to all shareholders for the assets and resources which are entrusted to them. Working inwards, boards should set corporate missions and objectives, and select, monitor, and compensate senior executives. The board should ensure timely and accurate financial and non-financial disclosure and present accounts to shareholders that reflect the true state of the company's financial position.

In recent years, boards around the world have switched from compliance-oriented bodies to active partnerships. There is a growing demand for independent and diversified boards, and the pay of executive directors is tied to stock options. Committees for different functions (e.g. executive, nomination, remuneration, audit, investment, and finance functions) are encouraged, and many of these committees should be composed mainly of independent, non-executive directors. (In this section, unless otherwise specified, the term 'directors' generally refers to executive directors.)

The Listing Rules of HKEx for the Main and Growth Enterprise Market (GEM) boards specify the duties and responsibilities of directors. Every director of a listed company must satisfy HKEx that they have the character, experience, integrity, and ability to demonstrate a standard of competence that is commensurate with their position. Directors are expected to fulfil fiduciary duties and the duties of skill, care, and diligence that may reasonably be expected of a person with their knowledge and experience. They should avoid actual and potential conflicts of interest, and fully disclose their interests in contracts with the company. However, the Listing Rules do not specify that directors must act in the interests of the shareholders. Under the Companies Ordinance, directors should fulfil their fiduciary duties to the company, but not to the shareholders.

Although directors' duties are stipulated in the Listing Rules, they lack statutory force, which makes any breach of duty difficult (and therefore more costly) to enforce under common law. In any case, for listed companies, it is directors, not managers, who are ultimately liable if company actions lead to the breaching of listing rules or company law. For corporate governance, directors also bear much more responsibility than managers.

According to a survey by the Hong Kong Institute of Company Secretaries (2002), less than forty per cent of directors in Hong Kong understand their fiduciary duties and legal responsibilities, and the rest give them low priority. In fact, many smaller company directors are ignorant of the concepts of corporate governance and directors' duties. The role of a director is sometimes mixed up with that of a senior manager. This is a common problem of many directors in Hong Kong (Mobius, 2002).

Regarding qualifications and training for directors, Hong Kong is far behind nearby countries in terms of preparation training, professional certification, and mandatory continuous professional education. Malaysia adopted professional training and examination schemes for candidate directors, and China has started running certificate courses for would-be directors. Although it could be argued that it is easier for these transitional economies to start new things from scratch, it is hard to believe that nothing has been done so far in this respect in Hong Kong. Although Hong Kong has an Institute of Directors, it has done very little towards pursuing professional certification or a self-regulatory scheme. As an international financial centre, Hong Kong should catch up in this regard to make its corporate directors more knowledgeable and accountable.

Recently, the Standing Committee on Company Law Reform's Consultation Paper contained proposals in relation to directors' duties and responsibilities. The key recommendations included the following:

1. An interested director should not vote at a board meeting on a transaction in which he or she has an interest, except for immaterial transactions.
2. The approval of shareholders should be obtained for transactions or arrangements of a requisite value that involve directors or connected persons.
3. Connected party transactions between a company and an 'associated company' should require the approval of disinterested shareholders (an associated company being one in which twenty per cent or more of the voting rights of the equity share capital is controlled by the first company).
4. Procedures for the nomination and election of directors should be improved in terms of, say, the timeframe within which a shareholder is allowed to submit a nomination, and the disclosure of nominees' biographical details.
5. The role and functions of non-executive directors should be made statutory. Independent directors should be entrusted with specific monitoring roles, for example, in cases where the company's board has breached its obligations to comply with the Listing Rules.
6. The development of a training programme for directors.

The HKMA also issued a revised corporate governance guideline for locally approved banks and deposit-taking institutions in July 2001. Under this guideline, the board should be ultimately responsible for the overall operation and financial stability of the bank, and should establish committees to take care of each specific area of duty. Further, banks should submit individual directors' board meeting attendance records to the HKMA one month before the end of the current financial year (Carse, 2002). The specific requirements included the following:

1. The board should ensure that the bank establishes policies, procedures, and controls to manage the various types of risk with which it is faced.
2. The board should ensure that the bank fully understands the provisions of section 83 of the Banking Ordinance on connected lending, and establishes a policy on such lending.
3. The board should ensure that it receives a management letter from external auditors without undue delay.
4. The board should maintain appropriate checks and balances against the influence of management and/or shareholder controllers, to ensure that decisions are made with the bank's best interests in mind.
5. Board meetings should preferably be held on a monthly basis, but in any event no less than once every quarter.
6. Individual directors should attend at least half of the board meetings that are held in each financial year, and all of the meetings at which major issues are discussed.
7. The HKMA will meet the full board of directors of each bank every year.

Independent Non-Executive Directors

Outside independent non-executive directors (INED) are perceived as a tool for monitoring management behaviour (Rosenstein and Wyatt, 1990). Ideally, an INED should function proactively, meet internal and external auditors, review business plans and budgets, visit business units, review management reports and financial statements, and ask and answer questions at annual general meetings. They should draft and sign part of the annual report, including the Corporate Governance Statement, the Report of the Audit Committee, and the Report of the Remuneration Committee. However, it is doubtful whether the appointment of INEDs in Hong Kong companies can provide effective checks and balances.

As in many other countries, the existence of INEDs on boards in Hong Kong is seldom voluntary. Since 1993, the Listing Rules of HKEx, as part of its Code of Best Practice, have required that every listed firm must have at least two INEDs. These INEDs must have no past or present financial or other interest in the business of the company or its subsidiaries, and no past or present connection with any connected person of the company who might affect the exercise of independent judgement. These conditions are critical due to the predominance of family ownership and control of firms in Hong Kong. However, other requirements of being an INED are not clear, such as the knowledge and experience that are needed, residency, number of directorships held, meeting attendance, and minimal time spent on firm business. The definitions of independence and the classification of directors as independent in some cases raise questions as to whether such people are truly independent.

Ho and Wong (2001b) found that the average proportion of INEDs on the boards of listed firms in Hong Kong was thirty-four per cent, and the average number was 2.45. Therefore, INEDs are still a small minority. However, it is required by the Listing Rules that at the committee level some committees, such as audit and remuneration committees, must have a majority of INEDs and be chaired by an INED. Clearly, the quality of INEDs is as important as the number in ensuring better governance. However, it is always difficult to find experienced and devoted INEDs, and most new appointees do not usually know enough about the realities of business to monitor inside executive directors effectively (Tricker, 1995).

Some argue that outside directors may not devote enough time to understanding the critical issues that are faced by a company. Many people agree that an outside director of a firm should be limited in the number of other boards they can be active on at the same time. For example, an average director of a publicly held company in the US spends only about 120 hours per year on board duties. This does not seem enough time to be able to protect the interests of outside parties. The same would be true in Hong Kong. Since the Enron incident, many institutional investors have requested that firms only appoint independent directors who are resident in the region, can attend meetings personally, and spend enough time on board business.

As most listed firms in Hong Kong are family-controlled, and in view of the low free float, it is generally perceived as being impossible to have truly independent directors. Real outsiders are usually not trusted, and friends or close contacts of the controlling family fill the independent director slots. In other words, these directors are less than fully independent. INEDs are often nominated by executive directors who represent controlling shareholders, who in turn hold the key votes at shareholders' general meetings on the election or re-election of those executive directors. Such INEDs can be replaced any time if they are not loyal to the controlling shareholders. Therefore, most INEDs are unable or unwilling to state the case of minority shareholders. Sometimes, when things go wrong, these INEDs simply resign early to avoid liability. Recently, there have been suggestions that independent directors should be elected directly by minority shareholders only.

Under the CG Consultation Conclusions of HKEx, some further guidelines would be issued by HKEx to help issuers assess the independence of INEDs. Issuers would be required to appoint at least three INEDs, one of which should have appropriate professional qualifications or experience in financial matters. In addition, the HKEx will recommend as a good practice that INEDs make up at least one-third of the board of directors (since 2003 in the US, INEDs must be the majority).

Again, HKEx seems put too much emphasis on the number of INEDs rather than their suitability for appointment. The introduction of more INEDs on Hong Kong's corporate boards does not seem to have improved practice (Ho and Wong 2001b).

The Audit Committee and Other Committees

The functions of an audit committee include ensuring the quality of the financial accounting and control system (Collier, 1993). As an audit committee consists mainly of non-executive directors, it can reduce the amount of information that is withheld. Agency theory predicts the establishment of audit committees as a means of attenuating agency costs. Forker (1992) found that the existence of audit committees improved internal control, and thus he regarded them as effective monitoring devices for improving disclosure quality. Ho and Wong (2001b) found that firms with an audit committee tended to have a significantly higher level of voluntary disclosure.

The Code of Best Practice of HKEx recommends listed firms to establish and disclose the existence of audit committees (or to give reasons why they do not exist) in their annual reports since January 1999. The Hong Kong Society of Accountants also issued guidelines on the formation and operation of an audit committee. The guidelines, which have been endorsed by the stock exchange, stipulate that an audit committee company should consist of a minimum of three INEDs with board business backgrounds (the majority of whom should be independent), with written terms of reference that deal clearly with the 'four responsibilities': financial and other reporting, internal control, internal and external audits, and the needs of management.

The revised Code of Best Practice will recommend the establishment of a remuneration committee and a nomination committee. Nomination committees make recommendations on the appointment or re-appointment of executive and non-executive directors by listed issuers. These committees should be composed mainly of INEDs.

Despite the fact that the oversight of audit committees contributes significantly to corporate accountability, most countries around the world mandate the adoption of audit committees for all listed companies. In Hong Kong, it is surprising that neither the Companies Ordinance, the Listing Rules, nor the SFC requires this adoption. Under the terms of the HKEx CG Consultation Paper, the establishment of an audit committee would be made a requirement for Main Board issuers (it is already a requirement for GEM companies). However, HKEx finally decided to leave it as a voluntary act. This leniency reflects how Hong Kong is still lagging behind international standards in the realm of CG.

Dominant Personalities (CEO Duality)

Firms in which one individual serves as both chairman and CEO/managing director (i.e. in which there is CEO duality) are considered to be more managerially dominated (Molz, 1988). People who occupy both roles tend to withhold unfavourable information from outsiders. As the chairman is also the CEO, the board tends not to criticize the CEO's performance and supports the chairman's recommendation on compensation for the CEO. However, Fama and Jensen (1983a) argue that any adverse consequences due to CEO duality could be eliminated by market discipline. Nevertheless, Forker (1992) asserts that a dominant personality in both roles poses a threat to monitoring quality and is detrimental to the quality of disclosure.

CEO duality is common in the US, although the world trend tends to decouple the two roles. In 1998, this separation existed in seventy-one per cent of listed companies in Hong Kong (Ho and Wong, 2001b). Currently most Chinese-owned banks in Hong Kong have no separation of the two roles. In early 2002, the HKMA recommended that these banks separate their board chairmen from their CEOs; some banks accepted the recommendation and made the separation. The HKEx CG Consultation Paper recommends that the roles of chairman and CEO should be segregated, but HKEx concluded that it would be sufficient to include it in the Code of Best Practice rather than making it mandatory.

Directors' Dealings

In the Enron incident, dealings by directors with linked and associated companies appear to have been one of the problems. One of the major areas that both the SCCLR and the HKEx Consultation Paper have concentrated on is directors' dealings with their companies, subsidiaries, and associated companies. This is an area where it is likely that abuses could easily arise. The aim of any new rules will be to prevent directors from deriving unfair advantage from their positions. In formulating proposals, the SCCLR will resolve whether the regulation will be achieved by statute or listing rules. Further, the scope of the transactions that are covered needs careful consideration, as an 'associated' company is an accounting term and is not defined in legislation. In the HKEx CG Consultation Paper, various proposals were made to clarify the rules concerning directors' dealings and their disclosure. Stricter rules on the disclosure of securities transactions by directors were also proposed. Under HKEx's Consultation Conclusions, HKEx will amend the Listing Rules to require shareholders' approval for a service contract that is to be granted to a director of the issuers or its subsidiaries for a period exceeding three years. Shareholders who are the directors with an interest in the services contracts and their associates will be required to abstain from voting at the general meetings approving the respective service contracts.

Directors' Remuneration

Executive compensation contracts that are designed on the basis of firm performance can be an effective mechanism for reducing agency costs by aligning the interests of a firm's executives with its shareholders. The level of executive compensation and the extent of pay-for-performance for senior executives has been a topic of considerable controversy in the academic and business communities. The debate on executive compensation is highly visible, political, and controversial in Hong Kong, with accusations of compensation being excessive and compensation policies being non-transparent and self-serving (see, for example, Crystal (1991), *Ming Pao* (5 April 2002), *Hong Kong Economic Journal* (1998)).

Between 1991 and 1998, the average director's salary went up by 350 per cent, yet profits increased by only about 180 per cent. In Hong Kong, the average pay of a listed firm director–CEO in 2000 was about HK$5.7 million, while the highest paid executive director in 2002–3 received HK$373 million. These payments include salaries, bonuses, stock options, and other allowances. Internationally, the US is ranked top and Hong Kong fifth in the world and first in Asia in terms of senior executives' pay. In 1990, the average top fifty company CEO was awarded US$2.8 million, while in 1999 it was US$9.3 million (Ho, 2002). The pay awarded to US CEOs in 2002 was less than that of 2001 by ten to fifteen per cent. The average CEO in Hong Kong makes fifty times as much as the average manufacturing worker; in the US, this gap is even bigger. Some people worry about whether such a large income gap might cause those on a low income to lose their motivation to work and create social conflict.

Reports in the media in recent years have alerted Hong Kong investors to the issue of excessive pay packages for company executive directors. The issue has become especially controversial because, at the same time, company profits have dropped. In an often-cited example, the directors at PCCW received a huge payment of HK$768 million in 2000 (fifty times that of 1999), despite the company's record loss of HK$6.9 billion and a seventy-two per cent fall in its share price (*South China Morning Post*, 2002). According to a *South China Morning Post* survey, the total directors' pay in 2001 amongst the thirty-three Hang Seng Index firms increased by sixty-three per cent, despite a thirty-three per cent fall in the combined net profit of these companies. Other Hong Kong firms paying high salaries despite poor performance include Century City, Dickson Concepts, Emperor International, Luk's Group, Far East Group, Sunday, and Sincere. Certainly, there are a few exceptions, such as the directors of the Shui On Group, who cut their own pay by ten per cent in 2002.

Based on corporate data in Hong Kong since 2001, it is found that the growth in pay for executive directors far exceeds the growth of stock prices, net profits, and wages. There is no evidence that executive pay is significantly linked to a firm's performance. In addition, executive pay has a higher association with accounting earnings than stock price.

Among those few firms that link pay to performance, blue chip companies without controlling shareholders tend to pay the most fairly. In family-controlled firms, pay for performance may not be important because the executives have contributed their own capital and personal reputation to the business. This union of ownership and management tends to lead to a difficulty in distinguishing personal and company assets. However, company directors in family firms might use their control to abuse the system and use compensation to benefit themselves at the expense of minority shareholders. In Hong Kong firms with controlling shareholders, small shareholders have very little say about directors' pay because the board can make a proposal to the shareholders' general meetings and obtain approval quite easily.

While executive directors are overpaid, it is commonly held that INEDs are underpaid. There have been suggestions that the pay given to INEDs should be commensurate with their quality, risk profile, and performance. There are also arguments that each INED should hold a very small percentage of a firm's stock (say, not more than one per cent) in order to show his or her commitment to the firm. The issue of shareholding by an INED is still controversial, although such practices are quite common in the US and UK.

Although strongly recommended, the formation of remuneration or compensation committees, composed mainly of INEDs and deciding on payments using objective benchmarking, are voluntary, and only forty per cent of listed firms in Hong Kong had such committees in 2000 (Ho and Wong, 2001b). As most INEDs are not truly 'independent' in Hong Kong, the real effect of a remuneration committee of INEDs on making executive pay awards more accountable may not be as significant as many policymakers believe. In the current regulatory environment and given the relative importance of minority shareholders, directors can get away with it. To win a better deal for shareholders, one suggestion for improving the situation is that only minority shareholders should be allowed to vote on company proposals to increase the pay of individual directors by more than a certain percentage. However, the relative influence of minority shareholders looks unlikely to increase in the foreseeable future. In the short term the only answer may be regulation aimed at directors' remuneration more accurately reflecting the realistic health of a company.

In the US and the UK, academics have long examined the relationship between senior executive compensation, firm performance, and other firm characteristics (see Main (1991) and Pavlik, Scott, and Tiessen (1993) for reviews). However, these findings are largely mixed and may not be applicable to the Hong Kong environment. In a recent Hong Kong study by Ho and Lam (2003), it was found that directors' ownership had a negative and moderating effect on the total amount of pay to the top five executives of a firm and the total cash bonus that is paid to executives. It seems that pay-for-performance compensation schemes are not major factors in setting top executive remuneration in Hong Kong. Moreover, board size, firm size, market to book assets, and the existence of a bonus plan have a positive and significant effect on the total amount of pay to top five executives.

Ezzamel and Watson (1997) found that changes in executive pay in the UK were more closely related to external market comparison pay levels than to changes in either profits or shareholder wealth. There was also a marked difference in treatment between executives who appeared to be underpaid and those who appeared to be overpaid. Executives who were underpaid received a large and highly significant upward pay adjustment in the next year, while no comparable downward adjustment was visible in the case of overpaid executives. These results are consistent with the complaints by shareholder groups that many boards and remuneration committees tend to bid up executive pay rather than making pay more closely linked to performance.

Hong Kong is also well known for its opacity on executive compensations. Local companies usually disclose very little about their policies on compensating their directors and senior executives, and they have resisted proposals to increase disclosure of directors' pay on the grounds of privacy. Disclosure requirements on executive pay in the US and UK are much stricter and more demanding than they are in Hong Kong. In recent years, steps have been taken to increase the disclosure of executive pay, in the hope that this will increase transparency and be more closely tied to the firm's health and performance of companies. The HKSA has proposed more detailed disclosure requirements of directors' incomes such as aggregate amount, analysis by components, analysis by bands, remuneration policy, fixed versus discretionary pay, the value of options realized, and amount by individual name.

In the HKEx CG Consultation Paper, listed firms would be required by the revised Listing Rules to disclose individual (unnamed) directors' remuneration, their computation method, and a list of decision makers. It is also hoped that the future Listing Rules will require the explanation of a company's executive compensation and stock option policies, including exercise price, effective period, and numbers, in their annual reports. Firms will also need to divide the total pay into fixed basic salaries and performance-based bonuses. Currently, all of these important disclosures exist on a voluntary basis. The CG Consultation Conclusions of HKEx will amend the Main Board Rules to require issuers only to disclose directors' remuneration on an individual basis, but they will not be required to disclose the directors' names due to the respondents' concerns about directors' privacy (similar to existing GEM requirements). It only recommends in the revised Code of Best Practice that issuers should be encouraged to disclose directors' remuneration on an individual, named basis in their annual reports.

Abuses of Stock Options

In theory, incentive-based compensation schemes should use a weighted combination of benchmarks such as company earnings, share price, and other factors. A trend to watch for is the increasing importance of stock options for directors and CEOs. Most US companies link their directors' pay strongly to the share price, mainly from options, which is in theory a legitimate and valuable form of employee compensation. A stock option gives an employee the right to buy a certain number of shares in the company at a fixed 'favourable' price for a certain number of years and then sell the stock later at a higher price. These companies believe that earnings are short-term but the share price reflects future earnings, so it is possible to measure the impact over a longer term. Yet this assumes that the market is efficient and that share prices cannot be manipulated.

Many people believe stock option compensations benefit executives to the detriment of shareholders. The heavy adoption of executive stock options and the practice of not treating them as an operating expense in a company's financial statement (instead showing them only in footnotes), leaning more in favour of a share price peg, has stimulated some senior executives to behave opportunistically so that the stock price can rise in a short time. One cause of the Enron collapse was probably its abuse of stock options. During the market boom periods, all market players made profits and were happy with the capitalist model. Good corporate governance practice and internal controls were treated as cosmetic. As has now become clear, much of this was a cover-up, and serious deficiencies existed in the system. The mostly unregulated practice of giving executives stock options to boost compensation remained popular with boards of directors in the US until 2002, when several executives were caught cashing in millions of dollars in salaries and bonuses from their overvalued firms. Since then, many in Congress have lobbied to limit the stock options given to corporate managers.

In recent years, only a few US firms, such as Boeing, have treated share options as operating expenses. In fact, since the early 1990s, the Financial Accounting Standards Board (FASB) has attempted to develop accounting standards requiring firms to treat share options as an expense. However, due to strong opposition from hi-tech firms such as Cisco, Microsoft, Intel, and Sun, who strongly lobbied Congress, the plan was suspended. These are firms that would have experienced substantial net losses or much lower net profits if their share options had been treated as expenses, and the suspension of the plan allows them to keep their valuable professional staff and not lose their competitive power. Some experts, however, point out that treating share options as an expense will not actually stop companies continuing to issue share options, it will only make their financial reporting more transparent. Investment guru Warren Buffet has indicated that not treating share options as an expense would be unethical accounting practice, inflating a company's earnings. US companies such as Coca-Cola, GE, General Motors, and IBM have agreed to treat share options as expenses in their accounting systems; in the short term, this may affect their earning figures negatively, but in the longer term it will increase investor confidence in them.

Research by Shevlin (2002) found little evidence of the widespread mistreatment of stock options by US top corporate executives, despite the highly publicized scandals involving former officials at Enron, Global Crossing, and Worldcom. Rather, a study of more than 1,000 companies showed that for every dollar stock option given to a company's top executives, the firm's earnings increased by an average of $2.85 over the following five years. The existing legal, financial, and accounting infrastructures should be further improved, with bold steps and executive compensation loopholes tightened up. Specifically, it is wise to reapportion the ratio of fixed to variable pay that executive directors receive so that the variable pay should not exceed, say, sixty per cent. Rules can also be introduced so that these options cannot be exercised within a certain number of years unless the performance of the firm exceeds the average of the stock price in the market or when these executives leave the company. Directors and executives should be excluded from selling their holdings of company shares while serving on the board. Some experts also suggest executives' net gain (after tax) after exercising their options should be held in the company stock until a certain number of days after leaving the company.

In Hong Kong, as most listed firms are family-owned and controlled, the offering of share options to directors and CEOs is not as common as it is in the US. Further, this factor, coupled with the adoption of the International Accounting Standard (IAS), helps reduce the temptation for executives to misbehave. Of course, the measures on stock options mentioned above may further avoid the possibility of abuse and manipulation.

There is no magic formula for calculating how much directors should be paid. However, there must be some theoretical linkage to show outside investors that the amounts paid are not random or controlled by the directors themselves, that they are based on reasonable models, and that they are transparent and acceptable to minority shareholders. From an outsider's point of view, if directors continue to enjoy higher levels of pay regardless of the profitability of the company, this is clearly not in the interest of the investing public.

Accounting/Disclosure Standard Setting and Corporate Reporting

The effective functioning of capital markets critically depends on effective information sharing among companies, securities analysts, and shareholders. One major element of good corporate governance is transparency—the provision of timely, true, and relevant corporate information to stakeholders (especially investors) to enable them to make decisions. Besides traditional financial statements, this information should cover discussions on overall company performance, future prospects and positioning, strategic planning and policies, risk management, remuneration policy, and performance assessment criteria, both in financial and non-financial terms. Dipiazza (2002), the CEO of Ernst & Young, indicated that there were six objectives of corporate reporting: completeness, compliance, consistency, commentary, clarity, and communication.

Improvements in information sharing should increase management credibility, analysts' understanding of the firm, investors' patience and confidence, and, potentially, share value (Eccles and Mavrinac, 1995). In a study by *CFO Asia* of the 116 largest listed firms in Asia, those which disclosed more extensively were found to perform much better in earnings and stock prices than those which disclosed less extensively (*Apple Daily*, 2002). Amongst the top ten companies in terms of disclosure quality, three were from Hong Kong. Sufficient information disclosure is an effective mechanism to reduce information asymmetry and increase market efficiency.

Disclosures are either mandatory, voluntary, or provided by intermediaries, and they complement each other to enhance market transparency and efficiency. As additional disclosures involve extra costs and benefits, sometimes it is difficult for companies to strike the right balance, and the management must always exercise its judgement carefully in voluntary disclosure decisions.

The mandatory disclosure requirements in Hong Kong are mainly stipulated by the Hong Kong Company, the SFO, the Listing Rules (Appendix 7A), the Statements of Standard Accounting Practice (SSAPs), and the Industry Accounting Guidelines for certain special sectors. Besides shareholding and significant transaction disclosure requirements, some of the important disclosure requirements in the Listing Rules include principal activities and segmented information, directors' interests in shares, directors' service contracts and interests in contracts and emoluments, substantial shareholders, published forecasts of results, details of borrowings, details of properties, five-year financial summaries, emoluments of the five highest paid employees, principal suppliers and customers, management discussion and analysis, and the profile of directors and senior management. The new Code of Best Practice requires listed companies to disclose whether an audit committee is in existence, and all financial statements must be prepared under approved accounting standards. Overall, the scope of disclosure requirements in Hong Kong is much narrower and less specific than that in the US and the UK (Eccles and Mavrinac, 1995). For instance, until recently only interim (mid-year) and year-end reports were provided. There was no need for listed firms to disclose their balance sheets in their interim reports, and the cost of goods sold was not available in income statements. Disclosure rules governing ownership interests, notifiable and related party transactions, and directors' interests and remuneration are much less stringent than in the US.

In terms of banking, prior to 1992 banks in Hong Kong maintained inner reserves and disclosed little balance sheet or profit and loss information. The rationale was to smooth out large fluctuations in profits and thereby help to maintain public confidence in the banking system. However, pressure for change became irresistible, and there were criticisms from rating agencies and analysts. The lack of inner reserve disclosure was seen as incompatible with Hong Kong's position as an international financial centre. The HKMA persuaded local banks to disclose transfers to inner reserves in their 1994 accounts and the accumulated amount of inner reserves in their 1995 accounts. The amount of disclosure has been increased each year through annual HKMA Guidelines.

The experience has been positive and the image of Hong Kong banks has improved. Announcements of losses by a few banks during the Asian crisis were absorbed by the public without strong reaction. To achieve transparency, the HKMA recommends that banks should disclose their financial performance, financial position, risk management strategies and practices, and risk exposures, accounting policies, and corporate governance information (Carse, 2002). Currently, the level of disclosure by banks in Hong Kong is rated as the best in the region by the IMF. However, there is room for further improvement, as international standards for disclosure are being strengthened all the time. The New Capital Accord that was announced by the Basel Committee on banking supervision is a prime example of this.

Financial Reporting Standards and Compliance

Much of the financial reporting information is prepared by management, endorsed by the audit committee, approved by the board, audited by the external auditors, and circulated widely via various channels. Each participant in this chain must play its role with high professional standards to ensure transparency, reliability, and integrity. It is also important to bear in mind that the quality of accounting and auditing standards and their enforcement have a direct bearing on the quality of the financial information that is disclosed.

Unfortunately, the manipulation of accounting standards, window-dressing, creative accounting, earnings management, and even fraudulent reporting have been the practice of some of the largest listed firms in the world. These practices include channel stuffing, recognizing exchanged-out network capacity as income, excluding executive stock options and other liabilities from balance sheets, and overemphasizing certain earning indicators, such as earnings before interest, taxes, depreciation, and amortization (EBITDA). Although the Enron case is an isolated incident, the local accounting profession has registered and takes seriously the public concerns that were expressed following the affair in the US. The US SEC promulgated the Sarbanes-Oxley Act in mid-2002, which requires the CEOs and chief financial officers of over 940 listed companies to swear that the financial statements of their companies are true and fair. In the case of incorrect specifications, these executives are personally liable for high financial penalties, and even up to twenty years in prison. The accounting scandals that have rocked American businesses have also sent shock waves around the world. The repercussions will be widespread and long-lasting as similar incidents happen in other countries.

As a former colony, Hong Kong's financial reporting or accounting system largely follows British accounting practices. The Statements of Standard Accounting Practice (SSAPs), the Accounting Industry Guidelines, the Statements of Audit Standards (SAS), and professional ethical standards are issued by a self-regulated professional body—the Hong Kong Society of Accountants. Although non-statutory, compliance with these standards is required of all HKSA members. In terms of accounting standards, Hong Kong SSAPs were in the main local adaptations of the UK SSAPs in the early years. However, at the end of 1992, the HKSA switched to International Financial Reporting Standards (IFRS, formerly IAS) that are issued by the International Accounting Standard Board (IASB) as models for the new Hong Kong SSAPs.

Amongst some thirty-five IFRS, about half are compatible with local SSAPs. If there is no Hong Kong SSAP on a particular issue (there were about seven such cases in 2002), the IFRS are usually followed. Many local standards have been converted to make them consistent with IFRS. The general policy is to produce totally originally statements only if no equivalent IFRS exist. For this reason, local statements have been restricted to mainly Accounting Industry Guidelines. This symbolizes Hong Kong's commitment to the international harmonization of accounting practices. As Hong Kong SSAPs are in line with IFRS, Hong Kong Main Board and GEM issuers with a primary listing can adopt IFRS (while overseas issuers with a secondary listing in Hong Kong can adopt US generally accepted accounting principles (GAAPs)). The international standards on which Hong Kong standards are modelled follow a principle-based approach as opposed to the rule-based approach that is adopted in the US. The principle-based approach, which emphasizes substance/spirit over form, is regarded as a more effective safeguard against abuse. In principle, the kind of off-balance sheet finance arrangements through special purpose entities (SPE) that were permitted under the US GAAPs are not permitted under IFRS or Hong Kong SSAPs.

The present accounting standard-setting process operates well, but a number of areas still need reform or improvement. For instance, international convergence means relinquishing local autonomy and authority in standard setting. IFRS are subject to different interpretations and are difficult to enforce. Although Hong Kong SSAP 32 follows IFRS on paper, it does not achieve the original intent and the detailed disclosure requirements. For instance, some companies in Hong Kong frequently exclude the business of their offshore associated firms from their consolidated accounts. Facing ever-changing financial markets, current local accounting standards are not sufficient to cope with new financial activities and instruments. And as the current IFRS focus on accounting treatments more than disclosure requirements, the simple adoption of more IFRS may not be sufficient to resolve the transparency problem. Whether the quality of actual corporate disclosures satisfies investor information needs is more important. Currently, the SFC is helping the International Organization of Securities Commission (IOSCO) with the evaluation of new draft international disclosure standards (IDS), which will ultimately help to improve corporate transparency and risk management.

The SCCLR consultation report asked the HKSA to reform the composition of its Financial Accounting Standards Committee and Auditing Standards Committee to cater for greater public involvement in the process. This will ensure the wide and balanced representation of different stakeholders, and that the standard-setting process is less vulnerable to business and political lobbying. The HKSA should develop new accounting standards and tighten disclosure requirements on new areas such as staff stock options, intangible assets, R&D expenses, and financial derivative instruments. The SCCLR also recommends the establishment of an independent body with the authority to investigate financial statements and their compliance with accounting requirements. Auditors should be allowed to report on any inconsistencies between audited financial statements and the financial information that is contained in directors' reports. These suggestions are supported by the HKSA.

Disclosure Practice and Effectiveness

Overall, conformity with the Listing Rules and accounting standards by Hong Kong firms is high (Tai *et al.* (1990); Hong Kong Society of Accountants (1997)). The only area that has a comparatively low standard of compliance is the disclosure of related party transactions (Hong Kong Institute of Company Secretaries, 1998), which is most likely to be due to the high proportion of family-controlled listed firms. The Judges' Report of the Hong Kong Management Association Best Annual Report Award noted that many Hong Kong companies still made only the minimum disclosures that were required by the accounting standards and statutory provisions. In addition, over the years, the quality and quantity of information that is disclosed in annual reports has varied, even though the degree of difference has been decreasing and the quality of Hong Kong annual reports has improved (*South China Morning Post*, 28 November 1998). Nevertheless, firms in Hong Kong still have to provide more in-depth analysis of their business and performance (e.g. management analysis and discussion). Mandatory disclosure rules ensure equal access to basic information (Lev, 1992), but this information has to be augmented by firms' voluntary disclosures and information production by intermediaries.

Gray (1988) suggested that although the 'Asian–Colonial' cultural group to which Hong Kong belongs has a system of accounting that is characterized more by transparency than by secrecy, it consistently lags behind the 'Anglo' cultural group. Williams and Tower (1998) found that Hong Kong companies appear to disclose more additional information than do companies in ASEAN countries including Singapore, the Philippines, Thailand, Indonesia, and Malaysia. In a recent survey by Standard and Poor's, Hong Kong was ranked the same as China, South Korea, Malaysia, and Thailand. Singapore was ranked top, and Indonesia, the Philippines, and Taiwan were rated the lowest (*Ming Pao*, 12 June 2002).

Many investors and auditors in Hong Kong have worried about company disclosure practices for related party transactions and other dealings, and they have called for greater financial disclosure for listed companies following the series of corporate fraud cases mentioned above (*South China Morning Post*, 30 July 1998). Some audit firm partners have suggested that the stock exchange should increase its disclosure requirements, while others have suggested the voluntary disclosure of more information (*South China Morning Post*, 30 July 1998). To avoid the danger of over-regulation, HKEx hopes to encourage such a culture of voluntary disclosure. It believes that the quality of a company's disclosures will be reflected in its stock price and its future ability to raise share capital (Hong Kong Institute of Company Secretaries, 1998). Nevertheless, disclosure requirements in Hong Kong are reviewed and extended regularly. Besides seeking increased regulation, investors are increasingly concerned with the communication and disclosure processes of listed firms (*South China Morning Post*, 30 July 1998).

As mentioned previously, the new SFO introduced additional disclosure requirements to combat market misconduct and empower investors further. It has put in place a disclosure regime that is more in line with international standards. The initial disclosure threshold for substantial shareholders has been lowered from ten to five per cent, and the notification period has been shortened from five to three business days. HKEx's consultation paper suggests that Main Board-listed companies should publish quarterly reports less than forty-five days after the quarter end, which would be consistent with the GEM requirement. However, due to pressure from some issuers, quarterly reporting will not be a requirement for Main Board issuers for the time being. HKEx will only encourage Main Board issuers to adopt quarterly reporting as recommended good practice in the revised Code of Good Practice, to promote transparency. The existing quarterly reporting requirement in the GEM will be retained.

Both Main Board and GEM issuers would be required to publish their half-year results announcements within two months of the relevant financial period. Issuers would be allowed to distribute summary half-yearly and annual reports containing the information that is required by HKEx, provided they have ascertained the wishes of individual shareholders. HKEx will abolish the existing two-phase publication arrangement for half-year results announcements of Main Board issuers and annual announcements of Main Board and GEM issuers. Issuers would also have to disclose the nature of the audit work that they engaged in, the amount of audit and non-audit fees, and directors' remuneration. It is expected with the advance of Internet technology that online corporate reporting will be made possible by the Extensible Business Reporting language (XBRL) format.

In the United Kingdom, progressive companies such as Body Shop and British American Tobacco have launched new reporting initiatives called corporate social reporting (CSR). These reports, following strict guidelines and auditing (similar to financial reports), are meant to disclose to stakeholders the issues, impact, and performance of a company's 'non-financial' activities—ranging from environmental concerns to how the business affects local communities. This form of reporting is seen as critical in presenting a full picture of corporate activities, and Hong Kong enterprises have begun to take steps towards disclosure in this area as well. Town Gas, China Light & Power, and MTRC are reporting on their non-financial activities in ways that should be a model for others as a first move down the road to world-class CSR.

Ho and Wong (2001a) conducted a comprehensive survey of the perceptions of chief financial officers (as preparers) and financial analysts (as external users) in Hong Kong about a variety of information flow, disclosure, and capital market efficiency issues. While both subject groups believed that a majority of firms adopted a conservative one-way disclosure strategy and that there was a communication gap, analysts perceived a much higher need than CFOs for increased financial reporting regulations. Both subject groups did not think that enhancing disclosure requirements alone would suffice to close this gap. Instead, they suggested an improvement in the quality of the communication and disclosure processes through means such as developing industry reporting guidelines, choosing more appropriate communication media, formulating a more proactive disclosure strategy, enhancing investor relationships, and voluntarily reporting more information.

Ho and Wong (2002) further investigate the perceptions of both preparers and external users of the values of selected voluntary disclosure items and compare these perceptions with the actual disclosure practice by preparer firms. Based on a survey of ninety-eight CFOs and ninety-two financial analysts in Hong Kong, it was found that, in voluntary disclosures, preparers perceived that the potential benefit of share price improvement was significantly larger than that of reducing cost of capital, while the preparation cost was not significantly different from the cost of possible loss of competitive advantage. From the perspective of analyst users, the most important voluntary disclosure items were discussions of factors affecting future financial results, future prospects of the company, main products market share, acquisition and disposal activities, and China business review. The top five items with the highest net benefits are future prospects of the company, financial summary for more than five years, market capitalization, responsibilities of directors/senior management, and corporate strategy and impact. Overall, there is no significant difference between mean total benefits and mean total costs.

Among the thirty-five voluntary disclosure items, Ho and Wong (2002) found that there was no association between preparers' net benefits and users' perceived importance. This provides empirical evidence that for more user-desired information, the net benefits to the preparer firms may be very low or even negative. Although there was a significant positive relationship between perceived net benefits and the actual disclosure percentage by firms, there was no such correlation between users' perceived importance and firms' disclosure percentage. Therefore, preparers are influenced more by their own cost–benefit concerns in disclosure decisions, not user requirements. Of course, it is not only the cost–benefit analysis that determines the disclosure policy and decision of a firm, but also the control over managers' actions that can be exercised through the corporate governance of the company. Ho and Wong (2001) have found that the existence of an audit committee is significantly and positively related to the extent of voluntary disclosure, while the percentage of family members on the board is negatively related to the extent of voluntary disclosure.

Overall, if we believe decision usefulness is the primary purpose of financial reporting, in order better to serve users, firms should review seriously those information items being perceived as very important by users with a view to seeing whether they can disclose more such information in a cost-effective manner. If not, in order to reduce the communication and expectation gaps, firms should explain to users why they cannot do so. Also, there may be a need for policymakers to make mandatory the disclosure of some important items (as perceived by users) that are always missing from annual reports.

In practice, firms should note that users always want more predictive financial information. This information reflects a firms' future development and is therefore highly demanded by investors. One problem of such disclosure is the difficulty of ensuring the accuracy of the financial prediction, and this may involve legal responsibilities with regard to the firm in question and its auditors. Since predictive information focuses on future information and the prediction is based on a series of assumptions, the final result is bound to deviate from forecasts. Many firms would try to give their best predictions but would still be afraid of committing serious forecasting errors and incurring subsequent legal burdens. It is suggested that in developing the regulations governing the disclosure of predictive information, the rules should specify that if a firm does not intentionally provide incorrect predictive information it should not be held legally liable for the accuracy of the forecasting, providing the forecast information is properly audited and the firm can give a reasonable explanation for the variance.

Auditor Independence and Accountability

Auditors are appointed by the shareholders of a company to audit and report on the financial statements that are submitted by the directors and laid before the company at annual shareholders' general meetings. The auditors can provide a 'reasonable assurance' on the annual accounts; they cannot guarantee the financial wealth of the company. In the audit process, if an auditor believes that the contents of a financial statement need to be amended and the firm refuses to do so, auditors cannot insist on the change and can only state their observations in their audit report. An auditor is required to exercise reasonable scepticism when reviewing the transactions that are presented by management, but they are not expected to perform an investigation into the authenticity of those transactions. Auditors should, however, be constantly alert to possible errors and misappropriation by the management of the client company to discharge their duty to present a 'true and fair view' of its financial position.

In recent years, there have been a number of accounting fraud cases involving the auditors and the audited reports. Although the HKSA has a set of ethical standards for auditors to follow—including guidance on independence, objectivity and integrity, practice promotion, fees, clients' monies, and confidentiality—some people believe that the Guangnan auditor failure in 1998 is similar to the Enron case in the US. They wonder whether the HKSA has an effective enforcement regime to safeguard its members' adherence to the stated principles. Fraudulent activities in some red chip firms were exposed after the economic boom in China, but their accounts were all approved by their auditors. This aroused people's suspicions about the quality of auditors in Hong Kong. Originally scheduled to be listed in July 2001, some information in Kit Wai International's IPO prospectus was found to be untrue, even after the company was given the green light by its auditors, the regulators, the underwriters, and the listing committee of HKEx. The company's auditor, Arthur Anderson, withdrew its audit report from the prospectus but did not explain why the false information was not discovered in the auditing process. Were there no reporting of such cases by anonymous people, public investors would be cheated. There have also been cases in which the earnings of newly listed firms have increased a thousand times after their IPOs, and this has caused worries about the reliability of audited financial statements. The fraudulent financial reporting case of Euro-Asia Agricultural (Holdings), a PRC private enterprise listed in Hong Kong, was described as the 'mini Enron' case of Hong Kong. The orchid grower was alleged in October 2002 to have inflated its revenue twenty-fold when it applied for a Hong Kong listing. Its listing was subsequently suspended, and the firm, its sponsor, and its auditors were investigated by HKEx and the SFC.

Auditor Independence

Auditor independence has become the focus of much worldwide attention in the wake of the Enron collapse. The controversial independence issues that have arisen in the US are generally attributed to the dramatic growth in the size of some audit firms' consulting businesses relative to audits, and the widespread provision of management consulting services to audit clients. In contrast, audit and other traditional professional services— such as tax advisory—are still mainstream services that are provided by certified public accountants (CPAs) in Hong Kong. As most family-controlled firms tend not to use independent consulting services, such conflicts exist to a lesser extent than in the US. Furthermore, as most of the consulting activities of audit firms in Hong Kong are conducted by independent divisions, auditors should face fewer independence issues than in the US. However, the HKSA has admitted that there are no statistics on how CPAs perform auditing and non-auditing services, and it has no idea about the potential for conflict of interest in the profession. Many in Hong Kong still believe that auditing should be totally separate from management consulting activities. If auditors also serve as financial advisors to client firms, they are less likely to report any fraud found in the audit process.

Another major issue of auditor independence is that although auditors are employed by a listed company and should be accountable to shareholders (especially minority shareholders) by conducting professional and independent audits on the company's accounts, in practice only corporate management has direct contact with the auditors, and these auditors are therefore inclined to be accountable to the management or the controlling shareholders more than to outside minority shareholders. As such, conflicts of interest often exist. Further, the Big-4 auditing firms monopolize the auditing market and thus control the structure and norms of the industry. These firms not only participate in relevant legislation and policymaking indirectly to protect the interests of practising accountants, but any local professional body formed by such an industrial structure would find it difficult to be self-disciplined and perform the role of monitoring the others. It is necessary to enhance the independence of the regulatory system and ensure that auditors can perform their independent auditing duties to protect minority investors' rights.

The International Federation of Accountants (IFAC) recently released an updated International Code of Ethics for Professional Accountants featuring new rules on independence. Following a principle-based approach, the updated Code is intended to serve as a model from which to develop ethical guidelines for accountants worldwide. Consequently, the HKSA has decided to adopt the IFAC Code, which does not ban certain services but provides guidance on specific circumstances and relationships that threaten auditor independence, and also suggests safeguards to mitigate threats. In case no safeguard can reduce the threat to independence to an acceptable level, a ban should be imposed by reference to the principles of the Code.

The HKSA's current standard recognizes the possible threat to independence that is created by a quantum of fees, and imposes a guideline that fees from any one client should not exceed fifteen per cent of the total fee income of the audit firm. It also deals in depth with other potential threats, such as personal relationships, financial involvement, and the provision of non-audit services such as management consulting. The standard requires audit firms to take care not to perform management functions. When the safeguards are insufficient to eliminate the threats to independence or reduce them to an acceptable level, the firm is expected to decline the work or withdraw from the assurance engagement. A disclosure requirement for fees paid to auditors with respect to other non-audit services would increase audit transparency, and although there is no such current requirement, voluntary disclosure by companies is encouraged before mandatory disclosure is imposed.

The new SFO also allows the SFC to gain access to an auditor's working papers, and provides auditors of listed companies who choose to report any suspected fraud or misconduct to the SFC with statutory immunity from civil liability under client confidentiality rules. Unfortunately, the SFO does not compel auditors to report fraud (which is obviously a crime) to the regulators but makes this voluntary. Some auditors argue that it would be sufficient for them to report fraud to the client company's audit committee, but this view ignores the fact that many audit committees in Hong Kong are not truly independent. It is argued that the failure to impose a positive duty to report fraud is a significant omission in the SFO. Although auditors have no duty to detect or investigate fraud, they should be mandated to report irregularities to the audit committee of a client company and the regulatory body if any are detected in the auditing process.

Despite the adoption of the new IFAC ethical codes, the concept of self-regulation is facing strong challenges. Auditors should care not only for their clients' interests but also the interests of the investing public. In an attempt to prevent more scandals, recent proposals to enhance the independence and quality of auditors in Hong Kong include the following:

1. Listed firms are required to disclose their audit and non-audit fees.
2. Audit firms are required to disclose the percentage of income gained from consulting activities; a ceiling ratio should be imposed.
3. Practice reviews should be conducted by independent parties rather than by the HKSA.
4. There should be a separate set of auditing standards for listed firms.
5. Auditors should be restricted from working in a client's firm after leaving an audit firm.
6. Auditors should be appointed by minority shareholders, the audit committee, or an independent body.
7. Auditors or audit firms should be rotated regularly (say, every five years).
8. A two-tier audit system of two audit firms to one company should be adopted.
9. A second audit firm should be appointed by the SFC to review certain aspects of the work of the first audit firm.
10. Audit committees should be required to make independent statements about external auditors.
11. The giving of false or misleading information by directors and management to auditors should be treated as a criminal offence.
12. Auditors of listed companies should be put on the SFC/HKEx registered intermediaries list for monitoring.
13. Auditors should be assigned duty of care to third parties (i.e. the investing public, banks, and creditors) beyond their client companies.
14. A separate independent regulatory body for monitoring auditors should be formed.

Self-Regulation versus Independent Public Oversight

The HKSA's self-regulation system relies on its own members to monitor other members' professional conduct. Naturally, conflicts of interests tend to arise. The effectiveness of a self-regulatory system like this has been the subject of ever-increasing scepticism and challenges. Since 1998, HKEx has submitted eleven suspected auditor misconduct cases to the HKSA for investigation. Other than four cases which were withdrawn due to insufficient information, the HKSA has not so far been able to inform the public of its progress with regard to its investigations or any action taken in the remaining seven cases.

In the US, the regulation of professional accountants is multi-layered and involves the SEC, the Financial Accounting Standards Board (FASB), and the American Institute of Certified Public Accountants (AICPA). AICPA and the Big-5 (now Big-4) audit firms always support the use of both the public oversight board and peer review to improve the professional standards of accountants. Since the Enron incident and other high-profile corporate failures, there has been a crisis of confidence both in the accounting profession and about audited financial reports. Besides promulgating the Sarbanes-Oxley Act for reforming public companies accounting, the chairman of the SEC expressed the SEC's strong determination to revise its rules-based accounting standards and reform the management of public accountants. The Big-5 leaders agreed with these reforms and pledged not to offer further consultancy and internal auditing services to their audit clients. Besides strengthening their auditing standards and professional ethical guidelines, they also agreed to open up their mechanism for monitoring member accountants, with moves such as setting up a new Public Accountability Board to regulate public companies auditors with government appointees. Currently, US auditors are monitored (including investigations and disciplinary actions) by the SEC Practice Section, which is independent of the accounting body. Although this Section is still composed of practising accountants, it is overseen by the Public Oversight Board comprising non-professional public individuals. In the UK, the various accounting bodies contributed to the setting up of a monitoring committee comprising public participants to oversee the operations of various committees under these professional bodies. The UK Financial Reporting Review Committee was also formed to investigate accounts of problem listed companies and audit reports. Since then, other countries have been considering adopting similar public oversight bodies to monitor public accountants and further protect public investor interests.

During the sixteenth World Congress of Accountants held in Hong Kong in November 2002, many professional bodies agreed with independent regulation of the accountancy profession and believed that supervision of the profession should rest with the government. The new president of the IFAC, Rene Ricol, repeated his call for accountants to realize that 'self-regulation is over' and appealed to the Hong Kong profession to give up self-interest in favour of following international practice and abandoning self-regulation. In contrast, the former officers of HKSA claimed in response to press queries that there was no need to make any changes to the current self-regulatory mechanism—later changing their view after pressure came from various sources, saying that the HKSA would consider further the possibility of independent regulation. The HKSA defended the existing self-regulatory mechanism, saying that it was less expensive than independent regulation, there was no strong public demand for independent regulation, and it would be sufficient to increase public participation in HKSA's committees. These arguments failed to convince, and many people went away with the impression that the HKSA treasured self-interest more than it did the public interest.

Subsequently, both the Secretary for Financial Services and the Treasury (SFST) and the SFC raised concerns about the current self-regulatory framework of the accounting profession in Hong Kong. Under pressure from the public and the government, the HKSA called urgent council meetings and rapidly submitted to the government, in late December 2002, some compromise reform proposals relating to its governance and self-regulatory framework. The proposals attempted to explain how the Society would enhance its self-regulatory regime to address the demand for greater transparency and the restoration of public confidence in the accounting profession, trying to strike a balance between enhancing public oversight and retaining self-regulation.

Currently, there are three committees under the HKSA Council which handle members' ethical and disciplinary matters: the professional ethics committee, the investigation committee, and the disciplinary committee. When the Council receives a complaint, it usually refers it to the professional ethics committee to ascertain whether further investigations are needed. The Council then decides whether to let the investigation panel carry out further investigations or the disciplinary committee make disciplinary decisions. In the first case, the investigation panel gives its results to the Council, and the Council decides whether it will make its own disciplinary decisions or let the disciplinary committee do so. Under this arrangement, the disciplinary committee has no powers of investigation and cannot take the initiative to follow up any complaint.

The HKSA asked for more lay members to be appointed by the government to the Council, the investigation panel, and the committees. The reorganized investigation panel would be increased in size from three to five members, of whom at least three (currently only one) would be non-accountants, with a lay member chairman. The reorganized disciplinary committee would increase the number of non-accountants on its five-member committee from two to three, and the chairman should also be a lay member. The HKSA believes that these moves will have the effect of increasing objectivity and confidence in the decisions made by the Society; however, since the HKSA has only ten full-time staff in its compliance division overseeing investigations, it expects the government to give them more power and resources to conduct investigations. It is also considering increasing its maximum fine, which is currently HK$500,000, and is thinking about other penalties, such as public reprimands and consent orders.

As an alternative to reforming the two committees, the HKSA also proposed the establishment of an Independent Investigation Board (IIB), with expanded authority and increased resources, to investigate accounting and auditing faults in listed companies. Under this option, IIB still has to refer proven cases to the HKSA for follow-up internal investigation and disciplinary action. It has proposed this additional option because most investigations take a long time and the current procedures prescribed by the Professional Accountants Ordinance (PAO) do not allow a high level of investigative power and transparency. Its existing authority lies only over HKSA's members, but many fraud cases involve other parties such as company directors and CFOs. The establishment of the Board should give the added benefit of additional funding (*Hong Kong Accountant*, April 2003), and under the plan, the Board would comprise independent non-accountant members.

The HKSA has effectively put forward two proposed options without mentioning the possibility of setting up an independent oversight body. In doing so, it has not given up its other regulatory functions, including discipline, because it believes that increasing lay participation in the Council and the two committees would have the effect of subjecting all of these functions to the supervision of lay members. Since the disciplinary process will be led by a lay chairman and be open to the public, the HKSA thinks that there is no need to devolve this crucial function, and that it should retain disciplinary powers over its members.

However, as long it wishes to retain powers of appointment over the lay members, the independence of the two committees involved will be in doubt. The SFC recently expressed the view that the proposals may not meet the requirements of the principles for the oversight of auditors of listed companies set out in the Technical Committee Report of the International Organization of Securities Commission (IOSCO). Although the government has in principle accepted the reform proposals of the Council and the two committees of the HKSA, it has not indicated that it will accept the formation of the IIB. It has also said that it will take some time for a decision to be reached.

Many market participants believe that, in the long run, Hong Kong needs an independent public oversight body which has the right to follow up and investigate an independent complaint or a case noted from public sources. This should have full investigation, prosecution, and disciplinary powers and should also monitor the way that the HKSA handles public complaints and member disciplinary matters. Before the government makes a decision, the HKSA Council should allow the disciplinary committee to handle and investigate any complaints directly and make final disciplinary decisions. This implies that the investigation and disciplinary panels can merge into a single committee.

Improving the independence of the regulation of the accounting profession by introducing more pubic participation is a worldwide trend.

It is believed that if the local accounting profession does not take the initiative to form an independent oversight board, it will not regain lost confidence in public accountants and their audited reports. Ultimately, the government will have to take over the profession in the interest of the public if more accounting frauds and scandals occur.

Market Intermediaries and Analysts

Intermediaries such as investment banks, sponsors, underwriters, financial advisors, lawyers, accountants, surveyors, and valuators are key advisors to listed companies about their activities. Serving as a bridge between issuers and public investors, they rely on their professional knowledge and independence to ensure the accuracy of the corporate data of issuers so that the interests of the issuer and public investors can be balanced. They are intimately part of the checks and balances involved in ensuring the quality of corporate governance.

Since the Kit Wai International and Euro-Asia Agriculture scandals in the early 2000s, the independence and integrity of IPO sponsors and other intermediaries have been subject to public criticism. The performance of some newly listed firms dropped rapidly after IPO and was significantly different from what was forecast in the IPO prospectuses. It was found that intermediaries had assisted these companies to apply for listing by decorating their accounts and 'repackaging' their IPO materials. Collusion between the issuers and some intermediaries to exaggerate IPO earning figures have been the subject of attention by the regulatory bodies.

IPO Sponsors

The responsibility of an IPO sponsor is to ensure that an issuer fulfils all of the listing requirements, and to employ relevant professionals to verify related information and documents so that investor interests can be protected. In theory, IPO sponsors are accountable to future shareholders, but in practice most sponsors are directly employed by the senior management of the issuer. Sometimes the sponsor also serves as the issuer's IPO underwriter, responsible for IPO packaging and promotions in order to get the best deals. This clearly leads to conflicts of interest. Even when these roles are separate, as long as IPO sponsors are directly employed by an issuer the independence problem cannot be completely resolved.

In a survey of 445 people carried out by the Democratic Party in late 2002, it was found that over seventy per cent of the respondents had worries about the accuracy of corporate accounts and the credibility of analysts (about thirty per cent expressed 'serious worries'). These findings show that the investing public lacks confidence in the market intermediaries. Almost ninety per cent of the respondents thought that the government should tighten up the regulation of related market intermediaries as soon as possible. In a survey carried out by HKEx of fund managers' views on the efficiency of regulating new issuers, the average response was 'just satisfied'. Further, only a quarter of respondents thought that IPO sponsors had good professional ethical standards: far below a similar perception of lawyers and accountants. These findings confirm the general views that the quality of IPO sponsors is quite diverse.

To improve market quality in Hong Kong, both HKEx and the SFC need to ensure the quality of newly listed companies, and must also effectively monitor the market intermediaries. The government, HKEx, the SFC, and the HKSA have all made suggestions for improving the situation. The SFC currently supervises these intermediaries through the Code of Conduct on registered corporate finance advisors and their licensing rules. It can suspend or terminate the registration of an intermediary in case of misconduct, but this practice has been criticized as lacking flexibility since it would be difficult to find out whether the management or the sponsors violate rules. For this reason, since 1997 the SFC has condemned only thirteen registered corporate finance advisors, seven of whom had their registrations temporarily suspended.

To come into line with the new SFO, The SFST asked the SFC in late 2002 to strengthen the regulation of IPO sponsors and ensure that these professionals fulfilled their duties with care, including verifying the accuracy of data contained in IPO prospectuses. Under the SFO, the SFC can impose financial penalties on intermediaries, which will help to deter misconduct. If an IPO applicant submits false or misleading IPO information to the SFC, this can be treated as a criminal offence. Even if such a company was listed, it would receive the same penalty. Strengthening the regulation of market intermediaries is one of five high priority tasks to be completed in 2003 by the SFST.

If IPO sponsors commit serious misconduct, the SFC will apply their extended investigative and disciplinary powers. The SFC will be allowed by the SFO to investigate IPO-related papers from the new issuer's sponsors, banks, and auditors and ask them to offer explanations. The chairman of the SFC also said in February 2003 that the level of sanctions against IPO sponsors who violate rules will be strengthened. The fines can be up to ten million Hong Kong dollars, or three times the amount gained as the result of misconduct, whichever is higher. The SFC can suspend or cancel the licence of an intermediary if it is proved to be violating rules. Under the current Companies Ordinance, only directors of a listed company or those authorizing the issuance of the IPO prospectus will be held both criminally and civilly responsible if misleading information is found inside an IPO prospectus. Market intermediaries will be held liable only if they offer misleading information in the IPO prospectus. The SFST has suggested revising the Companies Ordinance to expand the scope of responsibilities of IPO sponsors.

Following GEM practice, HKEx has planned to set up an approved name list scheme to put qualified IPO sponsors and other intermediaries on a central register. The scheme will spell out the qualifications, rights, and obligations of a qualified sponsor. Intermediaries who perform unsatisfactorily in an IPO case will be given a certain number of penalty points. On meeting a certain threshold, they will be removed from the list (i.e. they will be blacklisted) by HKEx via public announcements, and they will not be allowed to engage in any further IPO advisory activities.

With the support of the government and the SFC, HKEx issued a consultation paper on regulating market intermediaries in May 2003, three months later than its original schedule, as a result of pressure from some big issuers and investment banks. The paper suggests a common scheme for regulating market intermediaries in both the main board and the GEM board, and clearly spells out the responsibilities of IPO sponsors and the means of handling misconduct cases. However, other than some investment bankers, the Listing Committee of HKEx, dominated by issuers and intermediaries, has indicated some reservations on these new initiatives from HKEx and the SFC. They are also against the idea of following the GEM board to set up an approved IPO sponsor list on the Main Board. In particular, they cannot accept the proposal that IPO sponsors, similar to corporate directors, have a criminal liability for the accuracy of the data inside an IPO prospectus. They believe this is a wrong move, shifting all the responsibility from corporate directors to IPO sponsors. These market players worry that if an IPO sponsor is jailed, very few people will be willing to serve as sponsors and the sponsoring fee will rise.

One major difficulty in regulating IPO intermediaries is that it is difficult to ascertain the specific responsibilities of the different intermediaries involved, such as sponsors, lawyers, accountants, and valuators. When a new issuer is caught, each of these bodies will try to point their fingers at the other intermediaries. The regulators wish to ensure that each intermediary knows its responsibilities and is accountable to the investors.

Under the current Listing Rules of the GEM board, within the first two years of the IPO, an IPO sponsor must provide advice to a newly listed company on continuous compliance with the relevant listing rules. These include share placement, mandatory disclosures, and connected transactions. The IPO sponsor will be held accountable for these disclosures and documents. Investment bank Morgan Stanley suggested that the government introduce 'corporate governance advisors', which can be taken up by lawyers, accountants, management consultants, brokers, or investment banks. This could help separate the role of an IPO sponsor and a continuous corporate governance advisor, and will also help to reduce IPO sponsors' worries about their responsibilities after IPO. A listed company could also receive proper guidance on compliance with rules and corporate governance after IPO. The bank suggested that the government conduct a wide consultation on this proposal in Hong Kong.

Other suggestions on regulating market intermediaries include prohibiting IPO sponsors serving as IPO underwriters, and developing further channels for civil actions against intermediaries violating rules. In the near future, the monitoring of valuators, lawyers, and surveyors should also be improved.

· *Analysts*

In the financial markets, due to information asymmetry and complicated transactions, outside investors face difficulty in monitoring listed companies, relying usually on professional analysts for additional information, analyses, and advice when making investment decisions. These supplement other limited information sources and make the market more efficient.

Unfortunately, most analysts cannot survive on an independent self-employed basis, and they are usually employed by a stockbroking firm or investment bank. These stockbrokers and banks have close business relationships with many issuers—serving as IPO sponsors or underwriters, for example—and this easily affects the independence of analysts. Many investment banks release research reports on new issuers before IPO activities, and as there is a close relationship between analysts and the investment bank, many analysts would be affected by the views of the bank's financing or marketing department when putting together pre-IPO reports. These reports always become PR documents for new issuers, even though many of them have no earnings records or even real business activities. Since these research reports, many of which contain forecasted earnings data, are technically not part of the IPO prospectus, they are not subject to the requirements of listing rules. Many of the analysts are compensated with bonuses and share options according to the earnings of the bank employing them and if they, through personal interest, provide misleading or inaccurate information in their reports, investors could be seriously misled about investment decisions.

From early 2001 until the collapse of Enron in October of that year, the analysts of all major investment banks in the US still strongly recommended buying Enron's stocks and bonds, even when the company announced a huge loss of US$1,000 million in its third quarterly report after the resignation of its newly appointed CEO. Some of these analysts admitted in their private emails that many of the shares they recommended were in fact 'junk stocks'. After the collapse of Enron, many US Congressmen condemned these Wall Street analysts and reflected that there were conflicts of interest amongst analysts who were linked to investment banks or funds houses. Indeed, in the previous ten years, more than ten security firms and investment banks on Wall Street assisted Enron in sixty-nine completed or uncompleted acquisition transactions and the issuing of 138 bonds. At the same time, they also employed analysts to provide investment advice on Enron. Some Congressmen pointed out that most of these analysts wore two hats, at once being independent analysts of listed firms and insider analysts who assisted investment banks in attracting more businesses. Rules have to be tightened in order to regulate such conflicts.

Inexperienced or unprofessional analysts make subjective earnings forecasts on the basis of simple data that is supplied by listed firms. They do this without conducting their own surveys or analyses. Although their subjective predictions or expectations are always unrealistic, they can become market forces that drive the firms concerned to adjust their strategies. To match analysts' predicted earnings or to restrain their stock prices from dropping, these firms use creative accounting methods to 'fix' their account books. Many people believe that the business relationship between an analyst's investment bank and a client firm affects the independence of the analyst to the degree that they tend to not disclose, or delay disclosing, any negative news about the client firm. There were also some well-known international credit rating agencies that intentionally delayed their announcements of negative rating reports on Enron (and perhaps other listed firms?) because they received assessment fees.

These giant US investment banks initially refused to admit the charges put up by the SEC and did not co-operate with the regulatory bodies in the investigation process. In late 2002, ten investment banks agreed to pay US$140 million for compensating cheated investors, with the expectation of avoiding prosecution by New York Chief Prosecutor E. Spitzer. In April 2003, the New York Chief Prosecutor, the SEC, and other regulatory bodies settled the case outside court with two investment banks. Analyst H. Blodget of Merrill Lynch was fined US$4 million, and analyst J. Grubman of Salomon was fined US$15 million and not allowed to continue working as an analyst. These penalties were recorded as the highest under the Security Act. Other well-known analysts, such as M. Meeker of Morgan Stanley and F. Quattone of Credit Suisse First Boston, are still under investigation. The US authorities also announced a series of regulatory changes, such as separating the research and marketing departments of an investment bank, and acquiring independent analyses from outsiders for public reference.

Similar problems also exist in other markets, including Hong Kong, although there have been few official complaints filed with the SFC. Instead, investors usually get free advice from media commentators and analysts. One problem is the conflict of interest for Hong Kong's large institutional investors: most fund managers are attached to investment banks, and the companies that they would like to criticize are also clients that these banks would like to win. Some bankers, brokers, and credit analysts often do not write what they really think about some companies, fearing that critical commentary could hurt their access to information or prospects for future advisory business. One good example is the Euro-Asia Agriculture incident: analysts of several giant international investment banks still recommended buying shares in the firm up until the arrest of the firm's chairman in November 2002, even though there had been rumours about the firm since the beginning of the year.

In Hong Kong most individual investors are not able to obtain research reports from large investment banks. With the exception of a few independent press columnists, there are not enough independent voices to pressure regulators into making Hong Kong markets more transparent and improving corporate governance. Some media analysts, with or without disclosing their identity, are employed by security firms or investment banks. According to a survey by the Democratic Party, over seventy per cent of investors do not trust analysts' advice when making investment decisions. What is needed are independent analysts such as Terry Smith in the UK and Zhang Hua-qiao in China (both of UBS-Warburg), who assert their independence without fear of termination by their employers or legal action by the firms they criticize. The culture of accountability that values high-quality and objective research and reporting holds the key to future confidence in analysts.

A security firm can issue a 'caution statement' to the effect that it may hold or trade the securities that are recommended by its research department, and that investors should therefore exercise their own judgement in dealing with the recommendations. To protect the integrity of the price discovery system, an improved practice would be that when a security firm makes a recommendation, it should not deal in the securities for at least three trading days before and after the publication. Besides 'Great Walls of China', other mechanisms should be instituted to prevent collusive activities between the research and trading divisions of the same security firm.

There are few regulations covering the quality and independence of analysts. Both IOSCO and the SFC are investigating whether rules should be established regarding analysts' practice. The SFC conducted a survey of all security firms in Hong Kong in early 2003, investigating current practice and possible measures to regulate analysts. Similar to investment advisors and IPO sponsors, it is suggested that an SFC/HKEx registration scheme should be set up to register qualified analysts and monitor their professional conduct. In the meantime, the SFC should consider introducing a voluntary registration scheme requesting participating analysts to disclose their academic qualifications, work experience, personal investments, and so on for public reference. There should be disclosure requirements on analysts' interests in shares that they comment on and the association between their pay and their employers' income. They should also disclose the relationship between their employers and the companies that they recommend. There should be a statutory requirement requiring investment banks to separate their corporate financing department from the research department in order to avoid potential conflicts of interest, and analysts should be prohibited from involvement in marketing and trading activities. Other than analysts employed by securities firms or investment banks, the government should consider the need for regulating freelance analysts providing investment advice through the media.

Empowering Minority Shareholders and Shareholder Activism

Overall, Hong Kong's minority shareholders are not properly represented, have very little influence, and are open to potential abuses by controlling shareholders who extract unfair gains from them. There are low free floats of the shares of listed companies, and the local media rarely investigate questionable corporate activities. The dominant voting power of insiders also easily neutralizes public shareholder activism and creates apathy. Individual investors in Hong Kong are usually inactive and vote with their feet. According to the CLSA, the country scores on the treatment of minorities are Singapore 100, Hong Kong 84, the Philippines 35, Taiwan 34, and Korea 33.3. La Porta *et al.* (1999) found that common law countries (mainly the US, the UK, Canada, and Australia) appear to have the best legal protection of minority shareholders, while civil law countries—particularly the French civil law countries—have the weakest protection. The legal protection score of Hong Kong is five (six equals 'excellent'), which is the same as the UK and the US, but many people doubt the accuracy of such a high ranking.

In theory, unlike small individual investors, there is greater incentive for large institutional investors to monitor management and try to influence its decisions rather than simply selling their stocks when they are dissatisfied. Like Hermes in the UK (which manages most of the assets of the British Telecom Pension Scheme and those of the Royal Mail, worth US$65 billion) and CalPERS in the US (the California pension scheme), they are the responsible owners or owners' agents in action, and take responsibility for keeping an active watch on the companies in which they invest. They help to ensure that a proper balance of power exists on the boards of companies between those with executive roles and those who are there to ensure that the interests of the owners are fully represented. These long-term shareholders should act as catalysts to institute change within companies, including their strategies, management, or capital structure. In the UK and the US, if institutional fund managers do not carry out these monitoring tasks, a hostile takeover may ensue, which benefits no-one except professional advisers.

Although institutional investors count for forty per cent of the local market transactions, they mainly trade on blue chip stocks and are not active in monitoring the management of invested firms. Further, provident fund markets are just starting to develop in Hong Kong, which means that it will be a long time before the fund reaches a sufficient size to be able to behave like CalPERS, which is feared in boardrooms across America. Forms of market discipline such as takeovers are not effective mechanisms for monitoring managerial behaviour and corporate performance in Hong Kong. This is because most family-owned firms are controlled by cross-shareholding, and corporate raiders or interested parties are not able to perform takeovers through open-market purchases.

In its consultation document of July 2001, the SCCLR proposed a number of amendments to improve shareholders' rights. These proposals included amending the law to provide outside shareholders with a more meaningful procedure by which to nominate and elect directors, and the introduction of statutory derivative actions whereby the SFC would be empowered to bring derivative actions against wrongdoers in relation to listed companies. There would also be an independent corporate accounts review committee. Measures to protect shareholders are also contained in the new SFO. As mentioned previously, the provisions in the SFO have enhanced the investigatory powers of the SFC, including the power to seek assistance from a listed company's bank, auditor, or business counterpart to verify information that is obtained from an investigation. Other measures include expressly providing for a private right of civil action for a person to seek compensation for a pecuniary loss that is suffered as a result of relying on any false or misleading public communication. Such compensation may be sought from the people who are responsible for disclosing the information, such as the directors or senior executives of a company. There is also a tighter voting mechanism for connected transactions by interested shareholders. However, civil suits involve large legal fees, and most individual investors would not be able to afford the fees to put up a case. Derivative actions, which involve suing those caught up in misconduct in the name of the company, would therefore be a useful channel for minority shareholders to realize their legal rights.

With regard to improving the right to derivative actions, the relevant local laws need to be revised. We can learn from the US and Canadian models. In the US, according to the Corporate Law, the decision as to whether to allow minority shareholders to adopt derivative actions is made by a group of corporate independent directors appointed by the court. These directors consider the cost-effectiveness by using corporate resources to sue those involved in misconduct (including controlling shareholders) for compensation. If the potential legal fees are higher than the incurred losses, these independent directors naturally will not opt for such rights or actions. Some experts suggest that the decision about adopting derivative rights should be made by the shareholders' general meeting instead of independent directors. In Canada, such decisions are made by the courts, as it is considered that market misconduct involves the public interest. And, as mentioned earlier, the government should also consider the feasibility of class actions as soon as possible so that minor shareholders can sue collectively for compensation arising from misconduct.

Improved Decision Procedures at Shareholders' General Meetings

Stricter rules against the dilution of shareholders' interests through the placing of shares, rights issues, and share repurchases have been proposed by HKEx in its consultation paper. However, after consultations, HKEx will retain the existing twenty per cent limit on the issue of securities under the general mandate and will not impose any restriction on the number of refreshments of the general mandates, in light of the diverse views of respondents to the consultation exercise. HKEx will amend the Main Board Rules to require independent shareholders' approval for any refreshments of the general mandate after the annual general meeting. To protect minority shareholders further, HKEx will limit the placing of shares under a general mandate at a substantial discount (up to twenty per cent unless otherwise approved by HKEx) to the market price. It is believed by many corporate governance advocates that without restricting the number of times that a company can have a share placement in a certain period, other means would not be particularly effective in terms of minority shareholder protection. In view of the disappointing HKEx conclusions, independent market critic David Webb launched Project Vampire (Vote Against Mandate for Placings, Issues by Rights Excepted) in 2003. This campaign involved voting against the general placing mandate in its current form at all Hang Seng Index firms' general meetings.

Most listed companies communicate with larger institutional investors, always leaving retail investors in the dark and leading them to trade on random and incomplete information. Disclosure rules in Hong Kong also make it difficult for minority shareholders to receive information about important corporate activities in time to take action. To facilitate trading, shares are usually not held under investors' names, but through their brokers under the name of the Hong Kong Securities Clearing Company Ltd (HKSCC) nominees, the local clearing company. This means that beneficial shareholders do not automatically receive annual reports, corporate announcements, and proxy statements, and cannot vote at shareholders' meetings (unless arrangements are made beforehand). In many cases, the central registration and deposit system is a barrier to information flows, and voting by a show of hands added to low turnouts and planted shareholders at general meetings all mean that bad deals get passed even on 'independent' votes. This must be remedied if minority shareholders are to play a role in promoting good corporate governance. To facilitate the timely disclosure of and efficient access to quality information, the government's Steering Committee on the Enhancement of Financial Infrastructure will promote scriptless trading further and remove the custodian layer in the Central Clearing and Settlement System so that companies can communicate directly with shareholders and facilitate their voting.

Currently, by tradition, most if not all resolutions at shareholders' general meetings are decided on a one-person one-vote show of hands. Since most publicly held shares are represented by a single person from HKSCC Nominees Ltd (owned by HKEx), this single person can only raise a single hand on each resolution. In this situation most resolutions are passed quickly, since most employee–shareholders and other associates of the controlling shareholders will be in favour of the agenda items. As such, all proxy votes sent in by absent shareholders are not counted, and it is not possible to know for a fact how many shares would have voted for or against each resolution.

After the HKEx CG Consultation, since mid-2003 the Listing Rules require voting by way of a poll for connected transactions and transactions requiring controlling or interested shareholders to abstain from voting. However, a poll is not mandatory for 'less important matters'. This 'half-baked cake' will certainly not be acceptable to many corporate governance advocates. As independent critic David Webb pointed out in his Project Poll in 2003 (Webb, 2003), one-share one-vote is an essential principle of shareholder participation in all decisions in a general meeting, and Hong Kong's traditional 'showing by hands' system is incompatible with international best practice of corporate governance. Although the controlling shareholders always dominate the decisions by whatever voting mechanism, a one-share one-vote poll counting proxy votes could inform the public about the extent of 'for' and 'against' votes, regardless of the outcome. This would increase the transparency of the voting process and hold management accountable to shareholders.

Since HKEx did not fix the voting rules, in Webb's Project Poll a five-person team was organized, each member holding two shares, to attend the general meetings of all Hang Seng Index firms and request a poll for every item. Under Section 114D of the Hong Kong Companies Ordinance, five registered shareholders, present in person or represented by proxy, of a company can require a poll to be held. However, other corporate governance critics think that the one-person one-vote polling mechanism (by ballot, not by showing hands) may be more useful, as it would allow minority shareholders to shape the decision if most of them could attend general meetings in person. If a minority shareholder bothers to vote or send in his/her proxy, many of them could perhaps be further encouraged to vote in person.

To protect minority shareholders further, the HKEx Consultation Conclusions require issuers to disclose the procedures for demanding a poll in their circulars when voting by poll is not mandatory for approving the transaction outlined in the circular. In addition, HKEx will include in the revised Code of Best Practice the requirement for the chairman of a general meeting to announce the procedures for demanding a poll at the general meeting approving the transactions. However, there is nothing yet in the listing rules to require the results of a poll to be published.

Empowering Minority Shareholders

There are those who have focused on encouraging investors to take a greater responsibility in the monitoring of managerial behaviour. This assumes that if minority shareholders grow increasingly active and knowledgeable and become the 'first line of defence', more protection for minority shareholders will be put in place. For instance, disclosure requirements need investor vigilance to monitor actual practices, particularly in terms of related-party transaction disclosures. It is hoped that the introduction of the Mandatory Provident Fund will lead to more institutional investors (particularly overseas investors) demanding a higher standard of corporate governance from Hong Kong companies. These international institutional investors should become driving forces behind shareholder activism.

The SFC Shareholders Group has been upgraded to a standing committee, but its impact is still rather limited. Some people suggest the formation of a 'shareholder support fund' to protect the interests of minority shareholders. The initial funding could be grants from the government, the SFC, HKEx, and private donations/subscriptions. A small percentage of the levy that is imposed on securities and futures transactions could be assigned to the fund, and its operations would be overseen by a board that would consist of a cross-section of the community. The fund could be used to provide advice or support in litigation against the company and/or its directors on a 'sharing basis' (both costs and compensations awarded). In addition, investment in shares of companies could ensure the right of the fund to attend general meetings and ask questions of directors.

Following this idea, David Webb suggested establishing a shareholder activist group, the Hongkong Association of Minority Shareholders (HAMS), in 2002, and it was hoped that the body would be funded by a levy on stock market transactions (about 0.005 per cent each). HAMS will seek out companies that are guilty of misconduct, draw attention to their behaviour, and, in the worst case, sue them on behalf of the group's members—similar to a class action—as long as one of the members holds that company's shares. The group will also develop a corporate governance rating system for listed companies and publish its results to encourage good governance. It is expected that HAMS will be accountable to the Legislative Council. However, despite its merit and a number of supporters, the government and some industry leaders have deep reservations about the funding proposal. As a private association, they believe that the group should be funded by the investors themselves (both individual and institutional). Another problem is the conflict of interest for Hong Kong's large institutional investors, as many fund managers are attached to investment banks. Some market players also think that establishing an activist group like this will bring about more legal cases and make Hong Kong a litigious society, even without class actions.

While the government thinks that shareholder activism will occur naturally in time, some people believe that the government needs to catalyse this reaction, besides considering the possibility of class actions. Further discussions of legal protection for investors under the SFO can be found in the next chapter.

The Convergence of Corporate Governance Practices

Over half of the IPOs in Hong Kong in 2001 and 2002 were from Chinese state-owned and private enterprises. In these two years, the market capitalization and funds that were raised by Mainland IPOs exceeded those of Hong Kong local companies. The China Security Regulatory Commission (CSRC) is making a serious effort to address corporate governance problems in China, and is taking tough enforcement action. The next wave of IPOs in Hong Kong is likely to be from Chinese private companies. Quality assurance is a large part of the reason that Mainland companies are encouraged to list here. If quality is not delivered, then Hong Kong markets will suffer. Western governance measures such as INEDs, audit committees, voting requirements, board practices, and financial reporting standards have been widely adopted by the CSRC.

However, some market participants still believe that disclosure quality and rule compliance and enforcement are inadequate in China, although some people believe China has done more than Hong Kong to improve corporate governance over the last few years and is narrowing the gap with Hong Kong. For instance, besides requiring listed companies to file quarterly financial statements from 2002 onwards, the CSRC issued guidelines on independent directors and established a delisting mechanism for companies that make persistent losses for three consecutive years, among other initiatives. By comparison, Hong Kong still does not have a delisting mechanism based on performance. Some market experts even predict that China could become the leading Asian country in terms of corporate transparency. To compete with China in the long term, Hong Kong must speed up its efforts on the CG front.

With China's entrance into the WTO and the sheer amount of business that is conducted between Hong Kong and China, the Hong Kong SFC and the CSRC should further their co-operation and develop mutually beneficial measures to enhance the quality of listed state-owned enterprises in Hong Kong. Hong Kong's adherence to the rule of law, its high quality of accounting standards, and relatively good ethical standards are strengths, and areas in which the Mainland capital markets could learn from Hong Kong.

Lately there has been growing interest in the pressures on national systems of corporate governance to converge due to the globalization process. If nations are to take advantage of new investment opportunities because of freer capital flows, they need to observe good international corporate governance standards. In the competition for global capital, global institutional investors—which originate largely from the US—may force firms to adopt US corporate governance standards. Local firms that wish to list in London or New York also need to convert to UK/US governance practices.

In fact, there is a trend towards countries learning from each other to effect continuous improvement. Each country and each firm seeks a system that reflects its own institutions, values, and traditions. Hong Kong will adjust to its own corporate governance practice in view of the major thrust of changes, including market globalization and other political and institutional changes. Changes in local family control practice include more non-family members joining the board and the management, more monitoring from external shareholding and business partners, tighter accounting standards, and listing rules for connected party transactions, amongst other moves. However, many people do not believe that Hong Kong will ultimately move to a full UK/US market model, but that it will adopt more relevant internationally accepted corporate governance principles, such as the OECD Principles, 1999 or the Pacific Economic Cooperation Council Guidelines, 2001. Certain practices in corporate governance are moving towards an international standard, but there is still no consensus on a single model that all countries should follow. The requirement for firms in Hong Kong is that they must gain more overseas experience and come closer to an international standard of corporate governance.

Hong Kong will seek to retain its fundamental 'free to choose' values and avoid some of the harshness caused by administrative measures. There is no need for formal convergence by administrative means. The best way to reconcile or harmonize the market and family models is to encourage a global process of self-selection and migration (Coffee, 2000). Large family businesses that want to grow to a global scale are likely to adopt the US/UK model, and firms that want to retain tight control will continue with the family-type model. This self-selection process will minimize the social friction and even unrest that formal convergence could cause.

Conclusion

The 1997 Asian financial crisis and recent corporate scandals propelled the issues of corporate governance in Asia to the forefront of the investor agenda. Amongst the factors that contributed to the downturn, weak corporate governance was a major culprit. Although Hong Kong was hard hit by the turmoil, analysts suggested that one reason for the relatively limited effect on local businesses was the local corporate governance regime.

Good corporate governance is the key to improving economic efficiency, enhancing the attraction of our market and investors' confidence, and maintaining the stability of our financial system. Enhancing Hong Kong's corporate governance regime is a priority of the Hong Kong government, particularly in terms of protecting minority shareholders' interests. The government and all relevant sectors have attached much importance, and dedicated considerable efforts, to reforming our legislation, rules, and guidelines to keep them up to date (Stephen Yip, Secretary for Financial Services, 2002). Despite some who prefer retaining the *status quo* because of vested interests, the ongoing efforts of different interested parties have made some good progress towards building a sound and solid corporate governance foundation for Hong Kong.

Hong Kong still has a lot of work to do to improve corporate governance, although it is ahead in the region. We cannot rely on stringent legislation and enforcement alone to enhance corporate governance standards. The Enron case indicates that such incidents happen even in the US, notwithstanding its stringent legislation and advanced regulatory regime. Drawing from the experiences of other countries, this chapter has suggested a number of ways to improve standards of corporate governance in Hong Kong. It stresses that in the reform process, refining the regulatory framework, improving internal governance mechanisms, raising the ethical standards of market participants, securing top management's commitment, and cultivating a healthy corporate culture are all important. Amongst the many suggested measures, we need to determine our priorities.

Good corporate governance is the product of the concerted efforts and hard work of all market players and stakeholders, all of whom should be working towards the common objectives of creating values and wealth and furthering Hong Kong's status as a world-class financial and business centre.

Discussion Questions

1. Identify three different definitions of corporate governance from the literature and compare them with the one given in the chapter.
2. Why is corporate governance important to the development of a financial market?
3. What do you think are the attitudes of international institutional investors towards the corporate governance standards of Hong Kong, and how may such attitudes affect their investments in Hong Kong?
4. Does Hong Kong legislation provide sufficient protection to minority shareholders against the wrongful acts of management?
5. Do you agree that in Hong Kong there should be class actions and that the burden of proof should be shifted to the alleged market players? What are the disadvantages of these new measures?
6. How and to what extent do INEDs perform their duties in ensuring that the interests of all shareholders (i.e. majority and minority shareholders) are taken into account by the board of directors?
7. With the vast majority of listed companies in Hong Kong subject to dominant family or individual control, do you think an INED could act as a watchdog for the board and the executive management?
8. Identify at least seven major differences between the US and Hong Kong on board composition and practice.
9. Should board directors fulfil their fiduciary duties to their company or to their shareholders? Why?
10. Should Hong Kong set up a new independent body to monitor the quality of corporate financial reports and auditor behaviour?
11. Should auditors be mandated by law to report suspect management frauds to the SFC during the audit process? Why?
12. To what extent do minority shareholders in Hong Kong exercise their rights in shareholders' meetings to protect their own interests? What are the major limitations and barriers?
13. Do you agree to the setting up of a shareholder activist group in Hong Kong, to be funded by a levy on stock market transactions? Why or why not?

Keywords

agency theory
audit committee
auditor independence
board of directors
CEO duality

16. Protection of Investors under the Securities and Futures Ordinance

CLEMENT SHUM

Introduction

The long-awaited Securities and Futures Ordinance (SFO) was enacted by the Legislative Council on 27 March 2002. It has been in operation since 1 April 2003. The ordinance aims to consolidate and update the law relating to financial products, the securities and futures market and industry, and the protection of investors.

The need for a modern legal and regulatory framework has been brought about by the globalization of financial services, advances in information technology, and the introduction of new products, services, and trading methods. In fact the UK, the US, Australia, and the Chinese mainland have also seen the need for a comprehensive legal framework to facilitate the development of their securities markets.

The government published the white paper version of the Securities and Futures Bill (the White Bill) on 2 April 2000 for public consultation. The consultation led to amendments being incorporated into a new version of the Bill (the Blue Bill), which was gazetted on 24 November 2000. The new law forms an integral part of the government's plans for maintaining Hong Kong's position as an international centre. It consolidates and repeals the ten ordinances listed below (Table 16.1), which contained many outdated concepts and definitions, into one comprehensive and composite ordinance, and it introduces a number of significant changes to the existing regulation of the securities and futures market in Hong Kong. The new regime is on a par with international standards and compatible with international practices, with necessary adjustments to address local characteristics and needs.

Table 16.1   The Ten Repealed Ordinances

The Securities and Futures Commission Ordinance (Cap. 24)
The Commodities Trading Ordinance (Cap. 250)
The Securities Ordinance (Cap. 333)
The Protection of Investors Ordinance (Cap. 335)
The Stock Exchanges Unification Ordinance (Cap. 361)
The Securities (Insider Dealing) Ordinance (Cap. 395)
The Securities (Disclosure of Interests) Ordinance (Cap. 396)
The Securities and Futures (Clearing Houses) Ordinance (Cap. 420)
The Leveraged Foreign Exchange Trading Ordinance (Cap. 451)
The Exchanges and Clearing Houses (Merger) Ordinance (Cap. 555)

The composite ordinance has 409 sections in seventeen Parts, with ten schedules. The provisions contain, among other things, clearer regulatory objectives and more effective supervisory and investigative powers for the Securities and Futures Commission (SFC; also referred to as 'the Commission'), a streamlined licensing regime for market intermediaries (i.e., licensed corporations or registered institutions), and the establishment of an independent Market Misconduct Tribunal (MMT).

This chapter covers the main provisions in the newly enacted Securities and Futures Ordinance relating to the protection of investors. Whenever appropriate, relevant provisions are quoted verbatim. This has the added advantage of providing a useful reference for current Hong Kong law. The legal convention of citation has been retained, so that s1(1)(a) refers to section 1, subsection (1), paragraph (a). Words and expressions in the masculine gender include the female; words and expressions in the singular include the plural; and words and expressions in the plural include the singular.

Regulatory Objectives

Section 4 of the SFO sets out the regulatory objectives of the SFC. This has no counterpart in the repealed ordinance. The objectives are:

(a) to maintain and promote the fairness, efficiency, competitiveness, transparency and orderliness of the securities and futures industry;

(b) to promote understanding by the public of the operation and functioning of the securities and futures industry;

(c) to provide protection for members of the public investing in or holding financial products;

(d) to minimize crime and misconduct in the securities and futures industry;

(e) to reduce systemic risks in the securities and futures industry; and

(f) to assist the Financial Secretary in maintaining the financial stability of Hong Kong by taking appropriate steps in relation to the securities and futures industry.

General Duties of the Securities and Futures Commission

In performing its functions, the SFC will, as far as is reasonably practicable, act in a way which is compatible with its regulatory objectives and which it considers most appropriate for the purpose of meeting those objectives (s6(1)).

In pursuing its regulatory objectives and performing its functions, the SFC must have regard to the following factors set out in section 6(2) of the SFO:

(a) the international character of the securities and futures industry and the desirability of maintaining the status of Hong Kong as a competitive international financial centre;

(b) the desirability of facilitating innovation in connection with financial products and with activities regulated by the Commission under any of the relevant provisions;

(c) the principle that competition among persons carrying on activities regulated by the Commission under any of the relevant provisions should not be impeded unnecessarily;

(d) the importance of acting in a transparent manner, having regard to its obligations of preserving secrecy and confidentiality; and

(e) the need to make efficient use of its resources.

Again, these general duties of the SFC have no counterpart in the former ordinance.

The New Licensing Regime

Part V of the SFO introduces a new 'single licence' concept whereby intermediaries are issued with a single licence authorizing them to engage in a number of different regulated activities such as dealing in securities and futures contracts, leveraged foreign exchange trading, and advising on securities, futures contracts, and corporate finance. In other words, they do not need to apply for different categories of registration and file separate returns and documents in respect of the various registrations. Only corporations may be licensed to carry on business in a regulated activity. The SFC will refuse to grant a licence to carry on a regulated activity unless the applicant satisfies it that (1) the applicant is a fit and proper person to be licensed for the regulated activity, (2) the applicant will be able, if licensed, to comply with the financial resources rules, and (3) the applicant has lodged and maintains with the SFC the security as required by the Commission, and is insured in accordance with Commission rules (s116).

Part V also introduces a 'management responsibility' concept to enhance investor protection. Section 125 states that a corporation licensed under section 116 will not carry on any regulated activity for which it is licensed unless (1) every executive director of the licensed corporation who is an individual is approved by the Commission as a responsible officer of the corporation in relation to the regulated activity; and (2) not less than two individuals, at least one of whom must be an executive director of the licensed corporation, are approved by the Commission as the responsible officers of the corporation in relation to the regulated activity (s125). The SFC will not approve a person as a 'responsible officer' unless he is a fit and proper person and has sufficient authority within the corporation (s126). In determining such fitness and propriety, the Commission will take account of the applicant's (1) financial status or solvency; (2) educational or other qualifications or experience; (3) ability to carry on the regulated activity competently, honestly, and fairly; and (4) reputation, character, reliability, and financial integrity (s129(1)).

In order to assure the investing public that intermediaries and their representatives are financially sound and honest, and that they will treat their clients fairly, the SFO empowers the SFC to (1) make rules on technical details relating to areas of regulatory concern (Parts VI and VII), (2) conduct continuous supervision of its licensees with a view to ensuring their compliance with all relevant legal requirements and licensing conditions (Part VIII), and (3) impose disciplinary sanctions on intermediaries, including revoking or suspending their licenses, reprimanding them, or imposing a fine, in the case of misconduct (Part IX).

Those who have actively participated in, consented to, or connived in the criminal misconduct of the corporation which they manage, or whose recklessness has allowed the corporation's criminal conduct to occur, will be criminally liable under the management liability concept (s390).

Securities and Futures Appeals Tribunal

The SFO establishes a full-time judicial Securities and Futures Appeals Tribunal, which has the jurisdiction to review certain decisions of the SFC, the Hong Kong Monetary Authority, or a recognized investor compensation company. This includes decisions relating to licensing, discipline, intermediary supervision, investment products, and registration of prospectuses. The Tribunal is chaired by a judge or former judge of the High Court assisted by two lay members who are appointed by the Chief Executive from among well-respected market practitioners (s216).

Anyone who is aggrieved by a specified decision of the relevant authority made about him may, by notice in writing given to the Tribunal, apply to the Tribunal for a review of the decision. The Tribunal can confirm, vary, or set aside the decision; where the decision is set aside, the Tribunal can substitute any other decision it considers appropriate, or the matter can be remitted to the relevant authority along with any directions that the Tribunal considers appropriate. For the purposes of a review, the Tribunal may, on its own motion or on the application of any of the parties to the review, receive and consider any oral evidence, written statements, or documents (even if such material would not be admissible in evidence in civil or criminal proceedings in a court of law), or require a person to attend before it at any sitting to give evidence and produce any article, record, or document in his possession relating to the subject matter of the review (ss217–228).

A party to a review who is dissatisfied with a decision of the Tribunal relating to the review may appeal to the Court of Appeal against the decision on a point of law. The Court of Appeal may allow the appeal, dismiss it, vary or set aside the decision in question, and, where the decision is set aside, substitute for the decision any other decision it considers appropriate, or it can remit the matter in question to the Tribunal with any directions it considers appropriate (s229).

Investor Compensation Companies

Under the old law, the SFC administered the assets held in the Unified Exchange Compensation Fund and the Futures Exchange Compensation Fund, while the recognized exchange companies received and determined claims and made apportionment where necessary. This arrangement was cumbersome. The new legislation includes a provision that where the Commission is satisfied that it is appropriate to do so in the interest of the investing public or in the public interest, or to facilitate the management and administration of the compensation fund, it may, after consultation with the Financial Secretary, by notice in writing served on a company, recognize the company as an investor compensation company (ICC) (s79). The SFO allows for the recognition of more than one ICC. A recognized ICC may make rules for its proper and efficient management and operation (s82), but no rule shall have effect unless it has the approval in writing of the Commission (s83).

Before the new legislation came into operation, the compensation ceilings were $8 million per stockbroker and $2 million per futures broker. One of the main objectives of the new compensation arrangements is to enhance the existing level of investor compensation and increase investor confidence by providing a 'per investor level' of compensation for retail investors through a new and independent entity that includes industry and public interest representatives and is subject to appropriate checks and balances.

The Chief Executive in Council can make rules relating to the means of funding the compensation fund and the maximum amount of compensation that may be paid to a person making a compensation claim (s244).

Offers of Investments

The SFO deems that a person commits an offence punishable with fines and imprisonment if he issues, or has in his possession for the purposes of issue, in Hong Kong or elsewhere, an advertisement, invitation, or document which is or contains an invitation to the public to enter into or offer to enter into (1) an agreement to acquire, dispose of, subscribe for, or underwrite securities, or (2) a regulated investment agreement (which, according to Schedule 1 of the SFO, means an agreement the purpose or effect, or pretended purpose or effect, of which is to provide, whether conditionally or unconditionally, to any party to the agreement a profit, income, or other returns calculated by reference to changes in the value of any property, but does not include an interest in a collective investment scheme), or to acquire an interest in a collective investment scheme such as a unit trust or a mutual fund. Certain categories of document, the issue of which the SFC has authorized, prospectuses which comply with the Companies Ordinance, and licensed or exempt securities dealers and authorized financial institutions are exempted (s103).

However, the SFC may, where it considers appropriate, authorize the issue of the above marketing material as well as collective investment schemes ('collective investment schemes' is a new term which covers unit trusts, mutual funds, and investment arrangements with respect to any property). In doing so, the SFC may impose such conditions as it considers appropriate, amend or cancel these conditions, or impose new ones. It may later withdraw any authorization granted (ss104–106). It is said that these provisions 'provide the flexibility necessary to better ensure that the SFC's jurisdiction to authorize investment products keeps pace with developments in the market, thus allowing for better investor protection' (see *Consultation Document on The Securities and Futures Bill* (2000), p. 35).

Section 107 of the SFO prohibits and makes it an offence for a person to induce another, by fraudulent or reckless misrepresentation, to invest money. Both fraudulent misrepresentation and reckless misrepresentation have been widely defined.

'Fraudulent misrepresentation' means:

(i)   any statement which, at the time when it is made, is to the knowledge of its maker false, misleading or deceptive;

(ii) any promise which, at the time when it is made, its maker has no intention of fulfilling, or is to the knowledge of its maker not capable of being fulfilled;

(iii) any forecast which, at the time when it is made, is to the knowledge of its maker not justified on the facts then known to him; or

(iv) any statement or forecast from which, at the time when it is made, its maker intentionally omits a material fact, with the result that-

    (A) in the case of the statement, the statement is rendered false, misleading or deceptive; or

    (B) in the case of the forecast, the forecast is rendered misleading or deceptive.

'Reckless misrepresentation' means:

(i)   any statement which, at the time when it is made, is false, misleading or deceptive and is made recklessly;

(ii) any promise which, at the time when it is made, is not capable of being fulfilled and is made recklessly;

(iii) any forecast which, at the time when it is made, is not justified on the facts then known to its maker and is made recklessly; or

(iv) any statement or forecast from which, at the time when it is made, its maker recklessly omits a material fact, with the result that-

(A) in the case of the statement, the statement is rendered false, misleading or deceptive; or

(B) in the case of the forecast, the forecast is rendered misleading or deceptive.

The word 'reckless' is not defined in the SFO, but the Oxford English Reference Dictionary defines it as meaning 'disregarding the consequences of danger, etc; lacking caution; rash'.

The SFO gives investors a statutory right of action to recover compensation for any pecuniary loss sustained as a result of reliance on the fraudulent, reckless, or negligent misrepresentation (see s108).

'Negligent misrepresentation' means:

(i)   any statement which, at the time when it is made, is false, misleading or deceptive and is made without reasonable care having been taken to ensure its accuracy;

(ii)   any promise which, at the time when it is made, is not capable of being fulfilled and is made without reasonable care having been taken to ensure that it can be fulfilled;

(iii) any forecast which, at the time when it is made, is not justified on the facts then known to its maker and is made without reasonable care having been taken to ensure the accuracy of those facts; or

(iv)   any statement or forecast from which, at the time when it is made, its maker negligently omits a material fact, with the result that-

(A) in the case of the statement, the statement is rendered false, misleading or deceptive; or

(B) in the case of the forecast, the forecast is rendered misleading or deceptive.

For the purposes of section 108, where a company or other body corporate has made any fraudulent misrepresentation, reckless misrepresentation, or negligent misrepresentation by which another person is induced to invest money, any person who was a director of the company or body corporate at the time when the misrepresentation was made will, unless it is proved that he did not authorize the making of the misrepresentation, be presumed also to have made the misrepresentation (s108(2)).

Market Misconduct

Market misconduct harms market integrity and, therefore, the interests of investors. Part XIII of the SFO establishes (1) a civil system to address market misconduct and (2) the Market Misconduct Tribunal to hear market misconduct cases using civil procedures and imposing comprehensive civil sanctions on wrongdoers. It also creates a statutory cause of action for those who suffer pecuniary loss as a result of market misconduct. This will simplify legal proceedings for those seeking civil redress.

'Market misconduct' means (1) insider dealing, (2) false trading, (3) price rigging, (4) disclosure of information about prohibited transactions, (5) disclosure of false or misleading information inducing transactions, or (6) stock market manipulation. The term includes attempting to engage in—or assisting, counselling, or procuring another person to engage in—any of the above conduct (s245).

Insider Dealing

There is a comprehensive definition of insider dealing in section 270 of the SFO, which is reproduced below:

(1) Insider dealing in relation to a listed corporation takes place-
   (a) when a person connected with the corporation and having information which he knows is relevant information in relation to the corporation-
      (i) deals in the listed securities of the corporation or their derivatives, or in the listed securities of a related corporation of the corporation or their derivatives; or
      (ii) counsels or procures another person to deal in such listed securities or derivatives, knowing or having reasonable cause to believe that the other person will deal in them;
   (b) when a person who is contemplating or has contemplated making, whether with or without another person, a take-over offer for the corporation and who knows that the information that the offer is contemplated or is no longer contemplated is relevant information in relation to the corporation-
      (i) deals in the listed securities of the corporation or their derivatives, or in the listed securities of a related corporation of the corporation or their derivatives, otherwise then for the purpose of the take-over; or
      (ii) counsels or procures another person to deal in such listed securities or derivatives, otherwise than for the purpose of the take-over;
   (c) when a person connected with the corporation and knowing that any information is relevant information in relation to the corporation, discloses the information, directly or indirectly, to another person, knowing or having reasonable cause to believe that the other person will make use of the information for the purpose of dealing, or of counselling or procuring another person to deal, in the listed securities of a related corporation of the corporation or their derivatives;
   (d) When a person who is contemplating or has contemplated making, together with or without another person, a take-over offer for the corporation and who knows that the information that the offer is contemplated or is no longer

contemplated is relevant information in relation to the corporation, discloses the information, directly or indirectly, to another person, knowing or having reasonable cause to believe that the other person will make use of the information for the purpose of dealing, or of counselling or procuring another person to deal, in the listed securities of the corporation or their derivatives, or in the listed securities of a related corporation of the corporation or their derivatives;

(e) when a person who has information which he knows is relevant information in relation to the corporation and which he received, directly or indirectly, from a person whom he knows is connected with the corporation and whom he knows or has reasonable cause to believe held the information as a result of being connected with the corporation-

(i) deals in the listed securities of the corporation or their derivatives, or in the listed securities of a related corporation of the corporation or their derivatives; or

(ii) counsels or procures another person to deal in such listed securities or derivatives; or

(f) when a person having received, directly or indirectly, from a person whom he knows or has reasonable cause to believe is contemplating or is no longer contemplating making a take-over offer for the corporation, information to that effect which he knows is relevant information in relation to the corporation-

(i) deals in the listed securities of the corporation or their derivatives, or in the listed securities of a related corporation of the corporation or their derivatives; or

(ii) counsels or procures another person to deal in such listed securities or derivatives;

(2) Insider dealing in relating to a listed corporation also takes place when a person who knowingly has relevant information in relation to the corporation in any of the circumstances described in subsection (1)-

(a) counsels or procures another person to deal in the listed securities of the corporation or their derivatives, or in the listed securities of a related corporation of the corporation or their derivatives, knowing or having reasonable cause to believe that the other person will deal in such listed securities or derivatives outside Hong Kong on a stock market other than a recognized stock market; or

(b) Discloses the relevant information to another person knowing or having reasonable cause to believe that the other person or some other person will make use of the relevant information for the purpose of dealing, or of counselling or procuring any other person to deal in the listed securities of the corporation or their derivatives, or in the listed securities of a related corporation of the corporation or their derivatives, outside Hong Kong on a stock market other than a recognized stock market.

According to section 247(1), an individual will be regarded as connected with a corporation if:

(a) he is a director or employee of the corporation or a related corporation of the corporation;

(b) he is a substantial shareholder of the corporation or a related corporation of the corporation;[1]

(c) he occupies a position which may reasonably be expected to give him access to relevant information in relation to the corporation by reason of-

    (i) a professional or business relationship existing between

        (A) himself, or his employer, or a corporation of which he is a director, or a firm of which he is a partner; and

        (B) the corporation, a related corporation of the corporation, or an officer or substantial shareholder of either corporation; or

    (ii) his being a director, employee or partner of a substantial shareholder of the corporation or a related corporation of the corporation;

(d) he has access to relevant information in relation to the corporation and-

    (i) he has such access by reason of his being in such a position that he would be regarded as connected with another corporation by virtue of paragraph (a), (b) or (c); and

    (ii) the relevant information relating to a transaction (actual or contemplated) involving both those corporations or involving one of them and the listed securities of the other or their derivatives, or to the fact that the transaction is no longer contemplated; or

(e) he was, at any time within the 6 months preceding any insider dealing in relation to the corporation, a person who would be regarded as connected with the corporation by virtue of paragraph (a), (b), (c) or (d).

A corporation will be regarded as a person connected with another corporation so long as any of its directors or employees is a person who would be regarded as connected with that other corporation by virtue of subsection (1).

According to section 245, 'relevant information', in relation to a corporation, means specific information about: (1) the corporation, (2) a shareholder or officer of the corporation, or (3) the listed securities of the corporation or their derivatives, which is not generally known to the people who are accustomed or would be likely to deal in the listed securities of the corporation but which would, if it were generally known to them, be likely to affect materially the price of the listed securities.

Certain people, such as trustees and personal representatives, underwriters, liquidators, receivers, or trustees in bankruptcy, while performing their duties as such, will not be regarded as having engaged in insider dealing (ss271–273).

False Trading

According to section 274, false trading takes place when, in Hong Kong or elsewhere, a person does anything or causes anything to be done with the intention that, or being reckless as to whether, it has, or is likely to have, the effect of creating a false or misleading appearance: (1) of active trading in securities or futures contracts traded on a relevant recognized market or a relevant overseas market (if it is proved that the conduct would have been unlawful had it been carried out there) or by means of authorized automated trading services, or (2) with respect to the market for, or the price for dealings in, securities or futures contracts traded on a relevant recognized market or a relevant overseas market (if it is proved that the conduct would have been unlawful had it been carried out there) or by means of authorized automated trading services.

Where a person (1) enters into any transaction of sale or purchase of securities that does not involve a change in the beneficial ownership of them, (2) offers to sell securities at a price that is substantially the same as the price at which he has made an offer to purchase the same or substantially the same number of them, or (3) offers to purchase securities at a price that is substantially the same as the price at which he has made an offer to sell the same or substantially the same number of them, unless the transaction in question is an off-market transaction the person will be regarded as doing something or causing something to be done with the intention that, or being reckless as to whether, it has, or is likely to have, the effect of creating a false or misleading appearance

False trading also takes place when, in Hong Kong or elsewhere, a person takes part in, is concerned in, or carries out, directly or indirectly, one or more transactions (whether or not any of them is a dealing in securities or futures contracts), with the intention that, or being reckless as to whether, it or they has or have, or is or are likely to have, the effect of creating an artificial price or maintaining at a level that is artificial (whether or not it was previously artificial) a price, for dealings in securities or futures contracts traded on a relevant recognized market or a relevant overseas market, or by means of authorized automated trading services.

Price Rigging

Pursuant to section s275, price rigging takes place when, in Hong Kong or elsewhere, a person (1) enters into or carries out, directly or indirectly, any transaction of sale or purchase of securities that does not involve a change in the beneficial ownership of those securities, which has the effect of maintaining, increasing, reducing, stabilizing, or causing fluctuations in the price of securities traded on a relevant recognized market or a relevant overseas market (if it is proved that the conduct would have been unlawful had it been carried out there), or by means of authorized automated trading services; or (2) enters into or carries out, directly or indirectly, any fictitious or artificial transaction or device with the intention that, or being reckless as to whether, it has the effect of maintaining, increasing, reducing, stabilizing, or causing fluctuations in the price of securities, or the price for dealings in futures contracts, that are traded on a relevant recognized market or a relevant overseas market (if it is proved that the conduct would have been unlawful had it been carried out there), or by means of authorized automated trading services.

Disclosure of Information about Prohibited Transactions

Disclosure of information about prohibited transactions takes place when a person discloses, circulates, or disseminates—or authorizes or is concerned in the disclosure, circulation, or dissemination of—information to the effect that the price of securities of a corporation, or the price for dealings in futures contracts, that are traded on a relevant recognized market or by means of authorized automated trading services will be maintained, increased, reduced, or stabilized, or is likely to be maintained, increased, reduced, or stabilized, because of a prohibited transaction (which refers mainly to any conduct or transaction which constitutes market misconduct) relating to securities of either the corporation or a related corporation of the corporation or to the futures contracts (as the case may be), if he, or an associate of his, (1) has entered into or carried out, directly or indirectly, the prohibited transaction, or (2) has received, or expects to receive, directly or indirectly, a benefit as a result of the disclosure, circulation, or dissemination of the information (s276).

Disclosure of False or Misleading Information Inducing Transactions

Disclosure of false or misleading information inducing transactions takes place when, in Hong Kong or elsewhere, a person discloses, circulates, or disseminates—or authorizes or is concerned in the disclosure, circulation, or dissemination of—information that is likely (1) to induce another person to subscribe for securities, or deal in futures contracts, in Hong Kong, (2) to induce the sale or purchase in Hong Kong of securities by another person, or (3) to maintain, increase, reduce, or stabilize the price of securities, or the price for dealings in futures contracts, in Hong Kong, if (a) the information is false or misleading as to a material fact, or is false or misleading through the omission of a material fact, and (b) the person knows that, or is reckless or negligent as to whether, the information is false or misleading as to a material fact, or is false or misleading through the omission of a material fact (s277).

Stock Market Manipulation

Stock market manipulation takes place when, in Hong Kong or elsewhere:

(1) a person enters into or carries out, directly or indirectly, two or more transactions in securities of a corporation that by themselves or in conjunction with any other transaction increase, or are likely to increase, the price of any securities traded on a relevant

recognized market or a relevant overseas market, or by means of authorized automated trading services, with the intention of inducing another person to purchase or subscribe for, or to refrain from selling, securities of the corporation or of a related corporation of the corporation;

(2) a person enters into or carries out, directly or indirectly, two or more transactions in securities of a corporation that by themselves or in conjunction with any other transaction reduce, or are likely to reduce, the price of any securities traded on a relevant recognized market, or a relevant overseas market (if it is proved that the conduct would have been unlawful had it been carried out there), or by means of authorized automated trading services, with the intention of inducing another person to sell, or to refrain from purchasing, securities of the corporation or of a related corporation of the corporation; or

(3) a person enters into or carries out, directly or indirectly, two or more transactions in securities of a corporation that by themselves or in conjunction with any other transaction maintain or stabilize, or are likely to maintain or stabilize, the price of any securities traded on a relevant recognized market or a relevant overseas market (if it is proved that the conduct would have been unlawful had it been carried out there), or by means of authorized automated services, with the intention of inducing another person to sell, purchase, or subscribe for, or to refrain from selling, purchasing, or subscribing for, securities of the corporation or of a related corporation of the corporation (s278).

Civil Liability for Market Misconduct

A person who has committed a relevant act in relation to market misconduct will be liable to pay compensation by way of damages to any other person for any pecuniary loss sustained by the other person as a result of the market misconduct, whether or not the loss arises from the other person having entered into a transaction or dealing at a price affected by the market misconduct. However, nobody is liable to pay compensation unless it is fair, just, and reasonable in the circumstances of the case that he should be so liable. He is also liable if a corporation has committed a market misconduct with his consent or connivance as an officer of the corporation, or he assisted or connived with any other person in the perpetration of any market misconduct (s281).

Criminal Liability for Market Misconduct

Until now insider dealing has not been a criminal offence. It was dealt with through civil proceedings before the Insider Dealing Tribunal, which made decisions based on the civil standard of proof. It might impose a number of sanctions on those responsible for insider dealing, including fines of up to three times the profit made or loss avoided.

In the USA, the UK, and Australia insider dealing is a criminal offence. There are convincing reasons as to why it should be made a crime. First, where directors of companies are involved, insider dealing may be seen as a breach of their fiduciary duties as directors. Second, in extreme cases, insider dealing may be seen as a fraud. Third, insider dealing is simply unfair to outsiders, who are denied material information affecting the price of the securities (see Hartmann (2000), p. 70).

Under the new legislation, insider dealing and other forms of market misconduct are crimes as well as civil wrongs (see Part XIV). The criminal route is an alternative in cases where there is sufficient evidence for a criminal prosecution and the Department of Justice considers that prosecution is in the interest of the public. If a decision is made to prosecute for market misconduct instead of following the civil route, the penalties available on conviction will include (1) imprisonment for a period of up to ten years and (2) a fine of up to HK$10 million, as well as the sanctions that my be imposed under the civil regime. But a person will not be tried in both the civil Market Misconduct Tribunal (see below) and the criminal courts for the same misconduct.

Sections 300 to 302 of the SFO also set out other offences—an offence involving fraudulent or deceptive devices, etc., in transactions in securities, futures contracts, or leveraged foreign exchange trading (s300), the offence of disclosure of false or misleading information inducing others to enter into leveraged foreign exchange contracts, and the offence of falsely representing dealings in futures contracts on behalf of others.

Market Misconduct Tribunal (ss252–269)

The SFO creates an alternative civil route to the criminal route for dealing with the various forms of market misconduct. It has been built on the strength of the Insider Dealing Tribunal, which provided a means of dealing with insider dealing, and expanded it into a Market Misconduct Tribunal to handle, in addition to insider dealing, the other types of market misconduct on the civil standard of proof and using civil procedures.

The MMT is chaired by a High Court judge, assisted by two prominent market practitioners with market expertise. The chairman of the MMT is appointed by the Chief Executive upon the recommendation of the Chief Justice.

Market misconduct proceedings are initiated by the Financial Secretary. If it appears to the Financial Secretary that market misconduct has or may have taken place, he may institute proceedings before the Tribunal concerning the matter. The Tribunal then determines (1) whether any market misconduct has taken place, (2) the identity of any person who has engaged in the market misconduct, and (3) the amount of any profit gained or loss avoided as a result of the market misconduct. A Presenting Officer (a legal officer, counsel, or solicitor), appointed by the Secretary for Justice, conducts proceedings before the MMT. He presents the case to the Tribunal and initiates such further inquiries as necessary.

According to section 257, the Tribunal may at the conclusion of any proceedings make one or more of the following orders with respect to a person identified as having engaged in market misconduct:

(a) an order that the person shall not, without the leave of the Court of First Instance, be or continue to be a director, liquidator, or receiver or manager of the property or business, of a listed corporation or any other specified corporation or in any way, whether directly or indirectly, be concerned or take part in the management of a listed corporation or any other specified corporation for the period (not exceeding 5 years) specified in the order;

(b) an order that the person shall not, without the leave of the Court of First Instance, in Hong Kong, directly or indirectly, in any way acquire, dispose of or otherwise deal in any securities, futures contract or leveraged foreign exchange contract, or an interest in any securities, futures contract, leveraged foreign exchange contract or collective investment scheme for the period (not exceeding 5 years) specified in the order;

(c) an order that the person shall not again perpetrate any conduct which constitutes such market misconduct as is specified in the order (whether the same as the market misconduct in question or not);

(d) an order that the person pay to the Government an amount not exceeding the amount of any profit gained or loss avoided by the person as a result of the market misconduct in question;

(e) an order that the person pay to the Government the sum the Tribunal considers appropriate for the costs and expenses reasonably incurred by the Government, whether in relation or incidental to the proceedings or in relation or incidental to any investigation of his conduct or affairs carried out for the purposes of the proceedings;

(f) an order that the person pay to the Commission the sum the Tribunal considers appropriate for the costs and expenses reasonably incurred by the Commission, whether in relation or incidental to any investigation of his conduct or affairs carried out before the matter was referred to the Tribunal by the Financial Secretary or in relation or incidental to the proceedings;

(g) an order that any body which may take disciplinary action against the person as one of its members be recommended to take disciplinary action against him.

Appeal against the Tribunal's decision or determination may be made to the Court of Appeal on a point of law or, with the leave of the Court of Appeal, on a question of fact.

Conclusion

The SFO is one of the three proposals, announced by the government in March 1999, for reforming the securities and futures market in Hong Kong with a view to making Hong Kong a better international financial centre.

It was obvious that many of the concepts and definitions in use in the repealed ordinances were out of date. In particular, the core piece of legislation, the Securities Ordinance, was more than a quarter of a century old. The ordinances were unable to meet both the market and investors' increasing demands brought about by globalization, the use of computers, and new products and services.

The new regime is user-friendly. Among other things, it aims to streamline the regulatory framework for intermediaries and upgrade the quality of intermediary services for the better protection of investors. It reduces market malpractice and financial crimes, and therefore promotes market confidence. It is on a par with international standards and compatible with international practices. It has also taken into account local characteristics and needs. What remains to be done by the relevant authorities is to formulate as quickly as possible clear guidelines for the smooth operation of the provisions in the ordinance and an equally smooth transition from the old to the new regulatory framework.

Discussion Questions

1. Explain the background leading up to the enactment of the Securities and Futures Ordinance.
2. What are the general duties of the Securities and Futures Commission? What are the matters which the Commission has regard to when performing its functions?
3. The Securities and Futures Ordinance has introduced two new concepts—a single license concept and the management responsibility concept. Explain these two concepts.
4. What is the jurisdiction of the Securities and Futures Appeals Tribunal? What may a party do if he or she is dissatisfied with the decision of the Tribunal?
5. What are the changes that have been made to the investor compensation fund by the Securities and Futures Ordinance?
6. Section 107 of the Securities and Futures Ordinance makes it an offence for a person to induce another to invest money. Under what circumstances will (1) the offence be committed and (2) the investor be able to recover compensation for pecuniary loss?
7. What is insider dealing? Why should insider dealing be a crime instead of simply a civil wrong?
8. Under what circumstances will false trading of securities take place and what are the effects of false trading?
9. Critically discuss the provisions in the Securities and Futures Ordinance relating to civil liability as well as criminal liability for market misconduct.
10. Explain the composition and jurisdiction of the Market Misconduct Tribunal. What are the orders that the Tribunal may make?

Keywords

collective investment schemes
false trading
fraudulent misrepresentation
insider dealing
investor compensation company
market misconduct
Market Misconduct Tribunal
negligent misrepresentation
price rigging
reckless misrepresentation
Securities and Futures Appeals Tribunal
stock market manipulation

17. A Quarter of a Century on: A Survey of Hong Kong as an International Financial Centre

GEORGE W. L. HUI

Introduction

The Tomkins Report of the early 1960s (see Jao, 1974) found Hong Kong to be overbanked, and a series of bank runs followed shortly after. In 1965, the Hong Kong government imposed a moratorium on bank licences, and for the next thirteen years no more were granted, either to local or foreign entrants. The sole exception was made in 1972 when Barclays, one of Britain's clearing banks, was admitted. By the late 1970s, however, domestic and foreign pressures had prompted a reconsideration of the policy and the government slowly came to grips with the evolving banking and financial industry. In 1978, the moratorium was lifted (though re-imposed shortly thereafter) to let in forty-one foreign banks. Hong Kong quickly developed into an international financial centre of some repute.

This chapter surveys the developments in the quarter century since 1978. In her recent book, Schenk (2001) advances the thesis that Hong Kong was an international financial centre as early as after the war. That might or might not have been true, but her decision to limit her period of study to 1965 indirectly affirms my view that post-moratorium changes represented novel developments.

This chapter begins with a review of major events, followed by a discussion of developments in the 1980s—when Hong Kong's international banking was oriented towards Japan—and the 1990s, when Hong Kong played a role of some import in equity finance, raising funds for mainland Chinese companies. The global market shares of Hong Kong's various international financial activities are examined, followed by a comparison of Hong Kong and Singapore under similar schemes. Hong Kong's market of Chinese shares is juxtaposed with the Mainland market, and its long-term viability is examined. The conclusion contains some revisionist views of Hong Kong's past successes.

What is not covered is the little-asked but important question of how Hong Kong's status as an international financial centre contributes to its economy. Because of the particular way in which Hong Kong's international financial activities are entangled with its domestic ones, it is necessary to do more than simply calculate the value of a particular sector, and so this topic must be left for another occasion.

To survey actual economic activities, one almost always starts from the relevant academic literature. Though a collection such as Roberts (1994) contains upwards of seventy articles on international financial centres, there is a dearth of theory and models. A possible reason may be that there were few such financial centres historically, the extensive discussion of typology in Roberts and elsewhere notwithstanding, and their formation was at least partly influenced by chance elements and events. Charles Kindleberger, the economic historian, once bemoaned (1974) that the formation of financial centres was no longer studied in economics. He attributed this indifference to the subject's falling between urban and regional economics, which does not deal with finance, and financial and banking economics, which does not deal with geography. With the re-emergence of economic geography, we may be more hopeful, and it's possible that network economics (Shy 2001) will provide useful tools as well.

Major Events

The moratorium of 1965 denied entry to banks but not quasi-banks. Finance companies proliferated. These were not restricted by bank cartel arrangements and were able to offer higher deposit rates, and incumbent banks also established deposit-taking subsidiaries to protect their market shares. When the Deposit Taking Companies Ordinance was enacted in 1976, close to 200 entities registered, more than twice the number of extant banks. On the external front, over 100 foreign banks had set up representative offices in the territory; some had also set up deposit-taking companies. The government wrestled with these market developments well into the 1980s; it was only towards the end of the decade that the regulation and supervision framework took hold. The supervision of banks and near banks was combined under the Office of the Commissioner of Banking. Later in 1993, the Hong Kong Monetary Authority was established by merging this Office and the Office of the Exchange Fund by taking over the functions of the Monetary Affairs Branch of the government. In line with British practice, the separation of banks into commercial and investment varieties was due to custom and specialization rather than legislation.

The Hong Kong economy has gone through many speculative episodes. Former banking commissioner and stock exchange executive Robert Fell was impressed enough to remark in his memoirs (1992): 'The speculative element was everything.' For a long time, vulnerabilities caused by excesses have occurred in the banking system. As the banking system has gradually been put on a secure basis, vulnerabilities have been found in the stock and futures markets. In reaction, the government has been playing an increasingly active role in governing and managing these markets. The instinct that prompted the banking moratorium was probably the same as the one that halted the establishment of further stock exchanges in the early 1970s. The offsetting impulse that lifted the moratorium was apparently the one that pushed for the entry of foreign brokers and unification of the four stock exchanges in the 1980s. When the bull market of 1987 ended with the worldwide crash in October, the merged Stock Exchange of Hong Kong (SEHK) earned disrepute for its four-day closure. The government stepped in and assembled a financial package to bail out the futures exchange. It also undertook a review of the securities industry. Following through the recommendations of the Davison Report (Securities Review Committee 1988), the government established the statutory Securities and Futures Commission (SFC) and reorganized the exchanges and clearing houses.[1]

Even so, problems resurfaced and more reforms were undertaken in the aftermath of yet another speculative episode. Both the stock and property markets reached new highs around the changeover of sovereignty in 1997. The onset of the Asian financial crisis quickly put these markets as well as the Hong Kong dollar under pressure; for a few hours in October 1997, local interest rates went as high as 300 per cent. The markets came under selling pressure again in August 1998. The government alleged that market manipulators were at work: their 'double play' involved raising Hong Kong interest rates and benefiting from short positions in the stock and futures markets. Eventually, the government entered the stock market to set a floor to equity prices; they bought up to six per cent of the market, concentrating on several of the blue chips.

The intervention proved to be the straw that broke the camel's back, and the pendulum swung further towards regulation and order. In March 1999, the Financial Secretary announced reforms of the securities and futures markets 'to tighten up market discipline'. The SEHK and Futures Exchange would be demutualized so that ownership and trading rights would henceforth be separated. The two exchanges and the three clearing houses would be merged into the new Hong Kong Exchanges and Clearing Limited. These changes were completed in 2001. The new entity has been listed and its governing body has taken on more government-related personnel. It was the second time in two decades that a former government official was appointed to head the Exchange.[2]

In 1993, the SEHK and the SFC signed a Memorandum of Regulatory Cooperation with China's Securities Regulatory Commission and two Mainland exchanges to allow companies incorporated in the Mainland to obtain primary listing in Hong Kong's Exchange. This opened the door for Hong Kong to be a market for Mainland equities. But the back door had been ajar even before that.

International Financial Activities

The framework of a financial system provides a start for the study of international financial centres. On the right hand side of Figure 17.1a, we have ultimate lenders or suppliers of loanable funds, and on the left the ultimate borrowers or demanders of loanable funds. Through the financial system, loanable funds are transferred from the former to the latter and financial claims from the latter to the former. When the transfer is effected through financial markets, we have direct finance; when the transfer is effected through financial intermediaries, we have indirect or intermediation finance. Allen and Gale (2000) is the latest study to examine why some transfer is effected through one and not the other for an economy.

Figure 17.1a   The Framework of a Financial System

In the case of international finance, at least one of the parties involved should be non-resident (although see complications, below). In Figure 17.1b, loanable funds are transferred from ultimate lenders at home to ultimate borrowers abroad. This transfer may be effected through a domestic financial centre, a foreign financial centre, or both, as the different lines indicate. If the transaction between the ultimate lender and the domestic financial centre is denominated in a foreign currency, this is often considered an international financial transaction as well.

Figure 17.1b   The International Finance Model

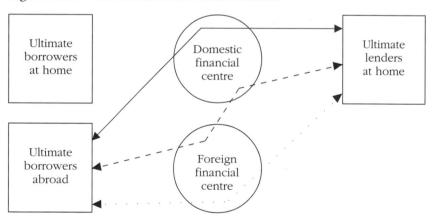

More could be learned from the figure. Why do domestic lenders lend to foreign borrowers instead of domestic ones, especially if transaction costs may possibly be like transport costs: increasing with distance? Analogously, why do firms borrow from abroad rather than at home? We may also turn our attention from the ultimate players to the intermediaries in between. Visualize more lines passing through the foreign financial centre from more groups of ultimate players. The players constitute the hinterland of the financial centre in question or, in the terminology of economic geography, the market potential region. Why do the lines pass through this particular centre and not others? That would be an issue of centre rivalry.

One can also see the difference between two types of international financial centre in the figure. The domestic financial centre may become an international financial centre by engaging in many international financial transactions. Generally, this involves transferring domestic financial resources to external borrowers. If so, the financial centre is (sited in) an exporter of domestic capital. Alternatively, the foreign financial centre may take financial resources from lenders of other countries and transfer to borrowers of other countries. In that instance, the centre is a financial entrepôt. Rarely are international financial centres importers of foreign capital.

The graphics aside, an international financial centre has a concentration of international financial transactions. Rose (1994(b), p.1), with London as the prototype, says:

> An international financial centre has at least two characteristics: a relatively high level of cross-border transactions of different kinds and a concentration of offices of foreign financial institutions (which until the late nineteenth century would have been predominantly merchanting firms). Today a fully-fledged centre will be several things: an international banking centre; a market for foreign issues; a secondary market in foreign securities, including derivatives; and an international market in other financial services, notably insurance and commodity transactions.

Correspondingly, with regard to Hong Kong and later Singapore, we will look at (1) international banking, (2) foreign equities, and (3) international bonds. Though Rose emphasizes the importance of foreign financial institutions, their presence serves as a precondition in this day and age and is not a sufficient condition in itself. There has been some past discussion on Hong Kong (Jao (1988) and Hui (1992)) devoted to this topic, and it does not have to be repeated here.

International Banking

International banking consists of 'cross-border' and 'eurocurrency' transactions. Banks located in one jurisdiction may transact with banks and non-banks in another jurisdiction. These are 'cross-border' or 'external' transactions. Alternatively, banks and counterparties may transact in a currency that is not the currency of the jurisdiction where they are located. These are 'eurocurrency', 'offshore currency', or simply 'offshore' transactions. So, for example, a bank in Hong Kong may lend US dollars to a party in Hong Kong. This is a eurocurrency transaction, but not a cross-border one. On the other hand, if a bank in Hong Kong lends US dollars to a party located in Indonesia, this is both a eurocurrency and a cross-border transaction. Landell-Mills (1986) provides details on these issues as well as on data sources.

According to Rose (1994(a)), there have been three phases of international banking in the post-war period. The first phase (1958–74) can be viewed as a catching-up process after the Great Depression and the war. Growth was sparked off by the relaxation of exchange controls in Western Europe, whereas restrictions and regulations in the UK and US domestic markets helped to determine the form of international banking by giving rise to eurocurrency markets. The second phase (1974–82) started after the first increase of oil prices in 1973. OPEC countries invested their surpluses in liquid assets, and banks acted as intermediaries in the balance of payments financing process. Bank lending to the less-developed countries dominated and syndicated lending grew strongly. The ratio of bank cross-border claims to world trade (proxied by imports), which had risen by about one-half between 1963 and 1973–4, more than doubled in the period to 1982. This phase came to an end with the moratorium on Mexican debt. In the third phase (since 1982), the ratio of bank cross-border lending to world trade continued to rise, but more slowly, and has been on something of a plateau since 1987. The share of syndicated lending in international financing also fell. A growing share of financing has been taken by the issue of international bonds. Over-the-counter currency and interest rate swaps have grown rapidly in response to the volatility of exchange rates and interest rates. The advance of information technology has greatly assisted the growth of all international transactions. The Asian financial crisis of 1997–8 has disrupted if not halted some of these patterns. Though it may be too early to tell, my judgement is that the third phase has come to an end.

Table 17.1a Hong Kong Banks' Cross-Border Transactions

	Claims on External Banks	Claims on External Non-Banks	Total External Claims	Liab. to External Banks	Liab. to External Non-Banks	Total External Liabilities	Net External Claims
Average Growth Rate							
1981–2000	16.3%	15.4%	15.4%	12.9%	n.a.	n.a.	n.a.
1981–1990	31.5%	31.6%	30.7%	30.1%	n.a.	n.a.	n.a.
1991–2000	1.1%	−0.7%	0.1%	−4.3%	13.2%#	−3.1%#	168.9%#
Proportion of Total External Claims							
1980	67.5%	32.5%	100.0%	94.4%	N/A	N/A	N/A
1985	80.6%	19.4%	100.0%	82.4%	N/A	N/A	N/A
1990	70.6%	29.4%	100.0%	86.8%	6.0%*	91.8%*	8.2%*
1995	53.7%	46.3%	100.0%	84.7%	9.9%	94.6%	5.4%
2000	77.9%	22.1%	100.0%	51.0%	19.9%	70.8%	29.2%

Note: n.a.: not available.
    # 1992–2000.
    * 1991 data.
Source of data: Hong Kong Monetary Authority, *Monthly Statistical Bulletin*; see Appendix
    17.1 for details.

Detailed data on Hong Kong's international banking transactions began to be collected towards the late 1970s and under the cross-border convention. Table 17.1a indicates that the growth rates in the 1980s were high (30.7 per cent in the case of total external claims) and those in the 1990s were low (0.1 per cent). Since 1996, growth has in fact been negative. The major partners of Hong Kong-based banks have been Japan, the UK, the US, China, and Singapore, displacing Korea and the Philippines, which were important in the early years. Since 1985 the 'big five' have accounted for 50 to 80 per cent of Hong Kong banks' total external assets (see Table 17.1b). Among these, Japan has been the most important, but its market share has been in decline since 1996.

Rose's global distinction between Phase 1 and Phase 2 does not apply as sharply in Hong Kong's case because of the moratorium. The growth in the early 1980s can be viewed as part of the catching-up with the level of international financial activities in the world and in Asia, and that level of international financial activities being commensurate with the level of international trade in Asia. Against this background, there was a big push in the mid-1980s, strictly due to transactions with Japan. Growth rates of over 200 per cent in 1986–7 pushed the decade average to a hefty 80.3 per cent (see Table 17. 1b). At its peak, Japan's share in the Hong Kong banks' total external assets was 66.7 per cent (in 1990), but it had declined to 29.5 per cent by 2000. Detailed time series provided in Table A17.1 (see Appendix 17.1) show certain characteristics. These are:

1. Hong Kong's banks have been a net creditor system to Japan. This is not surprising: Japan's banking system has been a net debtor

Table 17.1b Hong Kong Banks' Claims on Major Partners

	Claims on Banks and Non-Banks in Japan	Claims on Banks and Non-Banks in China	Claims on Banks and Non-Banks in UK	Claims on Banks and Non-Banks in US	Claims on Banks and Non-Banks in Singapore	Total External Claims
Average Growth Rates						
1981–2000	36.8%	20.7%	16.7%	15.1%	16.0%.	15.4%
1981–1990	80.3%	33.5%	20.9%	22.5%	25.5%	30.7%
1991–2000	–6.8%	7.9%	12.5%	7.8%	6.5%	0.1%
Proportions						
1980	5.7%	4.3%	9.7%	5.9%	10.2%	100.0%
1985	13.2%	3.9%	14.2%	6.6%	14.3%	100.0%
1990	66.7%	3.3%	4.2%	3.1%	6.1%	100.0%
1995	62.3%	5.7%	3.9%	3.4%	5.4%	100.0%
2000	29.5%	6.3%	13.3%	6.1%	10.5%	100.0%

Source of data: Hong Kong Monetary Authority, *Monthly Statistical Bulletin*; see Appendix 17.1 for details.

system to the rest of the world in spite of Japan's strong balance of payments position.

2. Transactions had been dominated by interbank borrowing and lending until 1987, when Hong Kong's banks started to lend to Japan's non-banks on a massive scale. These lending banks, generally Hong Kong branches of Japanese-owned banks, apparently obtained some (but not all) of their financing from their headquarters in Japan. So the Japanese-owned segment of Hong Kong's banking system became a conduit for Japan's banks to lend to Japan's non-banks.

3. The year 1996 was a turning point, when important variables started to decline unambiguously.

I remain ignorant of the exact details of the regulatory and exchange rate origins that prompted the above phenomena. Some features might not have been peculiar to Hong Kong, though. Japanese-owned banks in London also borrowed in the interbank market and lent to their head offices in Japan in the 1980s (Lamb, 1986). In a study of Japanese banking activity in the American commercial real estate market, Peek and Rosengren (2000) identified aggressive penetration in the mid-1980s and a steady decline from late 1991. The expansion of Japanese banking into these different areas might have reflected the same impulse initiated by the Plaza Accord of 1985, but they differed in the timing of the reverse. Peek and Rosengren attributed the reverse in the American market to the desire of the Japanese banks to replenish their capital requirements after the home equity market collapse. Beckerling (2000(a); 2000(b)) provided some possible reasons in the case of Hong Kong but did not cite capital requirements.

Mainland China has been the other banking partner of note. Again, there was strong growth in lending in the 1980s followed by reduced and even negative growth in recent years (see Table 17.1b again). Interbank lending and borrowing were close in volume, so that they more or less cancelled each other out. There was increased lending to China's non-banks from the mid-1980s on and this reached a peak in 1996–7 (see Appendix 17.1, Table A17.2). Many of these were enterprises and investment trusts owned by provincial and city governments—for example, Guangdong Enterprises Holdings and the 'Itics'. Japanese banks played a not insignificant part in this lending (Chan and Lai, 1998). As the borrowers eventually fell into financial distress due to austerity measures on the Mainland, the refusal of the central government to bail out these enterprises contributed to the general downturn (Beckerling, 2000(c)).

Finally, we should mention that Hong Kong's banks have been a net creditor system to the rest of the world—partly because local residents hold significant amounts of deposits in offshore currencies.

Foreign Equities

Historically, there have been overseas companies listed on Hong Kong's stock exchanges. Malaysian rubber growers dated back to at least as early as the 1950s, and some Japanese companies obtained secondary listing status in the 1970s. The trading of such stocks was nonetheless low, and no primary issues may ever have been launched. Overseas institutional investors have been significant players here from the 1980s and probably earlier, but it was only in the 1990s that Hong Kong began to become an important market for foreign issues, specifically Mainland-related equities. These have taken two forms.

In the first instance, Mainland interests acquire control of a listed company and reorganize the listed company to include Mainland businesses and assets. The resultant firms are referred to as red chip companies. More precisely, HSI Services Ltd, on their website, defines them as 'companies registered in Hong Kong with 35% or above of their shareholding directly and indirectly under the control of Mainland entities'. They must also 'derive at least 50% of their sales revenue from mainland China'. The red chip is an innovation of the Hong Kong market; Francis Leung Pak-to of the liquidated organization Peregrine has been the name associated with it. Given the restrictive nature of ownership in the Mainland in the 1990s, whereby sizeable firms were still under the control of the State, red chips provided opportunities for investing in the Mainland. In the days of the red chip boom (1995–7), the claim of *guanxi* (connections), which would presumably enable red chip companies to acquire undervalued assets on the Mainland, added to their allure and supposedly accounted for the hefty premium of their stock price over net asset value. Most red chip companies were formed in the early 1990s. The regulatory authorities of both the Mainland and Hong Kong have subsequently discouraged such back-door listings.

Second, Mainland companies may have their H-shares listed here and have another class of equities listed elsewhere; the latter are likely to be A-shares at the Shanghai or Shenzhen exchanges. (Typically, an A-share company chooses among (1) a B-share listing in an offshore currency market, either the US dollar in Shanghai or the Hong Kong dollar in Shenzhen, (2) an H-share listing in Hong Kong, or (3) an N-share listing in New York.)

Red chip companies are registered in Hong Kong and H-share companies are registered on the Mainland, so they are mutually exclusive categories. Collectively, they number about 110 and have become increasingly important in the Hong Kong market. Table 17.2 shows that they account for about a quarter of total market capitalization and over a quarter of the turnover.[3] Initial public offering (IPO) funds have also increasingly accrued to these companies, as these took up more than half of the funds in 2000 and 2001. Between them, red chip companies have a larger market capitalization.

Table 17.2   Hong Kong's Equity Market: Capitalization, Turnover, and
IPO Funds

	H-shares	Red Chips	Others
Share of Market Capitalization			
1992	0.0%	2.9%	97.1%
1993	0.6%	4.2%	95.2%
1994	1.0%	4.0%	95.0%
1995	0.7%	4.7%	94.6%
1996	0.9%	7.6%	91.5%
1997	1.5%	14.8%	83.7%
1998	1.3%	12.6%	86.1%
1999	0.9%	20.2%	78.9%
2000	1.8%	25.1%	73.1%
2001	2.6%	23.4%	74.0%
Proportion of Average Daily Market Turnover			
1992	0.0%	3.5%	96.5%
1993	5.3%	7.2%	87.5%
1994	3.0%	5.1%	91.9%
1995	2.1%	5.6%	92.3%
1996	1.8%	9.6%	88.6%
1997	7.9%	27.5%	64.6%
1998	4.3%	21.7%	74.0%
1999	5.4%	18.5%	76.1%
2000	5.4%	22.1%	72.5%
2001	12.6%	25.5%	61.9%
Proportion of Total Funds Raised Through IPOs			
1992	0.0%	14.9%	85.1%
1993	27.9%	3.3%	68.8%
1994	56.9%	8.9%	34.2%
1995	24.8%	19.4%	55.8%
1996	21.9%	11.0%	67.1%
1997	39.2%	48.2%	12.5%
1998	34.8%	2.4%	62.8%
1999	27.4%	12.8%	59.8%
2000	44.1%	37.6%	18.3%
2001	25.0%	56.4%	18.5%

Sources of data: Primarily Hong Kong Securities and Futures Commission, *Quarterly Bulletin,*
but see Appendix 17.1 for details.

Two other developments should be mentioned. First, a second board
of the Stock Exchange of Hong Kong, the Growth Enterprise Market (GEM),
was established in November 1999. This caters to start-ups and
technologically oriented companies and is also open to Mainland applicants.
But its size is minuscule when compared to the Main Board. Its own
mismanagement and the bursting of the Internet bubble have compounded
its difficulties. Second, since May 2000, the Exchange has enlisted a small
number of NASDAQ stocks to be traded locally. As could have been
predicted, the trading is low.

Hong Kong's futures exchange has experimented with many products: sugar, soya beans, and gold futures in the 1970s and 1980s, and interest rate and Sub-Index futures more recently. But the Hang Seng Index futures contract launched in 1986 has remained the single most important product. Some foreign products, such as forex and regional equity index (e.g., the Taiwan Index), have also been tried and have failed. Others, such as Dow Jones Index products, are planned, but there is no indication that they will be more successful. So, to the extent that Hang Seng Index futures are a domestic product, the futures market is a local one.

International Bonds

International bonds are classified into foreign and euro bonds. Foreign bonds are issued by foreign companies and denominated in the currency of the country where they are distributed. Eurobonds are distributed in several markets at the same time and are often denominated in currencies other than those of these markets. Data on the amount of foreign bonds denominated in Hong Kong dollars are collected by the Organisation for Economic Cooperation and Development (OECD) (although the sources of the data are not clear). There has been no drastic development, and the funds raised per year have rarely been more than US$1 billion (see Appendix 17.1, Table A17.3). The number of bonds listed at the stock exchange took a big jump in the early 1990s, increasing from the teens to over 200. The majority are eurobonds. However, most of the bonds are rarely traded at the exchange and the turnover amounts to less than one per cent of that of equities.

Hong Kong's bond market has not been a fully developed one. The local government has generally had budget surpluses and has not had to borrow. Government debt in the form of Exchange Fund bills and notes has been issued to serve as an instrument of monetary management, as well as to develop a benchmark yield curve for Hong Kong dollar bonds. Even so, Hong Kong dollar bonds, whether issued by domestic or foreign entities, have been few and far between. Emery (1997) suggests that high listing fees, stringent listing requirements, and tax on interest income are the major reasons; in my view, however, the predominant reason is the negative real interest rate. Until the bursting of the asset bubble in the aftermath of the Asian financial crisis, Hong Kong had had high inflation for two decades. Yet because of capital mobility and the quasi-currency board system, domestic interest rates had followed those of the US. In this environment, domestic investors simply would not hold Hong Kong dollar bonds; the cause of underdevelopment was first of all macroeconomic. On the other hand, there has been significant demand for eurobonds. Issues of dragon bonds distributed in the 'small dragon' countries (also called the 'tiger economies') have generally been successful. It is an irony that most of these have been issued by overseas corporations from the OECD and not Asian borrowers.

Global Position

To see Hong Kong's global position, we will now look at its market share under each of the activities covered in the previous section. International derivatives are left out, as Hong Kong does not have much of a market, but foreign exchange turnover is included: internationally comparable data is readily available under the auspices of the Bank for International Settlements (BIS). Table 17.3 presents the various time series.

Table 17.3   Hong Kong's Global Market Shares

	Ratio of (a) Hong Kong bank external claims plus liab. to (b) bank external claims and liab. of leading international banking countries*	Ratio of (a) Hong Kong bank external claims to (b) bank external claims of leading international banking countries*	Ratio of Hong Kong's foreign equities value to London's foreign equities value	Ratio of Hong Kong's foreign equities daily turnover to London's foreign equities turnover	Ratio of HK$ bonds to total international bonds	Ratio of Hong Kong's forex turnover to global forex turnover
1980	1.7%#	3.3%			0.0%	
1981	1.9%#	3.5%			0.4%	
1982	2.1%#	3.4%			0.3%	
1983	2.3%#	3.5%			0.2%	
1984	2.5%#	4.0%			0.3%	
1985	2.7%#	3.5%			0.5%	
1986	3.2%#	3.5%			0.6%	
1987	4.2%#	5.9%			0.4%	
1988	4.4%#	7.0%			0.2%	
1989	4.5%#	8.9%			0.2%	6.8%
1990	5.1%#	12.1%	0.0%	0.0%	0.3%	
1991	10.4%	15.6%	0.1%	0.2%	0.3%	
1992	10.6%	16.2%	0.2%	0.5%	0.1%	5.6%
1993	10.4%	16.2%	0.6%	2.3%	0.2%	
1994	11.2%	16.9%	0.4%	1.1%	0.4%	
1995	10.6%	16.2%	0.4%	0.7%	0.2%	5.7%
1996	9.7%	14.3%	1.0%	1.3%	0.2%	
1997	n.a.	n.a.	1.7%	7.6%	0.1%	
1998	n.a.	n.a.	1.0%	1.6%		4.0%
1999	n.a.	n.a.	2.2%	1.5%		
2000	n.a.	n.a.	3.1%	2.1%		
2001	n.a.	n.a.	3.5%	1.9%		4.1%

Notes: * Leading international banking countries include England, USA, Japan, France, Germany, Switzerland, Hong Kong, and Singapore.
  # Figures for Hong Kong banks' liabilities to external non-banks in the period 1980 to 1990 are not available and are not included.
  n.a.: not available
Sources of data: See Appendix 17.1

Under international banking, we examine two variables: (1) the ratio of Hong Kong banks' external claims plus liabilities to bank external claims plus liabilities of leading international banking countries, and (2) the ratio of Hong Kong banks' claims on external non-banks to bank claims of leading international banking countries on external non-banks. The countries are the UK, the US, Japan, France, Germany, Switzerland, Hong Kong, and Singapore. The pattern for both variables is an increase in market share in the mid-1980s and a decline in market share from the mid-1990s. As mentioned in the previous section, this rise and decline was due to the transactions with Japan.

Foreign equities in Hong Kong's context are Mainland-related stocks. There is some ambiguity with red chips, although these are included as well. Global data on domestic equities is presented in the *Emerging Stock Markets Factbook*, but there are no systematic data on foreign equities. Sporadic efforts of comparison—for example, Worthington (1991)—have established that London, New York, NASDAQ, Tokyo, and Paris are the bigger and more active markets. It is generally accepted that London's market is the largest; its market value of foreign equities and daily turnover is believed to be at least half of the entire global market of foreign equities. In the early 1990s, they might even have accounted for as much as two-thirds of trading reported (Neuberger, 1992). Since London's data is readily available, we will compare Hong Kong's value and turnover to London's variables. In terms of market value, Hong Kong made steady progress in the latter part of the 1990s. Turnover was more volatile; in 1997, the proportion reached a peak of over seven per cent.

Gross issues of Hong Kong dollar bonds have remained insignificant, although the SAR may be an active centre in the placement of eurobonds. The foreign exchange turnover figures do not include derivatives trading, although the general pattern is no different. There has been a decrease in Hong Kong's share from 6.8 per cent to 4.1 per cent. This has been due to reduced trading caused by the Asian financial crisis and the relocation of bank treasury departments to other Asian cities. London maintains a share of over 30 per cent and is significantly ahead of the US (15.7 per cent) and Japan (9.1 per cent).

Presumed Rivalry

Singapore has been viewed as Hong Kong's rival (Ho (1991) and Jao (1997)), probably because they operate in the same market segment, being geographically close to each other and belonging to the same time zone. They are similar in many ways. Both are of British imperial parentage, so they share the same quasi-global customs and institutions in language, law, banking, and so on. Both are small economies without large domestic markets. It would make less sense to compare them either with Tokyo or Zurich. The next section reviews the international financial activities of

Singapore, looks at the similarities and differences of the presumed rivals, and discusses some of their common difficulties.

Singapore

If Schenk's thesis that Hong Kong was an international financial centre as early as just after the war is valid, then Singapore was a laggard—but its entry into the business has been more deliberate, and in many ways more nimble. In 1968, there was a relaxation of exchange controls similar to those in western Europe. The government would henceforth allow the free movement of funds into the offshore market through the creation of Asian Currency Units (ACUs). It abolished withholding tax for ACU deposits and granted a concessionary tax rate of ten per cent instead of forty per cent to income derived from offshore loans. Conditions for the entry of foreign banks were established in the early 1970s. In the same period, the government also allowed for the launching of the first Asian dollar bond.

It was a vacuum that Singapore moved into. Prime Minister Lee Kwan-yew remarked in his memoirs (2000): 'In the early years from 1968 to 1985, we had the field all to ourselves in the region.' International banking statistics show that the eurocurrency transactions of ACUs grew at a high rate until 1982–83 when there was a lull, the moratorium on Mexican debt apparently having an impact. Strong growth resumed shortly thereafter, and continued throughout the 1980s. The growth rates in the 1990s were distinctly lower and have been negative since 1998. Less is known about Singapore's banking partners than Hong Kong's as the Monetary Authority of Singapore (MAS) has released such information only in aggregated form and only for recent years. China, Hong Kong, Japan, South Korea, Taiwan, and ASEAN (besides Singapore) are not separately identified but presented collectively as 'East Asia'. Claims on external non-banks grew strongly in 1987–90, but it is not obvious whether this had to do with reflexive flows concerning Japan or constituted loans to neighbouring corporations and governments, Indonesia in particular. On the whole, ACUs have borrowed from banks in Asia and Europe to lend to non-banks in Asia.[4]

Singapore's stock market started out as a unified one for Singapore and Malaysia. Some other foreign stocks were also listed. But cross-listing of Malaysian stocks on the over-the-counter CLOBOTL market was halted in 1998, weakening the broad characteristic of the market. Presently, some of the largest listings, such as the Jardines group and Shangri-la, are foreign companies and are traded in foreign currencies. This miscellaneous collection of companies, however, has not constituted a well-defined market segment. Singapore's domestic bond market is not well developed, though for reasons different from Hong Kong's: forced saving through the Central Provident Fund and low domestic (nominal) interest rates might be important reasons. Until recently, MAS has discouraged foreign borrowing in the domestic currency. Singapore's Asian bond market seems just as large as Hong Kong's. Even in recent years, when Hong Kong has begun to promote its own bond market, the nominal value of bonds listed at the Singapore exchange has been about twice that of bonds listed at the Hong Kong exchange. Singapore's futures exchange, the Singapore International Monetary Exchange (SIMEX), was established in 1984 on the basis of the then Gold Exchange. The first of its kind in Asia, it trades financial futures, such as Eurodollar interest rates and the Nikkei 225 stock index. Presumably, over eighty per cent of the trades originate from overseas, although a geographic breakdown is once again not available. The Straits Times Index future was only launched as in 2000—so the futures market has always targeted international investors rather than domestic ones.

In spite of a smaller economy and smaller domestic financial markets, Singapore has global market shares (presented in Appendix 17.1, Table A17.4) close to those of Hong Kong. In the early 1990s, the market value of its listed foreign equities was even higher than that of Hong Kong's. It has managed to hold on to its six per cent of foreign exchange turnover as a beneficiary of bank treasury relocations.

International banking seems most developed for both centres. Each serves as a node connecting its own and neighbouring economies to the global financial system. Less is known about Singapore's geographic partners than Hong Kong's, but there is reason to believe that Singapore's ACUs deal with ASEAN businesses and individuals. In that sense, neither Hong Kong nor Singapore has encroached on the other's hinterland. The complementarity of the two centres is most obvious in the case of dragon bonds. They co-operate to export Asian savings to OECD countries.

On the whole, while following a similar agenda, Singapore has implemented many changes in the financial sector earlier than Hong Kong. Its monetary authority was established in 1971; Hong Kong's in 1993. Abolition of the interest rate cartel among banks was completed in 1975 in Singapore, and only recently in Hong Kong. Singapore's second board, SESDAQ, was established in 1987, more than a decade ahead of Hong Kong's GEM. MAS launched the revamped government securities market in 1987 as one of the measures to develop a domestic bond market; Hong Kong started its Exchange Fund bills programme in 1990. The Stock Exchange of Singapore (SES) and the Singapore International Monetary Exchange (SIMEX) were demutualized and merged (together with clearing entities) in December 1999 to become the Singapore Exchange (SGX), a year ahead of similar developments in Hong Kong. Hong Kong's exchange may be switching to longer trading hours and lower brokerage fees, but Singapore implemented these long ago.[5] Even their propaganda emphasizes the same things: time zone advantage, excellent infrastructure, political stability, a strong and stable currency, and so on.

Ambitions and Limitations

When discussing Figure 17.1b, a distinction has already been made between exporters of capital and financial entrepôts. We now return to this distinction, choosing bank external assets as the basis of comparison. (In the case of Singapore, bank external assets are eurocurrency assets of ACUs.) This variable contains a large interbank element and may not have a simple relationship to bank claims on external non-banks, but it is subject to less fluctuation than the latter. Its ratio to exports of goods and services is calculated, as well as its ratio to GDP.

The results of the calculations are shown in Table 17.4. (Readers should be reminded that banking data apply to entire countries in the case of the UK, Japan, and the US, and not just their pre-eminent international financial centres of London, Tokyo, and New York.) The international lending of Hong Kong, Singapore, and London is out of proportion to their exports and hence to the international financial position of their domestic economies. The international lending of Tokyo and New York, on the other hand, is more modest when measured against exports. Among the places under comparison, the US has the lowest ratios. A strong financial system may well be the prerequisite for the development of an international financial centre, but a large and thriving domestic system probably induces too much inwardness for international finance to take centre stage. International finance will remain a sideshow. New York will be too self-absorbed to pose a direct threat to London as the world's foremost international financial centre.

Both Hong Kong and Singapore are also trade entrepôts and their exports contain a large re-export element. Some of the ratios in Table 17.4 have

Table 17.4   Two Types of International Financial Centre

	Financial Entrepôts			Exporters of Domestic Capital	
	Hong Kong	Singapore	United Kingdom (London)	Japan (Tokyo)	United States (New York)
Ratio of Bank External Assets to Exports					
1990	463%	574%	408%	211%	22%
	(1,603%)	(1,083%)			
2000	185%	294%	557%	154%	34%
	(1,940%)	(619%)			
Ratio of Bank External Assets to GDP					
1990	621%	1022%	98%	22%	2%
2000	278%	529%	152%	17%	4%

Notes: Exports include exports of goods and services.
      Percentages in parentheses are the ratios of bank external assets to domestic (merchandise) exports.
Sources of data: International Financial Statistics and others; see Appendix 17.1 for details.

therefore been recalculated using domestic (merchandise) exports, with more magnified numbers found.

Once we accept that both Hong Kong and Singapore are financial entrepôts, it follows logically that comparison is best made between them and London, not between them and centres such as Tokyo and New York. Though the activities of the latter are no longer directly based on the saving position of Japan and the US and are hence not literally exporters of domestic capital, the size and importance of their resident economies are not matched by those of the entrepôts, London's included. Rather, it is often observed that the fortune of the City of London is not dependent on the British economy. The pertinence of this remark is best seen in equity finance, where the differences between the pre-eminent financial entrepôt and the two Asian upstarts can be more easily highlighted.

London's market in foreign equities is an institutional one. The average value per trade is above £0.2 million. Important stocks from all over the world are traded, at times in volumes rivalling those in the home market. Trading is generally not denominated in sterling, yet this poses no difficulty to institutional investors. Some of the market infrastructure, such as settlement, has evolved naturally—that is, in accordance with market development. In part because of its institutional nature and in part because of the constitutional orientation of Britain itself, regulation has been easy and the 'benign neglect' of regulators is welcome.

Hong Kong's market of foreign equities, on the other hand, has three groups of investors: Hong Kong residents; Mainland money, part of which comes in through illicit channels (Kynge (2000(a)) and (2000(b)); O'Neill (2002)); and institutional investors. While careful analysis of the proportions and characteristics of the three groups is still lacking and investor behaviour concerning foreign equities remains a puzzle (Lewis, 1995; 1999), we can safely say that the market would not have flourished without the participation of the first two. Herein lies a major dilemma in Hong Kong's development. Without the retail element, the market would not have enough turnover and liquidity. Yet to accommodate the retail element, regulations, the trading currency, and other arrangements often have to cater to it primarily. There are other limitations. Hong Kong's range of equities is limited: foreign equities are exclusively Mainland stocks, and domestic equities are neither sizeable nor diverse. The entrepôt nature of the market turns out to be a disadvantage in some circumstances. Stocks may have no 'loyalty', as the entrepôt market is not its natural home market. When corporate insiders misbehave, regulators have no jurisdiction over them—as the cases of the China Logistics Group and Akai (Moir (2002) and Ogden (2002)) illustrate.[6]

Singapore's policymakers and regulators have apparently recognized some of these trade-offs and limitations, although they have not necessarily come up with better solutions. In some instances, they have tried to maintain barriers between the domestic sector and the external sector. ACUs are set up as accounting entities separate from domestic operations. Foreign borrowing of Singapore dollars has been restricted until recently.

Only where there is no obvious risk to its financial system would the Singapore government allow domestic financial resources to be used to promote Singapore. Domestic savings, for instance, are used to attract asset management firms to set up operations (Tan, 2000).

One Country, Two Markets

Since the five-party memorandum formally opened the door for Mainland listings, the dominant theme of Hong Kong's international financial activities has been China. Hong Kong's exchanges and regulatory authorities have repeatedly emphasized their role to be that of developing Hong Kong into the major fund-raising centre for China. Previously, the two forms to date have been outlined: red chips and H-shares. Yet both forms have difficulties and limitations and do not portend further development.

The one-time popularity of red chips was, as I have suggested, based on a certain degree of opaqueness of the Mainland economy. Part of the opaqueness is inevitable. China started as a planned economy and has been governed by a communist political party. Its political, social, and economic system has not been an open one. There is still much uncertainty concerning the course of the Chinese economy as well as its economic and political policies. Such opaqueness and uncertainty has, in the meantime, allowed for claims to be made which we can presently conclude to be exaggerated. The claim of *guanxi* has not been substantiated (Quak, 2002) and a second red-chip boom involving new Mainland companies looks well nigh impossible.

Table 17.5 can be used to discuss the future of H-shares. Three pairs of variables are presented: the capitalization of the Hong Kong and Mainland

Table 17.5   Hong Kong and China: Equity Markets (US$ million)

	Hong Kong's Market Capitalization	China's Market Capitalization	Hong Kong's Annual Turnover	China's Annual Turnover	Funds Raised by A-shares	Funds Raised by H- and N-shares
1991	121986	2028	38607	820	939	
1992	172106	18255	78598	16715	9066	
1993	385247	40567	131550	43395	33814	10575
1994	269508	43521	147158	97526	5757	21898
1995	303705	42055	106888	49774	2716	3767
1996	449381	113755	166419	256008	26996	10050
1997	413323	206366	489365	369538	79020	43427
1998	343394	231322	205918	284769	53514	4584
1999	609090	330703	247428	377099	69162	5697
2000	623398	580991	377866	721538	121668	67900

Sources of data: Emerging Stock Markets Factbook and *China Statistical Yearbook*; see Appendix 17.1 for details.

markets, their annual turnover, and the amount of funds raised by Chinese firms via A- and foreign-listed shares. China has two stock exchanges with just about equal market shares, so the Mainland variables are the total of those of the Shanghai and Shenzhen exchanges. In the case of market capitalization, we should note that a significant portion of the shares of listed Mainland companies, sometimes up to two-thirds, is non-negotiable and not traded. In the case of the third pair, funds raised externally have been predominantly through H-shares, as N-shares have not been important. We have excluded B-shares as the funds involved are small. The outstanding phenomenon is the dramatic growth of the Mainland market. At the beginning of the 1990s, it was two per cent of the Hong Kong market; at the end of the decade, it was roughly equal to Hong Kong's in spite of considerable growth on Hong Kong's part—a five-fold increase over the 1990s. The latest figures show that it is larger than Hong Kong's and is the largest Asian market after the Japanese market. The two flow variables indicate likewise: the Mainland's turnover has outpaced Hong Kong's consistently since 1998, and the volume of funds raised domestically has been greater than funds raised externally since 1996. The difference in (potential) size cannot be denied. Hong Kong may well remain the major fund-raising centre outside China, but when domestic savings are taken into account its role may be limited after all.

The size issue brings forth a matter of viability sooner than most of us had expected. A-shares and H-shares are similar claims to the underlying assets of a Mainland company. A-shares are restricted to Mainland residents and H-shares to Hong Kong-based investors, so the market is segmented. At the moment, the prices of H-shares are at a big discount compared to those of A-shares. If Mainland firms safeguard the interests of their shareholders, they probably should not issue further H-shares,[7] yet H-shares have continued to be issued. The following factors are suggested to be at work: some Mainland firms want to obtain an H-share listing ahead of an A-share listing so as to bypass the congestion on the Mainland market; some may want an overseas listing to build up a global image or to obtain foreign funds; some are pushed by the central government to do it. On the other hand, if the prices of H-shares are ever at more of a premium than those of A-shares, Hong Kong investors will probably not welcome additional H-shares. More than these 'micro' efficiency issues, we must also beware of any 'disequilibrium' concealed by market segmentation. It is high time that Hong Kong's policymakers and leaders start to think about the role and function of the H-share market and consider possible issues of convergence or non-convergence of the A- and H-share markets.

The Paradox of the Freest Economy

Global financial liberalization and the emerging role of Asia in international trade in the 1970s gave rise to increased financial activity and the need for international financial centres in Asia. Restrictions and regulations of the financial sector in the dominant Asian economy of the day, Japan, opened the door for the two city–states, Hong Kong and Singapore, to emerge. These have the advantages of British heritage in language, law, and banking; they also have good infrastructure, political stability, and clean governments, as official propaganda correctly acknowledges but dubiously exaggerates. Hong Kong's emergence was given a further boost by two sets of special circumstances, again due to restrictions and regulations. In the case of international banking *vis-à-vis* Japan, Japanese regulations and macroeconomic policy were important. In the case of Chinese equities, the window of opportunity opened because of China's lagging financial system amidst a fast-growing economy and the strong interest of foreign investors. This window may be closing. Further liberalization of the Mainland economy, such as that compelled by WTO membership, can only imply that foreign investors will henceforth partake of China's growth opportunities in numerous ways, and not necessarily through Hong Kong. There is now some urgency for Hong Kong to address the issue of its own market position. It needs to find a realistic compromise between ambition and reality. It also needs to strike a better balance between regulation and freedom, order, and dynamism.

Milton Friedman (1980) has long held up Hong Kong as the paragon of the success of free markets, a claim that is all too frequently echoed by the Hong Kong government. World rankings have further reinforced this claim: the Heritage Foundation, for example, has consistently ranked Hong Kong as one of the world's freest and most successful economies. This is not the occasion to determine the extent to which Hong Kong allows for free markets. But the paradox of the presumed free-market economy *par excellence* is that its successes have required—or, at very the least, have been greatly facilitated by—the presence of fettered economies. As these liberalize as part of a global trend, Hong Kong's role and status are under threat. If arguably what is true in international finance is also true in international trade and Hong Kong is no more than a financial-cum-trade entrepôt, then Hong Kong must now redefine itself in the era of China's direct engagement with the world. This will affirm or refute Friedman's free-market hypothesis, as well as determine Hong Kong's future.

Discussion Questions

1.   What is an international financial centre? How is it different from a domestic financial centre?
2.   Why aren't international financial centres simply importers of foreign capital?
3.   Give examples of eurocurrency transactions from Hong Kong's everyday life. Do residents of Shenzhen and New York also engage in eurocurrency transactions?
4.   Does London use sterling as the major currency in its international

financial transactions? Why do both Hong Kong and Singapore emphasize the importance of a strong and stable domestic currency in marketing themselves as international financial centres?

5. In the 1992 episode that made George Soros famous, the sterling was devalued and Britain exited the European Exchange Rate Mechanism. Did this devaluation have an impact on London as an international financial centre? If the Hong Kong dollar were to devalue, would the impact be the same, smaller, or larger?

6. The capitalization of Hong Kong's entire stock market is sometimes used as an indicator of its international financial activity. Find the Standard & Poor's website and see how London (UK) ranks by this indicator. Comment on this indicator.

7. Compare the prices of foreign equities in London and in their respective home markets. Are there disparities between them? Are there major disparities between the prices of Mainland equities in Hong Kong and on the Mainland?

8. If Shanghai ever develops into an international financial centre, would it be an exporter of capital or a financial entrepôt?

9. Though New York houses the largest equity market of the world, N-shares have not developed as a viable form of fund raising for Mainland enterprises. Hong Kong is smaller, yet H-shares have been more successful. Do you have any idea why?

10. R. C. Michie, historian of the London stock exchange, has often argued for the right balance between market development and market regulation. Have Hong Kong and Singapore generally found the right balance?

Keywords

Asian Currency Units (ACUs)
cross-border transactions
Davison Report
eurobonds
eurocurrency
exporter of domestic capital
Fell, Robert
financial entrepôt
foreign bonds
foreign equities
H-share companies
international banking
international bonds
international financial centre
loanable funds
London
offshore currency

Endnotes

Chapter 1

1. Several pages of this section on regulation were taken from Ho (1991), Chapter 5: 'The Regulatory Framework of the Banking Sector'.
2. Controls on time deposits maturing within one week were eliminated in July 2000, and those on current accounts and savings accounts were eliminated in July 2001. The HKMA interviewed banks about their preparedness for the added competition implied by the deregulation. See the article 'Deregulation of Interest Rate Rules-Summary of Self-Assessment Reports by Banks' (Banking Development Division of the HKMA, Quarterly Bulletin, August 2000, pp. 1–4).
3. In America, when the interest rate ceilings paid by banks on savings deposits under Regulation Q were up for removal under the Depository Institutions Deregulation and Monetary Control Act of 1980, the small savings and loan associations wanted to keep the rate they paid a quarter to a half per cent higher in order to achieve a competitive position *vis-à-vis* banks and attract more deposit business. In that case, being able to pay depositors a higher rate was considered to be a competitive advantage, not a competitive disadvantage, for the smaller depository institutions—exactly the opposite of the view taken by Hong Kong banks.
4. This paragraph is paraphrased from the inside front cover of the Hong Kong Monetary Authority's *Annual Report 2000*.
5. The names 'SEHK' and 'HKEx' are used interchangeably throughout this book, depending on the context.

Chapter 2

1. Another topic, on which there is a large body of literature relevant to Hong Kong's financial system, is 'dollarization'. In the spring of 2000 there was a conference on this subject held at the Federal Reserve Bank of Dallas. Former senator Connie Mack, who was Chairman of the Joint Economic Committee of Congress at the time, sponsored a bill that would authorize Argentina and other Latin American countries to adopt the dollar as their currency. With hindsight, it is unfortunate that the arrangements did not work out with Argentina. Ecuador did adopt the dollar unilaterally.

Chapter 3

1. Note that although tourism is frequently cited as an important account in the trade in services, Hong Kong actually has a net deficit in its tourist service trade—a fact that anyone witnessing the weekend exodus to Shenzhen can appreciate.
2. A single bank, HSBC, makes up three-quarters of this number. Note that two-thirds of the business of HSBC is non-Hong Kong-related. However, most banks doing business in Hong Kong are not listed on the exchange.
3. Calling the HKMA a central bank is consistent with the view of Robert Haney Scott in Chapter 1 that the functions of the HKMA—keeping the Hong Kong

dollar stable, managing the payments and settlements system, managing the Exchange Fund, supervising banks, and developing financial infrastructure— are central banking functions. This is in contrast with the views of some writers (e.g. Hanke, 1997) that the HKMA is not a central bank because the currency board system severely limits monetary policy discretion.

4. US banks, since 1987, have been defined as any 'insured bank as defined by section 3(h) of the Federal Deposit Insurance Act' (FDIC). The FDIC Act in turn defines an insured bank as 'a banking institution which is engaged in the business of receiving deposits, other than trust funds . . . and is incorporated as a bank under the appropriate jurisdictional laws'. The FDIC Act's definition of 'deposit' clarifies deposits as including sums from the receipt of monies 'in settlement of checks, drafts, or other instruments forwarded to such bank or savings association for collection'. Definitions of banking in the British tradition from which Hong Kong derives its system simply refer to the taking of deposits and making of payments. In no jurisdiction that the author is aware of does the act of lending by itself qualify an institution as a bank.

5. 'Investment banking' and 'merchant banking' can be used interchangeably. The term 'merchant banking' originated in the UK in the eighteenth century with the discounting of trade acceptances of the large merchants. From this wholesale money market activity, merchant banking houses expanded naturally into securities underwriting and trading. In modern UK parlance, 'merchant banking' encompasses services associated with the US term 'investment banking'. Americans, in contrast, often use 'merchant banking' in the specific sense of providing loans that bridge capital markets transactions.

6. Hong Kong's statutory liquidity requirement is broad and usually not binding, i.e. it is met usually by banks in the course of meeting their own prudential standards. This differs from US primary reserve requirements, which require banks to maintain non-interest-bearing clearing balances and function essentially as a tax on deposits. Hong Kong maintains no primary reserve requirement.

7. For a discussion of definitions of the money supply, see Chapter 1. In theory, any asset that exhibits little price volatility and is widely accepted for payment— or is readily translatable at low cost for an asset acceptable for payment—can be considered money. Some jurisdictions include money market mutual funds in definitions of money. Definitions of money evolve with changes in financial service provision. Retail electronic money will probably enter the definitions in the near future.

8. A bank will rarely have clearing accounts with two central banks. For at least one of the two legs in the foreign exchange transaction, it will use its correspondent banking account with a direct clearer in that currency. So, for example, Hang Seng Bank, which has a Hong Kong dollar clearing account with the Exchange Fund but does not have a US dollar clearing account with the Federal Reserve Bank of New York, may use a deposit account with Citibank in New York for receipt of the proceeds of US dollar purchases (from the sale of Hong Kong dollars).

9. These include nationally funded deposit insurance programmes in the USA, Canada, Japan, etc, and industry-sponsored programmes in Germany. Researchers, however, have demonstrated that in the absence of strong monitoring the implementation of deposit insurance increases the frequency and exacerbates the severity of financial crises (see, for example, World Bank (2001) and Barch, Caprio, and Levine (2001)).

10. Before 1994, banks followed the deposit interest rates set by the Hong Kong Association of Banks. Those cartel rates were gradually phased out from 1994 to 2001. The final phase of deposit deregulation occurred during a recession, when the banks were flush with liquidity; hence there was no competitive increasing in deposit rates. As David Carse, Deputy Chief Executive of the HKMA, expressed it (2001): 'As it has turned out, the final stage of deregulation

probably could not have happened at a better time—at least from the point of view of protecting the regulator's peace of mind. The ample liquidity in the banking system has reduced the risk of an aggressive price war for deposits, which was the HKMA's principal concern. So we have ended up with a Little Bang rather than a Big Bang.'

11. The term 'Lender of Last Resort' is used in banking in three different ways: (1) providing liquidity to clearing banks against the collateral of liquid reserve assets, (2) providing liquidity to solvent but illiquid banks, and (3) providing liquidity to insolvent banks. In this chapter, the term is used in the first sense (see HKMA, June 1999.)

12. In 1994, the HKMA published Guideline No. 5.9, which recommended that banks' total exposure to real estate loans should not exceed forty per cent of lending. In August 1998, in recognition of the amount by which property prices had fallen (approximately fifty per cent) and to relieve downward pressure on the property market caused by the Asian financial crisis, the HKMA withdrew the guideline.

13. The term 'domestic Hong Kong bank' as it is used here excludes Hongkong Bank (owned by HSBC of the UK), Hang Seng Bank (majority owned by Hongkong Bank), Bank of China (Hong Kong) Ltd, owned by Bank of China, and Standard Chartered of the UK.

14. Historically, many jurisdictions opposed the commingling of investment and commercial banking on the one hand and banking and insurance on the other. In the United States, for example, regulations prohibited commercial banks from carrying out investment banking activities for almost seventy years from the 1930s to the late 1990s. Currently, fewer and fewer prohibitions exist worldwide. Deregulation has spurred the development of 'universal banking' or 'alfinanz', by which all financial services are offered by a single financial institution, subject to appropriate regulatory registration.

15. A 'Bulge Bracket', narrowly defined, is the group of investment banks underwriting and placing the largest number of securities in a stock, bond, or syndicated loan placement. Here, the term is used in its wider sense to mean the top tier of investment banks such as Citigroup SSB, Credit Suisse First Boston, Deutsche Bank, Goldman Sachs, Merrill Lynch, Morgan Chase, Morgan Stanley, Nomura, Salomon Smith Barney, and UBS Warburg.

Chapter 4

1. See, for example, Reilly and Brown (1997).
2. In the UK, the unit trust—that is, a legal trust—has been popular, and in practical terms the two vehicles are similar.
3. Credit Suisse First Boston Tremont Index LLC uses the TASS database, which tracks over 2600 funds. The universe consists of funds with a minimum of US$10 million under management and a current audited financial statement.
4. UCI (an EU term): Assets held in an investment fund divided into units managed by a fund management company on behalf of investors.
5. Only eighteen per cent of Hong Kong fund management firms were found to be complying with the Association for Investment Management and Research (AIMR) Performance Presentation Standards and Global Investment Performance Standards, compared with seventy-three per cent in the US and twenty-seven per cent in Europe (PriceWaterhouseCoopers, 2001).
6. Figures include mutual funds/unit trusts and exclude investment companies, Tracker Funds, and iShares.
7. The Securities and Futures Ordinance, enacted on 27 March 2002, subsumed the various former securities-related ordinances. However, at time of writing,

the relevant subsidiary legislation had yet to be enacted. For convenience, references are given also to the respective sections of the former ordinances.

Chapter 5

1. Exempt people refers to (1) employees and self-employed people who, at the date the relevant provision in the Mandatory Provident Fund Schemes Ordinance is implemented, have attained 64 years of age, (2) domestic employees, (3) self-employed hawkers, (4) people covered by a statutory pension and provident fund scheme (such as civil servants and subsidized or grant school teachers), (5) members of occupational retirement schemes which are granted exemption certificates, (6) people from overseas who enter Hong Kong for employment for less than a year, or who are covered by overseas retirement schemes, and (7) employees of the European Union Office of the European Commission in Hong Kong.
2. As a comparison, Australia, which started a mandatory private retirement scheme in 1992, had a compliance rate of eighty per cent in 1995 (Yiu, 2001b).
3. The International Association for the Study of Insurance Economics, better known as 'The Geneva Association', has advocated a fourth pillar to supplement the other three pillars. The fourth pillar refers to gradual retirement, which encourages older people to remain working on a part-time basis with a partial pension, so as to continue to make an economic and social contribution to the (service) economies. See, for instance, Delsen and Reday-Mulvey (1996) and Reday-Mulvey (2001).
4. The name comes from Section 401(k) of The Revenue Act of 1978 of the US.
5. All benefits derived from the mandatory contributions must be preserved until the scheme member attains the age of 65, except for early withdrawals under the specific circumstances described in the MPF regulation.
6. In Singapore, money in the Central Provident Fund can be withdrawn upon reaching fifty-five years of age.
7. Bancassurance represents a strategy by which banks and insurers work together in an integrated way to work the financial markets. The core activity of bancassurance is the distribution of insurance products by banks. For various bancassurance models existing in Hong Kong, see Chun (2002).

Chapter 6

1. Data are from *Sigma*, No.6/2001. The industrialized countries, including countries of North America, Western Europe, Japan, and Oceania, have fifteen per cent share of global population, seventy-seven per cent share of GDP, and ninety-one per cent share of world insurance premiums.
2. A technical definition of risk aversion is the Arrow-Pratt measure of risk aversion, defined by, where $u(w)$ is the utility function of wealth. The numerator and denominator represent the second derivative and first derivative, respectively; see for instance Varian (1992).
3. The remaining nineteen are composite insurers that do business in both categories.
4. Using 1999 gross premiums data, Swiss Re (2001) calculated the life and non-life Herfindahl Index for twelve Asian insurance marketplaces. Hong Kong has the lowest figures on both indexes among the twelve. A Herfindahl index of 100 means a single-firm monopoly, while a value of 0 indicates an extremely atomized market. With the non-life index of 2.51, Hong Kong's non-life insurance sector is close to total fragmentation.

5. All of the other three biggest lines of general insurance showed positive underwriting results. In 2000, the Accident and Health, Goods in Transit, and Property Damage business recorded an underwriting *profit* of HK$162.5 million, HK$243.2 million, and HK$311.8 million respectively. In fact, according to the OCI (2001a) all of these businesses recorded a positive underwriting margin over the previous five years.

6. The reader should be cautioned that Harrington and Niehaus's opinions on EC systems focus on US conditions.

7. The Insurance Companies (Amendment) (No. 2) Ordinance 1994 came into effect in May 1995.

8. The Insurance Companies (General Business) (Valuation) Regulation was put into operation in December 1995.

9. Both the Insurance Companies (Margin of Solvency) Regulation and the Insurance Companies (Determination of Long Term Liabilities) Regulation went into effect in October 1995.

10. In December 1992, the OCI and the Hong Kong Federation of Insurers (HKFI) reached an agreement on the Code of Practice for the Administration of Insurance Agents. The following year, HKFI set up the Insurance Agents Registration Board as the self-regulatory body.

11. A brief account of HIH's Hong Kong subsidiary insurers' insolvency can be found in OCI's 2001 annual report.

12. The parent corporation of the second captive insurer domiciled in Hong Kong is actually a Chinese enterprise, China National Offshore Oil Corporation.

13. Ramos (2002) provides information about Asian companies deploying PDAs in their agency force. She also discusses the special characteristics, industry applications, implementations, and limitations of such new business tools.

Chapter 8

1. The Bank of International Settlements started its survey of exchange markets in 1989. The adjusted global foreign exchange average daily turnovers for April 1989, 1992, 1995, and 1998 were US$590, $820, $1,190, and $1,490 billion respectively. The daily turnovers increased from 1989 to 1998, but from April 1998 to April 2001 the turnovers decreased significantly by nineteen per cent. The decline was mainly due to the introduction of the euro, the growing share of electronic brokering in the spot interbank market, consolidation in the banking industry, international concentration in the corporate sector, and the decrease of risk tolerance in banks. The introduction of the euro reduced inter-Europe trading and thus reduced exchange market turnover. The decrease in the risk tolerance of banks was caused by the financial crisis in 1998, which led to banks' reduction of credit limits and thus reduced exchange market trading.

2. The compositions of the interbank exchange trading in Hong Kong were US$14.558, $2.623, and $32.518 billion in the spot, outright forward, and foreign exchange swap markets respectively.

3. The standard is set out in the Fifth Edition of the Balance of Payments Manual (BPM5) of the International Monetary Fund (IMF).

4. The explanation of current account and capital and financial account is drawn from related documents from The Hong Kong Census and Statistic Department's website (http://www.info.gov.hk/censtatd/eng).

5. Two other approaches to explaining the exchange rate are the monetary approach (sticky price version) and the portfolio balance approach.

6. The system requires the US to provide US dollars as reserves for other countries. As world trade grows, countries are requiring more and more US dollars to

serve as their reserves. In order to provide dollars for the growing reserves' needs of other countries, the US has to run balance of payments deficits. The more a US balance of payments deficit occurs, the more foreign countries worry about the ability of the US to convert dollars into gold at the official price. This paradox is called the Triffin paradox.

7. The pegged exchange rate system stopped operating for the four years between 25 December 1941 and 23 September 1945 because of the Japanese wartime occupation.

8. The Foreign Exchange Fund is an official organization of the Hong Kong government responsible for the maintenance of the Hong Kong dollar exchange rate and the management of the government assets in the Fund.

9. Coins are issued by the Hong Kong Monetary Authority through authorized agent banks. Transactions between the HKMA and the agent banks go through a similar procedure to the notes.

10. Since September 1998, licensed banks can convert Hong Kong dollars in their clearing accounts to US dollars at the fixed exchange rate of HK$7.75 to US$1 (the Convertibility Undertaking). From 1 April 1999, the exchange rate under the Convertibility Undertaking moved by one pip (i.e. HK$0.0001) per calendar day to converge with the linked rate of 7.80 on 12 August 2000 for the issue and redemption of certificates of indebtedness.

11. Some economists argue that the adjustment process is done through continuous government intervention rather than being automatic. The reason for this is that the elaborate mechanism automatically triggers sales of US dollars to banks whenever demand increases and *vice versa*. They therefore believe that the adjustment process is better viewed as automatic intervention.

12. Classical quantity theory of money states that:
    *money supply * velocity of money = prices * quantity of goods and services*
    If we assume that velocity of money and quantity of goods and services are largely fixed, an increase (or decrease) in money supply will result in higher (lower) price levels and lower (increase) the demand for the US dollar.

13. The date 17 October 1983 was the date that the pegged exchange rate system started; 7 July 1984 was when the draft agreement between the Chinese and British governments was about to signed. The Hong Kong dollar was pushed down to 7.90.

14. For example, Hsu (2001) finds that one can earn better than predicted profits, an earnings surprise, by investing in companies predicted to have low earnings. The finding casts doubt on EMH. Another example is a study by James (2001), which shows that the probability distribution against which the empirical studies on EMH are made is a shifting one, casting doubt on all of the findings reported.

15. Robert Haney Scott, one of the editors of this book, points out two fundamental questions about the validity of empirical analysis on the EMH. First, the EMH statement that prices reflect all available and relevant information is operationally meaningless in the sense that no hypothetical experiment could ever refute it. That is, a scientific hypothesis must be capable of refutation, so that if it were not empirically true the evidence could show that it were not. Any evidence purporting to refute the EMH would simply be dismissed as suggesting that the experiment was faulty in failing to introduce all the relevant information. Thus, it fails the scientific test of refutability. If one believes the hypothesis one must take it on faith since it is not scientifically testable. Second, in the economics of the allocation of resources, the paretian definition of an efficient allocation of resources is a paretian optimality condition—the condition that no-one can be made better off without someone being made worse off. The EMH, based as it is on the concept of available information, fails to impose this condition. Indeed, new and relevant information may simply reinforce a departure from paretian optimality. For example, information that a new drug has been approved by regulatory authorities may cause the stock price to rise.

But the drug company operates under a monopoly allocated by the government, and monopolized production of a good will be inefficiently priced. The new information therefore leads to support for inefficient enterprises. New information about government regulations may lead to investment in enterprises that are bad for efficiency in the sense of pareto when they result in a distortion of markets away from optimal allocation. Not all relevant new information leads to more efficient allocation of investment funds.

Chapter 9

1. In cases of declared bankruptcy, debt holders still have a higher priority than equity holders, although in reality neither may get anything because (1) both have a lower priority than the employees and the banks; and (2) by the time a firm declares bankruptcy, there is really not much left.
2. The formula for the price of a bond (P_B) with a fixed coupon payment (C) is P_B = $S_{i=1,n}[C/(1+r)^i]+X/(1+r)^n$, where r is the interest rate, X is the principal repayment, and n is the maturity of the bond. Thus, for any given change in interest rate (r), the longer the n, the greater the percentage change in P_B.
3. Another way is that the banks issue the bonds by themselves without going through the HKMC. Before the formation of the HKMC in March 1997, there were some MBSs issued directly by commercial banks.
4. See also Jiang *et al.* (2001) for a comparison of the relative sizes in Hong Kong and other economies.
5. In the debt market development reports by the HKMA (2000 to 2002), new debts issued instead of change in the outstanding amount of debt were reported. The former may not be a good measure of new funds raised because many of the new debts issued were used to refinance the maturing debts. This is particularly the case if there are a lot of short-term debts being rolled over through the issuance of new debts.
6. This is calculated as loans for use in Hong Kong by manufacturing, agriculture, and fisheries; transport and transport equipment; electricity, gas, and telephone; building; construction; property development and investment; wholesale and retail; mining and quarrying; as well as the hotel, boarding house, and catering sectors. Source: HKMA *Monthly Bulletin.*
7. The figures will remain large even if we exclude the figures for the H-shares market.
8. The first issue was made in October 1997 with a relatively small size of HK$0.65 billion. The second but more meaningful issue was made in August 1998 with a total of HK$3.5 billion.
9. For example, in the June 2002 issue by the HKMC, the interest rates for the one-, two-, and three-year renewable bonds before maturity were 2.75 per cent, 3.75 per cent, and 4.35 per cent respectively. Beyond the maturity, if the HKMC chooses to renew, say, the three-year bond for another two years, the interest rate in the fourth and fifth year will be 5.1 per cent.

Chapter 10

1. Listing Rule 8.24 defines the 'public'. It excludes people who are directors or chief executives, people with shareholdings of ten per cent or more, or people who are associates of any the above.
2. A sponsor can be a member of HKEx, an issuing house, a merchant bank, or a similar person acceptable to HKEx (Rule 3.01).

3. In Singapore since 1993, IPOs can be made either on a fixed price basis or on a combination of fixed price and tender offer. Under the combined method, IPOs are offered in two tranches: the first at a fixed price and the second in a tender offer. Hameed and Lim (1998) examined the relationship between the underpricing of first tranches and the proportion of shares offered in the second tranche.
4. Fads may arise in the IPO market due to the uncertainty of estimating the value of new stock, noise trading, market speculations, and high demand from over-optimistic marginal buyers during initial trading (Camerer (1989); Trueman (1988); Black (1986); Ang and Schwarz (1985); and Miller (1977)).
5. If the issuers could forecast the buoyancy in the market, IPOs could be timed to take advantage of investors' over-optimism by raising the offer prices (Loughran *et al.* 1994; Loughran and Ritter (1995); and Ritter (1991)).

Chapter 11

1. Exceptions are made if the client is a professional, already the owner of the securities, or has been represented by the dealer on at least three occasions over the previous three years.
2. An SI specifies the stock code, quantity of stocks, identity of counterparty, settlement date, and amount of payment.
3. Market capitalization is expressed as an average of the previous months.
4. Turnover is aggregated and individually assessed for eight quarterly sub-periods for the previous twenty-four months.
5. All HKEx-listed stocks are included in the AOI except: (1) stocks of overseas-incorporated companies whose principal activities are carried on outside Hong Kong and China; or (2) stocks which have been suspended for over one year; or (3) stocks which are not traded in Hong Kong dollars.

Chapter 12

1. Continuous discounting and compounding rely on the discount factor of e^{-rDt} and the compounding factor of e^{rDt}, where e is a constant equivalent to an approximation of 2.7183, r is a prevailing market interest rate, and Dt is the length of time between the discounting or compounding period.
2. Notice in Table 12.14 that the receipts and payments of cash flow for both counterparties can be easily traced by the difference in font faces: the normal font represents original portfolio cash flows, the bold face stands for the receipts from the swap arranger, and the italic font denotes the payments to the swap arranger.

Chapter 13

1. The existing number of members is 191.
2. Société Générale has taken the place of Credit Suisse First Boston.
3. Deutsche Bank AG gained its fixing seat in 1993 by acquiring the original London broker, Sharps Pixley. The use of the Sharps Pixley name was discontinued in 1996.
4. HSBC traces its fixing membership back to Samuel Montagu's traditional seat. Its gold business is now allied to the former Republic Bank of New York as HSBC Bank USA, which is also active in New York and Hong Kong.

5. Rothschild has been in the London gold market for 200 years. It has chaired the fixing since 1919, and is the sole independent survivor of the original fixing members.
6. Scotia-Mocatta is the global bullion banking division of the Bank of Nova Scotia, formed in 1997 by the bank's acquisition of Mocatta bullion from the Standard Chartered Bank in London. Mocatta itself dates back to 1671 as the oldest member of the London market.

Chapter 15

1. In its survey, the CLSA classified corporate governance according to seven criteria: discipline, independence, transparency, accountability, fairness, responsibility, and social awareness. It suggested that there are five key macro determinants of corporate governance: rules and regulations, enforcement mechanisms, the political and regulatory environment, international generally accepted accounting principles, and institutional culture.
2. Standard and Poor's used four criteria when assigning a company a corporate governance score: ownership and concentration, financial stakeholder rights and relations, transparency and disclosure, and board structure and process. There are also four elements in its country analytical structure: market infrastructure, legal infrastructure, regulatory environment, and information infrastructure.
3. Recent events surrounding the huge losses suffered by investors of Singapore-registered Asia Pulp and Paper, combined with the lack of progress in investigating this fraud case, is beginning to lead observers to question the leading position of Singapore on CG (see Mobius, 2002).
4. As SEHK became a subsidiary of HKEx in 2000, the two names 'SEHK' and 'HKEx' are used interchangeably in this chapter, depending on context.

Chapter 16

1. s247(3) defines a 'substantial shareholder' as a person who has an interest in the relevant share capital of the corporation, the nominal value of which is equal to or more than five per cent of the nominal value of the relevant share capital of the corporation.

Chapter 17

1. Coverage of some of the historical events may be found in Jao (1974), Fell (1992), and Hui (1994(a), 1994(b)).
2. The author is unaware of good documentation of the events of the summer of 1998. In contrast, the events of October 1997 were reviewed in the 'Report on the Financial Market Review' (April 1998). The market reforms subsequent to the stock market intervention were rationalized in the document 'A Policy Paper on Securities and Futures Market Reform' (March 1999). Both are available from the Financial Services and the Treasury Bureau's web pages at http://www.info.gov.hk/fstb/. Ironically, the 1998 Report denied the possibility of 'double play'.
3. In the case of H-share companies, only the market value of H-shares is counted towards Hong Kong's market capitalization and that of A-, B-, N-, and other shares is excluded.

4. See Bernauer (1983) for an early history of the ACUs and Tan (1999) for later developments.
5. Tan (1997) has a calendar of major events concerning Singapore as an international financial centre.
6. These limitations seem well understood by Singapore's commentators (Sivanithy (2002) and Wong (2002)).
7. Sito and Ng (2002) report that some red chip companies are bypassing Hong Kong to raise funds on the Mainland.

References

Chapter 1

Chapman, Stanley, *The Rise of Merchant Banking* (London, George Allen & Unwin, 1984).

Cetorelli, Nicola, 'The Role of Financial Services in Economic Growth', Chicago Fed Letter, Number 173, January 2002.

Cetorelli, Nicola and Michele Gambera, 'Banking Market Structure, Financial Dependence, and Growth: International Evidence from Industry Data', *Journal of Finance*, Vol. 56, No. 2, 2001, pp. 617–48.

Euh, Yoon-Dae and Alice H. Amsden, 'Korea's Financial Reform', *Journal of Management*, College of Business Administration, Korea University, Seoul, Vol. 33, 1990, pp. 45–84.

Ho, Richard Yan-Ki, Robert Haney Scott, and Kie Ann Wong (eds.), *The Hong Kong Financial System* (Hong Kong, Oxford University Press, 1991).

Ho, Simon S. M., 'Time We Set the Standard for Corporate Governance', *South China Morning Post*, 11 September, 2000.

Joskow, P. L., 'Inflation and Environment Concern: Structural Change in the Process of Public Utility Price Regulation', *Journal of Law and Economics*, October 1974, pp. 291–327.

Kane, E. J., 'Good Intentions and Unintended Evil: the Case Against Selective Credit Allocation', *Journal of Money, Credit, and Banking*, February 1977, pp. 55–69.

Kane, E. J., 'Incentive Conflict in the International Regulatory Agreement of Risk-based Capital', in S. G. Rhee and R. P. Chang (eds.), *Pacific-Basin Capital Markets Research*, Vol. 2, Elsevier, Amsterdam, 1991, pp. 3–21.

King, Robert and Ross Levine, 'Finance and Growth: Schumpeter Might be Right', *Quarterly Journal of Economics*, Vol. 108, No. 3, 1993, pp. 717–37.

Ma, Frederick, Speech delivered by the Secretary for Financial Services and Treasury at the 9th APEC Finance Ministers' Meeting on 5 September 2002, Mexico.

Scott, Robert Haney, K. A. Wong, and Yan-Ki Ho (eds.), *Hong Kong's Financial Institutions and Markets* (Hong Kong, Oxford University Press, 1986).

Scott, Robert Haney, 'Macao's Financial System and Its Future', in *Macao 2000*, edited by J. A. Berlie (Hong Kong, Oxford University Press, 1999, pp. 162–181).

Selgin, George A., *The Theory of Free Banking: Money Supply under Competitive Note Issue* (Totawa New Jersey, Roman & Littlefield, 1988).

Selgin, George A., 'Central Banking: Myth and Reality', *Hong Kong Economic Papers*, Hong Kong Economic Association, No. 19, 1988, pp. 1–13.

Stigler, G. J., 'The Theory of Economic Regulation', *Bell Journal of Economics*, Vol. 2, 1971, pp. 3–21.

Chapter 2

Caballero, Ricardo and Rudiger Dornbusch, 'Argentina Cannot Be Trusted', *Financial Times*, 8 March 2002.

Carse, David, 'Recreating the Financial Services Industry for the New Economy: A Regulator's Perspective', *Quarterly Bulletin*, Hong Kong Monetary Authority, February 2001, pp. 69–73.

Chan, Alex and Nai-fu Chen, 'An Intertemporal Currency Board', *Pacific Economic Review*, Volume 4 Number 2, June 1999, pp. 215–32.

Chan, Kenneth S. and Francis T. Lui, 'Foreword' to 'Special Section: Currency Boards and Exchange Rate Arrangements: Theories and Issues', Part I, *Pacific Economic Review*, Volume 3, Number 3, October 1998, pp. 201–2, and Part II, Volume 4, Number 2, June 1999, pp. 137–8.

Chan, Kenneth S. and Kee-Jin Ngiam, 'Currency Crises and the Modified Currency Board System in Singapore', *Pacific Economic Review*, Volume 3, Number 3, October 1998, pp. 243–63.

Cheng, Leonard K., Yum K. Kwan, and Francis T. Lui, 'Risk Premium, Currency Board, and Attacks on the Hong Kong Dollar', Working Paper Series No. 128, City University of Hong Kong, May 1999.

Cheng, Leonard K., 'An Alternative Approach to Defending the Hong Kong Dollar', Working Paper Series No. 129, City University of Hong Kong, May 1999.

Economic Research Division, 'Balance of Payments Statistics: Examining Some Received Wisdom', *Quarterly Bulletin*, Hong Kong Monetary Authority, February 2001, pp. 21–31.

Espinosa-Vega, Marco A., and Jang-Ting Guo, 'On Business Cycles and Countercyclical Policies', *Economic Review*, Federal Reserve Bank of Atlanta, Fourth Quarter 2001, pp. 1–12.

Hanke, Steve H., 'Some Reflections on Monetary Institutions and Exchange-Rate Regimes', *Zagreb Journal of Economics*, No. 5, 2000, pp. 77–92.

Hanke, Steve H., 'Who's Killing the Peso in Buenos Aires?', *The Wall Street Journal*, 30 November 2001.

Ho, Richard Yan-Ki, Robert Haney Scott, and Kie Ann Wong (eds.), *The Hong Kong Financial System* (Hong Kong, Oxford University Press, 1991).

Hong Kong Monetary Authority, *1998 Annual Report*, pp. 38–9.

Hong Kong Monetary Authority, 'Record of discussion of the Exchange Fund Advisory Committee Sub-Committee on Currency Board Operations on 2 November 2000', *Quarterly Bulletin*, February 2001, p. 88.

Jao, Y. C., 'The Working of the Currency Board: The Experience of Hong Kong 1935–1997,' *Pacific Economic Review*, Vol. 3, Number 3, October 1998.

Kwan, Yum K., Francis T. Lui, and Leonard K. Cheng, 'Credibility of Hong Kong's Currency Board: The Role of Institutional Arrangements', Working Paper Series No. 131, City University of Hong Kong, August 1999.

Latter, Tony, 'Why Blame the Peg?', *Quarterly Bulletin*, Hong Kong Monetary Authority, May 2002, pp. 39–48.

Lai, Kitty, Jiming Ha, and Cynthia Leung, *Quarterly Bulletin*, Hong Kong Monetary Authority, May 2002, pp. 1–8.

McCandless, George T. Jr. and Warren E. Weber, 'Some Monetary Facts', *Quarterly Review*, Federal Reserve Bank of Minneapolis, Fall 2001, pp. 14–24.

Monetary Policy and Markets Department, 'Implementation of the US Dollar Clearing System in Hong Kong', *Quarterly Bulletin*, Hong Kong Monetary Authority, February 2001, pp. 41–3.

Monetary Policy and Markets Department, 'Hong Kong's Real Time Gross Settlement System', *Quarterly Bulletin*, Hong Kong Monetary Authority, February 1997, pp. 30–7.

Nugee, John, 'A Brief History of the Exchange Fund', in *Money and Banking in Hong Kong* (Hong Kong Monetary Authority, 1995).

Scott, Robert Haney, *Money, Financial Markets and the Economy* (Singapore: Prentice Hall, 1995).

Scott, Robert Haney, *Saving Hong Kong's Dollar* (Hong Kong: University Publisher and Printer, 1984).

Tsang, Shu-ki, 'The Case for Adopting the Convertible Reserves System in Hong Kong', *Pacific Economic Review*, Volume 3, Number 3, October 1998, pp. 243–64.

Yam, Joseph, 'Chief Executive's Statement', *Annual Report*, Hong Kong Monetary Authority, 2000. pp. 4–9.

Yam, Joseph, 'Building Stability in Unstable Times', *Quarterly Bulletin*, Hong Kong Monetary Authority, November 2001, pp. 82–8.

Yam, Joseph, 'Open and Connected: Scaling New Heights', *Quarterly Bulletin*, Hong Kong Monetary Authority, February 2001, pp. 54–61.

Yam, Joseph, 'The Lender of Last Resort', *Quarterly Bulletin*, Hong Kong Monetary Authority, August 1999, pp. 120–6.

Yam, Joseph, 'Sustainability of Monetary and Exchange Rate Policies', *Quarterly Bulletin*, Hong Kong Monetary Authority, August 1999, pp. 96–102.

Yam, Joseph, 'Defending Hong Kong's Monetary Stability', *Quarterly Bulletin*, Hong Kong Monetary Authority, November 1998, pp. 75–9.

Yam, Joseph, 'Why We Intervened', *Quarterly Bulletin*, Hong Kong Monetary Authority, November 1998, pp. 1–4. A shortened version published in the *Asian Wall Street Journal*, 20 August 1998.

Yam, Joseph, 'The Development of Monetary Policy in Hong Kong', in Y. C. Jao (ed.), *Monetary Management in Hong Kong: The Changing Role of the Exchange Fund* (Charted Institute of Bankers, Hong Kong, July 1991).

Zarazaga, Carlos E. J. M., 'Building a Case for Currency Boards', *Pacific Economic Review*, Volume 4, Number 2, June 1999, pp. 139–64.

Chapter 3

Barth, James, Gerald Caprio, and Ross Levine, 'The Regulation and Supervision of Banks Around The World: A New Database', Policy Research Working Paper, World Bank Development Research Group, Washington DC, May 2001.

Beecham, B. J., *Monetary and Financial System in Hong Kong*, (Hong Kong Institute of Bankers, 1996).

Carse, David, 'Bank Consolidation in Hong Kong', *HKMA Quarterly Bulletin*, August 2001.

Carse, David, 'The changing Landscape of Banking in Hong Kong,' *HKMA Quarterly Bulletin*, 11, 2001, p. 96.

Financial Services Bureau, *Hong Kong: The Facts* (Hong Kong, Information Services Department, Financial Services Bureau, 1999).

Hanke, Steve H., 'Auto Pilot for Hong Kong', *Wall Street Journal*, 29 October 1997.

HKMA, 'HKMA Policy Statement on the Lender of Last Resort', HKMA press release, 29 June 1999.

HKMA, 'Enhancing Deposit Protection in Hong Kong', HKMA consultation paper, 24 October 2000.

HKMA, 'Hong Kong Banking into the New Millennium—Policy Response to the Banking Sector Consultancy Study', HKMA policy initiatives (booklet), July 1999.

KPMG Barents, 'Hong Kong Banking into the New Millennium—Hong Kong Banking Sector Consultancy Study', Consultancy study commissioned by HKMA, released December 1998. Available online at: http://www.info.gov.hk/hkma/eng/press/index.htm.

McCauley, Robert and Y. K. Mo, 'Recent Developments in the International Banking Business of Hong Kong', *BIS Quarterly Review*, June 1999, pp. 13–14.

Nakaso, Hiroshi, 'The Financial Crisis in Japan during the 1990s: How the Bank of Japan Responded and the Lessons Learnt', *BIS Papers*, No. 6, BIS Economic Department, October 2001.

2001 Hong Kong Venture Capital Yearbook (Asia, Thomson Financial Venture Economics, 2001).

World Bank, *Finance for Growth* (New York, Oxford University Press, 2001).

Chapter 4

Fama, Eugene F., 'Component of Investment Performance', *Journal of Finance* 27, No. 3, June 1972, pp. 551–67.

Hall, Alvin D., *Getting Started in Mutual Funds* (New York, John Wiley & Sons, 2000).

Hong Kong Monetary Authority, *Annual Report*, 2000.

Ho, Richard and Clement Wong, *The Role of Fund Management in Promoting Capital Markets Development in Asia Economies* (Hong Kong, Hong Kong Committee for Pacific Economic Cooperation, May 1998, p. 37).

Hong Kong Investment Funds Association, *The Hong Kong Investment Funds Yearbook*, 2000 and 2001.

Jensen, Michael C., 'The Performance of Mutual Funds in the Period 1945–1964', *Journal of Finance* 23, No.2, May 1968, pp. 389–416.

Investment Company Institute, '2001 Profile of Mutual Fund Shareholders', *Fundamentals* [Investment Company Institute's magazine], Volume 10, No.4, September 2001.

Markowitz, Harry, 'Portfolio Selection', *Journal of Finance*, No. 1, March 1952, pp. 77–91.

Markowitz, Harry, *Portfolio Selection-Efficient Diversification of Investments* (New York, John Wiley & Sons, 1959).

PriceWaterhouseCoopers, '2001 Hong Kong Survey Results', *Trends in Performance Measurement* (booklet produced by PriceWaterhouseCoopers, 2001).

Multiple Authors, *The Capital Guide to Offshore Funds* (Hong Kong, ISI Publications, 1996).

Multiple Authors, *A Capital Guide to Marketing Unit Trusts and Mutual Funds in Asia* (Hong Kong, ISI Publications, 1998).

Multiple Authors, *The Practitioner's Guide to Mutual Funds in Hong Kong* (Hong Kong, ISI Publications, 1999).

Reilly, Frank K. and Keith C. Brown, *Investment Analysis and Portfolio Management* (USA, The Dryden Press, 1997).

Securities and Futures Commission, *Annual Report*, 2000 and 2001.

Sharpe, William F., 'Mutual Fund Performance', *Journal of Business* 39, No. 1, Part 2, January 1966, pp. 119–138.

Treynor, Jack L., 'How to Rate Management of Investment Funds', *Harvard Business Review* 43, No. 1, Jan to Feb 1965, pp. 63–75.

Chapter 5

Ando, Albert and Franco Modigliani, 'The Life Cycle Hypothesis of Savings: Aggregate Implications and Tests', *American Economic Review*, Volume 53, Number 1, March 1963, pp. 55–84.

Bassett, William F., Michael J. Fleming, and Anthony P. Rodrigues, 'How Workers Use 401(k) Plans: The Participation, Contribution, and Withdrawal Decisions', *National Tax Journal*, Volume 51, Number 2, June 1998, pp. 263–89.

Baum, Stanley D., 'Renewed Availability of Section 401(k) Plans Gives Tax-exempt Employers Greater Options, *Journal of Taxation*, Volume 86, Number 4, April 1997, pp. 231–9.

Blanchard, Olivier J. and Stanley Fisher, *Lectures on Macroeconomics* (Cambridge, Massachusetts, MIT Press, 1989).

Bodie, Zvi and E. Philip Davis, *The Foundations of Pension Finance* (Northampton, Massachusetts, Edward Elgar Publishing, 2000).

Bodie, Zvi, Alan J. Marcus, and Robert C. Merton, 'Defined Benefit versus Defined Contribution Pension Plans: What are the Real Trade-offs?', in Bodie, Z., Shoven,

J. B., and Wise, D. A. (eds.), *Pensions in the U.S. Economy* (Chicago, Illinois, University of Chicago Press, 1988).

Chiu, Estella, 'The Mandatory Provident Fund Experience', seminar paper in the 11th East Asian Actuarial Conference, 2001, Hong Kong.

Chow, Nelson W. S., 'Care of the Elderly—Whose Responsibility?', *Hong Kong Journal of Gerontology*, Volume 8, Number 1, June 1994, pp. 12–18.

Chun, May, 'Hong Kong Life Insurers—Change Is Here!', *Asian Insurance Review*, August 2002, pp. 39–40.

Clay, Daniel C. and Jane Vander Haar, 'Patterns of Intergenerational Support and Childbearing in the Third World', *Population Studies*, Volume 47, Number 1, March 1993, pp.67–83.

Davis, E. Philip, 'Policy and Implementation Issued in Reforming Pension Systems', European Bank for Reconstruction and Development Working Paper No. 31, August 1998.

Delsen, Lei and Geneviève Reday-Mulvey (eds.), *Gradual Retirement in the OECD Countries*, (England, Dartmouth Publishing, 1996).

Diamond, Peter A., 'National Debt in a Neoclassical Growth Model', *American Economic Review*, Volume 55, Number 5, December 1965, pp. 1126–50.

Employee Benefit Research Institute, *EBRI Databook on Employee Benefits* (Washington, DC, EBRI, 2001).

Engen, Eric M., William G. Gale, and John Karl Scholz, 'The Illusionary Effects of Saving Incentives on Saving', *Journal of Economics Perspectives*, Volume 10, Number 4, Fall 1996, pp. 113–38.

Fabel, Oliver, *The Economics of Pensions and Variable Retirement Schemes*, (Chichester, England, John Wiley and Sons, 1994).

Harrington, Scott E. and Gregory R. Niehaus, *Risk Management and Insurance*, (Boston, Massachusetts, McGraw-Hill, 1999).

Ho, Lok Sang, 'A Universal Fully Funded Pension Scheme', *Contemporary Economic Policy*, Volume XV, July 1997, pp.13–20.

Hong Kong Federation of Insurers, *Monthly Brief*, Issue No. 66, June 2001.

Hong Kong Government, *Department of Social Welfare Report*, (Hong Kong, Department of Social Welfare, 1998).

Kotlikoff, Laurence J., Avia Spivak, and Laurence H. Summers, 'The Adequacy of Savings', *American Economic Review*, Volume 72, Number 5, December 1982, pp. 1056–69.

Lee, William K. M., 'The Feminization of Poverty among the Elderly Population of Hong Kong', *Asian Journal of Women's Studies*, Volume 7, Number 3, 2001, pp.31–62.

Logan, John R. and Fuqin Bian, 'Family Values and Coresidence with Married Children in Urban China', *Social Forces*, Volume 77, Number 4, June 1999, pp. 1253–82.

Lui, Francis T., *Retirement Protection: a Plan for Hong Kong* (Hong Kong, City University of Hong Kong Press, 1998).

MacPherson, S., 'Social Security in Hong Kong', *Social Policy and Administration*, Volume 27, Number 1, March 1993, pp.50–7.

Mastio, David, 'Lessons Our 401(k)s Taught Us', *Policy Review*, Issue 95, June/July 1999, pp. 37–45.

Milagros, Maruja, B. Asis, Domingo Lita, John Knodel, and Kalyani Mehta, 'Living Arrangements in Four Asian Countries: A Comparative Perspective', *Journal of Cross-Cultural Gerontology*, Volume 10, Number 1&2, April 1995, pp. 145–62.

Modigliani, Franco and Richard Brumberg, 'Utility Analysis and the Consumption Function: An Interpretation of Cross-section Data', in Kenneth K. Kurihara (ed.), *Post-Keynesian Economics* (New Brunswick, New Jersey, Rutgers University Press, 1954).

Ng, Anita C. Y., David R. Phillips, and K. M. William Lee, 'Persistence and Challenges to Filial Piety and Informal Support of Older Persons in a Modern Society: A Case Study in Tuen Mun, Hong Kong', *Journal of Aging Studies*, Volume 16, Number 2, May 2002, pp. 135–53.

Papke, Leslie E., 'Are 401(k) Plans Replacing other Employer-Provided Pensions? Evidence from Panel Data', *Journal of Human Resources*, Volume 34, Number 2, September 1999, pp. 37–45.

Pigou, Arthur C., *The Economics of Welfare*, (London, Macmillan, 1932, 4th Ed.).

Posner, Richard A., *Aging and Old Age* (Chicago, Illinois, The University of Chicago Press, 1995).

Poterba, James M., Steven F. Venti and David A. Wise, 'Saver Behavior and 401(k) Retirement Wealth', *American Economic Review*, Volume 90, Number 2, May 2000, pp. 297–302.

Poterba, James M., Steven F. Venti, and David A. Wise, 'How Retirement Saving Programs Increase Saving', *Journal of Economics Perspectives*, Volume 10, Number 4, Fall 1996, pp. 91–112.

Poterba, James M., Steven F. Venti, and David A. Wise, 'Personal Retirement Savings Programs and Asset Accumulation: Reconciling Evidence', in David A. Wise (ed.), *Frontier in the Economics of Aging*, (Chicago, Illinois, University of Chicago Press, 1998).

Reday-Mulvey, Geneviève, 'Studies on the Four Pillars: Editorial', *The Geneva Papers on Risk and Insurance: Issues and Practice*, Volume 26, Number 4, October 2001, pp. 515–16.

Samuelson, Paul, 'An Exact Consumption-Loan Model of Interest with or without the Social Contrivance of Money', *Journal of Political Economy*, Volume 66, Number 6, December 1958, pp. 467–82.

Strotz, R. H., 'Myopia and Inconsistency in Dynamic Utility Maximization', *The Review of Economic Studies*, Volume 23, Issue 3, 1955–56, pp. 165–80.

Tan, Paul, Fiona Loughrey, and David Clark, *Hong Kong Retirement Schemes*, (Hong Kong, Baker and McKenzie in association with Asia Information Associates Limited, 1995).

Wang, Jennifer L., 'An Analysis of the Substitution and Supplemental Effects between 401(k) and other Employer's Pension Plans', *Journal of Insurance Issue*, 2002, Spring Issue (March), pp. 24–46.

World Bank, *Averting the Old-Age Crisis: Policies to Protect the Old and Promote Growth*, (Oxford, Oxford University Press, 1994).

Yip, Paul S. F., Joseph Lee, Beda Chan, and Jade Au, 'A Study of Demographic Changes under Sustained Below-Replacement Fertility in Hong Kong SAR', *Social Science and Medicine*, Volume 53, October 2001, pp. 1003–9.

Yiu, Enoch (2001a), 'MPFA faces merger with Insurance Body', *South China Morning Post*, Business Main, Page 1, 4 June 2001.

Yiu, Enoch (2001b), 'Unhappy Birthday', *South China Morning Post*, Business 2, Page 1, 30 November 2001.

Chapter 6

Beenstock, Michael, Gerry Dickinson, and Sajay Khajuria, 'The Determination of Life Premiums: An International Cross-Section Analysis', *Insurance: Mathematics and Economics*, Volume 5, October 1986, pp. 261–70.

Brown, Jeffrey R. and Austan Goolsbee, 'Does the Internet Make Markets More Competitive? Evidence from the Life Insurance Industry', *Journal of Political Economy*, Volume 110, number 3, June 2002, pp. 481–507.

Browne, Mark J., JaeWook Chung, and Edward W. Frees, 'International Property-Liability Insurance Consumption', *Journal of Risk and Insurance*, Volume 67, Number 1, March 2000, pp. 73–90.

Browne, Mark J. and Kihong Kim, 'An International Analysis of Life Insurance Demand', *Journal of Risk and Insurance*, Volume 60, Number 4, December 1993, pp. 617–34.

Doherty, Neil A., *Integrated Risk Management: Techniques and Strategies for Reducing Risk* (New York, McGraw-Hill, 2000).

Harrington, Scott E. and Gregory R. Niehaus, *Risk Management and Insurance* (Boston, Massachusetts, McGraw-Hill, 1999).

Holloway, Richard and Heerak Basu, 'Annuities in Asia Pacific', seminar paper in the 11th East Asian Actuarial Conference, October 2001, Hong Kong.

Hong Kong Federation of Insurers, *Monthly Brief*, Issue No. 66, June 2001.

Koh, Wendy, 'Bancassurance in Asia to Grow Rapidly', *Asia Insurance Review*, Volume 11, Number 12, December 2001, p. 31.

Kreps, David M., *A Course in Microeconomic Theory* (London, Harvester Wheatsheaf, 1990).

Lui, Marina L. W., 'Towards Professionalism: Mandatory Education for Insurance Intermediaries in Hong Kong Special Administrative Region People's Republic of China', seminar paper presented in the 6th Asia-Pacific Risk and Insurance Association Annual Conference, Shanghai, July 2002.

Mas-Colell, Andreu, Michael D. Whinston, and Jerry R. Green, *Microeconomic Theory* (New York, Oxford University Press, 1995).

Mossin, Jan, 'Aspects of Rational Insurance Purchasing', *Journal of Political Economy*, Volume 76, Number 4, Part I, July to August 1968, pp. 553–68.

Office of the Commissioner of Insurance, *Annual Report*, 2000 and 2001(a).

Office of the Commissioner of Insurance, *Hong Kong: An Ideal Domicile for Captives* (OCI promotional pamphlet), 2001(b).

Pope, Nat, *A Report on the Australian Reinsurance Marketplace*, study commissioned by the Insurance Council of Australia, August 2000.

Ramos, Laura, 'Getting Serious about PDAs for Insurance Applications', *Asia Insurance Review*, Volume 12, Number 6, June 2002, pp. 26–8.

Rejda, George E., *Principles of Risk Management and Insurance*, (Boston, Massachusetts, Addison Wesley, 2001).

Swiss Re, 'World Insurance in 2000: Another Boom Year for Life Insurance; Return to Normal Growth for Non-Life Insurance', *Sigma*, No. 6/2001, November 2001.

Swiss Re, 'Insurance Markets in Asia: Sanguine Outlook despite Short-term Uncertainties', *Sigma*, No. 4/2001, June 2001.

Swiss Re, 'Asia's Insurance Markets after the Storm', *Sigma*, No. 5/1999, September 1999.

Swiss Re, 'The Global Reinsurance market in the midst of Consolidation', *Sigma*, No. 9/1998, October 1998.

Swiss Re, 'Asia's Insurance Industry on the Rise: Into the Next Millennium with Robust Growth', *Sigma*, No. 6/1996, August 1996.

Trowbridge Consulting and Deacons, *Review of Employees' Compensation System in Hong Kong*, (Hong Kong, Hong Kong Federation of Insurers, 2000).

Varian, Hal R., *Microeconomic Analysis*, 3rd edition (New York, W. W. Norton and Company, 1992).

Wong, Jim H. Y., 'Hong Kong's Insurance Industry', in Ho., Y. K., R. H. Scott, and K. A. Wong (eds.), *The Hong Kong Financial System* (Hong Kong, Oxford University Press, 1991).

Yip, C. W., *An Analysis of the Structure of Hong Kong Insurance Market and Its Commercial Prospects for Foreign Insurance Companies*, MA thesis, School of Accounting, Banking, and Economics, University of Wales.

Yu, Ben T., *Institutional Development of the Insurance Industry* (Hong Kong, City University of Hong Kong, 1997).

Chapter 7

Fabozzi, Frank J. and Franco Modigliani, *Capital Markets* (New Jersey, Prentice-Hall, 2003, 3rd Ed.; Chapter 20).

Hong Kong Monetary Authority, *Exchange Fund Bills Programme: Information Memoranda*, Hong Kong Monetary Authority, 1998, available online at: http://www.info.gov.hk/hkma/eng/public/index.htm.

Jiang, Giorong, Nancy Tang, and Eve Law, 'Hong Kong Dollar Debt Market Developments in 2001', Hong Kong Monetary Authority, *Quarterly Bulletin*, February 2002, pp. 1–7.

Lui, Y. H., *The Hong Kong Financial System* (Hong Kong, Hong Kong Commercial Press, 1989).

Scott, Robert Haney, *Money, Financial Markets and the Economy* (Singapore, Prentice-Hall, 1995; Chapter 8).

Scott, William L., *Markets and Institutions: A Contemporary Introduction to Financial Services* (Cincinnati, South-Western Publishing Company, 1999, 2nd Ed.; Chapter 14).

Stigum, Marcia, *The Money Market* (Homewood, Illinois, Dow Jones-Irwin, 1983).

Chapter 8

Allen, H. and M. P. Taylor, 'Chart Analysis and the Foreign Exchange Market', *Review of Futures Markets*, Volume 8, 1989, pp. 288–319.

Bank for International Settlements, 'Triennial Central Bank Survey: Foreign Exchange and Derivatives Market Activities in 2001', March 2002.

Bernhardsen, T., 'The Relationship between Interest Rate Differentials and Macroeconomic Variables: A Panel Data Study for European Countries', *Journal of International Money and Finance*, Volume 19, 2000, pp. 289–308.

Bilson, J., 'The Speculative Efficiency Hypothesis', *Journal of Business*, Volume 54, 1981, pp. 435–51.

Chen, J. and N. C. Mark, 'Alternative Long-Horizon Exchange-Rate Predictors', *International Journal of Finance and Economics*, Volume 1, No. 4, 1996, pp. 229–50.

Chiang, T. C., 'The Forward Rate as a Predictor of the Future Spot Rate—A Stochastic Coefficient Approach', *Journal of Money, Credit and Banking*, Volume 20, 1988, pp. 212–32.

Chinn, M. D. and R. A. Messe, 'Banking on Currency Forecasts: How Predictable is Change in Money?', *Journal of International Economics*, Volume 38, No. 1, 1995, pp. 53–69.

Diebold, F. X. and J. A. Nason, 'Nonparametric Exchange Rate Prediction?', *Journal of International Economics*, Volume 28, No. 3–4, 1990, pp. 315–32.

Dooley, M. P. and J. Shafer, 'Analysis of Short-run Exchange Rate Behavior', in D. Bigman and T. Taya (eds.), *Exchange Rate and Trade Instability* (USA, Ballinger, 1973).

Fama, E. F., 'Efficient Capital Markets: A Review of Theory and Empirical Work', *Journal of Finance*, Volume 25, 1970, pp. 383–417.

Froot K. A. and R. H. Thaler, 'Anomalies: Foreign Exchange', *Journal of Economic Perspectives*, Volume 2, 1990, pp. 179–92.

Frankel, J. A. and K. A. Froot, 'The Rationality of The Foreign Exchange Rate—Chartists, Fundamentalists, and Trading in the Foreign Exchange Market', *American Economic Review*, Volume 18, No. 2, 1990, pp. 181–5.

Hansen, L. P. and R. J. Hodrick, 'Foreign Exchange Rates as Optimal Predictors of Future Spot Rates: An Econometric Analysis', *Journal of Political Economy*, Volume 88, 1980, pp. 829–53.

Ho, Y. K., 'The Money Market and the Foreign Exchange Market', in R. H. Scott, K. A. Wong, and Y. K. Ho, (eds.), *Hong Kong's Financial Institutions and Markets* (Hong Kong, Oxford University Press, 1986; pp. 79–103).

Hong Kong Monetary Authority, *Monthly Statistical Bulletin*, various issues.

Hong Kong Census and Statistics Department, 'Balance of Payments for 1997', Press Release, April 1999.

Hong Kong Census and Statistics Department, 'Balance of Payments Accounts for 4th Quarter 2001', Press Release, March 2002.

Hong Kong Census and Statistics Department, *Interpreting the Capital and Financial Account of Balance of Payments Statistics*, Department Publication, January 2001.

Hong Kong Census and Statistics Department, *Interpreting the Current Account of Balance of Payments Statistics*, Department Publication, January 2001.

Hong Kong Census and Statistics Department, *Tables for Balance of Payments Account*, Department Publication, various issues.

Hsu, H. C., 'Earnings Surprises and Stock Returns: Some Evidence from Asia/Pacific and Europe', *B>QUEST [Business Quest* online journal], 2001.

Jao, Y. C., *The Future of Hong Kong's Economy* (Hong Kong, Joint Publishing (HK) Co, Ltd, 1993).

James, G. R., 'Empirical Implications of Efficient Markets Models', *Alternative Prospectives on Finance and Accounting*, Vol. 1, No. 4, 2001, pp. 1–8.

Kohlhagen, S. W., *The Behavior of Foreign Exchange Markets: A Critical Survey of the Empirical Literature*, (New York, New York University Press, 1978).

Lee, C. I., K. C. Gleason, and I. Mathur, 'Trading Rule Profits in Latin American Currency Spot Rates', *International Review of Financial Analysis*, Volume 10, 2001, pp. 135–56.

Lee, C. I. and I. Mathur, 'Trading Rule Profits in European Currency Spot Cross-Rates', *Journal of Banking and Finance*, Volume 20, 1996, pp. 949–62.

Levi, M. D, *International Finance* (USA, McGraw-Hill, 1990).

Levich, R. M., 'Are Forward Exchange Rates Unbiased Predictors of Future Spot Rates', *The Columbia Journal of World Business*, Volume 14, 1979, pp. 49–61.

Levich, R. M. and L. R. Thomas, 'The Significance of Technical Trading Rule Profits in The Foreign Exchange Market: A Bootstrap Approach', *Journal of International Money and Finance*, Volume 12, 1993, pp. 451–74.

Lui, Y. H., 'The Foreign Exchange Market', in Y. K. Ho, R. H. Scott, and K.A. Wong (eds.), *The Hong Kong Financial System* (Hong Kong, Oxford University Press, 1991; pp. 187–214).

MacDonald, R. and M. P. Taylor, 'Risk, Efficiency and Speculation in the 1920s Foreign Exchange Market: An Overlapping Data Analysis', *Weltwirtschaftliches Archive*, Volume 127, 1991, pp. 500–23.

Mark, N. C., 'Exchange Rates and Fundamentals: Evidence on Long-Horizon Predictability', *American Economic Review*, Volume 85, No. 1, 1995, pp. 201–18.

Mark, N.C. and D. Sul, 'Nominal Exchange Rate and Monetary Fundamentals: Evidence from a Small Post-Bretton Woods Panel', *Journal of International Economics*, Volume 53, 2001, pp. 29–52.

Martin, A. D., 'Technical Trading Rules in The Spot Foreign Exchange Markets of Developing Countries', *Journal of Multinational Financial Management*, Volume 11, 2001, pp. 59–68.

Messe, R. A. and K. Rogoff, 'Was it Real? The Exchange-Rate Interest Differential Relation over the Modern Floating-Rate Period', *Journal of Finance*, Volume 43, No. 4, 1988, pp. 933–48.

Raj, M., 'Transactions Data Tests of Efficiency: An Investigation in the Singapore Futures Markets', *Journal of Futures Markets*, Volume 20, 2000, pp. 687–703.

Sweeney, R. J., 'Beating the Foreign Exchange Market', *Journal of Finance*, Volume 41, 1986, pp. 163–82.

Sweeney, R. J., 'Some New Filter Rule Tests: Methods and Results', *Journal of Financial and Quantitative Analysis*, Volume 23, No. 3, 1988, pp. 285–300.

Schulmeister, S., 'Currency Speculation and Dollar Fluctuations', *Quarterly Review* (Banca Nazional del Lavoro), No. 167, 1988, pp. 343–65.

Taylor, S. J., 'Trading Futures Using a Channel Rule: A Study of The Predictive Power of Technical Analysis with Currency Examples', *Journal of Futures Markets*, Volume 14, No. 2, 1994, pp. 215–35.

Yam, Joseph, *Hong Kong's Linked Exchange Rate System*, Hong Kong Monetary Authority publication, November 2000.

Chapter 9

Greenspan, Alan, 'Global Challenges', Remarks at the Financial Crisis Conference, Council on Foreign Relations, New York, 12 July 2000.

Jiang, G.R., Nancy Tang, and Eva Low, 'Cost–Benefit of Developing Debt Market', *Quarterly Bulletin*, Hong Kong Monetary Authority, November 2001.

Hong Kong Monetary Authority, 'Hong Kong Debt Market Developments in 1999' (also 2000 and 2001), *Quarterly Bulletin*, May 2000, February 2001, and February 2002.

Chapter 10

Aggarwal, R. and P. Rivoli, 'Fads in the Initial Public Offering Market?', *Financial Management*, Volume 19, 1990, pp. 45–57.

Aggarwal, R., R. Leal, and L. Hernandez, 'The After-Market Performance of Initial Public Offerings in Latin America', *Financial Management*, Volume. 22, 1993, pp. 42–53.

Allen, F. and G. Faulhaber, 'Signaling by Underpricing in the IPO Market', *Journal of Financial Economics*, Vol 23, 1989, pp. 303–23.

Ang, J. and T. Schwarz, 'Risk Aversion, Information Structure: An Experimental Study of Price Variability in Securities Markets', *The Journal of Finance*, Volume 40, 1985, pp. 825–44.

Baron, D. P., 'A Model of the Demand for Investment Banking Advising and Distribution Services for New Issues', *The Journal of Finance*, Volume 37, No: 4, 1982, pp. 955–76.

Baron, D. P., 'The Incentive Problem and the Design of the Investment Banking Contracts', *Journal of Banking and Finance*, Volume 3, 1979, pp. 157–75.

Baron, D. P. and B. Holmström, 'The Investment Banking Contract for New Issues Under Asymmetric Information: Delegation and The Incentive Problem', *The Journal of Finance*, 35, No: 6, 1980, pp. 1115–38.

Beatty, R. P. and J. R. Ritter, 'Investment Banking Reputation, and the Underpricing of Initial Public Offerings', *Journal of Financial Economics,* Volume 15, 1986, pp. 213–32.

Black, F., 'Noise', *The Journal of Finance*, Volume 41, 1986, pp. 529–44.

Beckman, J., J. Garner, B. Marshall, and H. Okamura, 'The Influence of Underwriter Reputation, Keiretsu Affiliation, and Financial Health on Underpricing of Japanese IPOs', *Pacific-Basin Finance Journal*, Volume 9, 2001, pp. 513–34.

Block, S. and M. Stanley, 'The Financial Characteristics and Price Movement Patterns of Companies Approaching the Unseasoned Securities Market in the late 1970s', *Financial Management*, Volume 9, 1980, pp. 30–6.

Booth, J. R., and L. Chua, 'Ownership Dispersion, Costly Information, and IPO Underpricing', *Journal of Financial Economics*, Volume 41, 1996, pp. 291–310.

Brennan, M. J. and J. Franks, 'Underpricing, Ownership and Control in Initial Public Offerings of Equity Securities in the U.K.', *Journal of Financial Economics*, Volume 45, 1997, pp. 391–413.

Buckland, R., P. J. Herbert, and K. A. Yeomans, 'Price Discounts on New Issue in the UK and their Relationship to Investor Subscription in the Period 1965–75', *Journal of Business Finance Accounting*, Volume 8, 1981, pp. 79–95.

Cai, J. and K. C. J. Wei, 'The Investment and Operating Performance of Japanese Initial Public Offerings,' *Pacific-Basin Finance Journal*, Volume 5, 1997, pp. 389–417.

Camerer, C., 'Bubbles and Fads in Asset Prices: Review of Theory and Evidence', *Journal of Economic Surveys*, March 1989, pp. 3–41.

Carter, R. B. and S. Manaster, 'Initial Public Offerings and Underwriter Reputation', *Journal of Finance*, Volume 45, 1990, pp. 1045–67.

Cheng, T. Y. and M. Firth, 'An empirical analysis of the bias and rationality of profit forecasts published in new issue prospectuses', *Journal of Business Finance and Accounting*, Volume 27, 2000, pp. 423–46.

Cheung, Y. L., S. L. Cheung, and R. Y. K. Ho, 'Listing Requirements, Uncertainty, and Underpricing of IPOs', mimeo, City Polytechnic of Hong Kong, 1993.

Clarkson, P. M. and J. Merkley, 'Ex Ante Uncertainty and the Underpricing of Initial Public Offerings: Further Canadian Evidence', *Canadian Journal of Administrative Sciences*, Volume 11, No. 1, 1994, pp. 54–67.

Dawson, S. M., 'Secondary Stock Market Performance of Initial Public Offers, Hong Kong, Singapore, and Malaysia: 1978–1984', *Journal of Business Finance and Accounting*, Volume 14, 1987, pp. 65–76.

Dawson, S. M. and T. Hiraki, 'Selling Unseasoned New Issue Shares in Hong Kong and Japan: A test of Primary Market Efficiency and Underpricing', *Hong Kong Journal of Business Management*, 3, 1985, p. 125–34.

Davis, E. W. and K. A. Yeomans, 'Market Discount on New Issues of Equity: The Influence of Firm Size, Method of Issue and Market Volatility', *Journal of Business Finance and Accounting,* Volume 3, 1976, pp. 27–42.

De Bond, W. and R. Thaler, 'Does the Stock Market Overreact?', *Journal of Finance*, Volume 40, 1985, pp. 793–805.

De Bond, W. and R. Thaler, 'New Evidence on Investor Overreaction and Stock Market Seasonality', *Journal of Finance*, Volume 42, 1987, pp. 557–81.

De Bond, W. and R. Thaler, 'A Mean-Reverting Walk Down Wall Street', *Journal of Economic Perspectives*, Winter 1989, pp. 189–202.

Dimson, E., 'Risk Measurement when Shares are Subject to Infrequent Trading', *Journal of Financial Economics*, Volume 7 No. 2, 1979, pp. 197–226.

Finn, F. J. and R. Higham, 'The Performance of Unseasoned New Equity Issue-cum-Stock Exchange Listing in Australia', *Journal of Banking and Finance*, Volume 12, 1988, pp. 333–51.

Garfinkel, J. A., 'IPO Underpricing, Insider Selling and Subsequent Equity Offerings: Is Underpricing a Signal or Quality?', *Financial Management*, Volume 22, 1993, pp. 74–83.

Grinblatt, M. and C. Y. Hwang, 'Signalling and the Pricing of the New Issues', *Journal of Finance*, Volume 44, 1989, pp. 393–420.

Grossman, S. and O. Hart, 'Takeover Bids, the Free-Rider Problem and the Theory of Corporation', *Bell Journal of Economics*, Volume 11, 1980, pp. 42–64.

Hameed, A. and G. H. Lim, 'Underpricing and Firm Quality in Initial Public Offerings: Evidence from Singapore', *Journal of Business Finance and Accounting*, Volume 25, 1998, pp. 455–68.

Hamao, Y., F. Packer, and J. R. Ritter, 'Institutional affiliation and the role of venture capital: Evidence from public offerings in Japan', *Pacific-Basin Finance Journal*, Volume 8, 2000, pp. 529–58.

Hansen, R. S. and C. Crutchley, 'Corporate Earnings and Financing: An Empirical Analysis', *Journal of Business*, Volume 63, 1990, pp. 347–71.

Harris, M. and A. Raviv, 'The Design of Securities', *Journal of Financial Economics*, Volume 24, 1989, pp. 255–87.

Hin, T.C. and H. Mahmood, 'The Long-Run Performance of Initial Public Offerings in Singapore', *Security Industry Review*, Volume 19, 1993, p. 47–58.

Holmén, M. and P. Högfeldt, 'Corporate Control and Security Design in Initial Public Offerings, *Proceedings, ABN AMRO International Conference on Initial Public Offerings*, University of Amsterdam, July 2000.

HKEx/Stock Exhange of Hong Kong, *Annual Report*, 1997 to 2001.

HKEx/Stock Exchange of Hong Kong, *Fact Book*, various issues from 1986 to 2001.

HKEx/Stock Exchange of Hong Kong, 'The 1998/1999 Review of Certain Chapters of the Rules Governing the Listing of Securities on the Stock Exchange of Hong Kong Limited', Consultation Paper, available online at: http://www.HKEx.com.

HKEx/Stock Exchange of Hong Kong, 'Rules Governing the Listing of Securities', old edition (1991) and updated edition (2003).

How, J. C. Y. and J. G. Low, 'Fractional Ownership and Underpricing: Signals of IPO Firm Value', *Pacific Basin, Finance Journal*, 1(1), 1993, p. 47–65.

Ibbotson, R. G., 'Price performance of Common Stock New Issues', *Journal of Financial Economics*, Volume 2, 1975, pp. 235–72.

Ibbotson, R. G. and J. F. Jaffe, 'Hot Issues Markets', *Journal of Finance*, Volume 30, 1975, pp. 1027–42

Jain, B. A., and O. Kini, 'The Post–Issue Operating Performance of IPO Firms', *Journal of Finance*, Volume 49, 1994, pp. 1699–726.

James, C., 'Relationship-Specific Assets and the Pricing of Underwriter Services', *The Journal of Finance*, Volume 47, No: 5, 1992, pp. 1865–85.

James, C. and Peggy Wier, 'Borrowing Relationships, Intermediation, and Cost of Issuing Public Securities', *Journal of Financial Economics*, Volume 28, 1990, pp. 149–71.

Jegadeesh, N., M. Weinstein, and I. Welch, 'An Empirical Investigation of IPO Returns and Subsequent Equity Offerings', *Journal of Financial Economics*, Volume 34, 1993, pp. 153–75.

Jenkinson, T., 'Initial Public Offerings in the United Kingdom, United States, and Japan', *Journal of Japanese and International Economics*, Volume 4, 1990, pp. 428–49.

Jensen, M. and W. Meckling, 'Theory of The Firm: Managerial Behaviour, Agency Cost, and Ownership Structure', *Journal of Financial Economics*, Volume 3, 1976, pp. 306–60.

Johnson, J. M. and R. E. Miller, 'Investment Banker Prestige and the Underpricing of Initial Public Offerings', *Financial Management*, Volume 17, 1988, pp. 19–29.

Keasey, K. and H. Short, 'Equity Retention and Initial Public Offerings: The Influence of Signalling and Entrenchment', *Applied Financial Economics*, Volume 7, 1997, pp. 75–85.

Keloharju, M., 'The Winner's Curse, Legal Liability, and the Long-run Price Performance of Initial Public Offerings in Finland', *Journal of Financial Economics*, Volume 34, 1993(a), pp. 251–77.

Keloharju, M., 'Initial IPO Returns and the Characteristics of Post-IPO Financing in Finland', mimeo, Helsinki School of Economics and Business Administration, 1993(b).

Kim, J., I. Krinsky, and L. Jason, 'Motives for Going Public and Underpricing: New Findings from Korea', *Journal of Business Finance and Accounting*, Volume 20, 1993, pp. 195–211.

Kim, J., I. Krinsky, and L. Jason, 'The Aftermarket Performance of Initial Public Offerings in Korea', *Pacific-Basin Finance Journal*, Volume 3, 1995, pp. 449–8.

Koh, F. and T. Walter, 'A Direct Test of Rock's Model of the Pricing of Unseasoned Issues', *Journal of Financial Economics*, Volume 23, 1989, pp. 429–48.

Lee, P. J., S. Taylor, and T. S. Walter, 'Expected and Realised Returns for Singaporean IPOs: Initial and Long-run Analysis', *Pacific-Basin Finance Journal,* Volume 4, 1996a, pp. 153–80.

Lee, P. J., S. Taylor, and T. S. Walter, 'Australian IPO Pricing in the Short and Long Run' *Journal of Banking & Finance* Volume 20, 1996b, pp. 1189–210.

Leland, H. and D. Pyle, 'Information Asymmetries, Financial Structure, and Financial Intermediation', *The Journal of Finance,* Volume 32, No. 2, 1977, pp. 371–87.

Levis, M., 'The Winner's Curse Problem, Interest Cost, and the Underpricing of Initial Public Offerings,' *Economic Journal,* Volume 100, 1990, pp. 76–89.

Levis, M., 'The Long-Run Performance of Initial Public Offerings: The UK Experience 1980–1988', *Financial Management,* Volume 22, 1993, pp. 28–41.

Levis, M., 'Seasoned Equity Offerings and the Short and Long-Run Performance of Initial Public Offerings in the U.K.', *European Financial Management,* Volume 1, 1995 pp. 125–6.

Ljungqvist, A. P., 'Pricing Initial Public Offerings: Further Evidence from Germany', *European Economic Review,* Volume 41, No: 7, July 1997, pp. 1309–20.

Logue, D. E., 'On the Pricing of Unseasoned Equity Issues: 1965–1969', *Journal of Financial and Quantitative Analysis,* Volume 8, 1973, pp. 91–103.

Loughran, T. and J. R. Ritter, 'The Operating Performance of Firms Conducting Seasoned Equity Offerings', *The Journal of Finance,* Volume 52, 1997, pp. 1823–49.

Loughran, T. and J. R. Ritter, 'The New Issue Puzzle', *The Journal of Finance,* Volume 50, 1995, pp. 23–51.

Loughran, T. and J. R. Ritter, 'Why Don't Issuers Get Upset about Leaving Money on the Table in IPOs?', *The Review of Financial Studies,* Volume 15, 2002, pp. 413–43

Loughran, T. and J. R. Ritter, 'The Timing and Subsequent Performance of New Issues: Implications for the Cost of Equity Capital', Unpublished Manuscript, University of Illinois at Urbana-Champaign, July 1993.

Loughran, T., J. R. Ritter and Rydqvist, K., 'Initial Public Offerings: International Insights', *Pacific Basin Finance Journal,* Volume 2, 1994, pp. 165–99.

McDonald, J. G. and A. K. Fisher, 'New-Issue Stock Price Behaviour', *The Journal of Finance,* Volume 27, 1972, pp. 97–102.

McGuinness, P., 'Investor- and Issuer-Related Perspectives of IPO Underpricing', *Omega International Journal of Management Science,* Volume 21, 1993, pp. 377–92.

McGuinness, P., 'An Examination of the Underpricing of Initial Public Offerings in Hong Kong: 1980–90', *Journal of Business Finance and Accounting,* Volume 19, No: 2, 1992, pp. 165–86.

McGuinness, P., *A Guide to the Equity Markets of Hong Kong* (Oxford University Press, 1999).

Michaely, R. and W. H. Shaw, 'The Pricing of Initial Pubic Offerings: Tests of Adverse-Selection and Signalling Theories', *Review of Financial Studies,* Volume 7, 1994, pp. 279–319.

Michaely, R. and W. H. Shaw, 'Asymmetric Information, Adverse Selection, and the Initial Public Offerings', mimeo, Cornell University, 1992.

Mikkelson, W. H., M. M. Partch, and K. Shah, 'Ownership and Operating Performance of Companies that Go Public', *Journal of Financial Economics,* Volume 44, 1997, pp. 281–307.

Miller, R. E., 'Risk, Uncertainty, and Divergence of Opinion', *Journal of Finance,* Volume 32, 1977, pp. 1151–68.

Miller, R. E. and Reilly, F. K., 'An Examination of Mispricing, Returns, and Uncertainty for Initial Public Offerings', *Financial Management,* Volume 16, 1987, pp. 33–8.

Mok, Henry M. K. and Y. Hui, 'Ex-Ante Risk and Underpricing of IPOs in Shenzhen, China', *Hong Kong Journal of Business Management,* Volume XV, 1997, pp. 41–57.

Muscarella, C. J. and M. R. Vetsuypens, 'A Simple Test of Baron's Model of IPO Underpricing', *Journal of Financial Economics*, Volume 24, 1989, pp. 125–35.

Neuberger, B. M. and C. T. Hammond, 'A Study of Underwriters' Experience with Unseasoned New Issues', *Journal of Financial and Quantitative Analysis*, Volume 9, 1974, pp. 165–77.

Neuberger, B. M. and C. A. LaChapelle, 'Unseasoned New Issue Price Performance on Three Tiers: 1975–1980', *Financial Management*, Volume 12, 1983, pp. 23–8.

Pagano, M, F. Panetta, and L. Zingales, 'Why Do Companies Go Public? An Empirical Analysis', *The Journal of Finance*, Volume 53, No: 1, 1998, pp. 27–64.

Paudyal, K., B. Saadouni and R. J. Briston, 'Privatisation of Initial Public Offerings in Malaysia: Initial Premium and Long-term Performance', *Pacific-Basin Finance Journal*, Volume 6, 1998, pp. 427–51.

Ritter, J. R., 'The Hot Issue Market of 1980', *The Journal of Business*, Volume 57, 1984, pp. 215–240.

Ritter, J. R., 'The Long-Run Performance of Initial Public Offerings', *The Journal of Finance*, Volume 46, No: 1, 1991, pp. 3–27.

Rock, K., 'Why New Issues Are Underpriced', *Journal of Financial Economics*, Volume 15, 1986, pp. 187–212.

Saunders, A. and J. Lim, 'Underpricing and the New Issue Process in Singapore', *Journal of Banking and Finance*, Volume 14, 1990, p.291–309.

Scholes, M. and J. Williams, 'Estimating Beta from Nonsynchronous Data', *Journal of Financial Economics*, Volume 5, 1977, PP. 309–27.

Shleifer, A. and R. W. Vishny, 'Large Shareholders and Corporate Control', *Journal of Political Economy*, Volume 94, No: 3, 1986, pp. 461–88.

Slovin, M. B. and J. E. Yong, 'Bank Lending and Initial Public Offerings', *Journal of Banking and Finance,* Volume 14, 1990, pp. 729–40.

Slovin, M. B., M. E. Sushka, and Y. M. Bendeek, 'Seasoned Common Stock Issuance Following an IPO', *Journal of Banking and Finance*, Volume 18, 1994, pp. 207–26.

Smart, S. B. and C. J. Zutter, 'Control as Motivation for Underpricing: A Comparison of Dual- and Single-Class IPOs', *Proceedings, ABN AMRO International Conference on Initial Public Offerings*, University of Amsterdam, July 2000.

Spence, A. M., *Market Signaling* (Cambridge, Mass., Harvard University Press, 1974).

Truman, B., 'A Theory of Noise Trading in Securities Market', *The Journal of Finance*, Volume 43, 1988, pp. 83–96.

Uddin, Md. Hamid, 'An Investigation on Initial Public Offers in Malaysia', PhD Thesis, National University of Singapore, 2001.

Wasserfallen, W. and Wittleder, C. 'Pricing Initial Public Offerings: Evidence from Germany', *European Economic Review,* Volume 38, 1994, pp. 1505–17.

Welch, I., 'Seasoned Offerings, Imitation Costs, and the Underpricing of Initial Public Offerings', *Journal of Finance*, Volume 44, 1989, pp. 421–49.

Wong, K. A. and H. L. Chiang, 'Pricing of New Equity Issues in Singapore', *Asia Pacific Journal of Management*, Volume 4(1), 1986, pp. 1–10.

Wong, K. A. and D. Xie, 'Initial Underpricing and Long-term Performance of IPOs: Evidence from Shanghai Stock Exchange', Working Paper, National University of Singapore, 2001.

Wong, K. A. and Md. Hamid Uddin, 'The Aftermarket Performance of Initial Public Offerings in Malaysia: Where IPOs Outperform the Market in the Long Run', *Proceedings, ABN AMRO International Conference on Initial Public Offerings*, University of Amsterdam, July 2000.

Wong, K. A. and Md. Hamid Uddin, 'The Effect of Stock Listing Time Lag on IPO Initial Underpricing: Evidence from Malaysia', Working Paper, National University of Singapore, 2002.

Young, L. S. F. and R. Chiang (eds.), *Hong Kong Securities Industry* (The Stock Exchange of Hong Kong and The Chinese University of Hong Kong, 1997).

Zingales, L., 'The Value of Voting Right: A Study of the Milan Stock Exchange Experience', *Review of Financial Studies*, Volume 7, No: 1, 1994, pp. 125–48.

Zingales, L., 'Insider Ownership and the Decision to Go Public', *Review of Economic Studies*, Volume 62, 1995, pp. 425–48.

Chapter 11

Agrawal, A. and K. Tandon, 'Anomalies or Illusions? Evidence from Stock Markets in Eighteen Countries', *Journal of International Money and Finance*, Volume 14, 1994, pp. 83–106.

Ariel, R., 'A Monthly Effect in Stock Returns', *Journal of Financial Economics*, Volume 18, 1987, pp. 161–74.

Ariel, R., 'High Stock Returns before Holidays: Existence and Evidence on Possible Causes', *Journal of Finance*, Volume 45, 1990, pp. 1611–26.

Banz, R. W., 'The Relationship between Return and Market Value of Common Stock', *Journal of Financial Economics*, Volume 9, 1981, pp. 3–18.

Basu, S., 'Investment Performance of Common Stocks in Relation to their Price-Earnings Ratios: A Test of the Efficient Market Hypothesis', *Journal of Finance*, Volume 32, 1977, pp. 663–82.

Black, F., 'Capital Market Equilibrium with Restricted Borrowing', *Journal of Business*, Volume 45, 1972, pp. 444–54.

Black, F., M. Jensen, and M. Scholes, 'The Capital Asset Pricing Model: Some Empirical Tests', in M. Jensen (ed.), *Studies in the Theory of Capital Markets* (New York, Praeger, 1972; pp. 79–121).

Cadsby, C. B. and M. Ratner, 'Turn-of-Month and Pre-Holiday Effects on Stock Returns: Some International Evidence', *Journal of Banking and Finance*, Volume 16, 1992, pp. 497–509.

Cervera, A. and D. B. Keim, 'High Stock Returns before Holidays: International Evidence and Additional Tests', in Keim, D.B. and W.T. Ziemba (eds.), *Security Market Imperfections in World Wide Equity Markets* (Cambridge University Press, 2000; pp. 512–31).

Chan, S.-Y. and W.-M. Fong, 'Reactions of the Hong Kong Stock Market to the Publication of Second-Hand Analysts' Recommendation Information', *Journal of Business Finance and Accounting*, Volume 23, 1996, pp. 1121–39.

Chan, Y.-C., 'Multivariate Testing of the Capital Asset Pricing Model in the Hong Kong Stock Market', *Applied Financial Economics*, Volume 7, 1997, pp. 311–16.

Chen, D. F., 'The Month-of-the-Year Effect as a Profitable Trading Rule in the Hong Kong Common Stock Market', *Hong Kong Journal of Business Management*, Volume 7, 1989, pp. 19–23.

Cheung, Y.-L., 'A Small Cap: A Big Return', *The Securities Journal*, January 1995, pp. 14–16.

Cheung, Y.-L., Y. K. Ho, and K. F. Wong, 'Return and Risk Premium Seasonalities in Three Emerging Asian Markets: Hong Kong, Taiwan and Korea', *Journal of International Financial Management and Accounting*, Volume 5, 1994, pp. 223–41.

Chui, A. C. W. and K. C. J. Wei, 'Book-to-Market, Firm Size, and the Turn-of-the-Year Effect: Evidence from Pacific-Basin Emerging Markets', *Pacific-Basin Finance Journal*, Volume 6, 1998, pp. 275–93.

Constantinides, G., 'Optimal Stock Trading with Personal Taxes: Implications for Prices and Abnormal January Returns', *Journal of Financial Economics*, Volume 13, 1984, pp. 65–89.

Cross, F., 'The Behaviour of Stock Prices on Fridays and Mondays', *Financial Analysts Journal,* Volume 29, 1973, pp. 67–9.

Draper, P. and K. Paudyal, 'Microstructure and Seasonality in the UK Equity Market', *Journal of Business Finance and Accounting,* Volume 24, 1997, pp. 1177–204.

Fama, E. F., 'The Behaviour of Stock Market Prices', *Journal of Business,* Volume 38, 1965, pp. 34–105.

Fama, E. F., 'Efficient Capital Markets: A Review of Theory and Empirical Work', *Journal of Finance,* Volume 25, 1970, pp. 383–417.

Fama, E. F., *Foundations of Finance* (New York, Basic Books, 1976).

Fama, E. F. and K. R. French, 'The Cross-Section of Expected Stock Returns', *Journal of Finance,* Volume 47, 1992, pp. 427–65.

Fama, E. F. and K. R. French, 'Multifactor Explanations of Asset Pricing Anomalies', *Journal of Finance,* Volume 51, 1996, pp. 55–84.

French, K. R., 'Stock Returns and the Weekend Effect', *Journal of Financial Economics,* Volume 8, 1980, pp. 55–70.

Fung, A. K.-W., 'Overreaction in the Hong Kong Stock Market', *Global Finance Journal,* Volume 10, 1999, pp. 223–30.

Gibbons, M. R. and P. Hess, 'Day of the Week Effects and Asset Returns', *Journal of Business,* Volume 54, 1981, pp. 579–96.

Gultekin, M. N. and N. B. Gultekin, 'Stock Market Seasonality: International Evidence', *Journal of Financial Economics,* Volume 12, 1983, pp. 469–81.

Hawawini, G. and D. B. Keim, 'The Cross Section of Common Stock Returns: A Review of the Evidence and Some New Findings', in Keim, D. B. and W. T. Ziemba (eds.), *Security Market Imperfections in World Wide Equity Markets* (Cambridge University Press, 2000; pp. 3–43).

Ho, Y. K., 'Stock Return Seasonalities in Asia Pacific Markets', *Journal of International Financial Management and Accounting,* Volume 2, 1990, pp. 47–77.

Ho, Y. K. and Y. L. Cheung, 'Seasonal Pattern in Volatility in Asian Stock Markets', *Applied Financial Economics,* Volume 4, 1994, pp. 61–7.

Ho, Y.-W., R. Strange, and J. Piesse, 'CAPM Anomalies and the Pricing of Equity: Evidence from the Hong Kong Market', *Applied Economics,* Volume 32, 2000, pp. 1629–36.

Keim, D. B., 'Size-Related Anomalies and Stock Return Seasonality: Further Empirical Evidence', *Journal of Financial Economics,* Volume 12, 1983, pp. 13–32.

Kim, C. and J. Park, 'Holiday Effects and Stock Returns: Further Evidence', *Journal of Financial and Quantitative Analysis,* Volume 29, 1994, pp. 145–57.

Lakonishok, J. and S. Smidt, 'Volume and Turn-of-the-Year Behaviour', *Journal of Financial Economics,* Volume 13, 1984, pp. 435–56.

Lakonishok, J. and S. Smidt, 'Are Seasonal Anomalies Real? A Ninety-Year Perspective', *Review of Financial Studies,* Volume 1, 1988, pp. 403–25.

Lee, I., Pettit, R. R., and M. V. Swankoski, 'Daily Return Relationships among Asian Stock Markets', *Journal of Business Finance and Accounting,* Volume 17, 1990, pp. 265–84.

Lintner, J., 'The Valuation of Risk Assets and the Selection of Risky Investment in Stock Portfolios and Capital Budgets', *Review of Economics and Statistics,* Volume 47, 1965, pp. 13–37.

Lintner, J., 'The Aggregation of Investor's Diverse Judgements and Preferences in Purely Competitive Security Markets', *Journal of Financial and Quantitative Analysis,* Volume 4, 1969, pp. 347–400.

McGuinness, P. B., 'Inter-Day Return Behaviour for Stocks Quoted "Back-to-Back" in Hong Kong and London', *Applied Economics Letters,* Volume 4, 1997, pp. 459–64.

McGuinness, P. B., *A Guide to the Equity Markets of Hong Kong* (Oxford University Press, 1999).

Mok, M. K., 'The Lunar and Western New Year Effects and Influence from Major Markets: A Cross-Country Comparison', *Proceedings of the Third Symposium on Cross-Cultural Consumer and Business Studies,* Hawaii, USA, December 1990, pp. 80–91.

Poterba, J. M. and L. H. Summers, 'The Persistence of Volatility and Stock Market Fluctuations', *American Economic Review,* Volume 76, 1986, pp. 1142–51.

Reinganum, M. R., 'Misspecification of Capital Asset Pricing: Empirical Anomalies Based on Earnings Yields and Market Values', *Journal of Financial Economics,* Volume 9, 1981, pp. 19–46.

Reinganum, M. R., 'The Anomalous Stock Market Behaviour of Small Firms in January: Empirical Tests for Tax-Loss Selling Effects', *Journal of Financial Economics,* Volume 12, 1983, pp. 89–104.

Ritter, J. R. and N. Chopra, 'Portfolio Rebalancing and the Turn-of-the-Year Effect', *Journal of Finance,* Volume 44, 1989, pp. 149–66.

Rogalski, R. J., 'New Findings Regarding Day-of-the-Week Returns over Trading and Non-Trading Periods: A Note', *Journal of Finance,* Volume 39, 1984, pp. 1603–14.

Roll, R., 'Vas ist das? The Turn-of-the-Year Effect and the Return Premia of Small Firms', *Journal of Portfolio Management,* Volume 9, 1983, pp. 18–28.

Ross, S. A., 'The Arbitrage Theory of Capital Asset Pricing', *Journal of Economic Theory,* Volume 13, 1976, pp. 343–62.

Rozeff, M. and W. Kinney, 'Capital Market Seasonality: The Case of Stock Returns', *Journal of Financial Economics,* Volume 3, 1976, pp. 379–402.

Sharpe, W. F., 'A Simplified Model of Portfolio Analysis', *Management Science,* January 1963.

Sharpe, W. F., 'Capital Asset Prices: A Theory of Market Equilibrium under Conditions of Risk, *Journal of Finance,* Volume 19, 1964, pp. 425–42.

Wong, K. A., 'Is There an Intra-Month Effect on Stock Returns in Developing Stock Markets?', *Applied Financial Economics,* Volume 5, 1995, pp. 285–9.

Wong, K. A. and P. C. Ho, 'An Intra-Month Effect in Stock Returns: Evidence from Developing Stock Markets', Working Paper, National University of Singapore, 1999.

Wong, K. A., T. K. Hui, and C. Y. Chan, 'Day-of-the-Week Effects: Evidence from Developing Stock Markets', *Applied Financial Economics,* Volume 2, 1992, pp. 49–56.

Wong, K. A., T. K. Hui, and R. Tao, 'Re-Examination on Size and BTM in Cross-Sectional Stock Returns: Evidence from Hong Kong', Working Paper, National University of Singapore, 2002.

Wong, K. A. and S.-K. Koh, 'Anomalies in Asian Emerging Stock Markets', in Keim, D.B. and W. T. Ziemba (eds.), *Security Market Imperfections in World Wide Equity Markets* (Cambridge University Press, 2000; pp. 433–57).

Young, S. F. L. and R. C. P. Chiang, *The Hong Kong Securities Industry* (The Stock Exchange of Hong Kong Limited and The Chinese University of Hong Kong, 1997, 3rd Ed.).

Chapter 12

Chesterton, Josephine M. and Tushar K. Ghose, *Merchant Banking in Hong Kong* (Singapore, Butterworths Asia, 1998).

Crouchy, Michael, Robert Mark, and Dan Galai, *Risk Management* (New York, McGraw-Hill, 2000).

Fabozzi, Frank J., Franco Modigliani, and Michael G. Ferri, *Foundations of Financial Markets and Institutions* (New Jersey, Prentice-Hall, 1998, 2nd Ed).

Hull, John C., *Introduction to Futures and Options Markets* (New Jersey, Prentice-Hall, 1998, 3rd Ed.).

Kolb, Robert W., *Futures, Options and Swaps* (UK, Blackwell Publishers, 1999, 4th Ed.).

Rose, Peter S., *Commercial Bank Management* (New York, McGraw-Hill Irwin, 2001, 5th Ed.).

Stock Futures and Stock Options (Hong Kong Exchanges, 2001).

Terpstra, Robert H., *Manual of the Hong Kong Securities Industry* (The Stock Exchange of Hong Kong Limited, 1994, 2nd Ed.).

Understanding Stock Options (and Their Risks) (Hong Kong Exchanges, 2001).

Chapter 13

Dealer Training Course Manual, Trading Section (Hong Kong, Hong Kong Futures Exchange Ltd and ICCH, 1985).

Gold Field Mineral Services, 'Hong Kong—Market Introduction', information page on the GoldAvenue Gold Encyclopaedia website, maintained and updated by Gold Field Mineral Services. Available at: http://info.goldavenue.com/Info_site/in_mark/in_ma_hong.htm, last accessed May 2003.

Gold Field Mineral Services, 'London Fixing', information page on the GoldAvenue Gold Encyclopaedia website, maintained and updated by Gold Field Mineral Services. Available at: http://info.goldavenue.com/Info_site/in_mark/in_ma_lond_fix.htm, last accessed May 2003.

Green, Timothy, *The World of Gold Today* (New York, Walker and Company, 1973).

Hong Kong Futures Exchange Quarterly Bulletin, Research Department, Hong Kong Futures Exchange Ltd, March 1988.

Indices and Financial Futures Market Bulletin, Research Department, ICCH (Hong Kong) Ltd, October 1988.

Jastram, R., *The Golden Constant* (New York, John Wiley & Sons, 1977).

Lam, C. M., *Gold and Commodity Investment* (Hong Kong, Man Yuen Publication, 1988).

Man, K. Y., *Bullion Dealings in 24 Hours* (Hong Kong, Kam Ling Publisher, 1987).

Monthly Newsletter, Nos. 116–43, Research Department, Hong Kong Futures Exchange Ltd.

Sherman, Eugene J., *Gold Investment Theory & Application* (New York Institute of Finance, Prentice Hall, 1986).

Sun Hung Kai Securities, *A Survey of the Hong Kong Gold Market* (Hong Kong Sun Hung Kai Securities Limited, March 1981).

Tan, Ronald H. C., *The Gold Market* (Singapore, Singapore University Press, 1982).

Woo, W. F., *The Hong Kong Gold Market* (Hong Kong, Joint Publishing Co Ltd, 1988).

Chapter 14

Anderson, G. A., J. R. Barber, and C. H. Chang, 'Prepayment Risk and the Duration of Default-free Mortgage Backed Securities', *Journal of Financial Research*, Volume 16, 1993, pp.1–9.

Choudhry M., *Bond Market Securities* (London, Financial Times: Prentice Hall, 2001).

Davidson, A. S. and M. D. Herskowitz, *Mortgage-backed Securities* (Chicago, Probus, 1994).

Fabozzi, F. J., *Bond Markets, Analysis and Strategies* (Prentice Hall, 1996, 3rd Ed.).
Fabozzi, F. J. and T. D. Fabozzi (eds.), *The Handbook of Fixed Income* (Irwin, 1995, 4th Ed.).
Fabozzi, F. J. and F. Modigliani, *Mortgage and Mortgage-Backed Securities Markets* (Harvard Business School Press, 1992).
Henderson, J., 'Property Securitisation', *Australian Accountant*, Volume 63, pp. 44–5.
Henderson, J. and J. P. Scott, *Securitization* (Cambridge, Woodhead Faulkner Limited, 1988).
Hong Kong Monetary Authority, *Annual Report*,1993–2000.
Hong Kong Monetary Authority, *Quarterly Bulletin*, 1995–2001.
Hong Kong Mortgage Corporation, *Annual Report*, 1997–2000.
Hong Kong Mortgage Corporation, *Bi-Monthly Report*, 1998–2000.
Hong Kong Mortgage Corporation, *Mortgage Monthly*, Mar 2001 to Dec 2001.
Ming Pao, 'HKMA: A Large Jump in Negative Equities' (in Chinese), Economic Section, 10 July 2003.
Schwartz, E. S. and W. N. Torous, 'Prepayment and the Valuation of Mortgage Pass-through Securities', *Journal of Business*, Volume 65, 1992, pp. 221–39.
Schwartz, E. S. and W. N. Torous, 'Prepayment, Default, and the Calculation of Mortgage Pass-Through Securities', *Journal of Business*, Volume 44, pp. 375–92.
Tsang, S. F., 'Mortgage Backed Securities In Hong Kong', MBA Project, Hong Kong Baptist University, May 1997.

Chapter 15

Allen, J., 'Corporate Governance in Asia: Myth, Fad or Reality?', in *2002 Symposium on Corporate Governance and Disclosure: The Impact of Globalization*, The School of Accountancy, The Chinese University of Hong Kong, February 2002.
Anonymous, 'Corporate Governance in Hong Kong – the Road to Reform Following the Asian Financial Crisis', *International Financial Law Review*, 2001, pp. 53–9.
Apple Daily, 'More Corporate Disclosures, Better Stock Prices', 17 April 2002.
Berle, A. and G. Means, *The Modern Corporation and Private Property* (New York, Macmillan, 1932).
CalPERS, *Corporate Governance Principles and Guidelines* (California Public Employees' Retirement System, 1998).
Carse, D., 'The Role of Good Governance, Disclosure and Transparency in Banking Stability' in *2002 Symposium on Corporate Governance and Disclosure: The Impact of Globalization*, The School of Accountancy, The Chinese University of Hong Kong, February 2002.
Choi, F., 'Financial Report Dimensions of Asia's Financial Crisis', *Proceedings of the 10th Annual Conference of Accounting Academics* (Hong Kong Society of Accountants, 1998).
Chow, P., 'Invest in Corporate Governance: A Perspective from the HK Asset Management Industry' in *2002 Symposium on Corporate Governance and Disclosure: The Impact of Globalization*, The School of Accountancy, The Chinese University of Hong Kong, February 2002.
Claessens, S., S. Djankov, and L. H. P. Lang, 'The Separation of Ownership and Control in East Asian Corporations', *Journal of Financial Economics*, 58, 2000, p. 81.
Claessens, S., S. Djankov, J. P. H. Fan, and L. H. P. Lang, 'Expropriation of Minority Shareholders: Evidence from East Asian Corporation', Working Paper, The World Bank, 1999.

CLSA, *CG Watch: Corporate Governance in Asia* (CLSA, April 2003).

Coffee, J. C., Jr., 'The Future as History: The Prospect for Global Convergence in Corporate Governance', *Corporate Practice Commentator*, Wilmette, 2000, pp. 899–965.

Collier, P., 'Factors Affecting the Formation of Audit Committees in Major UK Listed Companies', *Accounting and Business Research*, Vol. 23, No. 91A, 1993, pp. 421–30.

Crystal, G., *In Search of Success: The Overcompensation of American Executives*, (New York, W. W. Norton and Company, 1991).

Dallas, G., 'Evaluating Asian Corporate Governance in an International Context', in 2002 Symposium on Corporate Governance and Disclosure: The Impact of Globalization, The School of Accountancy, The Chinese University of Hong Kong, February 2002.

Dipiazza, S. A., 'How to Gain The Public's Confidence Again—A Model for Future Corporate Financial Reporting' (in Chinese), *21st Century Economic Report*, 15 July 2002.

Eccles, R. G. and S. C. Mavrinac, 'Improving the Corporate Disclosure Process', *Sloan Management Review*, Summer 1995, pp.11–24.

Ezzamel, M. and R. Watson, 'Executive Remuneration and Corporate Performance' in K. Keasey and M. Wright (eds.), *Corporate Governance: Responsibilities, Risks and Remuneration* (London, John Wiley & Sons Ltd, 1997; pp. 61–92).

The Economist, 'Asian Business: in Praise of Rules', 7 April 2001, pp. 2–18.

Fama, E. F., 'Agency Problems and the Theory of the Firm', *Journal of Political Economy*, 88(2), 1980, pp. 288–307.

Fama, E. F. and M. C. Jensen, 'Separation of Ownership and Control', *Journal of Law and Economics*, 26, 1983(a), pp. 301–26.

Fama, E. F. and M. C. Jensen, 'Agency Problems and Residual Claims', *Journal of Law and Economics*, 26, 1983(b), pp. 327–49.

Fan, J. P. H. and T. J. Wong , 'Corporate Ownership and the Informativeness of Accounting Earnings', Working Paper, Department of Accounting, The Hong Kong University of Science and Technology, 1999.

Ferguson, N., 'Cleaning up Hong Kong's Companies', *International Financial Law Review*, London, May 2001, pp.66–8.

Forker, J. J., 'Corporate Governance and Disclosure Quality', *Accounting and Business Research*, Vol. 22, No. 86, 1992, pp. 111–24.

Gill, A., 'Corporate Governance in Emerging Markets—Saints & Sinners: Who's Got Religion?', in *2002 Symposium on Corporate Governance and Disclosure: The Impact of Globalization*, The School of Accountancy, The Chinese University of Hong Kong, February 2002.

Gray, S. J., 'Towards a Theory of Cultural Influence on the Development of Accounting Systems Internationally', *Abacus*, March 1988, pp. 1–15.

Guan, L. and A. Lau, 'An Empirical Evaluation of Environmental Factors Influencing the Adoption of IAS in Pacific Asia Countries', Paper presented at the 10th Asia Pacific Conference on International Accounting Issues, Melbourne, Australia, November 1999.

Hong Kong Economic Journal, 'Transparency of Hong Kong Blue Chips less than Australia and Singapore' (in Chinese), 16 November 2001.

Hill, J. G., 'Deconstructing Sunbeam—Contemporary Issues in Corporate Governance', *University of Cincinnati Law Review*, 1999, pp.1099–1127.

HKEx, 'Consultation Paper on Proposed Amendments to the Listing Rules Relating to Corporate Governance Issues', January 2002.

Ho, S. S. M., 'Design and Effects of Incentive Pay Scheme for Senior Executives' (in Chinese), *Hong Kong Economic Journal*, 11 November 1997.

Ho, Simon S. M., 'The Role of Ownership Structure and Disclosure in the Asian Financial Crisis' (in Chinese), *Communication in Finance and Accounting*, No. 1, 2000, pp. 22–5.

Ho, S. S. M., 'Companies Facing Loss but Directors' Pay Jumped 50 Times' (in Chinese), *The Apple Daily*, 28 January 2002.

Ho, S. S. M. and K. Lam, 'Family Ownership, Executive Compensations and Firm Performance', Working Paper, School of Accountancy, The Chinese University of Hong Kong, 2003.

Ho, S. S. M., K. Lam, and H. Sami, 'The Investment Opportunity Set, Director Ownership, and Corporate Policies: Evidence from an Emerging Market', *Journal of Corporate Finance*, 2002.

Ho, S. S. M. and K. S. Wong, 'A Study of Corporate Disclosure Practice and Effectiveness in Hong Kong', *Journal of International Financial Management and Accounting*, Vol. 12, No. 1, 2001(a), pp. 75–102.

Ho, S. S. M. and K. S. Wong, 'A Study of the Relationship between Corporate Governance Structures and the Extent of Voluntary Disclosure', *Journal of International Accounting, Auditing and Taxation*, Vol. 10, 2001(b), pp. 139–56.

Ho, S. S. M. and K. S. Wong, 'The Perceived Value of Voluntary Disclosure Items and Firms' Disclosure Practice', Working Paper, School of Accountancy, The Chinese University of Hong Kong, 2002.

Hong Kong Institute of Company Secretaries, 'The Limit of Governance', *Company Secretary*, January 1998, pp.15–18.

Judges Report of the HKMA Best Annual Report Award (Hong Kong Management Association, 1998–2000).

Hong Kong Society of Accountants, *Report of the Working Group on Corporate Governance* (Hong Kong Society of Accountants, January 1995).

Hong Kong Society of Accountants, 'Special Issue on Corporate Governance', *Hong Kong Accountants*, September/October 1996.

Hong Kong Society of Accountants, *Second Report of the Corporate Governance Working Group* (Hong Kong Society of Accountants, January 1997).

Hong Kong Society of Accountants, 'Statements prepared by Hong Kong Society of Accountants and Presented before the Legislative Council Panel on Financial Affairs', *Hong Kong Accountant*, April 2002, pp.13–20.

Ip, S., 'Corporate Governance in Hong Kong', speech given at the Hong Kong Institute of Directors' Speaker Luncheon Meeting, 16 February 2001.

Jensen, M.C. and W. H. Meckling, 'Theory of the Firm: Managerial Behaviour, Agency Costs and Ownership Structure', *Journal of Financial Economics*, 3, October 1976, pp. 305–60.

Lang, L. H. P., 'A Road to Serfdom', in 2002 Symposium on Corporate Governance and Disclosure: The Impact of Globalization, The School of Accountancy, The Chinese University of Hong Kong, February 2002.

Lang, L. H. P. and L. Young, 'Minority Interest, Majority Concern', *Corporate Governance International*, 1, 2001, pp. 44–9.

La Porta, R. L., F. Lopez-De-Silanes, and A. Shleifer, 'Corporate Ownership Around the World', *Journal of Finance*, LIV(2), April 1999, pp. 471–517.

La Porta, R. L., F. Lopez-De-Silanes, A. Shleifer and R. Vishny, 'Law and Finance', *Journal of Political Economy*, 106, 4, 1998, p. 1113.

Low, C. K., 'The Securities and Futures Bill 2000', *Company Secretary*, Vol.12, No. 1, January 2002, pp. 14–17.

Main, B. G. M., 'Top Executive Pay and Performance', *Managerial and Decision Economics*, 12, 1991, pp. 219–29.

Ming Pao, 'Financially Distressed Firms may be Required to Disclose more Financial Situations' (in Chinese), 25 July 1998.

Ming Pao, 'CEO King's Daily Pay 0.82 Million' (in Chinese), 5 April 2002.

Ming Pao, 'HK Corporate Governance Ranking Just behind Singapore' (in Chinese), 12 June 2002.

Mobius, J. M., 'Corporate Governance in Hong Kong' in C. K. Low (ed.), *Corporate Governance: An Asia-Pacific Critique* (Sweet & Maxwell Asia, 2002; pp.201–23).

Molz, R., 'Managerial Domination of Boards of Directors and Financial Performance', *Journal of Business Research*, 16, 1998, pp. 235–49.

Monks, R. A. G. and N. Minow, *Corporate Governance*, (US, Blackwell Publishing, 2001, 2nd Edition).

Morck, R., A. Shleifer and R. W. Vishney, 'Management Ownership and Market Valuation: An Empirical Analysis', *Journal of Financial Economics*, 20, 1998, pp. 293–315.

Murphy, K. J., 'Executive Compensation', Working Paper, Marshall School of Business, University of Southern California, April 1998.

OECD, *OECD Proceedings on Corporate Governance, State-owned Enterprises and Privatization* (Organisation for Economic Cooperation and Development, 1998).

OECD, *OECD Principles of Corporate Governance* (Organisation for Economic Cooperation and Development, 1999).

Pavlik, E. L., T. Scott, and P. Tiessen, 'Executive Compensation: Issues and Research', *Journal of Accounting Literature*, 12, 1993, pp.131–89.

Pacific Economic Cooperation Council, *Guidelines for Good Corporate Governance Practice* (Pacific Economic Cooperation Council, 2000).

Roe, M., 'Political Foundations for Separation of Ownership from Control', *Stanford Law Review*, 2000.

Shevlin, T., 'Stock Options Boost Company Earnings, Research Indicates', *News Online*, the University of Washington Business School, Winter 2003.

Shleifer, A. and E. W. Vishny, 'A Survey of Corporate Governance', *Journal of Finance*, 52, 1997, pp.737–83.

South China Morning Post, 'Newcomers Quick Off Mark with Honourable mentions', Best Annual Report Awards Special Supplement, 28 November 1998, Business Section, p. 7.

South China Morning Post, 'Accountants Want Better Disclosure', 30 July 1998, Business Section, p.2.

South China Morning Post, 'PCCW Directors' Pay Dwarfs Rivals', 4 January 2002, p. 1.

Standing Committee on Company Law Reform, *Corporate Governance Review by SCCLR: A Consultation Paper on Proposals made in Phase I of the Review* (Standing Committee on Company Law Reform, July 2001).

Stock Exchange of Hong Kong, *Best Disclosure Award 1996*, (Stock Exchange of Hong Kong, 1996).

Stock Exchange of Hong Kong, *The Rules Governing the Listing of Securities* (Stock Exchange of Hong Kong, 1997).

Sun, David, 'Effective Disclosure: The First Line of Defence', paper presented at the Symposium on Corporate Governance and Disclosure: The Impact of Globalization, School of Accountancy, The Chinese University of Hong Kong, 2 February 2002.

Tai, B. Y. K., O. K. Au-Yeung, M. C. M. Kwok, and L. W. C. Lau, 'Non-compliance with Disclosure Requirements in Financial Statements: The Case of Hong Kong Companies', *International Journal of Accounting*, 25 (2), 1990, pp. 99–112.

Tricker, R., 'Hong Kong, China and Corporate Governance—A Laboratory for the World', *Proceedings of the Seventh Annual Conference of Accounting Academics* (Hong Kong Society of Accountants, 1995; pp. A41–A53).

Webb, David, 'Webb-site.com Launches Project Poll', 23 March 2003, available online at http://webb-site.com, last accessed June 2003.

William and Tower, 'Voluntary Disclosure Practice: An Empirical Investigation of the Impact of Societal Variables', *Proceedings of the Eighth Annual Conference of Accounting Academics* (Hong Kong Society of Accountants, 1997; pp. 1–16).

Chapter 16

Burnett, B., *Australian Corporations Law* (Australia, CCH, Australia Limited, 1999).
Chung, J., 'The Securities and Futures Bill', *Hong Kong Lawyer*, May 2000, pp. 51–5.
Consultation Document on the Securities and Futures Bill (Hong Kong Special Administrative Region Government Consultation Paper), April 2000.
Hartmann, M., 'Insider Dealing', *Hong Kong Lawyer*, April 2000, pp. 69–74.
Legislative Council Brief, 'Regulatory Reform for the Securities and Futures Market: The Securities and Futures Bill.' File Ref.: SU B38/31 (2000).
Li, Paul, 'The Securities and Futures Bill and the Power of the SFC', *Hong Kong Lawyer*, May 2000, pp. 32–3.
Lipton, P. and A. B. E. Herzberg, *Understanding Company Law* (Australia, LBC Information Services, 1999, 8th Ed.).
Overview Guide to the Proposed Securities and Futures Bill, published by the Securities and Futures Commission, July 1999.
Securities and Futures Ordinance (Ord. No. 5 of 2002).

Chapter 17

Allen, Franklin and Douglas Gale, *Comparing Financial Systems* (Cambridge, Mass. and London, UK, The MIT Press, 2000).
Beckerling, Louis, 'Japanese Banks See Lending Dip', *South China Morning Post*, 17 July 2000(a).
Beckerling, Louis, 'Japanese Lenders Show Commitment to SAR', *South China Morning Post*, 24 July 2000(b).
Beckerling, Louis, 'GDE Debt Deal May be Right First Step', *South China Morning Post*, 27 December 2000(c).
Bernauer, Kenneth, 'The Asian Dollar Market', in *Federal Reserve Bank of San Francisco Economic Review*, Number 1, Winter 1983, pp. 47–63. Reprinted in Joseph G. Kvasnicka (ed.), *Readings in International Finance* (Chicago, Illinois, Federal Reserve Bank of Chicago, 1988).
Chan, Christine and Renee Lai, 'Japanese, Korean Banks Take Brunt of Gitic Closure: Japanese, Korean Banks Account for almost 50 percent of Gitic Loans', *South China Morning Post*, 15 October 1998.
Emery, Robert F., *The Bond Markets of Developing East Asia* (Boulder, Colorado, Westview Press, 1997).
Fell, Robert, *Crisis and Change: The Maturing of Hong Kong's Financial Markets, 1981–1989* (Hong Kong, Longman, 1992).
Friedman, Milton and Rose Friedman, *Free To Choose: A Personal Statement* (New York and London, Harcourt Brace Jovanovich, 1980).
Ho, Richard Yan-Ki, 'Hong Kong as an International Financial Centre', in Richard Yan-Ki Ho, Robert Haney Scott, and Kie Ann Wong (eds.), *The Hong Kong Financial System* (Hong Kong, Oxford University Press, 1991; pp. 381–405).
Hui, George W. L. Hui, 'Ranking Hong Kong as an International Financial Centre', *Hong Kong Economic Papers* 22, 1992, pp. 35–51.
Hui, George W. L. Hui, 'The Securities Markets of Hong Kong', in Robert Harold Terpstra (ed.), *Manual of the Hong Kong Securities Industry* (Hong Kong, The Stock Exchange of Hong Kong and the Asia-Pacific Institute of Business of the Chinese University of Hong Kong, 1994(a), 2nd Ed.), pp. 19–36.
Hui, George W. L. Hui, Review of Robert Fell's *Crisis and Change: The Maturing of Hong Kong's Financial Markets, 1981–1989*, *Hong Kong Journal of Business Management* XII, 1994(b), pp. 83–85.

Jao, Y. C., *Banking and Currency in Hong Kong: A Study of Postwar Financial Development* (London and Basingstoke, Macmillan, 1974).

Jao, Y. C., *Hong Kong's Banking System in Transition: Problems, Prospects and Policies* (Hong Kong: Chinese Banks Association, 1988).

Jao, Y. C., *Hong Kong as an International Financial Centre: Evolution, Prospects and Policies* (Hong Kong, City University of Hong Kong Press, 1997).

Kindleberger, Charles P., 'The Formation of Financial Centers: A Study in Comparative Economic History', *Princeton Studies in International Finance* No. 36, Department of Economics, Princeton University, Princeton, New Jersey, 1974. Reprinted in Charles P. Kindleberger, *Comparative Political Economy: A Retrospective* (Cambridge, Mass. and London, UK, The MIT Press, 2000).

Kynge, James, 'Capital Flight from China "Twice as High as Estimates"', *Financial Times*, 10 July, 2000a.

Kynge, James, '"You Don't Know where the Money Goes": China's Vanishing Foreign Reserves May Frustrate Plans to Relax the Country's Exchange Rate Regime', *Financial Times*, 10 July, 2000b.

Lamb, Andrew, 'International Banking in London, 1975–85', *Bank of England Quarterly Bulletin*, September 1986, pp. 367–378.

Landell-Mills, Joslin, *The Fund's International Banking Statistics* (Washington, D.C., International Monetary Fund, 1986).

Lee, Kuan Yew, *From Third World To First: The Singapore Story: 1965–2000* (Singapore, Singapore Press Holdings, 2000, Times edition).

Lewis, Karen K., 'Puzzles in International Financial Markets', in G. Grossman and K. Rogoff, ed., *Handbook of International Economics, vol. III* (Amsterdam, North-Holland, 1995), pp. 1913–1971.

Lewis, Karen K, 'Trying to Explain Home Bias in Equities and Consumption', *Journal of Economic Literature*, Vol. XXXVII, 1999, pp. 571–608.

Moir, Jane, 'Akai Aching for Investigation', *South China Morning Post*, 19 September 2002.

Neuberger, Anthony, 'London Stock Exchange', in Peter Newman, Murray Milgate, and John Eatwell (eds.), *The New Palgrave Dictionary of Money and Finance*, Vol. 2 (London and Basingstoke, Macmillan, 1992; pp. 615–17).

Ogden, Jon, 'Missing Millions Mystery: Cross-Border Vanishing Acts Do Little for Our Reputation as a Financial Centre', *South China Morning Post*, 18 September 2002.

O'Neill, Mark, 'China Share Trade Closer', *South China Morning Post*, 14 March 2002.

Peek, Joe, and Eric S. Rosengren, 'Collateral Damage: Effects of the Japanese Bank Crisis on Real Activity in the United States', *American Economic Review*, 90(1), 2000, pp. 30–44.

Quak, Hiang Whai, 'Can Guanxi Deliver Citic Pacific from its Woes?', *Business Times*, 17 January, 2002.

Roberts, Richard (ed.), *International Financial Centres: Concepts, Development and Dynamics*, Volume 1–3 (Aldershot, England, Edward Elgar, 1994).

Rose, Harold, *International Banking Developments and London's Position as an International Banking Centre* (London: London Business School City Research Project, 1994(a)).

Rose, Harold, *London as an International Financial Centre: A Narrative History* (London, London Business School City Research Project, 1994(b)).

Schenk, Catherine R., *Hong Kong as an International Financial Centre: Emergence and Development 1945–65* (London and New York, Routledge, 2001).

Shy, Oz, *The Economics of Network Industries* (Cambridge University Press, 2001).

Sito, Peggy and Eric Ng, 'Conglomerate Bypasses SAR in Seeking Funds', *South China Morning Post*, 2 April 2002.

Sivanithy, R., 'S'pore Still an Emerging Market?' *Business Times*, 2 September 2002.

Securities Review Committee, *The Operation and Regulation of the Hong Kong Securities Industry: Report of the Securities Review Committee* (Hong Kong, Government Printer, May 1988).

Tan, Chwee Huat, *Singapore Financial Sourcebook* (Singapore, Singapore University Press, 1997).

Tan, Chwee Huat, *Financial Markets and Institutions in Singapore* (Singapore, Singapore University Press, 1999, 10th Ed.).

Tan, Ee Ling, 'The Fund Management Industry in Singapore', Master's Thesis, Department of Economics, National University of Singapore, 2000.

Wong, Wei Kong, 'Getting out of No-Man's-Land', *Business Times*, April 16, 2002.

Worthington, P. M., 'Global Equity Turnover: Market Comparisons', *Bank of England Quarterly Bulletin*, May 1991, pp. 246–9.

Appendices

Appendix 4.1

A Brief History of Mutual Funds in the US

1924 to 1970

The first open-ended mutual funds, Massachusetts Investors Trust and States Street Investment Trust, emerged in the United States in 1924. Following the market crash of 1929 and the Great Depression, individual investors avoided all types of securities, including mutual funds. The entire industry was stagnant. Through the Investment Company Act of 1940, the authorities sought to provide a regulatory framework. Recognizing that bringing people back to the market was essential for the market's survival, the New York Stock Exchange and its member firms started the Monthly Investment Plan (MIP) in 1954. Combined with the rise in the stock market, the MIP successfully increased share ownership. However, the severe bear market of 1973–4 made mutual funds less attractive again.

1970 to 1980

During the mid-1970s, two events made investing in individual securities difficult for the small investor, and they consequently spurred the growth of mutual funds. First, the Federal Reserve Board (FRB) increased the minimum investment for Treasury Bills (T-bills). Interest rates on six-month T-bills increased to more than sixteen per cent. This caused investors to abandon the stock market and begin purchasing large amounts of US Treasury Bills directly from the FRB. To stem the demand, the FRB raised the minimum purchase amount for Treasury bills from US$1,000 to US$10,000. This placed T-bills out of the reach of many small investors. However, the small investor could access the T-bills market by buying the newly created money market mutual funds. Fidelity Daily Income Trust was the first money market mutual fund product created in 1974.

The second blow to the small investors came in 1975, when commissions on securities transactions became freely negotiable. The small investor became less attractive to the full-service brokerage firms, as the commissions to be earned were relatively insignificant.

1980 to Today

The elimination of fixed commissions was good news for fund management companies, and for a new type of brokerage firm—the discount broker. These companies saw the profitable opportunities in small investors' periodic purchases. Both sought to attract small investors who would regularly invest in the securities market either by buying mutual funds or by purchasing stocks and bonds. In doing so, they captured an ongoing stream of fees and commissions.

During the bull market of the 1980s, the number of mutual fund investors and the amount of money flowing into mutual funds increased rapidly. This growth was spurred by the creation of Individual Retirement Accounts (IRAs) under the Tax Act of 1981, and the public's increasing awareness of the benefits of mutual fund investing.

The amount of money Americans have poured into mutual funds illustrates this point. Assets held in US-based mutual funds rose from slightly less than $1 trillion at the beginning of 1990 to just under $7 trillion by the end of 2000 (Figure 4.19).

Figure 4.19 Mutual Fund Assets in the US, 1990–2000

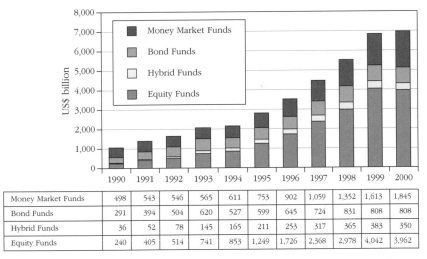

	1990	1991	1992	1993	1994	1995	1996	1997	1998	1999	2000
Money Market Funds	498	543	546	565	611	753	902	1,059	1,352	1,613	1,845
Bond Funds	291	394	504	620	527	599	645	724	831	808	808
Hybrid Funds	36	52	78	145	165	211	253	317	365	383	350
Equity Funds	240	405	514	741	853	1,249	1,726	2,368	2,978	4,042	3,962

Source of data: Mutual Fund Fact Book (www.ici.org/aboutfunds/factbook_toc.html)

Appendix 4.2

Rules and Regulations Relating to the Fund Management Industry

Relevant Ordinances (most now subsumed in SFO)
Securities Ordinance (now SFO)
Commodities Trading Ordinance (now SFO)
Protection of Investors Ordinance (now SFO)
Securities and Futures Commission Ordinance (now SFO)
Mandatory Provident Funds Schemes Ordinance

Codes of Conduct
Fund Manager Code of Conduct
Code on Unit Trusts and Mutual Funds
Code on Investment-Linked Assurance Schemes
Code on Pooled Retirement Funds
Client Identity Rule
Code of Conduct for Persons Registered with the SFC
SFC Code on MPF Products
Code on Takeovers and Mergers and Share Repurchases

Relevant Listing Rules for Listed Funds
Listing rules: Chapter 20, Chapter 21

Relevant Guidelines issued by the SFC
Management Supervision and Internal Control Guidelines for Persons
    Registered with, or Licensed by, the SFC
Guidelines for the Review of Internal Controls and Systems of Trustees/
    Custodians
Guidance Note on Internet Regulation
Guidance Note for Persons Advertising or Offering Collective Investment
    Schemes on the Internet
Guidelines for Registered Persons Using the Internet to Collect Applications
    for Securities in an Initial Public Offering
Guidance Note on the Application of the Electronic Transaction Ordinance
    to Contract Notes
Guidelines on Exempt Fund Manager Status under the Code on Takeovers
    and Mergers
Guidelines on Exempt Principal Trader Status under the Code on Takeovers
    and Mergers
Guidance Note on Competence
Guidance Notes issued by the SFC—Money Laundering
Guidance Note on Continuous Professional Training
Registration Guidelines for Intermediaries Advising on Securities Incidental
    to the Marketing of MPF Schemes Only

Appendix 17.1

International Banking

Data on Hong Kong's international banking are contained in the Hong Kong Monetary Authority's *Monthly Statistical Bulletin* and, before that publication began, were contained in the *Hong Kong Monthly Digest of Statistics*. There are two points to note. First, figures are denominated in Hong Kong dollars. The Hong Kong dollar suffered depreciation in the late 1970s and early 1980s. To offset this exchange rate effect, I have converted the Hong Kong dollar figures into US dollar figures by using the year-end exchange rate. The second point is that data on Hong Kong banks' liabilities to external non-banks were not collected before 1991.

World data is based on the *International Financial Statistics*, which terminated its coverage of international banking in 1996.

Singapore data are taken from the *Monthly Statistical Bulletin* of the Monetary Authority of Singapore, which follows the eurocurrency convention. The separation of banks into domestic currency units and Asian Currency Units (ACUs) facilitates data collection under this convention, but not the cross-border one.

Equities

Data on Hong Kong's equity market are taken from the *Quarterly Bulletin* of the Hong Kong Securities and Futures Commission (SFC). Much of this is also available in stock exchange publications and the *Digest of Statistics*, monthly and annual, of the Hong Kong Census and Statistics Department. Data on earlier years were presented in Hui (1994), which also gave sources of earlier periods.

World data is available in the *Emerging Stock Markets Factbook*, previously published by the International Finance Corporation and presently published by Standard & Poor's.

Information on London's foreign equities is based on data at the London Stock Exchange website.

Data on China's equity markets are taken from the *Emerging Stock Markets Factbook* and the *China Statistical Yearbook*.

Singapore data are taken from issues of the *Fact Book* of the Singapore Exchange as well as its website.

International Bonds

Data on bond issues at Hong Kong's exchanges in early years are taken from Hui (1994). Recent data are again taken from stock exchange publications.

World data are taken from OECD publications, specifically *International Capital Markets Statistics, 1950–1995*, for data before and including 1995, and *Financial Statistics Monthly: International Markets* thereafter. The limitations of the data are discussed in the Notes section of both of these publications.

Data on the nominal value of bonds at Singapore's exchange are taken from issues of the *Fact Book* of the Singapore Exchange. Data on gross issues of Asian dollar bonds are taken from Table 8-1 of Tan (1999), which in turn is based on the *Annual Reports* of the Monetary Authority of Singapore (MAS).

Foreign Exchange Turnover

World and country data are based on the Triennial Central Bank Survey of Foreign Exchange and Derivatives Market Activity conducted by the Bank for International Settlements (BIS). Similar data may also be found in the *Quarterly Bulletin* of the Hong Kong Monetary Authority (HKMA).

National Income Account Variables

Data on GDP and exports is mainly taken from the *International Financial Statistics* and is supplemented by data from the national publications of the countries and territories concerned.

Index